ADVANCE PRAISE FOR THIS BOOK

"Finally, an up-to-the-minute reference that parents and kids can use to find the gems and make the net a rich educational tool. If you've ever been frustrated, knowing that incredible treasures are out there, but without a clue about where to start, this remarkable collection points the way."

—Andrew Blau
Director,Communications Policy, Benton Foundation

" This book will save parents and teachers many hours of aimless searching, and provide the peace of mind that they are providing their kids with the highest quality of what's available on the Internet."

—Susan Calcari
Internet Scout, InterNIC Net Scout Services

"Jean Armour Polly has done a big part of what every parent wishes he or she had time to do—explored and assessed many sites for their suitability for K-8 use."

—Vint Cerf
Senior Vice-President, MCI Data Architecture; Internet Society Trustee and Internet pioneer

"Who better to help guide parent, teacher and pupil through the vast and ever-changing Internet than cyber-librarian Jean Armour Polly. Make this volume part of your home library."

—Keola Donaghy
Network Administrator, Hawaiian language immersion program

"Jean Armour Polly is one of the few people writing about the Internet who really knows what she's talking about! ...this book is just what the librarian ordered. I know it will be a big help to us at AskERIC."

—Mike Eisenberg, Ph.D.
Director, ERIC Clearinghouse on Information & Technology and the AskERIC
Internet Education Information Service

"Jean Armour Polly makes the Internet a lot more 'kid friendly.'"

—Ira Flatow
Host of public radio's "Science Friday"

"...a special peek below the waves at some of the incredible variety of resources that will help our children in their own explorations. "

—Rick Gates
Inventor of The Original Internet Hunt and Director of Development, Net Assets

"In today's world, people both young and old find themselves adrift in a 'Sargasso Sea' of information resources. This book provides a useful guide that will assist parents in helping their children navigate that sea, pointing the way to many of the safe harbors that exist along their journey."

—Dewayne Hendricks
Warp Speed Imagineering

"An indispensable and reassuring guide for parents who want to turn their kids loose on the Internet."

—Guy Kawasaki
Apple Fellow

"Amongst a flood of Internet books, Polly's stands out as instrumental and of true value."

—Brendan Kehoe
author of Zen and the Art of the Internet

"In the future, I'll plan on carrying it with me when I go 'on the road' as the K-12 'card catalog' for the Internet."

—Don Mitchell
frequent professional and personal presenter on the use of the Internet in K-12 education

"This book is an important work that will help youth—our most important resource and hope for the future—and their families more effectively and more quickly understand the power and potential of the communications medium represented by the Internet. "

—Mario Morino
Chairman, Morino Institute

"Jean Armour Polly has written an excellent guidebook to the Internet, enabling kids (and their parents) to find the digital treasures that await them in cyberspace."

—(Dr.) Michael R. Nelson
Information Technology Expert

"Jean Armour Polly's book is a worldwide online field trip for children! This educational travel guide enables students to become more globally aware through visits to other countries' school resources. This is a necessary reference for every classroom or home with Internet connectivity."

—Tracy LaQuey Parker
author, The Internet Companion and Education Market Development Manager, Cisco Systems, Inc.

"If anybody in the world is qualified to teach us about kid-friendly resources on the Internet, it's Jean Armour Polly. A librarian, a mother, a Net enthusiast for many years, she's been grappling with issues of usefulness, age-appropriateness, educational value, usability, for years."

—Howard Rheingold
author of best-sellers Virtual Reality and The Virtual Community, founding Executive Editor of HotWired

"This book redefines the concept of encyclopedia and teaching resource for the 21st century. Net-mom Jean Armour Polly has assembled and indexed an array of World Wide Web resources for children that makes fascinating reading in its own right."

—Tony Rutkowski
VP Internet Business Development, General Magic, Inc.; former VP and Executive Director, Internet Society

"This huge, current, and well-organized book is a unique and wonderful resource—a must-have for parents, children, teachers, and librarians, it is also terrifically fun to browse through even when you aren't online."

—Karen G. Schneider
freelance librarian and owner, Blue Highways Internet Services; Columnist, American Libraries
and author of The Internet Access Cookbook

"If kids need guidance on the Net at all, their parents should have that privilege. Not Internet Service Providers. Not governments. If this book helps keep kids on the Net where they belong, we like it."

—William L. Schrader
Chairman, President & CEO PSINet Inc.

"Kites, dinosaurs, astronomy, dogs...this book has given me all I need to take home to occupy my child on a rainy day...not to mention myself."

—Brad Spurgeon
newspaper librarian and cyber-writer at the International Herald Tribune, Paris, France

"The Internet frontier is changing from 'where can I click?' to 'who do you trust?' Here is a guide to children's Internet resources from someone worthy of that trust... "

—Stuart Weibel
Senior Research Scientist, OCLC Office of Research

"Jean Armour Polly has done it again—translated the obscure and difficult into something entertaining, understandable, and really useful. Get this book, get a kid, and beam into the information age."

—Jim Williams
Executive Director, FARNET, Inc.

"Jean Armour Polly has assembled a splendid sourcebook for introducing young people to the best the Internet has to offer. Kids: Try this at home!"

—Stephen Wolff, Cisco Systems
(formerly Division Director, Networking, National Science Foundation)

"How do you find your way to the White House without getting lost in downtown D.C.? Now you can turn to The Internet Kids Yellow Pages. This book transforms the entire Internet into a kid's encyclopedia. If your house has a kid and a computer, it must also have this book!"

—Steve Worona
creator of "CUInfo", the world's first Campus-Wide Information System, Cornell University

THE INTERNET KIDS YELLOW PAGES

SPECIAL EDITION

ABOUT THE AUTHOR

Jean Armour Polly is an internationally recognized expert on the Internet from a user's point of view. First to use the phrase "Surfing the Internet," she was one of the first two women elected to the Internet Society Board of Trustees.

She was formerly the director of Public Services and Internet Ambassador at NYSERNet, Inc. where she was co-principal investigator on the landmark *Project GAIN: Connecting Rural Public Libraries to the Internet* study (1994) and producer of the accompanying video. Jean has a special interest in telecommunications and Indian nations, and use of the Net to enhance the economic development of rural areas.

Prior to that, Jean was a public librarian for sixteen years. She now co-owns and co-moderates PUBLIB, the Internet discussion list for public librarians.

Besides the original "Surfing the Internet," available electronically, she has written two books on public technology and has been a columnist for *Library Journal* and contributor to *I*Way* magazine.

Jean received her BA in Medieval Studies at Syracuse University in 1974, and her master's in Library Science from the same university in 1975.

She is a member of the American Library Association and is a former director of the Library and Information Technology Association's Board. Jean also holds memberships in the Electronic Frontier Foundation, the Internet Society, and Computer Professionals for Social Responsibility.

A popular and entertaining regular on the demo and speaking circuit, Jean has jacked into the Net in places as diverse as: Alaska, the Czech Republic, Italy, Hawai'i, and historic booth number one at Roger's Frontier Bar in Old Colorado City, Colorado.

She lives on a hill in central New York, above a woods full of raccoons, fox, and deer. She is currently a freelance writer and independent contractor. Mom to a ten-year-old son, Stephen, Jean also enjoys her cats, ducks, and a garden pond full of goldfish and lilies. More about Jean is available at her home page: http://www.well.com/user/polly.

Communications about this book should go to feedback@pollywood.com.

THE INTERNET
KIDS
YELLOW PAGES
SPECIAL EDITION

Jean Armour Polly

Osborne McGraw-Hill

Berkeley New York St. Louis San Francisco Auckland Bogotá Hamburg London
Madrid Mexico City Milan Montreal New Delhi Panama City Paris São Paulo
Singapore Sydney Tokyo Toronto

THE INTERNET KIDS YELLOW PAGES

SPECIAL EDITION

OSBORNE MCGRAW-HILL
2600 TENTH STREET
BERKELEY
CALIFORNIA 94710
U.S.A.

For information on translations or book distributors outside the U.S.A., or to arrange bulk purchase discounts for sales promotions, premiums, or fundraisers, please contact Osborne **McGraw-Hill** at the above address.

1234567890 SEM 99876

ISBN 0-07-882197-5

Acquisitions Editor
Scott Rogers

Project Editor
Bob Myren

Copy Editor
Tim Barr

Proofreader
William Cassel

Computer Designers
Peter F. Hancik
Richard Whitaker

Illustrators
Roberta Steele
Leslee Basin

Series Design
Peter F. Hancik

Quality Control Specialist
Joe Scuderi

For my son Stephen
and my mother,
who both have a lot to teach about love,
and respect for children.

Put it before them briefly so they will read it, clearly so they will appreciate it, picturesquely so they will remember it, and, above all, accurately so they will be guided by its light

Joseph Pulitzer

Table of Contents

Acknowledgments

There are a number of people I want to thank, and this is the page where I get to do that.

You wouldn't be holding this book in your hands if it weren't for my husband, Larry Polly. He pulled the ethernet around the house, developed the database for the project, and ran the entire production side of the book manuscript. It was a mammoth task, and he never lost his sense of perspective and humor. Well, maybe he did *once*, when we found out you can't print formatted, styled text to disk out of *FileMaker Pro*. But I digress. Thanks, dear. Now that the book's done, maybe we can find time to take down the Christmas tree. Especially now that it's February.

And to my almost ten-year-old son, Stephen, a big hug and thanks for giving Dad and me the time to do something for kids all over the world.

Mario Morino, Chairman, Morino Institute, believed in this project from the start. I'd like to thank the Morino Institute for financial and moral support. Lots of people say they are behind children's issues, but Mario rolls up his sleeves and gets busy. Witness his help with the National Youth Center Network. Witness his involvement in the Potomac Knowledgeway. Witness his support of community networks as change agents for social and economic development. Watch the man closely—he's a visionary.

I would be remiss if I did not thank my friend Steve Cisler at Apple Computer, Inc., for continually pushing my thought and action toward finding my own Right Path.

Ted Nadeau, General Manager, PSINet/Pipeline New York, was very helpful in expediting a PSINet 56KB leased line installation to my house, during Thanksgiving week, despite the blizzard. You don't need a fast Internet connection to *use* this book, but you do need a fast connection to *write* something like this book. We're paying rack rate for our connectivity, so I don't *have* to give PSINet a plug at all. But Ted (and everybody else at PSINet connected with this install) did a great job and I want to express my thanks for fine service.

Thanks to Andra Schadt (and her husband Eric, and home schooled kids Kyle, Nikki, and Noah) for her help in my understanding of home schooling (and un-schooling) concerns and requirements. I hope this book is of special help to parents and kids who, for one reason or another, have chosen to educate at home. Take a bow, all of you!

Elaine Lyon, Head of Reference at Liverpool Public Library, was always helpful in answering my emergency fact-checking questions. You can get a lot of information on the Net, but you can't get everything (yet) and Elaine knows where it all lives on the Library shelves. Use and support your public library, and get to know your local library professionals. Thanks again, Elaine, and I promise I'll get that overdue book back real soon now. ;-)

While I am thanking people at Liverpool Public Library, I'd like to mention Kati Foley, for bringing a list of subject headings for children to my attention. They were useful in helping us create our own list. I'd also like to say that the Ladies' Night Group: Dorothy Morgan, Cheryl Cornell, Joyce Mills, Kathy Grosso, Marylou Matthews, and Judy Sibio provided encouragement throughout the life of this project. Peg Smallman, now of NYSERNet, should also be included in this group.

While I am mentioning NYSERNet, I wish to thank them for allowing one of their employees the use of corporate connectivity, on her own time, to help with the research on the book.

From Osborne McGraw-Hill, Scott Rogers, Executive Editor, Editorial Assistant Daniela Dell'Orco, and Project Editor Bob Myren should be praised for the time they took with the book, and the care and commitment they displayed toward making it right for families.

My gratitude also goes to my friend Harley Hahn, author of about a zillion computer and Internet books. Harley helped me through all phases of my own project, and was a wise source of counsel and encouragement. If there is a support group for Internet authors, Harley should be its president.

To Pat McManus, a tip of the wizard's hat, and a big thank you from Net-mom.

Thanks also to Ursula Braun for helping with some German words, the DHL guy for climbing through the snowbank, and Mom for providing support services and washing the dishes.

Finally, thank you to the research team, and especially their families, for giving up evenings, weekends, and holidays in order to meet deadlines.

Jean Armour Polly
Jamesville, New York
February, 1996

About the Research Team

Kitty Bennett is a news researcher at the *St. Petersburg Times* in Florida. She first journeyed into the Internet about five years ago, and now spends many hours a week there doing her work and having fun. A proponent of free community computer networks, she was one of a group of people who helped establish a Free-net in the Tampa Bay area.

Peg Elliott, MLS, is a fifth generation Californian. Just like her pioneer ancestors who walked across America in the 1840s, driven to conquer the western frontier, she has an avid interest in taming the new information frontier. As a reference librarian servicing children and adults, Peg is committed to developing the enhanced use of Internet resources for information and educational purposes in public libraries. Peg makes upstate New York her home, where she and her husband John parented his four children through their teenage years, and are now raising their three children, Liz, Katie, and Michael.

Ron Evry is a writer whose work appears regularly in *COMBO MAGAZINE* (where he writes about comics and the Internet), *The Comics Journal* and *Hogan's Alley Magazine*. He is often seen doing special reports on the nationally syndicated *Flights of Fantasy* TV show. He is the vice-president of Washington Apple Pi and learned how to create a web page using an Apple IIgs, writing HTML code using AppleWriter. He runs the computer lab at Antietam Elementary School in Woodbridge, Virginia, and you can drop in on the school's home page at *http://www.pen.k12.va.us/~revry/antietam.html*.

Jan France is a volleyball nut and ski bum wannabe, although in *real life* she's a Mac computer programmer in Colorado. She and her husband Ray, an information systems manager, have two teenagers who usually could care less about computers. But the kids do love to surf the Net! Jan owns a software company specializing in educational products for children, parents, teachers, and homeschoolers. Read the product descriptions and download demos at her home page: *http://www.elk-grove.k12.il.us/sperspect/france.html*

Brian M. Harris, Bachelor of Fine Arts, is a computer artist who has been tinkering with technology for as long as he can remember. Since direct exposure to the Internet in February of 1990, he has been diagnosed with a nasty case of online addiction. When away from his home workstation, he enjoys being a husband and father, and also enjoys drawing, home improvement, and traveling.

John Iliff is system administrator and head of reference at Pinellas Park Public Library in Florida. He co-owns and moderates PUBLIB, the oldest and largest listserv for public librarians around the world. A former chimney sweep, auto worker, and social worker, he became a librarian after obtaining a master's degree at the University of South Florida. He now lives in a beach shack on Coquina Key where he picks oranges off his tree almost every day of the year. His wife Karen (a nurse), and his son Michael, try to beat him to the modem every night.

Gayle Keresey is a school library media specialist at Goldsboro High School in Goldsboro, North Carolina. When she is not online, she enjoys spending time with her partner, Rebecca Taylor, and their four cats in Wilmington, NC. She also enjoys reading, and traveling to see lighthouses. Gayle has telecommunicated for eleven years and has spent the past five years working as a remote forum leader on America Online, in the computing and education forums. She is also a SYSOP for the Wayne node of FrEdMail. She holds a masters degree in Library Science from the University of Kentucky.

Vicki Kwasniewski is an ex-air traffic controller now doing circuit provisioning for NYSERNet, an Internet Service Provider. She met her husband, Michael, in the Air Force during her four year hitch. Their "children" are Beezer, a dachshund, Amadeus, an African Gray parrot, Mug-Y, a Moluccan Cockatoo, Whyumpa, a Severe Macaw, and Wedge, a hedgehog. You'll find Beezer and Wedge on the Web, at *http://www.newmexico.com/~hodges/hedgehogs/pics.html*. Vicki and Michael are also well known locally for their particularly lethal homemade salsa, made from ingredients home-grown in their central New York garden.

A former high school teacher and coach, Steven T. Marks is now involved in educational television production and distance learning applications. He sees the coming together of education and technology as a pathway to better learning, and also to much-improved communication. His television production experience has helped him identify ways to effectively reach students via the computer screen. Testing potential Net sites with his three school-age children gave him an additional advantage.

When he is not dodging Jean's cats, he enjoys soldering old electronic parts together with his son Stephen, age ten. He also enjoys travelling to exotic locales.

Stephen Jade Polly, ten, served as the Kid Advisor and arbiter of humor in the book. He likes to use the Net to learn things about science, and his favorite season is Hawai'i. His cat, Pooshka, is incredibly large.

Laurel Sharp is a children's and reference librarian who loves to play and hear music. She lives with her husband, three sons, and aging pets in central New York.

Bernie Sloan is a youth sports coach (soccer and basketball) who moonlights as senior library information systems consultant for the University of Illinois Office for Planning and Budgeting. He has two sons, Sam (17) and Zack (13), and lives with his wife, Sharon Stoerger (also a librarian!), and two African frogs (Froggio and Fabio) in Urbana, Illinois.

Mark A. Spadafore is proud to live in Syracuse, where he works at WCNY-TV 24, a PBS affiliate. When not rooting for the Tampa Bay Buccaneers (don't ask...) he is often seen surfing the Web and asking why he doesn't have a PowerBook at work, where he is the NYLink Coordinator—an online K12 telecommunications network. Mark is a graduate of Keuka College, which is located in the Finger Lakes region of New York State. "Some days you contemplate the great mysteries of life, other days, you just want a piece of chocolate cake." Spadafore original, 1988.

Diane Towlson is a graphic artist, with a bachelor of fine arts degree from the Rochester Institute of Technology. She is a staff artist and computer wrangler at Onondaga County Parks, where her very cool boss Jon helps her and her co-workers create "Special Places for Year-Round Adventure" in the central New York area. When Diane is not online, or hawking her fabric masks at art shows, she can be found vacationing in the land of sun, salsa, and Lime 'n' Chili taco chips (which for some reason are not sold east of the Mississippi).

Introduction

What's different about this book? Other books are collections. This book features *selections*. You're holding the first book of Internet resources for kids and families selected by a librarian. You'll find a thoughtful and intuitive organization of Internet knowledge here, which is driven by the types of questions I used to answer at the public library reference desk.

I selected these sites with care, respect, and yes, love. I was thinking hard about you, and your kids. I was thinking about inclusion, and tolerance, and disturbing events on the news. I believe that the Net can help humans learn to get along, and there is hope for a better world ahead.

WELCOME KIDS!

It's great to meet you! I can't wait to show you some of my favorite places on the Net! We're going all over the world, so you might want to pack a lunch, since we'll be gone all day. If you get tired, just turn off your computer, I'll be waiting here for our next fun adventure.

First, though, can I tell you something? Your parents and teachers have given you a great gift if they are letting you use the Net. And they trust me to help you find some terrific places to visit. But, the Net changes all the time. Some places I thought were cool when I wrote this book might not be the same by the time you follow in my footsteps. So please promise me one thing. If, on the Net, you get someplace that just doesn't "feel right" to you, or you are "talking" to someone and start to feel uncomfortable with what is going on, go get a parent, teacher, or caregiver. If there is no one around, just turn off the computer.

The good news is, while you're reading this, I'm still finding outstanding new places for the next edition of this book! Please think of me as your friend—come on, let's explore!

WELCOME TO PARENTS, TEACHERS, AND CAREGIVERS!

Thank you for allowing me the privilege of talking to your kids.

Because of my unique background as a public librarian, Internet expert, and mom, I wrote this book because I believe kids belong on the Net. There has been some movement to ban kids entirely, and I believe that is entirely wrong. Still, I know that there are places on the Net that I would not want my son to go without me. There are places in the city where I live that I wouldn't let him go alone, either.

So, I set out to find places on the Net that were either built expressly for children, or places where people of any age could find value. You're holding in your hands over 1,800 such locations. 98% of them are Web sites, the remainder are gopher, FTP, or other archives. They are located all over the world, from Washington, D.C. to the former Soviet Union. You'll visit servers on tiny Pacific islands, one inside the Vatican, and an Internet video camera aimed at a research station on Antarctica. You'll visit the Library of Congress, NASA, the British Museum, and even some school and family home pages.

SELECTION POLICY: WHAT YOU WILL FIND IN THIS BOOK

Every good library needs a selection policy, so naturally, we have one. Here it is:

This book selects resources for its collection that, in general,

° include compelling, engaging material for children from preschool through eighth grade. We also collect for adults in the FAMILY AND PARENTING section.

° display outstanding organization and navigation/search capabilities.

° use a judicious mix of graphics and text, so that they will be useful to a user with text-only Web access. Many times these resources will offer a text-only option.

° are authoritative and list their sources.

° are timely, and dated.

° exist on a stable Internet site with good connectivity.

SELECTION POLICY: WHAT YOU WON'T FIND IN THIS BOOK

I have explored all these sites myself, in great detail. This book does not knowingly include resources which contain violent, racist, sexist, erotic, or other adult content.

Additionally, I have not included resources involving sexuality and gender issues. In the "Families and Parenting" and "Health and Safety" sections, you will find information such as a text-based discussion on puberty. My research informs me that most parents want to decide how, and when, to introduce their children to these topics, so I have respected that. If you feel otherwise, please see the section of the book called "INTERNET—Search Tools and Indexes" for guidance on finding things on the Net.

You'll see that I have marked some annotations with a "Parental Advisory." Some sites contained too many links for me to follow to their ends. Please be sure to preview these sites yourself.

However, the Internet is always in motion, and resources may change. Something I found appropriate for inclusion in the book today may be inappropriate tomorrow. So, I cannot guarantee that your Internet experience, based on my recommendations, will always meet your needs.

I strongly recommend that parents, caregivers, and teachers always use the Internet alongside their children, and preview sites if at all possible.

Still, all that said, let me say that when in doubt, I left the site out. I was guided by the following, which I found on a server in Honolulu:

"You cannot make people see stuffs they no can see. So, jus worry about yourself ... no make hassles, treat everyone like how you like be treated, and everything should be okay dokey."

Bu La'ia

There is some outstanding material on the net, and over 1,800 compelling resources are in your hands. The Net is BIG, though, so if you don't find your favorite subject, or your favorite site, it's possible I haven't discovered it yet. You can e-mail me and tell me why it's your favorite, and maybe it will get into the next edition. (feedback@pollywood.com)

So, go have fun with the kids—I hope you like the book. Please write and let me know.

WHAT YOU NEED TO KNOW TO USE THIS BOOK

This book won't teach you how to use your Net browser. There are too many of them. I use Netscape, but you may use Lynx, or some other application. If you just know how to use your browser, you can find out how to use the Internet—just look at the "INTERNET— Beginner's Guides" section of this book.

You need to know what a "smiley" is. Here's one coming at you :-) now, put your left ear on your left shoulder and look at those characters again. See the little smiley face? This is a "winkie" ;-) and it means we're joking about something. We use these throughout the book. You can read more about smilies in the "INTERNET—Netiquette, Folklore, and Customs" section of this book.

ADDRESS UNKNOWN?

Unfortunately, I can't help you with connectivity problems. Contact your Internet Service Provider and ask them to help you with setting up your browser, or configuring other Internet software applications. They may also be able to help you with modem settings, or other hardware-related concerns.

However, I can help you with the following:

I typed in the address, but it doesn't work. I got "404 Not Found," or "Not found on this server," or "No DNS entry exists for this server," or some other cranky- sounding message. What should I do?

1. Try it again. The Internet isn't perfect. Along the way from where the information lives, to your computer, something may have blinked.

2. Check your spelling. Many of these addresses are long and complex, so it's easy to make a mistake. You might try having another person read you the address while you type it.

3. Make sure you are careful to use capital letters or lowercase when they are printed in this book. They are not interchangeable, and the computer won't recognize its file called "foo.html" if you have typed it "FOO.HTML."

4. The location or file name may have changed since I visited the page. That means its address will be different. Computer files (making up the pages you see on the World Wide Web) are stored in directories, on remote servers all over the world. Sometimes people move these files to different places, so you need to find where they have been moved.

But if you're pretty smart, and you are, because you've got this book, you'll know some tricks!

Trick #1—Solving File Name Change Problems

The first trick is to shorten the address and look there. Say that you've been looking for Dorothy and Toto's home page. It used to be at:

http://land.of.oz.gov/munchkinland/mainstreet/dorothy.html

Perhaps Dorothy changed the name of her home page, so let's go "back" a level and look around. Let's try:

http://land.of.oz.gov/munchkinland/mainstreet/

That takes you "higher" in the directory path, and you may be able to find where Dorothy has moved from there. On the "mainstreet" web page, we might see several new choices:

/the.scarecrow.html

/the.tin.man.html

/the.cowardly.lion.html

/dorothy.and.toto.html

Great! Dorothy's just changed the name of her home page to include her little dog, too. Choose that one, and make a note of it for future visits. Write the changes directly into this book—I won't mind. Another mystery solved!

If you still can't find what you're looking for, try going "back" another level. You may have to try several levels back until you locate what you want.

Trick #2—Solving Server Name Change Problems

It's also possible that the Wizard of Oz has ordered that the new name of the World Wide Web server containing everyone's home page will now be called "www.land.of.oz.gov," instead of just plain, old, "land.of.oz.gov." That creates a problem for people looking for home pages under the old server name, which isn't there any more. How are you supposed to find it?

Fortunately, the crafty old Wizard chose a common name change. If a computer server's name is going to be changed, it's often given a prefix to reflect the type of services it runs. Common prefix names are gopher (for those operating Gopher servers), or ftp (for those offering File Transfer Protocol), or www (for sites running Web servers.)

If you don't know what the new server name might be, try guessing, using one of these prefixes. For a Web server, try putting "www." in front of whatever name it originally had (unless it already had that prefix). Example:

old name:

http://land.of.oz.gov

Your guess at the new name:

http://www.land.of.oz.gov

Bingo! That was it! Be sure to make a note of the change in this book, so you won't have that problem again.

Trick #3—Another way of Finding Pages That Have Moved

If none of the above works, it's possible Dorothy took her home page someplace else. In that case, all the above tricks won't work, since you will no longer find an entry for her anywhere in the Land of Oz domain.

Your next trick involves trying one of the "Net Search" or "Net Directory" indexes, such as Lycos, Yahoo, Open Text, or Alta Vista. There are many of them listed under those "Net" buttons on Netscape's browser. If you are using another browser, there are probably similar choices to help you search the entire World Wide Web. Look in the section of this book called "INTERNET—Search Tools and Indexes" for more information on searching techniques.

Choose one, and search on the word "dorothy." Chances are, she's put up her home page on a computer server in her new domain. Wow, the search returns hundreds of pages containing the word "dorothy." How do you know which one you want, without having to look through all of them?

Look at the original entry for Dorothy's home page in this book. We have been very careful to print whatever Dorothy used as her home page's title. It is very possible that she is still using that home page title, even though it is located on a different computer server.

We don't really have a home page for Dorothy in this book, this is just an example:

Dorothy and Toto's Wicked Good Adventure

Go to one of the search indexes again. Instead of just searching on "Dorothy," try the page's title as it is printed in this book. You want to make the search engine look for the entire phrase "Dorothy and Toto's Wicked Good Adventure." You don't want to search on "Dorothy," "Toto's," Wicked," "Good," and "Adventure" separately. If you did that, you would get hundreds of items again, and we are trying to narrow it down. Searching on the entire phrase will help do that. Check the directions for the particular index you are using, there is usually a "help" button that will take you there. Many of them allow you to keep the entire phrase together by putting it in quotes. Example:

Search on: "Dorothy and Toto's Wicked Good Adventure"

Alternative guess: "Dorothy and Toto"

Another alternative guess: "Wicked Good Adventure"

If that doesn't work, a final trick is to guess what Dorothy might have said in the content of her home page. She probably talks about Toto, the Scarecrow, the Tin Man, and the Lion in there somewhere. Therefore, these words will be indexed, and you should be able to use that knowledge when you search using one of the indexes.

Go back to your search engine (we like the advanced mode of the Alta Vista search engine for this) and try the following.

Search on: Dorothy AND Toto AND Scarecrow

Alternative: Dorothy AND Lion

Another alternative: Dorothy AND Scarecrow AND Lion

Trick 5—When all else fails

Look on my home page (http://www.well.com/ user/polly) to see if this book is on the Net in electronic form yet. When that happens, I will have a pointer to it from my home page. The electronic version will have all the current locations of the resources, and you'll be able to get to them easily.

These are just some tips to help you find where Dorothy's gone—I know they will help!

JEAN ARMOUR POLLY'S
TOP FIFTY EXTRAORDINARY EXPERIENCES FOR INTERNET KIDS

1. CONNECT WITH OTHER KIDS!

Share your writing and artwork with other kids.
(http://plaza.interport.net/kids_space/)

Participate in a virtual, real-time chat.
(http://lcs.www.media.mit.edu/people/asb/
moose-crossing/)

Join a listserv discussion group.
(http://www.liszt.com/)

Learn how to make your own home page.
(http://web66.coled.umn.edu/Cookbook/
contents.html)

Save the world.
(http://www.kidlink.org/home-txt.html)

2. SCIENCE

Visit a volcano.
(http://volcano.und.nodak.edu/vw.html)

Dissect a frog.
(http://curry.edschool.Virginia.EDU:80/~insttech/
frog/)

Tread water in the Kelp tank at the Monterey Bay
Aquarium.
(http://www.usw.nps.navy.mil/~millercw/aq/
index.html)

Look inside a human heart.
(http://sln.fi.edu/biosci/heart.html)

See as far as the Hubble telescope does.
(http://www.stsci.edu/pubinfo/BestOfHST95.html)

3. GOVERNMENT

Check up on Congress.
(http://policy.net/capweb/congress.html)

Read historic documents.
(http://www.law.emory.edu/FEDERAL/)

Learn about Presidents and First Ladies.
(http://sunsite.unc.edu/lia/president/pressites/)

Take Socks' special VIP tour of the White House.
(http://www.whitehouse.gov/WH/kids/html/
home.html)

Tour the Kremlin and Red Square.
(http://www.kiae.su/www/wtr/kremlin/begin.html)

4. NEWS and REFERENCE

Get the latest news.
(http://pathfinder.com/@@q6KLAWF2NwIAQAhT/
News/news.html)

Monitor weather worldwide, including sea
conditions at floating buoys around the maritime
U.S. and Canada.
(http://cirrus.sprl.umich.edu/wxnet/,
http://thunder.met.fsu.edu/~nws/buoy/)

Read a Kidopedia, written by kids, for kids.
(http://rdz.stjohns.edu/kidopedia/index.html)

Learn a language from native speakers.
(http://www.willamette.edu/~tjones/
Language-Page.html)

Convert measurments and currencies.
(http://rdz.stjohns.edu/kidopedia/index.html,
http://bin.gnn.com/cgi-bin/gnn/currency/)

5. ARTS

Visit the Louvre.
(http://sunsite.unc.edu/louvre/)

Be awed by the Sistine chapel.
(http://www.christusrex.org/www1/sistine/
0-Tour.html)

Climb up a lighthouse.
(http://www.lib.utk.edu/lights/lights.html)

Hear instruments of the symphony, check out a
cello.
(http://tahoma.cwu.edu:2000/~michelj/
Cello_Introduction/Cello_Introduction.html)

Try some folk dance steps.

(http://lucas.incen.doc.ca/ifdo.html)

6. HISTORY

Explore an ancient archaeological site.
(http://www.ncl.ac.uk/~nantiq/menu.html)

Dig up dinosaurs.
(http://ucmp1.berkeley.edu/diapsids/dinosaur.html)

Tour Ellis Island and Gettysburg.
(http://www.i-channel.com/ellis/index.shtml,
http://gettysburg.welcome.com/)

Admire famous African Americans.
(http://www.webcom.com/~bright/source/
  blackfac.html)

Find out which famous people share your birthday.
(http://www.eb.com/bio.html)

7. FUN

Rattle down a roller coaster.
(http://www.marketsmart.com/Coasters/)

Color an online coloring book.
(http://www.ravenna.com/coloring/)

Make your own Slime.
(http://ucunix.san.uc.edu/~edavis/kids-list/
  crafts.html)

Learn to build a birdhouse.
(http://www.ces.ncsu.edu/nreos/forest/steward/
  www16.html)

Look in on a live picture of a research station in
Antarctica, or check the Giraffe Cam at a zoo in
Colorado.
(http://www.antdiv.gov.au/aad/exop/sfo/mawson/
  video.html,
http://www.ceram.com/cheyenne/giraffe.html)

8. EDUCATION

Drop in on a school.
(http://web66.coled.umn.edu/)

Drop in on a homeschool.

(http://www.alaska.net:80/~mteel/)

Download a copy of Peter Pan.
(gopher://wiretap.spies.com:70/00/Library/Classic/
  peter.txt)

Print (to disk) a googolplex, the largest number.
(http://www.uni-frankfurt.de/~fp/Tools/
Googool.html)

Explore the uplifting chemistry of bread.
(http://ericir.syr.edu/Newton/Lessons/bread.html)

9. SPORTS

Cheer your favorite team.
(http://espnet.sportszone.com)

Sail a boat around the world.
(http://www.oceanchallenge.com/)

Fly a micro kite.
(http://www.uni-frankfurt.de/~fp/Tools/
Googool.html)

Start an exercise program.
(http://www.vannet.com/WCF/WCFTEXT/
  KIDFIT.HTM)

Take a hike.
(http://moe.cc.utexas.edu/~susanw/inform/roe/
  index.html)

10. COMPUTERS AND THE INTERNET

Learn to be safe on the Net.
(http://www.discribe.ca/childfind/kidrule.hte)

Download educational software.
(http://remarque.berkeley.edu/~tigger/
  sw-kids.html)

Find e-mail adddresses.
(http://www.Four11.com/)

Learn search strategies.
(http://altavista.digital.com/)

Get the status on a net-connected Coke machine.
(http://www.dsu.edu/~anderbea/machines.html)

AFRICAN AMERICANS

Drum Web Server Home Page

Here you'll find links to the arts, historical sources, entertainment, and much more. Read Dr. Martin Luther King's "I Have a Dream" speech, or the words of Malcolm X. Explore the civil rights resources and think about Maya Angelou's poem, read at the Million Man March:

> …The ancestors remind us, despite the history of pain
> We are a going-on people who will rise again.
> And still we rise.

http://drum.ncat.edu/

The Universal Black Pages

This site collects African American spoken word, music, art, entertainment, and historical resources. You'll also find lots about *The Diaspora*, which refers to the spread of Africans around the world by slavery and other means. Now their descendants find themselves separated by geography, but joined by their cultural and historical roots. Prepare for a rich experience here!

http://www.gatech.edu/bgsa/blackpages.html

CULTURE

Melanet On-Line African Wedding Guide

Some couples are choosing to add touches of African culture to their wedding ceremonies. If someone in your family is getting married soon, make sure she or he sees this site. You'll find information on choosing African fabrics, using symbols, and incorporating African traditions into today's weddings.

http://www.melanet.com/melanet/wedding/

HISTORY

AFROAM-L Griot Online [Afrinet]

In Africa, a *griot* is a highly respected person who has memorized the history, culture, songs, lineages, and other details about a village or a people. In the same tradition, this site collects maps, text, pictures, and a timeline. Millions of Black people throughout the Caribbean, South America, and North America share a common history, which this site tries to retell in words and pictures.

http://www.afrinet.net/~griot/

Anacostia Museum Home Page

Did you know that February is "Black History Month?" This site will give you many examples of the contributions of African Americans to U.S. history and culture. You will discover online exhibits of inventions, art, music, and more. The museum is located in Washington, D.C.

http://www.si.edu/organiza/museums/anacost/
   homepage/anachome.htm

CNN Million Man March—Oct. 16, 1995

Nation of Islam leader, Louis Farrakhan called thousands of African American men to go to Washington, D.C. to make their voices heard. This historic event is chronicled here. CNN's site includes pointers to the "official" MMM site, but adds audio and video to the print record. Read many related stories, quotes, and support material such as biographies of some of the main participants.

http://www3.cnn.com/US/9510/megamarch/
   march.html

Selections from the African-American Mosaic

The Library of Congress is in Washington, D.C., and it has a huge collection of materials, some of which cover about 500 years of African history in the Western Hemisphere. They have books, periodicals, prints, photographs, music, film, and recorded sound. This exhibit samples these kinds of materials in four areas—Colonization, Abolition, Migrations, and the Work Projects Administration period. You'll be able to look at pages from original materials, such as an abolitionist children's book. Sometimes it's useful to look at these original materials, also called "primary sources," for yourself, rather than use books other people have written about these same sources. This way, you're closer to what really happened! Lots to use here for school reports!

http://lcweb.loc.gov/exhibits/African.American/
   intro.html

A B C D E F G H I J K L M N O P Q R S T U V W X Y Z

HISTORICAL FIGURES

These sites will give you short biographies of many important African Americans from the late 1700s to today. Many pictures are also available here.

African American Historical Figures

Twelve famous African American men and women from the nineteenth century.

http://www.webcom.com/~bright/source/
  blackfac.html

African American inventors, inventions, and patent dates

This is a list of some African American inventors and their patented inventions. These include a pencil sharpener, refrigeration equipment, elevator machinery, and railroad telegraphy discoveries.

http://www.ai.mit.edu/~isbell/HFh/black/
  events_and_people/009.aa_inventions

African American Online Exhibit Homepage

Profiles of significant African Americans in science, medicine, and technology developed by students at the University of California at Irvine. There's also a great timeline of events, inventions, and people, and you'll find educational opportunities and organizations in support of African Americans pursuing a career in the sciences.

http://pitcairn.lib.uci.edu/AA/AAhomepage.html

African Americans in the American Revolution

Read about Cyrus Bustill and Oliver Cromwell, of Burlington, New Jersey. Bustill, a baker, supplied American troops with baked goods during the Revolutionary War. His great-great grandson was Paul Robeson. Cromwell served in the war, and George Washington personally signed his discharge papers. Washington also designed a medal which was awarded to Cromwell. Read about the Oliver Cromwell Black History Society which operates today.

http://bc.emanon.net/hist/

Explore the past in ANCIENT CIVILIZATIONS.

NET FILES

In the famous painting by Da Vinci, what color are the Mona Lisa's eyes?

Answer: Brown. This painting is also known as La Gioconda, and you can read all about the woman in the picture at http://sunsite.unc.edu/wm/paint/auth/vinci/joconde/

The Faces of Science: African-Americans in the Sciences

This site gives you biographical information for about twenty African Americans who have made important contributions to science. The articles are well-documented, and their sources are cited. You can also see a selection of patents issued to some of these scientists.

http://www.lib.lsu.edu/lib/chem/display/faces.html

Dr. Mae C. Jemison

Dr. Jemison was the first African American woman in space.

http://www.gsu.edu/~usgacmx/jemison.html

Ronald E. McNair

Dr. McNair was mission specialist aboard the 1984 flight of the space shuttle Challenger.

http://128.32.252.18/Ronald_E._McNair.html

AMPHIBIANS

See also: PETS

Frogs and Other Amphibians

Ahh—the sweet singing of frogs in the springtime! But did you know that frogs are disappearing all over the world? This phenomenon has been linked to depletion of the ozone layer in the atmosphere. It lets too much ultraviolet light through, which harms the frogs. Recently, scientists have also discovered a connection between the health of frogs and a buildup of ozone in the lower atmosphere due to pollution. Watch your frogs carefully, everybody! They are important! Did you know that Australian tree frogs give off a chemical that helps heal sores when it's put on a person's skin? Doctors expect to find lots of other ways the chemical can be used. Stop by the Frogs and Other Amphibians page where you'll find additional links that lead to information about rainforest amphibians and Australian frogs. You'll even be able to make your way to the Interactive Frog Dissection Kit where you can test your knowledge of frog anatomy by playing the Virtual Frog Builder Game.

http://web.bu.edu/~ldaly/herps/frogs/index.html

FROGS AND TOADS

Froggy Page

Do you love frogs? Do you jump at playing a game of leapfrog? Would you leap at a chance to learn how to make an origami jumping frog? Want to meet some famous frogs and read froggy tales? This is the ultimate frog lover's site! Check out the frog jokes or visit the Cyberpond, home of Sue the Tadpole. Ribbit! Croak! Jugarum! Go to the Froggy page and hear all kinds of frogs singing.

http://www.cs.yale.edu/HTML/YALE/CS/HyPlans/
loosemore-sandra/froggy.html

Fly Air Internet in AVIATION.

The Interactive Frog Dissection

Did you ever wonder what's inside a frog? Now you can look for yourself. There's a special way to take animals apart to learn about them, and it's called dissection. Learn to identify the locations of a frog's major organs. Click on one button and watch movies of dissections. Click on another button and practice what you've learned. Only one frog had to lose its life for this Web page, and many dissections can be performed over and over, by kids all over the world.

http://curry.edschool.Virginia.EDU:80/~insttech/
frog/

SALAMANDERS AND NEWTS

Astro-newts home page

10, 9, 8, 7, 6, 5, 4, 3, 2, 1, BLAST OFF!! The space shuttle Columbia has lift-off, but some unusual passengers are on board. Four Japanese Newts, black and red-orange salamander-like creatures, are part of the Japanese "astro-newt" team and were in space for two weeks. Visit the Astro-newts home page and meet the extra-terrestrial travelers that are aiding in scientific research.

http://www.vetmed.vt.edu/0/Research/Newt/
newthome.html

AMUSEMENT PARKS

See also: DISNEY

Institute of Future Technology

If you've never had an opportunity to visit Universal Studios' world-famous theme park and production studio, here's your chance! An interactive tour of "Back to the Future: The Ride," Doc Brown's wild trip through time, will take you down into live volcanoes and bring you way too close to long-extinct dinosaurs! Hint: don't eat lunch before looking at this site!

http://www.univstudios.com/btf/index.html

A
B
C
D
E
F
G
H
I
J
K
L
M
N
O
P
Q
R
S
T
U
V
W
X
Y
Z

National Amusement Park Historical Association

Here's a group dedicated to saving old amusement parks, on the theory that a once-amusing ride can never, ever cease to be amusing. Read about the history of amusement parks and some of your favorite rides.

http://www.sgi.net/napha/

Paramount's Great America

This park, in northern California, has a lot going for it. It has the largest IMAX theater in the world, the largest and most expensive carousel in the world, and the only stand-up coaster west of the Mississippi. It also has award-winning roller coasters, such as the Top Gun—an inverted looping coaster—and our personal favorite, the Green Slime Mine Car Coaster!

http://tmb.extern.ucsd.edu/WOC/pga1/pga/index.htm

Santa Cruz Beach Boardwalk

The Santa Cruz Beach Boardwalk in Santa Cruz, California, lets you take a walk into America's past. Check the live videocam to see what the weather's like in Santa Cruz today. Maybe you'll see the classic 1911 Looff Carousel or the 1924 Giant Dipper roller coaster. If you are interested in going to Santa Cruz, you can plan your whole vacation (including hotel information) right from this page!

http://www.beachboardwalk.com/

Welcome to Huis ten Bosch

This is the largest theme park in Japan. For some reason, it's based on the theme of Holland, with its canals and historic buildings. Wander around and click on things—you may end up at a ride, a restaurant, or a palace!

http://www.bekkoame.or.jp/~suga/htbe1.html

CAROUSELS

1911 Looff Carousel Page

Along the Boardwalk in Santa Cruz, California, there's a National Historic Landmark. It's a hand-carved carousel, and you can read about its history here. See closeups of some of the horses, and download a QuickTime movie of the carousel in action.

http://www.beachboardwalk.com/looff.html

Carousel!

Everyone has seen carousel horses, but did you know there are also carousels with frogs, roosters, and fantastic creatures like sea monsters on them? Find out about the history of carousels, see some detailed wooden horses, and listen to carousel music—guaranteed to make you smile! This site tells you where antique carousels can still be found and ridden. They are something of a rare species, since many old carousels have been taken apart and the horses and other figures sold. Maybe you can help save an old carousel in your town!

http://www.access.digex.net/~rburgess/

ROLLER COASTERS

Roller Coasters and other Insanities

This is everything you did, and didn't, want to know about roller coasters. There are many different links to info on roller coasters, including coasters from other nations, books, and Usenet groups devoted to those twisty pieces of terror.

http://www.marketsmart.com/Coasters/

NET FILES

What planet would float if you could find a big enough pond to put it in?

Answer: Saturn is the lightest of all the planets. Since it's mostly made up of gas, it's actually lighter than water, and would float just like a beach ball. Read more at http://seds.lpl.arizona.edu/nineplanets/nineplanets/saturn.html

World of Coasters

It all starts innocently enough. You get into a little car, you slowly click-clatter-click-clatter up the track to the top of a HUGE DANGEROUS MOUNTAIN, when all of a sudden, you're at the top and the whole world is below you. It might be nice to be able to enjoy the view, but with a rush of wind, you're catapulted over the hill, screaming out your last breath, speeding towards certain doom at the bottom. You twist, you turn, you wish you had not eaten lunch. At last, the car slows and it's all over. You hear yourself yell, "AGAIN!" Roller coaster fans will love this page, complete with reviews of coasters all over the world. You'll also find frequently-asked questions, photos, statistics, and an overview of roller coaster history right here. This is a "no hands" Web site and remember, in cyberspace, no one can hear you scream!

http://tmb.extern.ucsd.edu/woc/

NET FILES

What did Nero, of ancient Rome, use to improve his viewing of the gladiators?

Answer: The Emperor was known to use a large emerald to give him a better view of "the games." Concave gemstones were discovered to be useful as a magnifying lense in ancient times. Beam over to http://www.duke.edu/~tj/hist/hist_mic.html to read more about the history of lenses and optics.

ANCIENT CIVILIZATIONS AND ARCHAEOLOGY

See also: HISTORY—ANCIENT HISTORY

ABZU

ABZU is a "guide to resources for the study of the Ancient Near East available on the Internet." This guide is based at the Oriental Institute in Chicago. Resources are indexed by author, directory, region, and subject. The resources also include online journals, online library catalogs, and museum collections online. Check out the 3-D models of the pyramids and the animated fly-throughs of the Palace of Ashurnasirpal II. Some of the other topics of interest to students include Alexander the Great, ancient Roman cooking, a list of Roman emperors, Pompeii, and the Vikings. Don't miss the illustrated history of ancient plumbing!

http://www-oi.uchicago.edu/OI/DEPT/RA/ABZU/
ABZU.HTML

The Ancient World Web: Main Index

This site is chock-full of links to information about the ancient world. Topics include ancient documents, architecture, and cooking. In addition, links are provided to information about geography, history, the history of science, military history, money, theater, towns, and cities. What a great surfing stop for students of ancient history!

http://atlantic.evsc.virginia.edu/julia/
AncientWorld.html

ArchNet: WWW Virtual Library—Archaeology

ArchNet, which is housed at the University of Connecticut, serves as the World Wide Web Virtual Library for archaeology. Access to archaeological resources available on the Internet is provided by geographic region and by subject. Searching can also be done by academic departments, museums, news, and other resources. This is a "don't miss" site for budding archaeologists! Indiana Jones probably stops here all the time.

http://spirit.lib.uconn.edu/ArchNet/ArchNet.html

A B C D E F G H I J K L M N O P Q R S T U V W X Y Z

Exploring Ancient World Cultures

Move the mouse, punch the buttons, and be prepared to enter a different world. Eight cultures from the past can help you to understand the cultural diversity of today. Go on a journey through time to visit the following ancient cultures: the Near East; India; Egypt; China; Greece; the Roman Empire; the Islamic World; and Medieval Europe. Although the text is very dense, you'll get a lot of information from the photos, and thoughtful links to other places on the net.

http://www.evansville.edu/~wcweb/wc101/

ANCIENT AMERICA

MesoAmerica

Who were the Mayans and the Aztecs, and what happened to their civilizations? This site tells you all about the history and cultures of these lost nations. The ancient Maya had an apparently healthy culture from around A.D. 250. They were masters of mathematics, building huge pyramids in the jungles of what is now Mexico and Central America. They had complex astronomical calendars and engineering for improving agriculture. During the ninth century, their civilization collapsed. No one knows exactly where they went or what happened to them. From this site, you can follow an expedition team called MayaQuest, searching the jungle for archaeological answers throughout 1995.

http://kira.pomona.claremont.edu/
  mesoamerica.html

Shawnee Minisink Site

How did people live 10,000 years ago? What did they eat? What were their houses like? This Web page features an archaeological dig in the Delaware Water Gap area near what is now the border of Pennsylvania and New Jersey. The dig, conducted by the American University Department of Anthropology, reveals the history of the region, exactly what was dug up, and how the artifacts were pieced together to show a picture of that time period's culture.

http://www.american.edu:70/l/academic.depts/
  cas/anthro/sms/sms.html

ANCIENT EUROPE

Flints and Stones

Do you have the "right stuff" to survive in Stone Age times? Meet the shaman, who will show you what life is like in his village of Ice Age hunters and gatherers. You'll also meet the archaeologist, who will show you how he interprets the lives of the village folk from the objects, art, and other signs they have left behind. Everyone thinks cave men were big hairy guys who carried clubs and dragged women around by the hair. This site explodes that myth, and others. You'll also be able to take a Stone Age food quiz—hmm, should you eat that mushroom or not? Caution: this machine, at the Museum of Antiquities, University of Newcastle upon Tyne, UK, appears to have a slow link. The site is well worth the wait, though.

http://www.ncl.ac.uk/~nantiq/menu.html

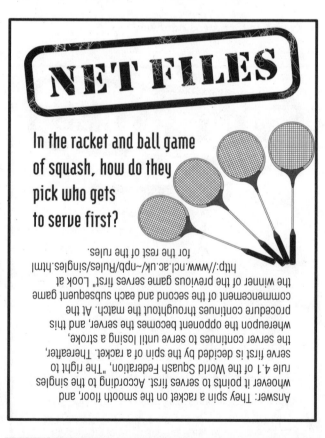

NET FILES

In the racket and ball game of squash, how do they pick who gets to serve first?

Answer: They spin a racket on the smooth floor, and whoever it points to serves first. According to the singles rule 4.1 of the World Squash Federation, "The right to serve first is decided by the spin of a racket. Thereafter, the server continues to serve until losing a stroke, whereupon the opponent becomes the server, and this procedure continues throughout the match. At the commencement of the second and each subsequent game the winner of the previous game serves first." Look at http://www.ncl.ac.uk/~npb/Rules/singles.html for the rest of the rules.

ANCIENT GREECE

Ancient City of Athens

This colorful site presents a photographic archive of the archaeological and architectural remains of ancient Athens, Greece. The owner of the Web page, Kevin Glowacki, is also one of the photographers. He gives rights to any students to use these images as long as the source is cited. The photographs are all GIF images and illustrate the topography and monuments of ancient Athens. Further details are given. This is a landmark site for any student studying ancient Greece. However, because there are a lot of color illustrations, be patient waiting for the page to load! It's well worth the wait!

http://www.indiana.edu/~kglowack/Athens/
  Athens.html

Perseus Project Home Page

The Perseus Project is "an evolving digital library on Ancient Greece" that is headquartered at the Classics Department of Tufts University. Art and archaeology information is offered as well as primary texts and Greek dictionaries. Included are pictures and descriptions of 523 coins, 1,420 vases, 179 sites, and 381 buildings. This is a "don't miss" site for anyone studying ancient Greece!

http://medusa.perseus.tufts.edu/

Time magazine's annual "Man of the Year" has also been a woman, or even an idea, from time to time. You're never going to guess who the first woman was. (Hint: a king loved her so much, he gave up his throne to marry her.

Answer: Wallis Warfield Simpson was Time's first "woman of the Year" for the year 1936. http://pathfinder.com/@@@jX*1VFB9AMAGF1Q/time/special/moy/1936.html.

ANCIENT ROME

ROMARCH List Home Page

Romarch, housed at the University of Michigan, is the home of Web resources about Roman art and archaeology from 1000 B.C. to 700 A.D.. General interest resources include central sources of information and images on society, culture, religion, law, and war. Resources that are especially good for students are marked. A geographic approach to the sources is available, but beware! You may accidentally stumble into a site in another language!

http://www-personal.umich.edu/~pfoss/
  ROMARCH.html

VIKINGS

The Viking Network Web

Experience the Viking way of life: raiding, trading, and exploration. This site is aimed at kids and teachers all over the world who are interested in Viking heritage and culture. You'll find some e-mail discussions to meet other kids interested in Vikings, too!

http://odin.nls.no/viking/vnethome.htm

ANTHROPOLOGY

UCSB Anthropology Cool Web Stuff

What's anthropology? Well, it's the study of families, cultures, and communities. That's called cultural anthropology. There's also physical anthropology, which includes archaeology. This colorful, well-designed page has unearthed many of the most interesting and important anthropological sites, and has annotated and organized them for easy accessibility. Here you'll find links described and cataloged in alphabetical order, by topical and geographical focus, and by departmental and museum sites. The museum sites are especially worth visiting.

http://www.sscf.ucsb.edu/anth/netinfo.html

A B C D E F G H I J K L M N O P Q R S T U V W X Y Z

AQUARIUMS

See also: FISH

Fish Information Service (FINS) Index

That little goldfish you bought has outgrown his bowl, so you're going to get him a new tank. Visit this archive of information about aquariums! It covers freshwater and marine, tropical and temperate fish tank culture. There's beginning to advanced information, especially on marine and reef tanks. Click on a picture to identify a fish and get more information, or use the glossary full of aquarium terms. Be sure to see the live video from a camera overlooking a garden pond, and check out the live "Fish Cam" activity at a saltwater tank in someone's office.

http://www.actwin.com/fish/index.html

The Florida Aquarium

WATCH OUT!!! Whew, didn't you see that stingray? You almost stepped on it! Because stingrays live in shallow offshore water, beach-goers often step on them by accident and get stung. Stingrays will lie partly buried in the sand, with only their eyes, spiracle, and tail exposed. Stingray stings are easy to avoid, though—just shuffle your feet as you wade. Learn more about stingrays and other creatures who inhabit Florida's waterways. Ask the Aquarium experts a question or check out one of many experiments and games available for kids of all ages.

http://www.sptimes.com/aquarium/Default.html

The Monterey Bay Aquarium Home Page

Did you ever wonder what it would be like to swim with fish, or even sharks? Would you dare feed them? Watch your hand, that shark looks hungry! Look at the sea otter pup—isn't it cute? Visit the Monterey Bay Aquarium Home Page and get a diver's-eye view of handfeeding the fish in the Kelp Forest tank. Watch the QuickTime movies as divers hand-feed various sharks, rockfishes, and eels that inhabit the underwater seaweed forests.

http://www.usw.nps.navy.mil/~millercw/aq/
  index.html

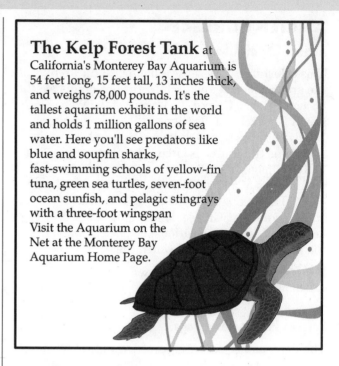

The Kelp Forest Tank at California's Monterey Bay Aquarium is 54 feet long, 15 feet tall, 13 inches thick, and weighs 78,000 pounds. It's the tallest aquarium exhibit in the world and holds 1 million gallons of sea water. Here you'll see predators like blue and soupfin sharks, fast-swimming schools of yellow-fin tuna, green sea turtles, seven-foot ocean sunfish, and pelagic stingrays with a three-foot wingspan Visit the Aquarium on the Net at the Monterey Bay Aquarium Home Page.

Sea World/Busch Gardens

Did you ever wish you could visit Sea World in either Florida, Ohio, Texas, or California? You can find out about all kinds of fish here, but also learn about parrots, polar bears, gorillas, lions, and more. Interested in setting up a tropical saltwater aquarium? This page tells you how to keep an aquarium as a hobby. Write, e-mail, or phone Shamu the Killer Whale to ask questions about the ocean and marine animals. Try your hand at the animal information quiz and receive a free animal information booklet. Check out the wide variety of educational programs and curriculum materials on endangered rain forests, ecosystems, and habitat. Surprise your grandmother with her very own pet coral reef—find out how to grow one at this site!

http://www.bev.net/education/SeaWorld/

Stars in your eyes? Try ASTRONOMY!

ARCHITECTURE

World Wide Web Virtual Library: Architecture

The resources here will guide you from the covered bridges of New Hampshire to the architecture of Islam. You'll find yourself looking at churches in Australia, contemporary buildings in Hong Kong, and Soleri's desert Arcosanti experiments. What a great way to experience many different architectural building styles all at once!

http://www.clr.toronto.edu:1080/VIRTUALLIB/ARCH/proj.html

BRIDGES

The Building of the Bay Bridge

The San Francisco-Oakland Bay Bridge opened to traffic in November, 1936. It was called "the greatest bridge in the world for the versatility of its engineering." This page contains the photos and text from a brochure printed in 1936, prepared by the U.S. Steel and Bay Bridges Educational Bureau. It's still a beauty of a bridge!

http://community.net/~jray/baybridg/baystart.htm

Covered Bridges

Why are some bridges covered? To avoid rot, according to Dr. McCain, who also says that the structures were once called "kissing bridges." Take the Northeastern Chester County Driving Tour and read about the renovation of Bartram's Bridge. Stop by the Covered Bridges page today and enjoy your virtual tour of the bridges of various counties in Pennsylvania, Oregon, and New Hampshire.

http://william-king.www.drexel.edu/top/bridge/cb1.html

Newton's Apple—Bridges

How do bridges stay up? London Bridge didn't. It was always falling down, falling down. What kind of bridge designs are there, anyway, and why would you pick one over another? If you're ready to build your very own bridge, better stop here first. Create a blueprint and model of your bridge before you begin construction. This *Newton's Apple* TV show will help!

http://ericir.syr.edu/Newton/Lessons/bridges.html

CASTLES AND PALACES

Castles on the Web

King Arthur, eat your heart out! If you want to know anything (and we mean anything) about castles, this is the page for you. You'll find Castle Tours, Castle of the Week, Castle Questions and Answers, the Castle Image Archive, and Castles for Sale. Maybe you can look up your family's ancestral castle. There's also a Glossary of Castle Terms so that even the novice castle lover can feel at home. Hey! Watch out for the... (splash) ...moat.

http://fox.nstn.ca/~tmonk/castle/castle.html

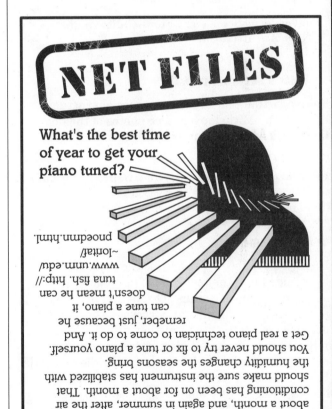

NET FILES

What's the best time of year to get your piano tuned?

Answer: According to the Piano Home Page, the best times are in the fall, after your furnace has been on for about a month, and again in summer, after the air conditioning has been on for about a month. That should make sure the instrument has stabilized with the humidity changes the seasons bring. You should never try to fix or tune a piano yourself. Get a real piano technician to come to do it. And remember, just because he can tune a piano, it doesn't mean he can tuna fish. http://www.unm.edu/~loritaf/pnoedmn.html.

ART is more than crayons and fingerpaint!

CHURCHES, MOSQUES, AND SYNAGOGUES

Dome of the Rock

Built in 692 A.D., the Dome of the Rock is one of the great monuments of the Muslim faith. The building looks like an enameled multicolored jewel, capped by a shining golden dome. The Dome protects and houses the Sacred Rock of Jerusalem sandstone at the summit of Mount Moriah. Muslims believe that the prophet Muhammad, guided by the archangel Gabriel, traveled to Jerusalem and rose to the presence of God from this Rock. The site is also sacred to other faiths, as it was formerly the location of the Temple of Solomon.

http://www.webcom.com/~zume/GallerySight/
   SN.Dome/Intro.html

St. Peter's Basilica, Rome, Italy

Take a virtual tour of this very special sanctuary, designed by Michelangelo. See photos of the domes, vaults, piazzas, and gardens at this multilingual site.

http://www.christusrex.org/www1/citta/0-Citta.html

GARGOYLES

Gargoyle Home Page

Have you ever seen a gargoyle? Gargoyles have been added into the roof lines of large buildings since the eleventh century. Originally, they were placed there for functional purposes—they helped drain water off the roof. But they also had symbolic religious significance. Today, gargoyles are still used as decorations on buildings. Tour the Gargoyle Home Page and find out more about the history and design of these little monsters. Be sure to keep an eye up as you walk down the street—you never know what may be looking back down at you!

http://ils.unc.edu/garg/garghp4.html

**Staring off into space?
Discover ASTRONOMY!**

GOVERNMENT AND PUBLIC BUILDINGS

Moscow Kremlin Online Excursion

The Kremlin is an architectural marvel located in Moscow, Russia. Its walled city is the site of Lenin's Tomb, Red Square, cathedrals, and many government buildings. Take a virtual tour and learn some fascinating facts about this complex.

http://www.kiae.su/www/wtr/kremlin/begin.html

Virtual Tour of the U.S. Capitol

This page lets you tour the U.S. Capitol in Washington, D.C. You can take a Guided Tour or explore using a Tour Map, which allows you to have control over what you visit. You'll learn the history of the building, too. On September 18, 1793, George Washington laid the first cornerstone for the Capitol. The dome is made of cast iron, and was erected during the Civil War. The pictures of the construction of the building are fascinating.

http://www.senate.gov/capitol/virtour.html

NET FILES

Do Fish Sleep?

Answer: According to Florida Aquarium, "Fishes don't sleep like we do, but reef fishes have active and inactive times. Some prefer days; others are active at night. The reef is like a motel with day guests who leave at dusk when night guests arrive." For more answers about fish and ocean life, check http://www.spitimes.com/Aquarium/FA.3.1.html

LIGHTHOUSES

Bill's Lighthouse Getaway

A foggy night, a ship is lost amid the black waves, shoals and rocks somewhere out ahead. Suddenly, the darkness is pierced by a friendly light in the distance. The lighthouse! Checking the navigational map, the ship's captain notes the location of the lighthouse on shore, and is able to steer clear of danger. Part of American lore and legend, lighthouses all over America can be visited via this home page. You'll find pictures and descriptions of lights from New England, through the Great Lakes, around the South Atlantic, to the West Coast. There are also links to Lighthouse Societies and something about the history of the fresnel lens, which produces the powerful light needed.

http://www.lib.utk.edu/lights/lights.html

The WWW Virtual Library: The World's Lighthouses, Lightships & Lifesaving Stations

Are there lighthouses all over the world? You bet—and this site will let you visit a lot of them. Learn all about the history of lighthouses and lightships from a real lighthouse keeper! Lightships are just that, very well-lighted ships, stationed at sea, guarding shoals and other navigational hazards.

http://www.maine.com/lights/www_vl.htm

TUNNELS

A Journey Through the Channel Tunnel

This is a tourist's-eye view of a trip through the tunnel under the English Channel. On December 20, 1994, the author traveled from London-Waterloo to Paris-Gare du Nord by Eurostar train, returning the same day. There are lots of pictures of the journey, as well.

http://www.elec.rdg.ac.uk/~stssjs/ctr.html

ARCHITECTURE, building blocks for grown-ups!

ART

Art Foundation of Michigan: Fresco Workshop

Do you know what a *fresco* is? It isn't a can of diet soda or a city in California. It's a form of artwork—and get this—painted right on the walls! Traditionally, plaster is poured in layers and is tinted as it dries. The end result is a lasting piece of art. The world's earliest known frescoes are the cave paintings of Lasceaux, France. They were made some 30,000 years ago—that's old! Historically, the technique was developed in Ancient Greece, and was incorporated into Minoan and Roman artwork. This series of pages takes you through the process step by step, as a group of people create a fresco of a playground scene.

http://www.tmn.com/Community/afmadams/fresco.html

The Art of Motion Control

Imagine having a robot that does your chores for you! How about a robot that cuts sheet metal or uses an airbrush? Artist Bruce Shapiro has designed a series of robotic tools that allow him to create artwork. He built an egg engraver, a plasma torch, and even an automated etch-a-sketch. With these tools, he makes metal sculpture, engravings, and more. See pictures of the tools and the artwork they've made. You can send Bruce e-mail—maybe he can build a robot that does your homework for you!

http://pluto.iaxs.net/bshapiro/

WWW Spirograph

Do you love to draw patterns? A mechanical toy that traces the path of one circle as it moves around another circle will draw complicated patterns for you. When your parents were kids, they had to draw these using toys that were actually geared tools. Their pens and gears were always slipping and it took forever to draw the final image. Now you can do it by typing in numbers and hitting the "Generate Image" button. Isn't technology wonderful?

http://juniper.tc.cornell.edu:8000/spiro/spiro.html

A
B
C
D
E
F
G
H
I
J
K
L
M
N
O
P
Q
R
S
T
U
V
W
X
Y
Z

CAVE ART

Discovery of a Palaeolithic painted cave at Vallon-Pont-d'Arc (Ardèche)

Admit it, you would love to draw all over the walls in your home. The only problem is that you would get in trouble. A long time ago, kids your age didn't have crayons or fingerpaint. In fact, ancient civilizations apparently encouraged drawing on the walls. At least 17,000 years ago, cave people drew all over this cave, and their artwork can still be seen today. These paintings were discovered by archaeologists in the Ardèche gorges of southern France. The photographs are gorgeous, too.

http://www.culture.fr/culture/gvpda-en.htm

CERAMICS

THE CRADLE OF KUTANI

Kutani is a very attractive form of Japanese pottery. The enameled vases look like jewels when they emerge from the kiln. The Kutani pages show the elaborate process that leads to a finished piece of ceramic art. You can view a map of Japan showing Terai-Machi (the cradle of Kutani) and see a picture of the tools of used in Kutaniware. Explore the history of the process and see examples of this beautiful art form.

http://www.njk.co.jp/kutani/

Virtual Ceramics Exhibit

What's the last thing you built with clay? What turns a piece of clay into art? The Virtual Ceramics Exhibit is an online art show for works in clay. Click on the pictures and read why the artists made the pieces. Warning: This site is very graphics-intensive and the pictures take a long time to load.

http://www.uky.edu/Artsource/vce/VCEhome.html

Wet or dry, give AMPHIBIANS a try!

DRAWING AND PAINTING

See Also: COLOR AND COLORING BOOKS

Kali

Math is fun! Kali is a geometry program written at the Geometry Center. It makes cool symmetrical patterns (suitable for framing or just coloring) based on your instructions, which are easily input through clicking on pictures and buttons.

http://www.geom.umn.edu/apps/kali/about.html

Sistine Chapel Tour

Have you ever been caught drawing on the wall? Can you imagine someone being paid to paint pictures on one? The ceiling of the Sistine Chapel in Rome, Italy is considered to be one of the most incredible works of art in human history. It was painted by Michelangelo in the 1500s. It took him many years to paint it. Take the tour, download the images, but please don't draw on the wall.

http://www.christusrex.org/www1/sistine/
   0-Tour.html

METAL AND JEWELRY CRAFT

ABANA Main Page

This is the home page of the Artist-Blacksmiths' Association of North America. Besides making common items, like nails and hooks, blacksmiths of long ago made ornate latches, gates, hinges, frames, handles, knobs, and more. Look at the "blacksmithing lessons" section to see some of the tools and how they are used today.

http://wuarchive.wustl.edu/edu/arts/blacksmithing/
   ABANA/

Gem of the Day™

Have you ever daydreamed about finding a hidden treasure? What would you buy if you had a million dollars? The Gem of the Day page features absolutely stunning jewelry. Although it isn't likely that you'll be wearing one of the selections to school, the gem of the day is a wonderful way to expose yourself to the finer things in life. Enjoy!

http://www.gemday.com/

There are over 37,500 works of art in the collection of the National Museum of American Art!

You can view over 500 artworks at its home page.

MUSEUMS

The American Museum of Papermaking

Young Roman students did their homework on wax tablets. Thanks to innovative thinking in China over 1,700 years ago, you turn your homework in on paper. By the time you are out of school, students will probably hand in their assignments on computer disks. The American Museum of Papermaking highlights the development of papermaking. From clay tablets to the modern paper mill, follow the winding history of paper. After all, without paper how would you make paper airplanes?

http://www.ipst.edu/amp/

Asian Arts

See the rich art of many cultures in this electronic journal devoted to Asian arts. You'll be linked to online museum exhibits, articles about new discoveries, and many graphics of traditional Asian art. Explore the different media that the artists used. Weavings, sculpture, metal engravings, masks, paintings, clay tablets, carvings, and more await you.

http://www.webart.com/asianart/index.html

Leonardo da Vinci Museum

You may know him as the inspiration for one of the Teenage Mutant Ninja Turtles. But the real Leonardo da Vinci didn't have a shell. Although famous for painting the Mona Lisa, he also designed a helicopter, a hang glider, a parachute, and several other contraptions that didn't actually get built until hundreds of years later.

http://www.leonardo.net/museum/main.html

National Museum of American Art home page

Look at all those paintings of yours that Mom has hung proudly on the refrigerator! One day you may become a famous American artist. Then your work would become part of a tradition of American art, and it might find a home in this museum. The museum boasts a grand collection of the best artwork produced by American artists. Which page will your artwork be on? Maybe the White House Collection of American Crafts, or part of the permanent collection? Browse these pages, and take a walk through history.

http://www.nmaa.si.edu/

Vatican Museum

The Vatican, an independent city-state, is located in Rome, Italy. It has its own postage stamps and souvenir coinage, but it is best known as being the worldwide center of Roman Catholicism. The head of the Catholic Church, the Pope, lives here. The world-famous Vatican Museums are here; the Popes have been collecting art since 1503, so there is a lot to see! If you go to the Vatican, you'll have to wait in line to get in, but here in the virtual museum, you can walk right in. View over 500 images of paintings, tapestries, and sculptures. The Sistine Chapel paintings are at *http://www.christusrex.org/www1/sistine/0-Tour.html*

http://www.christusrex.org/www1/splendors/splendors.html

Get to know some famous AFRICAN AMERICANS.

A B C D E F G H I J K L M N O P Q R S T U V W X Y Z

WebMuseum: Bienvenue! (Welcome from the curator)

Are you ready to treat yourself to the Louvre, in Paris, France? It's the most famous museum in the world! Browse through an incredible collection of famous paintings and other artwork. See the Mona Lisa, the most recognized piece of art in the world, or listen to some classical music in the auditorium. You can even take a mini-tour of Paris! The opening page of the WebMuseum includes a list of its mirror sites. Choose one close to you to provide a faster connection!

http://sunsite.unc.edu/louvre/

STAINED GLASS

The Chagall Windows

The Synagogue of the Hadassah-Hebrew University Medical Center, in Jerusalem, is lit by sunlight streaming through the world-famous Chagall Windows. Marc Chagall, the artist, worked on the project for two years. The Bible provided his main inspiration. The Chagall Windows represent the twelve sons of the Patriarch Jacob, from whom came the Twelve Tribes of Israel. Chagall's brilliantly colored windows also have floating figures of symbolic animals, fish, and flowers. See this beautiful example of stained glass art, without having to wait for a sunny day!

http://www1.huji.ac.il/md/chagall/chagall.html

NET FILES

What is a "Lama?"

Answer: An experienced and learned religious teacher. (Tibetans combine the words "la na me pa," meaning "insurpassable," plus "ma," meaning "mother." The combination means the compassion a mother has for her only child). http://www.fusebox.com/NYDG/glossary.html

TEXTILE ARTS

Textiles Through Time

What if there weren't any malls? Where would people go to buy their clothes? Throughout most of history, people have had to make their own clothes. This site links museum textile collections around the world. See hand-made fabrics, including clothing, quilts, ceremonial artifacts, and a whole lot more. There are links to the *Bayeux Tapestry*, Hmong needlework, and exquisite Japanese kimonos.

http://www.interlog.com/~gwhite/ttt/tttintro.html

Welcome to the World Wide Quilting Page

Of course you know what a quilt is, but do you know what goes into making one? Did you know that quilts can be computer-designed, watercolor-painted, tie-dyed, and even have pictures transferred onto them? The Quilting Page has a detailed "How to" section with every step of the process, from basic quilt design to advanced stitch technique. Peek in and see the shameful, losing quilt in the "Worst Quilt In The World Contest!"

http://ttsw.com/MainQuiltingPage.html

ASIAN AMERICANS

A. Magazine

"Inside Asian America" gives you a few articles from the print version of the magazine, as well as links to other Asian American sites on the Net. You'll find links to Asian music, newsgroups, and more! Explore this one with your parents—there is a lot here, you might get lost! This site is new, and promises to offer discussion areas in the future.

http://www.amagazine.com/

Know your ALPHABET? Now try someone else's!

CERN/ANU—Asian Studies WWW Virtual Library

Interested in the Pacific island of Tonga? Or maybe the country of Malaysia? Or perhaps Japan? Check this site for resources for school reports.

http://coombs.anu.edu.au/
WWWVL-AsianStudies.html

Kid's Window

This little window on things Japanese will bring a smile to your face. Learn several origami folded figures, select items from a Japanese restaurant menu, and hear some Japanese letters and words.

http://jw.stanford.edu/KIDS/kids_home.html

CULTURE
ASIAN ASTROLOGY

Find out about Chinese, Vietnamese, and Tibetan calendar and astrological systems here. There are also calendar conversion utilities and information on Asian divination. There is also an informative FAQ on *Feng Shui,* the art of locating buildings according to the most favorable geographic influences. Recently this practice has migrated to interior decoration. To find out whether you should relocate your bed or not, check here.

http://www.deltanet.com/users/wcassidy/
astroindex.html

Chinese Historical and Cultural Project, San Jose, CA, US

The Golden Dragon is reawakening! Discover how this 200-foot long historic creature appeared at Chinese festivals around the turn of the century. And now it's coming back! Have a look at the colorful modern photos as well as the historic photos and get a glimpse into Chinese history and culture. There are also complete lesson plans and materials for use in the award-winning Golden Legacy program.

http://www.dnai.com/~rutledge/CHCP_home.html

It never rains in cyberspace.

Hmong Textiles

The Hmong people of Vietnam and Laos have a language, but it is a spoken language, not a written one. So, their culture passes down its stories by telling them orally, or by telling them in cloths. Here are some cloths made by Hmong Americans and native Hmongs. What stories might they be telling?

http://www.lib.uci.edu/sea/hmong.html

WWW Hmong Homepage

The Hmong come from China, Thailand, and Laos. This is a collection of resources relating to the history, culture, and language of the Hmong people, many of whom have emigrated to the U.S. Check the photographic archives and the news links to read current information about the Hmong.

http://www.stolaf.edu/people/cdr/hmong/

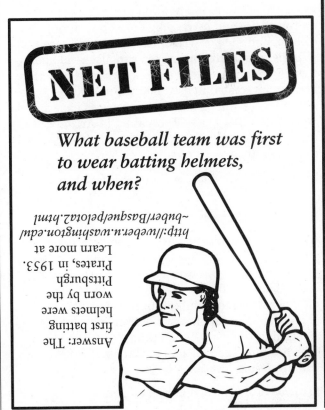

NET FILES

What baseball team was first to wear batting helmets, and when?

Answer: The first batting helmets were worn by the Pittsburgh Pirates, in 1953. Learn more at http://weber.u.washington.edu/~buber/Basque/pelota2.html

A
B
C
D
E
F
G
H
I
J
K
L
M
N
O
P
Q
R
S
T
U
V
W
X
Y
Z

ASTRONOMY, SPACE, AND SPACE EXPLORATION

The Astronomical Society of the Pacific

So, you think you might be interested in astronomy? Well, things are looking up! The Astronomical Society of the Pacific is here to help. This organization has been serving astronomers for over 106 years. They publish *The Mercury,* a monthly magazine, and *The Universe in the Classroom,* a free quarterly newsletter for teachers. Of course, there's also loads of information for astronomers here on their Web site.

http://www.physics.sfsu.edu/asp/asp.html

Dr. Odenwald's Guide Book to Astronomy

Do you have what it takes to be an astronomer? Do you have the same interests and curiosities that astronomers have? If you read this guide, you might just find the answers right here. Dr. Sten Odenwald starts by telling you about his childhood development and how a TV show sparked his own interests. He tells you how his knowledge of mathematics and astronomy developed through college, and then describes his career as a research scientist and astronomer. You can also read about the experiences of other astronomers and how they became interested in astronomy. Finally, the author takes you on a series of research experiences such as the Kitt Peak Observatory in Arizona. He describes his arrival at the sites, and about the experiments he performed while there.

http://www2.ari.net/home/odenwald/guide.html

Naked Eye Astronomy

If you're serious about learning about astronomy, you should read this introductory essay. It will give you older kids a good perspective on what astronomy is all about. It starts with the concepts of time and distance, which are important if you want to learn about the whys and hows of astronomy. If there's something you don't understand, try reading it with an adult, and then explain it to them. I'm sure they will appreciate it. ;-)

http://www.astro.washington.edu/strobel/
  naked-eye/naked-eye.html

SKYWATCHER'S DIARY

Are you interested in astronomy, but don't know where to look? Would you like to know what interesting events are happening in the night sky? Check out the Skywatcher's Diary for a day-by-day list of what to look for, and where to look for it. The list is updated each month and includes an archive of past diaries. Check out the archive near the end of the month to take a peek at next month's diary.

http://www.pa.msu.edu/abrams/diary.html

Space Calendar (JPL)

Keep this calendar on hand if you like to keep up with what's happening in space. If you check out June 27, 1996, you'll see that the Space Shuttle Columbia is scheduled to launch on flight mission STS-78. The astronauts will be performing microgravity experiments during the flight. The calendar also lists anniversaries of past space events, along with upcoming earthly meetings and conventions of space-related activities.

http://NewProducts.jpl.nasa.gov/calendar/

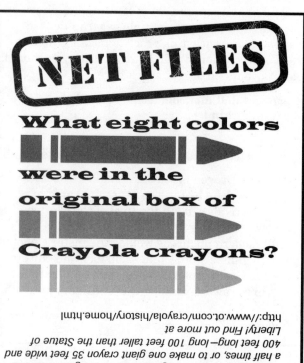

NET FILES

What eight colors were in the original box of Crayola crayons?

Answer: Black, brown, blue, red, purple, orange, yellow, and green.

Binney & Smith, maker of Crayola products, produces more than two billion crayons each year, an average of five million daily. That's enough to encircle the globe four and a half times, or to make one giant crayon 35 feet wide and 400 feet long—long 100 feet taller than the Statue of Liberty! Find out more at

http://www.crayola.com/crayola/history/home.html

Space Environment Laboratory

Check out today's space weather! Here's a partial listing for October 31, 1995: THE GEOMAGNETIC FIELD SHOULD REMAIN DISTURBED FOR THE NEXT THREE DAYS. GENERALLY ACTIVE TO MINOR STORM CONDITIONS ARE FORECAST. PERIODS OF MAJOR STORMING ARE EXPECTED FOR HIGH LATITUDES. ENERGETIC ELECTRON FLUXES AT GEOSYNCHRONOUS ORBIT SHOULD INCREASE TO HIGH LEVELS LATE ON 31 OCT.

Not exactly what you might hear on TV, but it's how the weather in space is described by the scientists that study it. You'll also find images of the Sun and charts showing how strong x-rays from space are today. Don't forget to wear your shades!

http://www.sel.bldrdoc.gov

The StarChild Project: Connecting NASA and the K12 Classroom

This is a wonderful beginner's guide to astronomy. It's written for smaller children and presents itself in an easy-to-read text. There are sections on general astronomy, Earth, planets, stars, galaxies, the Sun, and more. Use these pages to introduce a child (or brother or sister) to the wonders of space. You may even learn some new stuff yourself.

http://guinan.gsfc.nasa.gov/K12/StarChild.html

AURORA BOREALIS
The Aurora Page

Shimmering curtains of light in the night sky—it's the *Aurora Borealis*! Find out about Aurora Borealis sightings and forecasts. Various Aurora maps and images are here, including images taken from the Space Shuttle. Ever heard the Northern Lights? They also make sounds! Learn all about the theories on why this happens. There's even a survey for those lucky people who have "heard" one.

http://www.geo.mtu.edu/weather/aurora/

Try actual reality.

COMETS
Comet Introduction

Comets are just one of the "little guys" in our space neighborhood that turn up now and then to give us a show. They're made up of rock particles and frozen gases—it's cold out there in space! They orbit around the sun, but instead of traveling in a circle, like planets, their orbit takes them real close to the sun, then very, very far away. The show starts when they get close enough to the sun for their frozen gases to start to "boil" away. These boiling gases are part of what forms the bright tail that blazes across the sky. Find out more about comets, and look at pictures of some our recent visitors, including Comet West, Comet Shoemaker-Levy 9, Halley's Comet, and others.

http://bang.lanl.gov/solarsys/comet.htm

Comet Shoemaker-Levy Home Page (JPL)

For centuries, comets have been well known by the astronomers that scan the night skies, searching for their mysteries. Gene and Carolyn Shoemaker and David Levy spotted something on March 24, 1993 that was to become a major event. The comet they identified was found to have an orbit around Jupiter. Only this time, it was on a collision course! The fragmented comet, P/Shoemaker-Levy 9, after intense observation and study, collided with Jupiter between July 16 and 24, 1994. It took over a week for all the fragments to reach the planet, but provided a light show for anyone with a strong enough telescope pointed in the right direction. See the results here!

http://NewProducts.jpl.nasa.gov/sl9/

ECLIPSES
Educator's Guide to Eclipses

Have you ever seen an eclipse? It's certainly an eerie event. It takes the Moon, the Sun, and Earth to make an eclipse. A solar eclipse happens when the Moon gets between Earth and the Sun, and casts a shadow on Earth. A lunar eclipse happens when Earth gets between the Moon and the Sun, and casts a shadow on the Moon. All three objects have to be lined up just right in the sky for this to happen. Read about eclipses and discover the special words astronomers use to describe the event.

http://www.c3.lanl.gov/~cjhamil/SolarSystem/edu/eclipses.htm

A B C D E F G H I J K L M N O P Q R S T U V W X Y Z

May 10th, 1994 Eclipse

It was a dark day in New Mexico on May 10, 1984. No, the weather wasn't bad; there was a total solar eclipse! Scientists and astronomers traveled there from all over the world, just to get a good look. To see the rare event that caused all this excitement, check out this site!

http://www.ngdc.noaa.gov/stp/ECLIPSE/eclipse.html

PLANETARIUMS

Adler Planetarium & Astronomy Museum Home Page

The Adler Planetarium, in Chicago, opened in 1930 and was the first planetarium to open in the Western Hemisphere. This is a well-done page that tells you about the available shows and what's on exhibit. Read about their upcoming events and programs. If you're ever in the area, be sure to pay them a visit.

http://astro.uchicago.edu/adler/

Loch Ness Productions: Planetarium Web Sites

Have you ever been to a planetarium show? You sink back in your seat, the lights go down, and the stars come out across the domed ceiling of the planetarium. It's a special treat, each and every time you go. Here is a list of planetariums around the world, sorted by location. Find the planetarium closest to you to see what shows are available. If you're going on a trip, check out the schedule of a planetarium near your destination. Enjoy the show.

http://www.lochness.com//pltweb.html

SOLAR SYSTEM AND PLANETS

Mars Atlas home page

Fasten your seat belts. The Mars shuttle will be leaving just as soon as you get the courage to start clicking! You'll soon be served with a map of Mars that you can click to zoom in. Then move around by selecting directional arrows. You can either pack a lunch, or just go to the fridge if you get hungry. Stay as long as you like. Hint: the actual map link is down further on the page in the section labeled "To Get Started."

http://ic-www.arc.nasa.gov/ic/projects/bayes-group/
  Atlas/Mars/

The Nine Planets

Here's a place with pictures of all the planets and their moons, and much, much more. How did they get their names? Find out what planets are made of, which are most dense, brightest in the sky, and more. Many of the words are linked to a glossary that will tell you what they mean. Just click on a highlighted word for an explanation. Also find out which planets have the best prospects for having life on them. Earth is listed first!

http://seds.lpl.arizona.edu/nineplanets/nineplanets/
  nineplanets.html

NET FILES

On the Internet, nobody knows you're a frog. Craving some "Bee Grubs in Coconut Cream"? Where on Earth can a frog find a cookbook?

Answer: At the Froggy home page, of course! "Marinate bee grubs, sliced onions, and citrus leaves in coconut cream containing some pepper. Wrap in pieces of linen and steam. Serve as a topping for rice." It doesn't suggest where a frog might get some linen, though. http://www.cs.yale.edu/HTML/YALE/CS/HyPlans/loosemore-sandra/froggy/recipes.html

Primer on the Solar Space Environment

How well do you know our nearest star? Have you ever wondered how long the Sun will last before it burns out? How big are sunspots? Are they bigger than your school? Visit this site for a comprehensive description of the Sun as an energy source and its effects on life on Earth.

http://www.sel.bldrdoc.gov/primer/primer.html

Solar System Live

This is Solar System Live, and they mean it! You can tell the computer to draw a picture of the solar system almost any way you'd like it. You can even see what it looked like in the past, or what it will look like some time in the future, by giving it that date. If you're adventurous, you can even get a stereo view, but you need to train yourself how to look at the twin pictures. Now, this may take a bit of practice, or some help from someone older, but it's worth it. You can even include a comet to discover how it travels through the solar system on its long journey.

http://www.fourmilab.ch/solar/solar.html

Sun

It's big, it's hot, it's the brightest thing around. No, we're not talking about glow-in-the-dark Slime. We're talking about our very own star, the Sun. The Sun makes plants grow and keeps us warm. It's over 4.6 billion years old and is big enough to hold 1.3 million Earths. Read all about what it's made of and how it works.

http://www.c3.lanl.gov/~cjhamil/SolarSystem/sun.html

For happy hedgehogs see PETS AND PET CARE.

The Sun

It's pretty hot stuff! At 15 million degrees Kelvin at its center, the Sun is the source of energy for all life on Earth. Each second, the Sun burns enough fuel to produce 386 billion-billion megawatts of energy. That's a lot of light bulbs! But don't worry, it has enough fuel to burn another five billion years. There are many more interesting facts here to discover about the Sun.

http://seds.lpl.arizona.edu/nineplanets/nineplanets/sol.html

Views Of the Solar System

What do you think of when you hear the word "Mars"? Mars, ahh yes, one of my favorite candy bars. How about "Pluto"? Hey, that's Mickey's pet dog! "Saturn"? My dad's got one of those in the garage! OK, now, what do they all have in common? They're all planets, of course! Did you know there are volcanoes on Mars, and that the biggest is fifteen miles high (the biggest one on Earth is only six miles high). Or did you know that, at least until 1999, Pluto is closer to the sun than Neptune? Scientists also think that Pluto's atmosphere freezes and falls to the ground when it gets further away from the sun! Imagine shoveling clouds off your front walk! Did you know that you can drive a Saturn, but you can't make it sink? At least not the planet—it floats! There's lots more here, including many images and animations of planets, comets, and asteroids.

http://bang.lanl.gov/solarsys/

Welcome to the Planets™

This collection centers on images taken from NASA's planetary exploration program. There are different annotated views of each planet, including close-ups. You'll also find pictures and facts about the spacecraft NASA used to take these photos, including Mariner, Viking, Voyager, Magellan, Galileo, and the Hubble Space Telescope.

http://stardust.jpl.nasa.gov/planets/

A B C D E F G H I J K L M N O P Q R S T U V W X Y Z

SPACE EXPLORATION AND ASTRONAUTS

History of Space Exploration

Humans have been observing the stars for hundreds of years. It wasn't until 1959, with Luna 1, that we were able to actually break away from the gravity of Earth to visit another heavenly body—the Moon. In 1968, Apollo 8 made the first manned space flight around the Moon. Read about all the other spacecraft that we have launched in our quest for knowledge about our universe.

http://www.c3.lanl.gov/~cjhamil/SolarSystem/
history.html

Jim Lovell and the Flight of Apollo 13

This is a brief biography of astronaut Jim Lovell, from his childhood through to his retirement. Read about how his interest in rocketry developed into a love for flying and space travel. Jim's most famous mission was the ill-fated Apollo 13 flight to the Moon. This disastrous flight ended up with the crew "escaping" back to Earth by way of the lunar module that was supposed to land on the Moon. There are various links included that explain more about some of the terms used in the story.

http://www.mcn.org/Apollo13/Home.html

Space FAQ 12/13—How to Become an Astronaut

Being an astronaut must be a cool job. But how do you get to be one? Getting a Ph.D. and being a flight pilot are two very important qualifications for becoming an astronaut. Good eyesight and excellent physical condition are also a must. Also, don't be shy; astronauts need to be able to speak to the public. This page tells you all about how to impress NASA to get a job with them as an astronaut.

http://www.cis.ohio-state.edu/hypertext/faq/
usenet/space/astronaut/faq.html

Space Shuttle Clickable Map

Isn't it amazing how much stuff we recycle these days, when we used to throw it away? NASA is doing the same thing with their Space Shuttle. They recycle the booster rockets after they fall into the ocean, and fly the main cabin and cargo bay back to use again and again. This page has a clickable picture of a Space Shuttle that will take you on a descriptive tour of its different parts. Explore the Shuttle and find out what makes it click, er, tick.

http://seds.lpl.arizona.edu/ssa/space.shuttle/docs/
homepage.html

Space Shuttle Launches

Here's the official schedule for all upcoming Space Shuttle launches. It also describes each of the past flights. Find out about the crew and cargo for each of the missions. There are also descriptions of the scientific experiments the astronauts performed while in space. Some of these experiments include studying the growth of crystals in microgravity, and the effects of gravity on the growth of newt eggs (flight STS-65).

http://www.ksc.nasa.gov/shuttle/missions/
missions.html

The Ultimate Field Trip—Section 1

Here's a field trip that you're unlikely to forget. Astronaut Kathy Sullivan is your host and guide on this incredible journey. She tells you about her decision to switch careers from marine biologist to astronaut. As she talks about her experiences as Mission Specialist aboard the Space Shuttle, she guides you on a tour of Earth photos taken from the Shuttle. Kathy describes each photo in her own personal way, which gives the you a special insight into her own experience.

http://ersaf.jsc.nasa.gov/uft/uft1.html

Whooooooo will you find in BIRDS?

Read any good Web sites lately?

SPACE PHOTOS AND IMAGES

ASP List of NCG Images

Here is a list of space images, many of them with descriptions and sky locations. This collection includes images from the Hubble Space Telescope and observatories from around the world. Browse away and discover the wonders that exist out in the Universe!

http://www.physics.sfsu.edu/asp/ngc.html

Astronomy Picture of the Day

Today, there's a Hubble Telescope image of NGC 4261, a neighboring galaxy that has a giant black hole at its center. It says tomorrow there will be a picture called "24 hours from Jupiter." Guess we'll have to return tomorrow to see that one. They also have an archive of images that goes back to June 16, 1995.

http://antwrp.gsfc.nasa.gov/apod/astropix.html

Chesley Bonestell Gallery

Did you ever watch old Hollywood movies about outer space? You know, the ones where the rockets look like firecrackers! Since humans hadn't even started to explore space yet, the moviemakers had to rely on imagination when they wanted to show the surface of an alien planet! Most of those outer space scenes were actually filmed against painted backdrops. To film Martians in their natural habitat, movie directors dressed actors in silly costumes and plopped them in front of the paintings of Chesley Bonestell. His work wasn't just a great backdrop for 1930s movies...it helped shape the way scientists design spacesuits and rocket ships.

http://www.secapl.com/bonestell/Top.html

JSC Digital Image Collection

So many pictures, too little time! This is the Johnson Space Center's collection of space images taken from various space missions. Over 10,000 press release images and 300,000 Earth observation images are available. There are pictures here from the first Mercury flight to the latest Space Shuttle mission. If you know your latitude and longitude, you might be able to find a space photo of where you live here. (You can get your latitude and longitude for most places in the U.S. at the How Far Is It? page at *http://www.indo.com/distance/* if you want to check.)

http://images.jsc.nasa.gov/

SEDS Messier Database

This would definitely make E.T. feel homesick: 110 images of the brightest, most beautiful objects in the night skies. This is the Messier Catalog of star clusters, galaxies, and nebulae. Charles Messier started this catalog in the Eighteenth Century as a collection of objects that were most often mistaken for comets. It serves as an excellent reference list for both beginners and seasoned astronomers. You'll also find the celestial position for each object, which will help you locate it in the sky.

http://seds.lpl.arizona.edu/messier/Messier.html

STARS AND CONSTELLATIONS

Milky Way Description

Did you know that they named a galaxy after a candy bar? Or was it the other way around? Anyway, our Earth is part of the solar system that centers around the Sun, our closest star. Our sun is only one of a few hundred billion stars that make up the Milky Way Galaxy. And if you think that's big, the Milky Way (the galaxy, not the candy bar) is only one of millions of galaxies in the universe.

http://www.astro.washington.edu/strobel/
milkyway.description/milkyway.description.html

SLIME is a polymer, as anyone who's read CHEMISTRY knows!

Curl up with a good Internet site.

Out of This World Exhibition

You may have heard the names of some of the star constellations before. There's the Big Dipper, Taurus the Bull, and Aquarius, to name a few. You may have even seen their figures drawn along with the stars that form them. Probably not like the figures you'll find here! These pages are filled with etchings and drawings of star charts and maps from hundreds of years ago. They show the constellations drawn with detailed figures and objects. Early astronomers might not have had the fancy instruments we have now, but they sure had imagination!

http://www.lhl.lib.mo.us/pubserv/hos/stars/
   welcome.htm

The Universe in the Classroom, Spring 1986

Can you imagine weighing 10,000 tons? That's how much you would weigh if you were able to stand on one of our neighboring stars, Sirius B. Although this star is only about the size of our Earth, it weighs almost as much as our own Sun. That tremendous weight is what gives it such strong gravity. Our Sun is over 300 times brighter than Sirius B. However, Sirius A, its twin, is twice as big as our sun. It would look over twenty times brighter if it were in the same spot as our Sun. If these facts sound interesting, there's lots more here about these, and other, stars that share our corner of the universe.

http://www.physics.sfsu.edu/asp/tnl/05/05.html

TELESCOPES AND OBSERVATORIES

Binoculars and Telescopes

Have you always thought that you needed a telescope to look at the stars? Did you know that binoculars work just fine to help you find thousands of objects in the night sky that you can't see with just your eyes? It's a good way to get started in stargazing. Read this page to find out more about using binoculars, and learn how to choose a telescope.

http://www.cnde.iastate.edu/staff/jtroeger/
   binoc.html

HST Greatest Hits 1990-1995 Gallery

They say on a clear day, you can see forever. However, astronomers would rather do without the air, no matter how clear. Light waves get distorted as they travel through the air and it's hard to get a good picture when you're trying to see very far away. That's the idea behind the Hubble Space Telescope. With a powerful telescope in orbit above the atmosphere, scientists can get a much better picture of our universe. The images are sent back to earth electronically. This way they are not affected by the atmosphere. Be sure to check out their greatest hits!

http://www.stsci.edu/pubinfo/BestOfHST95.html

Telescopes

Read all about reflecting, refracting, parabolic mirrors, and spherical aberration. These are some of the definitions used to describe telescope features and how they are made. Telescopes need to magnify light from weak, distant sources and make the images visible to the observer. There's a lot more available on astronomy if you click on "Return to lecture notes homepage" at the bottom of the page.

http://www.astro.washington.edu/strobel/
   telescopes/telescopes.html

UNIVERSE

The Universe

What do you think of when you hear someone say the words "big bang"? You probably think that they are talking about fireworks on the Fourth of July! Astronomers use the phrase "big bang" to talk about the most popular theory of how the universe began—with a Big Bang! Read on to get an explanation of how it all started around 20 billion years ago. If you want to learn more, then you're well on your way to becoming an astrophysicist (someone who studies the universe).

http://www.ast.cam.ac.uk/RGO/leaflets/cosmology/
   cosmology.html

Crack open CODES AND CIPHERS.

Computers are dumb;
People are smart.

The Universe in the Classroom, Summer, 1993

You can check in, but you can't check out! As far back as 1793, astronomer Rev. John Mitchell reasoned that if something were big enough, its gravity would be so strong that even light could not escape. Since then, Einstein's Theory of Relativity has helped explain how this is possible. These objects are now called black holes. Some scientists think that black holes are formed from stars that collapse into themselves when they burn out. Well, that's hard to imagine, but we're finding out more and more about black holes all the time. Maybe you'll be the one who makes a big discovery someday about the mystery of black holes.

http://www.physics.sfsu.edu/asp/tnl/24/24.html

AVIATION AND AIRPLANES

Airport Information

Type in the three-letter airport code for the airport you want and you'll get detailed information back. If you don't know the code, you can just type in the name of the nearest city. You can try to look for nearby balloonports, gliderports, heliports, seaplane bases—pretty much everything but a starship dock! You'll get back a map of the airport, its radio frequencies, runway descriptions, yearly traffic statistics, and more. It will also list obstructions in the general area, such as tall radio towers or buildings. You'll also find out if there are sometimes migratory birds or animals on the runways.

http://www.cc.gatech.edu/db1/fly/airport-info.html

Aviation Enthusiast Corner

Whoa! Did you see that precision flying team, the U.S. Air Force Thunderbirds? Those F-16 Fighting Falcons sure do put on a great airshow! Want to learn more about this drill team in the skies, and see when they will be coming to your area? Check this Web site! You'll also find the schedules of lots of other air show performers, plus specifications on lots of different types of aircraft. There are also links to aircraft manufacturers and aviation museums.

http://146.245.2.151/rec/air/air.html

NET FILES

In the Chinese calendar, when is the Waking of Insects?

http://bronze.ucs.indiana.edu:80/~hyuan/newyear.html

Answer: It's from the fifth or sixth of March, as the earth awakes from hibernation, according to the Chinese New Year page at

The First General Aviation WWW Server

What in the world is a flight plan? Well, just like you should map out your summer vacation road trip, you should prepare for the best route of flight before taking off. A flight plan will include items such as departure and destination airports, navigation aids, fuel consumption rates, and wind information. This will aid in a safer flight for all. You can download software to assist with flight planning, or if you'd rather, you can stay on the ground and use the flight simulator games available here. Make your reservations now!

http://aviation.jsc.nasa.gov/

FLIGHT

Look, it's a bird! No, it's a plane! In fact, it's a whole bunch of things that fly. From the Montgolfier Brothers' hot air balloon (built in 1783) to the world's largest passenger airplane, the Boeing 747, you'll discover it here. You'll learn the history of flight and the people and technology behind it. Caution: this page is graphics-rich.

http://smdg2.nmsi.ac.uk/collexh/

National Air & Space Museum Home Page

See pictures and learn about milestones in aviation, such as the *Spirit of St. Louis*. This plane was built for Charles Lindbergh, one of the most famous pilots in history. In it, he was the first to cross the Atlantic alone. He took off from Roosevelt Field, in New York State, early on the morning of May 20, 1927. After thirty-three and a half hours, Lindbergh landed at Le Bourget Field, near Paris, welcomed by a cheering crowd. This was the first solo crossing of a major ocean by air, and it was a Very Big Deal at the time. Come in for a landing at this online museum, where you'll also see famous spacecraft and even a real moon rock! The National Air and Space Museum is part of the Smithsonian Institution, and it is located in Washington, D.C.

http://www.nasm.edu/

Tom's Home Page—The Airport

Wow—you're taking a flight lesson! The weather is nice, but there are winds from 15 to 20 MPH! That means plenty of practice with crosswinds. Yikes, too crooked, better go around! What's it take to be a pilot anyway? Read the diary of a student pilot and find out!

http://www.wolfe.net/~tegwilym/airport.html

Welcome to the Information Skyway™

Any airline with a Web page is collected here! Cruise links to all the big airlines (Delta, United, TWA, British Airways) plus check out the little ones. You'll find Tigerfly, the UK-based "world's smallest airline." Lots of airline statistics here too, like how much airlines spend per passenger on food, and current monthly statistics about which airlines generally took off and landed on time. Beware, though, this is a graphics-heavy site! You may want to try its "lite" version at *http://haas.berkeley.edu/~seidel/airline.html*.

http://w3.one.net/~flypba/AIRLINES/carc.html

See what's shakin' in EARTH SCIENCE-GEOLOGY-EARTHQUAKES.

Watch your step in DANCE.

BALLOONING

Morris's Ballooning Info Page

Up, up and away! Look at all the beautiful balloons. This is the place to go to discover the wonderful world of ballooning. You'll learn about the Kodak Albuquerque International Balloon Fiesta, the largest ballooning event in the world. You'll meet the pilots and crew of Serenity, a balloon based in Fort Collins, Colorado. Want to buy a used balloon? There's a resource here for that, too.

http://www.unm.edu/~mbas/BALLOON.HTML

NET FILES

"I hate it when he barneys it! I wish he'd get a case of Kodak courage!" Huh? Where might you hear these comments?

Answer: You just might hear these expressions on the ski slopes with some snowboarders. Snow boarders have just about created their own language! A rough translation is: "I hate it when he goes over the jump too slowly, and flattens it! Maybe he'll get braver if there's a camera around!" Meanwhile, the sport of snowboarding is growing, and gaining in recognition. Find out how to do it, and how to "speak" it, at http://www.jyu.fi/snw/.

BIOLOGY

The Heart: A Virtual Exploration

The heart is more than just a symbol for Valentine's Day. It's the pump that keeps your life's blood flowing throughout your body. Your blood distributes food to your cells and carries away the waste. Since it can't move on its own, it would be quite useless without the heart to keep it moving. Visit this page to read about the heart and all its functions.

http://sln.fi.edu/biosci/heart.html

Kids Web—Biology and Life Sciences

Biology is the study of life, and life is everywhere. Mammals, insects, dinosaurs, and frogs are all examples of life forms. Each includes part of the exciting field of biology. YOU are a life form too, and biology means studying how you work as well. If you want to learn more about life and biology, take a look here. You'll see pointers to biology information from all over the Internet.

http://www.npac.syr.edu/textbook/kidsweb/
biology.html

MICROSCOPES

Early History of the Lens

Sure, we could *tell* you all about the person who first thought of using a lens to magnify things. Or when eyeglasses came into vogue—earlier than you might think! Or about the dude who later invented the microscope. But wouldn't you rather check it out *yourself*? Lots of pictures and fascinating facts about early optics and scientists are here for you to explore.

http://www.duke.edu/~tj/hist/c1.html

Microscapes: Images From the Microscope

Yoo-hoo! I'm right down here. Right under your nose. No, silly, not on the floor! Under the microscope. Take a look at me and a bunch of other images on the Microscapes page. Find out how to set up a microscope. Honey, I blew up the cells!

http://micro.magnet.fsu.edu/

If you want to visit another world without leaving home, check out Microscapes: Images From the Microscope.

Microscopy

There's a great little diagram here with all the parts of a microscope, and links to info on lenses, electron microscopy, and more.

http://www.chem.vt.edu/chem-ed/microscopy/
microscopy.html

BIRDS

See also: FARMING AND AGRICULTURE—POULTRY, PETS AND PET CARE

The Aviary

Here's where you should join the flock for a large variety of information about birds. Whether you own a companion bird, or enjoy watching wild birds, this home page is a gathering place and resource center for all bird lovers. You'll find information about bird illness, how to keep your bird safe, and food and nutrition tips. You'll discover the importance of toys for your pet bird, and learn about wild bird rescue. Fly on over and ask an avian vet a question about your pet bird today.

http://www.master.net/aviary/

The Sun never sets on the Internet.

A B C D E F G H I J K L M N O P Q R S T U V W X Y Z

Common Birds of the Australian National Botanic Gardens

It's such a nice day for a walk in the garden. What beautiful birds! And listen—their songs are so pretty. The Australian National Botanic Gardens are so peaceful, it almost feels as if you are actually there. Watch out, though. During the spring breeding season, male magpies protect their territory by "swooping" intruders; a painful experience for those unlucky enough to be hit. Did you know that the tongue of the New Holland Honeyeater has a "brush" at the end, which helps it gather the sweet nectar in flowers? Visit the gardens and learn about the other fascinating birds in the sanctuary.

http://osprey.anbg.gov.au:80/anbg/birds.html

Have you ever heard a bird song and wondered who wrote the music? You might find its composer at The North American Breeding Bird Survey where they have over fifty of the latest bird tunes on file for your listening pleasure.

The National Audubon Society Sanctuary Department

Did you know that the greatest threat to wild birds is the loss of habitat? Imagine walking along and seeing a wood stork close up in a cypress tree, or a sandhill crane family talking a walk along the river sandbar. Visit The National Audubon Society Sanctuary Department home page and learn about sanctuaries across the United States that protect these wild birds and other wildlife. Take time out to enjoy the scenery and wildlife in these refuges.

http://www.igc.apc.org/audubon/xsanc.html

The North American Breeding Bird Survey—95.1

This survey says nearly 63% of wetland bird species are increasing in numbers! This site offers a large-scale survey and source of information about population changes of North American birds. It is also a tool for learning about birds, with pictures of common birds of North America. The coolest part, though, is over fifty audio files of common bird songs and calls.

http://www.im.nbs.gov/bbs/

The Pet Bird Page (Parrots)

Thinking about buying a bird for a pet? If so, this is the place to stop before making your purchase. They'll help you choose the bird that's best for you. You'll also find important information on what to feed your bird, how to train it, and guidelines to finding a good vet. You'll have an opportunity to talk to professionals and experienced breeders in the chat room, and you'll learn about the daily and periodic care required for your feathered friend.

http://hookomo.aloha.net/~granty/

Everybody loves budgies, those colorful little birds also known as parakeets. budgie is short for budgerigar, which is from an Aboriginal word which translates as "good eating!" If you'd rather admire and not eat your budgies, try perching on The Pet Bird Page (Parrots).

Satellite Tracking of Threatened Species

"Graak, #12345, last seen March 15, 1995 at 19:48:22." This is a sample of monitoring migratory, threatened species. The bird's activity, latitude, and longitude can be measured via satellite data transmissions. Discover why and how these birds are being tracked by visiting this interesting site!

http://outside.gsfc.nasa.gov:80/ISTO/
  satellite_tracking/

BIRD WATCHING
GeoGraphical Birding Guide

Shhh!—be very quiet—we don't want to disturb the golden eagle nest and its babies. Look, there are four baby eaglets! Watch out, here comes their mom to feed them! The GeoGraphical Birding Guide has information about the distribution and population changes of birds all over the world. It also has tools for learning about birds, with pictures and quizzes on bird identification. Use the clickable map to find out about birding hotspots in your state and other information.

http://www-astronomy.mps.ohio-state.edu/
  ~ignaz/birds/ABA/ABA.html

Virtual Birding in Tokyo

Wouldn't it be fun to see what kinds of birds are in other kids' backyards—say, in Tokyo, Japan? This site lets you compare your local birds to their counterparts on the other side of the world! Does the puddle duck mallard you have strutting around your park pond look the same as the ones in Japan? Find out here at this beautiful site!

http://www.st.rim.or.jp/~koike/

BIRDHOUSES
HOMES FOR BIRDS

Home, home on a metal pole? Sure, if you're talking about a birdhouse! Did you know that more than two dozen North American birds will nest in birdhouses? Stop by this Web site and you will discover very complete advice about how to design a birdhouse to attract different types of birds to your neighborhood.

http://www.bcpl.lib.md.us/~tross/by/house.html

HotSpot for Birds—Bird Houses, Feeders, and Supplies

Everyone needs a home, even our fine feathered friends, the birds! You'll find that different types of birds require different types and placements of their homes. A birdhouse is not only appreciated by its tenants, but boys and girls, young and old can enjoy the presence of a birdhouse, and no batteries are required!

http://www.lainet.com/hotspot/bhcare.htm

NC State University—Building Songbird Boxes

Did you know that you can build houses for specific kinds of birds? Just by varying the diameter of the entrance hole, you can make a house for bluebirds, flycatchers, or flickers. You also have to make the hole a certain distance above the floor of the bird-house, and there are other building considerations to keep in mind for various species. Check this site for plans and specifications for birdhouses and predator guards for them. Then place your new homes in the trees and fields in March or April, while the birds are still home-hunting! For larger birds, such as woodpeckers and owls, see the instructions for Woodland Wildlife Nest Boxes at *http://www.ces.ncsu.edu/nreos/forest/steward/www17.html.*

http://www.ces.ncsu.edu/nreos/forest/steward/
  www16.html

DUCKS, GEESE, AND SWANS
Carter's Rare Birds

Duck, Duck, Goose! You probably know Daffy Duck, and Donald Duck, and even Mother Goose, but let's look at some of the less famous ducks and geese, like the cackling Canada geese, the cinnamon teal, the American widgeons and wood ducks. Stop by Carter's Rare Birds site where you'll meet some of these birds and hear what they sound like. You'll also learn about their nests and eggs, and their status both in the wild and in captivity.

http://www.cei.net/~rarebird/index.html

Space Exploration is a blast. Check out Astronomy

A B C D E F G H I J K L M N O P Q R S T U V W X Y Z

North West Swan Study

Do you know what a cob is, besides something corn grows on? What's a pen, besides something you write with? A cob is an adult male swan and a pen is an adult female swan. The three to seven eggs the pen lays are called a clutch, and young swans are called cygnets. To learn more about swans, visit this page, and listen to the warning call swans give humans that get too close to their nest.

http://www.airtime.co.uk/users/cygnus/
   swanstud.htm

EAGLES, FALCONS, AND HAWKS
THE RAPTOR CENTER at University of Minnesota

You find a hawk with an injured wing. What do you do? You need to call a special kind of animal doctor called a *wildlife rehabilitator*. That's a long word, but it means someone who helps the bird get better, so it can be released to the wild again. This site tells you what to do in an emergency, but the most important rule is that the less contact you have with the bird, the better its chances of survival will be. You can also call the Raptor Center 24 hours a day to get advice. They treat many sick or injured birds of prey, also known as raptors. For example, a bald eagle was found with a severe bacterial infection. The Raptor Center cured it and released it the next month. Years later, the same lucky bird was found caught in a steel-jawed trap, and it had another visit to The Raptor Center. The injury was successfully treated and the eagle was, once again, released in February, 1995. Visit this Web site to find more materials about The Raptor Center and the birds they treat, including information about endangered/threatened birds and the environmental issues which affect them.

http://www.raptor.cvm.umn.edu/

Surf today, smart tomorrow.

SERRC's Home Page

Did you ever wonder how injured wild birds are rehabilitated? What if they don't fully recover? Visit the Southeastern Raptor Rehabilitation Center's Home Page and discover what it takes to rehabilitate injured birds before they can be released to the wild. Meet the special permanent residents that will never be released due to the severity of their injuries. Learn the importance of raptors and how you can help ensure that these birds get the finest care available. Maybe your class could participate in the Adopt-A-Raptor program!

http://www.vetmed.auburn.edu/raptor/

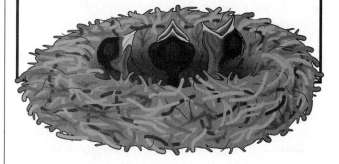

Adopt-A-Raptor today!
Find out more about how these birds of prey need your help, and what you can do for them, at SERRC's Home Page.

OTHER BIRDS
Hummingbirds!

Did you know that, in the spring, male hummingbirds start heading north as early as three weeks ahead of the females and immature birds? This is so the male can scout ahead for food for the females and young during migration. For more information on attracting hummingbirds to your yard, hummingbird feeders, the natural history of hummingbirds, and more, visit the Hummingbirds! home page.

http://www.inlink.com/~creative/hummers/
   welcome.html

the penguin page menu

We all know what macaroni and cheese is, but have you ever heard of a macaroni penguin? They live in the Antarctic and nearby islands, and they eat crustaceans, fish, and squid. Visit the penguin page menu and discover the difference between the "sideways stare" and the "alternate stare" given by penguins to other penguins and other animals. You'll also learn about various penguin species and their predators.

http://www.vni.net/~kwelch/penguin.shtml

OWLS

Jamie Stewart's Screech Owl Page

What a wonderful collection of photos, taken of a family of screech owls nesting near Jamie Stewart's house! Be sure to fill out the guest book, and tell Jamie you saw his page referred to in this book. When you do this, you get to see another cute owl picture!

http://www.voicenet.com/~jstewart/scrchowl/
scrchowl.html

NC State University—Owls

Do you know a barn owl from a screech owl? You will if you visit this site! A barn owl has a heart-shaped face, and can be between 15-20 inches tall. A screechie, on the other hand, has tufted ears and is much smaller—only about 10 inches long. You can learn to build owl houses here, and help increase the owl population where you live! Let's owl build some soon!

http://www.ces.ncsu.edu/nreos/forest/steward/
www22.html

Purdue On-Line Writing Lab Web Server Owl Info Page

Whoo, whoo is the largest of them all? With a wingspan of six feet, six inches, the eagle owls are the largest of the owl family. Stop by the Purdue On-Line Writing Lab Web Server Owl Info Page for an introduction to owls and check out the wonderful gallery of owl pictures. Did you know that the owl's eyes are almost immovable, and that some owls can turn their head completely upside down? Whoo, whoo knew?

http://owl.trc.purdue.edu/Images/
Picture-Gallery.html

BOATING AND SAILING

See also: OUTDOOR RECREATION

Age of Sail Page

Your *Treasure Island* book report is finished, but it would be great to put a graphic on that title page! Or maybe you've written your very own pirate story! If your report or story is on sailing, boating, tall ships, pirates, or adventure on the high seas, then here's your source for great clip art. There is also a quality list of links to related boat pages. "Aaaay, me bucko! Have at it!"

http://www.cs.yale.edu/homes/sjl/sail.html

Hoofer Tech Manual

If you don't know a dinghy from a dory, or a tell-tale from a boom vang, you need to visit this great page from the Hoofer Sailing Club at the University of Wisconsin-Madison. You'll learn, in words and pictures, how to control a sailboat, tie useful knots, and avoid the dreaded "turtling" maneuver.

http://rso.union.wisc.edu/Hoofers/sailing/
tech_manual/tech_manual.html

Interactive Marine Observations

This falls into the category of truly amazing. A network of sea buoys and CMAN (Coastal Marine Automated Network) stations is maintained by the National Data Buoy Center (NBDC), a division of NOAA (National Oceanic and Atmospheric Administration). The observations are updated continuously and an eight-hour history is usually available for each station. They report temperature, dew point, wind (sustained and gust) direction and speed, surface pressure, wave heights, and the period between waves. How are the waves off Maui, Hawai'i? What's the temperature off Anchorage, Alaska? Or check even closer to home, if you're going boating in the coastal waters of the U.S. or Maritime Canada.

http://thunder.met.fsu.edu/~nws/buoy/

A
B
C
D
E
F
G
H
I
J
K
L
M
N
O
P
Q
R
S
T
U
V
W
X
Y
Z

Navigation Information Connection (NIC)

The U.S. Army Corps of Engineers sponsors this informative site, which offers maps of navigable rivers in the U.S. as well as daily reports on the status of navigation locks along those rivers. Never seen a lock in operation before? They allow boats to go around waterfalls or rapids by providing a water "elevator" for the boat to climb or descend the river. There are diagrams and pictures of locks here; the shortcut is *http://www.ncr.usace.army.mil/ navdata/locpic.htm* if you wish to bypass the other interesting resources.

http://www.ncr.usace.army.mil/nic.htm

Ocean Challenge

What if your teacher told your class to go get your coats, because you're going on a field trip. You'd probably be pretty excited, right? What if she led you right onto the deck of a tall ship, and said to get comfortable, because you were all going on a round-the-world cruise! Still interested? What if she then told you that your class was going to be the crew, and that you'd be gone for months! That's exactly what's happening to 44 high school kids, their teachers, and only eight actual old salt crew members. You can follow the progress of their journey on the Net, and even ask them questions! Meet the kids, read their ship diaries, and enjoy this classroom afloat.

http://www.oceanchallenge.com/

Sailing Dictionary

Where's the *bow*? What if your *scupper* is plugged? And how do you know when to *luff*? If you're going to be talking to boaters or sailors (or if you're going to be one), then you'll have to check out this site! And you thought you were a sailor because you knew your "port" (left) from your "starboard" (right)! Sail on over and find the definition of any sailing word.

http://infoweb.magi.com/~nedcore/sos/diction.html

How fast does a glacier move?

http://www.whistler.net/glacier/

Answer: The fastest moving glacier, the Quarayaq in Greenland, moves about 2.7 to 3.3 feet per hour. Most of them move much slower than that! Surprisingly, science didn't know glaciers moved at all until 1827! A Swiss scientist built a small hut on a glacier. When he came back three years later, the hut had moved more than 100 yards downhill! Read more fun glacier facts at Blackcomb Glaciers—Main page.

The Semaphore Flag Signaling System

You want to say "Hi" to your buddy in a boat across the bay, but it's too far to yell. You could use the semaphore alphabet and two flags to send messages. How? Boaters spell words by holding a flag in each hand and moving them into different positions. An "H" is made by holding the right-hand flag out straight, and the left-hand flag down and across the body. You can learn the whole semaphore alphabet from the pictures and descriptions you'll find at this page. Get your flags and practice!

http://osprey.anbg.gov.au/flags/semaphore.html

Become one with the Net.

United States Power Squadrons®

Can you pass the online navigation quiz offered by the Power Squadron? Try it! You'll be asked which color running light is on the "port" side, and similar questions. You can compare your scores with others, and no, you don't have to sign your name! If your score could use some improvement, check to see if there is a local Power Squadron group near you. They offer free classes in boating and sailing safety and navigation. You can preview what will be taught in the classes here.

http://www.ronin.com/USPS/

BOOKS AND LITERATURE

Children's Literature Selections Page

This page features first chapters of some books selected by the American Library Association/ Association for Library Service to Children as Newbery Award and Honor Books Winners. It doesn't include all winners, just those published by Dial-A-Book. Links include background on the Newbery Awards, the terms and criteria used to select winners, and information about the committee that selects the books. There is an option to order some of the books online, but check your local library first!

http://dab.psi.net/ChapterOne/children/index.html

Children's Literature Web Guide

This is the FIRST place to look for Internet resources related to books for children and young adults! Here you will find online children's stories, information about authors and illustrators, children's book awards, and lots of lists. Also available at this site are lists of book discussion groups, sources for book reviews, online resources, publishers, booksellers, and Children's Literature Associations. David K. Brown updates this site frequently and provides a convenient What's New.

http://www.ucalgary.ca/~dkbrown/index.html

Visit the stars in Astronomy.

How a Book is Made

These pages give you an inside look at how a book is published. Illustrations from Aliki's book, *How a Book Is Made*, help to tell the story. Various cats pose as illustrator, author, and editor, as well as workers in production, advertising, and sales. They show the steps involved in the writing and publishing of a book!

http://www.harpercollins.com/kids/book.htm

Author, author, lend me your words. If you like writing, and want to find out more about what it's all about, check out How a Book is Made.

IPL Youth Division

Welcome to the Internet Public Library! Join the Story Hour and read from a selection of five stories, including "Do Spiders Live on the World Wide Web?," *The Tortoise and the Hare*, and "Molly Whuppie." Nine children's authors and illustrators are available to answer your questions, and seven more will be added soon. Biographical information is also available. Authors include Avi, Robert Cormier, Lois Lowry, and Charlotte Zolotow.

http://www.ipl.org/youth/index.html

Yogatta try Yoga.

A
B
C
D
E
F
G
H
I
J
K
L
M
N
O
P
Q
R
S
T
U
V
W
X
Y
Z

ADVENTURE STORIES

Choose Your Own Adventure

Sixth-graders wrote this interactive adventure! Cruise along with Buzz Rod in his candy apple red Dodge Viper, after a fight with his parents. He sees a bright flash of light! To find out what happens after Buzz loses control of his car, surf on over to Hillside Elementary School! Every time you click on the Random SpaceTime Warp button, you will find a different ending to Buzz's story. Not only will you find out what happens to Buzz, but you can also read about the author of each ending and hear sound effects recorded by the authors.

http://hillside.coled.umn.edu/class1/Buzz/Story.html

Read-along Stories

See the pictures; read the story; and listen to the words. Parents and kids alike will enjoy these some-times scary read-along stories from PARENTS AND CHILDREN TOGETHER ONLINE, A Project of the Family Literacy Center. There are also sections titled "things to do before reading the story" and "things to do after reading the story." Waiting for the audio to load takes a little patience, but it's well worth the wait. Check out this family resource from the ERIC Clearinghouse for Reading, English, and Communication.

http://www.indiana.edu/~eric_rec/fl/pcto/read.html

Theodore's Surprise Friend

Theodore Tugboat is the star of a Canadian television series. In this set of links, Theodore and part of the story appear on each page. At the end of each page, you get to choose which of two things Theodore will do next! This choice is offered on almost every page, so you'll be actively involved in the story and its ending.

http://www.cochran.com/theosite/IStory.html

Take a ride on a Carousel in AMUSEMENT PARKS.

CLASSICS

Kindred Spirits: The LM Montgomery Home Page

The Kindred Spirits WWW site is dedicated to the works and life of Lucy Maud Montgomery (or LMM for short), the Canadian author of the *Anne of Green Gables* series. Here you will find information about Cavendish, which is the model for Avonlea. A comprehensive FAQ contains a list of all of Montgomery's works, books about her, and other materials based upon her characters and her works. Other links take you to The Road to Avonlea Home Page, a LMM Art Gallery, as well as information about Ontario, where LMM lived as an adult, and PEI (*P*rince *E*dward *I*sland), where she grew up.

http://www.upei.ca/~lmmi/cover.html

Ozcot Home Page

L. Frank Baum, the author of the Oz books, called his California home Ozcot. This home page contains a list of Oz books by the author. The major feature of this site is a set of text-only HTML files of *The Wonderful Wizard of Oz* and *The Marvelous Land of Oz*.

http://www.best.com/~tiktok/

The OZ Piglet Press Tour Guide

Jump on this page and be prepared to be swept away by a Kansas twister and totally immersed in Oziana. Piglet Press has gone way beyond the call of duty in promoting their small collection of Oz audio tapes by putting together the most thorough collection of pictures, descriptions and notes to L. Frank Baum's beloved series of books. There are pages devoted to each and every Baum book, as well as material on those done by Ruth Plumly Thompson and other successors. It is possible to look up specific characters, places and things from the first fourteen books via the 878-page Encyclopedia Oziana, reference the movies (there have been plenty of them), get details about Baum himself, and find out about two different international Oz Clubs. There are also sample sound files from the Piglet tapes here, sections on Baum's songs and short stories, and a bibliography. To exit from the page, just click your heels together and say, "there's no place like home..."

http://www.halcyon.com/piglet

The Page at Pooh Corner

Somewhere in the Internet's Hundred-Acre Wood is The Page at Pooh Corner. It's the home of information about A. A. Milne's Winnie-the-Pooh books. Find general information about Pooh and facts about the author, A. A. Milne, and the illustrator, E. H. Shepard. Learn about the area in England where the Pooh stories are based, and the real Christopher Robin. Sing along with your favorite Disney Pooh songs or download pictures of Pooh and his companions. This page also gives you links to more sites that feature Pooh, that "tubby little cubby all stuffed with fluff."

http://www.public.iastate.edu/~jmilne/pooh.html

CONTEMPORARY FAVORITES
G-G-G-G-Goosebumps!

Are you a fan of R. L. Stine? His *Goosebumps* series is the subject of this home page. Follow links that lead you to Stine's biography, his photo, and the transcript of an online Halloween chat with Stine. Also read a chapter from *Deep Trouble*, the nineteenth book in his series. In addition, read all about the new Fox TV series based on the books. A link includes synopses of the TV episodes, identifying the book featured.

http://www.scholastic.com/public/Goosebumps/
  Cover.html

Go to G-G-G-G-Goosebumps! for a thrilling look at R.L. Stine's Goosebumps book and TV series.

HarperCollins Children's Books

The Big Busy House Web site gives you the latest news from this publisher of children's books. Read sample chapters from their new *X-Files* series, or from other new titles. Or, read information about how classics like *If You Give a Mouse a Cookie* were developed. Check out the author interviews and add that info to your next book report. There's a lot at this site—you might even enter and win one of the contests!

http://www.harpercollins.com/kids/index.htm

MYSTERIES
Booklover's Den: The Booklover's Virtual Reading Room

Links from the Booklover's Den give a mystery fan information about a ton of series books and other mysteries. Series featured include Nancy Drew, Trixie Belden, Judy Bolton, and the Dana Girls, as well as Hardy Boys, Encyclopedia Brown, and The Three Investigators. The author of these Web pages, Biblioholics, is also starting a free online newsletter about children's series.

http://members.aol.com/biblioholc/Den.html

ONLINE BOOKS

Many full-text, public-domain books appear on the Internet. Some are collected as part of Project Gutenberg (*http://jg.cso.uiuc.edu/PG/welcome.html*), while others are in the Online Book Initiative (*gopher://ftp.std.com:70/11/obi/book*). Another large collection is at Carnegie Mellon (*http://www.cs.cmu.edu/Web/books.html*).

Most of the books you will find are retrieved as flat text files. If you prefer reading them as HTML hypertext, try the archives at *http://www.cs.cmu.edu/Web/People/rgs/rgs-home.html* or *http://www.cs.cmu.edu/Web/books.html*. These resources tell you whether the files are text or HTML.

We have selected some classic children's books from these huge collections: look for your favorites!

Barrie, J.M.

Peter Pan
gopher://wiretap.spies.com:70/00/Library/Classic/
  peter.txt

> ## Origami: the fold to behold!
> ## Check out CRAFTS
> ## AND HOBBIES.

Burnett, Frances Hodgson

Sarah Crewe
gopher://wiretap.spies.com:70/00/Library/Classic/
  crewe.txt

The Secret Garden
gopher://wiretap.spies.com:70/00/Library/Classic/
  garden.txt

Burroughs, Edgar Rice

Tarzan of the Apes
http://www.cs.cmu.edu/Web/People/rgs/
  tarz-table.html

Irving, Washington

The Legend of Sleepy Hollow
gopher://wiretap.spies.com:70/00/Library/Classic/
  sleepy.txt

Kipling, Rudyard

The Jungle Book
gopher://wiretap.spies.com:70/00/Library/Classic/
  jungle.rk

London, Jack

The Call of the Wild
gopher://gopher.vt.edu:10010/02/117/6

Porter, Gene Stratton

A Girl of the Limberlost
gopher://wiretap.spies.com:70/00/Library/
  classic/limber.gsp

The BookWire Electronic Children's Books Index

Many online children's books are collected here,
including Hans Christian Andersen fairy tales.

http://www.bookwire.com/links/readingroom/
  echildbooks.html

Classics for Young People

Many books your parents read as kids are collected
here; some of the ones they may remember include
the *Wizard of Oz* books, *The Wind in the Willows*,
and *Treasure Island*. You'll also find the *Anne of
Green Gables* stories, and *Alice in Wonderland*.
Maybe you can read these books to your parents
just before you tuck them in for their naps!

http://www.ucalgary.ca/~dkbrown/storclas.html

Complete Online Works of Edgar Allan Poe

This home page collects Poe's complete works,
including his poetry and short stories. Some of the
works are available in HTML. All are available in
ASCII. Access to Poe's writings is alphabetical, so
you can quickly find what you're looking for. Surf
on over to read "The Raven" or another one of Poe's
122 poems and stories!

http://www.cstone.net/~wmm/VIRGINIA/people/
  Poe/index.html

NET FILES

What are the historical origins of the toy Frisbee?

Answer: It depends if you go with the "Pie Plate" or the "Cookie Tin" theory. But everyone agrees that the Frisbie Pie Company operating in New Haven, Connecticut in early 1870s, had a lot to do with the origin of the game. Yale college students had a lot to do with it, too. You can learn about the History of the Disc at http://www.upa.org/~upa/upa/frisbee-hist.html

FAIRROSA'S CYBER LIBRARY

Inside, you'll find lots of links to online kids' books, such as *A Little Princess*, *Peter Pan*, and *A Journey to the Center of the Earth*. One of the coolest things, though, is the selection of links to authors' home pages. Need some biographical author info to complete your book report? Try here!

http://www.users.interport.net/~fairrosa/

PICTURE BOOKS

Candlelight Stories

Storybooks right on the Web! The illustrations are beautifully done by the author of this site. It's amazing how preschoolers can learn to use the mouse when they are reading these stories. Try "Sally Saves Christmas" for a look at what happens when a little girl travels on a moonbeam. As you look at each page, try asking the preschooler what will happen next—will Sally decide to follow the Moon Queen?

http://users.aol.com/cimal/candlelight/candle.htm

Concertina—Books on the Internet

Concertina is a new Canadian children's publisher. Current titles featured include *Waking in Jerusalem*, *I Live on a Raft*, *My Blue Suitcase*, and *The Song of Moses*. Additional links tell the reader about the authors and illustrators as well as the design techniques used to create the online versions of the book. Each book includes the illustrations and all of the pages. *Waking in Jerusalem* is enhanced by the addition of sound clips for each page.

http://www.iatech.com/books/

Cool Dog Teddy

This page celebrates the life and times of Cool Dog Teddy (CDT), a puppy who has many different adventures. For example, "Good Neighbor Sam" is about the new cat who moves in next door and wanders into CDT's yard. Though Samantha the Cat is way different from CDT, that doesn't mean that she's not a good neighbor. These stories are meant to be read to younger children, who can look at the cute illustrations. You can also get on a mailing list to be notified when a new CDT adventure is up on the Web.

http://www.america.com/~stevesch/www/
  morningwalk.html

> ## Frisbee is the Ultimate in GAMES AND FUN.

Cyber-Seuss Page

Welcome to the world of "the great glorious and gandorious... Dr. Seuss!" Thirteen of the Dr.'s books are online (words only), including *The Cat in the Hat*, *How the Grinch Stole Christmas*, *Green Eggs and Ham*, *Fox in Sox*, and *Yertle the Turtle*. See a photo of Seuss, read quotes from him, and visit Dartmouth, where Ted (Dr. Seuss) went to college. Check out the Grinchnet and cast your vote in the Great Grinch debate! Admire the collection of Seuss images, and if you still want to read more, peruse the list of Dr. Seuss books in print!

http://www.afn.org/~afn15301/drseuss.html

> ***Green Eggs and Ham*** has been a favorite breakfast of ours since as far back as we can remember. Rumor has it that's a long time, so you know this is a tried-and-true feast. Read all about this and more recipes for treats you can enjoy at any meal at the Cybrer-Seuss Page.

> ## Lost your sheep? Count them in FARMING AND AGRICULTURE.

A B C D E F G H I J K L M N O P Q R S T U V W X Y Z

Chase some waterfalls in EARTH SCIENCE

Grandad's Animal Book Contents

Grandad, Thomas Wright, lives on the Hawaiian island of Maui. He's written an interactive animal English alphabet book. A picture of an animal is shown with each letter of the alphabet. You know the drill: "Z" is for Zebra. But you'll also find a vocabulary list, notes on classifying animals, and facts about various classes of animals. You can also choose a letter of the alphabet and then identify which animal begins with that letter of the alphabet.

http://www.maui.com/~twright/animals/
  htmgran.html

The Internet Public Library Story Hour

Bored? Parents not telling you any good stories anymore? Just want to read something new? Point your browser towards the Internet Public Library Story Hour. Many traditional stories are available, as well as newer ones. Illustrated by kids, too!

http://ipl.sils.umich.edu/youth/StoryHour/

Theodore Tugboat

Here's a tugboat with a smile and appealing eyes, straight from the Canadian TV series! Toddlers will love the interactive story where they get to choose what happens next. If you have a slower connection, be sure to set your browser not to autoload images. Downloadable coloring book pages sail via the Net to your printer or graphics program. Little ones can even get their own postcard in the mail from Theodore Tugboat himself!

http://www.cochran.com/TT.html

PLAYS AND DRAMA

The Complete Works of William Shakespeare

Ah, the Bard himself comes to the Net! Visit this site for the complete works of Shakespeare. You can search the texts, find lists of his plays (chronologically and alphabetically), read Bartlett's familiar Shakespearean quotations, as well as find a picture of William himself! The list of Shakespeare's works is divided into comedy, history, tragedy, and poetry. After you choose a play, you will move to a Web page where you can read one scene per page. The text includes hyperlinks to the glossary, making it easy to understand what Shakespeare was saying. This is a "don't miss" visit for all drama students!

http://the-tech.mit.edu/Shakespeare/

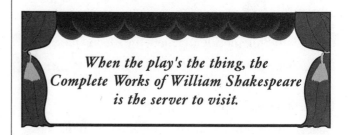

When the play's the thing, the Complete Works of William Shakespeare is the server to visit.

Reader's Theater Editions

Looking for a play you can perform with the rest of your class? This site has nine complete plays for grades 2-8. A wide range of subjects is covered, from folktales to science fiction. Most are adapted from short stories by Aaron Shepard.

http://www.ucalgary.ca/~dkbrown/readers.html

Theatre Central

All the world's a stage at this site, which contains links to theatre-related pages from all over the world. This site is dedicated to all kinds of theatre, from professional companies, to scholastic groups, to online magazines. It's updated weekly by its owner, Andrew Kraft. You can find schedules of theatre companies, information about associations, people involved in theatre, educational resources, stagecraft, publications, and film resources. This is a great site if you're interested in drama!

http://www.theatre-central.com/

POETRY

Electronic Poetry Center Home Page

Are you a poet? Want to make sure everyone else knows it? The Electronic Poetry Center is a central gateway to resources in electronic poetry on the Internet. The goal of the center is to make a wide range of contemporary poetry resources available. You can browse the libraries by author, small press, sound, or graphics. You can make a comment about what you've read, or collaborate on a poem. The sound archives contain sound files of the poems, as well as actual live broadcast readings.

http://wings.buffalo.edu/epc/

Grin's Message

Grin the dolphin will rhyme his way into any preschooler's heart. He conveys messages about ecology and kindness, via several aquatic animals. The poem is accompanied by lovely drawings. Put this site in your bookmarks, 'cause once you introduce children to it, they'll want to access it again and again!

http://www2.opennet.com/schoolhouse/grin/ Welcome.html

The Internet Poetry Archive

The Internet Poetry Archive is very new, but its plan is to make available selected poems from a number of contemporary poets. The goal of this project is to make poetry accessible at little cost, and to give poetry students new ways of studying these poets and their texts. Living poets around the world are eligible for inclusion. Currently the archive features only two poets, including Seamus Heaney, the 1995 Nobel Prize in Literature winner, and Czeslaw Milosz, the Lithuanian poet. Included in the collection are audio clips of each poet reading his works, the poet's comments upon his works, a photo of the poet, and graphics to help the reader understand the poem. Texts of the poems, a critical biography, and a short bibliography are available.

http://sunsite.unc.edu/dykki/poetry/home.html

Lost your marbles? Find them in GAMES AND FUN.

Online Songs and Poetry for Children

"The Naming of Cats is a difficult matter," begins *Old Possum's Book of Practical Cats* by T.S. Eliot. Did you know it was the basis for the famous musical *Cats*? You'll find the poems here, plus many other collections from poets such as Robert Louis Stevenson, Lewis Carroll, Walter de la Mare, and Edward Lear.

http://www.ucalgary.ca/~dkbrown/storsong.html

Poetry Gallery

Are you a poet, and want to publish your poetry so the world can read it? Then this is the place for you! Read poems written by other kids. Send in your masterpiece, and soon you can read your own poem on this page.

http://mgfx.com/kidlit/kids/artlit/poetry/index.htm

POETRY—HAIKU

Haiku Homepage

Haiku is a form of poetry which began in Japan, but is popular all over the world. Tips for aspiring haiku writers are given here. One of the links leads to The Haiku Attic, where you can post poems to share with others.

http://www.dmu.ac.uk/~pka/haiku.html

Get your hobby off the ground! Try Rockets in MODELS AND MINIATURES.

A
B
C
D
E
F
G
H
I
J
K
L
M
N
O
P
Q
R
S
T
U
V
W
X
Y
Z

The Shiki Internet Haiku Salon

Shiki Masaoka, a haiku poet, was born in Japan in 1867 and helped popularize the arts, as well as haiku, Japan's short poem form. Haiku consists of three lines of five, seven, and five syllables each, and usually has a special word which evokes the season. Here is a haiku we made up about the Internet:

> The Net's a garden.
> See, my modem light is on,
> Netscape slowly blooms.
> Now you try it!

http://mikan.cc.matsuyama-u.ac.jp/~shiki/

POETRY—JUMP ROPE RHYMES

JUMPROPE Hypertext archives

> *Cinderella, dressed in green,*
> *Went upstairs to eat ice cream.*
> *How many spoonfuls did she eat?*
> *One, two, three, ...*

Do you jump rope? You may want to look at this collection of old and new rhymes kids have used to keep rhythm while they were jumping rope. They have been contributed from all over the world, and you can add ones you know. Some are very old, some aren't considered "politically correct" any more, but all are interesting. Peek into the past of splits and red hot peppers, in the days before double dutch. For information on jump rope associations and competitions today, see the U.S.A Jump Rope Home Page at *http://www.ortech-engr.com/USAJRF/*. Do not miss the action photos, especially the Subway trick, which seems to defy gravity!

http://www.uwf.edu/~stankuli/jrope/jumprope.htm

POETRY—ONLINE

Angelou, Maya
"Inauguration Poem" January 20, 1993

> *A Rock, A River, A Tree*
> *Hosts to species long since departed,*
> *Marked the mastodon...*

gopher://english.hss.cmu.edu/00ftp%3AEnglish. Server%3APoetry%3AAngelou-Inauguration%20Poem

Carroll, Lewis (Charles Lutwidge Dodgson)
"Jabberwocky"

> *'Twas brillig, and the slithy tove*
> *did gyre and gimble in the wabe.*
> *All mimsy were the borogoves,*
> *And the mome raths outgrabe.*
> *"Beware the Jabberwock, my son!*
> *The jaws that bite, the claws that catch!*
> *Beware the Jubjub bird, and shun*
> *the frumious Bandersnatch..."*

gopher://english.hss.cmu.edu/00ftp%3AEnglish. Server%3APoetry%3ACarroll-Jabberwocky

Frost, Robert
"Stopping By Woods on a Snowy Evening"

> *Whose woods these are I think I know.*
> *His house is in the village, though;*
> *He will not see me stopping here*
> *To watch his woods fill up with snow...*

gopher://wiretap.spies.com:70/00/Library/Classic/ Poetry/woods.p

Kilmer, Joyce
"Trees"

> *I think that I shall never see*
> *A poem lovely as a tree...*

gopher://wiretap.spies.com:70/00/Library/Classic/ Poetry/trees.p

Kipling, Rudyard
"If"

> If you can keep your head when all about you
> Are losing theirs and blaming it on you;
> If you can trust yourself when all men doubt you,
> But make allowance for their doubting too...

gopher://wiretap.spies.com:70/00/Library/Classic/
Poetry/if.p

Lear, Edward
"The Jumblies"

> They went to sea in a Sieve, they did,
> In a Sieve they went to sea:
> In spite of all their friends could say,
> On a winter's morn, on a stormy day,
> In a Sieve they went to sea...

gopher://english.hss.cmu.edu/00ftp%3AEnglish.
Server%3APoetry%3AEdward%20Lear-The%20
Jumblies

Longfellow, Henry Wadsworth
"Paul Revere's Ride"

> Listen my children and you shall hear
> Of the midnight ride of Paul Revere,
> On the eighteenth of April, in Seventy-five;
> Hardly a man is now alive
> Who remembers that famous day and year...

gopher://english.hss.cmu.edu/00ftp%3AEnglish.
Server%3APoetry%3ALongfellow-Paul%20Revere

"The Song of Hiawatha"

> Should you ask me,
> whence these stories?
> Whence these legends and traditions,
> With the odors of the forest
> With the dew and damp of meadows,
> With the curling smoke of wigwams,
> With the rushing of great rivers,
> With their frequent repetitions,
> And their wild reverberations
> As of thunder in the mountains?
> I should answer, I should tell you...

gopher://wiretap.spies.com:70/00/Library/Classic/
hiawatha.txt

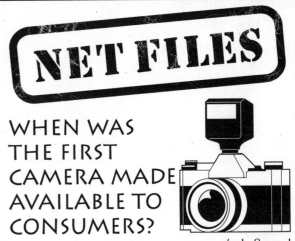

NET FILES

WHEN WAS THE FIRST CAMERA MADE AVAILABLE TO CONSUMERS?

Answer: The first consumer camera was marketed all the way back in 1888! The Kodak camera was priced at $25 and included film for 100 exposures. It was a little inconvenient to get your pictures developed, though. The whole camera had to be returned to Kodak in Rochester, New York for film processing! Click over to http://www.it.rit.edu:80/~gehouse/timeline/kodak1.html for more on the history of photography!

"The Village Blacksmith"

> Under a spreading chestnut-tree
> The village smithy stands;
> The smith, a mighty man is he,
> With large and sinewy hands;
> And the muscles of his brawny arms
> Are strong as iron bands...

gopher://wiretap.spies.com:70/00/Library/Classic/
Poetry/village.p

Moore, Clement
"The Night Before Christmas"

Is there anyone who doesn't know this beloved classic, which begins

> 'Twas the night before Christmas, when all through the house
> Not a creature was stirring, not even a mouse...

gopher://gopher.vt.edu:10010/02/125/1

Stevenson, Robert Louis
A Child's Garden of Verses

Many poems you can read to your little brothers and sisters. The first one starts

> *In winter I get up at night*
> *And dress by yellow candle-light.*
> *In summer quite the other way,*
> *I have to go to bed by day...*

gopher://wiretap.spies.com:70/00/Library/Classic/child.rls

Wordsworth, William
"The Daffodils"

> *I wandered lonely as a cloud*
> *That floats on high o'er vales and hills,*
> *When all at once I saw a crowd,*
> *A host, of golden daffodils...*

gopher://wiretap.spies.com:70/00/Library/Classic/Poetry/daffo.p

"Lines Written in Early Spring"

> *I heard a thousand blended notes,*
> *While in a grove I sate reclined...*

gopher://ftp.std.com:70/00/obi/book/William.Wordsworth/lines.in.spring

POETRY—NURSERY RHYMES
Mother Goose, Nursery Rhymes, & Children's Songs

Everyone loves these gentle rhymes of childhood. The rhymes are subdivided by subject, including animals, bedtime, folks and things they do, food, places to go, and weather and things around us. An alphabetical listing is available, as well as a list of recommended books. The rhymes chosen are favorites of the collector and her children. This is a useful site for finding those elusive words you can't quite remember from a long-forgotten nursery rhyme!

http://pubweb.acns.nwu.edu/~pfa/dreamhouse/nursery/rhymes.html

Nursery Rhymes for Our Times

According to Douglas Crockford, the nursery rhymes are archaic because of the language. He says the rhymes fail to teach kids about the one thing they need in order to live full, productive lives: technology. Crockford rewrites eleven nursery rhymes to make them relevant for modern children. A sample rhyme from his page rewrites Old King Cole:

> *Mister Cole has remote control*
> *And remote control has he*
> *He gets CNN*
> *He gets HBO*
> *And he gets his MTV.*

http://www.communities.com/paper/nursery.html

> *Are you beeping?*
> *Are you beeping?*
> *Brother Jack?*
> *Brother Jack?*
> *Get your pocket pager.*
> *Get your pocket pager.*
> *Call them back.*
> *Call them back.*

Poetry always reflects its cultural context, and this is one you can find in Nursery Rhymes for Our Times.

SCIENCE FICTION
The Good Reading Guide—Index

A comprehensive index to works by science fiction authors, arranged by author. Includes standard authors as well as many children's authors, including Lloyd Alexander, John Christopher, Madeline L'Engle, C.S. Lewis, and Ursula K. LeGuin. While not all of the lists are comprehensive, this is an excellent site for finding other titles by your favorite science fiction authors.

http://julmara.ce.chalmers.se/SF_archive/SFguide/

CARS

AutoZonLine Classic Car Museum

There are cars, and then there are "classic" cars. The AutoZonLine Classic Car Museum has pictures of the coolest classic cars ever. There's even a 1926 Nash and a 1926 Chrysler! Yes, they had cars in 1926! And they look just like the Viper. . . not!

http://xweb.com/autoweb/carbarn.html

Car and Driver

Cars are fun to look at, and interesting to talk about. *Car and Driver* talks about them every month in their magazine. Driving is fun too, unless you get stuck in traffic. You may not be a driver yet, but you know you will be. And no matter what the reason, everyone seems to have some interest in cars. They're big business, too. You can't watch TV without seeing lots of ads for cars. You need a place to find out what's happening in the world of cars this year, this month, *today*! This site has great resource information on every kind of car you can think of, but it also has "Daily Auto Insider" with today's news on cars. Drive on in, here's a parking space!

http://www.caranddriver.com/

Car Culture

Car Culture is an educational site that's fascinating and fun! "Whatzit" tells you all about those "car words" you hear on TV, like "anti-lock brakes." What are they? "How They're Built" is the story behind making a car, with pictures and an explanation we can all understand. "Crossing Six Continents with Tacoma Jim & Jo" takes us along on a drive around the world, starting February 1! And "Where to Drive" takes you on a drive through a different state each month. If you wish you knew more about cars, you'll love it! And you'll learn a lot about the world, too.

http://www.toyota.com/hub/carculture/

Ford Historical Library

If you need a great topic for your report, what about the history of the world-famous Ford Motor Company? What report? How about that history report? Or that technology report? Or that science report? Or … Wait a minute! You don't need to have a report due to go here! It's just awesome information, pictures, and stories about cars from 1903 right up to today. And, for the real sports car fan, there's the "Jaguar Historical Library" here, too!

http://www.ford.com/archive/intro.html

The PM Zone: Popular Mechanics

You can see next year's models, *now*? How about classic cars? Those too? This must be the PM Zone's Automotive section, where you can get the latest on all the cars out there, from *Popular Mechanics* magazine. *Popular Mechanics* surveys users and reports on cars. That means that you get the real story on how the cars perform from the people who drive them, not just from the manufacturer. They report on every kind of car—from Ferrari Spiders to Dodge Caravans—and they spy on the new models, so you can be the first to see them. Put the key in, start 'er up, and head into the "PM Zone."

http://popularmechanics.com/

Everyone is talking about the new car being unveiled next fall, but nobody has seen it. Is it just a revamp of this year's model, or really as hot as they claim? You might just get that sneak preview at The PM Zone: Popular Mechanics. Investigate the "Spy" section for the latest.

A B C D E F G H I J K L M N O P Q R S T U V W X Y Z

RACING

American Racing Scene

If you love those super-fast race cars, then make your next pitstop at "American Racing Scene." Here you can find all the latest information on Indycar and NASCAR racing. There's cool photography. And "Shop Talk" lets you "talk" with others who like cars that go fast. You can pick a topic to join in on the discussion, or start a new topic of your own. Revvvvvv-vroom!

http://www.racecar.com/

CATS

See also: MAMMALS-CAT FAMILY, PETS AND PET CARE

Cat Fanciers' Home Page

Crazy about cats? Then this is the place for you! It will give answers to questions you didn't even know you had. It contains information about cat breeds, colors, cat shows, the welfare of animals, and lots of other cat-related subjects. Are you concerned about Feline Leukemia Virus? Don't worry, you can't catch it—the virus is specific to cats only, and is considered to be the most common cause of serious illness and death in domestic cats. Lots of links to cat health information at veterinary schools around the world may be found here.

http://www.ai.mit.edu/fanciers/fanciers.html

Cats on the Internet

"Here kitty, kitty, kitty. There you are, of course, I should have looked at the Cats on the Internet home page first!" Here you'll find information about getting a cat, general cat care, basic health care, behavior problems in cats, pointers to other feline sites, and much more. Stop by today and Socks, the First Cat, will say hello.

http://http2.sils.umich.edu/~dtorres/cats/cats.html

Origami: the fold to behold! Check out CRAFTS AND HOBBIES.

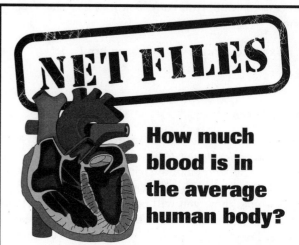

NET FILES

How much blood is in the average human body?

Answer: The average human has about 5 liters of blood. About 55 per cent of your blood is plasma. Check out the inside story on blood at http://sln.fi.edu/biosci/blood/blood.html

rec.pets.cats FAQ Homepage

This is the FAQ from the Usenet newsgroup, arranged in HTML so it's easy to read. Find out all about cat breeds, colors, health, training, and more!

http://www.zmall.com/pet_talk/cat-faqs/

World Wide CATS

Visit with cats around the world. You'll find it hard to resist laughing out loud when you read the "Bad Kitty/Bad Human List." Talk to a cat on the east coast, check out the "Cat-in-a-bag," or ask Mr. Puddy for advice. Stop by the World Wide CATS and claw your way through the world of cats.

http://www.timis.ac.jp/tcat/catcatalogue.html

CAT SHOWS
/OFF: Online Feline Fanciers

Your cat is so beautiful! Do you want to enter your pet in a cat show? Be sure and stop by this site first and find out about how to get started showing your cat under Cat Fanciers' Association (CFA) rules. Read up on breeder information and learn about CFA scoring and how titles are earned. If you think you are ready to enter the realm of cat shows, check out CFA's show schedule, and good luck!

http://www.clock.org/~ambar/off/

CHEMISTRY

General Chemistry

Do you love chemistry? Does the idea of equilibrium, states of matter, or quantum mechanics give you goose bumps? If that's the case, then the General Chemistry page is for you! Here you'll find a multimedia course on chemistry that should satisfy even the most intense chemistry nut.

**http://www-wilson.ucsd.edu/education/
  gchem/gchem.html**

Mathematics and Molecules

Everything around you is made of chemicals—from your computer, to your favorite book, to you! Scientists are learning more and more about how chemicals work by understanding the math of molecules. You may wonder why learning math, algebra, or geometry makes any sense, but these are the keys to understanding much of chemistry. To see how math is used in chemistry, check out this page. You'll never look at your math book the same way again!

http://www.nyu.edu/pages/mathmol/

Understanding Our Planet Through Chemistry

How do scientists know the age of the Earth, or when a meteor struck our planet? How can scientists predict and understand volcanoes when no one can look closely at an eruption and survive? The answer to these, and many other questions about the Earth, is in chemistry. To learn more, take a peek at Understanding Our Planet Through Chemistry.

http://helios.cr.usgs.gov/gips/aii-home.htm

EXPERIMENTS
Bread Chemistry

Everyone likes bread. It's great as toast, makes for good sandwiches, and sometimes is excellent for missiles in a food fight. Bread, though, is a good lesson in chemistry. Every time bread is made there are all kinds of interesting chemical reactions. Don't loaf around! Check out Bread Chemistry from the award winning *Newton's Apple* TV program for a lesson in bread as science.

http://ericir.syr.edu/Newton/Lessons/bread.html

Physical Science and Chemistry Lesson Plans

You have to do a science experiment, and you thought maybe a chemistry experiment would be the way to go. Problem is, what experiment should you do? Wouldn't it be great if you could get hold of a teacher's lesson plans for doing chemistry experiments? Well....you can! There is a whole slew of great experiments at the Physical Science and Chemistry Lesson Plans gopher page. Be careful, though, and always check with an adult before doing these experiments. You can never be safe enough when it comes to mixing chemicals.

**gopher://ec.sdcs.k12.ca.us:70/11/lessons/
  UCSD_InternNet_Lessons/
  Physical_Science_and_Chemistry**

Solving Dissolving Activity—Science Museum of Minnesota

How can rainwater make an acid and dissolve rock? Actually, that's how many caves are formed. Here is an experiment to try at home that will explain how, complete with pictures and instructions. Be sure to ask for help from a parent or teacher.

http://www.ties.k12.mn.us:80/~smm/sdact.html

**Frisbee is the Ultimate in
GAMES AND FUN.**

A B C D E F G H I J K L M N O P Q R S T U V W X Y Z

PERIODIC TABLE OF THE ELEMENTS

Periodic Table of the Elements

Chemistry is easy to understand—it's "elementary." Actually, chemistry is all about elements—the primary parts of all chemicals. For years, scientists have learned what the elements of chemistry are, and they've grouped the elements in a chart called the periodic table. To see all of the elements and what the properties of each element are, take a look at this page, presented by the Los Alamos National Laboratory. It's easy to use, and you'll learn much.

http://www.c8.lanl.gov/infosys/html/periodic/
    periodic-main.html

PLASTICS AND POLYMERS

Slime Time

Polymers are chemicals that we use all the time. Plastic is a polymer, nylon is a polymer, the keyboard of your computer is probably largely made of polymers. The greatest polymer of all, though, is SLIME!!!! No kidding. You can read all about slime, and polymers, on the Slime Time page produced by Mr. Lemberg's First Period Chemistry Class in Washington State's Battle Ground Public School.

http://152.157.16.3/phs/doc/chem/doc/slime.html

SOLIDS, LIQUIDS, AND GASES

Microworlds—Exploring the Structure of Materials

Scientists are learning more and more about the world by studying the tiniest parts. By looking at atoms and molecules, scientists are learning why some objects are hard, others brittle, and why some are strong. You can view this miniature world at the Microworlds- Exploring the Structure of Materials page. You'll see a new machine that is helping to explore inner space, and you can also view discoveries about materials you use every day.

http://www.lbl.gov/MicroWorlds/

**Chase some waterfalls in
EARTH SCIENCE**

Starch

OK, you mix equal parts of starch and water. Do you bet that the result will be a solid or a liquid? Think carefully. Still don't know? It's both! A thyxotropic substance is liquid under normal conditions. However, when it's under pressure, it becomes a solid! Find out why here! And, you'll find it's a lot of fun to play with this slime, er, thyxotropic toy.

gopher://schoolnet.carleton.ca:419/00/K6.dir/
    trycool.dir/starch

CIRCUS AND CLOWNS

See also: JUGGLING

CIRCUSTUFF

Interested in circus tricks? Start your clowning around here! Visit the CIRCUSTUFF page where you can download digital animations of juggling tricks. You can slow the animation down and even freeze the frames to be sure you "catch" every move. You'll also find juggling props to keep you busy for a long time!

http://www.demon.co.uk/circustuff/index.html

The FSU Flying High Circus Home Page

Did you know you can go to college AND be in a circus at the same time? At Florida State University, you can! Learn about lots of circus tricks performed by students. Some stunts—like triple somersaults on the flying trapeze, and seven-man pyramids—are so hard that lots of professional circus performers won't even try them. What's really surprising is that most of the students haven't had any circus training before joining the Flying High Circus. Don't miss the "cloudswings," especially the kind done without a net. Other circus schools around the world are also listed, as well as links to related sites, like unicycle and juggling home pages.

http://www.fsu.edu/~mpeters/fsucircus.html

Juggling Information Service

The three ingredients of becoming a juggler: practice, practice, and the Juggling Information Service web site. Here you'll find the home pages of fellow jugglers, a collection of juggling pictures in the gallery, juggling videos in the movie theater, and much more. Ask for juggling help and you'll get helpful suggestions from other jugglers. Have fun, and don't forget to check out "The Instant Jugglers' Manual"—warming up, 4 balls, 5 balls, you're on the way to being a juggler.

http://www.hal.com/services/juggle/

CLOTHING

Levi Strauss & Co.—Welcome!

Although Levi's jeans have been around for over a hundred years, they just got this web site up and running, and it is packed full of fun stuff. Explore the "jean-eology" historic timeline offered through the "faded" link. Rummage through the "Fifth Pocket" for hidden prizes. Take the "Inner-seam" tour to see how the company comes up with their television commercials. Check out what's happening in the world of fashion through the "street" link.

http://www.levi.com/menu

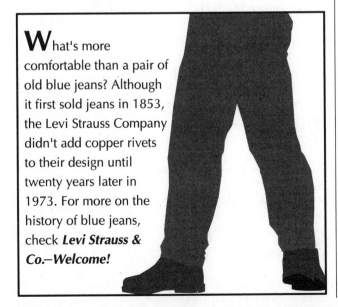

What's more comfortable than a pair of old blue jeans? Although it first sold jeans in 1853, the Levi Strauss Company didn't add copper rivets to their design until twenty years later in 1973. For more on the history of blue jeans, check *Levi Strauss & Co.–Welcome!*

Lost your sheep? Count them in FARMING AND AGRICULTURE.

COSTUME

Art Deco-Erté Museum

When you think of a special event costume, you probably think of Halloween. In Hollywood, movie stars put on costumes for special events, like parties or awards ceremonies. The costumes they wear today are usually just tuxedos and gowns. Long ago, famous people used to incorporate a lot more imagination into their costumes! Designers like Romain de Tirtoff, better known as Erté, went to great efforts to create one-of-a-kind costumes. Erté was an Art Deco fashion creator, and this site is full of great costume ideas.

http://www.webcom.com/~tuazon/ajarts/erte.html

CODES AND CIPHERS

The Beale Page

The Beale Ciphers hold the key to one of the greatest unsolved puzzles of all time. The story goes that around 1820, a fellow named Beale hid two wagon-loads of silver, gold, and jewels someplace near Roanoke, Virginia. He left three coded letters, supposedly detailing the location of the treasure, with a trusted friend. Then he left for the West, and was never seen again. One of the letters, describing the treasure, has been deciphered. It was in a code based on the Declaration of Independence. It is believed the other letters are similarly coded to the same document, or other public documents. You can read about the status of the Beale ciphers, and maybe try solving them yourself! If you find this treasure, please let us know!

http://www.ruhr.de/home/zaphod/beale.html

A B C D E F G H I J K L M N O P Q R S T U V W X Y Z

Morse Code

Morse Code was invented by Samuel Finley Breese Morse as a way to send messages over telegraph lines. Morse is known as the inventor of the "electromagnetic recording telegraph" although he had help from others. The first message transmitted over a telegraph line was in 1844. "What hath God wrought" went 36 miles, from Washington, D.C. to Baltimore, Maryland, in code sent by Morse himself. What happens if you make a mistake in sending code? You can't erase or backspace, so to indicate that a mistake has been made and tell the receiver to delete the last word, send .... (eight dots).

http://www.soton.ac.uk/~scp93ch/refer/
  alphabet.html

Morse Code Translator

Type in your name and get it translated into Morse Code! Or, if you're a real code wizard, type in the dots and dashes and have it translated back into readable text! .-- --- .-- or, "wow" in Morse code!

http://www.soton.ac.uk/~scp93ch/refer/
  morseform.html

National Cryptological Museum

Years ago, the road signs pointing to the CIA (the spy guys—the Central Intelligence Agency) building in Virginia said, "Bureau of Public Roads." Everybody knew what it was, but nobody was willing to admit it publicly. A lot of this has changed. The National Security Agency, a similar government agency that does all kinds of James Bondian things, opened up this public museum devoted to secret codes and codebreaking in 1993. This page has a nice sampling of Museum exhibits, complete with photographs. You'll see once-secret cryptology devices such as the Cipher Wheel, the Black Chamber, and Enigma. Museum hours and instructions on how to get to the place (including a map) are available here as well. Thank goodness they didn't put the directions in code!

http://www.nsa.gov:8080/museum

What is the Black Chamber?
Despite its ominous-sounding name, it was the name for a highly secret MI-8 code-breaking project during the 1920s. Herbert O. Yardley worked for the Army and the State Department and broke the diplomatic codes of several different nations, including Japan. Before the meetings of the Washington Naval Conference of 1921-22, the U.S. State Department would break the codes detailing the Japanese bargaining position. Everyone was dumbfounded because it seemed that the U.S. was reading the minds of the Japanese. They were, of course. The Japanese quickly figured this out, and changed their codes. Find out more at the National Cryptological Museum home page.

Some Classic Ciphers and Their Weaknesses

Using a "secret code" can add intrigue and excitement to the rather ordinary activity of sending a note or letter to a friend (especially via e-mail!). While personal computers have made it possible for anybody to have access to encryption programs, sometimes it's just more fun to use a code that you can scribble on a piece of paper. Some of these ciphers go back to the time of Julius Caesar, and a good handful of them can be found on this page. Each code is simply explained, and each is taken apart as well. What is even more fun than writing in code is breaking someone else's. Here, you can learn how to use the Caesar, Vigen-Augustus, and Playfair Ciphers, among others, and also find out what it takes to rip them up. Then for people who really want to keep a secret, there is a link to the modern cryptosystem for e-mail, PGP (Pretty Good Privacy).

http://rschp2.anu.edu.au:8080/cipher.html

COLLECTORS AND COLLECTING

Collectibles by Nerd World Media

The nerds at Nerd World have done it again! They have put together the most incredible set of links dealing with a cornucopia of collectibles! If you're looking for web sites about ship models, real or model railroads, gold coins, old magazine art, carousel horses, radio controlled vehicles, paper ephemera, cards, card games, signs, comics, phone cards, PEZ dispensers, historic newspapers and books, dolls, stamps, clocks, and much, much more, then be sure to drop in here! Parental advisory: this is a large site with many links, and they have not all been checked.

http://www.nerdworld.com/nw768.html

Collector's Universe

Collector's Universe claims to be "the largest collectible oriented site on the Internet." Whether this assertion is true or not, if you collect coins, stamps, comics, or trading cards, this page is not to be missed. Using professional-quality, vividly colored graphics, each separate "universe" link includes lists of dealers, shows, classified ads, news, and chat sections and clubs. They also have promised to be on the cutting edge with innovations that will "change collectibles on the Internet forever." This may be worth checking out every once in a while just to see what they mean by that!

http://www.collectors.com

COIN COLLECTING

See also: MONEY

Coin Collecting FAQ's

Have you got a nice collection of coins already, or did you just stumble into a few old ones in your change? Not really sure what to do with them? Roll on over to this page and get some of the more basic coin collecting questions answered. "How can I determine what a coin is really worth?" and "How can I sell my coins?" are two of the questions that are answered here, clearly and with logic and detail.

http://turnpike.net/emporium/M/mikec/gold3.htm

Numismatics Home Page

Coin collecting is an international activity, and this is a good place to look for information and links to numismatic hobbyists around the globe. Here you'll find links to discussion lists, news, pictures of coins, and a special link to an international web-based currency converter!

http://www.cs.vu.nl/~fjjunge/numis.html

You've got a good start on a coin collection, but some of them are pretty dirty. Should you clean your coins? Probably not. Collectors today value the originality of a coin, and any attempt to clean a coin may alter this originality and lower its value. Read more about this controversy, and many other questions about numismatics at the **Coin Collecting FAQ's page** *.*

One-Minute Coin Expert

Scott Travers' has excerpted one entire chapter from his popular book, *One Minute Coin Expert,* on this site. He answers many frequently-asked questions from both beginner and experienced coin collectors. Most of these questions are based on ones he has often been asked on radio and television programs. The information posted here is solid and useful, and of course, is designed to entice you to buy the book and get the rest of what you need to become a "one minute coin expert" yourself. One of the tips he recommends for kids is that they join the Young Numismatist coin collecting club (it's free). Send a postcard with your name, address, age, and telephone number to Lawrence J. Gentile Sr., 542 Webster Ave., New Rochelle, NY 10805. His program for kids includes "free seminars, free coins, free books, and a wealth of information that youngsters find helpful."

http://www.inch.com/%7Etravers/1min.htm

A
B
C
D
E
F
G
H
I
J
K
L
M
N
O
P
Q
R
S
T
U
V
W
X
Y
Z

SHELL COLLECTING

My Fourth Year Project—Sea Shell Modeling

Tony Printezis has graciously put together this page of detailed photographs of his shell collection. The unique thing about his collection is that it doesn't exist! Printezis devised a computer program from scratch that creates delicate, multicolored images of sea shells that look like they came off of a magical beach. Click on the thumbnails and see full-screen pictures of these shells.

http://www.dcs.gla.ac.uk/~tony/ss/default.html

Shell-a-rama

Shell-a-rama sells sea shells down by the sea shore, plus coral, shark teeth, sand dollars, starfish, sea fans, and lots of other goodies from the briny deep. Peek here at their color catalog, and be tempted to give them a call to get one. You can then use it for identification. And who knows, you might even order something. They say that nothing they sell is endangered.

http://www.gate.net/~quasisig/worldad/allen/

Shell-Bent on Sanibel

Florida's Sanibel Island's lack of offshore reefs and perpendicular heading, compared to its neighbor islands, make it a natural interceptor of shells from the south seas. People come from all over the world to comb Sanibel's beaches for washed-up natural treasures. Find out about the myriad sea shell-related activities here, such as the 60-year-old Sanibel Shell Show, the Bailey-Matthews Shell Museum, and other information for the traveler.

http://cypher.turbonet.com/finetrav/northa/usa/
    florida/SANIBEL/sanibel.htm

Lost your marbles? Find them in GAMES AND FUN.

SPORTS AND OTHER TRADING CARDS

B-Online: The Collector's Connection

For over a decade, Dr. James Beckett and his organization have tracked and published the prices of baseball, football, basketball, hockey, and many other sports trading cards. BeckWorld is a free membership organization that allows visitors to drop in and dig up information on selected popular cards. A paid subscription plan is also available for unlimited online searches in their extensive guides.

http://www.beckett.com

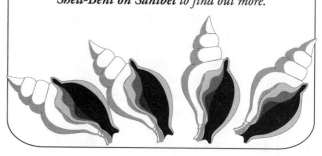

Can you do the Sanibel Stoop?
Stand on the shore, bend over, and scoop up a handful of rare and beautiful sea shells found on Florida's Sanibel Island.
Kick off your flip flops and head on over to Shell-Bent on Sanibel to find out more.

Sports Collectibles by Nerd World Media

Links to over a dozen sports collectible sites can be found here, many of them specializing in sports cards. The intriguing thing is that some of these pages on the Nerd World list are professional commercial sites, while others are strictly amateur, done for the love of the hobby. They're all great. This is the place to start looking for sports card information, whether you want to buy, sell, get questions answered, or just chew the fat with other collectors.

http://www.tiac.net/users/dstein/nw430.html

STAMP COLLECTING

postal page

Clicking on the crumpled envelope on this site's welcome page will bring you into one of the Smithsonian Institution's newest museums! It's organized into five major galleries that tell the story of postal history, and include a great collection of rare and wonderful stamp images. In many ways, the study of U.S. Postal Stamps is the study of American history and tradition. Whether you collect stamps, or just use them to mail letters, you'll find a visit to this site well worth the time.

http://www.si.edu/organiza/museums/postal/homepage

The Penny Black and the [Two] Penny Blue were the world's first adhesive postage stamps, issued in Great Britain, in 1840. They featured a portrait of a very young Queen Victoria. The U.S. issued its first postage stamps in 1847. Benjamin Franklin cost five cents, while George Washington was worth ten cents. **The Smithsonian Institution's National Postal Museum** *offers a glimpse into the intriguing—and sometimes sticky—world of stamps and stamp collecting.*

Stamps and Postal History Page

Bob Swanson has a collection of stamps, cancellations, first-day covers, and post cards that would make any collector drool, and he has put lots of the best images right here. He has a monthly "Mystery Cover" and links to the American Philatelic Society, the Military Postal Society, and plenty other fascinating stamp-oriented sites. If you want to try scanning in your own stamps, there is advice on that, too.

http://www.cris.com/~Swanson/posthist.html

COLOR AND COLORING BOOKS

See also: ART—DRAWING AND PAINTING

Carlos' Coloring Book Home

Did you ever use a computer and the Internet to color? At Carlos' Coloring Book you can color a birthday cake, a snowman, and other fun pictures on the World Wide Web with your computer! The best thing about this coloring book is that you can color over and over.

http://www.ravenna.com/coloring/

Crayola * Crayola * Crayola * Crayola

What's your favorite Crayola color? How do they make crayons anyway? In 1903, the Binney & Smith company manufactured the first box of "Crayolas." Explore the history of Crayolas, read the latest "Colorful News," and learn about Crayola trivia. Uh-oh! You left a bunch of crayons on the back seat of your Dad's car, and now they've melted! On the Crayola page, you can find out how to remove the stains. Make fun stuff from ideas right out of *Crayola Magazine*. You don't even have to color between the lines!

http://www.crayola.com/crayola/

Kendra's Coloring Book

Coloring used to be so hard. There's that "stay within the lines" thing. Plus, it can be tough to find the right color crayon or marker. When you do find it, it's always broken or out of ink. If you make a mistake, you might as well start over. These worries are over with Kendra's Coloring Book. All you have to do is pick a picture, select a color, and click where you want the color to go. No more worrying where you left the "Peach."

http://www.gcg.com/misc/colorbook/

Don't be a stick-in-the-MUD!

A B C D E F G H I J K L M N O P Q R S T U V W X Y Z

For happy hedgehogs see
PETS AND PET CARE.

Pocahontas Drawing Board

Would you like to make your own Pocahontas coloring book? Disney has created black and white pictures of Pocahontas, John Smith, Meeko, and Flit from the movie *Pocahontas*. You can copy them to your computer and color them in a paint program, or print them out and color them on paper.

http://www.disney.com/DisneyPictures/Features/
Pocahontas/ColoringBook/ColoringBook.html

COMICS AND CARTOONS

Collector's COMIX WORLD—Home Page

Are you an avid comic book reader? Have you ever daydreamed about being a superhero— webslinging, or flying up, up and away? If you count the days until the next issue of your favorite comic book hits the newsstands, then this link is for you! It offers a contest highlighting the best web sites for comics, a searchable calendar of comics shows and conventions, an extensive comics dictionary, and a searchable listing of dealers. This comics site has everything you need to stay on top of the comics scene.

http://www.comix-world.com/

The Comic Strip

Every week they make families around the world laugh. They have names like "Snoopy," "Dilbert," and "Marmaduke." Who are these wacky characters? They are the drawings that make up the comic strips in your newspaper. Catch up on your favorite comic strip characters, and see what they are doing on the Internet. Find out about the artists and how they thought up the characters, and play games based on the comic strip.

http://www.unitedmedia.com/comics/

Hergé

Let's go on an adventure! Tintin is a bold, youthful character who finds himself constantly in the middle of excitement. He travels around the world, with his pet dog Snowy, solving baffling mysteries. Tintin was created in 1929 by Belgian artist Hergé. Originally, it was a newspaper comic strip, but it has recently become an animated series. Read about the development of Tintin, and see some of the wonderful drawings.

http://www.netpoint.be/abc/herge/

How We Make Cartoons

Do you love to watch cartoons? Do you ever wonder how cartoons are made? At "How We Make Cartoons," Warner Brothers takes you on a tour of the process. Follow along as voices, sound effects, and music are added. See how the pictures go from pencil sketches to hand-painted art.

http://pathfinder.com/@@9rjXJtEm9AMAQGdz/
KidsWB/cartoon/cartoon.html

http://pathfinder.com/@@9rjXJtEm9AMAQGdz/
KidsWB/cartoon/cartoon.html

Cartoons sure have a lot of sound effects! Did you know that the ones they use over and over are stored on computers? Then, whenever they are needed in a cartoon, they are "played" with a special computer-connected piano keyboard. Other sound effects are created on the spot. Draw on How We Make Cartoons for more information.

Mother Goose & Grimm

Does your dog eat out of the garbage can? If so, it has something in common with Grimm! Mother Goose and Grimm are the lovable duo that appear in newspapers around the world, as well as Saturday morning cartoons. At this site, you can read biographical information about Mother Goose, Grimm, Atilla, and Mike Peters (the guy who draws these zany characters).

http://www.grimmy.com/

This week's Zany Zoo

If animals could talk, what would they say? The Zany Zoo is a weekly cartoon featuring a cast of zoo animals and the strange things they do. See the animals' perspectives on such things as Kangaroo Hiccups and Punk Penguins. Join zoo keeper John Johnson, his assistant Mike, and veterinarian Maria as they interact with this wonderful group of characters.

http://zeb.nysaes.cornell.edu/z/zz/

The Uncanny X-Page

X-Men? Look no further. All you could possibly want to know about X-Men comics (and other comics, too) is here. Somewhere. At least we think so, although we have not checked all the links.

http://www.students.uiuc.edu/~m-blase/x-page.html

You Can with Beakman and Jax

Put on your thinking cap and log into *You Can with Beakman and Jax*! This newspaper feature has become so popular there is now a *Beakman's World* TV series! Check out important historical facts in the "You Can Calendar." Discover the answers to important questions like "what are fingernails made of?" Help Beakman and Jax out with their research project. See pictures from the Hubble Space Telescope, and read about what the pictures show and what they mean.

http://www.nbn.com/youcan/

COMPUTERS

alt.folklore.computers List of Frequently Asked Questions

The word "folklore" generally conjures up images of Davy Crockett or Paul Bunyan. While not as rustic, the world of computers is just as rich in legends and lore. The Usenet newsgroup *alt.folklore. computers* has amassed a barrage of legends, and this site puts the most popular of them into easy-to-follow HTML format. Learn the truth about the NASA probe that rumors say was destroyed because of a computer typo. Who really wrote MS-DOS? Find out about the origins of Usenet and Unix, various computer firsts, and where in the world Jolt's high-caffeine cola is illegal.

http://www.best.com:80/~wilson/faq

Dave's Guide to Buying a Home Computer

How do you figure out which computer is the right one for you? What's an IDE? What size and speed of microprocessor do I need? You don't want to waste your money on a computer that is more than you need, but you do want a system that will be usable for a number of years. Read this guide for tips and suggestions on purchasing and installing a PC. Find out what to ask the store salesperson, and what to look for in features. The opinions expressed here are just that, opinions; but you'll find some invaluable information here.

http://www.css.msu.edu/pc-guide.html

Do Spiders Live on the World Wide Web?

Take your baby sister to the University of Michigan's Internet Public Library's story time! This picture book dictionary will help her learn the difference between the mouse on your desk and the mouse in your barn. In case you were wondering, the one in the barn eats up all the corn, while the one on your desk eats up all your time.

http://ipl.sils.umich.edu/youth/StoryHour/spiders/mousepg.html

Whooooooo will you find in BIRDS?

A
B
C
D
E
F
G
H
I
J
K
L
M
N
O
P
Q
R
S
T
U
V
W
X
Y
Z

Introduction to PC Hardware

Are today's computers a "RISC?" How much "cache" do you need to buy a computer? "IDE"'d like a bigger hard drive, but what kind do I get? Is our spelling that bad, or are we trying to make a point? Well, it so happens that those "misspelled" words are computer terms that you can read about on this page. You'll find out all about the different kinds of memory, and how they are used in a computer system. Read about what's inside a microprocessor chip, and about the different kinds of hard drives. By the time you're through, you'll be able to impress the salespeople in your local computer store— and maybe get a good deal to "boot."

http://pclt.cis.yale.edu/pclt/pchw/platypus.htm

THE JARGON FILE, VERSION 3.2.0, 21 MAR 1995

In the Beginning, computers were understood only by a small group of insiders. These insiders developed their own language and made up their own words, all of which served to further isolate them from the rest of the world, which was, after all, a distraction from computers and programming! ;-) For years, this hacker lore and legend has been collected into The Jargon File. It's even been published in book form as *The Hacker Dictionary*. Now it's made it to the Web, and you will laugh at the funny computing terms and lingo heard daily in machine rooms all over the Net. Some have even made it into popular conversation! You can search the file for specific terms, or just browse for fun. Parental advisory: some of these terms have mildly racy origins.

http://www.fwi.uva.nl/~mes/jargon/

RING!OnLine! Computer Advisor

Here's some advice on "How to Buy a Computer." This two-part column will help you if you're looking for your first computer, or looking to upgrade that old "slow-poke." How much RAM do you need, how big a hard drive should you get, what is a cache, anyway? Check this site out to find out.

http://www.ring.com/vts/advisor/main.htm

Did you hear about the guy who missed the chance to sell his operating system to IBM instead of Bill Gates's MS-DOS, because he was flying around in his airplane?

What is the longest thread ever in a newsgroup?

Where can you buy slide rules these days? Find out the fascinating answers to these and other questions at **alt.folklore.computers List of Frequently Asked Questions.**

The Virtual Museum of Computing

The world's largest museum devoted to computers is appropriately located in Downtown Hyperspace. Don't worry about putting coins in the parking meter. Just stroll around and check out the ever-growing collection. You'll find galleries featuring local virtual exhibits, corporate histories, and entire wings with histories of computing organizations and societies, plus general computer history. There are special exit doors here that will take you to a couple of dozen other online computing museums. While there is no virtual snack bar here yet, you can drop in on an assortment of selected computer-oriented newsgroups to chat about what you've seen. Parental advisory: this is a large site with many links, and they have not all been checked.

http://www.comlab.ox.ac.uk/archive/other/
museums/computing.html

Read any good Web sites lately?

ARTIFICIAL INTELLIGENCE

Howdy, Kids! Cog the Humanoid Robot

Back in 1921, playwright Karel Capek coined the word "Robot" and since then, books, movies, and television programs have all speculated about the form these mechanical creatures will take. Now a group of researchers at the Massachusetts Institute of Technology's Artificial Intelligence Lab are actually attempting this feat. Artificial intelligence is the process where a computer takes in information and uses it to create new knowledge—a simulation of human thinking. Cog the Robot is a collection of sensors and motors that attempt to duplicate the sensory and manipulative functions of the human body. Coupled with Artificial Intelligence programming, Cog may eventually succeed in bringing Science Fiction's Fantasies to reality. Move over Data, here comes Cog!

http://www.ai.mit.edu/projects/cog/cog-himself.html

NET FILES

What vegetable nicknamed the "King of American Crops" has its own palace ?

Answer: Corn. The Corn Palace is located in Mitchell, South Dakota. Read all about it at http://info.aes.purdue.edu/agronomy/cornguid.htm

HARDWARE AND SOFTWARE COMPANIES

Apple Computer

This is the computer "for the rest of us" that the PC has been trying to catch up with for years. While Windows 95 looks like tough competition, this is the company that introduced into the mainstream, the mouse, the graphical user interface, and the networked laser printer. Apple's home page has product information to help you choose a system, and a technical support area to help answer questions. You'll also find downloadable upgrades to Apple software and information on the "cool Apple technologies" that Apple is working on to improve its products for the future. Apple has been an advocate of the education market ever since 1977, with the introduction of the Apple II. Since then, it has continued to embrace education with its product lines, including the Macintosh and Power Macintosh. A 1993 *Technology in Public Schools* report showed that "93% of public school students attended institutions that use Apple computers." Additionally, the Apple Classrooms of Tomorrow (ACOT) research program is a collaboration among public schools, universities, research agencies, and Apple Computer, Inc., itself. For the past ten years, ACOT has studied technology's impact on education. A compilation of the lessons learned is available for a few dollars. It's called *Changing the Conversation About Teaching, Learning & Technology: a report on 10 years of ACOT Research*. The ordering information is at *http://www.atg.apple.com/acot/index.html*. Other research studies are also available. Find out more about Apple's educational programs at Apple's Education page in the Solutions area, or at *http://www.info.apple.com/education/*.

http://www.apple.com/

Have you hadrosaurus today? If not, try DINOSAURS AND PREHISTORIC TIMES.

A B **C** D E F G H I J K L M N O P Q R S T U V W X Y Z

Guide to Computer Vendors

Here they are: over a thousand computer hardware and software vendors with web pages ready to be accessed with a click. It's all filed with an easy-to-use alphabetical index, and as a bonus, there's a Telephone Directory here with several thousand computer companies listed. Want more? Link into the Computer Magazine list maintained on this page, and drop in on your favorite periodical's web site! Not all links have been viewed.

http://www.ronin.com/SBA

MicrosoftFocus on K-12

In February, 1975, Bill Gates and Paul Allen completed the first computer language program, a BASIC interpreter, written for a personal computer. For the next few years, Microsoft created products such as COBOL, BASIC, and FORTRAN compilers, and in 1981, shipped MS-DOS 1.0 for IBM's new personal computer. In the years to come, MS-DOS became the standard operating system that was bundled with the millions of PCs shipped to businesses and individuals. In 1985, Windows was introduced to the public. Since then, Microsoft has shipped over 100 million units of Windows. Did we mention that today, Microsoft is the largest software company in the world? Check out these K-12 pages and see what Microsoft is doing in the way of sponsoring programs to promote education, such as the Global Schoolhouse.

http://www.microsoft.com/k-12/

PC SoftDIR—Software Publishers

There are about "500 North American Software Companies" listed in this index. The companies are listed alphabetically, and each listing contains general company information, plus a list of their software products, along with descriptions and pricing. A link to the company's home page is also included, if one is available. ElJen Publishing, Inc., the publisher, also offers a Windows CD version of this directory that includes more in-depth descriptions for each product.

http://www.netusa.com/pcsoft/publshr.htm

MACINTOSH
The Cult of Macintosh TM

An unofficial evangelistic effort promoting the Macintosh is actively attempting to place page mirrors on every continent in the world. Frequently updated, it has become a friendly all-around resource for Mac users with hundreds of links to just about anything a Mac user could desire. Try one of these mirrors if you have trouble connecting:

> http://www.gulf.net/~stone/mac
> http://ucsu.Colorado.EDU/~jungd/cult
> http://www.dakota.net/~schnaidt/cult

http://cult-of-mac.utu.fi

Mac Vendor Web Sites

Eventually, every computer owner will run across a problem, and need some kind of support from a manufacturer. Mac users—here's a site with a huge list of Mac-oriented vendors. Many of the vendors here, in addition to product information, have technical support and downloadable upgrades for their products.

http://webcom.com/~level6/VendorWebSites.html

Macintosh Educators Page

Billed as an "Educators" page, anyone with a Mac (and even those without one) will have a blast visiting here. Short descriptions are provided for each of the links, which include all the major Macintosh archives, magazine pages, and help sites, as well as Science, General Education, and Fun pages, and a changing "Mystery Site."

http://www.netins.net/showcase/macintosh

The ULTIMATE Macintosh

Hundreds of Macintosh-related links are piled up on this one page, making it possible to conduct a search using your browser's "Find" command (on Lynx, use the "/" command). The best thing about this page is the "What's HOT!" section, that provides up-to-the-minute news and links to the latest information (including promotions from Apple and major vendors) and software updates. Not all links have been viewed.

http://www.velodrome.com/umac.html

MAGAZINES

Yahoo—Business and Economy:Products and Services:Magazines

Sorry for the long URL, but here's the direct link to Yahoo's online list of computer-related magazines on the Net. (Be sure to save the bookmark for this so you don't have to retype it.) Check out your favorite, or find some new interesting magazines to browse through. Of course, there's also a search function that can help you find a word, or topic of interest. Be sure to select the "Search only in Personal Computers" button, unless you want to search all of Yahoo.

http://www.yahoo.com/Business_and_Economy/
   Products_and_Services/Magazines/Computers/
   Personal_Computers/

OTHER COMPUTERS

Amiga Report Magazine

The Amiga may be the Phoenix of computers, rising out of the ashes to new heights. While never achieving the measure of popularity in the U.S. as it had in Europe, the purchase of the rights to the once-discontinued system by the Amiga Technologies group has created the possibility of new developments that may make the machine a major contender in the American market. Whether you already own an Amiga and are looking for sources of support and new software (there is a Mosaic for Amiga users!), or are just interested in keeping track of promised new machines, drop in on the *Amiga Report* regularly.

http://www.omnipresence.com/Amiga/News/AR/

The Amiga Web Directory

If you are an Amiga owner, you've found heaven! Here, you'll find links to Amiga news, software archives, and product information. There's free software, demos, user group information, Amiga magazines, hardware and software support, and links, links, links. If you can't find the solution to your Amiga needs here, it probably doesn't exist. Need we say more?

http://www.cucug.org/amiga.html

> ## Curl up with a good Internet site.

Apple II Resources

While Apple Computer may have discontinued the II line a few years ago, there are millions of these workhorse machines still in use in homes and schools everywhere. Plenty of new II hardware and software is still being developed. Nathan Mates has collected as many Apple II links as he could find, including Newsgroups, FTP sites chock-full of programs and information, lists of BBSs, and companies producing Apple II products. Once the corporate slogan for Apple Computer, "Apple II Forever!" seems to be a fact of life for a dedicated bunch of folks you'll find here.

http://www.ugcs.caltech.edu/~nathan/
   apl2.resource.html

NET FILES

What's the longest-lived mammal on Earth? If you guess that, then what's the second longest-lived mammal?

Answer: Man has the longest life of all mammals, but the Spiny Anteater comes in second, at fifty years of life expectancy. Read more about this unusual egg-laying mammal at *http://edx1.educ.monash.edu.au/~juanda/vcm/gary.htm.*

Atari 8-bits

The Atari 8-bit computer was a natural outgrowth of the company's phenomenally popular game cartridge machine. In fact, all of these machines, whether the 400, 800, or any of the XL or XE series, had a port or two for popping in game or program cartridges. There are plenty of folks still getting lots of mileage out of them, and this site is a great starting point if you're wondering what you can do with one. It includes plenty of links to active Atari 8-bit home pages, as well as the important "Atari 8-bit Omnibus."

http://zippy.sonoma.edu/~kendrick/nbs/
    what_is_atari.html

ZX81 Home Page

At first glance, the ZX81, more commonly known in the U.S. as the Timex Sinclair Computer, appears to be a sleek and snappy palmtop. Actually, this tiny, membrane-keyed desktop computer once sold like hotcakes. As the first computer in history to break the hundred dollar price barrier, over a million were sold. They came with a "whopping" one kilobyte of RAM, and used cassette tapes to store data. Writing programs for the machine was an exercise in precision coding. If you've found a ZX81 in the attic or at a garage sale, this is the page to turn to for lots of fascinating information about it, and where to go for help in using it. We had two of them. Dad often enjoyed showing us cool programs he wrote for it, while we were still figuring out the manual for our Apple IIe. Loading from cassette tape was quite a trick though. Back in the olden days... when we had to trudge through the snow to buy RAM....

http://www.gre.ac.uk/~bm10/zx81.html

SLIME is a polymer, as anyone who's read CHEMISTRY knows!

PC COMPATIBLES, MICROSOFT WINDOWS

The IBM world wide web home page

Here's where the personal computer (PC) all started. IBM introduced the PC in 1983. Today, computers based on the same design account for about 85% of the microcomputer market. Talk about popular! Before the PC, and even now, IBM's stronghold has been with big-business computers that run governments, corporations, banks, and other institutions. Explore this web site to see what this computer giant is up to these days, such as speech recognition. Hint: if you click "Stretch" on the home page, you'll find a surprise!

http://www.ibm.com/

Welcome to Gateway 2000

Did you know Gateway computers are shipped in boxes that look like they are part dairy cow? What's with those cows, anyway? Ted Waitt's family had been in the cattle business for many generations. When he created a new computer company, Gateway 2000, he brought some of his heritage with him. Apparently, he also brought some luck with him, because his company is now the largest seller of computers sold through direct marketing.

http://www.gw2k.com/

The Windows 95 QAID

"How much RAM is required to run Windows 95?" "I lost multiboot option, how do I get it back?" These are two of the many questions that are answered on this Question-Answer-Information-Database (QAID). The questions are listed by category, like CD ROM, Booting, Printers, and Sound. You'll also find news, tips & tricks, and other Windows 95-related areas to browse through. Some of the dialog can get quite technical, but then, computers can get that way sometimes. The QAID database is also available for download, allowing you to search for answers while offline.

http://www.whidbey.net/~mdixon/win40001.htm

> ## See what's shakin' in EARTH SCIENCE-GEOLOGY-EARTHQUAKES.

Windows95.com

Despite the name, this page is not owned and operated by Microsoft. Using the familiar Windows interface, visitors can click and get help on a variety of topics regarding Windows95, including the straight lowdown on what kinds of computers should, and should not, use it. There are discussion forums and live chat areas, links to 32-bit shareware, a glossary, and lots of information for beginners. You can download *Win95 Magazine* or a Windows95 Demo for Windows 3.1 users, and new users can purchase "Quick Tutors 95," an interactive online help program.

http://www.windows95.com

SOFTWARE ARCHIVES

Aminet at ftp.wustl.edu

"Aminet is the Internet's largest collection of Amiga software." Check out the recent uploads list to keep up-to-date with your favorite shareware. Visit the "Tree of Aminet directories" for a list of their archives sorted by category. There's also a search tool, and help files available for those in need.

http://ftp.wustl.edu/~aminet/

c/net resources—software central

This is an intro page to the shareware.com software archives. We've pointed to this page because of its three sections at the bottom of the page called "virus check?," "survival kits," and "beginner's guides." Each section has a Mac- and PC-specific selection that contains valuable information, especially for first-time users. For those "experts" out there, the direct link to the archive is *http://www.shareware.com/*. Enjoy!

**http://www.cnet.com/Resources/Software/
index.html**

CSUSM Windows World

All you Windows users—here's a great place to visit for shareware. This collection, maintained at California State University, has its software titles sorted by category for easy browsing. Each listing contains a short description, its file size, and date. There is also a search facility that will help you find that special program.

**http://coyote.csusm.edu/cwis/winworld/
winworld.html**

Happy Puppy's Front Porsche

Happy Puppy brings you a list of software and home pages of many of the game software companies on the Net. You'll find lists for Mac and PC games, and info on new versions of your favorite games as they are announced. Other software archives listed here have shareware, demos, and upgrades available for those in need of too much fun! Some of the categories at the bottom of the page are still under development, and at this writing, they don't work, but there's plenty of software here to keep you busy.

http://happypuppy.com/

INFO-MAC Hyperarchive ROOT

Over the years, info-mac has become the master list for Macintosh software archives, with mirror sites around the world. Now you can use your web client to search or browse this mirror collection at MIT. This is a great way to find shareware, demos, clip art, help, and information about Macintosh. If you own a Mac, this will become one of your best links.

http://hyperarchive.lcs.mit.edu/HyperArchive.html

Jumbo!—Shareware! Shareware! Shareware!

Shareware? What's that? You can try out shareware software before you buy it. Sometimes the shareware version will do everything that the full version will do! Jumbo also has lots of free programs for most computers and operating systems. It's easy to find what you want, since everything is classified by subject. The short descriptions will help you find that arcade game, er, math tutorial, you wanted!

http://www.jumbo.com/

A B C D E F G H I J K L M N O P Q R S T U V W X Y Z

Crack open CODES AND CIPHERS.

Oak Software Repository

Check out this grandfather archive site for access to just about all the DOS and Windows software available. Besides listing many of the other software archives, you can browse the legendary SimTel archives here with your web browser. The SimTel collection goes back to the early DOS years, and is the largest collection of PC programs and information in the world. Of course, a search function is available to help you find the "needle in the haystack" you might be looking for.

http://www.acs.oakland.edu/oak.html

Tigger's Children's Shareware Page

Families who drop in on this site will find it a severe test of the storage capacity of their hard drives. :-) There is a wealth of kids' software available on the Internet, and this is the place to look for it. This extensive, fully annotated collection gives each program its own page, including age recommendations, program sizes, and shareware fees, if there are any. The page is divided between Mac and PC archives and a third section devoted to downloadable commercial demo programs. This last section includes links to many pages of kids' software review sites.

http://remarque.berkeley.edu/~tigger/sw-kids.html

TotWare

Ready-made links to a couple of dozen downloadable shareware and freeware programs for both the Mac and PC can be found here. They are all for preschoolers, and capsule reviews give an idea what each one does. The programs are organized by categories, such as "Bangers," "Games," "Nature," and "Letters and Numbers."

http://www.het.brown.edu/people/mende/
totware.html

UNIX

UNIXhelp for users

Excuse me, but you "grepped" my file while I was "rm"ing it! Unix geeks like to talk like that, a lot. It establishes a "safe" distance between them and non-geeks. Well, just how close would you get to someone who said things like that? Unix is the operating system that is most often used by engineers and networking professionals, because of its power. Unix systems don't have to "add" TCP/IP to "plug" into the Internet, it's their native networking language. Now try to guess what operating system was used to expand the Internet into what it is today. You're right, it's Unix. Unix was even used to run *Jurassic Park*, and... oh, never mind.

http://www.eecs.nwu.edu/Unixhelp/

VIRTUAL REALITY

virtual reality

Watch out! There's a giant batwinged bird that's about to swoop down and talk to you. Does that sound impossible? Well, it's not impossible when you are wearing specially designed helmets and data gloves that allow you to view virtual worlds. *virtual reality* is an electronic magazine dedicated to virtual reality news, movies, books, arcade games, hardware, and software. Be careful, those spotted pigs look like they want to play.

http://Web.Actwin.Com:80/NewType/vr/index.htm

CONSUMER INFORMATION

See also: MONEY

Consumer Information Center

Got a limited allowance budget? Learn how to stretch it a bit further with publications from the Consumer Information Center. Many of them are right on this page in text or html format. Or you can order the publications online, and have them sent to you. You can also find pamphlets on how to learn to read, booklists of great reading for kids, and more!

http://www.gsa.gov/staff/pa/cic/cic.htm

Consumer World

OK, you bought that skateboard you've been wanting. Now it won't even roll! Hustle over to Consumer World to find out what you can do about it. It doesn't matter that you're a kid! You have consumer power, and manufacturers listen to consumers, regardless of their age. While you're there, you can also find out how to avoid online scams, determine if the skateboard has been recalled, and link to the Better Business Bureau. You'll also find out how to contact many companies, and other sources of consumer information. Be sure to show this site to your parents, they will love it!

http://www.consumerworld.org/

COOKING, FOOD, AND DRINK

CheeseNet 95

You can slice it, grate it, melt it, and of course you can eat it. What's your favorite way to eat cheese? How is cheese made? Read about the cheesemaking process, or tour the cheese picture gallery. Read about the differences among cheeses around the world. If you have questions you can send them to "cheeseologist Dr. Emory K. Cheese" in the "Ask Dr. Cheese" section. You might be amused by the "Cheese Poetry," then again, maybe not.

http://www.efn.org/~kpw/cheesenet95/

EPICURIOUS: FOOD DRINK, COOKING AND RECIPES

You still can't find that extra-special recipe for your dinner party. Your family just found a great restaurant that you want everyone to know about. And, just how *do* you eat an artichoke in public? The publishers of *Bon Appetit* and *Gourmet* magazine give you recipes and a restaurant forum, and share tips on how to make being in the kitchen a rewarding experience. Check the explanations on how to eat awkward foods in public without having them land in your lap.

http://www.epicurious.com/

Watch your step in DANCE.

Food and Cooking

Everything you ever wanted to know about pork, but were afraid to ask Mom, is here. Get some free recipes sent to you by mail. (Go to "You're Invited" to get these freebies.) While you're at this site, look around at all the recipes and pictures. Yum!

http://www.nppc.org/food&cooking.html

Food Lover's Glossary

Have you ever read a recipe in a cookbook and come across an ingredient that's unfamiliar? The Food Lover's Glossary is a collection of terms to make reading recipes easier. From "Abalone" to "Zuppa Inglese," the glossary provides mouth-watering definitions. The terms cover all types of food from all walks of life. There are recipes for every meal of the day and every course of the meal, plus some delightful extras. Check your knowledge against the glossary, but be warned—don't do it on an empty stomach.

http://foodstuff.com/pearl/gloss.html

HomeArts: Food Table of Contents

Who doesn't like food? When you think about food, do you think about what is on the plate, or how it got there? HomeArts puts together information about food from *Redbook, Good Housekeeping, Country Living,* and other great sources of food news. There are tons of hints on cooking and food preparation for you to explore. Warning: this site requires the ability to download big graphics.

http://homearts.com/depts/food/00dpfdc1.htm

Find your roots in GENEAOLOGY.

A
B
C
D
E
F
G
H
I
J
K
L
M
N
O
P
Q
R
S
T
U
V
W
X
Y
Z

NET FILES

Who is credited with inventing the concept of computer programming?

Answer: Ada Byron Lovelace (1815-1851) is credited with the invention of programming, for her work with Charles Babbage's Analytical Engine. A military programing language, Ada is named after her, in commemoration. Read more about this mathematician at http://www.scottlan.edu//riddle/women/love.htm

Mycelium Welcome

Does the thought of Shiitake-Leek Quiche make your mouth water? Is your idea of a perfect weekend roaming the woods and fields in search of small fungi so you can whip up some Cajun Glazed Mushrooms? Discover how to identify the good from the bad while in pursuit of the elusive wild 'shrooms. And if you would prefer to stalk shiitake in the supermarket instead of hunting chanterelles in the great outdoors, you can learn about the different types found in the produce section, and pick up some some great mushroom recipes, plus techniques of preserving mushrooms.

http://www.igc.apc.org/mushroom/welco.html

The Pie Page

When is the best time for pie? If you answered anytime, you are definitely going to enjoy The Pie Page. The Pie Page has recipes for all of your favorite dessert pies and even one for venison pie...mmmmmmmmm. Seriously, The Pie Page has tips for better pie making. There's also a step-by-step tutorial of how to make a pie crust.

http://www.teleport.com/~psyched/pie/pie.html

This Page Stinks!

You know that smell from a mile away—it's garlic! Garlic has a wonderful flavor. It makes spaghetti and pizza taste great. Garlic is also legendary for repelling vampires. It's also good at chasing away garden pests, and it may even be helpful in avoiding cancer. Find out more about this fascinating food. The Garlic Page has recipes, health facts, growing tips, and, of course, garlic news. Don't, please *don't* choose the link from this page labeled "Surprise." We warned you. Although perhaps there might be one of you out there interested in the effects of garlic on medicinal leeches.

http://broadcast.com/garlic/index.html

FOODS AND DRINKS

Ben & Jerry's Home Page

Admit it. How many times have you run to the grocery store because you needed a Ben & Jerry ice cream cone? Now you can get it here without leaving your seat. If you love their ice cream, you will love their site. It's chock-full of the philosophy and wit that makes them so popular. Find out who these guys are, and play with their fun stuff. If you still grieve over the discontinuation of your favorite flavor, make sure to visit the flavor graveyard, and find peace of mind knowing that at least they have gone to the Great Web Page on the Net. But if you start to get a craving for the real thing, don't even try to lick the screen—just go to the store like everyone else.

http://www.benjerry.com/

Butterball

Which do you prefer light, or dark meat? ("Hey!!" says the turkey, "It's all the same meat to me!!") Turkey is not only a very popular food during the holiday season, it's a great meal any time of the year. ("Yeah, well so is Vegetarian Pizza!") Turkey is great because after the first meal, there are usually leftovers good for a zillion sandwiches and a delicious soup. ("Ever heard of falafel, pita, and hummous??") At this page, you will find great stuffing recipes, gravy recipes, carving tips, and creative garnishing ideas. ("I'm outta here!")

http://www.butterball.com/

Chocolate Town U.S.A.

Crunchy, creamy, drippy like hot fudge, or steaming like cocoa—what could be more delicious than chocolate? Where do they make chocolate? Lots of places, but one of them is in Hershey, Pennsylvania, at Hershey's Chocolate Town, U.S.A. This site has fun facts about chocolate and a tour of the largest chocolate factory in the world. This site offers a text-only option for those with slower connections.

http://www.hersheys.com/~hershey/

The Dinner Co-op Home Page: for cooks and food-lovers

What's for dinner? The next time you have *no* idea, try the links on this page. For one thing, there are recipes. LOTS of recipes! And we haven't checked all the links, but there is certainly some interesting stuff here. For example, can the *color* of food suppress your appetite? Have you ever noticed that besides blueberries, no blue food exists in nature? Our brains are just not keyed into seeing a blue thing as a food source. If you want to eat less, put a blue light in your dining room, or eat off a blue plate. This page suggests you put a little food grade food coloring into the water the next time you cook some spaghetti, and try it out on yourself! Don't forget the blue M&M "meatballs!"

http://gs216.sp.cs.cmu.edu/dinnercoop/
    home-page.html

Did you know that the first meal on the moon was—turkey??? Astronauts Neil Armstrong and Buzz Aldrin feasted on roast turkey from foil packets. They apparently didn't have any cranberry sauce though. Stuff yourself with more facts at the Butterball page!

Dole's 5 a Day

Do you mind your peas and carrots? Learn the nutritional values of the fruits and vegetables that you eat every day. Then fun stuff awaits when you meet Adam Apple, Bobby Banana, and their friends. Try the 5 A Day Game along with them, as they point out how important they are to your well-being. Try some of the delicious recipes provided, and you'll want to bring these friends to your dinner table every day! There's also a virtual tour to the Dole Salad factory, oops, watch out for that radicchio!

http://www.dole5aday.com/

Frito-Lay Main Menu

Frito-Lay is more than just corn chips! Their site offers fun, interactive advertising games. You can create your own "dream date"—"is your dream date punk or preppie?" Use corn chips to spice up your recipes, and create Chili Pie or a Fiesta Burger. Ever wonder who invented the pretzel? It was invented by a monk in 610 A.D.! These pages are good munching for snack fanatics!

http://www.fritolay.com/

A B C D E F G H I J K L M N O P Q R S T U V W X Y Z

It was a breakthrough, back in 1913. Henry Ginaca, engineer and inventor, unveiled his masterpiece! It could peel, core, and pack 35 pineapples per minute. Wow, the people at the Dole factory were ecstatic! The Ginaca Machine is still used in pineapple canneries today. But Dole is more than pineapples, check out the Dole·s 5 a Day home page.

Godiva Online Home Page

See how sweet life can be! Godiva Chocolate welcomes you to their playground for chocolate lovers. They tempt your palate with chocolate recipes, trivia, and an online catalog for instant gratification. If only the Web would implement those aroma attribute protocols! You will never forget another anniversary or birthday if you register with their free gift reminder service. And if that still isn't enough, they have plenty of links to other chocolate sites to help satisfy your cravings.

http://www.godiva.com/

Kellogg Clubhouse

Let hosts Snap, Crackle, and Pop take you around the Kellogg Clubhouse. Snap shares nutrition tips and some recipes for sweet treats, including everybody's favorite, rice crispy squares. Crackle has some fun activities in the recreation room. Share a game with Pop in the lounge. This colorful web site is beautifully designed, but watch out, the graphics may take a long time to load. Also, it asks for your e-mail address, but if you just click "DONE" it seems to let you in anyway.

http://www.kelloggs.com/

People are the true treasures of the Net.

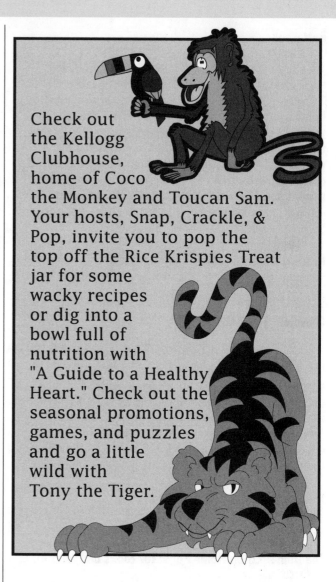

Check out the Kellogg Clubhouse, home of Coco the Monkey and Toucan Sam. Your hosts, Snap, Crackle, & Pop, invite you to pop the top off the Rice Krispies Treat jar for some wacky recipes or dig into a bowl full of nutrition with "A Guide to a Healthy Heart." Check out the seasonal promotions, games, and puzzles and go a little wild with Tony the Tiger.

M&M'S Chocolate Mini Baking Bits

When you eat M&M's, which colors do you eat first? Which colors do you avoid? M&M Baking Bits are tiny M&Ms. They are probably made tiny so they can be easily sprinkled atop cookies and cupcakes. The fun thing about them is that because they are smaller, you can fit more of them in your mouth at once! Here on the World Wide Web, you can see how the Mini Baking Bits are created on the "personalized tour." There are also recipes and baking tips for those who can resist eating them long enough to cook with them.

http://www.baking.m-ms.com/

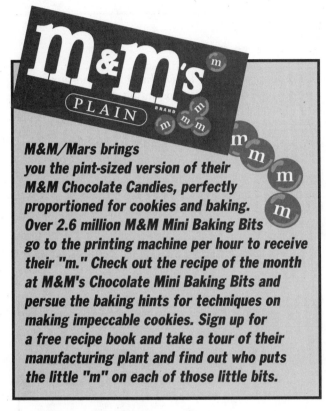

M&M/Mars brings you the pint-sized version of their M&M Chocolate Candies, perfectly proportioned for cookies and baking. Over 2.6 million M&M Mini Baking Bits go to the printing machine per hour to receive their "m." Check out the recipe of the month at M&M's Chocolate Mini Baking Bits and persue the baking hints for techniques on making impeccable cookies. Sign up for a free recipe book and take a tour of their manufacturing plant and find out who puts the little "m" on each of those little bits.

Nabisco, Inc. on the Web

Are you a twister or a dunker? Find out where you fall in the Oreo cookie survey, and discover the stories behind your favorite snacks like Fig Newtons, Barnum's Animal Crackers, and Chips Ahoy cookies, and how they came about. Nabisco also offers a section for healthy living, cooking tips, and recipes and challenges you to find the Nabisco "Thing" in "where's Waldo"-type crowd pictures.

http://www.nabisco.com/

Oscar Mayer CyberCinema

If you wish you were an Oscar-Mayer wiener, you'll want to spend a lot of time at this site. There are the usual recipes, contests, and company jabbering, but what caught our eye was the interactive History of the Wienermobile. With or without Real Audio, it's hot! The first hot dog on wheels toured the streets of Chicago in 1936. It was only 13 feet long. By the 50s, the wienermobile had grown to 22 feet. It had a sound system, and a sunroof. By 1958, though, it finally got what it had been lacking all these years. No, it wasn't mustard, but it was a bun! Six "Wienebagos" were touring the world by 1988, with the comforts of on-board microwave ovens and other conveniences. In 1995, the latest model is 27 feet long and 10 feet high. We cannot do any better than to quote from the home page: "The model underwent tests in the wind tunnel at the California Institute of Technology in Pasadena and could really, theoretically speaking, haul buns as it reached speeds in excess of 90 miles per hour." Hot dog!

http://www.oscar-mayer.com

Welcome to Burlingame On-Line's PEZ Exhibit

Have you ever had a PEZ? PEZ are a fruit-flavored candy, and are best known for their famous collectible dispensers. The first PEZ dispensers didn't have any heads at all, and now there are over 250 different models. The PEZ Exhibit has detailed pictures of all of the dispensers, with the date of manufacture for each one. You can see which dispensers were made when your parents, and maybe even your grandparents, were born!

http://www.spectrumnet.com/pez/

Welcome to the Land of Snapple

It's a soft drink bottled in all colors of the rainbow, and comes in exotic flavors, such as Black Cherry Jubilee Cider. It's sold all over the world—what is your favorite Snapple flavor? The Land of Snapple web site is full of fun, games, and contests. Who are those kids in the Snapple commercials? Hear audio and video of their experiences! Enter your favorite Snapple story, and maybe you'll be the subject of their next commercial!

http://www.snapple.com/

A
B
C
D
E
F
G
H
I
J
K
L
M
N
O
P
Q
R
S
T
U
V
W
X
Y
Z

INTERNATIONAL

EXPO Restaurant Le Cordon Bleu

Are you hankering for some French cooking? Do you want to try some recipes for true gourmet chefs? These recipes are for expert cooks, so don't ask your parents to help you whip up some *Feuilletde Saumon aux Asperges* after they've just come home from a hard day at the office. These recipes are for special days when everyone is ready for a treat! The site includes recipes for seven special days of cooking. Imagine, a whole week of French food—bon appetit!

http://sunsite.unc.edu/expo/restaurant/
restaurant.html

GUS Gourmet Cookbook

Is your mouth watering for some Chinese food? Here's something even better than take-out! Each week, this site presents one new Chinese food recipe that you can make at home. It even shows you how it will look. Get out your soy sauce and chopsticks for a great time!

http://www.gus.com/cook/cook.html

Hawaii's Favorite Recipes

Come tune into Aunty Leilani's Cooking Show and find recipes for tasty Hawaiian dishes. Check out the Internet Island Fruit Salad, or the Pineapple Cream Cheese Pie. Although it is more fun to cook these recipes while wearing a traditional Hawaiian print shirt, a lei, sandals, and a straw hat, the results are just as good if you don't.

http://hisurf.aloha.com/Recipes.html

Mama's Cookbook

Do you want to be a great cook? Mama's Italian cookbook is a great place to start! It has recipes for all your favorite Italian meals, plus cooking and pasta glossaries for beginners. If you're not sure which one you want, you can let Mama pick "one of her favorites." There is also a searchable database of recipes if you know what you want and don't want to hunt through the list to find it.

http://www.eat.com/cookbook/index.html

> ## Ask not what the Net can do for you, ask what you can do for the Net.

Mexican Cuisine and recipes

You probably already knew that tacos and burritos are Mexican dishes. Would you have ever guessed that chocolate and vanilla are also of Mexican origin? There are some delicious recipes for Mexican meals at this site, plus literature on Mexican influence on the world's cooking and "What people believe is Mexican, but it is not!"

http://csgrs6k1.uwaterloo.ca/users/dmg/mexico/
cocina/cocina.html

Did you know that the hard shells most frequently associated with tacos are not Mexican?

And that Chili con Carne is not a traditonal Mexican dish?

Find out more about this delicious cuisine at Mexican Cuisine and recipes.

Recipes for Traditional Food in Slovenia

Can you point to Slovenia on the world map? Can you name any Slovenian foods? Would you eat dandelion salad? Check out the recipes for traditional food in Slovenia. There are pictures of the foods and downloadable sound files of the names for many of the dishes. There are recipes for all kinds of foods, including a wonderful spring soup and a delicious fish stew.

http://www.ijs.si/slo-recipes.html

Become one with the Net.

Rolling Your Own Sushi

Do you know how to eat with chopsticks? If not, don't worry, sushi is a wonderful finger food. Sushi is a Japanese delicacy that is fun and relatively easy to make. A common misunderstanding about sushi is that it is raw seafood. There is a form of sushi called *sashimi* that does have raw seafood, but this is different than sushi. Sushi is delicious and (don't tell your parents) it's good for you. Warning: making sushi involves the use of a sharp knife, be sure to let your parents help you prepare your sushi.

http://www.rain.org/~hutch/sushi.html

SPECIAL DIETS
Asian Kashrus Recipes

Cooking Kosher is a very precise and delicate operation. Finding recipes can be a tedious task. With this collection of Asian Kosher Recipes, the job is made easy. There are dozens of recipes for cooking food in a variety of cuisines. Thai, Chinese, and Vietnamese are just a few of the delicious styles listed.

http://www.kashrus.org/recepies.html

Low-Fat Lifestyle Forum Home Page

Do you hate to eat food that is classified as "good for you"? The truth of the matter is that "good for you" isn't all liver and spinach. There are a lot of arguments about what "healthy eating" means, but most agree that a low-fat lifestyle is best. The Low-Fat Lifestyle Forum has cooking and eating tips, as well as recommended cookbooks and loads of easy recipes.

http://www.wco.com/~mardiw/lowfat.htm

What are the ingredients for a California Roll?

If you said imitation crab, avocado, cucumber, rice, and nori toasted seaweed sheets, you'd be a winner! Find out all about Rolling Your Own Sushi!

The Vegetarian Society UK

Ewwww! Do you dread being told to eat your veggies? Do Brussels sprouts make you hide in the closet? Vegetarian cooking doesn't have to mean tons of icky green food. The Vegetarian Society of the United Kingdom has assembled a list of tasty recipes for every meal, from breakfast to dessert. These pages are also loaded with important facts about nutrition.

http://www.veg.org/veg/Orgs/VegSocUK/info.html

The Sun never sets on the Internet.

A B C D E F G H I J K L M N O P Q R S T U V W X Y Z

How many onions should you put in an asparagus and peanut strudel?

One, yum! Find out about this and other delicious vegetarian recipes at the Vegetarian Society UK.

COUNTRIES OF THE WORLD

Arab Countries' WWW Sites

Web pages from 21 Arab countries have been assembled here for those of you looking for information on this part of the world. Each country page has a list of links to servers around the world with information related to that country.

http://www.liii.com/~hajeri/arab.html

City.Net Countries & Territories

World geography homework never had it so good! Now you can actually enjoy touring the world, looking for interesting places to study-up on for that class project. Inside each country link are links sorted by categories such as country information, culture and language, maps, and travel. At the bottom of each country page is an additional link that lists links to all the countries in the same region, or continent. Happy trails.

http://www.city.net/countries/

Space Exploration is a blast. Check out Astronomy.

Visit the stars in Astronomy.

K-12 Africa Guide

If you're trying to gather information for a homework assignment, or a project about an African country, take a good look at this site. Find information about Africa's languages, customs, governments, environment, and people. You'll discover and learn about the heritage of the different African countries and their rich history. The Multimedia Archives offer maps, images of animals, flags, satellite images, and pictures of African face masks. This site is sure to give that "extra" you need for an "A" in that next project.

http://www.sas.upenn.edu/African_Studies/
    Home_Page/AFR_GIDE.html

W3C/ANU—Asian Studies WWW VL

The World Wide Web Virtual Library at the Australian National University has, at last count, 61 countries listed here to search through. Links to and about all the Asian countries, from Turkey to Japan, are waiting here to be discovered. If you don't have a project that needs any of this information, browse around anyway, and discover some of the exciting marvels of this side of the world.

http://coombs.anu.edu.au/
    WWWVL-AsianStudies.html

The World Factbook 1995

It's the job of the Central Intelligence Agency (CIA) to know what's going on in the world. This involves gathering information about each country's government, its people, economy, and transportation facilities, including maps of each country. There are also some regional reference maps at the bottom of the home page, and appendices that explain some of the abbreviations used in the country descriptions.

http://www.odci.gov/cia/publications/95fact/

Yahoo—Regional:Countries

Brazil has its rain forests, Morocco has its desert, Chile has its mountains, and Yahoo has them all. Browse the world's countries here to your heart's content. Each country's links are sorted by up to 36 categories, such as government, health, libraries, culture, and more. Indices are also listed separately. These are sites that collect specialized links pertaining to that country.

http://www.yahoo.com/Regional/Countries/

EMBASSIES

The Embassy Page

Countries that are friendly toward each other often set up embassies in each other's countries, to help continue their good relationships. The embassies provide a place for businesses and individuals to get accurate and authoritative information about the other country. Embassies also provide a place for their own citizens to get help when they are away from home, and for travelers to get visas (not credit cards, entry permits) to the other country. Since embassies are in the information business, they can also be a valuable resource for researching facts about their country.

http://www.globescope.com/web/gsis/embpage.html

TOURISM

See also: TRAVEL

Lonely Planet online

Although this is a tourist-oriented service, Lonely Planet can be an excellent source of information about a country. They publish some of the most popular travel books in the world. You'll find facts on the environment, history, culture, and more about each of the world's countries here. Of course, since it's for tourists, there's even info on "getting there," "attractions," "events," and "travelers reports." All this adds up to some of the best stuff for reports and homework assignments. Not to mention interesting reading for that "virtual trip."

http://www.lonelyplanet.com.au/

Virtual Tourist II World Map

Virtual Tourist II is a map server front-end for the City.Net library of country information. Once you zoom in and click on a country, the map here takes you to City.Net, which has a list of links to sites with information *about* that country or region.

http://www.vtourist.com/vt/

NET FILES

Where is the Plimsoll Line, and why shouldn't you cross it?

Answer: These days, it's more of a pictograph than a line! It's painted on the hull of a merchant ship, showing the safe load limit for that ship. In 1870s England, Samuel Plimsoll, a Member of Parliament, proposed this "line" to help halt the number of shipwrecks and casualties caused by overloading. If this line was under water, the ship was overloaded, and unsafe. Calculating the placement of the line is not easy! It's dependent on the type of ship, cargo, season, and geographic area of operation. So there are really several "Plimsoll Lines" painted on every merchant ship. See a picture of one at http://pacifier.com/~rboggs/PLIMSOLL.HTML.

Virtual Tourist World Map

Virtual Tourist is a map server front-end for the W3C's web server directory. You're first presented with a clickable world map. Click on a continent or region, and you zoom in to a more detailed map showing the countries. Click once more on a country, and you're off to W3C with a list of web servers *located in* that country. These servers may have information about that country, or any other subject matter.

http://www.vtourist.com/webmap/

A
B
C
D
E
F
G
H
I
J
K
L
M
N
O
P
Q
R
S
T
U
V
W
X
Y
Z

CRAFTS AND HOBBIES

Aunt Annie's Craft Page

She won't pinch your cheeks and go on about how much you've grown! Aunt Annie WILL give you ideas, patterns, and great directions for making interesting crafts. She has a new project for you each week, and it's not the usual "handprint-in-the-plaster" craft. Many are paper crafts, like table decorations, paper hats, or toys. Who could ask for a cooler aunt?

http://mineral.galleries.com/annie/

Kid's Crafts

This is it! Recipes for imitation Play-Dough, fake GAK, finger paint, slime, pretend silly putty, and cinnamon ornament dough. It's all here! There is also a recipe for something you can *eat*, called "Singing Cake." We haven't tried it, but it "sounds" like fun! Sure, there are tons of craft ideas here, too.

http://ucunix.san.uc.edu/~edavis/kids-list/
  crafts.html

You Can Make Paper

Have you ever seen homemade paper? That rough, uneven edge (called a *deckle*) gives it that homemade look. You can recycle old newspaper or other printed materials into paper pulp. You can even throw in a bit of yucca, lawn grass, flowers, or other plants. Then make your own homemade, natural paper! Try it here!

http://www.nbn.com/youcan/paper/paper.html

NEEDLECRAFT AND SEWING

Welcome to the World Wide Quilting Page

Who would be crazy enough to take something whole, cut it up into a lot of little pieces, and then sew it all back together again? Quilters! But what they end up with usually looks pretty spectacular. Unless you are Ami Simms, who created the winning quilt in WORST Quilt in the World contest—see it here! This site provides you with all the information and resources needed to keep *you* from winning next year's contest.

http://quilt.com/MainQuiltingPage.html

Wonderful Stitches WWW

Are you hooked on cross-stitch or needlepoint? If the answer is yes, then this site is guaranteed to keep you in stitches! Check out what other stitchery enthusiasts have been creating with their busy fingers, then try out some of the decorative stitches featured in the monthly sampler. If you are in need of supplies, or want to join a needlework group, put down your needle and look here!

http://www.webcom.com/~stitch/

ORIGAMI

See also: PEACE

Joseph Wu's Origami Page

You don't care if you ever see another folded paper crane in your life! OK, relax, you don't have to fold any more cranes. Now you're ready for some intermediate and advanced origami projects. From Joseph Wu's Origami Page you can download incredible diagrams and instructions for a windmill, butterfly, or basket.

http://www.cs.ubc.ca/spider/jwu/origami.html

Kids School Arts & Crafts Class

Origami is the Japanese art of paper folding. The word literally means "to fold" (*oru*) "paper" (*kami*). Find a few sheets of square paper, and you can get started with some easy paper-folding projects. Here's an origami crane and a *yakko* (yes, a *yakko* and that's not someone who talks too much!). The Kids School Arts & Crafts Class will show you how to fold them with graphics and helpful instructions.

http://jw.stanford.edu/KIDS/SCHOOL/ART/
  kids_arts.html

Let balloonists take you to new heights in Aviation and Airplanes.

PAPER AIRPLANES

DSW Games

"Next time someone tells you to go fly a kite, you can fly a paper airplane instead!" This graphically amusing site gives you two airplane templates to print out and fold, "guaranteed to make you the Red Baron of the office!" You may need a paper clip and some tape to help trim your flyer, too.

http://www.dsw.com/airplane.htm

Paper Airplane Hanger Page

This site is the ultimate site for learning about, building, and—best of all—flying paper airplanes! You'll find step-by-step instructions, safety tips, and of course, LINKS!

http://www.cs.man.ac.uk/~bulmerr/p_planes/
  p_plane.html

CREATION STUDIES

Creation Science Home Page

How did life on Earth begin? Some scientists believe life evolved over millions of years. Others believe there are some real problems with the theory of evolution. For instance, how did life originate from dead chemicals? How could man have come from the apes? To see the arguments against the theory of evolution, go to this site.

http://emporium.turnpike.net/C/cs/

Evolution vs. Creation Science

Have you ever thought about how Earth began? Or how all the plants and animals came to be? Creation scientists are those who believe that it all came about as described in the *Bible*. To help form your own theories, investigate the Evolution vs. Creation Science site.

http://limestone.kosone.com/people/ocrt/
  evolutio.htm

Yogatta try Yoga.

CULTURAL DIVERSITY

Diversity

What you need is a little culture! How about a LOT of culture? Check this site for loads of links about African Americans, Latinos, Asian Americans, Native Americans, and more. Parental warning: preview links, this site changes often.

http://latino.sscnet.ucla.edu/diversity1.html

NET FILES

Dad says I can eat dessert first "once in a blue moon." What's a Blue Moon, and when is the next one?

ANSWER: Calendar months are either 30 or 31 days long. But the lunar month is twenty-nine and a half days. Every now and again, there are two full moons in the same month. The second full moon in the same month is called a Blue Moon. According to the Old Farmer's Almanac, the next one will be in June of 1996. Both June 1 and 30 will have a full moon, so get your dessert spoon ready! Look for more interesting weather lore at http://www.nj.com/weather/faq.html

A B C D E F G H I J K L M N O P Q R S T U V W X Y Z

Guide to Museums and Cultural Resources on the Web

The Natural History museum of Los Angeles County invites you to take a virtual tour of all the continents (including Antarctica) and explore museums in each. You may peek inside the Wool Museum in Australia, check out the Information Highway exhibit in Canada, or visit an art museum in Singapore. This will give you a good idea of how many different cultures there are in the world, and an understanding of what each has to teach.

http://www.usc.edu/lacmnh/webmuseums/

CURIOSITIES AND WONDERS

Birthstones

Did you know that if you were born in April, your lucky birthstone is the diamond? To find out more about various gemstones and their properties, check this site!

http://mineral.galleries.com/birthsto.htm

The Jackalope Page

Have you ever seen something that looks like a rabbit with antlers? Chances are good that you've never seen such a beast! Do they really exist? Some kids in Wyoming have put together some information on jackalopes, so check it out and see what you think! Here's a hint, though: you can only hunt jackalopes on June 31.

http://monhome.sw2.k12.wy.us/projects/
  jackalope.html

Take a ride on a Carousel in AMUSEMENT PARKS.

Lose yourself in a Museum. SCIENCE has them all.

NET FILES

How many pounds of steel are used to make a mid-size car body?

Answer: The mid-sized Toyota Camry has 550 pounds of steel in its body (in 970 different parts). How a car like the Camry is built and painted is all explained, in words and pictures, at http://www.toyota.com/hub/carculture/. Drive on over and learn all about auto-making and lot more!

Seven Ancient Wonders of the World

Everyone's heard about them, but who can name them? Well, there are the Pyramids, of course, and uh...hmmm. Luckily, there is whole list of all of them here, along with pictures and links. Since there are not many of the ancient wonders of the world around anymore, you'll also find a list of the Modern Wonders of the World, as well as the Natural Wonders of the World. There are also pictures and links for wonders such as these: the Great Wall of China, Victoria Falls, and the Eiffel Tower.

http://ce.ecn.purdue.edu/~ashmawy/7WW/

DANCE

Dance Clipart—Introduction

What fun! If you are doing a newsletter or article for your school paper, or maybe want to try making your own stationery at home, here are over 130 dance-related images you can download. There are even dance cartoons, symbols, and organization logos with dancers to choose from. So clip away!

http://www.cs.unc.edu/~leech/dance/clipart.html

The Performer's Edge Magazine

Are you interested in dancing competitively but don't know how to get started? Or are you already performing but still get nervous during auditions? How about foot and ankle problems in dance, or how to sew those beautiful costumes you want to wear? This site may answer some of these questions for you. Performer's Edge started in 1991 as a regional publication. Now, it's internationally circulated as an invaluable "how to" resource guide for students and their parents, and teachers of dance. The online site includes excerpts of the news briefs and articles from the most recent bimonthly issue, and lists the Table of Contents from all prior issues. Each issue contains information about dance performance and auditions, professional career possibilities, costuming, dance medicine and more. If you are a serious dancer, you won't want to miss this one.

http://arts-online.com/edge.html

The World Wide Web Dance Server

Try to keep your feet still while you explore this page—we dare you! You'll find links to ballroom dancing, square dancing, round dancing, and contra dancing. Try a highland fling, or maybe a samba. Dance through cyberspace, and start here!

http://www.net-shopper.co.uk/dance/index.htm

Surf today, smart tomorrow.

AFRICAN DANCE

African Music and Dance Ensemble

"The Africans Are Coming, The Africans Are Coming" is the largest seasonal, professional African cultural arts extravaganza in the U.S. Directed by C. K. Ladzekpos, the African Dance Ensemble has been performing since 1973 and continues to stand for tradition and creativity. Dance, especially ethnic dance, is characterized by music and costume and tradition, and you'll find all of that here! There are lots of video (and audio) clips featuring the colorful and vibrant dance and percussion ensemble music of West Africa.

http://cnmat.cnmat.berkeley.EDU/~ladzekpo/l

BALLET

Body and Grace: the American Ballet Theatre

Here you can learn about the history of the American Ballet Theatre (ABT) through photographer Nancy Ellison's electronic exhibition, "Body and Grace." This is a wonderful collection of photos which starts with the ABT's beginning in 1940 and includes such historical greats as Agnes de Mille, as well as portraits of the current ABT hierarchy: Principals, Soloists, and Corps de Ballet.

http://www.i3tele.com/photo_perspectives_museum/
   faces/abt.html

CyberDance—Ballet On The Net

If ballet is your life, you may want to take a break from your barre exercises long enough to check out this wonderful collection of U.S. and Canadian classical and modern ballet resources. There is a complete list of professional, regional, and school-affiliated ballet companies. You'll find their addresses and phone numbers, ticketing information, and their touring schedules. The link to the Boston Ballet, among others, even includes a spotlight on their solo and principal dancers. Find out what motivates 20-year-old Pollyana Ribeiro to keep trying new things. It doesn't stop there; you'll find articles, reviews, FAQs, e-zines and lots of great links, including one to the New York Public Library, which boasts the best dance collection in the world!

http://www.thepoint.net/~raw/dance.htm

A
B
C
D
E
F
G
H
I
J
K
L
M
N
O
P
Q
R
S
T
U
V
W
X
Y
Z

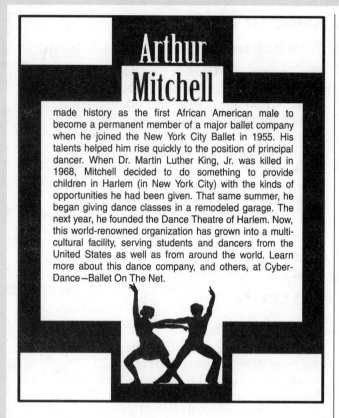

Arthur Mitchell

made history as the first African American male to become a permanent member of a major ballet company when he joined the New York City Ballet in 1955. His talents helped him rise quickly to the position of principal dancer. When Dr. Martin Luther King, Jr. was killed in 1968, Mitchell decided to do something to provide children in Harlem (in New York City) with the kinds of opportunities he had been given. That same summer, he began giving dance classes in a remodeled garage. The next year, he founded the Dance Theatre of Harlem. Now, this world-renowned organization has grown into a multi-cultural facility, serving students and dancers from the United States as well as from around the world. Learn more about this dance company, and others, at Cyber-Dance—Ballet On The Net.

WebMuseum: Degas, Edgar

Edgar Degas was a French impressionist painter in the late 1800s, and he's acknowledged as a master of drawing the human figure in motion. And what better subject for his paintings than the ballet dancer? This special Degas exhibit includes works from the Fogg Museum in Cambridge, Massachusetts, the Metropolitan Museum of Art in New York, the National Gallery in Washington, and the *Musèe d'Orsay* in Paris. So come browse and enjoy these wonderful pastel drawings and oil paintings which portray the grace and form of ballet dancers on stage and off. And while you're in the WebMuseum, be sure to check out the works by other famous painters as well.

http://www.emf.net/wm/paint/auth/degas/

Become one with the Net.

FOLK DANCING

The Bassett Street Hounds Morris Dancers

As early as the 1500s, groups of dancers in the Cotswold region of Western England were donning their bells and colorful ribbons and welcoming in the spring with this ritual folk dance. Morris dancing on the Net now boasts a worldwide representation from well over 100 teams. Read more about the history of Morris dancing and its various styles (Cotswold, Border, Longsword and Northwest), all of which are part of the Hounds' repertoire. From this site you can connect to a searchable archive of the Morris Dance Discussion List and "all-known" other Morris-related Web pages.

http://web.syr.edu/~rsholmes/morris/hounds/
  index.html

IFDO Home Page

Folk dancing is both fun to watch and fun to do. The International Folk Dancers of Ottawa bring together the traditional social dances and authentic music of many countries and cultures. Here you can find schedules and other information about folk-dancing in Ottawa and then link to lots of other folk dance resources on the WWW. Check out Chang's Folk Dancers HomePage and step-hop-step to the Salty Dog. Song Chang was born in Sweden and began his International Dance Group in the basement of his San Francisco home in 1938. Then go halfway around the world (without even leaving your chair) to dance the Hopak with the Volya Ukrainian Dance Ensemble.

http://lucas.incen.doc.ca/ifdo.html

Web Cloggers

OK, now you shuffle, step, step...then shuffle, step, shuffle, step...right foot then left. Traditionally associated with the Southern Appalachian Mountains, clogging or clog dancing is becoming more popular with young and old all around the world. This site is a great place for cloggers to find out "what's happenin'." There are lists of (and links to) upcoming events, clogging-related merchandise, books and videos, and lots of space for clogging instructors and dance groups to post their own information. So, come on, let's dance!

http://www.clogging.com/

HULA AND POLYNESIAN DANCING

Hawaii's H4—Hula From The Merrie Monarch Festival 1995

Aloha from Hawai'i! The Hula, Hawaiian word for dance, expresses the culture of the islands in a unique combination of colorful costumes and rhythmic hip and arm movements. This "photo album" contains screen shots from the TV coverage of the 20th annual Queen Liliuokalani Keiki Hula Festival and Competition. You don't have to cross the *moana* (ocean), *kai* (sea), or *mauna* (mountain) to enjoy the spirit of the Hula, just grab your lei (wreath of flowers worn around the neck) and point your browser toward this colorful site!

http://www.hotspots.hawaii.com/hula.html

Hula, Hawai'i's Art and Soul

The origin of Hula is a mystery, but everyone agrees that it began as a sacrament, not an entertainment for tourists. You can read about how goddesses brought Hula to the Hawaiians, and how it is performed with reverence today in many Hula schools around the islands. You can also hear a chant accompanied by traditional instruments, such as the pahu hula drum. It is constructed from a partially hollowed-out tree trunk with a shark skin stretched over the top.

http://www.aloha-hawaii.com/c_hula.html

MODERN AND JAZZ DANCE

Minnesota Modern Dance

"...While I cry I will feel. While I feel I will dance. While I dance I will laugh. While I laugh I will live..." This is part of a poem by Claudia Schmidt titled "While I Live." What a great way to lead off a home page for dance groups! This site acts as a clearinghouse for information on the seven modern dance companies in the Twin Cities, Minnesota area. Modern dance schools, upcoming dance events, and performances throughout the state are listed. And what would any Web page be without its links? This one will take you to two sites loaded with dance information from around the world. Check out both the WWW Dance Library and Dance Links. In each of these you need to select "type" and then "modern/contemporary" for information specifically about other modern dance companies.

http://freenet.msp.mn.us/arts/dance/modern/
  md.home.html

TAP DANCE

Tap Dance Homepage

Did you know that May 25 is National Tap Dance Day, signed into law by President Bush in 1989? But don't wait until then to find all the neat information about tap dancing at this site. If you're getting your Shim Sham confused with your Paddle and Roll, then refer to the Tap Steps Glossary (and instructions!) to set you straight. Sites and Sounds of Tap include video clips and recordings. There's an events calendar, book list, tap trivia, and lots more. The Who's Who section lists tap companies and has bios of some of tap's greatest from today and yesterday, like Gregory Hines, Hank Smith, Fred Astaire, and Bill "Bojangles" Robinson, whose birthday was—you guessed it—May 25, 1878!

http://www.hahnemann.edu/tap/

"My toes are the sticks, and the floor is the drum," says Ira Bernstein, dancer. Not just any dance, though. Ira does tap dancing, Appalachian clogging, English clogging, French-Canadian step dancing, Cape Breton step dancing, jitterbug swing dancing, and Cajun and Zydeco dancing. Because the sound of each dance is just as important as the look of it, he wears a variety of footwear when he performs: tap shoes, wooden clogs, fiberglass-tipped shoes, and rubber boots. These produce different tones, volumes, and dynamics of sound necessary for the different dances. You can hear a brief audio clip of Ira clog dancing in the Sights and Sounds of Tap area on the Tap Dance Homepage.

A B C D E F G H I J K L M N O P Q R S T U V W X Y Z

Tapestry Dance Company

First, get in the mood by downloading a video of some hoofin' by Ira Bernstein. Then read about this multidimensional dance ensemble from Austin, Texas. Now in their 7th performance season, they combine their love of dance with a dedication to community involvement and educational outreach. Last fall they offered a special Back-to-School Rock'n'Roll Tap Class. A large part of the proceeds went to the Muscular Dystrophy Association. Their unique lecture demonstration series, Rhythm, Dance, Music & You!, teaches elementary and secondary school kids about the history of dance in America. Make sure you dig deep enough to find the "tapping" shoe!

http://tapestry.org/site/tapestry.html

DINOSAURS AND PREHISTORIC TIMES

Dino Art Page

Now here's something different! If you really LOVE dinosaurs, you won't want to miss these exhibits. Here are the works of the world's most well-known dinosaur artists and model-makers, including animatronic model-makers, known for creating the moving dinosaurs in movies! Lifelike paintings, action sculptures, and life-sized models created for museums are all included here.

http://www.indyrad.iupui.edu/dinoart.html

Dinosaur Hall at UC Berkeley Museum of Paleontology

Can we start making new live dinosaurs like in the movie *Jurassic Park*? No way! There are a lot of good scientific reasons why cloning dinosaurs would be impossible. Visit "Dinosaur Movies and Reality" at this site to find out why. Packed with scientific information about dinos and prehistoric times, some of the exhibits here are narrated by scientists.

http://ucmp1.berkeley.edu/diapsids/dinosaur.html

Field Museum of Natural History

Virtually visit the "Life Over Time" exhibit at the Field Museum of Natural History! Watch movies of the Albertosaurus, the Moropus, the Triceratops, the camel, and the sabertooth cat. Test your knowledge of the prehistoric age. Enter the sweepstakes to start a new species and listen to mammoth bone music. A teachers' guide to the exhibits provides a bibliography, so you can read more about the dinosaurs and other prehistoric animals.

http://www.bvis.uic.edu/museum/

Field Museum of Natural History Exhibits

Where can you see pictures of dinosaurs, hear their names pronounced, and then watch them run? You can do all of this and more by visiting the exhibit pages at the world-famous Field Museum of Natural History. Here you can see birds dodge Jurassic dinosaurs and listen to the Triassic forecast on the dinosaur weather report! Tours include the following: "Life Before Dinosaurs"; "Dinosaurs!"; and "Teeth, Tusks, and Tarpits: Life After Dinosaurs." Go see it!

http://rs6000.bvis.uic.edu:80/museum/exhibits/
    Exhibits.html

Hadrosaurus

Where in the world was the first nearly complete skeleton of a dinosaur found? It was in Haddonfield, New Jersey! In the summer of 1858, vacationing fossil hobbyist William Parker Foulke led a crew of workmen digging "shin deep in gray slime." Eventually he found the bones of an animal, larger than an elephant, that once swam and played about the coastline of what is now Pennsylvania. Read about the discovery that started our fascination with dinosaurs!

http://tigger.jvnc.net/~levins/hadrosaurus.html

The Sun never sets on the Internet.

Honolulu Community College Dinosaur

Sometimes it's great to read all about dinosaurs. But sometimes it's more fun to look. Hey, how about looking at all kinds of fossils and sculptures while someone tells you all about them? At the HCC Dinosaur Exhibit you can see the dinosaur bones and sculptures, and listen to one of the exhibit's founders talk about them! These fossils are replicas of the originals at the American Museum of Natural History, in New York City.

http://www.hcc.hawaii.edu/dinos/dinos.1.html

Mammoth Saga

This page loads first in Swedish, but you can click on the British flag to get the English version. This virtual exhibition of mammoths, other animals, and plants of the ice ages is based on an exhibition held at the Swedish Museum of Natural History, Stockholm, Sweden. In it, you'll explore the U.S. Midwest 16,000 years ago, take a look at a woolly rhinoceros, a sabertooth cat, and an ancient reindeer. Siberian nomads lived in huts made of mammoth bones, and you can see a recreation of one here! There are also nice links to other places on the Web that will help you learn more.

http://www.nrm.se/virtexhi/mammsaga/
   mamintro.html

Royal Tyrrell Museum

Take a virtual tour of this famous museum in Alberta, Canada. You can stay on the guided tour, or use the virtual maps to go from exhibit to exhibit in any order you want! There are fantastic dinosaur exhibits with lots of pictures, and information all over the second floor in "Dinosaur Hall." In addition to all of the dinosaurs, you can visit a *Paleoconservatory,* which is a greenhouse full of primitive plants. Try the link to Dinosaur Provincial Park, from where most of the museum's exhibits have been excavated.

http://www.cuug.ab.ca:8001/VT/tyrrell/index.html

Yogatta try Yoga.

DISNEY

See also: AMUSEMENT PARKS, MOVIES

A Visit to Yesterland

Disneyland hasn't always been as it is now. New attractions have been added, and old ones have been replaced. Some of those old attractions were really good, and it's too bad they are gone. With the magic of the Internet, though, you can visit many of those attractions in A Visit to Yesterland. Here you can wander into Adventure Through Inner Space, take a ride on the Flying Saucers, or mosey down the People Mover. You'll learn when these and other rides started and ended, and get a good idea of what Disneyland was like for your parents, or maybe your older brothers and sisters.

http://www.mcs.net/~werner/yester.html

Disney Records Pages

"Be Our Guest" at this treasure chest of sounds from Disney movies. Whether you're in the mood for just "The Bare Necessities" (*The Jungle Book*), or something a little more exotic like "Hakuna Matata" (*The Lion King: Rhythm of the Pride Lands*), you'll find it here. All the latest music is available, but don't forget about the music from oldies like *Fantasia* and *Mary Poppins*. Also, you'll find information about each movie and how it was made.

http://www.disney.com/records/
   Disney_Records_Pages/Downloads.html

John's Mostly Mermaid Page

John's collected just about everything on Disney films such as *The Lion King*, *Sleeping Beauty*, *Aladdin*, and *Beauty and the Beast*. He has complete scripts for many of these movies, so you can print them out and follow along with the movie when Ariel (*The Little Mermaid*) says, "Walking around on those...what do you call them... feet?" The main focus here is on Ariel, but he does try to give other movies some equal time. Lots of graphics here for you to download, audio files, and links to other Disney sites around the Net.

http://http.tamu.edu:8000/~jvs6403/

A
B
C
D
E
F
G
H
I
J
K
L
M
N
O
P
Q
R
S
T
U
V
W
X
Y
Z

Let balloonists take you to new heights in Aviation and Airplanes.

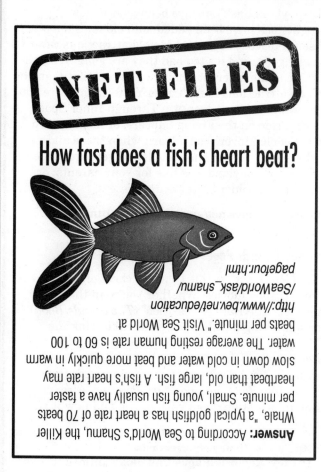

NET FILES

How fast does a fish's heart beat?

Answer: According to Sea World's Shamu, the Killer Whale, "a typical goldfish has a heart rate of 70 beats per minute. Small, young fish usually have a faster heartbeat than old, large fish. A fish's heart rate may slow down in cold water and beat more quickly in warm water. The average resting human rate is 60 to 100 beats per minute." Visit Sea World at
http://www.bev.net/education/SeaWorld/ask_shamu/pagefour.html

Spacecoast Hidden Mickey List for Walt Disney World

Did you know that the people who designed the Disney theme parks hid Mickey Mouse all over the place? It's true. At the Magic Kingdom, Epcot Center, Disney/MGM Studios, even in the Disney Hotels, Mickey Mouse's image is hidden in all kinds of unusual places. Look at a picture of Mickey Mouse: notice that his head is made of three circles—a big one for the head and two smaller ones for his ears. At Disney World these three circles are concealed everywhere, from lakes to ceiling fans. Check this site to find out where Mickey is hiding!

http://www.iu.net/tshaw/trs/HiddenMickey.html

The Ultimate Disney Link Page

Disney is all over the Internet. The Ultimate Disney Link Page is a good place to begin exploring Disney Internet sites. Here you'll find links to Disney theme parks, a hodgepodge of Disney fan pages, and connections to just about anything else that's Disney. Created by Disney World cast member Ed Sterrett, this truly is the Ultimate Disney site!

http://www.america.com/~dcop/tudlp/tudlpns.html

Walt Disney Pictures

The folks who brought you *Pocahontas, The Lion King, A Goofy Movie*, and *Toy Story* have their home page here. There's a bunch of video, sound, and color images of movies that have been released and also of movies currently in production. If you're hopelessly "techno-clueless," and can't get your audio or movie files to play, Disney's help files can really help. Find out how to see the video and hear the movie themes by linking to whatever software you need. Guess what else? This site has the graphics turned off by default—you'll have to turn on the pictures if you want to see them.

http://www.disney.com/DisneyPictures/Disney/DisneyHome.html

Welcome to Walt Disney

Oh yes, the Magical World of Disney!!!! The Walt Disney Company produces movies, television shows, and music, and they are nearly all fun. If you want to keep up on the latest from the folks at Disney, take a look at their official home page. You'll find clips from recent Disney movies you can play on your computer. You can listen to recordings from the Disney Channel. You also can get all kinds of great graphic images of your favorite Disney characters. There is much, much more. If you like Disney, this is a must-see.

http://www.disney.com/

Space Exploration is a blast. Check out Astronomy

THEME PARKS

Disneyland Paris, Introduction

Disneyland Paris gives folks in Europe a more convenient opportunity to visit a Disney park. A picture tour of Disneyland Paris and information about the park are available here. If you'd like to visit EuroDisneyland, this is the Web page for you!

http://www.informatik.tu-muenchen.de/cgi-bin/
   nph-gateway/hphalle1/~schaffnr/etc/disney/

Disneyland Park, Anaheim, California

Disneyland is the first of all the Disney parks, and some claim it has a special charm no other can match. At this Web site, dedicated Disneyland fan Doug Krause has pulled together a slew of information and pictures for anyone interested in visiting Disneyland.

http://www.best.com/~dijon/disney/parks/
   disneyland/

Tokyo Disneyland

Disneyland's Japanese cousin is called Tokyo Disneyland. With all the appeal of other Disney parks, you can see the sights of Disneyland—the Far East version.

http://www.toyo-eng.co.jp/NewHome/Messe/
   Useful-Info/Play/TDL/index-e.html

Walt Disney World Home Page

Going to Disney World? At this site, you'll find out everything you need to know about The Magic Kingdom, Epcot, Disney-MGM Studios, plus other attractions in the Orlando, Florida area.

http://www.travelweb.com/thisco/wdw/
   wdwhome/wdw.html

Take a ride on a Carousel in AMUSEMENT PARKS.

Lose yourself in a Museum. SCIENCE has them all.

DOGS AND DOG SPORTS

See also: MAMMALS—WOLVES AND DOG FAMILY, PETS AND PET CARE

The American Kennel Club

The AKC is the largest registry of purebred dogs in the United States. Here, you'll find a list of the breeds they recognize, a roster of recent obedience and show winners, and information on the AKC's many educational activities. You'll also find a list of breed clubs and contacts, as well as a breeder's directory.

http://www.webpress.net/akc/

Belgian Games

Stupid dog tricks! Sure there are some really silly ones here, but there are some useful ones, too. How about teaching your dog to start pawing you when he hears your alarm clock go off? Or teaching him to run around the house collecting your toys, then put them away for you? You could teach your dog to look for your mom's lost car keys, or how to nod on command. Then when you ask your furry friend to respond to a question like "Aren't I the best, smartest, and best-looking owner you could ever have?" he'll always nod an enthusiastic "YES!" The directions for how to teach these tricks are at *http://www.hut.fi/~mtt/training.html.*

http://www.hut.fi/~mtt/belg_tricks.html

Origami: the fold to behold! Check out CRAFTS AND HOBBIES.

A
B
C
D
E
F
G
H
I
J
K
L
M
N
O
P
Q
R
S
T
U
V
W
X
Y
Z

Dog Breeders Network

Gee, those puppies in the pet store look awfully cute! But wait. Before you buy a registered dog, you should know a lot more, and you may not find the answers in the pet store. Some breeds have medical problems that are genetically passed on to the pups. How do you know you won't be getting a puppy with these health problems—many of which can be expensive to treat, if not life-threatening to your best pal? The best way to avoid these problems is to buy from a trustworthy dog breeder. These folks will often let you meet your pup's mom and dad, as well as show you their medical test results and health records. A good breeder will know about and discuss any genetic problems with the breed you're investigating. Maybe you're looking for a quiet dog, or an energetic dog. Breeders often "temperament test" their puppies, and they can help match you with a dog that fits your personality.

This site lists breeders for various recognized dog breeds, but you could also find a list in an established dog magazine at the bookstore or public library. You should know that there are "good" pet stores as well as "bad" dog breeders. But the important thing is that you need to know a lot about where the dog's been, and his parents' health background. At this page, you'll also find information about the many "breed rescue clubs" around the world. These are people who love, for example, Golden Retrievers. They "rescue" these dogs from animal shelters and try to place them in adoptive homes. You'll also learn about groups that try to find homes for retired racing Greyhounds.

http://www.breeders.com/

rec.pets.dogs FAQ Homepage

This comprehensive site will give you information on everything from picking the best breed for you, to showing your dog in obedience trials, to health care. The Working Dogs area will tell you about sled dogs, search and rescue dogs, and even narcotics-sniffing dogs! Don't bark up the wrong tree, curl up with your puppy and this Web site!

http://www.zmall.com/pet_talk/dog-faqs/

Don't try to get your sled dogs running by yelling

"MUSH!"

*The word the dogs are expecting is "HIKE!" Now you're moving! Mushers know that to turn teams right, they yell "Gee," and for a left turn, it's "Haw!" You'll have to check the Working Dogs area of the **rec.pets.dogs** FAQ to find out how to get them to slow down!*

Service Dogs

Have you ever seen a blind person and guide dog team? Ever wondered how dogs for the blind are trained? How about hearing or signal dogs, who team up with deaf people? These animals go to their owners to signal when a noise is heard. They will signal on ringing doorbells and phones, smoke alarms, crying babies and much more. There are also therapy dogs, and special canine companions who know how to help disabled people. Find out about this very interesting class of working dogs here!

http://www.zmall.com/pet_talk/tittle/pets/dog-faqs/service.html

EARTH SCIENCE

GLOBE Home Page

GLOBE stands for *G*lobal *L*earning and *O*bservations to *B*enefit the *E*nvironment. It's an environmental education and science partnership of students, teachers, and scientists initiated to increase environmental awareness throughout the world and to contribute to a better understanding of Earth. Students take measurements and make observations of the weather at their schools and share their data via the Internet with other students and scientists around the world. All the details are patched together to make a view of the world as it's seen through the student findings at 1,900 schools in over 20 countries.

http://www.globe.gov/

GSC Atlantic's Earth Science Site of the Week

This is a growing one-stop earth science shop where you'll find links to everything from atmospheric studies to volcanology. Check out the current site of the week or visit the past site archive. There's an easy-to-use subject index as well as chronological listings. You can nominate your favorite earth science site for inclusion, too!

http://agcwww.bio.ns.ca/misc/geores/sotw/sotw.html

Sam's Page/GeoScience: K-12

Curious about science? Sam's Page/GeoScience: K-12 has link after link pointing you to interesting science sites. Whether you're a rockhound or go gaga over glaciers, you'll find something here that will excite you, but watch out for those drifting plate tectonics.

http://www.cuug.ab.ca:8001/~johnstos/geosci.html

Lose yourself in a Museum. SCIENCE has them all.

CLIMATE—ACID RAIN
You Can & Acid Rain

How can rain be an acid? It starts out as regular rain, but then falls through air pollution. It becomes a weak acid which can dissolve marble, kill trees, and ruin entire lakes. You can help. Here's how to make an acid finder and how to test rainwater. Let Beakman and Jax explain to you this phenomenon, first identified in England in 1872. Smoke from burning coal was the cause then, as it remains now.

http://pomo.nbn.com/youcan/acid/acid.html

CLIMATE—GREENHOUSE EFFECT
Air

Someone in a colder climate might think the "greenhouse" effect is a good thing. Especially for those who don't like the cold. However, there are consequences. And this doesn't just mean less snow to play in. Find out all about the greenhouse effect and its consequences at the Australian Environmental Resources Information Network.

http://kaos.erin.gov.au/air/air.html

DAY AND NIGHT
Earth Viewer

When it's 10 A.M., bright and sunny in Florida, what's it like in Japan? Stop by the Earth Viewer site and query their server. View a map of the Earth and it will show where it's light and dark in the world. You can choose the satellite to view from, or tell it to view from the Sun or Moon. You can even create a custom request and specify the longitude and latitude you want to view.

http://www.fourmilab.ch/earthview/vplanet.html

ECOLOGY AND ENVIRONMENT
The Green Page

Developed by high school students, this is an annotated guide to many of the best environmental science Web pages and projects out there. They don't hold back on their opinions of the ones they don't like, either!

http://www.vcomm.net/enviro/greenpg.html

Harlem Environmental Access Project Home Page

Did you know that a family of four throws away 80-150 pounds of garbage a week? If we recycle objects, rather than buy new ones, we can generate less garbage. The Harlem Environmental Access Project Home Page has Fast Facts on Recycling and many other resources on environmental issues such as rainforests and renewable energy. Don't miss the link to The Wild Ones, a resource on animals and zoos.

http://www.edf.org/heap/

National Wildlife Federation: Education, Teacher Resource

Looking for projects and information on a variety of environmental subjects? Check these out: Air, Habitat, People and the Environment, Wildlife and Endangered Species, and Water. Sound good? Each topic includes general background information, class activities, fun facts, and a glossary of terms. There are also suggestions of things you can do to help!

http://www.igc.apc.org/nwf/ed/

Teacher and Student Home page

Earthwatch takes ordinary people on extraordinary research expeditions. Of course, you pay for the privilege of counting katydids, or helping save a coral reef. But when you get back, you'll have a great story to tell about how you spent your summer vacation! This page archives some of the field notes and lesson plans developed from past trips, and it's interesting to see which ecological "hot spots" they will attend to next.

http://www.earthwatch.org/WWW/ED/home.html

Origami: the fold to behold! Check out CRAFTS AND HOBBIES.

GEOLOGY
Ask a Geologist

Have you ever wondered why earthquakes happen in some places but not in others? Why does Hawai'i have volcanoes when you never get to see one in Florida? Just "Ask a Geologist." This page tells how to e-mail your questions to a United States Geological Survey scientist for an answer. Be sure to read about what kinds of questions to ask, and how to ask them, before you send your mail. Over 2,000 answers served!

http://walrus.wr.usgs.gov/docs/ask-a-ge.html

GEOLOGY—EARTHQUAKES
NBC 4 SEISMO-CAM

Want to know what's shaking in L.A.—literally? Live shots of a seismograph tracking activity in the Los Angeles, California area can be monitored here. If nothing's happening while you're watching, you can look at some archived shots from past events, including a 5.8 temblor. There's also lots of great links to sites with info on earthquakes.

http://www.knbc4la.com/seismo/index.html

NET FILES

I like to keep track of all the different kinds of birds I've seen. Where can I find the rules I have to follow for counting birds on my lifelist? I was on the U.S. side of the Rio Grande and I saw a new bird across the river on the Mexican side. Can I count this on my American Birding Association Area list?

Answer: No, the bird may be counted on your Mexican list, but not on your American Birding Association Area list. Go to the GeoGraphical Birding Guide Page and learn about the other listing rules.

http://www-astronomy.mps.ohio-state.edu/~ignaz/birds/ABA/ABA.html

Recent Seismic Event Bulletins

How many earthquakes do you think occur in the world every day? Probably a lot more than you realize. Seismic activity is monitored day and night, and any recorded activity is posted to this site within 48 hours of the event. Check here and you'll be surprised to find there's a whole lot of shakin' goin' on.

http://www.cdidc.org:65120/web-bin/recentevents

Record of the Day

Where in the world was there an earthquake today? The answer is just a click away. This site will show you the most recent earthquake recorded by the Caltech Seismological Laboratory in California. You can look at the actual graph that was recorded by their seismograph. Pictures of the earth, showing where the earthquake happened, are also included. Be sure to check often. Earthquakes are happening around the world all the time.

http://www.gps.caltech.edu/~polet/recofd.html

GEOLOGY—FOSSILS

Teeth, Tusks, and Tarpits

Early scientists thought fossils were carved by ancient artists, or were seeds dropped from stars. Chicago's famous Field Museum of Natural History explains fossils and gives out a recipe for making your own. 'Course you'll need a dead animal or plant, and a million years or so to wait, but go ahead, try it at home!

http://rs6000.bvis.uic.edu:80/museum/exhibits/ttt/
    TTT1b.html

The Vermont Whale Directory of Exhibits

Just how did a whale get in Vermont, which has no seacoast? Find how the bones of this 12-foot beluga whale ended up buried in Charlotte, Vermont about 10,000 years ago. Very nice descriptions with drawings show how the whale probably died and was eventually preserved and fossilized in the sediment.

http://mole.uvm.edu/whale/TableOfContents.html

GEOLOGY—GEMS AND MINERALS

Rock 'U'

Rocks are our friends, says this tutorial on various types of minerals. It explores diamonds, oxides, and silicates, though not in too great detail. Still, you'll find out interesting stuff, like how to turn amethyst into citrine, and how quartz was used to detect submarines during WWI.

http://www.ucs.usl.edu/~amg6262/rocku.html

Do you know the difference between a rock and a mineral?

A mineral is always the same, the world over. A rock, on the other hand, may be made up of a few or many minerals. And you can pick up similar rocks right next to each other, and they may be made of different minerals. Mine Rock 'U' for more gems of knowledge!

Smithsonian Gem & Mineral Collection

Gems and jewels! Before they become treasures, they look like, well, rocks. You might be able to spot a diamond in the rough if you study this site. It's a collection of pictures and descriptions of rocks and minerals from the Smithsonian's National Museum of Natural History. This is a long Web page with lots of small pictures, but it's worth the wait. You can also click on each small picture to get a larger picture of that mineral. Hint: If you have a slow connection, turn images off before you open the page. Then click on the name of the mineral to see the picture.

http://galaxy.einet.net/images/gems/gems-icons.html

GEOLOGY—GEYSERS

Geysers

A geyser is simply a hot spring that erupts, shooting water into the air. There are only about 700 geysers left in the world! Four hundred of them are located in Yellowstone National Park, but they can also be found in such far-away places as Siberia and Chile. You can find out how a geyser builds up steam, and discover why geothermal energy production has destroyed many of the geyser fields and threatened some of the few remaining ones. See what happens when they leave the water running? ;-)

http://www.wku.edu/www/geoweb/geyser.html

GEOLOGY—VOLCANOES

Geology—Volcanoes

From here, it's safe to explore three different volcano labs: Cascades Volcano Observatory, Alaska Volcano Observatory, and Hawai'i Volcano Observatory. You might feel some heat, but that's probably just your computer monitor! In Alaska, things are hot this winter. They are monitoring several active volcanoes on both sides of the North Pacific, including Karymsky Volcano, in Kamchatka, Russia. It began erupting on January 1,1996, producing an ash and steam plume which reached 23,000 feet. The chief hazards are to aircraft, from the ash plumes which you can track on the air route maps. No villages are threatened, since this is in a remote area. You'll see satellite maps of activities almost as they occur!

http://geology.usgs.gov/

Learning about Volcanoes

How do you become a volcanologist? Just ask Mr. Spock for lessons, of course! Well, not quite. You could look at this site. Find out what becoming a volcanologist is all about and what courses you'll need to take. Also learn about computers. Hey, you're halfway there since you wouldn't be reading this if you didn't know about computers. Oh yeah, there's also information here about volcanoes, including lessons and activities for teachers and students.

http://volcano.und.nodak.edu/learning.html

Mount St. Helens Images/Stories/Curriculum

You've been living near a sleeping volcano for years, and suddenly, it blows up! There's dust and debris everywhere, mud slides, and boulders shooting into the air. Read exciting stories from people who were there. Sponsored by Educational Service District 112, in Vancouver, WA, this graphics-heavy site provides maps, photos, and classroom projects which help bring this devastating eruption to life. The site is also supported by NASA, the National Forest Service, and Volcano World.

http://volcano.und.nodak.edu/vwdocs/msh/msh.html

LAND FEATURES—CAVES AND CAVING

Mammoth Cave National Park

Captain, Spock here. According to the informative sign, I am exploring the longest recorded cave system in the world. There seem to be more than 336 miles mapped, but sensors indicate there is much more to this labyrinth. I chart my location as Kentucky. My Star Fleet tricorder reads ambient temperature at 53 degrees F. Here is a sign, I will read it aloud. "Violet City Lantern Tour, 3 hours, 3 miles (strenuous). A nostalgic tour into a section of the cave that is not electrically lit. The tour features saltpeter mining, prehistoric exploration, historic tuberculosis hospital huts, and some of the largest rooms and passageways in the cave. The first half-mile follows the Historic Tour route. Do not bring flashlights. Restrooms not available." No restrooms! Illogical! Beam me up! No, wait! It says there are other tours, some handicapped-accessible, and some short, fun walks for kids, too! And they have restrooms!

http://www.nps.gov/maca/

Frisbee is the Ultimate in GAMES AND FUN.

The Virtual Cave

Now you can explore the mineral wonders of the perfect cave, without leaving your house or school! This site has pictures of many geologic features besides stalactites and stalagmites! For example, you'll see popcorn, bathtubs, and cave pearls. For a bat-free cave experience, try spelunking here!

http://www.cruzio.com/~gooderth/virtcave/
    virtcave.html

LAND FEATURES—DESERTS

An Inside Look at the Arizona-Sonora Desert Museum

When you hear the word "desert" does it conjure up visions of sand dunes? Even Africa's Namib, perhaps the sandiest desert in the world, is only about 30 percent dunes! In Arizona's Sonoran Desert, sand covers only one or two percent of the area. And desert doesn't mean there are no plants, either. Sloping and flat desert lands host so many plants, you can't walk without bumping into bushes! And flowers bloom most of the year. Learn more about the interrelationships of the plants, animals, and geology of this arid environment, as presented by the Arizona-Sonora Desert Museum.

http://Ag.Arizona.EDU/ASDM/inside.html

LAND FEATURES—GLACIERS

Blackcomb Glaciers—Main

Did you know that 75% of the fresh water in the world is trapped in glaciers? And glaciers are not just found near the polar caps. They also exist along the equator, although only at the high altitudes. Find out how a glacier forms and what happens when glacier meets volcano.

http://www.whistler.net/glacier/

Did you know that **75%** of the world's fresh water supply is locked up in glaciers? That's equivalent to sixty years of nonstop rain, all over the world! Dig into the **Blackcomb Glaciers—Main page**, and watch out for the ice worms!

LAND FEATURES—MOUNTAINS

Shangri La Home Page

Welcome to a real life Shangri La! Around long before there were man-made boundaries, the Himalayas are not just rock and snow, but a breathtaking range of mountains, teeming with life. The exclusive home of the Spiny Babbler bird, they also lay claim to some impressive records, including the highest mountain and the deepest canyon. Learn more about the geography and inhabitants of this beautiful region and discover how man has left his mark on these majestic peaks.

http://aleph0.clarku.edu/rajs/Shangri_La.html

Chase some waterfalls in EARTH SCIENCE.

Lost your sheep? Count them in FARMING AND AGRICULTURE.

A
B
C
D
E
F
G
H
I
J
K
L
M
N
O
P
Q
R
S
T
U
V
W
X
Y
Z

LAND FEATURES—POLAR REGIONS

AntDiv Home Page

Discover why these Australian scientists put on their parkas and went way down under to set up shop in Antarctica. Their research includes studying issues of global change, management of the marine ecosystem, and protection of the Antarctic environment. It's tough to go to the Pole for a research season, and you can read all about life there to see if it's for you. Learn more about their expeditions, and find out why they are so interested in what those penguins just had for lunch.

http://www.antdiv.gov.au/

April's Antarctic Adventures

Join April Lloyd, a third grade teacher from Charlottesville, Virginia, on an adventurous trip to Antarctica. April describes her journey to New Zealand and then on to McMurdo Station in Antarctica. Her journey takes her all the way to the South Pole where she takes part in the first ever live television broadcast from that site.

http://pen1.pen.k12.va.us:80/~alloyd/AAA.html

International Arctic Project Home Page

On March 7, 1995, Will Steger and his team began a trek across the top of the world, on an expedition to the North Pole. Huskies and dog sleds hauled their gear over 2,000 miles of frozen tundra. Their mission took four months. They wanted to raise awareness of the global importance of the Arctic. Their journey is chronicled in this informative site. You'll see maps of the trip, read entries from the diaries, and never think about the North Pole the same way again!

http://www.scholastic.com/public/Network/IAP/
  IAP-Home.html

The Polar Regions

Dress up warm to visit this site, which covers the Arctic and Antarctic regions. You'll find everything from Santa Claus (who lives at the North Pole) to information on dog mushing. Follow various polar expeditions, and explore scientific research stations and projects involving schoolchildren all over the world. You'll find lots about wildlife and polar land forms here. Truly a labor of love, this site welcomes you to learn more about all things arctic.

http://www.stud.unit.no/~sveinw/arctic/

Virtual Antarctica

A slick site, with audio and cool Web graphics sure to grab your attention. Lots here on geology, weather, and wildlife, as well as history. A don't-miss-it site!

http://www.terraquest.com/

LAND FEATURES—RAINFORESTS

Rainforest Action Network Home Page

You may have already heard that there are more kinds of plants and animals in tropical rainforests than anywhere else on Earth. And you probably already know that about half of all the world's species live in rainforests. But did you also know that in the rainforest you can find an antelope that's as small as a rabbit, a snake that can fly, or a spider that eats birds? The Kids' Corner at the Rainforest Action Network is packed with just this kind of wild information about the rainforest, and has lots of pictures of the creatures and native people that live there. But there's a big problem: without our help rainforests might be gone by the time you grow up. They're already disappearing at the rate of 150 acres per minute! Find out what you can do to help.

http://www.ran.org/ran/

Don't be a stick-in-the-MUD!

Lost your marbles? Find them in GAMES AND FUN.

For happy hedgehogs see
PETS AND PET CARE.

LAND FEATURES—SWAMPS AND BOGS

Okefenokee Swamp ~ Information

Between northern Florida and southern Georgia lie the 700 acres of the Okefenokee Swamp, home to critters as diverse as coral snakes, alligators, and—yes, TOURISTS! You'll be amazed at the dark, mirror-like water of the swamp, with its overhanging trees draped in swaying strands of Spanish Moss. Explore old Seminole canoe routes and learn about the fragile ecology of this very special area. Don't miss hearing the swampwise music of "Okefenokee Joe" while here, but don't turn your back on that 'gator!

http://www.companet.net/gravity/joinf.html

Think that just because you're a kid, you can't do anything to help save the rainforest?
Wrong.
Here's one way: protect endangered species in the rainforest by asking your family not to buy anything made of ivory, coral, reptile skins, tortoise shells, or cat pelts. Go to the Rainforest Action Network Home Page to find out more ways.

Get your hobby off the ground! Try Rockets in MODELS AND MINIATURES.

WATER

Wise Use of Water—Brochures

The world is three-quarters water, isn't it? That means there is plenty to go around, right? Well, if you're talking about water that's healthy for us to drink, it's really in short supply. Consider the millions of people in the world, all of them thirsty. Now think of all the animals and birds in the world, all of them thirsty. Hmmm—better use that water wisely. Here's a list of tips and ideas to help you conserve this natural resource for future dried-out kids on hot, summer days.

http://www.cciw.ca/glimr/metadata/
water-wise-pamphlets/intro.html

WATER FEATURES—OCEANS AND TIDES

Education Center Activities: Let's Make Waves

If you have ever sailed, you know the windier the day, the more waves there are. It is often mistakenly believed that waves are produced from within the water, when they are actually caused by the wind. Through some simple experiments designed with kids in mind, you can use a fan and marbles to create waves and model energy moving through water. These activities should help you sailors remember that the wind in your sail also causes the waves beneath your boat!

http://gnn.com/gnn//edu/curr/rdg/gen_act/ocean/
wave.html

Ocean Planet Homepage

How many forests grow in the deep sea? Plenty—of kelp and other seaweed forests. Did you know that these kelp forests are home to many sea creatures? Just like the trees on land that shelter and provide homes for many birds and animals. The kelp forests also need good quality water to survive. Pollution and over-harvesting is a threat to them. Visit the Smithsonian Institution's National Museum of Natural History in Washington D.C. This is their Ocean Planet exhibit, where you can read about the kelp forests and much more.

http://seawifs.gsfc.nasa.gov/ocean_planet.html

A
B
C
D
E
F
G
H
I
J
K
L
M
N
O
P
Q
R
S
T
U
V
W
X
Y
Z

Whooooooo will you find in BIRDS?

Tomorrow's Forecast

What's controlling tomorrow's weather? Winds? Air pressure? Nope. The answer is the oceans, which cover two-thirds of our planet. They affect our weather more than anything else on Earth. Their existence is what makes life itself possible. This site has a number of lesson plans for teachers (or enthusiastic students). The lesson plans include projects and experiments all centered around how the ocean affects our lives and our planet.

http://educate.si.edu/art-to-zoo/oceans/cover.html

ENDANGERED AND EXTINCT SPECIES

Endangered Species

In the United States, 526 plants and 430 species of animals are currently on the threatened and endangered lists. That means they may soon be gone from planet Earth forever. Threatened species are animals and plants that are likely to become endangered in the future. Endangered species are animals and plants that are in danger of becoming extinct. Learn which species are listed as threatened and endangered where you live, both in the United States and internationally. Find out how each animal or plant became endangered and what you can do to help prevent their extinction.

http://www.nceet.snre.umich.edu/EndSpp/
  Endangered.html

Endangered Species Home Page

Why is it so important to protect the various species of fish, wildlife, or plants facing extinction? They have educational, historical, recreational, and scientific value to all of us, that's why! Stop and learn about the different recovery activities for species on their way back from the brink of extinction. You can also check the current status of endangered and threatened plants and animals here.

http://www.fws.gov/~r9endspp/endspp.html

It's not all bad news at the **Endangered Species** page. California condors are coming back! In 1987, there were only 27 of these huge birds left in the whole world. By 1993, there were 75, and a successful captive breeding program continues to offer encouragement that the species will survive.

Have you hadrosaurus today? If not, try DINOSAURS AND PREHISTORIC TIMES.

Read any good Web sites lately?

Crack open CODES AND CIPHERS.

ENERGY

ENERGY QUEST—Energy Education from the California Energy Commission

What was Ben Franklin's energy-saving invention? Join Ben in a word game to find out the answer. He also has other games, crafts, and even a Declaration of (Energy) Independence. This site has activities and games about all different kinds of energy, from wind, to solar, to nuclear, to hydroelectric! This site is a must for the energy-efficient!

http://www.energy.ca.gov/energy/education/
    eduhome.html

"Every time you look up at the sky, every one of those points of light is a reminder that fusion power is extractable from hydrogen and other light elements, and it is an everyday reality throughout the Milky Way Galaxy." Carl Sagan, *the famous astronomer, said that. How are we doing on producing fusion power here on Earth? Get an update at the Fusion Energy site!*

Curl up with a good Internet site.

FUSION ENERGY

Did you know that the Sun is a fusion power plant? Solar energy is produced by a 15-million-degree-Celsius reactor in the Sun's core. It would be great to be able to produce energy this way on Earth. Scientists are working on it, but they have a long way to go. They have already achieved the necessary temperatures, as high as 510 million degrees, more than twenty times the temperature at the center of the Sun. Now, the problem is keeping the deuterium-tritium fuel magnetically suspended inside the reactor. Say that ten times! Who knows, maybe you'll be the one to solve this problem. Will fusion power plants be the energy source of the future?

http://www.pppl.gov/oview/pages/
    fusion_energy.html

Maine Solar House

This is Bill Lord's solar house. He built this house in southern Maine, on a property specially chosen for the project. Everything was planned with the goal of constructing a house that would make the most out of solar energy. There are descriptions and diagrams that show how he uses heat from the sun to warm the house and produce his own electricity. He even sells electricity back to the power company when he has a surplus!

http://solstice.crest.org/renewables/wlord/
    index.html

Renewable Energy Education Module

For sale to a good home: five types of renewable energy. Choose yours today, before the world runs out of energy! Your choice of solar, wind, hydroelectric, geothermal, or biomass energy. Shots and history included, suitable for a beginner!

http://solstice.crest.org/renewables/re-kiosk/
    index.shtml

SLIME is a polymer, as anyone who's read CHEMISTRY knows!

Watch your step in DANCE.

Rocky Run Energy Projects

There are all kinds of things kids can do for energy! Drink more soda? No—that's not the kind of energy we have in mind! These students from Virginia have an energy-efficient house online, part of a village that they're designing. You can click on a room in the house and get energy-saving tips. In Virginia, there are three different kinds of power plants. How many do you have where you live?

http://k12.cnidr.org/gsh/schools/va/rrms/energy.html

ETIQUETTE AND CUSTOMS

See also: INTERNET—NETIqUETTE, FOLKLORE, CUSTOMS

EttiquettEmail FAQ

While it seems that formal etiquette no longer plays the role in today's society it once did, there are certainly occasions where the intricacies of social interaction call for hard and fast rules. This page includes the Frequently Asked Questions (FAQ) file of the EtiquettEmail list, a moderated forum for people who want to know which fork goes where on the table, and how to properly word an invitation or thank-you letter. While the primary focus of the list is on wedding formalities, it also frequently covers discussions of business and social etiquette. Information on subscribing to the list is included here as well, and plans are being formulated to post digests of the list at this site.

http://www.wam.umd.edu/~sek/wedding/
  etiquette-email.txt

See what's shakin' in EARTH SCIENCE-GEOLOGY-EARTHQUAKES.

Trans-Cultural Study Guide

It's all too easy to assume that people in other countries have the same customs as you do. But once you've found yourself saying or doing something that seems innocent at home that provokes anger somewhere else, you may wish you'd studied a bit more before traveling. This guide was put together by a group called Volunteers in Asia, but it works well for just about anywhere. Before you go traveling, try to get as many of these questions answered as possible, or possibly keep them in mind to ask the locals. This is a commercial publisher.

http://www.moon.com/trans.cultural/
  trans.cultural.html

NET FILES

Who bought the first car?

Dr. Pfennig, from Chicago, bought the first car. It was sold by the Ford Motor Company in 1903. In 1903 they didn't name cars after fast animals and reptiles. They just started naming models of cars after the letters of the alphabet! Henry Ford started what is today one of the largest corporations, and his Model N was a big success, but the Model K....well....
Find out all about the fascinating history of Ford at
http://www.ford.com/archive/intro.html

Find your roots in GENEAOLOGY.

EVOLUTION

Evolution Entrance

The University of California, Berkeley has set up a separate "exhibition area" for the subject of Evolution in its online Museum of Paleontology. Here you are greeted by Charles Darwin speaking of the course of evolution being much like a "great Tree of Life." From there, a visitor can link into sections on Dinosaur Discoveries and Systematics (the classification system used in charting the families of species), and find out about the most important scientists to develop this field.

http://ucmp1.berkeley.edu/exhibittext/
   evolution.html

Mutant Fruit Flies

Great, now it's teenage mutant ninja fruit flies! The basis for evolution is the ability of some individuals to adapt and change. This may result in a genetic mutation of the species. To demonstrate the varieties of genetic mutation, San Francisco's Exploratorium has transferred this amazing exhibit to their Web site. Detailed color illustrations of naturally mutated fruit flies graphically demonstrate better than pages of text how this phenomenon works. Just when you thought it was safe to go near the fruit bowl....

http://www.exploratorium.edu/imagery/exhibits/
   mutant_flies/mutant_flies.html

The Sci.Bio.Evolution Home Page

There are two Usenet News Groups that have rousing discussions of evolution; this one and *talk.origins*. You'll find links to the archives of each group here, ready to download. Check the link to Niel's Geologic Timelines at *http://xalph.ast.cam.ac.uk/public/niel/ geohist1.ascii* if you're always confused about whether the Paleozoic came before the Cenozoic. There are also links to two of Darwin's most important texts,*Voyage of the Beagle* and *The Origin of Species*. But you may like the formatting better at *http://www.wonderland.org/Works/ Charles-Darwin/*.

http://weber.u.washington.edu/~jahayes/evolution/
   index.html

The Talk.Origins Archive

People love to argue about whether the theory of evolution is "true" or not. This newsgroup is one of the places this discussion goes on. Check the entries for CREATION STUDIES in this book for more information. Though you probably won't want to enter into this newsgroup's conversation, the FAQs are interesting, and you can check out a nice collection of fossil images and other related links. An interactive browser and a keyword file searcher are included here, just to make things easy.

http://rumba.ics.uci.edu:8080/origins/faqs.html

EXPLORERS AND EXPLORING

1492 Exhibit

This Library of Congress display examines Columbus, the man and the myth. Why do we talk about the "discovery" of America when there were people living there all along? What was life like in the "America" Columbus encountered? And what changes, immediate and long-term, befell both the Europeans and the people of the Americas?

http://sunsite.unc.edu/expo/1492.exhibit/Intro.html

Exploration of the Americas Title Page

This shows that kids can create a Web site where no other exists! A fifth-grade class in New York has created an encyclopedia of exploration that has no rivals on the Net. It's divided into sections: Northeastern North America, Southeastern North America, Mexico and Western North America, and South America. Some of the explorers you'll read about include Cabot, Hudson, La Salle, Ponce de León, and Cortéz.

http://pen1.pen.k12.va.us/Anthology/Div/Albemarle/
   Schools/MurrayElem/ClassPages/Prud homme/
   Explorers/exploretitle.html

People are the true treasures of the Net.

A
B
C
D
E
F
G
H
I
J
K
L
M
N
O
P
Q
R
S
T
U
V
W
X
Y
Z

A History of South Pole Exploration

"The New South Polar Times" offers a dramatic account of man's touch on the Antarctic continent, from the earliest dog sled explorers to modern scientists in airplanes. Fascinating stuff, the story is better than Saturday superhero cartoons, and it's all true!

http://139.132.40.31/NSPT/HistSPExpl.html

The Heroic Age: A Look at the Race to the South Pole

Soon after the North Pole was reached by Robert E. Peary in 1909, the race was on to see who could first get to the South Pole. This page looks at three explorers: Ernest Shackleton, Robert Scott, and Roald Amundsen. All three attempted to reach the South Pole in the early 1900s, but only Amundsen and Scott made it. Investigate their strategies and what went wrong, or right, in each case. There is still more detail at *http://magic.geol.ucsb.edu/~geo10/Students/race.html*.

http://magic.geol.ucsb.edu/~geo10/Students/
  heroic.html

Lewis & Clark Trail

This is an ambitious project from Washington State which began in October, 1995. It has begun to collect information about the lives and times of Meriwether Lewis and William Clark. During the years 1804–1806, Lewis and Clark led the first transcontinental expedition to the Pacific coast. In commemoration of the 190th anniversary of the explorations, the journey is being recreated online. Their most fascinating travel journals are here, as well as some suggested classroom projects. What was life like on the trail before hiking boots and lightweight backpacks?

http://134.121.112.29/wahistcult/trail.html

> **Never give your name or address to a stranger.**

Random House Kid's Encyclopedia—Explorers

There's not a lot of content here, but there is info on Cook, Columbus, Magellan, and a few others, as well as maps and politically correct commentary. For more on Magellan, try *http://www.nortel.com/english/magellan/ferdinand/MagellanBio.html.*

http://www.adventure.com/WWW/reference_files/
  rhke/rfiexplo.html

Rune Stone

Columbus was a latecomer to the Americas; the Vikings had been here long before. Want proof? Look at the Heavener Rune Stone, in a state park near Heavener, Oklahoma. A Viking land claim was apparently made there about 750 A.D. It is believed that these Norse explorers crossed the Atlantic, sailed around Florida into the Gulf of Mexico, and entered the Mississippi River. From there they explored its tributaries, the Arkansas and Poteau Rivers, leaving five or so rune stones along the way.

http://admin.hps.osrhe.edu/hps/htmls/runtest.htm

> **Not everything on the Net is true.**

> **Ask not what the Net can do for you, ask what you can do for the Net.**

FAMILY AND PARENTING

Arm Yourself with Facts and Solutions

This page points out some alarming statistics. Homicide is the second-leading cause of death for all youths aged 15 to 24. It is the leading cause of death for young African American males in this age group. What can parents do to help stop the violence? One of the most powerful concepts found at this site is the following: "Help your child to adopt healthy responses to conflict. Avoid situations in which 'losing face' becomes an issue by recognizing the kind of behavior which leads to a fight. Assess the conflict for what you want, not for what the other person wants." Some good suggestions are found here, plus pointers to organizations and other resources across the Net.

http://www.dnai.com/~children/violence/
  arm_yourself.html

CyberKids Home

Monster In The Park, Mixed-Up Zoo, Beyond The Barrier Of Time, Scary Stories That Make Your Mom Faint—these are only some of the great stories, written by kids like you, that you and your family can read together in this online magazine. And like any magazine, there are writing and art contests, software and product reviews written by kids for kids, and cookie recipes, too. In addition to the fictional stories, the feature articles have crossword or word search puzzles along with them, to make learning about something new even more fun. The CyberKids Launchpad will link you to lots of other neat sites listed by subject area; and if you have thoughts or ideas you want to share with other CyberKids readers, be sure to send them in.

http://www.mtlake.com/cyberkids/

Family Explorer: Home Page

Ever wondered how to make butter at home? Maybe you'd like to experiment with some kitchen chemistry, or try some nature crafts? This is a magazine you can have sent to your house, but they do have a good number of their projects up on the Web. There's an incredible assortment, too: invisible ink, an oatmeal box "camera," and how to make your own "Surf in a Bottle"—the 90s version of the Lava Lamp. This is a fun site for families to explore together.

http://www.parentsplace.com/readroom/explorer/
  index.html

Check out what other kids are writing about at CyberKids Home. This site will inspire those of you who might think writing is hard, and even show you that it can be fun.

Whoooooooo will you find in BIRDS?

Have you hadrosaurus today? If not, try DINOSAURS AND PREHISTORIC TIMES.

A
B
C
D
E
F
G
H
I
J
K
L
M
N
O
P
Q
R
S
T
U
V
W
X
Y
Z

Family Internet Home Page

OK, where do you go if you need to find out how to make porcupine salad, learn whether or not to feed your Akita soybean dog food, read recent movie reviews, figure out how your family can save for your college education, and check today's headlines from the *Jerusalem Post*? That's right, the Family Internet Home Page has answers to all these questions and lots more. If you and your family are new to the Internet, this is a great starting place. You can just click the buttons for categories including Arts & Leisure, Medical Corner, Cooking With Blondee, Kids Corner, Daily News, and Education, to name a few. So, everyone pull up a chair and start surfing!

http://www.familyinternet.com

NET FILES

How many miles does a Cotter High School Marching Band member (Winona, Minnesota) march in a year? And how many total bars of music are played by a Cotter Band member each year?

Answer: They march 95 miles, give or take a few, er, feet, and they play 21,434,058 musical bars. By the way, there are 250 members in the band. The number of hamburgers consumed by Cotter Band members in an average summer is 6,324, and there are at least 12 T-shirts unclaimed on the band bus after every road trip.
Find more funny facts about this band at http://www.mps.org/~chsband/marching/HTML/facts2.html

Family World HomePage

Kids, if your family is planning a vacation to another part of the country, be sure to check the great events calendars at this site. Broken down into four regions, the calendars include information about museums, county fairs, and other fun activities for families to do in different cities across the United States, including Alaska. And if you're not planning a trip, maybe reading about some of these events will spur your interest! Family World is really an interactive magazine with color graphics, sound, and hypertext links to lots of resources families need. More than forty regional monthly parenting publications contribute feature articles on topics as diverse as connecting Dads with play groups and recipes for summer parties. You'll also find talk about educational issues and book and software reviews. Make sure you bookmark this site so you can check it each month for new features.

http://family.com

Kids' Space

What fun—Kids' Space is everybody's home page! Here you and your family (or teacher) can submit music or drawings and hear and see what other children around the world have done, too. The Story Book is where you can write your own stories, using the pictures and themes provided each month. There is even a beanstalk that keeps growing each month in the Craft Room. You can pick an artwork and create a story for it, or pick a story already written and draw a picture for it. All commands at Kids' Space include pictures with them, so even the youngest child who may be still developing reading skills can enjoy this interactive learning experience.

http://plaza.interport.net/kids_space/

Read any good Web sites lately?

KidsCom Home Page

In order to protect the integrity of this site, kids, you and your parents will have to register here, but it's worth it. It's free, by the way. One fun thing is you get to pick which language you want—English, French, Spanish, or German. If you are learning a foreign language in school, try picking that one and see how much you can understand! KidsCom is especially for kids ages 8-14. You can look here for a pen pal, post pictures and stories about your pets, or ask the expert, Scott Yanoff, anything you want to know about the Internet, and where to find things you are interested in. Try guessing the country capitals in the Geography Game, and then read more about each country by clicking on the map. Parents, you can get support from your peers on how to cope with bringing up kids, and, if you're feeling technologically challenged yourself, there's a spot for you to ask the computer expert, too.

http://www.kidscom.com/

NET FILES

What is a "Storm Chaser"?

Answer: A "Storm Chaser" is a person who chases tornadoes! Not that they want to catch them, you understand. They just want to record information about them and study them. Meteorologists, college professors, students, and curious citizens can all be storm chasers! Training is strongly encouraged, and you can find out how to get it at http:// www.weather.com/ weather/2bmet.html

Things with Kids

This site is for parents in a traditional family setting, as well as single moms or dads who are the primary parent. It was developed by a New Zealand dad who is separated, and has four kids. It's not a fancy site, but you'll find a lot of things you can do here. For example, try some of the games, which require almost no equipment. Or prepare some of the recipes, which range from the simple ("popcorn") to the bizarre ("Green Cake"). There are puzzles, crafts, and lots of rainy-day ideas here. This is a thoughtful and useful site; be sure to say hi and tell Stuart you found his site in this book.

http://www.massey.ac.nz/~KBirks/kids/kids.htm

ADOPTION

Faces Of Adoption: America's Waiting Children

If you are a family thinking about adopting, but still have lots of unanswered questions, then be sure to check out this site. First browse the photolistings of American children waiting for adoption. Then check the AdoptionQuest section for useful information on how to begin the adoption process, what kinds of questions to ask the agency, and articles on key issues such as single parent and older parent adoptions, tax credits, and the latest court rulings. There are book reviews and lists of books for both adults and children, lists of state agency contacts and links to the National Adoption Center (NAC) and Children Awaiting Parents (CAP) for additional information.

http://www.inetcom.net/adopt/

Internet Adoption Photolisting by Precious In HIS Sight

Miguel is a one-year-old born in Paraguay. Van Hoa was born in Vietnam and will be two in September 1996. Jeevan was born in India in 1992. Natasha was born in Russia in 1991. What these children all have in common is that they are among the hundreds of children waiting for a loving family to adopt them. At this site you can browse the international photolistings of children by country, age, or gender. You'll also find answers to frequently-asked questions about international adoption, general articles about adoption issues and concerns, and a comprehensive listing of agencies to contact for more information.

http://nysernet.org/cyber/adoption

A B C D E F G H I J K L M N O P Q R S T U V W X Y Z

BABIES

The Baby Booklet

Hey, you've got a new brother or sister! It is so adorable when it is sleeping, but what do you do when it wakes up and cries, and wets, and needs a bath, and is hungry, and gets diaper rash, or some other kind of rash, and... ? If you and mom and dad are feeling a little overwhelmed and need answers to even the most basic baby care questions, this is a good place to look. Written by Dr. Lewis Wasserman, a pediatrician from Florida, this booklet provides a guided tour to baby, with useful information about baby skin care, normal growth patterns (including weight tables), colic, and other common concerns of new parents (or "old" parents who may have forgotten!). Also useful is the health care schedule which includes a complete list of vaccinations and the ages at which they should be given.

http://www.gate.net/~lewis/booklet.html

Baby Care Information

Wow! Are you experiencing information-overload with nurses and doctors and well-meaning relatives and friends, all giving you information and advice about caring for your family's new baby? It's hard to sort it all out! And you don't want to call your pediatrician with every little question. Do your eyes glaze over when you walk into the baby stores and look at row after row of undershirts and sleepers and neat baby stuff, wondering how many of what size to buy? Are you wondering about all the immunizations your baby needs and if there are side effects to these vaccines? When do you introduce solid foods? How do you select safe toys for your baby? Relax, the Baby Care Corner is loaded with useful information ranging all the way from psychologically preparing for baby's arrival, to the challenge of potty training. If you have specific questions, there's even an interactive Q&A with Dr. Kathleen Handal, MD.

http://www.familyinternet.com/babycare/
  babycare.htm

The HALLWAY At Tommy's House

If you are a parent or grandparent of a premature baby (a *preemie*), or if you have friends going through this experience, you won't want to miss this site. You'll find emotional support, as well as valuable information and insight about what families go through when their baby is born too early. The information here is written by a father whose son was born at 25 weeks, more than 3 months early, and his family's experiences in the Neonatal unit at the hospital. The section Babies On The Web provides links to other parents' personal stories about their special baby. Want information on the special feeding needs of preemies or a knitting pattern for a preemie hat? It's all here.

http://www.xmission.com/~gastown/cking/
  index.html

Naming Baby

Your new family addition is on its way, or maybe even already here, and you think it will be a fun, family experience to help select a name for your new brother or sister. Think again! Here is a light-hearted look at one family's experience: their third child went nine days without a name, while the family tried to agree on one! Be sure to read the ten tips for involving everyone in the baby-naming process while avoiding a family feud!

http://family.com/Features/Baby/BABYNAME.HTML

BABYSITTING
Babysitting Safety Tips

You got a job babysitting!!! It's a very big and important job, but there is so much to remember! Learn how you can be a safe babysitter by taking a look at the Phoenix, Arizona Police Department's Babysitting Safety Tips page. You'll get loads of common sense tips that will make your babysitting job easier and more fun!

http://www.getnet.com/silent/babysit.html

BROTHERS AND SISTERS
MelnikNotes, 10/95

Parents—if sibling rivalry is a daily concern in your household, and you feel like a United Nations peace keeper much of the time, then read this overview of Faber and Mazlish's book, *Siblings Without Rivalry*. Tips are provided on how to foster cooperation between your children, rather than competition. There are also recommendations on how you can develop a better sense of compassion and acceptance of each child's right to have envious and negative feelings about its brother or sister.

http://family.starwave.com/reviews/melnik/archive/me100195.htm

DEATH AND GRIEF
C_12: Life Changes And Family Options

The topic of death and dying is a very difficult one to talk about for parents and for kids. Here is a great list of books that may help you through the grieving process and also help you understand each other's feelings better. Two good titles on the adult list are: "The Grieving Child: A Parents Guide and Talking About Death" and "Dialogue Between Parent and Child." The list of books for kids includes two stories about coping with the death of a pet.

http://family.starwave.com/resource/pra/C_12_2.htm

Children And Grief

Grief is a painful experience for both kids and grownups, and sometimes parents will try to protect their children from this pain by not allowing them to participate in the funeral of a loved one. Read about one little girl's struggle with the loss of a close family friend. The author of this article delivers some very useful advice on helping kids through a "healthy" grief process. Kids need the support of friends and family too, and attending funeral services is often an important part of saying good-bye.

http://www.funeral.net/info/chilgrf.html

Children And Grief

Coping with the death of a family member is a really hard thing to do. It's OK to be sad, though, or even angry. The most important thing is to share your thoughts and feelings with your other family members. This article lists some of the common emotions that grieving kids (and their parents) might experience. Parents, there is also mention of some warning signs to watch out for so that you can better help your child cope with and understand the loss.

http://www.psych.med.umich.edu/web/aacap/factsFam/grief.htm

Pets Grief Support

Loss of a beloved pet is a difficult time for both kids and parents. Many people like to remember their pets with the "Monday Candle Ceremony" which is described at this site. Another place to find information, including a list of books for kids and families, is at the Pet Loss—A Reference to References page, at *http://www.rahul.net/hredlus/pet-loss.html*.

http://ourworld.compuserve.com/homepages/edwilliams/

NET FILES

What sport uses the following apparatus: a ball, a rope, some clubs, and a ribbon?

Answer: Rhythmic gymnastics combines acrobatic and ballet movements with these pieces of equipment. Visit *http://www.geopages.com/colosseum/1082/rhythmic.html* to see the beautiful results!

Rainbow Bridge—Pet Loss

Kids, if you had a very special pet that has died, be sure to read this wonderful short story about Rainbow Bridge, a place just this side of heaven. The author knows that even though your pet may be gone from your life, it is never absent from your heart. Thinking about the animal you loved waiting for you at Rainbow Bridge may make your loss a little easier.

http://www.pcix.com/abap/rainbow.html

DIVORCE

CRC Catalog of Resources

Do you think divorce stinks? Well, so does Marcia Lebowitz, and she has written a book about divorce just for kids. So have lots of other authors, so check out this link from the Children's Rights Council for a good list of books for children, parents, step-parents, and grandparents. Find out how you can subscribe to *Kids Express*, a newsletter especially for kids ages 7-12 about divorce and separation. The newsletter includes a kid-to-kid advice column, puzzles, and lots of answers to frequently-asked questions.

http://www.vix.com/crc/catalog.htm

Family Law Advisor

Kids, this one is really for your parents, because it presents lots of legal and other factual information about divorce. The On-line Newsletter covers all aspects of divorce including child custody issues, visitation, and child support. There is an interactive bulletin board where parents can post questions and read about the concerns of other families in similar situations. Separation and divorce are situations which have effects on all family members, so be sure to also check sites like ParentsPlace at *http://www.parentsplace.com/*, and Facts For Families at *http://www.psych.med.umich.edu/web/aacap/factsFam/*, which periodically carry articles about children and divorce.

http://www.divorcenet.com/law/fla.html

FAMILY HOME PAGES
The Cain Family's Home Page

John and Joann live in Maryland with their four-year-old son, David. They are very interested in home schooling and their page includes a hotlist of home school resource links as well as some great music links. If you are interested in quilting, follow some of Joann's special links. David even has his own home page called SnakeNet, so you know what his main interest is!

http://www.charm.net/~jcain/

The foil, the épée, and the sabre refer to what?
a) Essential items for your next barbecue.
b) Those little bones in your ear.
c) The three weapons of fencing.

Answer: C. Fencing is that sport where the players, well, swordfight. You know, with those cage-like masks on their faces. Fencing is a sport, and to many, an art. Concentration, quickness and agility are all very important to the fencer. At http://www.ii.uib.no/~arild/fencing.html, find out how fencing started, how it is done, scored, and won. It's not just for swashbucklers!

Children's Stories, Poems, Pictures and Sounds

This is a great place to start your Internet searching. From their home in England, the Bowens have included links to a variety of resources. You'll find resources from writing children's books to chocolate, from teddy bears to the Smithsonian Museum. And the list goes on! Both daughters (Emma, age seven, and Alice, age nine) have individual home pages that include their own stories and artwork and other things they are especially interested in. Also, there are even more links to other family home pages!

http://www.comlab.ox.ac.uk/oucl/users/
jonathan.bowen/children/

Elizabeth's Snow White Page

Elizabeth says, "surfing the Internet lets me be free and go anywhere I want! Without my wheelchair or walker." Ten-year-old Elizabeth has Down syndrome and cerebral palsy, but from her wheelchair, she travels all over the world. With the help of her two big brothers, Chris and Ryan, she has developed her own home page. Elizabeth helps prove how computers can help challenged kids really express themselves and become more independent.

http://www.ecn.bgu.edu/users/gjmuzzo/lizzie1.htm

NET FILES

What do comedians, animals, lost articles, and snake bite victims all have in common?

Answer: They all have a patron saint! Here's a page where you can find these saints and more. http://www.catholic.org/saints/patron.html

Curl up with a good Internet site.

Heather's Happy Holidaze Page!! For Kids Only!!

Heather is not yet six years old and she came up with the concept and design of this neat home page all by herself! With a little help from her Dad and Mom, it's been up and running since September 1995. There are pictures that go with each of her favorite holidays, so children of all ages can enjoy this site. You'll find scary Halloween links and a search for Tom Turkey for Thanksgiving. For some little-known Christmas tree facts, traditions, and folklore, be sure to try the link to the National Christmas Tree Association. Heather's thirteen-year-old brother has his own Web page too. He is already saving for college by getting local corporate sponsors for his page on Snakes And Reptiles, which is full of everything you'd ever want to know about these cold-blooded creatures.

http://www.shadeslanding.com/hms/

Jackson's Page For Five Year Olds

Jackson has pictures with each of his links to help preschoolers "read" his page—which includes things most kids will be interested in (like Legos, Hot Wheels, and Power Rangers). But don't stop there. Be sure to look at the Signal Flag and Semaphore game. Then keep digging until you get to the Ports and Harbor Pilots Home Page. Buried in the "other interesting maritime sites" is a fun link to the Pirate Page with information on real pirates and their ships.

http://www.islandnet.com/~bedford/jackson.html

Jessica's Home Page

Jessica is a seven-year-old from Montclair, New Jersey. Her home page includes stories that she has written and illustrated. She says she has three brothers, but one of them is really her cat, Chester!

http://www.itp.tsoa.nyu.edu/~student/mags/
  jessy/jessy.html

The Petry Family Home Page

The Petry family is from Kentucky. You can listen to Megan, age ten, playing her violin! You can read about Japanese culture and customs because younger brother Douglas has a penpal from Japan. The many links to other family pages from around the world are great, and don't forget to check out the parent/teacher resources listed here, too.

http://www.thepoint.net/~michele/

A
B
C
D
E
F
G
H
I
J
K
L
M
N
O
P
Q
R
S
T
U
V
W
X
Y
Z

Rachel's Page

Rachel lives in Chicago, Illinois and is a typical eleven-year-old. She is in her school chorus and she loves cats. She has a "cool site for the time being" which doesn't change daily, but only when she finds another cool site. Kids' WB cartoon site was her cool site for two months until she discovered BHI TEENS 90210, a site that offers free personal Web pages to kids under eighteen, and will include things such as a monthly newsletter and music page. Along with links to other fun places for kids, Rachel includes a long list of links to other kids' pages, especially ten- to fourteen-year-olds with similar interests.

http://www.mcs.net/~kathyw/rachel.html

Steve and Ruth Bennett's Family Surfboard

Here's another great place for you and your family to start surfing the Net! As Steve and Ruth state, this site is for both the Web novice and the seasoned surfer. There is definitely something for everyone here. And what would any site be without its "best picks" list? Bennett's Picks include annotations to help you decide if you want to check them out or pass them by. Besides lots of links to museums, kids' publishing projects, and family vacations, you can also download some fun demo software in Kidding Around The Keyboard. There are even Public Service Announcements which are neat things the Bennetts have found in literature and then converted to electronic format to include on their page.

http://www.familysurf.com/

Teel Family Home Page

The Teel family is obviously proud of their home state of Alaska! They have included information about the animals that live there, a list of books with Alaskan themes for preschoolers and older, and many links to other Alaskan sites. Matthew and Susan are homeschoolers, so their home page has useful curriculum links, art and crafts projects, and lots more. And if you like to fish, you won't want to miss nine-year-old Caleb's page.

http://www.alaska.net:80/~mteel/

Tessa's Cool Links For Kids

Tessa shares some of her favorite Web sites, with pictures and descriptions. One of them shows ice and snow sculptures by sculptors from around the world. They were created for Winterlude, Ottawa's annual mid-winter fun-fest. There is more than just pictures here, though, so be sure to check it out.

http://www.islandnet.com/~bedford/tessa.html

TnT—Tristan and Tiffany's Daily Cool Stuff For Kids

This brother and sister team live in British Columbia, Canada. They have taken turns picking children's Web sites and then rating them so many "poodles" out of five. A site rated five poodles is really great! Tristan is nine years old and Tiffany is six. Some of their previous TnT selections include Miss Piggy's Home Page, *Sports Illustrated For Kids*, and The Gargoyles Home Page.

http://www.polar7.com/tnt/

MOVING

C_12: Life Changes And Family Options

Kids, are you worried that a gila monster is going to meet you at the airport when you get to your new town, or maybe even worse? To ease some of those fears, read Marjorie Sharmat's book and some of the others from this list of children's books dealing with moving. Families, find out how to order "Smooth Moves For Families And Kids," a resource packet filled with brochures, checklists, articles, and more to help your family adjust to relocating.

http://family.starwave.com/resource/pra/C_12_1.htm

Children And Family Moves

Is your family getting ready for a move? Whether it's to a new neighborhood or a new state, it still means leaving your old friends behind and having to adjust to a whole new school, right? Yes, but having e-mail so you can stay in daily touch with all your friends helps a little! Families, here are some helpful suggestions for making the move easier on all of you and helping your kids through the transition.

http://www.psych.med.umich.edu/web/aacap/factsFam/fmlymove.htm

PARENTING

Cute Kids Page

When his Mom told him to eat more vegetables because they would put color in his cheeks, one boy replied, "But Mom, I don't want green cheeks." Here's a family site where you can read what funny things other kids have said, and then contribute your own family stories. Plus, there are links to all sorts of other family interests, like reading lists for kids and their parents, several children's book sites, reviews of all your favorite family entertainment activities (like movies and video games), and more.

http://www.prgone.com/cutekids/

D.O.S.A. PARENTING HOME PAGE

Allan Hawkins, M.A. Psychologist, introduces this site with a humorous look at parenting kids and teens excerpted from Dr. Frank's article in *Psychology Today* magazine. Be sure to read both the "21 Tricks For Taming Children" and "21 Tricks For Taming Adolescents." Parents, you don't have to look too far, though, to see the truth and wisdom in many of these "tricks." Besides the treasure pick of the month, there are lots of links to other parenting sites and discussion groups and several psychology links, including *Practical Psychology Magazine*, which routinely carries articles on family life issues. Caution, though, the outside links have not been viewed.

http://www.mbnet.mb.ca/~ahawkins/

Facts For Families

The American Academy of Child and Adolescent Psychiatry provides 46 information fact sheets here. They provide concise and up-to-date material designed to educate parents and families about a wide variety of psychiatric disorders affecting children and adolescents. Issues covered include bedwetting, stepfamilies, learning disabilities, grief, adoption, AIDS, and much more. This material is revised and updated regularly, and is offered in three languages: English, Spanish, and French.

http://www.psych.med.umich.edu/web/aacap/
    factsFam/

NET FILES

What are Mancos Milk-vetch, Clay-loving Wild-buckwheat, Dudley Bluffs Bladderpod, and Penland Beardtongue?

Answer: Well, they are not the names of new rock groups! They are all plants on the endangered species list for Colorado! Find more about endangered and threatened species at http://www.fws.gov/~r9endspp/endspp.html (the Endangered Species Home Page)!

Family Planet

Your fourth-grader wants to subscribe to *Odyssey Magazine,* but you've never heard of it and wonder what it's about. Is the bargain software you saw at the store really something your kids will enjoy? What kind of toys are appropriate and safe for three-year-olds? You've got a business meeting in Chicago on Friday and you decide to take the whole family for the weekend, but what are they going to do while you're at the meeting? This site has it all! The regular features include advice columns on a wide range of family-related topics, or you can e-mail T. Berry Brazelton with your specific questions. The movie reviews include a "fidget factor" to help you decide if your seven- and ten-year-olds will really sit through the same movie. The Oppenheim Toy Portfolio has authoritative reviews of children's books, toys, and media. There are daily and monthly local activity calendars of family events for many U.S. cities. Families, you won't want to miss this site!

http://family.starwave.com

> ## SLIME is a polymer, as anyone who's read CHEMISTRY knows!

FatherNet

OK, Dads, here is a parenting site especially for you which confirms the important role you play in your kids' lives. Check out the electronic bulletin board to read what other Dads are thinking about, or read bimonthly issues of *ModernDad Newsletter* for feature articles on topics as diverse as youth sports, potty training, summer hiking (including trail mix recipes), taking baby pictures, and planning for college expenses. Then you'll find even more information when you link to other WWW resources on fatherhood, including two great quarterly newsletters—*FatherTimes* and *At-Home Dad*. In response to Vice President Al Gore's call to action, a Father-to-Father national effort to unite men and provide them with information, support and encouragement in their roles as fathers has been initiated in many states. Read how you can get a Community Starter Kit and join this movement.

http://www.fsci.umn.edu/cyfc/FatherNet.htp

Foster Parent Home Page/Foster Care Providers

Whoever said "I never promised you a rose garden" must have been referring to foster care. So says one dedicated foster parent who shares her personal story here. Foster parents, this is a wonderful site for you to find lots of information and support on all issues relating to foster care and the child welfare system. There are feature articles on topics such as foster care and the news media, medical, addiction, and educational concerns, plus transracial/cross-cultural issues. Intended as an interactive forum specifically for foster parents, there is enlightening information here for all parents.

http://www.worldaccess.com/~clg46/

KidSource OnLine Welcome Page

A grandparent wonders if he should put his philodendron plants up out of reach before his grandson-who-puts-everything-in-his-mouth comes to visit. An educator would like to post a request for donations of used computer equipment. This site has something for both folks, and more! Families, be sure to check out the reviews of kid-tested software—written from a family perspective, with both negative and positive comments. The Education section includes articles and book lists and, best of all, links and more links! And what about that philodendron? The list of the twenty most commonly ingested plants, and which ones of these are toxic, is only one of the articles in the Healthcare section. The ComputingEDGE is a way to match needy schools with computer equipment.

http://www.kidsource.com/

National Parent Information Network

Kids, are your parents stressed out? Do they yell at you all the time, and does it seem like they just don't understand you? Then be sure to have them check out this site, which is especially for parents. Parents, you are not the only ones out there struggling with issues like how much TV your child should be watching, or how to get your kids to clean up their rooms or develop better study habits. The NPIN is sponsored by the ERIC Clearinghouses on Urban Education and on Early Childhood Education. There are lots of choices: a parenting discussion list, and a Q&A service through AskERIC are only two. You can search the ERIC database on all topics relating to child development, child rearing, and parenting children from birth to adolescence. *Parent News* monthly newsletter offers feature articles on a wide range of topics, and periodically lists information about organizations of special interest to parents and how to subscribe to other publications such as *Pp* (Parents & Preschoolers) *Newsletter* and *Single Mother Newsletter*.

http://ericps.ed.uiuc.edu/npin/npinhome.html

Parenting: PARENTS PLACE.COM

Parents, whether you are on your first child, your 10th, or somewhere in-between, join the hundreds of other parents who come to ParentsPlace to get support and share information on the adventures and challenges of child-rearing. Whether you are looking for directions to make invisible ink, or the latest in toy safety-labeling requirements, you'll find it here. Feature articles include information on parenting twins, step-parenting, at-home dads, and single parents; but that's just the beginning. You can "Ask the Pediatrician" questions about children's health or look at sample articles from the Family Explorer Newsletter for some fun science and nature activities to do with your kids. And the S.O.S. (Search Our Site) feature is great! This Web site is sure to be one of your favorites.

http://www.parentsplace.com/

Parents Helping Parents

PHP—The Family Resource Center provides links to many other sites of interest to parents and their children. If you haven't found what you are looking for at any of the other sites mentioned in this section, be sure to try this one. There are links to disability, health, and child care information, legal, parents' rights, and support services, the Electronic School House and other educational sites for families, and lots, lots more. You should know that we have not previewed all links.

http://www.portal.com/~cbntmkr/php.html

Parents' Resource Almanac: Table of Contents

Beth DeFrancis has compiled this lifesaver for moms, dads, and other caregivers as a guide through the labyrinth of information on parenting and caring for children. Here you can find lists of the best books, magazines, products, and services as recommended by various child development experts. The information is arranged in broad topics, including Parenting Approaches and Techniques, Child Safety, Education, Work and Childcare, and so much more. The more you dig, the more you'll find! What to do about separation anxiety…how to raise "purchasing savvy" kids…fun activities to do on rainy days, like building forts…free resources and catalogs for homeschoolers…travel agencies specializing in travel planning for kids and their grandparents…and more and more….

http://family.starwave.com/resource/pra/
  Table_of_Contents.htm

SmartParenting (tm) On-Line

Parents, if you feel you need some fun and useful ways to reduce the stresses and strains of parenting in today's hectic world, then try some of Dr. Favaro's techniques. At this site, the child psychologist provides an electronic edition of *The Parent's Answer Book: 101 Solutions To Everyday Parenting Problems*. You can also download free copies of the *SmartParenting Electronic News* and the SmartParenting Catalog. If you are a single parent, Dr. Favaro also gives advice on managing custody and visitation issues.

http://www.smartparenting.com/parents

NET FILES

*Every year
The Worshipful Companies
of the Vintners and Dyers participate in
an unusual and ancient ritual
on the River Thames
in London.
What is it?*

Answer: They are charged with the Royal duty of rounding up and taking a census of all the swans! For many centuries, mute swans in Britain were raised for food, like other poultry. Individual swans were marked by nicks on their webbed feet or beak which indicated ownership. Somewhat like cattle brands in the American West, these markings were registered with the Crown. Any unmarked birds became Crown property. The swans are rounded up at a "swan-upping," and although they are no longer used for food, the Royal Swanherd continues the tradition to this day. Check *http://www.airtime.co.uk/users/cygnus/swanstud.htm* for more information.

FARMING AND AGRICULTURE

See also: GARDENS AND GARDENING, HORSES AND EQUESTRIAN SPORTS

OSU's Breeds of Livestock

Oklahoma State University's breed archive is extensive! You'll be able to find pictures and info on breeds of the following animals: horses, cattle, swine, sheep, goats, and poultry. Oh, yes, did we mention the "other" category? There you'll find llamas, donkeys, and—buffalo! But let's talk cattle. Everyone's heard of the Jersey cow: "With an average weight of 900 pounds, the Jersey produces more pounds of milk per pound of body weight than any other breed." And there's a nice photo here, too. But have you ever heard of the Australian Friesian Sahiwal? It's a breed being developed in Australia for use in tropical areas. How about the Florida Cracker/Pineywoods, the Florida equivalent of the Texas Longhorn? Visit this site for a virtual barnyard of breeds!

http://www.ansi.okstate.edu/breeds/

WWW Library—Livestock Section (Youth)

Are you interested in 4-H, or maybe even a career in animal science? This is the place for you! You can learn about sheep and wool, check out the National Dairy Database, or get information on your favorite breed of livestock. Maybe you'd like to attend the Judging Camp this summer, for hands-on experience. Not sure about the livestock-judging thing? Kids gain a lot from competing on a livestock evaluation team. It builds character, and may even give you confidence if you are shy, or tone you down a bit if you are a little less reserved! Don't forget about the genetics simulation called Cowgame. You can download a DOS program that lets you pick the bulls and cows you want to breed, then shows you the calf results.

http://www.ansi.okstate.edu/library/youth.html

BEEKEEPING
Beekeeping Home Page

To bee or not to bee, but the question is, what do you know about bees? Worker honeybees have many jobs in taking care of their hives. They do the feeding, cleaning, guarding, the long distance and short distance flying; they carry pollen, produce honey, and build the honeycomb. To learn more about beekeeping, visit the Beekeeping Home Page, and bee careful!

http://weber.u.washington.edu/~jlks/bee.html

CATTLE
Big Dave's Cow Page

Cow lovers alert! People's fascination with cows tends to mooove in the direction of humor, using pictures, sounds, poetry, and songs. This site contains all of that and more, including information for that udderly serious scholar in search of bovine research.

http://www.gl.umbc.edu/~dschmi1/links/cow.html

CROPS, PRODUCE, AND ORCHARDS
The Corn Growers Guidebook (Purdue University)

The corniest people in the United States bring you everything you need to know about the King of Crops—corn. Maybe you want to raise corn. Or need a corn recipe. Or a corn song. Or want to find out what products have corn in them. Or what ancient civilizations used corn. Well, you've corn to the right place. And when you have had your fill of corn, you can link to the maize page and read about—more corn.

http://info.aes.purdue.edu/agronomy/cornguid.htm

Crack open CODES AND CIPHERS.

Don't Panic Eat Organic

Farm, don't harm your environment. Nature's pesticides include a ladybug who eats an aphid, or an owl that catches a rodent. By understanding and using the natural biological systems on a farm, you can leave the sprays and chemicals on the store shelf, and let nature do most of the work. Let these certified organic farmers show you how to cultivate in harmony with your surroundings.

http://www.rain.org/~sals/my.html

GOATS

Goats

She has some quirky habits, quite a personality, smells a little, and has been hanging around you all day. Do you call the police? No, all the poor goat wants is good scratch between the shoulders! The Irvine Masa Charros 4-H Club raises dairy and pygmy goats and knows what a rewarding experience raising goats can be. With the dedication and knowledge demonstrated at this site, how can anyone not approve of these kids raising kids?

http://www.ics.uci.edu/~pazzani/4H/Goats.html

LLAMAS

LlamaWeb

Is it going to rain all day long? Well, let's check the llamas. If they rush to their shelter when it starts raining, then it will not rain long. If they remain where they are when it starts to rain, plan on bringing your umbrella, because it's going to keep on raining. Although llamas don't know when to come in out of the rain, they are very intelligent animals and make wonderful pets. They are used as pack llamas, golfing caddies, and watch or guard animals, and their coat fiber is used to produce rugs, ropes, sweaters, and other clothing. Stop by the LlamaWeb site and help them name the baby llama.

http://www.webcom.com/~degraham/

NET FILES

What year was the first commercial radio broadcast?

Answer: Although experimental radio broadcasts took place between 1910 and 1917, formal "broadcasting" is usually considered to have begun in 1920. One of the first important uses was on November 2, 1920, when Westinghouse's KDKA-Pittsburgh broadcast the Harding-Cox Presidential election returns (Harding won). Why the gap between 1917 and 1920? When the U.S. entered World War I in 1917, all radio was taken over by the U.S. Navy, to prevent possible use by spies. After the War ended in 1918, radio began to develop for consumer use.

POULTRY

Feathersite Poultry Page

If you are more interested in what *breed* of chicken crossed the road rather than why it crossed the road, then strut on over to the Featherside Farm and inspect their collection of colorful chick pics and descriptions. If you say there is more to poultry than fowl chickens, you're right! They've also included ducks, geese, turkeys, and peafowl guaranteed to smooth your feathers. (Hint: take the link back to the home page to view a dancing chicken.)

http://www.cyborganic.com/People/stefan/brkpage/Poultry/BRKPoultryPage.html

See what's shakin' in EARTH SCIENCE—GEOLOGY—EARTHQUAKES.

A B C D E F G H I J K L M N O P Q R S T U V W X Y Z

SHEEP

Sheep

If you are looking for a farm animal to raise, take a good look at the multipurpose sheep. Stay warm with wool sweaters made from their fleece. Feast on feta cheese produced from their milk. Stop mowing the lawn, let sheep keep your grass closely clipped. Get your daily exercise by walking a mile a day with your lamb. Make a profit when you take them to the market. BAAAAAA. (OK, the sheep request that you skip that last one.) Here is where 4-Hers show you how fun and rewarding sheep raising can be.

http://www.ics.uci.edu/~pazzani/4H/Sheep.html

SWINE

Did you know

President Harry Truman once said "No man should be allowed to be President who does not understand hogs." Even if you don't have political aspirations, you can learn a lot about pigs here. Peruse pig trivia, discover pithy porcine sayings, and meditate on the history of pork. Hogwash? Not here.

http://www.nppc.org/hog-trivia.html

What city became so strongly associated with pork production it was nicknamed **Porkopolis**? "Porkopolis" was another name for Cincinnati, Ohio. Read more intriguing pig facts at the Did You Know page.

Watch your step in DANCE.

The Pig Sty

Does the thought of swine make you swoon? Does having a pig as a pet make your day? Then a pot-bellied pig is the way to go. Read about where the pot-bellied pig came from, see other people's pigs, and join the Pot-Bellied Pig List where you can talk to others who think hogs are heaven.

http://www.waverider.co.uk/~grant/

Pigs

Are you interested in raising pigs for fun and/or profit? The 4-Hers at this site learn integrity, sportsmanship, and communication through raising hogs. Investigate the steps required to start your own pig raising venture, what breeds are available, and how to care for these large but gentle swine. And the added bonus—forget the health spa—unlimited free mud baths!

http://www.ics.uci.edu/~pazzani/4H/Pigs.html

FESTIVALS AND FAIRS

The Gathering of the Clans

'Tis a stirring sight, indeed, the Gathering of the Clans at the Highland Games, marching in behind the drums and blaring bagpipes. You can sample Scots recipes, admire clan tartans, listen to some folk tales, or watch a dancer step nimbly over crossed swords. Try the caber toss if you're very strong, throw the stone, or pitch the sheaf in these traditional games of Scotland. Learn about them here, as well as Gaelic culture in general.

http://www.discribe.ca/world/scotland/

Find your roots in GENEAOLOGY.

Internet 1996 World Exposition

Remember hearing about all the world's fairs and expositions that happened in the last century? The idea was to show people what new inventions—like railroads, telephones, lights, and cars—could do for them. Well, if you've been wondering what this new invention—the Internet—could do for you, welcome to the Internet 1996 World Exposition. It's a world's fair for the information age. One of the most important parts of this expo is the Global Schoolhouse Pavilion, linking schools around the world, showcasing young artists, and featuring activities that help kids learn (and like) the Internet. You won't want to miss the ToasterNet Pavilion, where new and unusual devices on the Internet are introduced, or the online dairy farm from the Netherlands, where you can monitor the position of your favorite cow using the World Wide Web.

http://www.town.hall.org/fair/

PowWow

Please rise as the flags and eagle staffs enter the arena for the powwow. It's OK, everyone is welcome at Native American powwows. Why not get to know your neighbors? Learn about the dance, regalia, drums, and song of powwows. If you're thinking about attending a powwow, this page will teach you its ways. Learn more by reading the NATIVE AMERICANS AND OTHER INDIGENOUS PEOPLES entries in this book.

http://www.mnonline.org/ktca/powwow/index.html

Shrewsbury Renaissance Faire

Art thou off to the faire? Don't forget your Renaissance-era costume and your muffin hat. You can learn to make one here. Yum, those gingerbread cookies look good! Care for some fried dragon scales? What is your U.S. currency worth in Elizabethan English pounds? See what goes into a reenactment of a 16th Century Welsh village, this one located near Corvallis, Oregon. Remember to learn history by playing faire, anon!

http://www.peak.org/~kiyose/Shrewsbury.html

FISH

See also: AQUARIUMS, OUTDOOR RECREATION—FISHING, SHARKS

Fish FAQ

Did you know that salmon generally lay from 2,500 to 7,000 eggs, depending on the species and its size? And that some lobsters hardly move more than one mile? What is the most common fish in the sea? Why do scientists classify fish? How long do fish live? How is the age of a fish determined? Visit the Fish FAQ home page where you'll find the answers to all these questions and more, and you'll discover how porcupine fish inflate themselves, too!

http://www.wh.whoi.edu/homepage/faq.html

*W*hen you're giving an opinion, sometimes you say that's "my two cents' worth!" Where did that phrase originate?

ANSWER: According to Evan Morris, "Two cents' or two-center has been a slang synonym for 'very cheap,' since the middle of the 19th century, when the cheapest cigar available was literally a two-center. The U.S. Treasury Department actually issued a two-cent coin in 1864, which was, incidentally, the first U.S. coin to bear the motto 'In God We Trust.' The government, evidently feeling frisky in a monetary sort of way, also issued coins in three-cent and twenty-cent denominations during the same period." Read more at *http://www.users.interport.net/~words1/index.html – the Words, Wit, and Wisdom Page.*

Surf today, smart tomorrow.

A B C D E F G H I J K L M N O P Q R S T U V W X Y Z

Underwater World Home Page

Want to go on an underwater diving adventure in the Galapagos Islands? Go to Underwater World, and don't forget your fins! You'll escape the deadly chomp of the scariest sharks in the sea. You can help some freaky fishes finish their family album by matching names with pictures, then add your name to the freaky fishes' friends hall of fame. Did you know that fish have no eyelids? They can't blink, wink, or close their eyes to sleep. Learn what a lobster eats, how a clam shell grows, how oysters make pearls, and answers to other fishy questions.

http://pathfinder.com/@@K2PmRxF18AAAQMhb/
   pathfinder/kidstuff/underwater/

FITNESS AND EXERCISE

Aerobics!

One, two, three—kick!! Aerobic exercises get your heart beating and your lungs heaving, and make your muscles strong. Many aerobic exercises are fun when done to music, as dance steps that tone your body. You can learn some new aerobic steps, and learn a ton about aerobics, by checking out the Aerobics! Web page.

http://grove.ufl.edu/~evilgreg/aerobics.html

Fitness Fundamentals

The President of the United States wants you to be physically fit! The President's Council on Physical Fitness and Sports is an organization whose single goal is to help Americans become fit—to aid citizens in learning how to be physically healthy. One of the many resources the Council provides is this booklet called "Fitness Fundamentals." It provides all the basics in starting an exercise and fitness program for people of all ages, including figuring out what your target heart rate during exercise should be.

http://www.hoptechno.com/book11.htm

Fun—the Key to Kid Fitness

The best way to exercise is to have fun. Duhhh, everybody knows that! Having ideas on *how* to keep exercise fun can be difficult, though. At the Fun—the Key to Kid Fitness page you'll see tips on how to keep exercise sessions more fun. Written for parents to get their kids exercising, you can use it to exercise with your parents, brothers and sisters, or friends. Best yet, you'll have fun while you are doing it! Here's a sample: 4 minute walk in a straight line. Tell each other 2 jokes. 3 minute walk in a zigzag fashion. 2 minutes of speed-walking. Child tries to catch parent. Doesn't that sound like fun?

http://www.vannet.com/WCF/WCFTEXT/
   KIDFIT.HTM

Reebok Guide to Fitness

Good ol' walking—putting one foot in front of the other—is a great way to stay fit. Extensive walking for exercise, though, requires preparation, including stretching exercises and goal-setting. It's all illustrated for you here! Check out the Reebok Guide to Fitness to get some ideas on how to plan to walk your way to fitness! (Take your dog out with you, he'd like some fresh air, too!)

http://planetreebok.com/walkreebok1.html

STRETCHING AND FLEXIBILITY

When you exercise, whether it's going for a run, a short jog, or dancing up a storm, stretching your muscles before you begin is important. At the Stretching and Flexibility page on the World Wide Web you'll learn *everything* there is to know about stretching. And how muscles contract. And fast and slow fibers, connective tissue, and cooperating muscle groups. As a matter of fact, if you read all this, you'll be a foremost expert on this subject!

http://www.ntf.ca/NTF/papers/rma/stretching.html

> **People are the true treasures of the Net.**

FLAGS

An Incomplete Collection of World Flags

Despite the modest title, this site features just about every flag from every nation in the world, each as a separate, downloadable, full-color, inline GIF image. Black-and-white versions are also available, and other information for each nation from the *World Factbook* can be found here as well.

http://www.adfa.oz.au/CS/flg

Ausflag—For Further Information

Vexillology is, of course, the study of flags, and there are many people who find it a topic of deep consequence. This site gives some general flag terms, plus worthwhile links to flag resources all over the Net. Also try the Vexillology and Heraldry page at *http://www.cesi.it/flags/vexilla.html*. There, you'll find out about why flags are flown at half mast, which flags get to fly higher than others, and more.

http://www.ausflag.com.au/info/info.html

Flags

Dyed-in-the-wool flag fans will find some delightful goodies on this Australian page. Besides a fine selection of international flag images, you'll find sections featuring motor racing flags, international maritime signal flags ("I am discharging explosives!"), and the complete semaphore flag code—all graphically displayed.

http://osprey.anbg.gov.au/flags/flags.html

Microscopic Flag Icons for the KIDLINK WWW

Here you will find 75 tiny flag icons representing countries participating in the KIDCAFE and KIDLINK discussion list projects. This page loads rapidly, since the GIFs are so small.

http://www.kidlink.org/WWW/miniflags.html

Never give your name or address to a stranger.

Pirate Flags

If you ever see one of these flags on a ship headed your way, better warp out of there, fast! Variations on the "skull and crossbones" theme were flown by famous pirates, such as Blackbeard and others.

http://www2.ecst.csuchico.edu/~beej/pirates/flags.html

The United States Flag Page

For a country that is barely over two hundred years old, the United States has a vast and rich accumulation of lore and tradition regarding its flag. Old Glory gets its due from this page in red, white, and blue embellishment. Images of every single official and unofficial U.S. flag are stored here, as well as a variety of documents, songs, poems, speeches and letters. Red Skelton's famous version of the Pledge of Allegiance can be found here as well as the information you'll need if you'd like to acquire a flag that has flown over the Capitol. A series of intriguing questions and answers are posted here, along with the (complete!) words to the National Anthem. The site also carries "opposing views" about flags, national symbols, and patriotism.

http://www.elk-grove.k12.il.us/usflag/

Did you know you can buy a flag that has flown over the U.S. Capitol?
It doesn't stay up there very long, just a minute or so, but think of the tradition and history and, heck, the fun of having a flag like that! You can even request a flag that has flown over the Capitol on your birthday or another special occasion.
The flags cost between $7.50 and $19.00 plus shipping, and the ordering information can be found at The United States Flag Page.

USPS and other Nautical Flags

Have you ever seen a tall ship "dressed"? That means it has all its colorful flags and pennants flying for a special occasion. Those flags also represent a common maritime language. Some flags stand for letters, numbers, or words. Some combinations of flags have special meanings, too. Check this site to see messages like "I am on fire" or "I need a tow." You'll also learn a lot about nautical flag etiquette, as well as international and U.S. flag customs in general. This excellent site is prepared by the U.S. Power Squadron.

http://www.ronin.com/USPS/f_stuff/flag.html

Welcome to Flags of the World

Chances are good that your local mall doesn't have a flag store. This site is where you will probably want to go when the occasion calls for purchasing a flag, whether it's the Stars and Stripes, a state flag, the Jolly Roger, or flags from any of over 175 nations. You can even get the flag for Vatican City here! Flag poles, mounting brackets, and indoor display equipment are all available here as well. All their flags are made in the USA, from top quality fabrics and dyes.

http://www.mallmart.com/flags

FOLKLORE AND MYTHOLOGY

Gryphons, Griffins, Griffons!

This page is dedicated to gryphons, mythological beasts who have the head, forelegs, and wings of an eagle, and the hindquarters, tail, and ears of a lion. They are symbols of strength and vigilance in mythology. Sections of this home page include gryphons in literature, in art and architecture, and other gryphon sightings on the Internet. Fly over to this site to check out these wondrous beasts!

http://sashimi.wwa.com/~tirya/gryphon.html

Reed Interactive's Online Projects

Creation stories and traditional wisdom as told by school children from around the world is the focus of this WWW page. Included are animal legends, creation stories, the environment, and other stories. Stories have been submitted by children from Australia, Iceland, Canada, Alaska, and Israel.

http://www.ozemail.com.au/~reed/global/mythstor.html

Welcome to MYTHTEXT: Mythology Site

Welcome to Mythtext: home of the Godfiles! Available at this site are a short list of gods and goddesses with biographical entries, a collection of FAQs about mythological topics, and bibliographies about mythology and history. Pointers to major texts available on the Net are here, as well as a collection of smaller mythological works. Also included are WWW and FTP sites related to mythology, as well as listservs and newsgroups on the subject. There is some material for sale here, but much of it is free.

http://www.the-wire.com/culture/mythology/mythtext.html

FABLES
Fluency Through Fables

Welcome to Fluency Through Fables! Each month, The Comenius Group provides a fable and a variety of exercises to assist students of English. The types of exercises include vocabulary matching, true or false comprehension, vocabulary completion, and written discussion. Five fables are presented. These are "The Donkey and the Grasshopper," "The Father and His Sons," "The Kingdom of the Lion," "The Musical Fisherman," and "The Tortoise and the Hare." Brush up on your skills here!

http://www.comenius.com/fable/index.html

Not everything on the Net is true.

Stories/Fables/Legends

Welcome to NativeWeb! The purpose of this site is to provide a cyber-place for Earth's indigenous peoples. One of the sections of the NativeWeb houses Stories/Fables/Legends. Here you will find the Fables of the Mayas. Included in the fables collection are stories of the rabbit, the jaguar, and the coyote. Each animal's page is attractively accompanied by lifelike animals. Hop on over to read rabbit stories and other fables!

http://kuhttp.cc.ukans.edu/~marc/natlit/stories.html

FAIRY TALES

Cinderella Project: Home Page

You have seen Disney's animated story of *Cinderella,* but you may not know there are lots of other pictures and stories about her. Here is a collection of twelve different versions of the story, some with illustrations. She's really an old lady! The earliest version here is dated 1729!

http://www.usm.edu/usmhburg/lib_arts/english/
   cinderella/cinderella.html

Tales of Wonder

Tales of Wonder features folk and fairy tales from around the world. Geographic areas represented include Russia, Siberia, Central Asia, China, Japan, and the Middle East. Tales from Scandinavia, Scotland, England, Africa, and India, and Native American tales, are also included. The source used for the stories is listed. This is an excellent site for exploring the world of folk and fairy tales.

http://www.ece.ucdavis.edu/~darsie/tales.html

Ask not what the Net can do for you, ask what you can do for the Net.

KING ARTHUR

Avalon: Arthurian Heaven

Avalon is "the mystical isle to which King Arthur was taken after being mortally wounded by his son Mordred in battle." According to legend, Arthur is still sleeping in Avalon until a hero can awaken him. This home page offers lots of information for beginners, including a FAQ, a list of Arthurian names, the ten rules of chivalry, and some Arthurian shields. Other types of references you can find here are books, articles, and other media, including *First Knight.* Don't forget to read the link to information about copyright of this home page if you're going to use this information in a school report!

http://reality.sgi.com/employees/chris_manchester/
   arthur.html

Cinderella fans—drive your carriage immediately over to the Cinderella Project: Home Page! This site is a text and image archive containing a dozen English versions of Cinderella. The texts may be read horizontally, one version at a time, or vertically, one episode at a time, for comparisons among the versions. You can also choose to look only at the images. This is a good site to visit if you'd like to read variations on a common fairy tale!

A B C D E F G H I J K L M N O P Q R S T U V W X Y Z

FREE THINGS

AT&T PreTest

There's a free mousepad waiting for you after you play a Movie Mania trivia quiz. You don't even have to ace the quiz in order to have AT&T mail the mousepad to you! While you're becoming a movie trivia master, you can go to some movie sites. Want to see *The Brady Bunch*?

http://www.att.com:80/hotquiz/

e-Coupons

You open up the newspaper. All of the coupons slip out and fall on the floor. Not only do you have to pick them up, you have to cut them out, sort them, go shopping, and haul it all home. No more of that nonsense with e-coupons! These electronic coupons change often. You just fill out a form and choose the free items you want. Then the freebies are mailed right to you! Keep in mind that your name will probably be added to a mailing list, and you may get more material than you requested!

http://www.e-coupons.com

Flint River Ranch—Super Premium Health Food for Pets

Is your dog's coat looking a little ragged? Or perhaps your cat seems a little pokey? Get a free sample of health food for your pet by calling an 800 number or by sending e-mail.

http://www.snni.com/ferguson/flint-rr.htm

FREE TRAVEL BROCHURES—INFOSYSTEMS' TRAVEL RESOURCES

Are you dreaming of a sunny beach, on an island far away? Or how about a cruise along the route of explorers Lewis and Clark? Get free travel brochures to your dream destination! And now that you're on the Net, maybe your parents will let *you* plan the family vacation.

http://mmink.com/infosystems/trc.html

Become one with the Net.

The Sun never sets on the Internet.

The Freebie Update

We don't know who Julie is, but she puts together a great list of freebies and low-cost items! The deals change every week—you can keep your eye out for crafts, videos, stickers, and more. Some of the things are free only if you buy at least one, so read carefully! Maybe your grandfather is turning 80 years or older? Request a free birthday card for him from the White House!

http://www.winternet.com/~julie/freebie.html

HarperCollins Children's Books

Did you ever want to try out a book before you read it? HarperCollins will let you download a free chapter from some of their books, including *A Very Personal Computer*. It's about a boy named Conner and his know-it-all computer, which...well, you can download it yourself! After you give the first chapter a read-through, you can buy a copy, or pick up the book at your local public library, where books are always free.

http://www.harpercollins.com/kids/

National Pen WWW Home Page

It's just like a scavenger hunt! Have a look through this online catalog and take note of the clues that are there. Then take a little quiz, and you could win a free pen with your choice of message imprinted on it.

http://www.pens.com/

ORIENT MAGAZINE

Orient Magazine celebrates the Asian-American experience. You can get a free issue of their print version! From Asian cooking to acupuncture, this magazine thoroughly covers the Asian scene!

http://www.eyec.com/orientmag/

GAMES AND FUN

Build-a-Monster

This is a sweet little game to amuse the little kids in your family. Pick a head for your monster—how about this frog? OK, now let's pick a body—you like that chicken? Now, which feet should we pick? Yikes, that makes a very strange-looking monster, but it won't scare anyone!

http://www.rahul.net/renoir/monster/monster.html

The Electric Origami Shop

Actually, it's not really about origami at all, but the stuff here will bend your mind. Check the Fridge Gallery, where you can display your art in cyberspace. None of those tacky magnets needed—just a bit of cyber-glue and your imagination. Or take the temperature of the mood of the Internet today—is it blissfully unaware, grumpy, or happy? Add your mood. Be sure to seed some alien snow, and watch it grow into drifts before your eyes!

http://www.ibm.com/Stretch/EOS/

I Spy

Before we all wondered where Waldo was, we loved a game called "I Spy." Now that game's come to the Web, and it's perfect entertainment for young children. Choose a picture, say, a screenful of colorful postage stamps. Then the first player looks at the picture and says "I spy a rocket!" Player two points to the stamp with the rocket on it, if he can find it! Then it's player two's turn: "I spy a stamp with a dog!" And so on. See if you can find the stamp with Mt. Rushmore!

http://www.lexmark.com/data/spy/ispy07s.jpg

Mr. Edible Starchy Tuber Head

If you are a big fan of Mr. Potato Head, this is the next best thing. Select online options for eyes, ears, hair, etc. to determine what your Mr. ESTH looks like. The author of the page also has created stories about Mr. ESTH, as well as places he's been spotted in the movies and on TV!

http://winnie.acsu.buffalo.edu/potatoe/

Oasis * Here & There * Kid's Corner

Ever want to star in your very own story? Here's your chance! Fill in your name and your best friend's name, and get a personalized story online! Kid's Corner also contains some other fun games including a puzzle and a hangman game.

http://www.ot.com/kids

Zarf's List of Interactive Games on the Web

You'll find links to all kinds of Internet games here. You'll find games you can play against other kids over the Net, as well as things you can play by yourself. Besides interactive games, try some of the "web toys" Zarf's collected!

http://www.cs.cmu.edu/afs/andrew/org/kgb/www/zarf/games.html

BOARD GAMES

Connect Four

Tired of the same old tic-tac-toe? Then maybe you'd like to try Connect Four! Play against the computer and see if you can outsmart it—we couldn't! The best thing about playing over the Net is that you never lose the game pieces!

http://csugrad.cs.vt.edu/htbin/Connect4.perl

Marcel's Web Mind

This is the Web version of the popular Master Mind game. You can play this game right over the Internet! The objective is to break the "code" by finding the right combination of colors. The computer will show a black peg, meaning that you have the right color in the right position, or a white peg, which means that you have the right color, but it's in the wrong position. You can play at several different skill levels, too.

http://einstein.et.tudelft.nl/~mvdlaan/WebMind/WM_intro.html

Surf today, smart tomorrow.

A B C D E F G H I J K L M N O P Q R S T U V W X Y Z

San Jose Scrabble® Club No. 21

Did you know that "a'a" is an acceptable Scrabble word? It's a type of rough, cinder-like lava. If you're a fan of the game, this page would go a long way to settling arguments and food fights over what word is legal or not. This page provides links to other Scrabble pages on the Web and even has information on the World Championships!

http://www.yak.net/kablooey/scrabble.html

The Gateway to Othello

This Swedish site lets you play Othello, or Reversi, against the computer. You can also read about rules, strategy, and tournaments, and view a list of the world's best (human) players at some of the linked sites.

http://www.pt.hk-r.se/~roos/othello1/

CARD GAMES
Card Games

This page is an excellent place to get the rules of many different types of card games from all over the world. If you have a question about which way the turns should go in Go Fish, then this is the page for you!

http://www.cs.man.ac.uk/card-games/

Did You Know

Jokers were added to American card decks in the 1870s? You can learn about different types of decks, plus try out lots of fun card games at The House of Cards!

The House of Cards

Do you ever just sit alone on a rainy day and wish you could start playing solitaire! If you only knew HOW to play solitaire! Think of The House of Cards as the place you can go to learn rules of card games new, old, and never-before-heard-of!

http://www.sky.net/~rrasa/hoc.html

DARTS
CyberDarts

Do you see bull's eyes when you surf the net? Maybe you'd better turn off the computer and take a walk outside, in *actual reality*!? If you're looking for bull's-eyes, though, you've come to the right place. This is the page for those who are obsessed with the game of darts. This page includes press releases from the American Dart Association, a listing of dart groups—find one near you—and wild and crazy dart stories. It's a must for dart enthusiasts!

http://www.cyberdarts.com/

FRISBEE
Flying Disc Dog Home Page

Don't leave your dog home when you want to play—take him along! This page features world-class disc dogs in action photos! Bone up on how to train your dog to catch and fetch a flying disc!

http://www.vais.net/~krobair/discdog.html

Freestyle Frisbee

Ever notice how Frisbees never come with directions? How do you learn those cool tricks? Now you can visit this Web site, and learn from the experts. Put a spin on it, and don't forget the silicon spray!

http://www.frisbee.com/index.html

Visit the stars in Astronomy.

The History of the Disc

Ever wondered who invented the toy Frisbee? It began life as either a pie plate or a cookie tin lid from the Frisbie Pie Company, in New Haven, Connecticut, long ago in the early 1870s. You can read the incredible history of this toy here, and even see the original patent. Never heard of a patent? This page explains it all!

http://www.upa.org/~upa/upa/frisbee-hist.html

An Introduction to the Sport of Ultimate

"When a ball dreams, it dreams it's a Frisbee!" And you thought it was just a "simple" game! This stuff is serious fun. Ultimate had a modest beginning back in 1968 at Columbia High School in New Jersey. By 1972, the game had escalated to an intercollegiate sport, and today it's played in over thirty countries around the world. As with any sport, there are rules, but the list is short and the play is simple. Check it out!

http://radon.gas.uug.arizona.edu/~hko/upa/
  intro.html

GRAFFITI

CyberSight's Graffiti Wall: Let's Go

Let's be honest. Graffiti is ugly: it makes buildings and signs look hideous. On the other hand, it is kind of fun to be able to leave a mark somewhere. The problem is that graffiti makes whatever is marked look ugly. Now, through the wonder of the Internet, you can leave your mark and never worry about defacing property. It's CyberSight's Graffiti Wall. Spray paint, scratch, do what you like. It's designed for fun with no unsightly mess to clean up! Just like real graffiti, though, you may see that some of the messages left here aren't so nice.

http://cybersight.com/cgi-bin/cs/gw?main

The Sun never sets on the Internet.

Yogatta try Yoga.

HORSESHOE PITCHING

Horseshoe-Pitching

You can't just borrow some shoes from the pony in the paddock, you've got to use regulation horseshoes if you want to play with folks from the National Horseshoe Pitchers Association! According to their home page, the horseshoes used by the NHPA are very different from shoes actually used on horses. They are much bigger! Any shoe used in a tournament must not exceed 7 $\frac{1}{4}$" wide, 7 $\frac{5}{8}$" in length. The opening of the horseshoe can't be wider than 3 $\frac{1}{2}$" from just inside both points of the shoe. Most of them weigh about 2½ pounds. For more of the fine points of horseshoe-pitching, trot on over here!

http://www.holli.com/~tsears/
  Horseshoe-Pitching.html

Horseshoes on the Net

Here are the court dimensions, rules, and how the scoring works for the game of horseshoes. It's everything you'll need to set up the game. Add two steel stakes, a set of horseshoes, some sand for the pits, and a yard. A partner is also a must!

http://www.mindspring.com/~jlock/shoes.html

MAZES

The Maze

Hang a left—NO, A RIGHT!! Now you're lost!! But don't worry, there's always that "BACK" key on your browser! Have fun exploring these interactive mazes, but watch out for The Minotaur! Don't worry, though, every now and again The Wumpus will turn up and show you where you are on his map. Unfortunately he runs away again and takes the map with him!

http://www.pb.net/usrwww/w_tglenn/maze.htm

A
B
C
D
E
F
G
H
I
J
K
L
M
N
O
P
Q
R
S
T
U
V
W
X
Y
Z

NET FILES

In modern times, what famous people were born on December 25th?

Answer:
Rod Serling, creator of The Twilight Zone.
Conrad Hilton, founder of the Hilton Hotel chain.
Louis Chevrolet, auto racer and designer, whose name is on General Motors cars.
Clara Barton, founder of the American Red Cross, and many others.
Find out who shares your birthday at
http://www.eb.com/bio.html

PeterCat's Treasure Mazes

Gosh—which way should we go? We have a choice of three directions. Should we try the Twisting Little Maze of Passages, the Maze of Little Twisting Passages, or the Twisty Maze of Little Passages? Sometimes when you choose a direction, a "treasure" Web site is selected, and you can choose to go "off-maze" to check it out. Choose the right directions and angels and leprechauns will escort you to the exit! Parental advisory: not all the "treasure" sites have been checked, please use this with your kids.

http://web.syr.edu/~pjkappes/maze/index.html

POGS AND MILKCAPS
The POG Page

This no-frills page tells you how to play POGS the usual way. But did you ever think of playing POGS Baseball? How about POGS Football? Check this page for these new variations!

http://www.macshack.com/johns/pog.html

The Story of Milkcaps

Has the game of Milkcaps, or POGS, hit your school yet? Don't worry, it will! This very easy game has kids everywhere clamoring for POGS, POGS, and MORE POGS! But did you know that they may have started 600 years ago, in Japan? This page is advertising a book on milkcaps, but it will give you a history of the game and its travels around the world!

http://www.directnet.com/wow/books/pogs/pogchap.htm

STONE SKIPPING
North American Stone Skipping Association

"If you can throw a stone at the water and make it touch down and lift off, just once, you have skipped a stone and thereby join one of the most ancient recreational activities of humankind," says Jerdone. He's the current Guinness World Record Holder for stone skipping! In 1994, he made a small piece of flat black slate jump 38 skips, on the Blanco River, in Texas. This site tells you all about the history of stone skipping, also known as "Ducks and Drakes" in England, "ricochet" in France, and "stone skiffing" in Ireland. It even tells you how to challenge the world record holder, and asks you to send in your favorite stone skipping locations so they can be mapped worldwide.

http://www.ccsi.com/yeeha/nassa/a1.html

Space Exploration is a blast. Check out Astronomy.

STRING FIGURES
World-wide Webs

Everybody's taken a loop of string and played Cat's Cradle with a friend. Here's a collection of string figures from around the world to keep you busy all afternoon! Try "The Banana Tree" or "Four Boys Walking in a Row," both from Pacific islands.

http://www.ece.ucdavis.edu/~darsie/string.html

GARDENS AND GARDENING

See also: FARMING AND AGRICULTURE

The Butterfly Guide

You love butterflies, especially when they visit your own yard. You wish they'd stay around longer, though. This Butterfly Guide tells you what kinds of plants you need in your garden to attract caterpillars and butterflies, especially the really pretty and unusual ones. For example, if you want the beautiful light blue Spring Azure butterfly to hang around, you need to plant aster, butterfly weed, and dogwood trees.

http://www.butterflies.com/guide.html

Canoe Plants / Introduction and Contents

When early Polynesian explorers set out for Hawai'i, a journey of thousands of miles, they traveled in wooden canoes. With them they took, among other things, twenty-four plants thought to be essential to life. These "canoe plants" of ancient Hawai'i included awapuhi kuahiwi (shampoo ginger), ko (sugar cane), and niu (coconut). They were all the new settlers needed for their food, rope, medicine, containers, and fabrics. Here's a guide to these life-sustaining plants.

http://hawaii-nation.org/nation/canoe/canoe.html

Don't be a stick-in-the-MUD!

Lose yourself in a Museum. SCIENCE has them all.

Carnivorous Plant Database

Imagine this if you can: a little fly takes a break from buzzing around by coming to rest on the leaf of a beautiful pink plant. What the fly doesn't know is that the leaf is very sticky. Unfortunately for him, he's not going to be leaving anytime soon. Slowly the leaf edges curl up around the fly. Gulp! He's been eaten—by a plant! Trapping insects for food is what "carnivorous" plants do. They live in poor soil, so they have to get their nutrition from somewhere (or something!). Here's where you can see what they look like. A fun thing to do at this site is to click on "Database Entry Formats" to find out the right abbreviation for where you live. Then enter the abbreviation into the search box to see if carnivorous plants are anywhere near you. Keep your pet flies inside if they are. There are also links to other sites on the Net with even more information and pictures of carnivorous plants.

http://www.hpl.hp.com/bot/cp_home

Hydroponic Society of America

Okay, you've got no dirt, no sunshine, and no space. No way can you start a garden, right? Wrong. Hydroponics to the rescue. Hydro-what? "Hydro," as in water, and "ponics," as in the Greek word *ponos*, which means labor. But you don't have to work very hard to grow plants hydroponically, which just means growing them in water mixed with fertilizer—no dirt required. Plants use a lot of energy tunneling their roots into the dirt to get food. With the hydroponic method, vegetables, fruits, flowers, and herbs get big and fat by lying back and letting their roots hang down in some very nutritious water. Imagine making strawberry shortcake in the middle of January, with organic strawberries grown from your own "water farm" in your bedroom closet! Take a look at this site to find out how.

http://www.intercom.net/user/aquaedu/hsa/ index.html

A B C D E F G H I J K L M N O P Q R S T U V W X Y Z

Hypergarden

So what if you've got a black thumb—you can always go hang out in the Hypergarden, created by the students at the Electronic Imaging Lab of Metropolitan Community College in Omaha, Nebraska. Here you'll find a weird but beautiful bunch of images using parts of actual gardens—like trellises—and fractal forms. Huh? What's that? A fractal is a geometric shape—like certain kinds of triangles, snowflakes, trees, clouds, and mountains—that can be divided into parts that each look like the shape you started with. If the spooky Addams Family has a garden, this is what it looks like.

http://www.unomaha.edu/~gday/hypergarden.html

Search Horticultural Factsheets

Yikes! Your carrots have weevils all over them, and the bottoms of your tomatoes are covered with black spots. Who ya gonna call? Ohio State University's WebGarden Factsheet Database, that's who. It's a mega-collection of over 4,000 links to gardening factsheets from the United States, Canada, and the Netherlands, complete with a handy little search form. In the case of your weird tomatoes, for example, all you have to do is type "tomatoes" and "black spot" into the title part of the form, and choose "vegetables" as the category for expert advice and instant relief. (Hint: bet you're watering too much or too little.)

http://hortwww-2.ag.ohio-state.edu/hvp/Webgarden/
   FactsheetFind.html

The Tele-Garden

Now here's a garden for the 90s, where Web cruisers gather to plant seeds and water plants by remotely controlling an industrial robotic arm. Called the Tele-Garden, this is a real garden at the University of Southern California, where the idea is to bring together a community of people to help tend a "shared garden." You can explore the Tele-Garden by clicking on a drawing of the robotic arm. This moves the arm—and a camera—to give you an up-to-the-minute picture of what's going on.

http://www.usc.edu/dept/garden/

Take a ride on a Carousel in AMUSEMENT PARKS.

The *Time Life* Gardening Library

OK, you live in Colorado and have a shady front yard. You really like red flowers, but your soil is very poor. Is there anything you can plant? Search this database of thousands of plants to find out which ones will work, what they look like, and how to take care of them. Maybe you already know the name of the plant you want to grow and are just looking for some watering or pruning tips. Everything you need to know is here! When nothing can grow outside, search for a house plant. If your parents find out about this site, watch out: you may get to do some weeding. But remember, a weed is just a plant for which a use has not yet been discovered.

http://pathfinder.com/@@CetUtoGA5wMAQKlM/
   vg/TimeLife/

The Virginia Cooperative Extension Gopher

This is a treasure trove of gardening projects just for kids and families, brought to you by 4-H and the Virginia Cooperative Service. Whether it's growing a salad on your windowsill, or sprouts in an egg shell, you'll find easy-to-understand instructions here. There's even more: games, puzzles, family projects, and advice on the best gardening books for kids.

gopher://gopher.ext.vt.edu:70/11/vce-data/hort/
   consumer/general/children

Let balloonists take you to new heights in Aviation and Airplanes.

BOTANIC GARDENS

Australian National Botanic Gardens

Ever hear a kookaburra laugh? The call of this bird is one of the most famous sounds of the Australian bush. You can listen to the calls of the kookaburra, the currawong, the peewee, and a bunch of other very strange birds at the Australian National Botanic Gardens. Birds love the gardens because it's a safe place, filled with lots of native plants and habitats that give them food and shelter. You can also find out how Aborigines—who have lived in Australia for at least 40,000 years—gathered everything they needed to live a healthy life from the land. At least half of what they ate came from plants, and one of the ways they encouraged new plants to grow was to burn all the old plants to the ground! And speaking of plants, don't miss the Kangaroo Paws and the Wattles, just two of the many different kinds of plants grown halfway around the world.

http://osprey.erin.gov.au/anbg/
anbg-introduction.html

Boyce Thompson Southwestern Arboretum

If you're one of those people who think a cactus is just a prickly, ugly weed, and the desert is a dry wasteland of sand, may we suggest taking a cyberwalk through Arizona's Boyce Thompson Southwestern Arboretum? There's not very much water to go around in the desert, but most deserts are not deserted! Many scientists think that the variety of life in the desert is second only to that found in the tropics. You won't want to miss the cactus garden, with its 800 different cacti, including skyscraper saguaros, paddle-shaped prickly pears, and squat, branched hedgehogs. So the cactus can conserve what little water it has, some of its flowers last only one day—and that day happens to be captured here in lots of beautiful pictures.

http://ag.arizona.edu:80/BTA/btsa.html

Origami: the fold to behold! Check out CRAFTS AND HOBBIES.

The Butchart Gardens

A garden in an old rock quarry? Come to Vancouver Island, off the west coast of Canada, and see for yourself. Over a million bedding plants are used each year, to ensure continuous bloom. And they plant 100,000 bulbs every fall to make a spectacular Springtime display!

http://vvv.com/butchart/

NET FILES

How do you say "Where is the bathroom?" in Klingonaase?

Answer: nuqDaq 'oH puchpa''e';
Say that six times fast!
http://www.kli.org/kli/phrases.html

The New York Botanical Garden

Back before there was a New York City, a forest covered the whole island of Manhattan. Of course, there isn't much of a forest left these days, but 40 acres of the natural, uncut, 200-year old forest has been saved at the New York Botanical Garden just as it was. The garden, one of the oldest and biggest in the world, also has 27 specialty gardens featuring everything from rocks to roses, all of which you can visit online. Make sure you read all about the garden's scientists, who travel the world looking for medicinal plants that may help to fight cancer and other diseases.

http://pathfinder.com/@@ONBf*cHKMwIAQBRT/
vg/Gardens/NYBG/index.html

A B C D E F G H I J K L M N O P Q R S T U V W X Y Z

HOUSEPLANTS

Time Life's House Plant Pavilion

Some scientists think we humans have a natural urge to make our houses like the surroundings of our earliest ancestors: lots of clean, warm, humid air, and a green landscape. Time-Life's House Plant Pavilion is a good place to get started if you want to turn your house into a jungle. Newbies will learn how to grow everything from acalypha (otherwise known as a copperleaf) to zantedeschia (that's a golden calla lily). You'll also learn a lot about the history of houseplants, which goes back a long, long ways.

http://pathfinder.com/@@*SaWpLENJgMAQIJh/
vg/TimeLife/Houseplants/index.html

GENEALOGY AND FAMILY HISTORY

Everton's Genealogical Helper: Online Edition

Here's the online version of the world's largest genealogical magazine, *Everton's Genealogical Helper*. Sure, it's not the print version, which usually runs around 300 pages, but some great features and lots of help for beginning genealogists are available—for free! Recent issues explained how to find your Scandinavian ancestors and talked about Jewish resources on the Internet.

http://www.everton.com/ghonline.html

Family Associations and Whom to Contact

Ever wonder what it would be like to go to a huge family reunion and meet relatives from all over the country? Maybe there's one being planned right now for your family name. To find out, just go to this site and click on the first letter of your last name. If there is an association for your family, the name and address for the person in charge will be listed.

http://www.magibox.net/~tfc/socmain.htm

Family History Centers

Where's the biggest collection of genealogical material in the world? The Family History Library in Salt Lake City, Utah is the biggest one of its kind. The library is part of the Church of Jesus Christ of Latter-day Saints. The church thinks it's very important to find out about your family history, so they send researchers around the world to copy family records. You can see these records in person by going to a Family History Center—a branch of the Family History Library—near you. There's at least one in every U.S. state, and there are others in the British Isles, New Zealand, Australia, and Canada. They're free and open to the public. Take a look at this list to find one close to you.

http://ftp.cac.psu.edu/~saw/FHC/fhc.html

NET FILES

Why would you want to play a medieval *krummhorn* with a blanket over your head?

Answer: According to "The strangest thing you have been asked to do at a gig," at Windplayer Online, it's impossible to play the krummhorn softly! The only way to quiet it down a little is to throw something over the player's head! Try http://www.windplayer.com/wp/strangesthl.html for more strange tales.

Lost your sheep? Count them in FARMING AND AGRICULTURE.

The Genealogy Home Page

Ever thought about drawing your family tree? No, not the one in your front yard! We're talking about your relatives. Picture a tree with you at the bottom. On the first two branches are your parents. On the next highest branches are their parents, who are your grandparents. Farther up the tree are THEIR parents, your great-grandparents. Guess what—that tree reaches up higher than you can see!! Get started here with help from experienced family researchers called genealogists. Computers and the Internet are two of the most important tools being used today by genealogists. You can get your own free family-tree-tracking software here and learn how to be part of a project to share family histories over the Net. The project already includes over one and a half million names! Wouldn't it be amazing if someone's already working on your family history? Find out here!

http://ftp.cac.psu.edu/~saw/genealogy.html

Genealogy Toolbox

Sure, your dog has a pedigree, but do you? Search for your family name and history here. You may find out your friends should be calling you "Duke," "Prince," or "Princess"! Would you like to see what your grandparents' (or maybe even great-grandparents') birth or death certificates looked like? Find out how to send away for your own copies. And if your family has its own coat of arms, the section on Heraldry will explain what all those colors and symbols mean.

http://www.outfitters.com/~helm/si.html

Chase some waterfalls in EARTH SCIENCE

Guide for Interviewing Family Members

"Who was your best friend?" That's just one of the questions you need to include on a family-history questionnaire. What are the other 118? Check this site, print out the questions, then go visit grandma and grandpa for some amazing stories.

gopher://ftp.cac.psu.edu/00/genealogy/roots-l/
  genealog/genealog.intrview

GEOGRAPHY

MAPS

The Map Case

The Map Case is a project presented by the Bodleian Library Map Room in Great Britain. The Bodleian Library is one of the oldest libraries in the world, and it contains the seventh largest collection of maps. This is a perfect site if you have to do a report on British history, but there are some unusual maps from the New World, too. For example, there's "Part of Virginia Discovered ... by John Smith 1612"—maybe Pocahontas helped him draw it!

http://www.rsl.ox.ac.uk/nnj/mapcase.htm

Mapmaker, Mapmaker, Make Me a Map

If you wanted to get to your friend's house but didn't know the way, how would you get there? One way would be to have your friend write the directions on a sheet of paper. That might work if she only lived a few blocks away, but it could get very complicated and wordy if she lived farther away. The answer: draw a map! This page tells you about how maps are made and explains some of the terms used in mapmaking. You'll also find out about the different kinds of maps and how they are used.

http://loki.ur.utk.edu/ut2kids/maps/map.html

Get your hobby off the ground! Try Rockets in MODELS AND MINIATURES.

For happy hedgehogs see PETS AND PET CARE.

NAISMap WWW-GIS Home Page

If you ever wanted to make a detailed map of a country, this is the perfect place for you. You'll use your forms-capable browser to instruct a Graphical Information System (GIS). Here you can build many different maps of Canada, and learn tons about geography in the process. Want to know the Canadian range of the Grizzly Bear, or the location of wetlands? Try this site!

http://ellesmere.ccm.emr.ca/naismap/naismap.html

The Perry-Castañeda Library Map Collection

Available from the University of Texas Library, this collection includes maps from around the world, and links to some of the best map collections on the Internet. Check out the historical maps, and the current-events maps of Bosnia and Kashmir. If you need a map, start here!

http://www.lib.utexas.edu/Libs/PCL/Map_collection/
Map_collection.html

Rare Map Collection at the Hargrett

Of course, maps have been around for a long time. You can view one of the finest collections of historic maps on the Internet at this Web site in Georgia. Included are some great maps of U.S. Civil War battlefields, as well as material on Colonial and Revolutionary America.

http://scarlett.libs.uga.edu/darchive/hargrett/maps/
maps.html

Lost your marbles? Find them in GAMES AND FUN.

TIGER Map Server

This experimental server will give you color maps with cities and other features clearly marked, based on 1992 data. Try searching by ZIP code, latitude-longitude, as well as city name. You can mark your maps with a variety of symbols. Since this is an experiment, not all cities are included, but it's a good start. It's also linked to the Census Bureau's U.S. Gazetteer, with information on population.

http://tiger2.census.gov/cgi-bin/mapbrowse

What Do Maps Show—Teacher's background

This site has comprehensive lesson plans and hands-on student activity sheets for students— all related to understanding maps. You can also download student map packets which you can print out for use with the lessons. A great geography teaching and learning tool.

http://info.er.usgs.gov/education/teacher/
what-do-maps-show/index.html

Xerox PARC Map Viewer

Quick! You need an emergency map of Idaho to complete your homework! Relax, this site gives you public domain, copyright-free maps on demand, for the United States and world regions, using several different projections. The maps show only coastlines, rivers, and borders; they don't have marked cities or roads. The map data is based on *CIA World Factbook* information from 1985-1990, so don't look for countries newer than that. 60,000 line-drawing maps are requested per day, so this site may be slow to draw a map on your computer. For those using a text-only browser, the following hint is suggested by XEROX's Palo Alto Research Center: select the Map Viewer's "Hide Map Image" option and then the "Retrieve Image for Separate Viewer" option. Some browsers will then allow you to save the image to a file on your computer.

http://www.xerox.com/map

Whooooooo will you find in BIRDS?

Have you hadrousaurus today? If not, try DINOSAURS AND PREHISTORIC TIMES.

GIFTED CHILDREN

FishNet

Who said smart kids aren't cool? Take a look at FishNet (one of the best sites on the Internet) and notice it's designed for bright teenagers. You'll find the Weird Fact of the Day, Edge (a fantastic e-zine), great threads of discussions amongst kids from all over, Street Talk, and much more. You haven't experienced the Internet until you've seen FishNet. Remember, it's cool to be smart!

http://www.webpress.net:80/jayi/Open.html

Gifted Resources Home Page

Being gifted is being blessed—it means having special talents beyond the average. While being gifted is good, it can also lead to complications. Sometimes school can be boring and unchallenging for gifted kids. Finding other kids who share the same interests sometimes can be difficult. The Internet offers a way for gifted children to explore the world in a challenging environment, and to find other kids with similar gifts. A good place to find information useful for gifted children!

http://www.eskimo.com/~user/kids.html

Southern Regional Maxtap Independent Study Program

Gifted kids need to be challenged. The Internet is the perfect vehicle to help bright kids branch out, and to experience world-wide sources of intellectual challenges. With an eye toward Internet resources that can captivate gifted kids, the Southern Regional Maxtap Independent Study Program page is an excellent launching point for gifted kids to explore the Internet.

http://dune.srhs.k12.nj.us/WWW/maxtap.html

NET FILES

What do ice, a thick layer of honey, petroleum jelly, and a thick paste of baking soda and water all have in common?

Answer: They are all suggested as first aid for minor burns, at First Aid Online. The best advice for you comes from your family doctor, but this site may also interest you:

http://www.symnet.net/Users/afoster/safety/

Read any good Web sites lately?

HEALTH AND SAFETY

Bugs in the News!

What is microbiology? It's the study of really, REALLY, little "critters" that can only be seen under a microscope. This includes stuff like bacteria and viruses. Ick, you say? Well, you might be surprised to know that bacteria are our friends. In fact, bacteria are absolutely necessary for all life on this planet. But not too many of them. And not the "wrong" kinds in the "wrong" places. You'll learn what an antibiotic does, and what to expect from viruses like the flu. And you'll read the very latest on breaking "bug" news stories, such as that *Jurassic Park* live bacteria they found in an insect trapped in amber for millions of years.

http://falcon.cc.ukans.edu/~jbrown/bugs.html

Facts for Families

The American Academy of Child and Adolescent Psychiatry has an answer for almost any kind of family challenge you can imagine, from dealing with divorce to welcoming an adopted child. Parents will want to use this page with their children.

http://www.psych.med.umich.edu/web/aacap/
    factsFam/

Family Health Home Page

Staying healthy means learning all kinds of facts. One fun way to learn some facts about staying healthy is to LISTEN to doctors giving good information on how to be healthy. At the Family Health Home Page, you can listen to physicians discussing tips on staying healthy. Here you'll find sound files, lasting approximately two minutes, on health topics from acne to weight loss. Give these a listen, it'll be good for your health! You might want to have a parent listen, too!

http://www.tcom.ohiou.edu/family-health.html

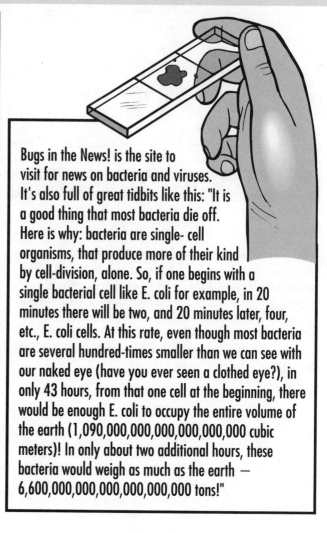

Bugs in the News! is the site to visit for news on bacteria and viruses. It's also full of great tidbits like this: "It is a good thing that most bacteria die off. Here is why: bacteria are single- cell organisms, that produce more of their kind by cell-division, alone. So, if one begins with a single bacterial cell like E. coli for example, in 20 minutes there will be two, and 20 minutes later, four, etc., E. coli cells. At this rate, even though most bacteria are several hundred-times smaller than we can see with our naked eye (have you ever seen a clothed eye?), in only 43 hours, from that one cell at the beginning, there would be enough E. coli to occupy the entire volume of the earth (1,090,000,000,000,000,000,000 cubic meters)! In only about two additional hours, these bacteria would weigh as much as the earth — 6,600,000,000,000,000,000,000 tons!"

Lynn Gazis-Sax's Children's Health Home Page

There is a lot to consider when you're a kid, and you are trying to stay healthy. How do you pick a doctor? What are some of the ailments that affect kids? Where do *really* sick children get help? A good place to look to get answers to these questions is here. While there's nothing like Mom's chicken soup to help you stay healthy, this is a pretty good place to look for kid's health information.

http://www.best.com/~gazissax/chealth.html

Yogatta try Yoga.

PEDINFO Home Page

This is an archive of information for pediatricians and others interested in children's health. Its keeper is a doctor at the Lister Hill Library of the Health Sciences at the University of Alabama at Birmingham. You'll find current information (and links!) on disorders, diseases, and syndromes. Visit many Pediatrics Departments in teaching hospitals all over the world, and examine some interesting information you won't find elsewhere. For example, here's a letter to pediatricians everywhere from a mother and pediatrician who adopted a child in China. The letter describes conditions in Chinese orphanages and reasons that pediatricians might prescribe antibiotics and other medications to be taken to China by the adoptive parent, with appropriate instructions on if, and when, to administer them, since delay in treatment could be counter-productive. There is also a very useful collection of info on parental control of Internet access.

http://www.lhl.uab.edu:80/pedinfo/

Welcome to Health Issues

What happens when students in Ms. Seno's sixth grade class, at Madison Wisconsin Middle School, write about health issues? You get some really great articles about all kinds of important ways to stay healthy.

Find out about:

Acupuncture—an ancient Chinese medical art;

Hydrocephalus—a disease of fluid build-up in the skull;

Prostate Cancer—cancer in the prostate gland in men;

Basketball Injuries—ever heard of jumper's knee?

Steroids—drugs that are killing and hurting athletes;

Tennis Elbow—it's a lot more painful than you think;

Hunting Dangers and Safety—it's not only unsafe for animals in the woods during hunting season!

Check out these health topics written by other kids!!

http://198.150.8.9/healthissues.html

ACUPUNCTURE
Acupuncture

Nobody likes seeing needles at the doctor's office—that usually means getting a shot or vaccination! The Chinese, though, have been using needles to EASE pain and cure diseases in an ancient medical art called *Acupuncture*. Learn the story behind this 5,000-year-old medical practice in a report by sixth grader, Paul Braun. Who knows, maybe you'll want to get poked by needles in a doctor's office after you read this!

http://198.150.8.9/acupuncture.html

BEDWETTING
Bedwetting

Bedwetting is EMBARRASSING! Did you know that 15% of all kids older than three wet the bed? It's true, and there are reasons for this. To learn more about bedwetting, check out the Bedwetting page produced by the American Academy of Child and Adolescent Psychiatry.

**http://www.psych.med.umich.edu/web/aacap/
  factsFam/bedwet.htm**

DENTAL CARE
General Dentistry

There is nothing better than a beautiful set of choppers. After all, how can you eat corn on the cob, or bite into a big juicy apple if your teeth aren't in tip-top shape? At the General Dentistry Web pages, Dr. O. Nestor Reyes will give you pointers on the best way to floss and brush your teeth. You can also look at some pictures of teeth and gums that have gone bad. Real gross, but that will keep you brushing after every meal!!

http://www.iquest.net/dentistry/

Take a ride on a Carousel in AMUSEMENT PARKS.

A B C D E F G H I J K L M N O P Q R S T U V W X Y Z

The Tooth Fairy's Home Page

Some children believe that when they lose a tooth, it should be left under their pillows for the Tooth Fairy. She takes the tooth and may leave behind some coins! Alas, there's nothing about that gentle story at this web site. But, you will find quick tips on how to keep your teeth healthy and cavity-free. How often should you brush your teeth, and what's that gunky stuff called plaque? Learn how to floss, and remember, the only teeth you have to floss are the ones you want to keep!

http://redwood.northcoast.com/~megmcc/
    dental.html

DISABILITIES

Apple's Disability Solutions

Now we're talking MICE! Mice of different sizes and speeds, remote-controlled mice, and head-controlled mice. But don't look here for information about cute, little furry rodents, or toys, or the latest on hypnosis; this site is for you and your family if you're looking for assistive technology solutions for your computer. The Mac Access Passport is a comprehensive database of access products. You'll find expanded keyboards and other neat gadgets if you are physically challenged, innovative software if you are visually impaired, and lots of special education software. There is a list with links to popular shareware for you to download, and a list of organizations that provide other assistive technology resources.

http://www.apple.com/disability/welcome.html

Assistive Technology On-Line

This site is probably more for the older kids and grown-ups, but, hey, you're going to be one of them some day yourself! This site is so loaded with information about all kinds of assistive technologies (AT) that you won't want to miss it. Look for links to specific disability Internet resources, products and companies, U.S. government policy, and federally funded programs relating to AT. There's even information on regional and local programs, including local branches of national organizations, volunteer groups, etc. The Lists of Lists is very comprehensive and a great place to start research on any particular type of disability.

http://www.asel.udel.edu/at-online/assistive.html

NET FILES

Does the word "vexillology" leave you vexed? What is it, anyway?

Answer: "Vexillology" is the study of Flags. Find out more about them at http://www.cesi.it/flags/vexilla.html

Autism Network International

"To me it means sadness (for causing me so many misunderstandings) and protection (from not having to understand peoples evilness) and it means satisfaction (because I don't have a problem with spending a lot of time in my own company), and isolation (because I don't know how to get close to people when I want)...." A personal view of autism by Gunilla.

Autism Network International (ANI) is an organization run "by and for autistic people." They promote peer support, information sharing, self-help, and help with educating the public about autism.

http://www.students.uiuc.edu/~bordner/ani.html

Autism Resources

This resource is a collection of autism-related sites on the Net. It includes a FAQ (frequently-asked questions) about autism, autism mailing lists, advice to parents, treatment methods, research information, and organizations. If you know someone with autism, do a good deed and tell them about this wonderful resource.

http://web.syr.edu/~jmwobus/autism/

Cerebral Palsy Tutorial

Cerebral Palsy, also known as CP, is a medical condition causing uncontrolled muscle movements. It's not a disease, and you can't "catch" it from someone who has it. People with CP have it all of their lives. Many times kids who have CP use wheel chairs around school, and sometimes they can't speak clearly. To learn more about CP take a look at the Cerebral Palsy Tutorial.

http://galen.med.virginia.edu/~smb4v/tutorials/cp/cp.htm

Children and Adults with Attention Deficit Disorder

ADD—ADHD—it's all just a bunch of letters to you. All you do know is that you really have trouble paying attention in school and you always want to start a new game or project, but never seem to finish any. You're not alone! 3.5 million kids in America have been diagnosed with Attention Deficit Disorder. At this site you can click on the map of the United States and see if there is a CH.A.D.D. (Children and Adults with ADD) chapter near you. CH.A.D.D. is a non-profit, parent-based organization, providing family support, advocacy, and education. There are articles and information here on upcoming events and current laws relating to students with ADD.

http://www.chadd.org/

Deaf World Web's Deaf CyberKids

If you are a "hearing" child, did you ever wonder how a deaf person could phone in a pizza order? If you are a deaf or hearing-impaired child, you know you are a child first, with all the same interests and activities as your friends. So this site has just what other sites have—a way to connect up with pen pals, a place to share your pictures and stories, and a chance to read about what some older deaf kids are doing at the Model Secondary School for the Deaf Performing Arts. Be sure to read Mel's Page to find out how to order pizza! And then tell your parents to check out all the great information in the Parents Guide section, which includes articles from the Deaf Children's Society Newsletter. The key topics covered are literacy tips, inclusion, and special technologies for the deaf.

http://deafworldweb.org/dww/kids/

Origami: the fold to behold! Check out CRAFTS AND HOBBIES.

Down Syndrome WWW Page

The information here has been compiled by members of the Down listserv. It includes information about support organizations, conferences, educational issues, medical resources, and parenting (and brother- or sister-ing) your special child (or sibling).

http://www.nas.com/downsyn/index.html

Future Reflections

The biggest hassle with being blind is not the lack of eyesight. It's a lack of understanding. Any blind kid knows that! For anyone interested in what's happening with blind kids, *Future Reflections* is THE magazine for blind children and their parents. It is available on the Internet, sponsored by the National Federation of the Blind. What color is the sun? How do you do arithmetic in braille? Know what blind kids know!

http://nfb.org/reflects.htm

How Can I Help? (CP Booklet)

What's it like to raise a child with a disability? If you have not shared that unique experience, it may be hard for you to understand and imagine how it feels. "It's just a different place," says Emily Kingsley in her article, "Welcome To Holland." For friends or relatives of a child with cerebral palsy, this site offers valuable advice on how to provide empathy and support for the family, as well as information on what they may be experiencing, and other ways you can help.

www.iinet.com.au/~scarffam/cpa.html

Lose yourself in a Museum. SCIENCE has them all.

A B C D E F G H I J K L M N O P Q R S T U V W X Y Z

National Sports Center for the Disabled

If you love outdoor recreation, adventure, and freedom, then read about all of the fun programs sponsored by the National Sports Center for the Disabled. The NSCD, a non-profit organization located in Winter Park, Colorado, celebrated its 25th year of "enabling the spirit through sports" in 1995. If you're a winter sports fan, you can join their Ski Pals Program, where disabled and able-bodied kids ages 8 to 14 hit the slopes. But if skiing isn't for you, how about the Family Camp in June? You and your family can enjoy white-water rafting, or hiking on nature trails designed to accommodate any special needs. There's even a rock-climbing course for the blind and visually impaired.

http://www.nscd.org/nscd/

Our Kids

Yum! You mean I can drink something that tastes great and is good for me, too? Peanut Butter Smoothie is just one of the high-calorie recipes listed here under nutritional tips. For a little support, and a lot of information, browse the Our Kids archives and then join the hundreds of others on this e-mail discussion list who are sharing stories about their children's accomplishments and challenges with other families who are facing similar situations. If you are a parent, relative, or friend of a child with any kind of developmental delay, this site also provides a great reading list of books for kids and grown-ups. For the "differently abled" child, there's a good list of adaptive technologies and how to contact the manufacturers. Be sure to try some of the links to special education institutions, medical research organizations, and others for more valuable information.

http://wonder.mit.edu/ok/

Frisbee is the Ultimate in GAMES AND FUN.

Chase some waterfalls in EARTH SCIENCE.

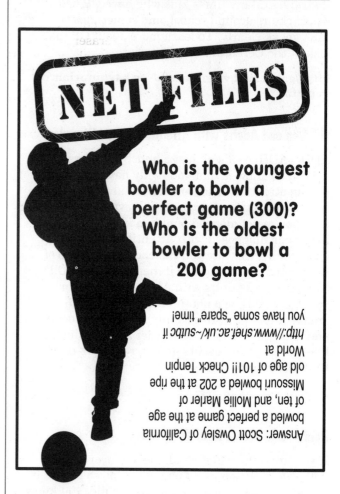

NET FILES

Who is the youngest bowler to bowl a perfect game (300)? Who is the oldest bowler to bowl a 200 game?

Answer: Scott Owsley of California bowled a perfect game at the age of ten, and Mollie Marler of Missouri bowled a 202 at the ripe old age of 101!! Check Tenpin World at http://www.shef.ac.uk/~sutbc if you have some "spare" time!

DRUG ABUSE

Growing Up Drug Free: A Parent's Guide to Prevention

Kids using drugs! It's bad news. Everybody knows that, but sometimes it's hard to know all the facts about drugs. Learn about why kids take drugs, what the effects of the drugs are, and how to "just say no." Show your mom, dad, or some other trusted adult the information at Growing Up Drug Free. Then, with that adult, read this information. It will help you to stay drug free and healthy all of your life!

http://www.seamless.com/talf/ftc/drgfree.html

FIRST AID
First Aid Online

Ouch! Insect bites, scrapes, cuts, sprained ankles, nose bleeds, and other injuries are never fun. When these bumps and bruises happen, always go to a trusted adult. Then, take a look at First Aid Online. You'll learn how to bandage a cut, how to help your baby sister if she puts an eraser in her ear, or how to take the sting out of a sunburn! Remember that no online service is a substitute for your doctor, but for minor injuries First Aid Online is a good place to remember.

http://www.symnet.net/Users/afoster/safety/

HUMAN BODY
Anatomy

Your body is so amazing. It's a combination of muscles, bones, arteries, and various organs, including your great brain. To get an inside peek at some parts of your incredible body, take a look at the Anatomy page from Levit Radiologic-Pathologic Institute. Your body looks a whole lot different from the inside!

http://rpisun1.mda.uth.tmc.edu/se/anatomy/

anatomy

What's your body's biggest organ (and we don't mean pipe organ)? It's your skin! You probably don't think too often about your skin, but it's there holding your body like a great wrapper. To see your skin from the vantage point of an electron microscope, take a look at the "ultrastructure of skin," from the anatomy page at the Mie University (Japan) School of Medicine. Get a close-up look at the various skin layers and see what happens if they get infected.

http://www.medic.mie-u.ac.jp/derma/anatomy.html

GVA Image Browser

Did you ever wonder what your body would look like with transparent skin? Did you ever wonder what your heart looks like while it's beating inside your chest? You don't have to wonder any longer! At the GVA Browser you can see images (including moving pictures) of these parts of your body and lots of others!

http://www.vis.colostate.edu/cgi-bin/gva/gvaview

The Heart: A Virtual Exploration

Probably the only time you think about your heart is when you run fast and you feel it beating in your chest. Or maybe you think about your heart when you put your hand over it and you feel it go thump, thump. Even if you don't think much about your heart, everybody knows the heart is important. After all, without hearts, what shape would valentines be? To learn all kinds of cool things about the heart, check out the Franklin Institute's info. You'll never take your heart for granted again!

http://sln.fi.edu/biosci/heart.html

Natal Care: Development of the Baby

You heard the news. Your mom, an aunt, someone else is PREGNANT. What the heck is happening? The answer is available at FamilyWeb's Development of the Baby page. Learn the stages in pregnancy, and what it feels like for a woman to be pregnant. Ask mom or dad to help you understand the technical terms here, while you look at the pictures of the baby's growth.

http://www.familyweb.com/pregnancy/natal/
natpt103.html

Puberty in Boys

It happens to every boy. All of a sudden, his voice starts croaking, his Adam's apple starts growing, and peach fuzz turns into whiskers. These changes are due to puberty. To learn more about puberty in boys read the text-only information provided by Planned Parenthood of Ontario. You may want to talk this over with someone you trust, like a parent, teacher, or pastor.

http://www.ncf.carleton.ca/freenet/rootdir/menus/
social.services/ppo/info/sex/s103.txt

Lost your sheep? Count them in FARMING AND AGRICULTURE.

A
B
C
D
E
F
G
H
I
J
K
L
M
N
O
P
Q
R
S
T
U
V
W
X
Y
Z

Puberty in Girls

As a girl grows into a woman, her body changes in many ways. This change is puberty, and sometimes it can be scary and confusing. To learn about puberty read the text-only information here, provided by Planned Parenthood of Ontario. You may want to talk this over with someone you trust, like a parent, teacher, or pastor.

http://www.ncf.carleton.ca/freenet/rootdir/menus/
    social.services/ppo/info/sex/s101.txt

ILLNESS AND DISEASE

Allergy Facts

Itchy skin, red eyes, runny nose, or headache are all symptoms of allergies. You may wonder why Mother Nature would ever let people suffer with allergies, but according to Dr. Russell Roby, allergies happen because your body is working extra hard to keep you healthy! Get the facts about allergies, so the next time you sneeze after the lawn is mowed you can understand why. Click on the On-Line Allergy Center graphic to get more information.

http://www.sig.net/~allergy/facts.html

Asthma Tutorial

Asthma is no fun. Wheezing, coughing, struggling to breathe; anyone with asthma knows what problems this illness causes. To learn about asthma, take a look at the Asthma Tutorial provided by the Children's Medical Center of the University of Virginia. You'll see cool graphics and hear some great audio files, including what the doctor hears when she listens through the stethoscope.

http://galen.med.virginia.edu/~smb4v/tutorials/
    asthma/asthma1.html

CELLS Alive!

You get a bad case of the sniffles, and your doctor gives you a shot of penicillin. OUCH! That hurt, but in a few days you feel better. What happened? To see how penicillin works, and to learn plenty of information about cells, take a look at CELLS Alive!

http://www.comet.chv.va.us/quill/

Consumer Health Info

Ahhchooo! Nobody likes getting sick. Chicken pox, mumps, influenza (that's the long way to say the flu) are among many illnesses you can catch. Sicknesses you catch are called *communicable diseases,* and you can learn about lots of these from this info provided by the New York State Department of Health. So, remember to always cover your face when you sneeze, wash your hands before you eat, and be health-smart by reading about the ways you can get sick.

gopher://gopher.health.state.ny.us/11/.consumer/
    .factsheets

Cystic Fibrosis

It used to be kids who had *cystic fibrosis,* a lung disease, rarely lived long enough to become adults. That has changed. Many people with cystic fibrosis (it's also called CF) can look forward to a long life. If you have CF, or you know someone who does, you have to take a look at the Cystic Fibrosis page. You'll find some easy-to-understand information about CF, and also the latest news about this disease.

http://www.ai.mit.edu/people/mernst/cf/

Head Lice

LICE!!!! Head Lice (some people call them "cooties") are small insects that attach themselves to human hair. They itch and they make you feel terrible. The thing to know is that many people get head lice, and getting them doesn't mean you're an unclean person. To learn more about head lice, and how to stop them if you get them, take a peek at the Head Lice page on the University of Illinois Health Resource Center's gopher site.

gopher://gopher.uiuc.edu:70/00/UI/CSF/health/
    heainfo/diseases/contag/lice

KidsHome

Cancer is almost always a serious illness. Fortunately, many very smart doctors are finding better ways to treat and even cure cancer. Some of the people working to fight cancer are part of the National Cancer Institute. They have set aside part of the Internet just for kids who have cancer and other illnesses. Meet other kids who hate taking their medicine. Share some stories and poems: welcome to KidsHome.

http://wwwicic.nci.nih.gov/occdocs/KidsHome.html

Med Help General Library

Let's face it—we all get sick once in a while. Sometimes it can just be annoying and other times it can be scary. At the Med Help General Library you can learn about all kinds of sicknesses. While reading this information won't cure an illness, it can let you know what's going on with your body when you're ill. Sometimes just knowing what's happening can help make you feel better.

http://medhlp.netusa.net/general.htm

NUTRITION

Ask the Dietitian™

Staying healthy means practicing good nutrition, but it's hard to know what's good or bad for you. Some say some fat is good, others say it's all bad. Some say sugar is unhealthy, others say it's OK for you. What to do? You can Ask a Dietitian! Here, you'll find information on many frequently asked questions about nutrition—from an expert who *knows* what foods are good for you.

http://www.hoptechno.com/rdindex.htm

IFIC Foundation

Is a big, gooey, pepperoni pizza part of a healthy diet? For pizza lovers, thank goodness, it is! According to the International Food Information Council Foundation, pizza can be used with other foods to keep you healthy. "10 Tips to Healthy Eating for Kids" is only the beginning. You'll also learn how to evaluate food advertising, so you won't be fooled into eating the prize and playing with the cereal!

http://ificinfo.health.org/10tipkid.htm

SAFETY

Child Safety Forum

It's rough out there! So many things can be dangerous. From bathtubs to exercise walkers, just about anything can be harmful. To get the scoop on how to be safe (and to learn what can be unsafe), get your mom, dad, or some other trusted adult to look at the Child Safety Forum with you. You'll see monthly features on safety for kids, updates from parents around the world on child accidents, and great links to kid's safety all over the Internet.

http://www.xmission.com:80/~gastown/safe/index.html

NET FILES

What's the hottest-selling CD in Tokyo?

Answer: Maybe it's the same as the hottest-selling CD in your town! As a matter of fact, it often is. But sometimes what "catches fire" in Japan is different than what's hot in Europe or America. Find out what's selling big in Tokyo, as well as what's not so cool, at *http://www.infojapan.com/JWAVE/*, a radio station in Tokyo!

Jeff Sam's Child Safety & Parenting Page

Everything from rollerblade safety, to tips on how to keep your baby brother amused in the store while your dad shops for groceries.

http://www1.usa1.com/~furball/jeffsam/jeffsam.html/

KIDestrians™

Did you know you have KID BRAKES? How do you learn to use them? They are what keeps you from stepping off the curb before looking both ways. Learn how to be safe on the streets, when crossing railroad tracks, and in many other traffic situations by practicing these activities with your parents.

http://tdg.res.uoguelph.ca/g-police/kid_intr.html

Lost your marbles? Find them in GAMES AND FUN.

A
B
C
D
E
F
G
H
I
J
K
L
M
N
O
P
Q
R
S
T
U
V
W
X
Y
Z

My 8 Rules for Safety

What are "checking first," "using the buddy system," and "trusting your feelings"? These are three of the "My 8 Rules for Safety" developed by the National Center for Missing and Exploited Children. To stay safe, it's important to stay with friends when you are outside, to always tell your parents or caregiver where you are going, and to trust your feelings if you think something is wrong. This site is presented by Child Find Canada.

http://www.discribe.ca/childfind/8tips.hte

Natural Disaster Program for Families

Tornado! Flood! Hurricane! Forest Fire! Earthquake! Natural disasters are those times when Mother Nature seems to go a little crazy. You, and everyone in your family, can learn how to be prepared for natural disasters by looking at the Natural Disaster Preparedness pages from the North Carolina Cooperative Extension Service. Take the time and learn how to set up a Family Disaster Kit (remember to pack games for kids!), how to cook without electricity, how to save your saltwater-soaked plants, and much more helpful information.

http://www.ces.ncsu.edu/disaster/contents.html

OUDPS Kid Safety Topics Menu

Sometimes it may seem it's hard to stay safe and play safe. What do you do if a bully starts picking on you? What do you do if you are in an accident? What do you do if some stranger contacts you on the Internet? Find the answer to these and many other safety questions on the Kids Safety Topics Menu provided by the University of Oklahoma Department of Public Safety. If you read all the information here, you'll be a safety expert!

http://www.uoknor.edu/oupd/kidsafe/kidmenu.htm

The Missing Kids Database

Who are Lamoine Jordan Allen, Marianthi Cassandra Basdaras, and Rachel Eugenia Kent? They are all missing children. Check their photos. Have you seen any of these kids? Maybe you can help! This site lets you search by state, physical description, and other characteristics.

http://www.missingkids.org/search.html

SLEEP DIFFICULTIES

Children's Sleep Problems

Sleep is a good time for dreams, when your body rests for a new day of fun. Sometimes, though, sleep is interrupted by nightmares, sleepwalking, or even real bad dreams called sleep terrors. If you would like to learn more about sleep problems that kids have, take a look here.

http://www.psych.med.umich.edu/web/aacap/factsFam/sleep.htm

NET FILES

1, Rue Sesame

What, or where are Sesam, Sesamstrasse, Plaza Sasamo, and 1, Rue Sesame?

Answer: They are all foreign language versions of *Sesame Street!* Kids in Sweden watch *Sesam*, while German kids enjoy *Sesamstrasse*. Latin American children watch *Plaza Sasamo*, and *1, Rue Sesame* is the favorite of the kids in France. You can learn more about the early history of the Muppets and this show at

http://www-leland.stanford.edu/~rosesage/MMM/MMM.html.

HISTORY

1492 Exhibit

"1492: An Ongoing Voyage" is an exhibit at the Library of Congress. Explore the "New World" before the Europeans got there, what happened when they arrived, and how both the Old and New Worlds were forever transformed by contact. This is a hypertext exhibit that includes both text and gif images. This is a good resource for information about Columbus and the early history of America. Read more in the EXPLORERS AND EXPLORING section of this book.

http://sunsite.unc.edu/expo/1492.exhibit/Intro.html

History Channel

Who says history's boring? If you get this cable channel, you know the truth is out there! Even if you don't have cable, you can visit this web site. There are activities for kids (including contests!) and classrooms. Plus, explore listings to places where you can see historic events and time periods re-created, and background info on many of the History Channel's special programs. Try This Day in History (type the date you want), and get historical facts, plus the top ten in music for past years. Even if you think you have no interest in history, stop in—we think you'll be pleasantly surprised.

http://www.historychannel.com/

History/Social Studies Web Site for K-12 Teachers

Wow! Finally, an easy way to learn and teach social studies! Subjects available in the menu include archaeology, diversity sources, electronic texts, genealogy, geography, government, and kids and students. Also included are general history, non-western history, European history, American history, and news and current events. Announcements and relevant TV specials are also listed. Impress your social studies teacher by introducing her to this excellent site!

http://www.execpc.com/~dboals/boals.html

ANCIENT HISTORY

See also: ANCIENT CIVILIZATIONS AND ARCHAEOLOGY

Exploring Ancient World Cultures

Exploring Ancient World Cultures is an introduction to ancient cultures in cyberspace. Eight cultures are represented, including Near East, India, Egypt, China, Greece, the Roman Empire, the Islamic World, and Medieval Europe. Anthony Beavers, an assistant professor at the University of Evansville, has tried to provide a variety of resources with balance among the cultures. Some of the Internet sites included in this home page are materials for the study of women in the ancient world, world art treasures, a collection of world scripture, and The International Museum of the Horse. This home page is rich in information for the student of ancient history.

http://www.evansville.edu/~wcweb/wc101/

HISTORIC DOCUMENTS
Declaring Independence: Drafting the Documents

You know the Declaration of Independence, written July 4, 1776. It begins "When in the course of human Events, it becomes necessary for one People to dissolve the Political Bands which have connected them with another...." Did the colonies just one day decide to send this letter back to the English King George III, telling him, hey—it was big fun, but now we're going to try it on our own, thanks very much. As it turns out, this wasn't an overnight decision. This Library of Congress exhibit presents a chronology of events. You'll find fascinating information about how the documents were drafted, plus photos of important objects. Some of these include fragments of the earliest known draft, the original draft, and various prints relevant to the exhibit, as well as correspondence from Thomas Jefferson. Did you know he was the one who wrote the original? For the actual text, see the National Archives at *http://www.nara.gov/exhall/exhibits.html*, or *http://www.law.emory.edu/FEDERAL/independ/declar.html*, if you want a transcription with the orginal "Dunlap Broadside" capitalizations preserved.

http://lcweb.loc.gov/exhibits/declara/declara1.html

A B C D E F G H I J K L M N O P Q R S T U V W X Y Z

EuroDocs: Western European Primary Historical Documents

The links at this Brigham Young University Library home page connect to Western European historical documents that are transcribed, scanned-in, or translated. The documents are in the public domain. The page is organized alphabetically by geographic region and then by time period within each country. Collections of many documents are found at the end of the national list. This home page is an excellent starting place for students who are researching Western European history, and want to use primary source material.

http://library.byu.edu/~rdh/eurodocs/
  homepage.html

THE GETTYSBURG ADDRESS

The Library of Congress has devoted this page to President Abraham Lincoln's Gettysburg Address. Lincoln was invited to dedicate the Union cemetery only three weeks before the ceremony, so he did not have much time to write the speech. View the working drafts of the eloquent speech Lincoln eventually delivered. You'll also see the only known photo of Lincoln taken at Gettysburg, Pennsylvania. These precious original documents have been preserved for future generations: find out how! The text of the Gettysburg Address is at *http://www.msstate.edu/Archives/History/USA/19th_C./gettysburg-address*.

http://lcweb.loc.gov/exhibits/G.Address/ga.html

Historical Text Archive

Choose the area of the world you're interested in—click—wow, here is an archive of that country's, or region's, important documents and resources. Try this for elusive information you haven't found anywhere else. The Women's Studies links contain several *Godey's Lady's Books* from the 1850s. Parents: not all links have been checked.

http://www.msstate.edu/Archives/History/
  index.html

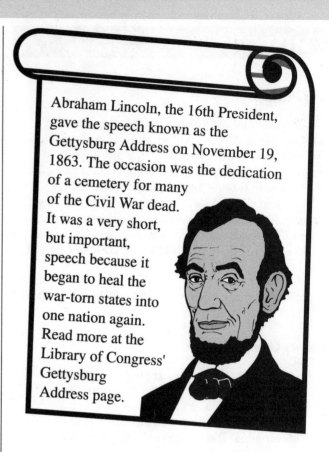

Abraham Lincoln, the 16th President, gave the speech known as the Gettysburg Address on November 19, 1863. The occasion was the dedication of a cemetery for many of the Civil War dead. It was a very short, but important, speech because it began to heal the war-torn states into one nation again. Read more at the Library of Congress' Gettysburg Address page.

Inaugural Addresses of the Presidents of the United States. 1989

George Washington's second term inaugural speech remains the shortest on record, requiring only 135 words. William Henry Harrison delivered the longest, speaking for an hour and 45 minutes in a blinding snowstorm. He then stood in the cold and greeted well-wishers all day. He died a month later, of pneumonia. Read the speech here, but make sure you keep your hat on! Project Bartleby, at Columbia University, houses a home page containing the Inaugural Addresses of the Presidents. Also included is an article about presidents sworn in but not inaugurated, and the Oath of Office itself. This is a good site for finding inaugural factoids, such as the revelation that Geronimo, the great Apache, attended the inauguration of Teddy Roosevelt, and that attendees at Grover Cleveland's second inaugural ball were all agog at the new invention: electric lights!

http://www.columbia.edu/acis/bartleby/inaugural/

What were women reading in the 1850s? Many of them loved to look through the Godey's Lady's Books, and now there are several online. Here' s part of an etiquette column, regarding proper behavior in the theater: We may as well mention here,for the sake of the other sex, that loud thumping with canes and umbrellas, in demonstration of applause is voted decidedly rude. Clapping the hands is quite as efficient, and neither raises a dust to soil the dresses of the ladies, nor a hubbub enough to deafen them. You can find more at *http://www.history.rochester.edu/ godeys/*, which is a link off the **Historical Text Archive** page.

Magna Carta

In 1215, the English Barons were fed up. They thought that the King had gone too far, on more than one occasion. They wanted a line drawn that would explain the difference between a King and a tyrant. They defined laws and customs that the King himself had to respect when dealing with free subjects. That charter is called the Magna Carta. It's made it all the way from 1215 to the Net, as part of the Treasures Digitisation Project at the British Library. You can view the whole manuscript, or a translation of the Magna Carta. A brief history and further reading are included.

http://portico.bl.uk/access/treasures/
  magna-carta.html

Have you hadrosaurus today? If not, try DINOSAURS AND PREHISTORIC TIMES.

National Archives Online Exhibit Hall

The National Archives and Records Administration (NARA) is a nationwide system that preserves the permanently valuable records of the United States government. The online exhibits help to bring to the public some of the rich and varied holdings of the National Archives. In the Exhibit Hall you will find some cool special exhibits: "The Charters of Freedom," features the Declaration of Independence, the Constitution of the United States, and the Bill of Rights. You'll also find a special exhibit on the Emancipation Proclamation, issued by President Abraham Lincoln, which ended slavery Other featured documents include the 19th Amendment, and Japanese Surrender documents. Visit this site for first-hand looks at the historic documents of the United States, several of them written in longhand!

http://clio.nara.gov/exhall/exhibits.html

U.S. Founding Documents

We particularly like this archive of U.S. documents for its searchable version of the Constitution of the United States. Do you know where your 19th Amendment is?

http://www.law.emory.edu/FEDERAL/

For happy hedgehogs see PETS AND PET CARE.

A
B
C
D
E
F
G
H
I
J
K
L
M
N
O
P
Q
R
S
T
U
V
W
X
Y
Z

US Historical Documents

The University of Oklahoma Law Center hosts A Chronology of United States Historical Documents. The chronology begins with the Pre-Colonial Era with the Magna Carta and the Iroquois Constitution, and concludes with the Inaugural Address of President Bill Clinton in 1993. Along the way, you'll find The Mayflower Compact, the famous "Give Me Liberty or Give Me Death" speech by Patrick Henry, The Monroe Doctrine, The Emancipation Proclamation, and Martin Luther King's "I Have a Dream" speech. Take a peek at the "other" verses of the National Anthem, too:

Oh! thus be it ever, when freemen shall stand
Between their loved homes and the war's desolation!
Blest with victory and peace, may the heaven-rescued
*   land*
Praise the Power that hath made and preserved us a
*   nation.*
Then conquer we must, for our cause it is just,
And this be our motto: "In God is our trust."
And the star-spangled banner forever shall wave
O'er the land of the free and the home of the brave!

http://www.law.uoknor.edu/ushist.html

Various Historical Documents

Jon Shemitz, who runs a Home Schooling web site, has put the U.S. Declaration of Independence, the Constitution of the United States, and the United Nations Convention on the Rights of the Child, into HTML (HyperText Markup Language) so that the documents can be read easily with a web browser. This presentation also makes the documents easy to search.

http://www.armory.com/~jon/historic-docs.html

HISTORIC SITES

Boston History Freedom Trail

It's only 2.5 miles long, but you'll be walking through years of Boston's history. Check out the Paul Revere House, and the Old North Church ("One if by land, two if by sea..."). Don't miss the Boston Massacre site, or the Bunker Hill Monument. Bring a cup of tea and take the virtual tour.

http://www.cybercom.net/~kiwicove/vboston/
   boshstry.htm

Ford's Theater NHS Home Page

The theater where President Lincoln was shot is now a National Historic site. If you scroll all the way down to the bottom of the page, you will learn some fascinating facts about the assassination. Why was there no guard—or was there? Where is the chair Lincoln was sitting in? And where is the bullet that killed him? The surprising answers are all here.

http://www.nps.gov/parklists/index/foth.html

Historic Mount Vernon—The Home of Our First President, George Washington

Seeing where our first President lived makes him more real to us. Walking up his front steps, lounging on his lawn—these things connect us to a real person instead of an historical figure. Maybe you can't visit Mount Vernon, Virginia, in person, but you can stop in via the Net. At Mount Vernon, you can take a tour, read some astounding facts, and even work out a Washington word search puzzle. You can also learn about archaeology at Mount Vernon, and explore related links. The Mount Vernon virtual tour includes the East Front, the large dining room, study, master bedroom, gardens, the Washingtons' tomb, and a slave memorial. Washington was the only one of the founding fathers to free his slaves.

http://www.mountvernon.org/

I-Channel Ellis Island

Between 1892 and 1924, Ellis Island, in the New York Harbor, was the gateway to America for over12 million immigrants. Before they could set foot in America, they had to be "processed." This meant a three to five hour wait, and medical and legal questions and inspections. Some were eventually turned away. Learn about the journey, the processing center, and life in the new land at this excellent example of multimedia education. You will hear audio recollections of some of the immigrants themselves. There is also an "immigrants' cookbook" with recipes such as cabbage rolls and ginger snaps.

http://www.i-channel.com/ellis/index.shtml

Moscow Kremlin On-line Excursion

Tour the Moscow Kremlin Exhibition! This field trip is on a server in the ex-Soviet Union (.su domain). Some of the sites you will see and read about are the Cathedral of Annunciation, Lenin's Mausoleum, Red Square, the Residence of the President, the Senate Building, and the Tsar-Cannon. This exhibition is organized by the State Museums of the Moscow Kremlin. Surf on over to see Moscow's historic sights!

http://www.kiae.su/www/wtr/kremlin/begin.html

National Civil Rights Museum

The National Civil Rights Museum is located at the Lorraine Motel (Memphis, Tennessee) where Dr. Martin Luther King, Jr., was assassinated April 4, 1968. Here you will find continuing exhibits, events, and links of interest. The virtual tour is arranged in chronological order. You'll learn about the Montgomery Bus Boycott, The Freedom Rides, Dr. Martin Luther King, Jr., The Student Sit-Ins, The March on Washington, and the Chicago Freedom Movement. You can take a chronological tour or choose the exhibit you want to see. Each exhibit has a short paragraph about the subject and why it is important in civil rights history.

http://www.quest.net/archermalmo/ncrm/

National Trust for Historic Preservation

Many historic sites are *old*—so how come they look so nice? Because people like you care enough about them to save them from deterioration. This is called historic preservation. This resource will help you find out how to save historic sites in your area. For international sites, a more direct source is the International Council on Monuments and Sites at *http://www.icomos.org/*.

http://home.worldweb.net/trust/

Don't be a stick-in-the-MUD!

Whooooooo will you find in BIRDS?

Did Washington really chop down a cherry tree?

How about that "throwing the silver dollar across the Potomac River" story—is that bogus?

True or false— wooden teeth?

All of these are false. One thing is true though. Many people wanted to crown Washington King. He declined, and accepted the Presidency. Read more facts you never knew at the pages of Historic Mount Vernon—The Home of Our First President, George Washington.

The Presidential Libraries IDEA Network

"PresidentS" is located at the University of North Carolina at Chapel Hill. Its mission is to help to bring presidential library materials to the Internet for improved public access, and to link America's past to her future. Presidential Libraries from Herbert Hoover, through President Clinton and Vice-President Gore, are included. Some of the more recent libraries have their own home pages. The earlier Presidential papers are available via gopher. Photographs are also housed at the newer libraries. This is an excellent site for accessing info on the 20th century Presidents, their First Ladies, and links to their homes, libraries, and other resources.

http://sunsite.unc.edu/lia/president/pres.html

A B C D E F G H I J K L M N O P Q R S T U V W X Y Z

ROME REBORN: THE VATICAN LIBRARY AND RENAISSANCE CULTURE

Rome is one of the most glorious cities in the world. Today, millions of visitors come to admire its architecture, art, and history, and find peace in St. Peter's Basilica. It has not always been that way, though. Once it was a miserable village! Explore the past in this exhibit of materials from the Vatican Library's most precious manuscripts, books, and maps. This exhibit was at the Library of Congress in 1993, but it lives on—on the Net!

http://sunsite.unc.edu/expo/vatican.exhibit/
   Vatican.exhibit.html

The Statue of Liberty

"Give me your tired, your poor,
Your huddled masses yearning to breathe free,
The wretched refuse of your teeming shore.
Send these, the homeless, tempest-tost to me,
I lift my lamp beside the golden door!"

This is part of the poem inscribed on the Statue of Liberty. It was written by Emma Lazarus. The Internet needs a good resource on the Statue of Liberty! There are a few factoids at this site: *http://freezone.com/WWW/reference_files/rhke/rfistatu.html*, and don't forget to check out magician David Copperfield's amazing "vanishing" of the statue, at *http://freezone.com/WWW/reference_files/rhke/rfistatu.html*.

http://www.parasoft.com/ahicken/docs/liberty.html

The United States Capitol Exhibit

Visit the Capitol, courtesy of the Library of Congress! The United States Capitol was envisioned as a "Temple of Liberty" by George Washington and Thomas Jefferson. Read the proposals about how people thought this most important of all U.S. public buildings should look. Then, study the approved plans and visit the porticoes and the wings of our Capitol as built. The original building took thirty-four years, six architects, and six presidents to build. When you're finished touring this historic site, you'll be an expert, and your feet won't be tired!

http://lcweb.loc.gov/exhibits/us.capitol/s0.html

United States Holocaust Memorial Museum

The United States Holocaust Memorial Museum in Washington, D.C., offers general information on this painful chapter of world history. The education page offers a guide to teaching about the Holocaust, a brief history, FAQs, a heartbreaking article about children in the Holocaust, and a videography. An online reservation form for groups is available. Parental advisory: descriptions may be too graphic for youngsters.

http://www.ushmm.org/

Did you know that although George Washington, the first President of the United States, directed the construction of the White House, he never got to live in it? It was our second President, John Adams, elected in 1796, who first lived there. His term was almost over by the time he moved in, and only six rooms had been finished. Take the tour, led by Socks, the First Cat, at the Welcome to the White House for Kids page.

Vietnam Veteran's Memorial

The U.S. National Park Service administers this site, which is in Washington, D.C. Over 58,000 American men and women died in this war, which was so controversial it divided the generations, as well as the country. All their names are engraved on a mirror-like granite wall. People leave flowers, poems, military gear, and other objects around the wall. It is a very moving place to visit, and we guarantee you will never forget your experience there.

http://www.nps.gov/nps/ncro/nacc/vvm.html

Welcome to the White House for Kids

Let Socks, the First Cat, take you on a fascinating kid's-eye tour of the White House, in Washington, D.C. You'll learn about how the White House was built (bricks were made on the front lawn), tour the rooms, and find out what First Family pets have lived there (don't miss President Harrison's goat, or Caroline Kennedy's pony!). We learned something we didn't know: the President's desk was once part of a ship, abandoned north of the Arctic circle in 1854! The HMS *Resolute*. was later found by the crew of an American whaling ship. It was repaired and refitted, and sent to Queen Victoria as a gesture of goodwill. Later, when the ship was taken out of service and dismantled, a desk was made from some of its timbers. Queen Victoria presented the desk to President Hayes, in 1880. The desk has been used by most Presidents since then. Socks never gets to sit on it though. Well, maybe he does, late at night when no one is around.

http://www.whitehouse.gov/WH/kids/html/home.html

MIDDLE AGES

Labyrinth Home Page

Welcome to the Labyrinth, a World Wide Web server for medieval studies, located at Georgetown University! The Middle Ages are those years after the Fall of the Roman Empire and before the Renaissance, so think 500-1500 (some authorities say 1300 or 1400). You can navigate the Labyrinth by selecting a main menu item, or by using the search engine to search all Labyrinth files. Sources available include bibliographies, text, images, and archives. Also offered are Daedalus's Guides to the Net and Web. Find your own Ariadne's thread to hold on to as you surf the Labyrinth!

http://www.georgetown.edu/labyrinth/
   labyrinth-home.html

Read any good Web sites lately?

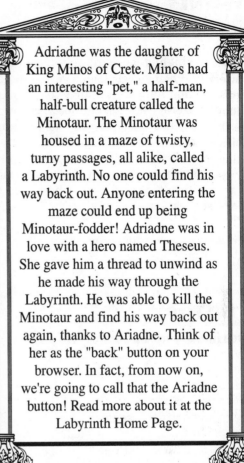

Adriadne was the daughter of King Minos of Crete. Minos had an interesting "pet," a half-man, half-bull creature called the Minotaur. The Minotaur was housed in a maze of twisty, turny passages, all alike, called a Labyrinth. No one could find his way back out. Anyone entering the maze could end up being Minotaur-fodder! Adriadne was in love with a hero named Theseus. She gave him a thread to unwind as he made his way through the Labyrinth. He was able to kill the Minotaur and find his way back out again, thanks to Ariadne. Think of her as the "back" button on your browser. In fact, from now on, we're going to call that the Ariadne button! Read more about it at the Labyrinth Home Page.

RENAISSANCE

The Atrium

The Atrium houses articles, period texts, and manuscripts about Medieval/Renaissance subjects. Here you will find articles about Celtic culture, Christmas in the Middle Ages, the Renaissance in Italy, Joan of Arc, medieval and Renaissance weddings, and Renaissance mathematics. Manuscripts available include the illuminated Book of Hours, the Bayeux Tapestry, a Vatican exhibit of early music, a *Beowulf* manuscript, and the Dead Sea Scrolls. Interested in the history of the table fork? Dig in here! This is an excellent source for students of medieval and Renaissance history.

http://www.honors.indiana.edu/~atrium/
   atrium.html

A B C D E F G H I J K L M N O P Q R S T U V W X Y Z

TIME LINES
Modernism Timeline, 1890-1940

This time line highlights significant events from 1890 to 1940. When you click on a year, you get a list of events that happened in that year, including political and literary events, and social customs. For example, in 1917, bobbed hair was popular, the Senate rejected Wilson's suffrage bill, Freud's *Introduction to Psychoanalysis* was published, and there was a famine in Germany. The question of "what is significant" is up for grabs here, and you can make suggestions for additions to the list.

http://weber.u.washington.edu/~eckman/
   timeline.html

U.S. HISTORY
American Memory from the Library of Congress

You have memories of your own life. Your parents have memories of their lives, and your grandparents have memories of theirs. Wouldn't it be great to find a place to archive all those memories, so they wouldn't be lost when someone died? You could call it the American Memory Project! Look no further. How about browsing through 25,000 turn-of-the-century postcards, maybe some are from your home town! Look in the Prints and Photographs Division under Detroit Publishing Company. (Show this to your parents, they will love it!) Check old movies of New York City made by Edison himself, in 1903. Look into the eyes of these immigrants coming to America—so much hope is expressed there. The historical periods covered are from the Civil War to World War II. Each collection is annotated, and broad topics are listed. This is an excellent source for students who are looking for non-print sources to accompany an American history report. Don't forget to try out American Memory.

http://rs6.loc.gov/amhome.html

Curl up with a good Internet site.

The American Revolution and the struggle for Independence

The main body of this home page comes from the booklet, "An Outline of American History," distributed by the United States Information Agency. The text is illustrated with stamps! It has very dense text, so you may want to look at this site only for heavier research. Additional original sources with hypertext links (that go all over the Net) have been added. This site covers American history from the colonial period until World War I. Check it out, it's fun just to know there was a stamp with the Carolina Charter on it!

http://grid.let.rug.nl/~welling/usa/

What happened on 23rd Street, during the summer of 1901, in New York City? Move over, Marilyn Monroe! Inventor Thomas A. Edison was experimenting with films that year. The film is now in the Library of Congress' American Memory collection, and it's also on the Internet! "From a contemporary Edison film company catalog: The scene as suggested by the title is made on 23rd street, New York City. In front of one of the large newspaper offices on that thoroughfare is a hot air shaft through which immense volumes of air is forced by means of a blower. Ladies crossing these shafts often have their clothes slightly disarranged, (it may be said much to their discomfiture). As our picture was being made a young man escorting a young lady, to whom he was talking very earnestly, comes into view and walks slowly along until they stand directly over the air shaft. The young lady's [ankle-length] skirts are suddenly raised to, you might say an almost unreasonable height, greatly to her horror and much to the amusement of the newsboys, bootblacks and passersby This subject is a winner. Class B. 50 ft. $6.00." It should be noted that the dress blows up "almost" to her knees. It was shocking, for those times! To see the film, go to *http://rs6.loc.gov/papr/paprquery.html* and search on the term twenty-third (don't forget the hyphen). For more, remember American Memory from the Library of Congress.

Library of Congress World Wide Web Home Page

The Library of Congress, founded in 1800, uses the World Wide Web to present materials from its collections, so that people all over the world can see them without traveling to Washington, D.C. You can view exhibits, search and view documents in digitized historical collections, search the LC card catalog, and learn about Congress and the government by using the collection known as Thomas. This is an excellent starting point to find information about the United States government and history, both present and past.

http://lcweb.loc.gov/

Life on the Prairie

In the 1800s, many settlers left the east coast and headed west to make a better life for themselves. Trying to carve out places of their own from wilderness prairie wasn't easy. This excellent site shows, in pictures and words, the struggles of the Dakota pioneers. You'll read a diary written by a physician in the 1870s Dakota Territory. And you will be fascinated by a series of "Then and Now" photographs, comparing photos of long ago to the same spot in a photo from today. How things have changed!

http://www.gps.com/life/life.htm

Selections from The African-American Mosaic

This exhibit is a sampler of materials found in the Library of Congress illuminating the last 500 years of the African-American experience in the Western Hemisphere. This exhibit covers only four areas—Colonization, Abolition, Migrations, and the WPA (Work Projects Administration) era. This is an excellent starting point for searching for materials about African-American history. Be sure to check the AFRICAN AMERICAN section of this book, too.

http://lcweb.loc.gov/exhibits/African.American/
intro.html

> ## Crack open CODES AND CIPHERS.

Wm. Murray's Time Page

Murray categorizes the generations in American history based upon his reading of the book *Generations*. You can then trace his links by eras, generations, and the future. One of the most valuable aspects of this site is the collection of links to resources in American history, although his take on who the visionaries were in each era is also interesting.

http://www.seanet.com/Users/pamur/time.html

CIVIL WAR

Civil War

Will Krieger's a fourth grader in Oregon, and he's also very well-informed about the Civil War. Read his report here, part of the Kidopedia Project.

http://vose.demos.com/will.html

WORLD WAR II

See also: PEACE

D-Day

This archive of World War II facts, pictures, movies, and memories was built by students at Patch American High School, located at the United States European Command, in Stuttgart, Germany. You'll find battle plans, newsreel footage, and famous speeches connected with D-Day and W.W.II.

http://192.253.114.31/D-Day/Table_of_contents.html

Enola Gay Perspectives

War is an ugly thing, and it's hard to understand how people could want to harm other people. In 1945, the United States dropped an atomic bomb on the Japanese city of Hiroshima. This Web resource, developed by library school students as part of a project for the University of Maryland, tries to make sense of it all. You'll find out the reasons government leaders decided to drop the bomb. You'll learn about the crew of the plane "Enola Gay," and the consequences of their mission. There is also a section on the controversy surrounding the Enola Gay exhibit at the Air and Space Museum. For an objective look at the issue, try this site. Look in the PEACE subject heading for more on this subject.

http://www.glue.umd.edu/~enola/welcome.html

A B C D E F G H I J K L M N O P Q R S T U V W X Y Z

Iwo Jima

Read Anthony Clark's report about the most famous battle of World War II. This is part of the Kidopedia Project. Anthony is in fourth grade in Beaverton, Oregon.

http://vose.demos.com/anthony.html

U.S. HISTORY—CIVIL WAR

U.S. Civil War Center—Civil War Links Index

The Civil War is a fascinating event in American history. Many people have spent a great deal of time studying the war and collecting material on it. The "Civil War related Web Links Index" will lead you to any of hundreds of sites. Diaries, forts, miniatures, maps, music, and much more, are all a click away. This is your starting point for any topic on the Civil War that you need information on. Pictures? Oh yes, there are plenty of those too!

http://www.cwc.lsu.edu/civlink.htm

Welcome to Gettysburg

It was the turning point of the Civil War. On July 1, 2, and 3, 1863, at Gettysburg, Pennsylvania, more men fought and died than in any other battle on North American soil. There were a total of 51,000 killed and wounded. Today, the battlefield is a National military park, with over 1,000 monuments. Follow the maps of the battles, and explore other Civil War links from this site.

http://gettysburg.welcome.com/

WORLD HISTORY

Gateway to World History

The Gateway provides "Internet resources for the study of world history and in support of the struggle for social progress." Resources offered include an archival document collection, online resources, and searching tools for online resources. You can search by keyword or by subject. In addition, Internet discussion lists, and pointers to History Departments online are included. Reference works, resources about navigating the Internet, and other favorite places are offered by Haines Brown. This is a good launchpad for world history students, and parents, we have not checked all these links.

http://neal.ctstateu.edu/history/world_history/
  world_history.html

WORLD CULTURES

Welcome to the Internet portion of WORLD CULTURES to 1500, taught by Richard Hooker at Washington State University! While this site is background for a college course, it also offers much information for the world history student. You can find a glossary of world cultures, including concepts, values, and terms, readings about the world, and Internet resources. This is a good supplemental starting point for world history students. Parents: not all links have been explored.

http://www.wsu.edu:8080/~dee/index.html

World History to 1500

This excellent site contains links to resources on the Internet dealing with world history prior to 1500. This material was collected as a supplement to materials covered in a course at Brigham Young University—Hawai'i. The information is mostly arranged geographically. Geographic regions covered include Mesopotamia, India, Rome, Europe, Egypt, China, Greece, Africa, Eurasia, and East Asia. Topics addressed include prehistory, cultural evolution, Islam, Christianity, Judaica, and cultural diffusion. This is a good beginning site for world history reports that cover the early years of civilization.

http://www.byuh.edu/coursework/hist201/

The World-Wide Web Virtual Library: History

This home page contains history indexes, conferences, world news, historical news groups and discussion lists, and Carrie: An Electronic Library. Kansas students will particularly like the Kansas Sites! You can explore history by era, subject, or world region.

http://history.cc.ukans.edu:80/history/
  WWW_history_main.html

SLIME is a polymer, as anyone who's read CHEMISTRY knows!

HOLIDAYS

World Birthday Web

This site is kind of silly and cool at the same time. Who's birthday is today? Find out here. You can go there and enter your own name and birthday. You can also enter your e-mail address and your home page, if you want. The info gets added to the database immediately. When your birthday rolls around, you'll get e-mail greetings from all sorts of well-wishers. This year, we got one from the Klingon Language Institute!

http://www.boutell.com/birthday.cgi/

ASIAN HOLIDAYS

Annual Events in Japan

Let's see, on May 5, there is CHILDREN'S DAY! (learn a little more about it at *http://www.wakhok.ac.jp/~nobuaki/japan.html*). You'll also find the beautiful Star Festival (July 7) when children tie their wishes to tree branches, and audio of the tolling New Year's bells. You can see photos of many of these festivals at this site, offered by a Japanese newspaper: *http://www.mainichi.co.jp/photogallery/omatsuri/index-e.html*. Learn even more about traditional festivals and holidays in Japan here: *http://fumi.eco.wakayama-u.ac.jp/English/Kishu/festival.html* and here: *http://w3.lab.kdd.co.jp/japan/*.

http://www.jnto.go.jp/07annualevents/
annualevents.html

China

Dragon and lion dances are a big part of Chinese festivals. The dragon dance was once done to stop the spread of epidemics. The lion dance was once a rain dance. Watch as the lion chases a clown that is making fun of him! Stop in and learn about other Chinese festivals.

http://zero.com.hk/hkta/culture.html

Watch your step in DANCE.

Chinese Holidays & Festivals

June 1 is when China celebrates its Children's Day. Kids are showered with presents, and their schools give them big parties. Sound like fun? Read about this, and more Chinese traditions here. Another fascinating place to look is *http://198.111.253.141/festivals/chinese.html*, where you'll find photos and descriptions of interesting holidays like the Dragon Boat Festival, as well as learn about the Hungry Ghosts festival.

http://bronze.ucs.indiana.edu/~hyuan/holiday.html

Chinese New Year

The Chinese calendar is based both on the Gregorian and a lunar-solar system. It divides a year into 12 months, each with $39\frac{1}{2}$ days. There are also 24 poetic solar terms describing seasonal changes, for example, the Beginning of Spring, the Waking of Insects, Grain in Ear, Frost's Descent, Great Cold, and so on. There is also a system that names the years in a 12-year cycle: Rat, Ox, Tiger, Hare, Dragon, Snake, Horse, Sheep, Monkey, Rooster, Dog, and Boar. Find out how the Chinese New Year is celebrated, and read some predictions for 1996!

http://bronze.ucs.indiana.edu:80/~hyuan/
newyear.html

Festivals and Culture

Learn the traditions of the Taiwanese Dragon Boat Festival, the Birthday of the Goddess of the Sea, and the Lantern Festival, among many others. You'll also read a bit about Chinese knots, rice-dough figures and candy sculpture, and lion dances.

http://peacock.tnjc.edu.tw/ADD/TOUR/keep.html

Festivals of India

Click on any of the months, then see a text description of the festivals celebrated that month. Wish there were photos and multimedia, the descriptions are intriguing! November 14th is Children's Day in India.

http://sunsite.sut.ac.jp/asia/india/jitnet/india/
festivals/fest-in.html

NET FILES

What's "short track"?

http://web.mit.edu/jeffrey/speedskating/asu.html

Answer: Nope, not track and field for little kids! This is a sport kids can participate in, though. It's speed skating, usually skated on indoor hockey rinks. "Long track skating" is the older sport, skated on huge ovals, usually outdoors. These two sports are fast, hard work, but lots of fun and terrific exercise. Find out more about it at

Hawaii's Greeting of the Season

Many folks in Hawaii come from a Japanese, Chinese, or other Asian heritage. As in many countries, the coming of the New Year deserves a big celebration. One of the symbolic Japanese decorations you might see is the *kadomatsu* (gates of pine). It's a graceful arrangement of pine and bamboo, symbolizing good wishes for a long, prosperous life. They are displayed for several days before January 1, then burned or tossed into flowing water. The Chinese celebrate New Year's Day according to another calendar system (see TIME-Calendars in this book), and in 1996, The Year of the Rat begins in February. One of the exciting traditions is the lion dance, many of which are performed by martial arts clubs in Hawaii. The lion is a symbol of life, luck, and health. Colorful costumed lion dancers parade down the streets, accompanied by the sounds of gongs and drums. Merchants and others throw firecrackers at the feet of the "lions," symbolically chasing away bad luck. Read more about these happy Asian celebrations here.

http://www.aloha-hawaii.com/c_greetings.html

CHRISTMAS
Christmas Around The World

Here's a trip you can take without even packing your suitcase! Travel through cyberspace to countries in Asia, Eastern Europe, Latin America, and the United Kingdom to learn the different ways children celebrate Christmas. The spirit of the Christmas season, of giving and goodwill toward everyone, is shared by many countries worldwide, each with its own unique traditions and customs. You'll learn which countries have a Santa or Santa Claus-like figure as part of the holiday celebration. Sometimes he is called a different name—like St. Nicholas, Svaty Mikulas, Hotei Osho, Grandfather Frost, Lan Khoong-Khoong, or Father Christmas. And when you return from your trip, you can even send e-mail to Santa Claus!

http://www.christmas.com/christmas.html

The Christmas Page

It's the night before Christmas, and, boy, are you sick of reading that poem! It's time for some new holiday stories, and here's a collection in the St. Nick of time! You'll find the complete text of *How the Grinch Stole Christmas* as well as lesser-known tales from European and other cultural traditions.

http://www.ucalgary.ca/~dkbrown/christmas.html

The Grinch Net

Do you remember the Grinch and how he "stole" Christmas from Whoville in the TV movie, *How the Grinch Stole Christmas*? Well, if you are a Grinch fan, then this site is for you! The complete text of Dr. Seuss's book is here along with images. The Grinch Song lyrics are also here, as well as lyrics from the movie, *The Year Without a Santa Claus*. If you just can't get enough of Dr. Seuss, jump to the Cyber-Seuss Page at *http://www.afn.org/~afn15301/drseuss.html*.

http://lamar.colostate.edu/~ddave/grinchnet.html

Santa's Holiday Bookmarks

If you want to send e-mail to Santa, you can do that here! You can even get some yummy holiday recipes, read charming holiday stories, and find out about Christmas in other lands. For those who can't wait, there's a special countdown clock that tells you exactly how many months, days, hours, minutes, and seconds it is until Christmas! There's also an Advent calendar to help you count down the days.

http://www.america.net/christmas/christmas.html

Welcome To Santa's Workshop

"'Twas the night before Christmas and all through the house..."—wait a minute, you don't have to wait until Christmas Eve to visit this site. It's fun any time of the year, especially if you enjoy reading this poem made famous by Clement Moore in the 1820s. Santa's Workshop is a great place to find answers to lots of Santa Claus FAQ's (frequently-asked questions), as well as other holiday traditions and fun historical facts about Christmas. Have you ever wondered about the origins of Santa Claus? Well, it was the Dutch settlers in New Amsterdam (later renamed New York) who actually brought the idea of Santa Claus, or *Sint(e) Klass*, to America. Even though Christmas songs date way back to the fourth century, the lighter and more joyous Christmas songs that we know today as carols came from Renaissance Italy. The word "carol" comes from the French word *caroler*, meaning "to dance in a ring." And for the Scrooge in your family, you'll find that famous Charles Dickens story, *A Christmas Carol*.

http://www.cyberspace.com/santa/

Welcome to the North Pole

If you want an interactive version of *The Night Before Christmas*, complete with sound effects, try this holiday site. And don't forget to try decorating a digital tree!

http://north.pole.org/santa/

> **People are the true treasures of the Net.**

CINCO DE MAYO
Cinco de Mayo

Do you like a really good party? Well, every fifth of May, many Latino Americans and citizens of Mexico celebrate a grand event, and have a great party in the process. In 1862, on *Cinco de Mayo* (that's Spanish for the fifth of May), a handful of Mexican troops defeated a much larger and better armed force of soldiers from France. This victory showed that a small group, strengthened by unity, can overcome overwhelming odds. Ever since, *Cinco de Mayo* is celebrated with music, tasty food, parades, and a party. Read about the history behind this celebration on the *Cinco de Mayo* page.

http://latino.sscnet.ucla.edu/cinco.html

DAY OF THE DEAD
The Day of the Dead

On November 2, Mexicans celebrate the annual Day of the Dead. But it's not a sad occasion. They make special foods and prepare a feast to honor their ancestors. They have picnics on their relatives' graves so the dead can join in the festivities, too. One of the special foods is called "Bread of the Dead" (*pan de muerto*). The baker hides a plastic skeleton in each rounded loaf, and it's good luck if you're the one to bite into the piece holding it! People also give each other candy skeletons, skulls, and other treats with a death design. The holiday has complex social, religious, and cultural meanings. Learn more about this celebration here!

http://www.public.iastate.edu/~rjsalvad/scmfaq/muertos.html

> **See what's shakin' in EARTH SCIENCE-GEOLOGY-EARTHQUAKES.**

A
B
C
D
E
F
G
H
I
J
K
L
M
N
O
P
Q
R
S
T
U
V
W
X
Y
Z

EARTH DAY

EcoNet's Earth Day Resources

Do you worry about whether there will be clean streams for you to fish in 20 years from now? Or if there will even be fish in the stream at all? If you are concerned about the environment, and want to do something about it, then join the millions of people worldwide who celebrated the 25th anniversary of Earth Day in 1995. Read about subscribing to the Earth Day listserv and ways you and your family or classmates can help preserve the environment for years to come. The slogan in 1995 was "more than just a day—a way of life," and the promoters of Earth Day celebrations around the world want to encourage every individual and organization to make awareness of environmental issues part of their daily lives. This site provides great links to Earth Day information, state by state in the U.S., as well as in Canada and many foreign countries. Read about our Allies in the Rainforest and how you can support international efforts to preserve this natural habitat. You'll even find a list of endangered species.

http://www.econet.apc.org/earthday/

Here's a fun way you and your school can celebrate Earth Day and raise environmental awareness in your community.

Check out Earth Day Groceries! at
http://www.halcyon.com/arborhts/earthday.html
to see what children in 115 schools in U.S., Canada, and Australia did with paper bags, markers, a little imagination, and a lot of energy. Find out more at EcoNet's Earth Day Resources.

NET FILES

A **junior** is an athlete who is less than 20 years old on December 31 in the year of the performance. Who remains the holder of the **U.S. junior record** for the mile, 30 years after the race?

http://www.hkkk.fi/~niininen/wrjm.html
There are more junior records listed at world records in his career. become an Olympic medalist, and held many 1966. He was 19 at the time. He went on to pace of 3 minutes, 51.3 seconds on July 17, holds the U.S. junior record for his blistering Answer: Jim Ryun of Lawrence, Kansas, still

EASTER

A Lesson In Easter Celebration and Traditions

OK, Christmas is always on December 25, Valentine's Day is on February 14, and St. Patrick's Day is always celebrated on March 17, so what about Easter? Why is it always on a different date each year? The answer is a long one, but here goes. Easter is observed on the first Sunday following the first full moon after the first day of spring (vernal equinox) in the Northern Hemisphere. This can occur any time between March 22 and April 25. Many of the Easter customs we practice today (like Easter baskets filled with grass and even the Easter bunny himself) are thought to come from activities related to the ancient goddess of spring, Eostre. The hare, a larger relative of the rabbit, was the animal sacred to Eostre. Find out more interesting facts about the history of Easter festivals at this site.

http://family.com/Features/Entertainment/
  Easter.html

How to Make Ukrainian Easter Eggs

This page explains everything you need to know about the art of Pysanky, the Ukrainian Easter egg. You need an adult to help, because this process involves a candle and hot wax. First, you must decide on the designs you're going to use. Many geometric patterns have traditional meanings, such as curlicues meaning protection, diamonds signifying knowledge, and so on. There are suggested beginner designs, so get your equipment and get started! Apply wax to the egg using a special stylus, called a *kistka*. (The page lists several sources for materials.) Put it everywhere you want to remain white. Then dip the egg in colored dyes. Wherever you apply wax, the color the egg is currently will appear in the final design. When completed, you melt the wax off, and all of the colors appear! It takes a long time to make one of these, but you'll have a true work of art. If handled carefully, you'll be able to give these eggs to your children, and maybe even your grandchildren! This may be eggs-actly the hobby you've been looking for!

http://www.isisnet.com/amorash/ukregg.htm

GERMAN HOLIDAYS
German

This cultural gem originates at the Patch American School, on a U.S. military base in Germany. Because a lot of American kids, living there with their military families, find some of the local customs unusual, this site attempts to explain them. For example, it explains the differences between a German Christmas and an American one. You'll also learn all about St. Martin's Day, the witches of May, and the beautiful candlelit traditions of the Advent season.

http://192.253.114.31/German/Ger_Home.html

Never give your name or address to a stranger.

GROUNDHOG DAY
Groundhog Day—February 2, 1996

Long before we had weather satellites, and Doppler radar, and the Weather Channel, we got our winter weather forecasts from a rodent. Yes, and it's part of what has made America great. And the tradition continues in Punxsutawney, Pennsylvania. Now you can get an up-close-and-personal look at Punxsutawney Phil, Groundhog extraordinaire. Now some may call him a Woodchuck, some may call him a Gopher. We call him a great publicity stunt, but we always pay attention to his predictions for an early or late Spring. As the legend goes, if Phil comes up out of his hole and sees his shadow, he'll be frightened back for six more weeks of winter. If, on the other hand, it's cloudy, we'll get an early Spring. Will he see his shadow? Film at 11.... If that is not enough, try the following Groundhog Day pages for more Phil trivia: *http://www.penn.com/~ezra/ghog.html#anchor154577*, or *http://www.csh.rit.edu/~jones/ghd.html*.

http://warren.penn.com/PunxsyPhil/

Wiarton Willie's Homepage

Lest you think Canadians don't have a weather rodent (En Français, MÉTÉO MARMOTTE) of their own, meet Wiarton Willie, an albino Marmot. "Born on the 45th parallel, exactly midway between the Equator and the North Pole, this white groundhog has the uncanny ability to signal the end of winter. Weather watchers around the world look to Willie's shadow and its 90 percent accuracy rate to see just how long winter is going to continue!" The statue of the critter is not to be missed, and Willie has fun games and mazes to play with, too. You can even send him e-mail, he must have a modem in his burrow. Come join in the fun in southwestern Ontario, on Lake Huron.

http://www.wiarton-willie.org/~willie/index.html

Not everything on the Net is true.

A B C D E F G H I J K L M N O P Q R S T U V W X Y Z

HALLOWEEN
A Dark and Stormy Site

Tricks and treats abound at this great Halloween site! Enter the haunted house if you dare, but watch out for the morphing monsters, vampire bats, ghosts, and hobgoblins. Stroll through the pumpkin patch and play some ghastly games, but if you fall into the cauldron, the prank's on you! You can create a crazy Halloween story with wacky, wicked words. Download scary sound effects or share costume ideas with other kids by ghost writing on the wall.

http://www.delphi.com/edukids/hallow/

"Groundhog Day— Half your hay."

That's an old saying connected with February 2, Groundhog Day. New England farmers knew, despite how sunny or cloudy the day was, that there was still a lot of winter to come. If there was less than half the year's store of hay left in the hayloft, the cows were in for a stretch of rationing before Spring rains brought the new grass. Discover the strange and fanciful traditions of this unusual holiday, at the Groundhog Day— February 2, 1996 page, which celebrates the weather forecasting abilities of a rodent.

The Penny Whistle Halloween Book

From blood-curdling beverages (with insects in the ice cubes) to devilish desserts (with chocolate spiders), your Halloween party is sure to be ghoulish if you follow some of the ideas here. There are Halloween decorations and activities that any witch, wizard, or goblin will love. Don't forget to tip-toe through the Pumpkin Patch for design do's and don'ts about carving and lighting the best jack-o'-lantern ever!

http://family.starwave.com/funstuff/pwhallow/
  index.htm

Did you know that the first carved jack-o-lantern was not a pumpkin?

Find out what other large vegetable was used for this purpose during the Middle Ages, and learn about other Halloween lore and legend at A Dark and Stormy Site.

INDEPENDENCE DAY
America's Birthday

This patriotic site features a message from Vice-President Al Gore, an audio file of the National Anthem, links to lots of government resources around the Net, and last but very important: fireworks safety tips!

http://banzai.neosoft.com/citylink/usa

NATIONAL FOREIGN HOLIDAYS

The United States celebrates its birthday on July 4th. There are parades, picnics, and at night—fireworks! Most countries celebrate national holidays that are their equivalents of the American Fourth of July. Here's a list of them.

http://www.worldculture.com/holidays.htm

JEWISH HOLIDAYS
A–Z of Jewish & Israel Resources

Search the subject index or browse alphabetically in the A–Z of Jewish and Israel Resources for topics like "Hebrew children's songs for the holidays" and "choreographic descriptions of Israeli folk dances."

http://www.ort.org/anjy/a-z/festival.htm

Ben Uri Art Society

Here is a great site to learn about art, history, and the Jewish holidays, all rolled into one! The Ben Uri Art Gallery is a collection of over 700 paintings, drawings, prints, and sculpture by Jewish artists—selections from which are shown regularly in the gallery in London, England. The first two art selections show the *Shabbat*, the Hebrew word for Sabbath, which begins at sundown each Friday. Because the Jewish calendar is based on the lunar calendar (cycles of the moon), the new "day" begins at this time. *Rosh Hashanah*, the Hebrew phrase for the "Head of the Year," is the Jewish New Year celebration, and so our illustrated tour begins with this holiday in September. Continue through the Gallery, and the months of the year, to learn more about the other Jewish holy days and festivals, and the food, songs, and dances that are part of these traditional celebrations.

http://www.ort.org/links/benuri/home.htm

Calendar of Jewish Holidays

This resource, offered by B'nai B'rith, gives the dates for all important Jewish holidays through the year 2,000. Mark your calendars in advance.

http://israel.nysernet.org/bbrith/caln.html

> Ask not what the Net can do for you, ask what you can do for the Net.

Hanukkah—Festival Of Lights

Imagine it's the year 165 B.C., and after a three-year struggle, you and all the Jews in Judea have successfully defeated the Syrian tyrant, Antiochus. Now you are ready to hold festivities and celebrate the reclaiming of your Temple, but there is only a very small bottle of oil left with which to light all the holy lamps. Miraculously, this small amount of oil lasts for eight days. Hanukkah, the Jewish Festival of Lights, involves the lighting of candles for eight days in a special ceremony. In late December every year, Jewish families celebrate Hanukkah by lighting candles on a *Menorah*, a candle holder with nine branches. And, just like the holiday celebrations of other cultures, there are special foods and music for Hannukah. It's all here, the history, the goodies, and three traditional Hanukkah songs with music and lyrics, in both English and Hebrew. There is even a pattern for making a *dreidel* (a four-sided spinning top), which is part of a traditional children's game of luck.

http://www.ort.org/ort/hanukkah/title.htm

JOHN MUIR DAY
John Muir Day Study Guide

Every April 21, students in California celebrate the life of John Muir, and his contribution to conservation and appreciation of the environment. He founded the Sierra Club, and pushed the U.S. Government to establish the National Parks system. The first National Park, designated in 1890, was Yosemite in California. You can visit it via this site, as well as read a biography of Muir and accounts of his travels around the world.

http://ice.ucdavis.edu/John_Muir/John_Muir_Day_Study_Guide/

JUNETEENTH
JUNETEENTH: Freedom Revisited

Celebrate freedom! African Americans recall June 19, 1865, as the date when many slaves in the state of Texas learned that they had been freed, over two years earlier, by President Abraham Lincoln. This celebration is known as *Juneteenth,* and is usually marked by historical displays, feasts, songs, and dancing. Learn about the origins of Juneteenth at the Anacostia Museum, Washington, D.C.

http://www.si.edu/organiza/museums/anacost/homepage/june.htm

KWANZAA

Kwanzaa Information Center

The symbolic lighting of candles is associated with many holidays. And so it is with *Kwanzaa*, an African American spiritual holiday, emphasizing the unity of the Black family and encouraging a festive celebration of the oneness and goodness of life. Learn how the seven candles, the *Mshumaa*, represent seven principles of *Nguzo Saba*. Read about the history and meaning of the other symbols used in the celebration of this holiday. A list of children's books about Kwanzaa is also provided here.

http://melanet.com/melanet/kwanzaa/kwanzaa.html

The Meaning of Kwanzaa

In 1966, a man named Maulana Ron Karenga and the U.S. Organization invented a new American holiday, based on harvest celebrations in Africa. They called this celebration *Kwanzaa,* which is a Swahili word meaning "first," signifying the first fruits of the harvest. Many Americans of African heritage celebrate this holiday from December 26 to January 1.

http://www.si.edu/organiza/museums/anacost/
   homepage/kwanz.htm

ST. PATRICK'S DAY

RCA Victor: I Am Irish

They say that on St. Patrick's Day, everyone is Irish! Come join the parade as you march through this site to find answers to questions like: Are potatoes Irish? Why do people kiss the Blarney Stone? Which city boasts the very first St. Patrick's Day parade in North America? Learn more about the legend of St. Patrick, along with other Celtic lore. Yes, there are leprechauns here too! If you're a history buff, there's even more here for you with a great list of famous Irish Americans throughout history. If you think the shamrock is the official emblem of Ireland, guess again. It's the harp, a favorite musical instrument in Ireland, dating back hundreds of years.

http://www.irish.com/irish/irish-stuff.html

A Wee Bit O' Fun

Have you ever wondered who St. Patrick really was and why we celebrate St. Patrick's Day? And is there really such a thing as a leprechaun? Americans have been celebrating this holiday for over 200 years. Read all about the history of St. Patrick's Day at this site. Also check out the list of other web sites dominated by the color green, including one called 40 Tips To Go Green, which has ideas for saving the environment.

http://www.nando.net/toys/stpaddy/stpaddy.html

NET FILES

What do you get if you walk the dog correctly on your first try?

Answer: Five points when competing in the American Yo-Yo Association Competition.
http://www.pd.net/

THANKSGIVING

The First Thanksgiving

Would you like to fix the perfect Pilgrim-style Thanksgiving dinner? Check this site out to learn about the Pilgrims and the first Thanksgiving in 1621. Great recipe ideas will help you recreate that seventeenth-century harvest feast. The interpretive guides, dressed in historic period costumes, will take you on a virtual tour of Plimouth Plantation, the first permanent European settlement. You'll also see Hobbamock's Homesite, a reconstructed Native American hamlet, complete with a wigwam and a bark-covered longhouse.

http://media3.com/plymouth/thanksgiving.htm

DON'T want to eat your Brussels sprouts? What would you do if your Mom made you finish all your furmenty, a dish from colonial times? You'd probably be happy! Furmenty is a delicious dish containing cracked wheat, milk, and brown sugar. It's sort of like a sweet oatmeal. Find the recipe and others from the first Thanksgiving at The First Thanksgiving.

Zia Thanksgiving

This site has tasty recipes, directions for carving the turkey, and even instructions for making table decorations. If you've ever wondered how to make a cornhusk doll, look no further!

http://www.zia.com/thanks.htm

VALENTINE'S DAY

ZIA Valentines

At this site, you can send a fun or a sappy e-mail valentine to your friend or your true love. You can also find valentine party ideas, recipes, and crafts, and read all about the history of this love-ly holiday. This site is designed for kids, too.

http://www.zia.com/holidays/valentine/

HORSES AND EQUESTRIAN SPORTS

See also: MAMMALS—HORSE FAMILY

Aberdeen University Riding Club World Equestrian Information

This U.K. site is the most comprehensive collection of equine resources we've seen, We like the arrangement better at Hay.net, but this one has more links. Stories, clubs, newsletters, events, loads of personal pages, and more. We haven't checked all the links here, so parents, do your thing!

http://www.abdn.ac.uk/~src011/equine.html

A
B
C
D
E
F
G
H
I
J
K
L
M
N
O
P
Q
R
S
T
U
V
W
X
Y
Z

The Hay.net: A comprehensive list of almost all the horse sites on the Internet

This site is the Internet equivalent of Sweet Feed for horse owners: all sorts of delicious grains, dripping with molasses, each crunchier than the last! Start with the Pick of the Week—maybe it's something on x-raying large animals, or perhaps an interactive guide to horse health care. Let's move into the barn and see all the different breeds—Arabians, Quarter Horses, Thoroughbreds, sure. But you'll also find Icelandic ponies, Halflingers, and all kinds of drafts. What's this little one here, not moving at all? Oh, it's a model horse! Lots here on them, too. Check the Olympic events, the Denver Stock Show, and lots of racing and driving information. Pull up a hay bale and make yourself comfortable!

http://www.freerein.com/haynet/

Haynet Home Page

There are TWO horse sites with similar names, but this is the one for Model Horse enthusiasts. If you love horses, we mean *really* love horses, chances are you have a model horse or two. Did you know there are horse shows for model horses, too? You can find out where they are, and what classes you and your model horse can enter. There are also tips about painting and otherwise reworking your Breyer or other collectible horse models. You won't believe the photos of the detailed models here.

http://nehalem.rain.com/haynet/

Horse Country

The ultimate horse site for juniors! Horse history, care, stories, sounds, images, and associations are all here! There's a fantasy game where you can create your own dream stable, "buy and sell" virtual horses, "compete" in virtual horse shows, and share the results with your fellow dream stable owners! Other musts here are the Junior Riders Mailing Digest and an International Pen Pal List for horse lovers.

http://www.pathology.washington.edu/Horse/
Carroll_horse.html

Become one with the Net.

International Museum of the Horse—Lexington, Kentucky

"Our history was written on his back," says this site, dedicated to the history of horses and horsemanship. Learn about horses in war, in sport, in work, and in recreation. There are also some fascinating special exhibits: "The Draft Horse In America: Power for an Emerging Nation"; "The Buffalo Soldiers on the Western Frontier"; and the famous Thoroughbreds at "Calumet Farm: Five Decades of Champions."

http://www.horseworld.com/imh/imhmain.html

Do you love horses?

Are you into rodeo or racing?

Did you know that the horse evolved from an animal no bigger than a modern-day fox? If horses are your thing, then this is your page. Everything from the history of horses, to a gallery of breeds, to horse sports, will be found here. Gallop on over to the **International Museum of the Horse –Lexington, Kentucky**.

The Sun never sets on the Internet.

Janet's Horse Links

It's raining, and you hate to ride in the rain! It's a pain to clean the mud off your tack afterwards, to say nothing of making your horse look presentable again! Why not give your horse an apple and the day off, and ride the trails of this great web site, instead? Janet's pulled together a nice group of web sites, including breed home pages, horse health, sports, wild horses, and electronic horse magazines. The back issues of these "e-zines" alone will keep you busy for hours! Hey, it's stopped raining!

http://www.interealm.com/p/ratzloff/jan/horse.htm

The Wild Horse, Mustang, & Burro Page

Ever thought of adopting a wild horse? This site tells you all about what you have to do to adopt one from the U.S. Bureau of Land Management. There are requirements though, and remember, these are wild animals who have never been around people before, so folks sometimes have difficulty getting the horses tamed. This site has a schedule of adoption locations and dates, and plenty of information for the potential adoptive family.

http://iquest.com/~jhines/mustang/

NET FILES

How many people are there on Earth?

Answer: Quite a few! For the latest estimate, check the world population clocks at http://sunsite.unc.edu/lunarbin/worldpop

FOXHUNTING
Horse Country Hunting Pages

Nowadays, many hunts don't actually hunt foxes, they follow a scent of fox urine that has been dragged over the ground hours before. Still, the sight of hounds running across a field, with a herd of bold horses and riders galloping behind, is pretty exciting! Here you'll find some interesting history about foxhunting, and learn some of the special jargon you'll need to know in the hunt field. You can also hear some hunting horn fanfare, and learn why those obviously bright red hunting jackets are called "Pink Coats."

http://www.pathology.washington.edu/Horse/hunting.html

POLO
PoloNet

Polo is a four-person, four-horse team sport, requiring a mallet, and a ball about the size of a baseball. The object is to score points by hitting the ball to a goal. The outdoor variation of polo is played on a grass surface measuring 300 by 160 (or more) yards, about the size of six football fields! Learn about the tactics and strategy of the game, and link to polo clubs and other players around the world.

http://www.cts.com/browse/polonet/

A B C D E F G H I J K L M N O P Q R S T U V W X Y Z

INSECTS AND SPIDERS

The Butterfly WebSite

Do you know what the first butterflies of spring are? Here's a hint—they have a blue sparkle about them. Give up? The Azure butterflies are the first, followed by the Sulphurs and Whites. But you don't have to wait for spring to see butterflies. There are hundreds of butterflies and moths waiting for your discovery year round. Find out how to locate moths and butterflies during any time of the year. Learn about butterfly gardening, and which flowers and plants attract butterflies and encourage them to lay eggs.

http://mgfx.com/butterflies/

BALLOONS look so pretty against the sky– but those massive balloon launches aren't a good idea. The balloons travel on high speed winds, high in the sky. Eventually they lose their helium, and come down. Sometimes, that can be in the ocean. According to the Butterfly WebSite, up to 100,000 whales and seals die each year from eating plastic objects floating in the sea. Seals, dolphins, whales, sea turtles, fish and marine birds all mistake balloons for food. All seven species of sea turtles are seriously endangered, partly due to swallowing balloons. Check out The Butterfly Website to find out about the conservation of these and other animals.

Gordons Entomological Home Page

Did you know that insects were often used as medical treatment? Bedbugs were thought to be a cure for malaria, beetle grubs were used as a cure for toothaches, and acid from ants was often used as a cure for neurotic troubles. Others perceived insects as a delicious addition to their diet. In case you were wondering how to make "banana worm bread" or "rootworm beetle dip," you can find the recipes here. On the other hand, insects make great pets! OK, so you may have to do some convincing with mom and dad. Well, not only are insects smaller and less intrusive than other pets, but generally they are quieter, and cheaper to feed. Yeah, that's it! You can even learn how to care for your pet tarantula or cricket.

http://info.ex.ac.uk/~gjlramel/welcome.html

The Insects Home Page

UGH, it's a bug! Bugs aren't really so bad. Butterflies are pretty, ladybugs are cute, and praying mantises are helpful in a garden. Insects produce valuable items too, such as honey, silk, wax, and dyes. Some insects are used for human food, and others have proven to be very useful in scientific and medical research. Explore the world of insects here—they are the most successful lifeform on the planet!

http://info.ex.ac.uk/~gjlramel/six.html

See the Live Ants!

Steve's Ant Farm is a happenin' place. In fact, it's a crawlin' place. Steve's got an ant farm, and he's got a camera pointed at it. Every five minutes, the camera posts a new picture to this Web site. You can watch ants build tunnels, construct bridges, and make molehills out of mountains.

http://sec.dgsys.com/antfarm.html

Surf today, smart tomorrow.

Let balloonists take you to new heights in Aviation and Airplanes.

Spiders of the World

Help a real scientist in her research! Help Dr. Rosie Gillespie, a professor in the department of Zoology at the University of Hawai'i, answer this question: Why do the Tetragnatha and other families of spiders in Hawai'i live in such diverse habitats, in comparison to families of spiders on the mainland? Look at various species of spiders and learn how to identify them. Then go on a spider hunt! Find out the kind and number of families of spiders in your neighborhood, then submit your spider data to Dr. Gillespie online. See your spider data graphed with other information from students and teachers worldwide.

http://seawifs.gsfc.nasa.gov/JASON/HTML/
   SPIDERS_HOME.html

University of Kentucky Entomology Youth Facts

Have you ever been to the Olympics? How about the insect Olympics? See a flea go for the gold in the high jump competition! Watch a Bolus spider go for a "bolus-eye" in archery. Check out insect world records, and discover which insects are the ugliest, have the longest legs, or the smallest wings. Is your class looking for a mascot? How about an insect? Here you'll find some guidelines to help pick the best choice for your classroom. Interested in an insect treat? How about "ants-on-a-log"? Come on, it's just a stalk of celery spread with peanut butter, and sprinkled with raisins!

http://www.uky.edu/Agriculture/Entomology/
   ythfacts/entyouth.htm

Welcome to Cockroach World

Betty the Bug Lady is the host of the yuckiest site on the Internet, Cockroach World! You can ask her about cockroaches and other yucky bug stuff. Take the Cockroach World quiz, or tell your cockroach story to the rest of the forum. Did you know that if you cut off a cockroach's head, it will run around for a week, then die of thirst? That's right, a cockroach can live a week without its head. It only dies because without a mouth, it can't drink water. Stop by Cockroach World's multimedia library for yucky sights and sounds! Hear the hiss of the Madagascar Hissing Cockroach or watch the Smelly Roach QuickTime movie. You'll also learn that cockroaches spend 75 percent of their time resting up for those late night snack runs!

http://www.nj.com/yucky/roaches/index.html

You Can Spider Webs

Why doesn't a spider stick to its web? Try this experiment with Beakman and Jax to find out! Then look at the many different kinds of spider webs, and maybe even collect some using the method described here. But be sure to wait until Charlotte's done with hers before you take it home!

http://pomo.nbn.com/youcan/spider/spider.html

INTERNET

Hobbes' Internet Timeline

How did all this get started, anyway? The unofficial official history of the Internet is here.

http://www.isoc.org/guest/zakon/Internet/
   History/HIT.html

Hobbes' Internet World

Everything you need to know about the Internet is probably on this page. We haven't checked every possible link, but we're pretty sure everything is here. If you're looking for an Internet service provider, try the POCIA link. Want to control your own domain name? The forms are here. Curious about Internet organizations, including The Internet Society? Looking for beginner's guides, standards documents, or security alerts? Told you it was all here. Links galore and even MORE!

http://info.isoc.org/guest/zakon/Internet/

ILC Glossary of Internet Terms

Confused on all those new Internet terms? Can't tell an IMHO from a TTFN? Don't SLIP in the MUD, come on over to this terrific glossary and All will be revealed.

http://www.matisse.net/files/glossary.html

The Sun never sets on the Internet.

in the can? No, SPAM on the Net! On the Internet, people sometimes send out e-mail messages to many, many people on electronic conferences like listservs and Usenet. Usually these messages advertise some product or service, having nothing to do with the topic of the discussion. This is called SPAMming. This is just like junk mail, and you can throw it away.

Internet Companion

One of the best books ever written about the Internet is called *The Internet Companion* by Tracy LaQuey. The entire book is available on the Internet FOR FREE! If you want to learn how the Internet came about, see what you can do with the Internet, and become more familiar with the Internet in general—take a look here.

http://www.obs-us.com/obs/english/books/
   editinc/obsxxx.htm

The Scout Toolkit Homepage

The Internet Scout has put together a page that will help you. If not today, tomorrow. Trust us when we say this: you will need this page. All the tools you need are right here in the toolbox: browsers, search options, specialized applications like Real Audio (radio and other audio over the Net) and CU-SeeMe (video over the Net). There's also a great section on how to keep up with what's current on the Net. Remember, if you don't have the newest stuff in your toolkit, everything looks like a *This Old Net* rerun.

http://rs.internic.net/scout/toolkit/

The Unofficial Internet Book List

Obviously, you know that reading about the Internet is one way to learn about it, otherwise you wouldn't be holding this book. There are many other books about the Internet, and they cover a wide range of information. If you're eager to do more book reading, you can get a complete catalog of Internet books from The Unofficial Internet Book List. Then look at your local public library to see if they can get the ones that interest you. If you read all of the books listed you'll know as much about the Internet as anyone. That will take a while, though: there are several hundred books on the list!

ftp://rtfm.mit.edu/pub/usenet/news.answers/
   internet-services/book-list

WWW History

A big part of the Internet is the World Wide Web, or WWW, or the Web. The World Wide Web makes it easier to use pictures (or graphics), and also helps to link information together on the Internet. To better understand the WWW, and get a good dose of Internet history in the process, take a peek at the WWW History page.

http://k12.cnidr.org:90/web.history.html

BEGINNER'S GUIDES
Beginner's Guide to URLs

From the inventors of Mosaic comes this brief guide to URLs, or *Uniform Resource Locators*. If something's out there on the Internet, you can "point to it" using a URL and your favorite Net browser. This will give you the syntax for pointing at gopher servers, ftp archives, news, and of course, Web resources!

http://www.ncsa.uiuc.edu/demoweb/url-primer.html

Become one with the Net.

EFF's (Extended) Guide to the Internet—Table of Contents

Do you want to be an Internet expert? Do you want to know where much of the good information is, what all the Internet terminology means, and how you can find plenty of information on the Internet? The EFF Guide to the Internet is probably as good a source as there is to achieve these goals. Parental advisory: this site gives addresses, but does not link to, various resources that may be inappropriate for your family.

http://www.nova.edu/Inter-Links/bigdummy/
bdg_toc.html

Internet Help

When you use the World Wide Web on the Internet, it's like taking a voyage. Each page you link to and every new computer you access are like the twists and turns of a fun road trip. But, just like learning to drive a car or ride a bike, you need to practice. You need to learn the rules of the road. To get some practice in your World Wide Web travels, take a spin over to Mouse Travel Tips.

http://www.internet-for-kids.com/help.html

Introduction to the Internet

The Internet is confusing. It is BIG, people use all kinds of strange words when talking about it (such as telnet, HTML, or the Web), and it is changing all the time. How can you learn about it? You're doing it right now—you're reading about it. Another thing you can do is explore it by looking at the Introduction to the Internet page. Be patient—you won't learn all there is immediately, but with practice you'll be a Net expert before you know it!

http://www.sils.umich.edu/~fprefect/inet/

**Strike up the bandwith
in Music.**

FINDING PEOPLE

As you use the Internet, you may start wondering if people you know have Internet accounts. Maybe you have a favorite uncle who lives on the other side of the country, or a friend from a town where you used to live, and you'd like to communicate with them via the Net. Problem is, how can you determine if they are on the Internet? The surest way is to call the person, or write him or her via a postal letter, and ask. There are a variety of experimental programs on the Internet, though, that you can use to track people down. Listed here are a few places you can look that provide links to different people-finding tools. Happy hunting, but be sure to read the instructions for these programs. Some are much easier to use than others.

Finding Internet E-mail Addresses

A general introduction to the problem, and some solutions.

http://www.sil.org/internet/email.html

Four11 White Page Directory

FINALLY. It's new, it's easy. Though similar to "WhoWhere?" below, this one has a few more nifty features, and you can search for people with similar interests or backgrounds to your own.

http://www.Four11.com/

Jean's People—Finding Internet Resources

Another general one, with the added strategy of checking college Web phone books, and more.

http://www-leland.stanford.edu/~csdismas/find.html

WhoWhere? PeopleSearch

It's also new, and it's linked into Netscape, under the Net Search button. Finding addresses should always have been this easy.

http://www.whowhere.com/

A
B
C
D
E
F
G
H
I
J
K
L
M
N
O
P
Q
R
S
T
U
V
W
X
Y
Z

MACHINES ON THE NET
Anthony's List of Internet Accessible Machines

For some time various folks on the Internet have attached computers to all kinds of machines. With the machines hooked up, the owners are then able to give updates on those machines live on the Net. Soft drink vending machines, refrigerators, toasters, and cameras (with live pictures) are among the types of devices connected. For example, you can learn how many cans of soda are available in a machine, what the temperature in a refrigerator is, and you can see students live in a college dorm room. Why have people done this? Probably best to ask, "Why ask why?" Take a look at Anthony's Internet Accessible Machines to see what it's all about!

http://www.dsu.edu/~anderbea/machines.html

MUDs AND MOOs

MUDs and MOOs (you'll also hear of similar MUSHes and MUSEs) are programs that let you explore, and sometimes create, computer-generated, text-based worlds. For example, you can build a stream next to a mountain, and maybe put a magical fish in it. You can talk live, via your computer keyboard, to kids from all over the world, and learn about science, history, and computers. Best of all, these are a ton of fun!

FredNet MOO

FredNet MOO is a fun learning experience, and an excellent place to learn how to move around in a MOO environment. At FredNet, you'll explore (among many other things) a biochemical lab, Ancient Rome, Ford's Theater (where President Lincoln was assassinated), and more. You can also practice exploring MOOs by using the excellent tutorial.

http://www.fred.net/cindy/frednet.htm

telnet://fred.net:8888

Space Exploration is a blast. Check out Astronomy.

The Never Ending Story

You've probably heard of, or maybe read, *The Never Ending Story*—a wonderful book (and movie) about a young boy and a thrilling fantasy world. You can sample that world, to a certain extent, by telnetting to *The Never Ending Story* MUD. If you liked the book or the movie, this may be the perfect MUD for you!

telnet://snowhite.ee.pdx.edu:9999

SchoolNet MOO

You've never seen a school like the SchoolNet MOO. Housed in a computer in Canada (it's a multilingual system for French and English speakers), SchoolNet MOO is a place where you can build all sorts of things while interacting with kids from all over. To connect to SchoolNet MOO you'll need telnet capability, so ask your parents or teachers if you have that.

http://schoolnet2.carleton.ca/english/adm/office/ help/MOO2.html

telnet:// schoolnet.carleton.ca:7777

NET FILES

Where is the Rainbow Bridge?

Answer: Some people believe it is a very special place "just this side of heaven." It is where beloved pets go when they die, and it's a wonderful happy place. There is always enough to eat and drink, and the pets play together and have a lot of fun. They wait at Rainbow Bridge until one day their owners follow them. There is a rush of barks and meows and waving tails! Then owner and pet cross Rainbow Bridge together. Read the story at http://www.pcix.com/abgp/rainbow.htm and check out more Pet Grief resources at http://ourworld.compuserve.com/homepages/edwilliams/

Welcome to 1848's Home Page

Imagine going back to 1848 and striking out for the Wild West in America. You'd find frontier towns, Native Americans, and frontiers-people. At this MOO, you don't have to stretch your imagination too far—America 1848 awaits if you have access to telnet software. Ask your parents or teachers if you do.

http://www.1848.musenet.org/1848/

telnet://bridges.usmee.maine.edu:1848

Welcome to MOOSE Crossing!

Would you like to build your own world with kids from around the world? Would you like to work on special projects with kids thirteen and under? Would you like to work on a computer at MIT—the foremost center of computer innovation? Do you own, or have access to, a Macintosh computer? If you answered yes to these questions, then MOOSE Crossing is the place for you!

http://lcs.www.media.mit.edu/people/asb/
  moose-crossing/

NETIQUETTE, FOLKLORE, AND CUSTOMS

Electronic smiles won't shock your lips

When writing e-mail messages sometimes it's hard to express what you are really feeling. This has been a problem for folks on the Internet for a long time, and to help better express emotions something called *smileys* were created. For example, turn your head sideways to the left, and look at this —> :-). Do you see this makes a little smiley face? There are many variations of these smileys—to see more, take a peek at this page. Note to parents: there are lots of smiley lists on the Net that are more comprehensive, but this one is family-oriented.

http://aleph0.clarku.edu/~mfourche/scarlet030295/
  electronic-smiles-won-t-.html

Take a ride on a Carousel in AMUSEMENT PARKS.

A smiley, or emoticon, is a way of expressing your feelings through typed characters. Look at this sideways :-D does that look like a really happy face?

Find more at the Electronic smiles won't shock your lips page.

The Net: User Guidelines and Netiquette

Everybody knows that politeness and good etiquette make life easier. Waiting your turn in line, keeping your locker in order, or being nice to your friends helps you as much as the people around you. The same is true on the Internet. There are some basic rules of etiquette (on the Internet it's called netiquette) that help keep things running smoothly. Check out some of these basic rules of Internet good behavior.

http://rs6000.adm.fau.edu/rinaldi/net/index.htm

Origami: the fold to behold! Check out CRAFTS AND HOBBIES. Yogatta try Yoga.

A
B
C
D
E
F
G
H
I
J
K
L
M
N
O
P
Q
R
S
T
U
V
W
X
Y
Z

PARENTAL CONTROL

Parental Control Product Review

The Internet is great—you can learn a lot, make new friends, and have a whole new world opened to you. However, there may be parts of the Internet your parents don't want you to see. Just like with some television programs, or books, or magazines, or parts of town, your parents decide what you can or cannot view. There are a variety of software products your parents can place on your computer to help you better use the Internet, and to help them guide what you see. Show this page to your mom, dad, or some other adult in charge. They'll see what is available and also get answers to questions about what they can do to make your Internet experiences great! We support these types of products because we believe that this type of guidance should come from the home, not be imposed by the government.

http://www.neosoft.com/parental-control/

PEDINFO Parental Control of Internet Access

There's been a lot of talk in the news about the Internet having stuff on it that is inappropriate for kids. The overwhelming majority of information is OK—but the news stories can make your parents and teachers nervous. Some people are even talking about keeping kids off the Net entirely! That would be terrible! We think that access to information is a good thing. But we also recognize that parents may want to participate and guide your selection of information resources. There are ways for your parents, school, or other adult to help you select the best of the Net, and this page is a good place for those folks to look and see what's available.

http://www.lhl.uab.edu/pedinfo/Control.html

SAFETY

OUDPS: Notes, Advice and Warnings for Kids

The Internet is a fun place to be. It is important, though, that you learn to use the Internet safely and wisely. What if they ask for your phone number? What if they ask for your password? What if you stumble into something that's "too old" for you? The University of Oklahoma Department of Public Safety gives loads of great tips on using the Internet in a good way.

http://www.uoknor.edu/oupd/kidsafe/warn_kid.htm

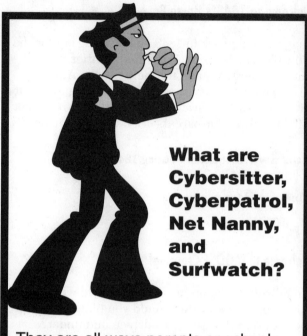

What are Cybersitter, Cyberpatrol, Net Nanny, and Surfwatch?

They are all ways parents or schools can help guide your Internet experience and make sure you're safe. Read more at the **Parental Control Product Review** page.

Rules for Kids on the Internet / Information Highway

It's OK to keep a secret, especially when you meet people on the Internet! Never give anyone personal information about yourself, and never send a picture to someone or agree to meet someone without talking to your parents or your teacher about it first. To learn many other safety rules of the road on the Information Superhighway, view this site!

http://www.discribe.ca/childfind/kidrule.hte

Lose yourself in a Museum. SCIENCE has them all.

SEARCH ENGINES AND DIRECTORIES

There is a lot of treasure out there on the Internet, but the problem is trying to find exactly the gold you want, hidden somewhere in the millions of grains of sand. *search engines* and *Internet directories* can help. Usually, you can find both by selecting them on your Net browser. On Netscape, for example, there are buttons called "Net Search" and "Net Directory."

What's the difference? Maybe this example will help. Say you want a tuna fish sandwich for lunch. But there's a problem. You don't have any tuna fish! Think of a search engine as a way to go catch your own fish in the ocean. You hope to cast out your net and get a nice tuna. You may even catch one. But you may also catch some dolphins, some sea turtles, and maybe some floating sea trash.

A directory, on the other hand, is more like a grocery store, where you can just walk over to the CANNED GOODS aisle and pick out a can marked "Tuna." Someone has already caught the correct kind of fish for you, marked the can the right way, and put it in the right store aisle!

There are reasons you'll want to know about and use both types.

A search engine (the "fishing net") is a computer program that will search through millions of resources looking for the appearance of the words you've used to describe your topic. But it won't search all those actual places while you wait. It's only looking through its own list of words, in its own index. Where does it get the words? Special software is always working in the background, combing the Net, looking for new sites (and words) to harvest. These harvests are used to create the search engine's word index. So, if a resource was put up on the Internet an hour ago, you probably won't be able to find it yet, whether you use a search engine or a directory. It won't turn up in an index until it's harvested by one of the search engine's robots.

Just knowing that a word appears in a document doesn't mean the document will really be about the topic you want! Searching on the word "CAT" will pull up thousands of *hits*. (A hit is an answer the computer sends back in response to your question. Sometimes a question is also called a *query*.) Asking for a search on CAT will return information on CAT and CATS, but also CATalog, CATapult, and CATacombs.

(Remember the sea turtles and the dolphins? These are hits you don't need.) There are advanced ways of using search engines which will pare down the number of unwanted hits, and narrow the focus more towards what you want. The best way to learn how to do this is to read the searching tips each search engine offers. They are all different.

Guess what? There have also been instances of people stuffing their Web resources with keywords, so they will turn up in more searches. One guy wanted to sell his new product. He reasoned that if more people saw his product, he'd sell more of it. So, he put his ad on an Internet Web page. Then, he padded the Web page with about a thousand extra keywords! The keywords had nothing to do with the product, but that trick did make his ad turn up in millions of searches (see "floating sea trash," above)!

A directory ("grocery store shelf"), on the other hand, takes Internet information resources and puts them in some kind of logical subject order. In other words, a *real person* looks at the resources, then decides what they are about, and where they should go on the directory's subject "shelves." A directory will return hits which should be precisely on-target. But, because the Internet is growing so fast, and there are so many documents, most subject directories are not fully up-to-date.

Another thing to notice is that some search engines and directories, are concerned with only part of the Internet. Some deal with Web resources only. Some include Web, gopher, and maybe ftp or Usenet newsgroup information. Pay attention and know what region of the Internet you're really searching.

There is one more thing you need to know. Not everything on the Net is true. Some of the information is out-of-date. Some of it is just plain wrong. And some of it is put there as a way to mislead you. How do you tell the good stuff from the bad stuff? One of the ways is to use this book, which you're holding in your hands. We've found some of the good stuff for you. Other authorities in which to place your trust will vary. Ask your parents, a teacher, or a trusted adult. They may help you to decide if the information you find on the Net is right for your purpose.

A good Internet searcher knows how to use lots of searching tools to advantage. Read on for some tips on using some of the best so far. We'll pretend we're looking for information on cat care, and we'll see how the various servers handle the same simple request.

A B C D E F G H I J K L M N O P Q R S T U V W X Y Z

Alta Vista

The newest of the bunch, Alta Vista claims to have the largest index. They all claim they are the best, to one extent or another. Your best bet is to use several of them! One thing you can say for this one is that it is FAST! And you can almost always connect to it; they seem to have a lot of servers to handle the load. Our straightforward "cats" search pulled 70,000 items. In the first ten, we found an ad for a Maine Coon Cat cattery, several personal pages showing off their pets, a humane association with cats available for adoption, and several off-topic hits. Alas, nothing about pet care. To find something more specific we'd have to use the "Advanced Query" options. For example, let's try the following search: cats NEAR care AND health. That makes the computer look for the words "cat" and "care" occurring near each other. Our query also requires the word "health" to be present somewhere in the resource. OK, with that search, we got only about 400 hits. That's still too many, but it's not too many for our example, since we easily found what we wanted. In the first ten hits, we had two references to the same Usenet FAQ on cat care, an ad for a book about cat care, two purebred cat organizations, and several others that applied, or did not, in varying degrees.

http://altavista.digital.com/

excite

This directory has something a little different. It gives you a "confidence" rating alongside your hits, and it gives you what it thinks are its "best" hits first. Search on words either as "concepts" or as "keywords." Our "concept" search on cats led to five good hits out of ten. All ten were rated at a 75-76% confidence level. A search on "cats" as a keyword returned the identical hits. Another nice feature is the ability to just look at the hits on excite's version of the page, without having to leave excite and surf over to the resource itself. That's a quick way to see if the resource is of any value to you, without wasting time connecting to it. There are also other things to do at excite. You can use the subject directory listing, and just search reviewed sites. Or, read columns on Net topics, or read some current news stories. There is also a weekly interactive political cartoon, which didn't, er, "excite" us very much. We do use their directory service a lot though, because we like the confidence ratings and the advanced searching capabilities.

http://www.excite.com/

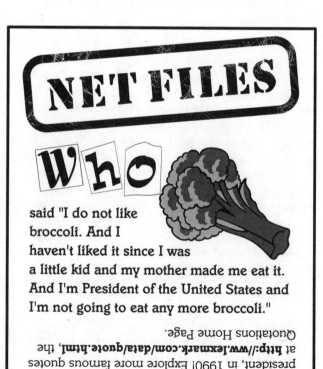

NET FILES

Who said "I do not like broccoli. And I haven't liked it since I was a little kid and my mother made me eat it. And I'm President of the United States and I'm not going to eat any more broccoli."

Answer: It was George Bush, the 41st U.S. president, in 1990! Explore more famous quotes at **http://www.lexmark.com/data/quote.html**, the Quotations Home Page.

Chase some waterfalls in EARTH SCIENCE.

InfoSeek Guide

This directory service looks for the number of times your keywords appear in the resources. For our "cats" example, the more times "cats" were mentioned in the resource, the higher it scored. InfoSeek gives you the "high score" items first. We got 100 hits. In the first ten, six were direct hits on cat care and health, two more were specialized on various health aspects, and two more were a cattery and a cat items company.

http://guide.infoseek.com/NS

Lycos, Inc. Home Page

Lycos is a very big search engine, and has been around a relatively long time. The folks who make it available claim that they have harvested 91% of the Web. That's a lot of information! They also offer The Lycos 250, which is a list of 250 of the most-visited sites on the Web, sorted by subject. The index found 9,876 hits for our little search on "cats." Of the first ten, there were three huge archives of CAT pictures, a university CATalog, a company selling CAT items, someone's personal page about her pet CAT, something about CATS (Citizens for an Alternative Tax System), and four useful CAT care Web sites. You can also get news and reviews at the Lycos server; they come from the Point (see separate listing.)

http://www.lycos.com

Get your hobby off the ground! Try Rockets in MODELS AND MINIATURES.

Magellan Internet Directory

This directory of reviewed sites has another twist, "green light" sites. If, at the time of review, "no objectionable material" was found, the site gets a green light—safe for kids—rating. Our "cats" search was limited to "green light" sites only. We got thirty-five hits from the green light area. The first ten included a cattery or two, several feline personal pages, and an exotic cat sanctuary. From the surface descriptions, nothing appeared to be about cat care. Inside one of the links was the Usenet cat care FAQ.

http://www.mckinley.com/

The Open Text Index

The Open Text Index is another very big search engine, and one of our favorites. Our search on "cats" found over 8,900 hits. Of the first ten, eight of them led us to the same Usenet FAQ on cat care. The other two were off-topic. As you use Open Text, you'll find there are options available to refine your searches. Practice will make your research perfect!

http://www.opentext.com:8080/

Lost your marbles? Find them in GAMES AND FUN.

Don't be a stick-in-the-MUD!

A B C D E F G H I J K L M N O P Q R S T U V W X Y Z

Point Communications Corporation

Point claims to just list the "top 5%" of the Internet. They say they only list the very best things, based on their selection criteria. They do have some nice things in their collection, but it seems very uneven to us. However, we do like to set our Web browser's start-up home page to go to the "Now" version of the Point at *http://www.pointcom.com/now/*. It's an easy way to read current news stories, follow weather news, and in general keep up with everything all at once.

http://www.pointcom.com/

NET FILES

What is the function of "The Hat" in the card game called Hungarian Tarokk?

ANSWER: Only on the Net would you learn this one! Tarokk is played with a deck of forty-two cards." An important part of the apparatus of this game is the hat, which should look as silly as possible. The original version is a sort of Austrian hunting hat with too many large feathers stuck into it at odd angles, but anything ridiculous-looking will do. Any player who has the XXI of trumps captured by an opponent's Skíz must wear the hat until someone else suffers the same misfortune." For a description of the deck, and the rules, go to *http://www.cs.man.ac.uk/cardgames/tarot/paskiev.html* off the Card Games home page!

Yahoo!

Yahoo! was originally a student project at Stanford University. This directory is fun and easy to use. Information is broken down into broad categories, like Science, or Education. By selecting any of these categories, you'll find more detailed sub-categories, like Education—K-12 (for kindergarten through 12th grade). Every so often you'll see a pair of sunglasses next to a listing. That means the folks who create Yahoo! thought the resource was way cool. Yahoo! is an excellent place to begin to explore the Internet. Trying our search on "cats" here found over 200 items Yahoo! thought were relevant. Some of the first ten led us to further collections of companies trying to sell cat supplies, as well as a directory of individual cat home pages. But within that ten we also found feline pet care and magazines on cats. There was one hit on CATskill Mountains, and one on sailing Hobie CAT sailboats.

http://www.yahoo.com

WEBWEAVING AND HTML
A Beginner's Guide to HTML

Itching to write your own cool home page? You'll need to learn Hypertext Markup Language (or HTML), so you can write the code to amaze the world with your Web creation. A very good place to learn HTML, and learn how to weave your Web pages, is A Beginner's Guide to HTML. Here you'll find step-by-step descriptions and instructions.

http://www.ncsa.uiuc.edu/demoWeb/html-primer.html

Read any good Web sites lately?

HTML Tutorial

Would you like to be a Webweaving expert, a person who knows the ins-and-outs of HTML? Then this HTML Tutorial is for you! Here you'll follow an extensive course in learning how to make the most rad World Wide Web pages anywhere. NOTE: This tutorial was created for one of the earliest Web browsers—Mosaic—but the information here is good for any Web browser such as Netscape, or whatever.

http://fire.clarkson.edu/doc/html/htut.html

Web 66: Cookbook

Wouldn't it be great to have your very own home page on the World Wide Web? You could write funny stories, talk about your pets, or discuss your favorite hobby. Creating a Web page is not too hard—it requires learning a simple computer language called Hypertext Markup Language (or HTML for short). There are many FREE tutorials to help you learn HTML, and the Web 66: Cookbook is a good one (especially if you have a Macintosh). Now that you've got a home page, where are you going to put it? Did you know you can also run your own server? Well, you'll want a direct line to the Internet to do that the most effective way, and that can be pretty expensive. Maybe you can help your school create its own Web server, instead. Those directions are here, too.

http://web66.coled.umn.edu/Cookbook/
contents.html

Curl up with a good Internet site.

INVERTEBRATES

The Cephalopod Page

An octopus is more than just any tentacled cephalopod that squirts ink and runs. It is the smartest of the invertebrates, with both a long- and a short-term memory. It learns through experience, and solves problems using trial and error. Check out this site about the octopus and its relatives, and you'll soon realize that these octopi are not just a bunch of suckers.

http://is.dal.ca/~wood/www.html

NET FILES

Who invented the world's first skateboard?

Answer: It may have been the world-famous female flyer, Amelia Earhart! See what you think at http://web1.si.edu/resource/150th/150trav/discover/d513a.htm, and check the entry for U.S. TERRITORIES, Howland Island, for more information on Earhart and her mysterious last flight.

Whooooooo will you find in BIRDS?

A
B
C
D
E
F
G
H
I
J
K
L
M
N
O
P
Q
R
S
T
U
V
W
X
Y
Z

The Lobster Institute

Can lobsters bite? No, they may be able to pinch you with their claws, but their teeth are in their stomachs. Take the lobster quiz and learn more about the King of Seafood. Then if you want, join a lobster chat. But if you feel the only way to appreciate a lobster is to eat it, the Lobster Institute proudly presents their cookbook pages, with recipes and tips for choosing the perfect lobster.

http://inferno.asap.um.maine.edu/lobster/info/info.html

NET FILES

In Greece, do they celebrate Christmas by decorating a tree?

Answer: Christmas trees are seldom seen. More common is a wooden bowl containing a cross wrapped in a sprig of basil (an aromatic herb). There is some water in the bowl to keep the plant fresh. According to the Christmas around the World home page, "Once a day, a family member, usually the mother, dips the cross and basil into some holy water and uses it to sprinkle water in each room of the house." This ritual is done to keep pesky sprites, called Killantzaroi, away from the house. They do things like put out hearth fires, make milk sour, and generally cause trouble. Luckily, they only come out for the twelve days of Christmas, and since they come down the chimney, keeping the fire burning the entire time is also a good deterrent. Read more at http://www.christmas.com/christmas.htm about Christmas traditions.

Sea Urchins Harvesters Association—California

Sea urchins may look spiky and threatening, but when you come right down to it they have no backbone. Harvested by divers, these colorful invertebrates are part of a growing industry, as they have become a popular food source. You can find out more about these creatures and how they saved the economy of the North Coast of California.

http://seaurchin.org/

WORMS

The Worm Page

Tractors and earthworms both plow the land, but you don't have to gas up a worm. Just give them some garbage or organic material and watch them go! Learn more about the different types of worms and how slimy, yet beneficial they are. Then choose your side as notable worm minds debate the greatest unsolved mystery of all—why are there so many worms all over the pavement after it rains?

http://www.en.com/users/wibble/worm.html

There can be more than one million worms in an acre of land!
Visit The Worm Page to learn about our friend, the worm.

The Worm Web

Just the dirt please. This is the techno-worm place. This is the place where worms are referred to as *C. elegans*, and the topics range from worms in space to "Immunologic Detection of Cytoplasmic Components that Segregate with the Germline Throughout the Life." If you just want to compost with worms, wiggle away from this site. But if you are into serious worm study you can dig deep here.

http://hyrax.bio.indiana.edu:8080/

JOKES AND RIDDLES

Kaitlyn's Knock-Knock Jokes and Riddles

Kaitlyn's only five, but she has dreams of being a children's doctor or maybe a figure skater! She's got some jokes and riddles here on her home page that may make you chuckle! Example: Q: Why did it take the monster ten months to finish a book? A: Because he wasn't very hungry. You can also send Kaitlyn your jokes and riddles, and she'll add them, giving you credit!

http://www.usa.net/wolfBayne/kaitlyn/
  default.html#nok

Kids' Humor

"Most books now say our sun is a star. But it still knows how to change back into a sun in the daytime." This is a little collection of things kids have said on class exams, and you may think they are pretty funny! Don't use any of these on your next test, though, unless your teacher has a good sense of humor!

http://www.cts.com/~netsales/herc/khumor.htm

Riddle du Jour

This site offers a new riddle or brainteaser every day and archives the last week's worth of riddles. Parental advisory: The site contains some fantasy/science-fiction artwork that may not be appropriate for your children. Since it has no impact on the other content, we've suggested they change it, because sometimes Webmasters just don't think about a young audience. Please preview this site.

http://www.new3.com/riddle/today.shtml

JUGGLING

Juggling Information Service

Believe it or not, the first thing a new juggler learns is how to juggle only one ball! But it gets much harder after that. The Juggling Information Service is for every juggler from beginner to experienced. There are tips and tricks, links to jugglers' home pages, a photo gallery, and even a movie theater with great performances and demonstrations!

http://www.hal.com/services/juggle/

NET FILES

What are the ten most endangered species in the world (not counting your little brother)?

ANSWER: Find the answer at http://envirolink.org/arrs/endangered.html. The list includes the tiger, the giant panda, the Asiatic black bear, and the black rhino, among others. The only plant on the list is the Himalayan Yew, "a slow growing conifer occurring throughout sections of Bhutan, Afghanistan, Pakistan, India, Nepal, Burma, and possibly China." It is used for extraction of a special drug that might help cure cancer, but people are cutting down too much of it and its habitat.

Juggling Jukebox Home Page

The worlds of technology and entertainment really come together here! If you ever run into the Juggling Jukebox, put your money in the machine and then watch and listen. Depending on your selection, you see a variety of juggling routines, and the "wired" juggler makes hi-tech music your ears won't believe. It's a fascinating real-life invention you can see and hear on the Net!

http://www.eskimo.com/~bret/jukebox/

KARTING AND SOAP BOX DERBY

THE Karting Website

Karting is a worldwide sport that hardly resembles the "go-cart" races of yesteryear. If you watch an old movie or TV show, you might see a kid rolling down the hill in a "go-cart." Go-carts were home-made little "cars," put together by kids with mom or dad's help. Sometimes the wheels came from a baby stroller or an old wagon. And other parts came from almost anywhere else. Well, times have changed! Today's "karts" are complicated, streamlined racing vehicles. Here, you'll find out all about the various forms of this racing hobby practiced all over the world. Latest news, track listings, organizations, and pictures are all here.

http://biggulp.callamer.com/~pete/karting/

KITES

Japan Close-up

Japanese kites have the most spectacular designs in the world! They are painted to look like fanciful birds, animals, insects, and fierce warriors. A kite isn't just a toy in Japan. It's closely tied to good luck and special occasions. Kites often have symbolic meaning, and were once associated with prayer. See some beautiful kite pictures and learn all about the history of kites, including miniature kites that fit inside a clam shell!

http://www.sumitomocorp.co.jp/closer/index.html

Let balloonists take you to new heights in Aviation and Airplanes.

Cheerful kites

against the sky, like confetti, or willful fish, pulling towards some bottomless sea. Did you know that once, some kites were illegal? The tsugaru, a strong, heavy kite made in Japan, was actually banned during the Second World War. These kites are noisy! They have a slim bit of rice paper on them that produces a deep scream in flight, remarkably similar to that of an approaching aircraft engine. Find out more about kites on the Web!

Kel's MicroKite Site... (MN_KiteNut)

"Any day is a good day to fly a kite," says Kel, "If you remember to put one in your pocket!" At this site you'll see the world's smallest kite ($1/16$ sq. inch) and learn how to make microkites of your own! You can fly these sub-one-inch kites indoors, or outside on windless days. Or tie one to your wheelchair and take off down the hospital hallways!

http://www.millcomm.com/~kitenut/

Kite Aerial Photography — Home Page

Ever wonder what your kite sees, as it soars high above your head? It gets a good view up there, and now there's a way for you to see it, too! Check the tools and techniques at this site, then go fly a kite!

http://www.ced.berkeley.edu/~cris/kap/

Origami: the fold to behold! Check out CRAFTS AND HOBBIES.

Lost your sheep?
Count them in FARMING AND
AGRICULTURE.

Kite Flier's Site

Did you know that some people use kites for fishing? Or that you can make a tetrahedral kite from drinking straws? Maybe you want to attend a kite festival, or just get some online tips for flying technique. This is the site you'll want to visit!

http://www.kfs.org/kites/cool.html

KNOTS

The Knotting Dictionary of Kännet

Clear black-and-white drawings and explanations of how each knot should be used (and not used) make this a must-see page for kids wanting to improve their rope skills. Besides common ones like Reef Knots, the Fisherman's Knot, and the Sheet Bend, here you'll find the Round Turn, the Prussick, and the Jug Sling Hitch, among others. The page is also available in Swedish, and Jan Andersson (who put the page together) is looking for people to help translate to lots of other languages. Also look for a link to Swedish Scouting's Home Page here.

http://www.ida.his.se/ida/~jan/knopar.eng.html

Frisbee is the Ultimate in
GAMES AND FUN.

A lot of us learned to tie a bowline by thinking of the end of the rope as a rabbit, and making a loop to represent his burrow-hole. We memorized this little speech by Elmer Fudd:

"The wabbit goes up, out of his hole, 'wound the back of the twee, and back down into his buwwow."
Visit **The Knotting Dictionary of Kännet** if you want to learn the ropes!

Some Useful Knots

Are you all thumbs when it comes to tying knots? You try to follow diagrams in books, but your fingers get tangled up like pretzels! Here's a site with some remarkably clear live-action MPEG movies that make the Bowline, Sheet Bend, Clove Hitch and Tautline Hitch knots seem as easy as tying a shoelace!

http://www.pcmp.caltech.edu/~tobi/knots

Lose yourself in a Museum.
SCIENCE has them all.

Chase some waterfalls in
EARTH SCIENCE.

A
B
C
D
E
F
G
H
I
J
K
L
M
N
O
P
Q
R
S
T
U
V
W
X
Y
Z

LANGUAGES AND ALPHABETS

ALPHABET

This site teaches "A" is for apple, "H" is for horse, then asks you to read the word "apple" and pick out the correct picture from among the several offered. This site has nice graphics but plays very slowly.

http://www.csn.net/children/

ALPHABET SOUP

When you're eating alphabet soup, have you ever tried to spell your name on the edge of the soup bowl? Ever notice you never have the right assortment of letters? We're including this site as an example of two things: one, it's amazing the type of information you can find on the Net; and two, some people have way too much time on their hands if they have time to count the letters in a can of soup!

http://www.gigaplex.com/wow/food/soup.htm

El Alphabeto Español

Do you know the alphabet? "Sure," you say, "I learned that in nursery school." However, every language has a different alphabet. Sometimes the letters are completely different from English, and other times the letters may be the same but pronounced differently. With Spanish, the alphabet is the same as English, but the pronunciation is different. You can learn how a good part of the Spanish alphabet is pronounced by taking a glimpse at the Ralph Bunche School *El Alphabeto Español* page. Each letter also has a nice drawing.

http://mac94.ralphbunche.rbs.edu/spanish.html

Ethnologue Database

What languages do they speak in Croatia? Did you know that in Kenya, at least fifty-eight languages are spoken, including Kenyan Sign Language? You can find any country on this page, and then discover which languages are spoken in that country. Also find out how different languages are related using the language family tree. The Inuit language, Aleut, is related to the Russian Siberian language, Yupik. Do you know why that could be?

http://www.ala.doc.ic.ac.uk/~rap/Ethnologue/

For Spelling Out Loud

You might find this one interesting. Enter a word or a phrase, and a sound file is built for you that spells it back. You can get the words "spelled" back in a male, Midwestern-American accent. You can even get the word spelled back to you using the phonetic radio alphabet (Alpha, Bravo, Charlie). Save the sound files and build your own Web-based spelling bees!

http://medlib.jsc.nasa.gov/cgi-bin/sp.snd

Human-Languages Page

Do you like to amaze people by saying things in a different language? Here's the place to get some more vocabulary words in your favorite language. There are tons of links to every imaginable tongue. You'll also find lots of translating dictionaries, including a project called The Internet Dictionary, a multi-lingual dictionary created by Internet users!

http://www.willamette.edu/~tjones/
  Language-Page.html

Morse Code and other Phonetic Alphabets

Besides Morse Code, various United States and other military alphabets are here. Words are sometimes easier to understand than letters when broadcast over radios. It's clearer for a listener to hear "Victor" when you mean "V." "V" by itself sounds like "E" or "B" or "D," and may be misunderstood. So many military and civilian radio broadcasters use an alphabet made of words rather than letters.

http://www.soton.ac.uk/~scp93ch/refer/
  alphabet.html

Right to Left Software Home Page

What would happen if alien dinosaurs came to explore our planet? With all the languages spoken here, they would surely wonder how to communicate. If you are a Windows user, you can download the shareware version of "Earth Words" to see what the aliens recorded with their dino-flex movie camera! Even if you don't use Windows, you can learn how to speak words for common objects in many languages online. Compare the sound of "bicycle" or "tree" in different languages from all over the Earth. Become a Net citizen!

http://www.execpc.com/~rtls/

Yamada Language Guides

Wow! From Afrikaans to Yiddish, this is a set of guides to 103 languages! (Guess they don't have a language starting with Z.) But, let's say you wanted to learn some Italian. You could look up phrases that you would need to know if you were traveling to Italy, find information about Italian culture and history, get the daily news in Italian, even dissect a frog in Italian! Now, that last one is REALLY useful! Besides languages, though, this gives links to cultural and historical information about the people who speak these languages. Check the Lakota home page for example, or the Inuit, or even pages for Klingon or the languages from J.R.R. Tolkien's books.

http://babel.uoregon.edu/yamada/guides.html

BRAILLE

General Braille Information

Imagine reading words by the way they feel to your touch. That's one of the ways blind people read, by feeling the little bumps, which represent letters. This is Braille, and you can learn about it at the General Braille Information page. It also includes a cool tutorial that shows how all the Braille letters look.

http://disserv.stu.umn.edu/AltForm/brl-guide.html

CYRILLIC

Friends and Partners—Cyrillic Text

The Russian alphabet is very different from the one we use in English, the Latin alphabet. To get a look at it, and learn how to pronounce the letters, try this site. You'll also find links to Cyrillic fonts on the Net, and instructions on how to view Web pages in Cyrillic. Also check *http://ASUdesign.eas.asu.edu/places/Bulgaria/cyr/* for more, as well as *http://www.vostok.com/RUS_FONT/FONT_ENG.htm* for the fonts.

http://solar.rtd.utk.edu/friends/cyrillic/cyrillic.html

NET FILES

On May 18, 1980, Mount St. Helens erupted in Washington State. It was a violent explosion that resulted in massive changes in the landscape. Most dangerous were the huge mud slides, which traveled at up to 30 miles per hour, carrying boulders measuring twenty feet across. The mud slides flattened everything in their paths. They often took houses and bridges miles downstream from where they belonged. Wait—volcanoes erupt lava, don't they? So, where did all the water and mud come from.?

Answer: Mount St. Helens did erupt hot lava and volcanic gases, as well as rocks, ash, and other debris. These combined to trigger enormous avalanches. Most of the water that poured across the surface of the mountain came from the debris itself. This included water that had been trapped inside the volcano, and melting blocks of ice that had been glaciers before the mountain erupted. Find out more at http://volcano.und.nodak.edu/vwdocs/msh/msh.html.

DAKOTA

The Dakota Language Homepage

As you were growing up, you learned your language. Most likely, you heard other people speak it, and then you spoke the sounds yourself. Here's a way to do just that while you learn the Dakota language, one of many Native American Indian languages. Native speakers help you make the sounds of the Dakota language as you explore a color-coded language "keyboard."

http://swcc.cc.sd.us/daklang/maps/
langmap.map?73,49

Let balloonists take you to new heights in Aviation and Airplanes.

A
B
C
D
E
F
G
H
I
J
K
L
M
N
O
P
Q
R
S
T
U
V
W
X
Y
Z

ENGLISH
English as a Second Language

A new family has moved into your neighborhood. You and your sister decide to visit them and invite them to play. As you knock on the door, three kids race to it and greet you. They don't speak English, but they want to learn! Here's a page to help you teach them. One of the best ways to learn a language is to hang around other kids! Bet you'll pick up some of their language, too.

http://www.ed.uiuc.edu/edpsy-387/rongchang-li/esl/

FRENCH
French Lesson Home Page

A language can really come in handy! Sometimes it's hard to learn a foreign language if you can't hear a real native speaker of the language. Here's a way to learn how to pronounce French without having to go to a foreign country. You'll also discover how to write common words. Papa? That's French for daddy! See, it's not so hard!

http://teleglobe.ca/%7Eleo/french.html

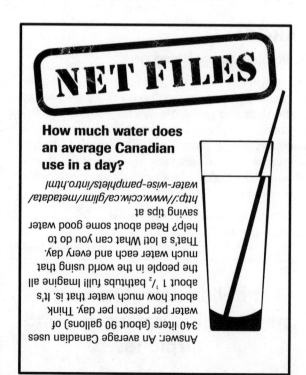

NET FILES

How much water does an average Canadian use in a day?

Answer: An average Canadian uses 340 liters (about 90 gallons) of water per person per day. Think about how much water that is. It's about 1 ½ bathtubs full! Imagine all the people in the world using that much water each and every day. That's a lot! What can you do to help? Read about some good water saving tips at http://www.cciw.ca/glimr/metadata/water-wise-pamphlets/intro.html

GAELIC
Gaelic and Gaelic Culture

If you're interested in Irish or Scottish variants of Gaelic, or other Celtic languages, check this site. You'll find lots on the various Gaelic languages, plus links to music, products, literature, and more. One of the links has a tutorial in Welsh.

http://sunsite.unc.edu/gaelic/gaelic.html

HAWAIIAN
Ernie's Learn to Speak a Little Hawaiian

Mahalo nui loa (thank you very much), Ernie, for this page, which teaches just a little Hawaiian. You'll find pronunciation notes and a little glossary.

http://www.mhpcc.edu/otherpages/ernie/ernie1.html

Native Tongue—Discover the Hawaiian Language

Learn about petroglyphs—ancient pictographs found on rocks all over the Hawaiian Islands. What do they mean? Who left them there for us to discover? Listen to audio clips of Hawaiian vowels, and many common words and phrases. Check out this site *wiki-wiki* (fast)!

http://www.aloha-hawaii.com/a_speaking.html

HEBREW
Sounds Of Israel — The Hebrew Alphabet

You can see and hear pronunciations of the Hebrew alphabet letters at this site. There are pictures of what each letter looks like in its script and print forms. Check the links to Hebrew stories and other language notes, and to the page for numbers and counting in Hebrew.

http://www.macom.co.il/hebrew/the.alphabet.html

ICELANDIC
Icelandic Alphabet

If you're wondering what those strange runes in Icelandic words are, check this page. There's also a handy pronunciation guide.

http://www.cs.rpi.edu/~ulfar/
    IcelandicAlphabet.html

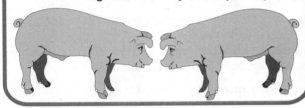

ODAY OUYAY ETGAY A ICKKAY OUTAY OFAY EADINGRAY IGPAY ATINLAY?

enThay ointpay ouryay rowserbay otay The Web in Pig Latin! andAy avehay unfay!

MIDDLE EGYPTIAN

Middle Egyptian

Want to be Indiana Jones someday? Better learn about hieroglyphics so you can read the markings inside the pyramids! Hey, where's the EXIT sign? This is just the site for that, and you can even type in your name and get it back in hieroglyphs!

http://weblifac.ens-cachan.fr/Portraits/
  S.ROSMORDUC/EgyptienE.html

PIG LATIN

Pig Latin Converter... or something

Now here's something to confuse your teacher. Go to this site and enter the location of a familiar Web page you've seen a million times. You'll get to the site, all right. But the whole thing will be in Pig Latin! "Oh, teacher, there's something wrong with my browser!" Worse, every link you follow from that site will be in Pig Latin too! Your only hope is to open a new site. Avehay unfay!

http://voyager.cns.ohiou.edu/~jrantane/menu/
  pig.html

RADIO ALPHABET

Radio Alphabet

Here's the radio alphabet, used in international aviation and other applications. What makes this page special is the addition of pronunciation files, so you can hear how to say the words properly. <SQUAAAAWK!> Roger that, ALPHA BRAVO CHARLIE! <SQUAAAWK!>

http://aviation.jsc.nasa.gov/alphabet.html

Deaf World Web's Deaf CyberKids

Are you a member of the deaf community? Here's a place where you can find a pen-pal, read stories, and see art created by other deaf kids. Steer your parents to the parent's guide, too. It has ways for them to understand the deaf culture in which you live.

http://deafworldweb.org/dww/kids/

Interactive ASL and Braille Guide

Fingerspelling is one way to communicate with folks who can't hear. Or it's a secret language you and your friend can use when the teacher says "No Talking!" Here's an interactive fingerspelling guide, and a quiz. See how fast you can "sign" your name! There's also a Braille guide at this site.

http://www.disserv.stu.umn.edu/AltForm/

SIGN LANGUAGES

Sign Language

Input any word, and see it spelled in the sign language finger alphabet! This works better for some words than others. Remember that finger-spelling is done in three dimensions; sometimes the letters have associated hand motions. Maybe this site will put up some QuickTime movies someday. Still, try it out!

http://www.mathart.com/signs/sign.html

A
B
C
D
E
F
G
H
I
J
K
L
M
N
O
P
Q
R
S
T
U
V
W
X
Y
Z

"What matters deafness of the ear, when the mind hears. The one true deafness, the incurable deafness, is that of the mind."

—— *Victor Hugo, 1845*

Visit Deaf World Web's Deaf CyberKids page and open your mind!

SPANISH

Web Spanish Lessons, by Tyler Jones

Sometimes it's tough to learn a new language if you don't know how it sounds. Here are some Spanish lessons, complete with the pronunciations which you can hear! This page will also test you on translations of written phrases. It's like having your own built-in Spanish teacher! There are links to similar pages teaching French and Italian.

http://www.willamette.edu/~tjones/Spanish/
    Spanish-main.html

LATINO

Azteca Home Page

Did you know many kids in the United States are of Mexican descent? They are proudly called *Chicanos y Chicanas.* Understanding what it means to be a Chicano means many things. It's music, history, culture, and language. For anyone wanting to understand about being Chicano, the Azteca Home Page is a good place to start.

http://www.directnet.com/~mario/aztec/

LatinoWeb

BIENVENIDO! That's Spanish for "Welcome," one of the first things you'll see on the LatinoWeb, one part of the Internet set aside for things Latino. If you want to see what's hot on the Internet for Latinos, LatinoWeb has much to see. News, music, cool sites—they are all here.

http://www.catalog.com/favision/latnoweb

Niños y Niñas

For many Latin American kids, surfing the Internet can be tough. Just about everything is in English, and for Spanish speakers, this can be difficult. Fortunately, there is a good starting point for Spanish-speaking kids learning to use the Internet. It's called *Niños y Niñas,* and all instructions and descriptions of some great Internet sites are in Spanish. *Es* cool!

http://www.internet.com.mx/naveg/ninos.html

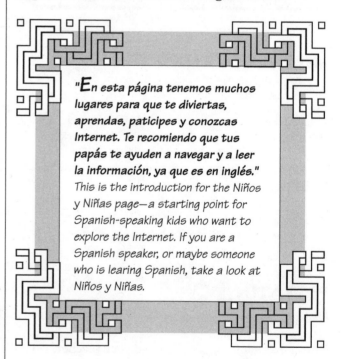

"En esta página tenemos muchos lugares para que te diviertas, aprendas, patícipes y conozcas Internet. Te recomiendo que tus papás te ayuden a navegar y a leer la información, ya que es en inglés." This is the introduction for the Niños y Niñas page—a starting point for Spanish-speaking kids who want to explore the Internet. If you are a Spanish speaker, or maybe someone who is learing Spanish, take a look at Niños y Niñas.

¿Quien o Que es El Maga?

El Maga is a very special computer. It survives by eating words written in Spanish. This might be a strange way to stay alive, but it's true! If you want to practice Spanish, give El Maga a visit. If you're lucky, El Maga might give you an answer.

http://communication.ucsd.edu/LCHC/LCM/
    letterspage.html

CULTURE

Chicano Mural Tour

Can you picture an art museum that's completely outside? Murals are paintings on buildings, and they turn the outdoors into an art gallery. Some of the best mural artists are Latino. In the past, many Latino artists couldn't get their work placed in art museums. Instead, they painted walls, hallways, all kinds of places, producing some beautiful murals. In Los Angeles, with its large Latino population, there are many, many murals. Take a tour of some of the best of these murals, and see what an outdoors art museum looks like!

http://latino.sscnet.ucla.edu/murals/Sparc/
sparctour.html

Lotoreia Mexican Bingo Games

Latinos like to play a fun game called *Lotoreia*. It's like Bingo, but has colorful pictures with Spanish names instead of numbers and letters. Would you like to play the game? You can! Go to the *Lotoreia* page on the World Wide Web. It's fun!

http://www.mercado.com:80/juventud/loteria/
loteria.htm

HISTORY

Hispanics in the American Revolution

Who is Marshall Bernardo de Gálvez? Well, among other things, he is who the city of Galveston, Texas is named for, and he is a hero of the American Revolutionary War. This Web page says, "between 1779 and 1785, Marshall Bernardo de Gálvez... defeated the British in Baton Rouge, Mobile, Pensacola, St. Louis and Fort St. Joseph, Michigan. These victories relieved British pressure on General George Washington's armies and helped open supply lines for money and military goods from Spain, France, Cuba and Mexico." There might not have been a United States of America if de Gálvez hadn't helped. Learn more about this American hero at the Hispanics in the American Revolution page.

http://www.clark.net/pub/jgbustam/galvez/
galvez.html

Hispanos Famosos

What do Roman Emperor Hadrian, Nobel Prize-winning scientist Luis Leloir, and painter Pablo Picasso have in common? They are all famous Hispanics—people with a Spanish heritage. Throughout history Hispanic people have been great scientists, soldiers, political leaders, artists, and musicians. Read about many famous and accomplished Hispanics here—and this page is in both English and Spanish!

http://www.clark.net/pub/jgbustam/famosos/
famosos.html

Landmarks of Hispanic LA

What do you think of when you hear someone say Los Angeles, California? Maybe movie stars come to mind, or surfers, or rock musicians. Los Angeles, though, is a very old center of American Hispanic and Latino culture. To understand Los Angeles, you have to understand its Latin roots. The Landmarks of Hispanic LA page is a good place to begin. Here you'll read about some of Los Angeles' earliest history, and see the landmarks where the history took place.

http://www.usc.edu/Library/Ref/Ethnic/
la_landmarks_hispan.html

LIBRARIES

The CIC Electronic Journals Collection

You've got a tough school assignment, and you might be wondering if you can find an article in some publication that can help you. There are e-zines (electronic magazines) and journals available on the Internet. The problem is—how to find these resources? A good place to start is the CIC Electronic Journals Collection (EJC). Here you'll find a good number of quality electronic magazines and journals on a variety of subjects. Most of the material is written for college-level research, but it sure can't hurt your research to get the most current material available!!

http://ejournals.cic.net/

A B C D E F G H I J K L M N O P Q R S T U V W X Y Z

Internet Public Library

Wouldn't it be great to have a public library available twenty-four hours a day? Well, you have one! The Internet Public Library is a project by the library school at the University of Michigan, and you'll find a whole host of material available to you for research projects. There are links to many useful resources on the Internet, guides to help you use the Internet, and librarians are available to help you with your studies in a really cool MOO (a MOO is a type of software that lets you interact live with other people in a computer-created world).

http://ipl.sils.umich.edu/index.text.html

Library of Congress World Wide Web Page

The U.S. Library of Congress is the world's largest single collection of library materials anywhere. It would be great if everything in the library was available to view on the Internet, but that's not possible right now. However, the folks at the Library of Congress have made a large amount of information available here. From their home page on the World Wide Web, you can view beautiful graphic images of exhibits such as original photographs from the U.S. Civil War, or see replications of documents from Columbus' voyages to America. You can also connect easily to the Library of Congress online catalog (if you have telnet software,) and there are also convenient links to many U.S. government sites.

http://lcweb.loc.gov/

SJCPL's List of Public Libraries with Gopher/WWW Services

Public libraries all over the world are active on the Internet. Some have their library online catalogs available, others have gopher sites, and yet others have great World Wide Web home pages. To see a list of many public libraries with Internet services, take a look at the SJCPL List of Public Libraries with Gopher/WWW Services. On most of the public library sites you'll find links to great resources on the Internet, and maybe you'll see your own neighborhood library on the list!

http://sjcpl.lib.in.us/homepage/PublicLibraries/
  PubLibSrvsGpherWWW.html#wwwsrv

Did you know that the longest held, confirmed POW (Prisoner of War) in U.S. history was **Lt. Everett Alvarez**? He flew a jet plane from an aircraft carrier, was shot down, but somehow landed safely. He was then captured as a POW and held for eight long years. Read about other famous folks by taking a peek at Hispanos Famosos.

LISTS

The List Server Page

In an attempt to make the whole discussion list subscription process easier, this site makes it all as easy as point and click! So far, there are only about a thousand lists available here. New lists are being added all the time, though, so keep looking if you don't find one of interest the first time.

http://www.cuc.edu/cgi-bin/listservform.pl

ListWebber II

Have you ever read something on a discussion list months ago, and wished you could find that information again? Or maybe you want to search the archive library of a list you don't subscribe to. This site makes that process fairly easy. Not all lists archive old messages, and some require that you be a subscriber before you can read the archives. ListWebber supports only Listserv and Listproc. The LWGate is another that does this, and supports mailing lists provided by Listserv, List Processor 6, Majordomo, and SmartList servers. It's at *http://www.netspace.org/users/dwb/lwgate.html* if you want to try it, but there are only a small number of lists in the database so far.

http://www.netspace.org/users/dwb/lwgate.html

Liszt: Searchable Directory of e-Mail Discussion Groups

Need a mailing list or a newsgroup? There are over 23,000 lists and 13,000 newsgroups here, all searchable by word or phrase. Your Internet service provider may not give you access to all these newsgroups, but at least you'll know they exist. Maybe you can ask your provider to carry them for you. Parental advisory: many of these lists are not for children.

http://www.liszt.com/

Publicly Accessible Mailing Lists

This mega-list of discussion groups is arranged by subject, for your searching pleasure. Parental advisory: many of these lists are not for children.

http://www.neosoft.com/internet/paml/

Search for Mailing Lists

You ought to be able to find a discussion list of interest here: there are over 12,000 choices! Just enter a word, such as "penpal" or "horse," and you'll get a list of items containing that word. For example, your "horse" search will pull up EQUINE-L and a Model Horse Digest, among several others. To get more information on a particular list, follow the instructions on the screen.

http://scwww.ucs.indiana.edu/mlarchive/

tile.net/listserv

Want to know what the most popular mailing list is? It's the e-mail version of David Letterman's "Top Ten List!" Here, you'll find a list of all the Listserv lists with over 1,000 subscribers. You can also find all the lists sponsored by a particular organization, or see lists arranged by host country, or subject. It's important to note that this site only contains lists run by Listserv software. Listproc, Majordomo, and other mailing lists are not included. This is unfortunate, but maybe by the time you read this, they will keep statistics on those lists, too.

http://tile.net/listserv/

Usenet Newsgroups

Usenet is a huge electronic e-mail messaging system. Created almost fifteen years ago, it now covers almost every imaginable topic. The topics discussed range from the banal to the bizarre. Obtaining access to Usenet depends on your Internet service provider, and not all Usenet discussions (called newsgroups) are available through all providers. You can read newsgroups through many World Wide Web browsers, or you can use a separate application. Ask your provider for suggestions. Here are some potentially worthwhile Usenet newsgroups for parents and caregivers:

misc.kids If you have a question about kids, this is a good place to post a message. This is a very active newsgroup, and many good ideas are exchanged.

misc.kids.computers This is a more focused newsgroup, with participants sharing ideas and tips on kids and their computers. This is also a good place to learn about software, CD-ROMs, and multimedia titles for children.

misc.kids.consumers If you want to learn about products for kids, this is a good newsgroup to read.

misc.kids.health If you have questions about your child's health, first contact your doctor. After that, you might find this newsgroup helpful.

Who said the following:

"If you would not be forgotten as soon as you are dead and rotten, either write things worth reading or do things worth the writing."

Answer: Benjamin Franklin, who, as an inventor, scientist, and statesman, certainly followed his own advice! Learn more about this famous American at *http://sln.fi.edu/franklin/rotten.html.*

A
B
C
D
E
F
G
H
I
J
K
L
M
N
O
P
Q
R
S
T
U
V
W
X
Y
Z

LISTS—DISCUSSION AND NEWSGROUPS FOR CHILDREN

Usenet Newsgroups for Kids

Usenet is like a huge e-mail party where people get together to exchange messages on all kinds of subjects. Part of Usenet is just for kids. However, it is IMPORTANT TO REMEMBER THE FOLLOWING: Even in areas set aside for kids, adults can send messages. You might even find adults pretending to be kids. Also, sometimes the kids in these discussion groups can say things you might not like. On Usenet, you never have to read, or believe, everything you see. Access to Usenet depends on your Internet service provider, and not all Usenet discussions (called newsgroups) are available through all providers. You can read newsgroups through many World Wide Web browsers, or you may use a separate application. Ask your provider for suggestions, and ask your parents or teacher for help.

Here are a few Usenet groups for kids:

k12.chat.elementary   Here kids, mainly between the ages of 11 and 13 years, exchange messages. Many are looking for keypals.

alt.kids-talk   Another newsgroup for kids, but this area can include high schoolers and younger kids.

alt.tv.nickelodeon   This newsgroup is dedicated to the first TV network just for kids.

DEAFKIDS

One problem with being deaf is that not everyone understands what it is like. With DEAFKIDS, though, there are always other kids who know exactly what it is like to be deaf. Take a little time and get in on the written conversation!

List Address: deafkids@sjuvm.stjohns.edu

Subscription Address: listserv@sjuvm.stjohns.edu

Take a ride on a Carousel in AMUSEMENT PARKS.

NET FILES

Why do tropical cyclones winds rotate counter-clockwise in the Northern Hemisphere, but clockwise in the Southern Hemisphere?

Answer: The reason is that the earth's rotation sets up a force—called the Coriolis force—that pulls the winds to the right in the Northern Hemisphere and to the left in the Southern Hemisphere. So when a low pressure area starts to form north of the equator, the surface winds will flow inward trying to fill in the low pressure area and will be deflected to the right. A counter-clockwise rotation will start. The opposite will occur south of the equator. Find out more at the hurricanes, typhoons, and tropical cyclones FAQ at ftp::/downdry.atmos.colostate.edu/pub/TCfaq/

Discussion Lists: Mail Server Commands

Your pen-pal in Michigan says you should subscribe to his favorite discussion group mailing list on snakes. That's great, but how the heck do you subscribe? And does it cost money? You'll be glad to know that, usually, list discussion groups are free. To subscribe, you send a mail message to a computer running the mailing list software. Because the subscription process is done by that remote computer, you need to send your request in a way the computer can understand. This means you have to use certain common commands to tell the computer what you want to do. That wouldn't be too hard, except that discussion lists use different software packages to distribute their mail—some popular ones are called Revised Listserv (also called BITNET Listserv), Unix ListProcessor (or Listproc), Mailbase, Mailserv, and Majordomo. And they all use different commands! James Milles has sorted it all out. Check this site to learn how to talk to all the major discussion group list mailers!

http://lawlib.slu.edu/training/mailser.htm

FISH-JUNIOR

If you like fish and want to learn about marine science, then FISH-JUNIOR is an online conversation you'll want to join. Marine scientists from around the world are monitoring FISH-JUNIOR to help kids learn about fish and marine science. This is almost as good as a snorkeling trip to the Bahamas!

List Address: **fish-junior@searn.sunet.se**

Subscription Address: **listserv@searn.sunet.se**

Kidlink and Kidcafe

You know the world's got some big problems. Why not talk to other kids and see if you can help solve some of them? Make new friends, and have some fun with kids from 72 different countries on the Kidcafe discussions. Take a look at the Kidlink mailing list page, and start e-mailing new friends. Show this to your teacher and parents, too. They'll find lots of good information about how to share a project with a class in another country.

http://www.kidlink.org/home-txt.html

KIDZMAIL

How would you like to contact kids from around the world and share messages? You could ask them about life in their country. Make a new *keypal* (that's like a pen pal, but one you send e-mail to, using a *key*board rather than using regular mail). KIDZMAIL is a good place to connect with kids the world over, and to maybe make friends from places you've never even heard of!

List Address: **kidzmail@asuvm.inre.asu.edu**

Subscription Address: **listserv@asuvm.inre.asu.edu**

Talknow

Arabs and Jews have been in conflict for many years. Things are changing, though, and just by talking together, Jews and Arabs are establishing friendships. Talknow is an Internet mailing list just for Arab and Jewish kids to talk to each other. Adults may lurk, that is, they may look at the messages, but only kids can participate!

List Address: **talknow@csf.colorado.edu**

Subscription Address: **listproc@csf.colorado.edu**

Y-Rights

Kids have rights, too! The question is, what rights do they have? Y-Rights is an electronic mailing list where discussion of the rights of kids and teenagers is front and center. Parents, teachers, kids, and others talk about the give-and-take of minors and their legal status. Younger children may have a hard time keeping up with the conversation, but teens may find this very interesting. For parents, keeping tabs and providing input on the rights of kids is essential.

List Address: **y-rights@sjuvm.stjohns.edu**

Subscription Address: **listserv@sjuvm.stjohns.edu**

LISTS—DISCUSSION AND NEWSGROUPS FOR PARENTS AND CAREGIVERS

DAYCARE-L

Running a daycare operation, whether from the home or in a center, is a challenging endeavor encompassing business skills, child psychology, parent psychology, and fun. To get in contact with other daycare operators, subscribe to DAYCARE-L, and learn with other professionals.

List Address: **daycare-l@io.org**

Subscription Address: **majordomo@io.org**

DTS-L (Dead Teachers Society)

Education is the key to so many things, including our children's and nation's future. The Dead Teachers Society, and its spin-off electronic discussion list, DTS-L, is a forum to discuss education. The conversations here are freewheeling and wide-ranging, but if you care about education, you will want to take part. Share your thoughts and learn from others.

List Address: **dts-l@iubvm.ucs.indiana.edu**

Subscription Address: **listserv@iubvm.ucs. indiana.edu**

May the force be with you in Physics.

A
B
C
D
E
F
G
H
I
J
K
L
M
N
O
P
Q
R
S
T
U
V
W
X
Y
Z

FATHER-L

FATHER-L is an e-mail conference dedicated to discussing the importance of fathers in children's lives. The American family is now rarely like *Father Knows Best*. Roles are changing, families are being reconfigured, and the role of a father is not always clear. Father-L gives dads a chance to discuss how best to help raise kids as the paternal role changes.

List Address: father-l@vm1.spcs.umn.edu

Subscription Address: listserv@vm1.spcs.umn.edu

HOME-ED and HOME-ED-POLITICS

Lots of kids don't walk very far to go to school. In fact, it's right in their own homes! Home schooling is growing by leaps and bounds. With approximately one million students in home school programs (up from a few thousand in the 1960s), there are increasingly more and more home school parents and caregivers to share ideas with. HOME-ED is one Internet mailing list that gives parents a chance to do this. HOME-ED-POLITICS focuses on legislative and other governmental issues of concern for home school providers.

List Address: home-ed@mainstream.com or home-ed-politics@mainstream.com

Subscription Address: listproc@mainstream.com

IECC, International E-Mail Classroom Connections

One of the great aspects of the Internet is that it provides children with the opportunity to reach well beyond their community to kids just about anywhere. International E-Mail Classroom Connections, or IECC, is a list for teachers to find other teachers and classes to enable interaction between students. While this is not a list for individuals to make contact one to another, it is a way for teachers to find classes their students can write to. If you are a teacher, definitely take a look. If you are a parent or caregiver, mention IECC to your child's teacher. A whole new way of communicating may well open up.

List Address: iecc@stolaf.edu

Subscription Address: iecc-request@stolaf.edu

NET FILES

What can weigh more than 600 pounds, measure more than 12 feet long, and eat the equivalent of 64 McDonald's hamburgers in one day?

Answer: A Siberian tiger, according to the Rhinos and Tigers and Bears—Oh My! page. In the wild, Siberian tigers eat large animals such as deer and cattle. In captivity at the Knoxville, Tennessee Zoo, they eat about six pounds of raw meat a day. Find it at http://loki.ur.utk.edu/ut2kids/zoo/zoo.html

KIDSPHERE

KIDSPHERE is a mailing list with the fundamental goal of establishing an international network for children. Some kids may find the discussion useful, but most of the people participating are adults. If your intention is to learn what tools are available on the Internet for working with children, KIDSPHERE is a good discussion to drop in on.

List Address: kidsphere@vms.cis.pitt.edu

Subscription Address: kidsphere-request@vms.cis.pitt.edu

Our-Kids

Parents and caregivers of children with developmental delay can benefit from sharing with other parents and caregivers. Our-Kids is an Internet mailing list that gives this opportunity. It's called "Our-Kids" to avoid any labeling, just to provide a place where adults can interact about the special kids they love.

List Address: our-kids@tbag.osc.edu

Subscription Address: majordomo@tbag.osc.edu

MAGIC TRICKS

Hocus Pocus Palace

Dare to challenge The Great Mysto in a game of mind-reading and clairvoyance! Through magical and as yet unexplainable Internet protocols, The Great Mysto will astound you with his long-distance feats. Doubters may scoff and say these are simple "magic square" tricks, but we're not so sure. (How did he know we were thinking of Marge Simpson?) You'll laugh out loud at the catalog of old magic trick apparatus, revealed and explained. O Great Mysto, you have a truly fun site!

http://www.teleport.com/~jrolsen/index.shtml

Magic Show

Abracadabra! The magic trick amazes the audience. You hear them whisper to each other "That's impossible! How do they do it?" Everyone loves a magic show. The only thing better than watching a magic show is being the magician yourself. This Web magazine has articles about professional magicians who amaze people, show after show. Each issue also contains secrets of how to perform tricks yourself! There are even movie clips of tricks being performed. Whether you want to learn magic or just enjoy it, this site has something for you. Don't forget the hat (and the rabbit)!

http://www.uelectric.com/magicshow/

Math Magic Activities

Put one end of a rope in each of your friend's hands and ask her to tie a knot without dropping the rope. Or amaze your friends with card tricks or other stunts. It's not magic, it's math!

http://www.scri.fsu.edu/~dennisl/topics/
  math_magic.html

The Unofficial David Copperfield Homepage

A lot of people think David Copperfield is the greatest magician and illusionist alive today. After all, he "vanished" the Statue of Liberty in front of a live audience (even its radar "blip" went away), and he also walked through the Great Wall of China. We attended one of his stage shows and it sure looked like he was *flying* around the stage to us! This page will tell you about David's childhood, his current schedule, and his illusions; but it does not give away any of his secrets!

http://www.rit.edu/~dbh6913/DavCop/copidx.html

MAMMALS

See also: CATS, DOGS, FARMING AND AGRICULTURE, HORSES, PETS AND PET CARE

California Department of Fish and Game

Look at that cute little dog! Wait, that's not a dog, it's a San Joaquin Kit Fox! They look just like small dogs with big ears. This endangered species is about 32 inches long, but 12 inches of that is its luxurious tail! You can see one at this site, along with great photos of lots of other mammals, like bobcats, porcupines, and raccoons.

http://darkstar.delta.dfg.ca.gov/species/
  mammal.html

The Electronic Zoo

This page is the best place to start your search for animal info on the Web. For zoo animals and wildlife, check in the "Exotics" category under the "Animals" selection. Other mammals (dogs, cats, ferrets, pigs, cows, horses, etc.) have their own sections.

http://netvet.wustl.edu/e-zoo.htm

For happy hedgehogs see PETS AND PET CARE.

Get your hobby off the ground! Try Rockets in MODELS AND MINIATURES.

A
B
C
D
E
F
G
H
I
J
K
L
M
N
O
P
Q
R
S
T
U
V
W
X
Y
Z

Mammals Home Page

Mammals are divided into three subclasses. They include the pouched mammals (look, it's a kangaroo!) known as marsupials. Another kind of mammal is in the subclass Placentalia. Most mammals are in this category. The third subclass includes egg-laying mammals (OK, a platypus, anything else?) such as the Spiny Anteater! See pictures of these unusual mammals here. Stop by today.

http://edx1.educ.monash.edu.au/~juanda/vcm/
    mammals.htm

Sounds of the World's Animals

Everybody knows that when a dog barks, he's saying "woof-woof," right? Well, not *everybody* knows that! A French dog says "ouah ouah," while a Japanese dog says "wanwan!" In Sweden, the dogs say "vov vov" and in the Ukraine, you'll find them saying "gaf-gaf"! This is a Web page full of what the world thinks various animals sound like. There's an audio sound file for each animal, so you can hear and decide for yourself which language "says it best."

http://www.georgetown.edu/cball/animals/
    animals.html

BEARS

North Cascades National Park: Grizzly Bear

Think you can tell the difference between a grizzly and a black bear? Guess what, black bears are not always black, and grizzly bears are not always grey-grizzled—making it very difficult (at times) to tell which is which. Learn the distinguishing characteristics that set these highly intelligent animals apart. Discover what precautions you can take to avoid a confrontation when you are camping or hiking in the places they call home. Will you know what to do if an encounter becomes unavoidable? You will if you stop in here.

http://www.halcyon.com/rdpayne/
    ncnp-grizzly.html

Polar Bears

Do polar bears really like winter? You bet they do! In fact, polar bears would rather live on ice than on land. Discover more about their chilly lifestyle and learn why you can't sneak up on a polar bear. (They can smell you coming up to twenty miles away.)

http://www.bev.net/education/SeaWorld/
    polar_bears/pbindex.html

CAT FAMILY
The BIGGER Big Cats Info Page

Have you ever known of a cat that swims? The fishing cat is the best swimmer of all cats. Not only that, as its name implies, it fishes, too! By using its long claws as fishhooks, it can catch fish, crayfish, mollusks, rodents, reptiles, and other small animals. To learn more about wild cats, visit The BIGGER Big Cats Info Page and discover (among other things) what strange sleeping habits the Margay has.

http://sys3.cs.usu.edu/faculty/cannons/cats.html

International Tiger Information Center

Why is this server's domain named "5tigers"? It's because there are only five subspecies of tigers on Earth today. Three other subspecies have disappeared into extinction in the last 70 years. There are only about 5,000 wild tigers left. This organization will teach you something about conservation efforts, and how you can help. You can also take a quiz and see how much you already know about the natural history of tigers.

http://www.5tigers.org/

ELEPHANTS
A day with the Elephants

Did you ever wonder what an elephant does all day in the zoo? Elephants demand instruction and guidance to flourish in a man-made environment and the Indianapolis Zoo strives hard to provide the psychological, physiological and social fulfillment needed to keep elephants happy and healthy. Spend a virtual day with the elephants and the trainers as they go about their busy schedules.

http://aazk.ind.net/ema/emaday/day.html

"Tyger! Tyger! burning bright
In the forests of the night,"

begins the poem
by William Blake. Besides
those forests of the night,
tigers inhabit both the snowy woods of Siberia
and the steamy jungles of Sumatra. Visit the
International Tiger Information Center and
see some tigers close-up.

An Elephant HomePage

Can you tell the difference between an Asian and
an African elephant? While Asian and African
elephants have a lot in common, each species looks
a bit different, and each faces different threats to
its survival. Asian elephants are "endangered,"
meaning they are in danger of extinction. African
elephants are "threatened," which means they are
on their way to becoming endangered. Neither
situation is a good one. Find out more about the
different species, and what efforts are being taken
to protect these precious pachyderms, at this site.

http://raptor.csc.flint.umich.edu/~mcdonald/

GIRAFFES

Giraffe Cam

You've gotta see the giraffes at the Cheyenne
Mountain Zoo in Colorado Springs, Colorado.
Sometimes they are in, sometimes they are out, but
keep tuning in and you're bound to see a giraffe or
two eventually. We did! They are normally visible
from 10 A.M. to 4 P.M. Mountain Time. This zoo is
famous for their success in breeding giraffes in
captivity!

http://www.ceram.com/cheyenne/giraffe.html

Giraffes

Tall and majestic, giraffes cruise the grasslands of
Africa with grace and style. But don't even think of
messing with them! These 15-foot reticulated
wonders are into neck wrestling and head banging,
and if threatened, can kill a predator with a single
kick. You definitely want to keep on the good side of
this 4,000-pound animal! Even the babies are six
feet tall at birth.

http://www.wolfe.net/~ohwell/giraffe.html

HORSE FAMILY AND ZEBRAS

See also: HORSES

Animal Bytes: Grevy's zebra

Did you know that every zebra's stripe pattern
is as unique as a fingerprint? Zebras help other
plant-eaters on the grassland plains, since they eat
off the coarse forage at the top of plants, leaving the
tender new growth for other animals.

**http://www.bev.net/education/SeaWorld/
animal_bytes/grevysab.html**

For some fun facts about many
mammals (and other animals and
birds) try **Animal Bytes**
at *http://www.bev.net/
education/SeaWorld/
animal_bytes/
animal_bytes.html* for
fast information.
This site, from
Busch Gardens
in Florida, is
growing rapidly.

A
B
C
D
E
F
G
H
I
J
K
L
M
N
O
P
Q
R
S
T
U
V
W
X
Y
Z

Equus burchelli

Meet some Damaraland zebras at Seattle's Woodland Park Zoo. They not only have black and white stripes, but also brownish "shadow" stripes. This camouflage helps them disappear in the sun-on-shifting-grasslands habitat of their native Africa. Unfortunately, fewer than a half million of these herd animals remain in the wild. You'll learn a lot about the natural history of zebras, and also something you probably did not know about legendary rock star Jimi Hendrix, and why there is a plaque in his honor at the Seattle Zoo. If you want more pictures of zebras, try Bexley's Zebra Page, at *http://www.wildfire.com/~ag/zebras.html*.

http://www.zoo.org/science/animals/zebra.html

MARINE MAMMALS
THE MARINE MAMMAL CENTER

This San Francisco area wildlife rehabilitation center specializes in pinnipeds: California sea lions, northern elephant seals, and harbor seals. Do you know why the elephant seal's eyes are so big? It's so they can see when they dive deep. They get most of their food this way. They prefer to be offshore, up to 35 miles, diving to over 4,000 feet and possibly even deeper! On land, because they have non-reversible rear flippers, the elephant seal must slide, wriggle, and roll, using movements that resemble those of a caterpillar. To learn more about other marine mammals, visit this home page.

http://www.well.com/user/tmmc/index.html

West Indian Manatee in Florida

Have you ever heard of the manatee? Found in waters around Florida, throughout the Caribbean, and into South America, manatees are gentle vegetarians that are also called sea cows. They are, believe it or not, related to elephants, and some think the myth of mermaids may have come from sailors who saw these graceful creatures swimming. To learn more about manatees, take a look at the West Indian Manatee page.

http://www.dep.state.fl.us/psm/booklet.html

Whale Adoption Project Home Page

Whale Patrol Report—July 1994, now that's a whale of a story! Wouldn't it be neat to be on the observation platform of a whale patrol looking for whales? As you watch the ocean, a whale crashes through the surface, jaws bulging with food and water, and off to your right, four other humpbacks are blowing the underwater bubble clouds they use to help capture fish. Interested in more exciting adventures? Stop by and read about Sickle, the humpback whale, and her baby that weighed in at more than one thousand pounds and measured about thirteen feet at birth! You can adopt a humpback whale, take a look at the Great Whale Order Catalog, or find the hidden words in the Whale of a Word Find and learn a fun fact about the humpback baby. Parental warning: behind several warnings, there is a graphic sequence showing the death and butchering of a Minke whale. This area is described as not for children or other sensitive individuals.

http://www.webcom.com/~iwcwww/whale_adoption/waphome.html

Whales

Have you ever heard of friendly whales? No, not "Baby Beluga" or "Shamu"! The term "friendly whale" usually refers to the gray whale. In the lagoons in Mexico, sometimes gray whales will approach small boats. Scientists are unsure why the whales do this, since most wild animals are too wary to approach people or allow people to approach them. Maybe they just want to be friendly! Is a whale a fish? Although they share the same environment, there are important differences between a fish and a whale. Visit the Whales page to discover differences in the way fish and whales breathe, swim, and eat. This page is full of references for teachers, activities for students, and whale projects for all!

http://curry.edschool.virginia.edu/~kpj5e/Whales/

Have you hadrosaurus today? If not, try DINOSAURS AND PREHISTORIC TIMES.

WHALETIMES

Did you ever look for a dolphin in a tree? WHAT, you ask? That's right, if you're looking for a *Bouto* or Amazon River Dolphin, that's the place to look. They live in South America. During the rainy season, the rivers flood and the water gets as deep as 40 or 50 feet! When this happens, the dolphins, and other animals that swim in the river, can actually swim through the trees. Have you ever wondered how to tell the difference between a shark and a whale? Many sharks have two dorsal fins. A whale, on the other hand, would only have one dorsal fin, if any at all. Also, a shark's tail is vertical and a whale's tail is horizontal. If you're fishing for fishy facts, you can ask Jake the SeaDog. He'll answer questions online! You can even help write an ocean story! Take a swim to the Whaletimes Web page and see for yourself.

http://www.lightspeed.net/~whaletimes/

MARSUPIALS (POUCHED MAMMALS)

Koala's page

What seldom drinks, has a big rubbery nose, large fluffy ears, little or no tail, and looks like a cuddly toy? Why, a koala bear, that's what! Koalas live in trees, eat eucalyptus leaves, and are categorized as marsupials because they nourish their young in abdominal pouches. A mother koala only has one baby at a time and she carries it around in her pouch for seven months, after which the baby clings to its mother's back until it is about one year old! An old Australian story tells how koalas came about from a little boy. Stop by the Koala's page and check it out.

http://www.ocf.berkeley.edu/~jpeng/koala.html

Ruth's Sugar Glider Page

Sugar Glider? Never heard of it. Do you eat it or fly it? Neither. It's only the cutest marsupial to come up from "down under." About the size and shape of a flying squirrel, these creatures are soft, striped, and captivatingly cute. Native to Australia, they are considered exotic to the U.S., so you need a license to buy and own one. But owners will tell you they make great pets and are well worth any paperwork hassle. CAUTION! Think twice before checking out this site, because once you see one—you're going to want one.

http://www.rtis.com/nat/user/regrove

MONKEYS AND PRIMATES

Jane Goodall Institute

Chimpanzees are biologically close to humans; there is only a 2% genetic difference. This is why they are so frequently used in research. The Jane Goodall Institute is committed to improving the lives of chimpanzees both in the wild and in captivity. Her wildlife research in Africa is internationally known and respected. You can get involved with her Roots and Shoots program, or the Youth Summit sponsored by the Institute.

http://gsn.org/gsn/jgi.home.html

Orang Utan—Indonesia Business Center Online

The current number of orangutans left in the wild is estimated at between 20,000 and 27,000. They are an endangered species, and are the only big ape found in Asia. Unlike other primate species, they do not live in groups, preferring a solitary life. They feed on fruits, bark, leaves, and insects—like ants, termites, and bees. Male orangutans feed at ground level; however, the females never leave the trees. Stop by this page and meet Grungy the orangutan, and learn more about projects in support of their rehabilitation and preservation around the world.

http://www.indobiz.com/orang.htm

Primate Gallery

What's all the monkeying around? Why it's the Primate Gallery Web site, that's what! You'll find information on over 200 living primate species, including links to images and primate audio files. Stop by and see which primate is being featured this week. This comprehensive site will lead you to other monkey business on the Net.

http://www.fhcrc.org/~ialwww/PrimateGallery/
    PrimateGallery.html

Whooooooo will you find in BIRDS?

A B C D E F G H I J K L M N O P Q R S T U V W X Y Z

RHINOCEROS

Animal Bytes: Black Rhinoceros

Fewer than 3,000 of these animals exist on the planet today. Some people believe that the rhino "horn" has medicinal properties, and the animals are killed by poachers who want to harvest the horn. The horn isn't attached to the skull, and it's made out of keratin, the same substance found in fingernails, so it is not a true "horn" at all. Some zoos, such as the San Diego Wild Animal Park, have had some success breeding these animals, but they will never return to the wild, since their habitat is mostly gone.

http://www.bev.net/education/SeaWorld/
  animal_bytes/black_rhincerosab.html

Save the Rhino Home Page

He may be a little thick-skinned, but his reputation for aggressiveness is totally overblown. Normally timid, a white rhino will charge only when confronted. He has no natural enemies, yet the loss of his home and poaching of his horns has nearly destroyed his population. Here you can learn more about this rhino and his relatives, and see how one organization is attempting to keep the 97% extinction rate from becoming 100%.

http://www.cm-net.com/rhino/

In the last thirty years, 97% of the world's rhinoceros population has been wiped out. There are only about 10,000 left!

What can kids do to make sure their kids get to see live rhinos?

Check the Save the Rhino Home Page.

RODENTS

The Capybara Page

What would you get if you crossed a guinea pig and a hippopotamus? Probably something that looks like a capybara. These large, friendly rodents are rather vocal, making a series of strange clicks, squeaks, and grunts. Although they adapt easily to captivity, mice and rodent collectors will have to pass this one by as a pet. Capybaras are the largest living rodents on Earth, weighing in at 100 pounds or more. Our Great-Grandma calls them "outdoor hamsters."

http://www.access.digex.net/~rboucher/capybara/

Guinea Pigs on the Net

We loved this page and it wasn't just because of the "surfing guinea pig" pictures. There is a FAQ for care of your pet cavies, plus links to other guinea pig pages, and loads of "family portraits" of beloved "pigs" everywhere. This pig page is on a server in Italy.

http://www.ing.unico.it/carlo/cavie.html

RMCA Home Page

Move over, Mickey—it's the Rat and Mouse Club of America home page! These pages are absolutely stuffed with more information and resources about mice and rats than you can ever imagine. Show standards, photos, pet info—this site is a pack rat's dream come true.

http://www.rmca.org/

VARIOUS ANIMALS

Adam's Fox Box

When Fox went out on a chilly night, he was probably heading to this home page. Learn to fox trot, view some great fox photos, and read stories, songs, and poems about foxes. Links off the "fox fringe" have not been checked, and the fox hunting section is not for the sensitive.

http://tavi.acomp.usf.edu/foxbox/

Bat Conservation International Top Page

Did you know that the world's smallest mammal is the bumblebee bat? It weighs less than a penny. Nearly 1,000 different kinds of bats account for almost 25 percent of all mammal species. Most bats are very good to have around. One little brown bat can catch 600 mosquitoes in just one hour. Visit the Bat Conservation International site to learn more about bats and bat houses, or stop in at the world's largest urban bat colony.

http://www.batcon.org/

HRS Home Page

WANTED: A patient human with a sense of humor who spends a lot of time at home and doesn't mind hanging out on the floor with me. I am a bunny rabbit that is in need of a good home. I am inquisitive, sociable, litterbox trained, and would make a wonderful companion for the right person. I need to be protected from predators, poisons, temperature extremes, electrical cords, and rough handling. I may even purr when I am happy. Stop by to find out what life would be like if you adopted me. Please hurry, my friends and I need your help! This is the page of the House Rabbit Society, and they have rabbits for adoption all over the U.S. You'll also find out a lot about rabbit care and handling, so hop on over!

http://www.psg.lcs.mit.edu/~carl/paige/
  HRS-home.html

The Wonderful Skunk and Opossum Page

What would you do if your dog got sprayed by a skunk? Does a tomato juice bath really work? The answer is, sort of, but it may turn your dog pink for awhile! You can also try a newer remedy, involving hydrogen peroxide, baking soda, and liquid soap (the recipe is here). There's advice on keeping skunks as pets, plus loads of lore on both skunks and opossums. Opossums are marsupials, meaning they carry their babies in a pouch. Another little-known fact is that a 'possum has 50 teeth, more than any other North American mammal.

http://elvis.neep.wisc.edu/~firmiss/
  mephitis-didelphis.html

The World Wide Raccoon Web

Who's that bandit prying off the lid of your garbage can? It's a family of raccoons! Their nimble paws, black masks, and long ringed tails make them unmistakable. Visit this home page to meet a true fan of raccoons and their natural—and unnatural—history! You'll find lots of photos, legends, and links, and read the incredible story of how one raccoon saved a student's life at Cornell University!

http://www.loomcom.com/raccoons/

What causes the distinctive odor of skunks?

About a century ago, T.B. Aldritch published his analysis, which said that it was primarily 1-Butanethiol (also known as n-Butyl Mercaptan). Many books still think Aldritch got it right. However, a 1990 analysis of the volatile components of skunk musk reveals it's actually made of seven chemicals. The Wonderful Skunk and Opossum Page says "One component had never before been seen in nature and another had never been reported anywhere (natural or man-made), yet none of them were 1-Butanethiol!"

Did times change or did skunks?

Read any good Web sites lately?

WOLVES AND THE DOG FAMILY

Desert Moon's Wolf Page

Wolves are large, powerful, wild canines that depend on large prey such as deer, elk, moose, and bison for survival. Some of their prey weigh more than a thousand pounds! The wolf has powerful jaws, capable of exerting about 1,500 pounds of force per square inch, or about twice that of the domestic dog. It is a highly social animal, generally living within the same pack for most, if not all, of its life. To learn more about wolf natural history, lore, and legend, visit Desert Moon's Wolf Page—and listen for the howling wolves.

http://www.scs.unr.edu/~timb/desertm.html

Welcome to the Wolf HomePage

You are supposed to be home by now! You decide to take a shortcut through the woods. As you enter the forest, the night gets darker. You start hearing things. Suddenly, you hear an animal howling nearby. You're sure it's a wolf and you're convinced it is getting closer. You didn't notice the full moon and now you're afraid the wolf is going to attack you! Should you be afraid of wolves? No! In fact, wolves are very shy around people and try very hard to avoid them! They do not eat people. By the way, wolves will howl any time of the day, but are most often heard at night when they are most active. Wolves will howl to defend their territory or reunite pack members. And they will howl whether there is a full moon or not! Visit the Wolf HomePage and learn more about wolf communication and how wolves live. Hope you get home OK, now!

http://www.usa.net/WolfHome/

MATH AND ARITHMETIC

Ask Dr. Math

Mom and Dad don't understand your math homework. Neither does your best buddy. But you can ask Dr. Math! You'll enjoy finding out the answers to some of the questions that kids have already asked Dr. Math. For instance, "Can one infinity be larger than another?" or "Why can't you divide a number by zero?"

http://forum.swarthmore.edu/dr.math/dr-math.html

Can you guess this riddle?

In a marble palace white as milk,
Lined with skin as soft as silk,
In a fountain crystal clear,
A golden apple does appear.
There are no doors to this stronghold,
Yet thieves break in to steal the gold.

The answer is: an egg!
Find more at the Riddle du Jour!
http://www.new3.com/riddle/today/.shtml

Brainteasers

If you're looking for some cool puzzles to stretch your brain cells, try this site. Every week you'll find new brainteasers, arranged by grade level. Typical puzzles include map reading, word problems, and puzzles that require a genuinely different outlook. Stumped? Get a hint! If you need a clue, the solutions are also provided.

http://gnn.com/gnn/meta/edu/curr/math/brain/
  index.html

Chapters of the MegaMath Book

Kids from nine to ninety will have hours of fun playing the thinking games here that involve Flat and Topological Geometry, as well as other math and logical concepts. Everything is presented in a colorful, simplified manner that almost belies the complexity of thought that is needed for some of these games. The Most Colorful Math of All, Games on Graphs (that can be played on a table or playground), Algorithms and Ice Cream for All, and The Hotel Infinity are some of the activities awaiting you here.

http://www.c3.lanl.gov/mega-math/workbk/
  contents.html

Geometry Forum—Student Center

Part of a larger forum devoted to geometry, this page focuses on links that would be useful or of interest to students. Lots of games, projects and downloadable software can be found here. Most interesting is the High School/Elementary Partnership program, which allows high school kids to act as Math Mentors for younger kids. There is also an Elementary Problem of the Week posted as a companion project.

http://forum.swarthmore.edu/students.html

MathMagic!

There's some world-class math puzzles here, for K-12 students and teachers. But don't worry, you can join a team of other kids around the Net, all trying to solve the same puzzles! You'll be paired with an expert who will help guide your journey towards the solution. You can also enjoy the puzzles, without the team element, if you wish.

http://forum.swarthmore.edu/mathmagic/

CALCULATORS
TI-85 Games Page

Whatever use you might have for the Texas Instruments TI-85 programmable calculator, you know deep down that the best thing about it is all the nifty games you can play on it. Here you can download versions of *Simon*, *Tetris*, Bonk, and Gladiators for your calculator, and link to up to half a dozen other TI-85 game sites.

http://www.mv.com/ipusers/lynk/ti-85/ti-85.htm

COUNTING
Blue Dog Can Count

Painter George Rodrigue's famous character Blue Dog has appeared in paintings, books, and an animated film. Now Blue Dog will solve simple math problems for you! Simply enter the problem on this page, then listen to Blue Dog bark out the answer! Actually, your browser will download and play a sound file of Blue Dog—the more barks, the longer it will take to load. Make sure your cat isn't around!

http://kao.ini.cmu.edu:5550/bdf.html

Print A Googolplex

Mathematician Edward Kasner's nine-year-old nephew coined the name for a very large number. That number, ten to the power of 100, otherwise written as a one with a hundred zeroes trailing it, was named a GOOGOL. While this was a very large number indeed, perfect for trotting out at parties to impress people, another mathematician was unimpressed, and came up with something even more immense: GOOGOLPLEX, a 10 to the power of GOOGOL. This page examines exactly what this incredibly huge number is, and explains why no computer could ever print out something that large. There is a downloadable program here that will store a much-abbreviated version of a GOOGOLPLEX in about ten hours on a ten gigabyte hard drive. The program is only 1,235 bytes in size and is triple zipped so your Web browser won't try to unpack it automatically! Be the first (and probably the last) on your block to have your very own pet GOOGOLPLEX!

http://www.uni-frankfurt.de/~fp/Tools/Googool.html

FORMULAS AND CONSTANTS
Appendix F: Weights and Measures

You'll find a lot more about this topic in the REFERENCE section of this book. Still, we thought you'd find some of this Central Intelligence Agency resource interesting. For example, you've heard of megabytes (1,000,000) of hard drive space, right? The next step is a gigabyte (1,000,000,000), but did you know the next largest threshold is a terabyte (1,000,000,000,000)? And after that, well, we can't count that high, but this site says it's a petabyte (1,000,000,000,000,000). A petabyte of hard disk storage: bliss!

http://www.odci.gov/cia/publications/95fact/appendf.html

Curl up with a good Internet site.

A
B
C
D
E
F
G
H
I
J
K
L
M
N
O
P
Q
R
S
T
U
V
W
X
Y
Z

Erdos for Kids Web Site

Did you know there are a number of math problems that have *never* been solved? Paul Erdos, one of the greatest mathematical minds of the century, has challenged young people to help come up with the solutions! In the past, Erdos has given cash prizes as incentives, and found kids who have been able to solve puzzles on the very frontiers of mathematical knowledge. He promises to offer prizes through this site, and will include background information on the unsolved problems and the mathematicians who originally posed them.

http://www.csc.uvic.ca/~mmania/

Pi Mathematics

What good is Pi anyway? This page answers that question and provides activities to help you learn about this most interesting mathematical constant. The Indiana State Legislature once voted to make the value of Pi equal to 3.2. This was hailed as a "new mathematical truth." The Senate, however, postponed indefinitely its vote on the act! (You can get the full story at *http://www.cis.ohio-state.edu/ hypertext/faq/usenet/sci-math-faq/ specialnumbers/lawPieq3/faq.html.*)

http://www.ncsa.uiuc.edu:80/edu/RSE/RSEorange/
   buttons.html

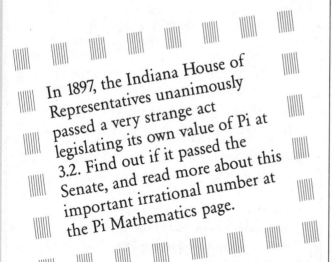

In 1897, the Indiana House of Representatives unanimously passed a very strange act legislating its own value of Pi at 3.2. Find out if it passed the Senate, and read more about this important irrational number at the Pi Mathematics page.

FRACTALS
The Fractal Microscope

This page explains the Fractal Microscope, a tool devised by the National Center for Supercomputing Applications which enables schools to link to supercomputers via the Internet. This procedure allows schools to run fractal-generating programs much faster than can be done with a stand-alone desktop computer. The ideas behind fractals are clearly explained here, and a number of images are presented, including a group designed by students at an Illinois elementary school.

http://www.ncsa.uiuc.edu/Edu/Fractal/
   Fractal_Home.html

Sprott's Fractal Gallery

What is a "Julia set," a "Strange Attractor," or an "Iterated Function System"? They are all math equations which generate beautiful fractal images. A fractal drawing is the picture a computer makes as it maps out one of these equations. Sprott's Gallery includes sample programs to download and run on your computer so you can see fractals for yourself. There is a "frequently asked questions" section and also lots of cool fractal pictures to download.

http://sprott.physics.wisc.edu/fractals.htm

MAGIC SQUARES AND TRICKS
Magic Squares

Magic Squares are those pesky little grid puzzles that require you to fill in the boxes with numbers that add up the same in every direction. Visitors to this site will not only find out what a Magic Square is, and generate odd-numbered squares with a click, but will also find out the amazingly simple solution for creating and solving your own. With a little practice, you can mystify your friends with the ease in which you write out magic squares with any odd number per side!

http://www.auburn.edu/~harshec/WWW/
   MagicSquare.html

MODELS AND MINIATURES

See also: RAILROADS AND TRAINS

Miniatures WWW Archive

Maybe you like wargame miniatures. Maybe you like collecting and painting them. Maybe you even like playing with them! See the pictures of some very detailed models, check out the painting tips, and learn the moves for your favorite game. It's all here!

http://biochem.dental.upenn.edu/Mosaic/
    miniatures.html

rec.models.scale Home Page

Did you know that an old dental pick is great for cleaning up filler and carving plastic when you're building a model? It feels great to know you started with pieces, put it together, painted it, and finished it off yourself! It doesn't matter if you like model ships, vehicles, figures, or fighter planes, it's all assembled here. Find out what new kits are available, and read reviews before you buy them. And learn how to build your model from the excellent online beginner's course. Get building!

http://meteor.anu.edu.au/~dfk/scale_model.html

AIRPLANES
Introduction to Model Aircraft

Flying your own airplane might have to wait until you're just a little older—unless you have a radio controlled model airplane. Yes, then you can fly! Here you can find out how to get started in this fun hobby, but even if you already fly, there's so much information here that you're bound to learn something new. It starts with practical material about the planes, and then covers everything from building them to flying them. There are extensive sections on the parts, the words that the hobbyists use, and the specialized accessories. So what are you waiting for? Prepare for take-off!

http://www.peinet.pe.ca/ECMC/intair.html

RAILROADS
Model Railroad Information

Everything, from garden trains (larger than O scale [1:48], but smaller than the trains that are large enough to ride on), to tiny Z gauge (1:220) trains, is collected here. Want a track layout that does more than go around your Christmas tree? It's here! Painting scenic backgrounds or sculpting your own figures to dress up the stations will be a breeze with these lessons! All aboard! The track's clear as far as you can see on the Net!

http://www-cse.ucsd.edu/users/bowdidge/
    railroad/rail-models.html

A
B
C
D
E
F
G
H
I
J
K
L
M
N
O
P
Q
R
S
T
U
V
W
X
Y
Z

ROCKETRY

Model and High-Powered Rocketry

Thinking about blasting off into the wide world of model rocketry? At this site you can learn some, see some, and explore this exciting hobby. There's basic information on small, large, and high-powered rockets, and some great picture samples to give you a look at what you can do. Now that you're this far, you may want more, and so plenty of links to other rocketry resources are listed. Just consider this your launch pad to model rocketry!

http://www.irving.org/rocketry/

Model Rocket FAQ Page

Model rockets can actually take off? Sounds like you have some basic questions, like: how do you do it? Where do you do it? Is it dangerous? Is it legal? Here are the answers to almost any question you might have about model rocketry. Now, what if your questions are more like: where can I find engines that are discontinued? How can I prevent body tube damage from the shock cord? Or, should I invest in a piston launcher? Then you must be experienced in model rocketry. Well, come on in, too! This site has categorized questions and answers for every level of rocket enthusiast. Now, should I use a thermalite fuse...?

http://www.dtm-corp.com/~sven/rockets/
  rmrfaq.toc.html

MONEY

See also: CONSUMER INFORMATION

Currency Comparison

Can you believe there's a project on the Internet dedicated to finding out just how much food you can buy for five dollars? And they mean you! The idea is to compare the value of your five dollars to the same amount of money in other countries. It's fun, and the interactive currency conversion chart lets you compare different money from all over the globe. If you're not from Albania, you might still be interested in just how much lunch the "lek" (Albanian monetary unit) will buy! You'll have to contribute your own data before you can see everyone else's, though.

http://stan.wimmera.net.au/gorokep12/
  curcomp1.html

GNN/Koblas Currency Converter

When is a dollar not a dollar? Wait a minute! Where did you get that dollar? Is that a U.S. dollar, or an Australian dollar, or a Namibian dollar? Because if it's a Namibian dollar then it is likely worth less than half the U.S. Dollar. But,the Australian dollar is worth more than the Namibian dollar, but still not worth as much as the U.S. dollar. Confused yet? What about the German mark, the Japanese yen, or the Slovenian tolar? Whoa! This stuff *can* get confusing. Luckily, at this site, just a couple of clicks and you can compare currencies from all over the world. Try it! Another site that does this is The Olsen Currency Convertor at *http://www.olsen.ch/cgi-bin/exmenu*, and it has more countries (like Namibia).

http://bin.gnn.com/cgi-bin/gnn/currency/

Money Curriculum Unit

Money! You see it every day. You probably have some in your pocket right now. But how much do you know about its history and how it's made? Recently, the government has made many changes in U.S. money to make it harder for it to be copied. See what the new tricks are to stop counterfeit cash. And, if you don't know what all the symbols on U.S. bills mean, and whose portrait is on each one, you will by the time you finish "spending" some time at this site!

http://woodrow.mpls.frb.fed.us/econed/curric/
  money.htm

Printing money

It takes sixty-five distinct steps to print a U.S dollar bill. You can follow the process here at *Newton's Apple*, and also learn how to make and print your own "pretend" money!

http://ericir.syr.edu/Newton/Lessons/money.html

Crack open CODES AND CIPHERS.

NET FILES

Yummm—chocolate!
Think you really know a lot about candy? How much did the largest Hershey's Kiss weigh?

ANSWER: The largest Hershey's Kiss weighed 400 pounds, was 30 inches tall and measured three feet in diameter. It was used in a 1987 marketing promotion in Hong Kong. Check it out at: http://www.hersheys.com/~hershey/fun-facts.html

Street Cents Online

Young people make money, save money, and spend money, just like everyone else! But sometimes there just isn't much advice for young people about handling their money. Do you spend money on entertainment, sports, music, food...your hair? Well, all of these topics and more are covered in *Street Cents*, a popular Canadian television show. And now the "show" is online in an informative and fun Web page. Spend some time there!

http://www.screen.com/streetcents.html

U.S. National Debt Clock

Did you know that if you're an American citizen, you owe the government about $18,000? That is currently every citizen's share of the National Debt. What's that? The U.S. government spends more money than it takes in. When this happens, it has to borrow money from someplace else. The amount it owes to other sources is called the National Debt. This site explains more about how this happened and what the government is trying to do to pay off the debt and keep this from happening again. Canada's also got a National Debt clock, which is linked here too.

http://www.brillig.com/debt_clock/

MONSTERS

A Yeti Tale: Introduction

The Abominable Snowman has been spotted high up in the Himalayan Mountains by a number of respectable mountaineers. To folks in Nepal and Tibet, where he has been sighted countless times for hundreds of years, he's known as Yeti. If Yeti does exist, chances are the creature is not possessed of magical powers, but legends about them persist. Read some of those legends here.

http://www.kei.com/homepages/surya/ytale1.html

Alt.fan.dragons: information and files on dragons

There are real dragons, you know! The Komodo Dragon is the world's largest lizard, and it lives (among other places) on Komodo Island, which is part of Indonesia. Other dragons live in the fantasy worlds of literature, lore, and legend. This home page celebrates all kinds of dragons. You'll find dragon art, stories, and riddles. Dragons love to ask people riddles. Here is one, from J.R.R. Tolkien's *The Hobbit*:

It cannot be seen, cannot be felt,

Cannot be heard, cannot be smelt,

It lies behind stars and under hills,

And empty holes it fills.

It comes first and follows after,

Ends life, kills laughter.

A parental advisory goes on this site because we haven't explored all the links, and some fantasy dragon art is graphic. The riddle's answer is *darkness*.

http://icecube.acf-lab.alaska.edu/~fxdlk/

Watch your step in DANCE.

A
B
C
D
E
F
G
H
I
J
K
L
M
N
O
P
Q
R
S
T
U
V
W
X
Y
Z

Nessie, the Loch Ness Monster

Mark Chorvinsky has put together a remarkable Web site exploring the controversies surrounding Scotland's world famous Loch Ness Monster. Nessie, as the lake monster is affectionately known, has been the subject of numerous credible sightings over the past 63 years, even though extensive scientific efforts to track her down have been a lesson in frustration. This page presents well-researched and clearly written essays on the sightings, the searchers, and the debunkers, as well as investigations into other, lesser-known lake monsters from around the world, such as Canada's "Ogopogo," spotted regularly since 1926.

http://www.cais.com/strangemag/nessie.home.html

The Western Bigfoot Society

These folks take their Sasquatches seriously! Back issues of their newsletter, *The Track Record*, which include plenty of up-to-date Bigfoot sightings, are available here, as well as information about the ongoing Digital Bigfoot Conference. Links to other Bigfoot sites are also included. One of the best is The Bigfoot Research Project, which coordinates many of the efforts to gather solid evidence of the existence of this large, hairy, elusive creature. Other links (in the "Skeptics" area) lead to places you may want to preview for your family.

http://www.teleport.com/~caveman/wbs.shtml

MOVIES

See also: DISNEY

Babe

Babe is a pig who marches to the beat of a different drummer—he wants to be a sheepdog! Find out about the movie production and see some video clips from the film, which is based on Dick King-Smith's children's book, *The Sheep-Pig.*

http://www.mca.com/universal_pictures/babe/
  index.html

Casper

Whatever you do, don't scream! Casper's a friendly ghost! See what happens when a little girl and her dad move into spooky old Whipstaff Manor. Casper and his ghostly uncles star in this popular movie from MCA/Universal Studios. You'll learn how the movie was made, and the secrets behind the special effects!

http://www.mca.com/home/casper/TorTanim.html

Disney's *Pocahontas*

The story of an independent Native American girl and her relationship with Captain John Smith in 1607 Jamestown, Virginia. Download the film clips and coloring pages. Don't forget to use your "Colors of the Wind" crayons!

http://www.disney.com/DisneyPictures/Features/
  Pocahontas/PocahontasHome.html?LO=D&GL=T

A Goofy Movie

What happens when Goofy and his teenage son Max decide to drive cross-country to spend some "quality time"? Max isn't thrilled. He'd rather spend time with his new girlfriend. In fact, he's got some cool concert tickets, and would like to take her with him—but Dad wants him to go fishing! This animated film features detours, cliff-hangers, "rapid" transit, and some wild driving you won't see on your street! What happens when they meet up with Bigfoot? Will Max ever get to the rock concert? Download pictures and clips from the movie, including a music video!

http://www.disney.com/DisneyPictures/Features/
  GoofyMovie/GoofyMovieHome.html?LO=D&GL=T

Hollywood Online

Parental advisory: this site lists all movies, not just "G-rated" ones. Hollywood Online's the place for the latest on all the hottest movies. It's got all the video, soundbites, pictures, and production notes you could possibly want—but what makes it really special is the stuff you can download and keep to play around with later. For every movie, you can download an interactive multimedia kit, a complete package of goodies about the movie. Every one includes a neat interactive game for Macintosh or Windows systems. The *Goldeneye* game, for example, challenges you to put an exploding pen's pieces back in their correct order. The game that comes with *The American President* kit has you try to figure out which gift will win the heart of the President's new love interest.

http://www.hollywood.com/

The Indian in the Cupboard

A toy Indian comes to life after being put inside a magic cupboard, and amazing things begin to happen! How did this Iroquois youth from the 1800s get transported to a nine-year-old boy's room of today? Even more curious—how did they make a grown man look like he was only three inches tall? Find out how they did it, download clips from the movie, and learn about Native American lore.

http://www.paramount.com/Indian.html

The Lion King

Young lion cub Simba prepares to follow in his father's footsteps to become king of the vast African plain. After his father's death, Simba blames himself, and runs away. Will he come back to the Pride Lands and take up his destiny in the "circle of life"? Find out at this site, with music and clips from the popular movie.

http://www.disney.com/DisneyPictures/Features/
    LionKing/LionKingHome.html?LO=D&GL=T

People are the true treasures of the Net.

Mighty Morphin Power Rangers: The Movie

Power Rangers Tommy, Kimberly, Billy, Rocky, Aisha, and Adam have been busy practicing their martial arts moves for their next battle with Ivan Ooze and the evil he is cooking up. But if you send them a quick note of encouragement, they will make sure to take a break and write back! You can even send a note to the monsters if you want to see what they have in store!

http://www.delphi.com/power/powrhome.htm

MovieLink 777FILM Online

Okay, let's go to the movies—but which one? And where's it playing? If you live in a major American city, the best place to find out is here, at MovieLink, which calls itself "America's online source for movie information." Type in your city or ZIP code and find out what's playing near you and what the showtimes are. From there, you can read movie reviews and even let your family check out the Parents' Guide ("Look, Mom, it's rated PG!"), so they can put their stamp of approval on your choice. Once you've settled on a movie you'd like to see, you can reserve your tickets online. If you loved the movie, you can download posters and movie trailers as electronic souvenirs.

http://www.777film.com/

Pocahontas for American Indian Students

For a view of the popular Disney movie through native eyes, check this Web page. The true history of Pocahontas and Captain John Smith might make less of a story than the Disney version, since she was only about eleven or twelve years old when she begged for his life. See what some Native American kids and adults think about the cartoon and its look at their culture and history.

http://www.fdl.cc.mn.us/~isk/pocahont.html

Welcome to Toy Story

This is Disney's first completely computer-generated movie! What happens in Andy's room once he gets a new toy? This exciting adventure features the voice of Tim Allen as Buzz LightYear—Space Ranger, Annie Potts as Bo Peep, and Tom Hanks as Woody the Cowboy. Download coloring books, games, computer screen wallpaper, icons, film clips, and more!

http://www.toystory.com/

A
B
C
D
E
F
G
H
I
J
K
L
M
N
O
P
Q
R
S
T
U
V
W
X
Y
Z

REVIEWS

The Dove Foundation's Home Page

Free Willy 2: The Adventure Home, The Babysitter's Club, and *Babe* are just three of the movies that have won the Dove Foundation's Seal of Approval for being "family friendly." So far, this group, whose motto is "Families everywhere deserve a choice," has approved over 1,400 movies. You can get the list just by signing the guest book here. Don't miss film critic Holly McClure's reviews of the top ten new movies and videos for family viewing. If you still can't decide what to see, just fill out a simple online form and search by viewer age group or type of movie, including action, adventure, classic, and lots more.

http://www.dove.org/dove/dove.htm

The Internet Movie Database

WOW! This international volunteer effort covers over 54,000 movies! You can find info on the following: biographies of actors; plot summaries; character names; movie ratings; trivia; famous quotes from the movie; goofs and things that went wrong, but didn't get cut out; soundtracks; filming locations; sequel/remake information; advertising tag lines; and Academy Award information. If the movie is based on a book, you'll get that information here too! Butter up some popcorn and enjoy this site!

http://www.msstate.edu/Movies/welcome.html

The Movie Mom's List of the Best Movies for Families

Nell Minow is an author and a critic, but most importantly a mom. She calls herself "Movie Mom," and gives lots of advice to kids and families on the best movies to see. According to Movie Mom, no one should grow up (or be a grown-up) without seeing *The Muppet Movie, Tom Thumb, The Absent-Minded Professor,* and *Captains Courageous,* among others. Take a look at this site to read her reviews and to find out other movies you must see. The authors of a new book called *The Practical Guide to Practically Everything* liked her opinions so much they included them in their book!

http://pages.prodigy.com/VA/rcpj55a/list.html

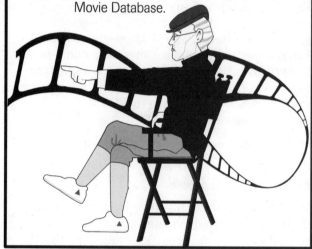

Viewers around the world have voted **Star Wars** as their all-time favorite movie! Did you know part of it was filmed in Tunisia? There are a lot of famous mistakes in it too, such as the part where a stormtrooper hits his head on a door. To see famous quotes from the movie other than "Use the force, Luke!" and to learn lots of great trivia, be sure to check the Internet Movie Database.

SOUNDS AND THEMES

Internet Movie Database Soundtrack Search

You loved a song you heard at the movies last night, but you have no idea what it's called or who sang it. Here's what you do: pop a word from the movie title into this searching machine to get all the details in a flash. You can do the same thing with your favorite group. For example, if we type the word "Mozart" into the search box, we find out his music has been in lots of movies, even *Operation Dumbo Drop*!

http://www.msstate.edu/M/search_songs

www.filmmusic.com: Music

Whether you're looking for movies with bagpipe music, the theme to *Jurassic Park* (Watch out! It's 1.5 megabytes!), or music to shoot aliens by, this is the place. Movie music composers, collectors, and fans will find all the reviews, music clips, discussions, and guides they could ever possibly want at this site.

http://www.filmmusic.com/music.html

STUDIOS AND PRODUCTION COMPANIES

The Lion's Den

Parental advisory: all of Metro Goldwyn Mayer's movies are here, not just the "G-rated" ones. The world-famous MGM lion welcomes you to his den! Just click on a movie poster to find out everything you've wanted to know about the cast, the story, and the filmmakers. Click on "multimedia" and you can get a glimpse of a newly released movie by downloading some clips from the QT (QuickTime) library. Songs and sounds of the latest movies are also here for the taking, along with hundreds of still pictures. If it's just too confusing, you're invited to cruise over to the Tech Center, where the hottest Web tools—like QuickTime, Real Audio and Liquid Reality—are ready and waiting to be downloaded.

http://www.mgmua.com/

MCA Home Entertainment Playroom

Kid's Playroom will keep your little sister entertained. She'll love the "Casper the Friendly Ghost" treasure hunt and the "Timmy the Tooth" interactive adventure. Make sure she doesn't find her way back into the movie previews section of this page without mom or dad, or another adult, to help guide her to other kid sites.

http://www.univstudios.com/home/playroom/

Paramount Pictures Online Studio

Lots of good movies and TV shows come out of this studio, but not everything here is for kids. "A computer is to life what a credit card is to your wardrobe—the ultimate accessory," says *Clueless*'s Cher Horowitz, who has her own PG-13 home page at this site. Yep, there's a ton of goodies about Paramount movies, past and present, but one of the coolest things here might just be the interactive area for one of Paramount's most popular television series, *Star Trek: Voyager*. Trekkers won't want to miss the descriptions of the Voyager's missions and alien encounters, not to mention the Starfleet personnel records for the crew. Kids with slower modems will really appreciate the "graphics-lite" options.

http://www.paramount.com

> **Never give your name or address to a stranger.**

Sony Pictures Entertainment Home Page

Are you game? Game for what? *Jumanji,* the Internet adventure, that's what. It's based on the Sony Pictures movie about an ancient, magical board game. If you take the challenge, you'll be navigating through alligator-infested swamps, dodging stampeding elephants, and escaping a spider's web. Help yourself to a free *Jumanji* Screen Saver as a souvenir. Don't miss the sneak peeks of upcoming movies or the studio tour of Imageworks, Sony's visual effects company. Parental advisory: this site contains many Sony movies, some of which may not be suitable for your family.

http://www.spe.sony.com/Pictures/index.html

MUPPETS

The Fabulous Miss Piggy Page

Miss Piggy says "Not everyone can be a superstar, but anyone can be a semistar, a starette, or a teensyweensystar." She, herself, is a true supernova! Thrill to her fascinating and glamorous lifestyle, described in loving detail at this one-of-a-kind Web page.

http://www-leland.stanford.edu/~rosesage/Piggy.html

Muppets Home Page

Bill Sherman's unofficial Muppets Home Page is about as close to an "official" site as there ever will be. All images, sounds and scripts here are present with permission of Jim Henson Productions, and there are episode guides for *The Muppet Show*, *Fraggle Rock*, *Dinosaurs*, and even *Sesame Street*! Look for press releases from Jim Henson Productions to be posted here, and lots of lists and reviews.

http://www.ncsa.uiuc.edu/VR/BS/Muppets/muppets.html

Muppets, Monsters and Magic

In 1994, as a tribute to Jim Henson, an exhibit called "Muppets, Monsters and Magic" was mounted at the Bay Area Discovery Museum, near San Francisco, California. A virtual tour of this exhibit is still on display here. You'll find all sorts of Muppet history and trivia, from the earliest days to the more current monsters we see in movies (*The Dark Crystal*, *Labyrinth*) and on TV (*Dinosaurs*). Find out what gives Miss Piggy her blush and dazzling hair-do!

**http://www-leland.stanford.edu/~rosesage/
 MMM/MMM.html**

When Jim Henson started producing short television programs and commercials for a local Washington, D.C. station back in the fifties, he could not have dreamed what an international phenomenon they would become. Visit the **Muppets Home Page** tribute to Kermit, Miss Piggy, Fozzie, and friends.

MUSIC AND MUSICIANS

CDnow : welcome

This is an online store, where you can get your parents to order cassettes and CDs, but it's also the new home of the volunteer-built All Music Guide. The AMG is a huge review archive for—guess what—ALL MUSIC. You can search for albums by artist, title, or subject genre. The "Children's" genre is inside the "Other" directory. This site also links to Real Audio files, so you can listen to some albums. Lots of artist home page and concert links, so we need to put a Parental Advisory on this one. Point lists this site as one of the Internet Top Ten, and we have to agree. Hint: for slower connections, pick the text option.

http://cdnow.com/

The Instrumental Music Resource Page

Here's help for "students, parents, and teachers of Instrumental Music." And it's a good gathering place for much musical information. Click on The Brass Page (Western Illinois University), and learn why it's not such a great idea to smile and play the trombone at the same time. Try the Internet Resources for Brass Players. You'll find the French horn home page, as well as a site on Mahler Symphony recordings, the Classical Music Home Page, and others. Under "Instrumental Music Information" are a clickable trumpet, trombone, sax, clarinet, and flute. Each leads to a brief essay on instrument care, e-mail lists, embouchure, tips on technique, and links to home pages for the given instrument. The flute has an additional link to an extensive project on the history and practice of flute-playing. And have you ever needed a great excuse for not practicing? Get inspiration from "Great Excuses," collected by music teachers over the years.

http://www.fcasd.edu/per-hom/traugh/imrp.html

J.S. Bach Home Page

The home page of J. S. Bach really does lead you to his home. Under "Biography," a clickable hypermap shows you the relatively limited geographical space he inhabited from 1685 to 1750. You can travel through time and space from Eisenach, Germany, where he was born, to Leipzig, Germany, where he died. Either click on the map, or go from link to link in the right order. You'll see portraits of significant people, and photos of buildings. Also, the entry for his birth in the official birth registry in Eisenach has been scanned in. Quite a time capsule! You'll also find directory information on his complete works here, by catalog number, category, instrument, and title. There is a similar listing for Bach recordings.

http://www.tile.net/tile/bach/

Not everything on the Net is true.

K-12 Resources For Music Educators

When you hear your music teacher say, "oh, there's nothing on the Web for me..." you can just show him or her this page. There are resources collected in categories for band, orchestra, and choral music teachers. You'll also find links for classroom music teachers. And the selection is really interesting for The Rest of Us, too. You'll find composer biographies, newsgroups, MIDI resources, and hints on how to really *listen* to music. We also liked one of the links from here, the Music Education Online page (*http://www.geocities.com/Athens/2405/index.html*) for general excellence and being right on key.

**http://www.isd77.k12.mn.us/resources/staffpages/
    shirk/cindys.page.k12.link.html**

The Mammoth Music Meta-List

This site is like one of those nesting Russian dolls. Every link opens up a new world of music. Where else could you find Morris dancing, the San Francisco Symphony, and a sight and sound demo of different renaissance consorts and instruments? The Webmaster hopes to keep the site a relatively complete set of all music resources available. If you have an interest in Christian music—or Indian, or Russian, or reggae (pick your subject)—it's probably here. The pop/rock section is huge, with bands both well-known and obscure. Also there are links to the home pages of specific bands and musicians, as well as reviews and "top-40" and other countdown charts. The links to specific instruments are very complete. For whatever information you need or want on any aspect of music, start here.

http://www.timeinc.com/vibe/mmm/music.html

Ask not what the Net can do for you, ask what you can do for the Net.

Musi-Cal

So you want to go to a concert (or a festival, or a coffeehouse). You like acoustic music (or blues, or ska) and you're willing to travel up to ten miles from your home. Musi-Cal will pinpoint the very concert you seek. The site strives to provide easy access to current world-wide music information. They promise no weird pictures, no old information, no 200K graphics to download. Search right off by performer, city, venue, or event, or go to "Options" for a detailed search form. It includes artist(s), event, city, radius around city (up to 200 miles, or 400 km), dates, venue, musical genres, even keywords. You can also contribute concert information. There are sometimes links to performers' Web pages as well.

http://calendar.com/concerts

The San Francisco Symphony

This site has specific information about the SF Symphony (tickets, concert hall, and so on) but it also has real Web Value. There are messages from, and press releases about, Michael Tilson Thomas, the new conductor. You can also meet some of the 106 musicians—you'll see what they look like, why they chose their instruments, who likes baseball, and what other kinds of music they like. The Web links lead you to searchable archives of listservs, reference guides to composers, music and recordings, and an array of other symphonic ensembles.

http://www.hooked.net/sfsymphony/sfshome.html

The Ultimate Band List

Parental advisory: this is a good place to preview lyrics for CDs your kids want to buy. For other uses, please explore this with your children. Prepare to spend the day sifting through this vast list. It's an "interactive guide" to band Web pages, and digitized music and lyrics servers. There are also listings by genre such as pop/rock/alternative, metal/hard rock/industrial, country/western, jazz/blues/R&B, even classical and new age. You can browse by ABCs, type of music, or resource. "Resource" includes newsgroups, mailing lists, FAQ files, lyrics, guitar tab, digitized songs, and many, many WWW pages. Persist. Try early in the day. This busy site is sometimes hard to get to, but worth your effort for its depth.

**http://american.recordings.com/wwwofmusic/
    ubl/ubl.shtml**

A B C D E F G H I J K L M N O P Q R S T U V W X Y Z

BRASS INSTRUMENTS

The Canadian Brass

A review in the *Columbus Dispatch* called this group "the best thing to happen to brass music since the invention of the spit valve" (Barbara Zuck). They play music from Bach to blues, and some say they put brass music "on the map." Their witty arrangements, vast repertoire, and humorous commentary beguile their audiences. Here you'll find biographies of each member, a history of the group, and brass-related articles from the *New York Times* and other sources. You can read mostly glowing reviews, check out the popular, classical, and Christmas discographies, and find out about their line of brass instruments and arrangements.

http://www.canbrass.com/

The Home Page of the Trombone

A picture of the Three Stooges sets the stage nicely for this sometimes goofy page. Here you can explore the soul of the trombonist. Read about the 500 trombone players (over 6 times 76!) who descended upon Las Vegas for the 24th International Trombone Workshop in late May, 1995. Did you know there's an International Women's Trombone Choir? You'll find a picture to prove it here. There are also sound clips, a mouthpiece chart, and selected bibliographies. The Trombone-L listserv is a discussion list dedicated to "any aspect of the trombone"—even messy slide treatments. The archives are here, too. If you like what you read, sign on for daily reports from the Land of Trombone. The links include other brass Web sites, like trumpet, French horn, and euphonium.

http://www.missouri.edu/~cceric/index.html

Trumpet Players' International Network

Trumpet players of the world, unite! At the TPIN site you'll find advice, lists of literature, facts about jazz and orchestral playing, and notes (so to speak) on improvisation. If you want a daily dose of trumpet lore, sign up on the e-mail Trumpet List. There's also an online chat server at this site. The graphics file includes pictures of performers like Dizzy Gillespie, as well as trumpets, old and new. And go through the more than two dozen Web pages for individual trumpet players, some famous, some not. There's also a miscellaneous section on valve alignment, humor, performance anxiety, and trumpet myths. How do you get to Carnegie Hall? Practice, practice, practice—then stop, and read essays on practice routines you might try, by famous performers and teachers. Even non-trumpeters can benefit from these specific ideas.

http://trumpet.dana.edu/~trumpet/

NET FILES

Everyone's heard of the 4-H Club. What, exactly, are the four H's?

Answer: In 1911, they stood for "Head, Heart, Hands, and Hustle . . . head trained to think, plan and reason; heart trained to be true, kind and sympathetic; hands trained to be useful, helpful and skillful; and the hustle to render ready service, to develop health and vitality." Now, however, they signify Head, Heart, Hands, and Health. The 4-H "four-leaf clover" emblem was patented in 1924.
http://www.fourhcouncil.edu/

Surf today, smart tomorrow.

Become one with the Net.

CHILDREN'S MUSIC
Children's Music Listing

Here you can find *mucho* info on children's performers, recordings, kids playing music, and where to order stacks of tapes and CDs. Run down all those links—Resources, Children's Musicians, Record Labels, Retail Outlets, and Children's Musical Theater. They'll lead you to yet more musical information!

http://www.cowboy.net/~mharper/Chmusiclist.html

Judy and David Online

This Canadian duo started performing in 1993, and recently had their first TV special. Are they the next Raffi(s)? Time will tell. In the meantime, they've put together a sweet home page. If you are in the audience when Judy and David perform, you'll find that every song they sing also has a part for you. Their online presence is similar. There's an Online Songbook, with the words, and some sound clips of traditional children's songs, and their original songs as well. After you listen to or sing "Alice the Camel," go to the coloring page, print out a picture of her, and color her to your liking.

http://www.io.org/~jandd/

CLASSICAL
BMG: Classics World

You know, there is a Beethoven other than the St. Bernard movie star (pant, pant, drool, drool). Here's where you find out when the other one lived, and what he did. This is also the place to satisfy your raging curiosity about Early Music, the Romantic period, or what's happening today in classical music. "A Beginner's Guide to Classical Music" is an online music mini-encyclopedia. It covers both eras (no, not ears) and famous composers, with good graphics and solid information. You can get a little background on the composer of that new piece you're playing in orchestra this week.

http://www.classicalmus.com/

Classical Net Home Page

People new to classical music have two questions—what do you listen to? And what are the best recordings of those pieces? This dense site answers both questions. The "List of Basic Repertoire" is a tutorial on styles and forms of music, organized by period, from Medieval to Modern. You'll also learn about each composer. Then there are reviews of recommended CDs. There's even a "Composer Data" section, with birthdates, further links to home pages, lists of works, and more classical links. "Classical music" spans nearly a thousand years. This site will give you a good start at understanding it.

http://www.webcom.com/~music/

RCA: Idiot's Guide to Classical Music

Did you know that when you listen to the Elmer Fudd Theme Song ("Kill da wabbit! Kill da wabbit!") you're really tapping your foot to *Ride of the Valkyries*, by Wagner? You probably recognize more classical music than you'd think! Take a listen to some of the sound bites at this site, and see which ones you know from TV commercials, shows, and movies. You'll also find a "Beginner's Guide to Classical Music" at this site.

http://www.rcavictor.com/rca/hits/idiots/cover.html

COUNTRY
Country Connection

This is the busiest, biggest, most-visited country music site on the Web. And no wonder! You can search the Country Connection Archives for songs and singers, and look at country music news. Then look at one of the most comprehensive collections of links to the topic—the Artist Archives. An entry for an artist might include a performer's home town, birthdate, roots and influences (sometimes with links to them), a discography, fan club address, lyrics, tablature and chords to songs, reviews, pictures, sound bites, and Web sites. There are further links to related sites, including fan pages, record labels, and "fun stuff." There's a little bit of radio and TV information too. And if you're in the mood to see your favorite performer live, look at the Tour Information. There's a link to the very detailed Musi-Cal search engine. You can enter performer's name, city, or type of event to customize your concert preferences.

http://digiserve.com/country/

A B C D E F G H I J K L M N O P Q R S T U V W X Y Z

COWPIE News

That's COuntry and Western Pickers of the Internet Electronic Newsletter. Look here to find country music songs—lyrics, tablature, and chords. They were gleaned from various newsgroups and other Net sources. Take a look at the archives of the newsletter. If you like it, and have an e-mail address, you can subscribe for free, and new issues will be e-mailed to you. The country music archives are worth a look, too. You'll find such gems as Jimmy Buffett's "Love in the Library" ("Surrounded by stories/Surreal and sublime/I fell in love in the library/Once upon a time").

http://www.realtime.net/~bleonard/cowpie.html

FOLK

Arlo Guthrie: Welcome to Arlonet!

Arlo calls himself a "folkperson and part-time thinker." He made it big in the '60s with "Alice's Restaurant," a 20-minute song that eventually became a feature film. He's been around ever since, touring, writing songs, producing albums, hanging out. Recently, he acquired the church that used to be Alice's Restaurant. Now it's home to the Guthrie Foundation (a charitable organization), the Guthrie Center, and Arlo's record label, Rising Son Records. The site has lots of lyrics, album covers, and some liner notes. You can link up to Pete Seeger, Bob Dylan, Bonnie Raitt, and other folk singers here. What does Alice Brock (of Alice's Restaurant fame) serve the night before Thanksgiving? "The Night Before Seafood Soup," of course! Get the recipe at *http://www.clark.net/pub/downin/cgi-bin/rbr.html?rbr17.*

http://www.clark.net/pub/downin/cgi-bin/arlonet.html

FolkBook: An Online Acoustic Music Establishment

FolkBook is the place to be if you're looking for info on acoustic music and musicians. There are artist biographies, collections, pictures, audio, lyrics, guitar tablature, tour schedules, and more! Want to see Mary-Chapin Carpenter in person? Try the festival and concert listings, and information organized by date and by region. You'll also find pointers to other folk-related World Wide Web and Internet information. Parental advisory—we have not chased down all the links, so you should use this site with your kids.

http://www.cgrg.ohio-state.edu/folkbook/

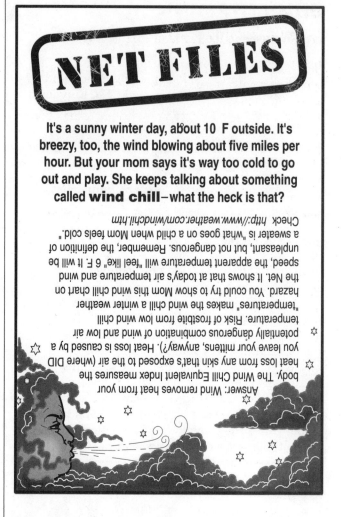

NET FILES

It's a sunny winter day, about 10 F outside. It's breezy, too, the wind blowing about five miles per hour. But your mom says it's way too cold to go out and play. She keeps talking about something called **wind chill**—what the heck is that?

Answer: Wind removes heat from your body. The Wind Chill Equivalent Index measures the heat loss from any skin that's exposed to the air (where DID you leave your mittens, anyway?). Heat loss is caused by a potentially dangerous combination of wind and low air temperature. Risk of frostbite from low wind chill "temperatures" makes the wind chill a winter weather hazard. You could try to show Mom this wind chill chart on the Net. It shows that at today's air temperature and wind speed, the apparent temperature will "feel like" 6 F. It will be unpleasant, but not dangerous. Remember, the definition of a sweater is "what goes on a child when Mom feels cold." Check *http://www.weather.com/windchill.htm*

Richard Robinson's Tunebook

Haul out your fiddle (or flute, sax, or tuba) and try some of these great tunes. This is real sheet music! If you hang out with acoustic or traditional musicians, you'll recognize some of these tunes. Jigs, reels, polkas, schottisches, and more were selected from France, Finland, Turkey, and Cape Breton, as well as lots from the British Isles. There's bound to be some *bourree* or other you've never played before. And the real fun comes when you share the tunes with other players. Anybody can play them. If you've been taking Suzuki Method lessons for a while, try something new. It's the 32-bar pause that refreshes! More tunes at *http://celtic.stanford.edu/pub/tunes/RRTunebook/tunebook.html.*

http://www.leeds.ac.uk/music/info/RRTunebk/country.html

JAZZ

Jazz: Welcome to the World of Jazz Improvisation

How does jazz work? This site can tell you. Not for performers only, lessons on jazz theory and practice fill you in on history, fundamentals, and playing with others. You'll get new insights into the heart of jazz. Also take a look at the shorter "Jazz Improvisation Primer." The rest of this site is an entire jazz library. The photograph *A Great Day in Harlem* is in the Other Music Places/Jazz-Net West section. Check out this wonderful clickable photo: it's a group picture of 57 jazz greats, taken in 1958 by Art Kane of *Esquire* magazine. Jean Bach used it in 1994 as the basis for *A Great Day in Harlem,* one of the best films ever made about jazz music. See it if you get the chance. Until you do, you can find out about most of the people in the photo, their music, and "Choice Cuts"—recommended recordings. Other links are to Pop and Commercial Music, Jazz Education resources, and World Music. There you'll find Chinese, Russian, and Bulgarian sounds, and the Mbira Home Page! Also European jazz, more photos, and jazz literature. Bring a sandwich and spend the day here.

http://gopher.adp.wisc.edu/jazz/

NET FILES

What is the sound of one cow mooing?

Answer: We're not sure, but you'll find it at Big Dave's Cow Page. Besides solo cow sounds, you'll find a cow duet, a cow chorus, and cacophony of cowbells. Mooove over, Garth, here comes Bossie! At http://www.gl.umbc.edu/~dschmil/cows/sounds.html you can hear what we mean.

Marsalis on Music Online

Wynton Marsalis, the great jazz and classical trumpet player, says, "We play at music, we don't work at it." This site is a great place to play with music. It's an overview of the four-part PBS special "Marsalis on Music." Marsalis taped this show at Tanglewood, Massachusetts, in front of a live, young audience. Yo Yo Ma and Seiji Ozawa also appeared on the show. You'll get an idea of what each episode is about; for example, "Why Toes Tap" introduces rhythm and meter. You'll get some background on wind bands and early jazz in "From Sousa to Satchmo." Marsalis also has advice on taming the "monster"—how to practice productively, and enjoy it. You can take the interactive quizzes for each show. The "Blow Your Horn" link allows you to express yourself—ask a question, share a musical anecdote, talk about your favorite performer. "Musical Accompaniments" has software you can download so you can listen to the audio examples. Ordering information for the video and book of the series is also included. On the "Welcome" page is the complete transcript of a live chat appearance in early November of 1995. Marsalis answers questions about the television series and his experiences, and he gives advice to aspiring musicians. As Wynton Marsalis says "The world of music always accepts new citizens. It's never too early or too late."

http://www.wnet.org/mom/

WNUR—FM Jazz Web (Northeastern University)

Look in "The Styles of Jazz" at the clickable hypermap. It's a chart that somehow manages to place everything from blues to bebop in the proper perspective, both time- and place-wise. When you click on "ragtime" (or whatever), you are given a fascinating article on the history and particulars of that style of jazz. You'll find artist biographies, discographies, and reviews in "Artists." In "Performance," you'll find out about festivals, venues, and regional jazz information. You can also pick an instrument, like the guitar, organ, trombone, or violin, and find more information on resources and musicians. There are also links to "media"—radio stations on the Web, magazines, and a few books. Remember books?

http://www.nwu.edu/WNUR/jazz

A
B
C
D
E
F
G
H
I
J
K
L
M
N
O
P
Q
R
S
T
U
V
W
X
Y
Z

KEYBOARD INSTRUMENTS
Piano Education Page

Have fun while practicing the piano? Isn't that a contradiction in terms? Maybe not. The "Just for Kids" section of the Piano Education Page features piano-related advice from Taz, tips for practice fun (really!), and an interview each month with a famous, sometimes dead, composer. There's even a Virtual Keyboard—it's just like a real piano, only very slow, very small, and very silly, and it sounds terrible. You'll be delighted to get to 88 real keys after that!

http://www.unm.edu/~loritaf/pnoedmn.html

LYRICS
Digital Tradition Folk Song Database

What makes a song a folk song? Folks sing them, of course! The Digital Tradition Folk Song Database is a "not-for-profit, not-for-sale, not-for-glory" collection. The 5,000+ (and growing) songs are searchable by keyword, title, and tune. For about half of these songs, you can even hear their tunes, played on a beeper. If you're interested, look at the detailed notes on how to search, and how songs get included on the database.

http://pubWeb.parc.xerox.com/digitrad

Tower Lyrics Archive

At Tower Lyrics Archive, you'll discover lyrics to Broadway and Disney shows. Take a look at Andrew Lloyd Webber's *Cats*. Since it's based on T.S. Eliot's "Old Possum's Book of Practical Cats," you'll find wonderful cat poetry there. The Disney archive has words to songs from *Aladdin, Beauty and the Beast, The Jungle Book,* and *The Little Mermaid.* If Gilbert and Sullivan delights you, *Pirates of Penzance* and three other entire plays, with dialogue as well as lyrics, are available. *Pirates* has "Modern Major General" in it. The rock opera *Tommy,* and movies like *The Nightmare Before Christmas* and *Grease*, are also here.

http://www.ccs.neu.edu/home/tower/lyrics.html

MARCHING BANDS
Marching Bands

Do you love a parade? If you're a *Music Man* fan, or if you're in a band yourself, this is the site for you. Bands by the score, of every description, abound. You can see pictures, statistics, contest standings, and lots of homecoming celebrations from all over the U.S. You can download sound clips too. "Professional" bands, like the Right Reverend All's Screamin' Hypin' Revival Band ("dedicated to the production of camaraderie and volume") vie with the 60 or so college bands. There's a great variety here, from the straight-laced traditional bands like Michigan State, to the newer "scramble bands" of the Ivy League schools. Take a look at "The World's Worst Marching Band," or the International bands (especially if you read Norwegian). Even if you don't play the glockenspiel, these links are good fun. Links to Instrument Jokes for every instrument and musical style are fun (although a few may be mildly racy).

http://seclab.cs.ucdavis.edu/~wetmore/camb/
     other_bands.html

NEW AGE
Music for a New Age

Just what is New Age Music, you might ask? What else can you call electronic synthesizers combined with the droning of the ancient Aboriginal didgeridoo? All this, and more, can be found here. "Record Company Web Pages" starts with Windham Hill and has links to many more. The personal selection of links includes one to the Audium in California. It bills itself as the First Theatre of Sound in the World. Builders of the Audium pioneered the exploration of space in music with 169 speakers that move sound around, past, over, and under the audience to make "sound sculptures." In "Artists" you can find out about Kitaro, a Japanese "National Living Treasure." He once gave a free concert specifically for 2,000 pregnant women. Yanni, Ancient Future ("world fusion music"), Enya, Andreas Vollenweider, and many other artists have home pages. Other music sources include links to jazz sites, CD sources, a database of ambient musicians (including John Cage) and reviews of 100 artists.

http://www.his.com/~fjp/music.html

PERCUSSION INSTRUMENTS
The Bodhrán

Just what is a *bodhrán*? How do you even pronounce it? Find out here—it's "the heartbeat of Irish music," and it rhymes with "cow brawn." A large wooden round frame is loosely covered with goat skin (or donkey, or greyhound skin!). The resulting large shallow drum is played with a double-headed stick. The head can be damped with the player's hand to make different tones. Look here for advice about making, buying, playing, and caring for the bodhrán. The usual assortment of tasteless musician jokes is also included. Example: What do you call a bodhrán player with a broken wrist? A huge improvement. Chieftains fans, Irish music lovers, check it out!

http://www.panix.com/~mittle/bodhran.html

The Drums and Percussion Page

Is there a drumming circle near you? If so, this site will lead you to it. You'll also find specifics about drumming, like choosing and caring for drums, drum etiquette, and percussion folktales. The standard methods of drumming are included. And there are grooves—transcriptions and patterns, like paradiddle, Latin rhythms, and ska. Check out the hand drum grooves, from *Abakua* (Cuban) to *Zebolah* (Congolese). There's an illustrated encyclopedia of percussion instruments, and lots of other drum-related sites linked here, too. Once you find one, you're on to them all.

http://www.cse.ogi.edu/Drum

REGGAE
Jammin Reggae Archives

Immerse yourself in this deep reggae site—you'll find a huge archive of articles, including a sketch of Rastafarian history; .au and .wav audio; books; graphics; interviews; and biographies of artists. Find reggae radio stations near you. Check out tour schedules. Look at all six Bob Marley Web pages, plus many other artists' home pages. And there are associated Web sites on ska and Jamaica.

http://orpheus.ucsd.edu/jammin.html

ROCK GROUPS
The Internet Beatles Album

A splendid time is guaranteed for all! Look here for Beatles history, interviews (sometimes as audio files), lots of photos, and some gossip. The information is classified using Beatles song titles. For instance, the section called "I want to tell you" debunks (or verifies) certain Beatles rumors. Is "Lucy in the Sky with Diamonds" about drugs? Well, no. Four-year-old Julian Lennon's drawing of the same name gave John the inspiration. You can look at the picture here.

http://www.primenet.com/~dhaber/beatles.html

Rock & Roll Hall of Fame + Museum

Are these really the 500 songs that shaped rock & roll? Well, it's a start, and if you have other ideas, you can always vote in the Ballot Box for your personal choice. The Rock & Roll Hall of Fame + Museum is in Cleveland, Ohio, and is a little bit like the Baseball Hall of Fame in Cooperstown, New York. Read profiles of the rock legends who have been inducted into the Hall of Fame, and listen to their audio files. You can also read about and listen to the 500 songs themselves. If you "Visit the Rock Hall of Fame" you'll see photos of the building and those celebrities who have visited lately. In "Win Free Stuff" you can submit your best rock & roll memory (in 75 words or so). You may win a T shirt. Even if you don't win, look at the sweet memories of previous winners. What rock star was born on your birthday? There's a file in "Rock News" that will tell you. And there are searchable archives, and articles (from the *Cleveland Plain Dealer*) about "Cities that Formed Rock & Roll," like Detroit, LA, and Liverpool, England.

http://www.rockhall.com/

The Sun never sets on the Internet.

SACRED

Christian Artists List

Maintained for a Christian radio station in Ohio, you'll find a great variety of artists at this site. Some of the pages are more unofficial than others. You may be interested to learn why Alice Cooper is on the Christian Artists List. He's reportedly found God, and you can read some first-hand accounts here. Read about the Benedictine Monks of Santo Domingo de Silos for a history of Gregorian chant. The Webmaster says these are not necessarily all "Christian" artists, but defines them as "artists that have been found to be of interest to Christians...."

http://linus.cs.ohiou.edu/~wlhd/alight/cartists.html

Christian Music Online

For rock and other popular music with a message, look here. You'll find album covers, long biographies, and lyrics for artists like Amy Grant and Guardian. You can browse the artists alphabetically. There's also a link to two Christian magazines. *Christian Calendar* magazine has sample interviews with William Bennett and others. *Release* is specifically about Christian entertainment.

http://www.cmo.com/cmo/

NET FILES

Where did the word **geyser** originate?

ANSWER: The Geysir, which means "gusher," is a geyser located in Haukadalur, Iceland. All other geysers in the world were named after it! It erupts only rarely these days, but when it does, the water and steam may reach two hundred feet in the air! Go to *http://www.wku.edu/www/geoweb/geyser/location.html* and read all about geysers around the world. There's also a colorful map of worldwide geyser locations.

STRINGED INSTRUMENTS

Cello Introduction

Cellists young and old, amateur and pro, will love this site! Here's an introduction to the instrument, including an "interactive multimedia presentation." You'll find out about repertoire, history, and famous artists and teachers. If you're a young cellist, there's a special section just for you on getting started, picking what to play, and what to listen to. In a photo tour, Baby Alec will introduce you to the parts of the cello. Don't miss the sound samples in the "Guide for the Clueless"; the harmonic bugle call would make a great start-up sound! The Tutor includes a few goofy exercises—hey, everyone, time to hug your cello!

http://tahoma.cwu.edu:2000/~michelj/
    Cello_Introduction/Cello_Introduction.html

The Classical Guitar Home Page

Suppose you've been playing classical guitar since three weeks ago last Tuesday. Is there any place you can find quality guitar music, with fingerings? Try the Classical Guitar Beginner's Page at this site. Whether you're a beginning or experienced classical guitarist, you'll have fun browsing here. The Beginner's Page suggests recordings, books, and videos to get you off to a good start. Suggested Playing includes pieces by Carulli and Sor in GIF format, with MIDI files to go along with them. More complicated music is available in "Guitar Music," with pieces by Bach and Satie, and a flamenco exercise. If you like the flamenco exercise, look at the Flamenco Guitar Home Page. There are links to guitar organizations, with reviews of concerts and recordings, and guitar-related articles.

http://www.teleport.com/~jdimick/cg.html

TEJANO

The New Tejano Home Page

Tejano (you pronounce this word Tay-Yawno) is a cool new music style that is a combination of Mexican sounds, American rock 'n roll, and a little bit of country music. If you are a fan of Tejano, or if you'd like to see what all the excitement is about, take a look at the New Tejano Home Page. All the best groups and solo artists are here, including birthdays of the stars, some great pictures, and the latest news on the Tejano scene.

http://www.OndaNet.com:1995/tejano/tejano.html

WIND INSTRUMENTS

The Recorder: Instrument of Torture or Instrument of Music?

Nicholas Lander, Webmaster of this site, ponders this same question. While mulling it over, he imparts information on history, technique, and repertoire of the recorder. His notes on fingerings and vibrato techniques are very complete. He also has links to recorder makers, catalogues (this is an Australian site), MIDI files, and references to journals and books. And then there's the link to his Crumhorn page.

http://www.iinet.net.au/~nickl/torture.html

Windplayer Online

Woodwind and brass musicians, take note. At Windplayer Online, you'll find tips and advice from those in the know—professional musicians. The featured instruments are an unlikely quintet: trombone, trumpet, sax, clarinet, and flute. In each category you'll find player profiles (of artists like clarinetist Don Byron). Then you might take a master class from Herbie Mann on Brazilian flute playing. New products from many instrument makers are presented. And if you're in the market to buy or sell an instrument, check out the classified ads.

http://www.windplayer.com/

WORLD MUSIC

Ceolas Celtic Music Archive

Celtic music can be defined rather loosely as music from Ireland, Scotland, Wales, Brittany (France), and Galacia (Spain), with the U.S. and Canada also contributing. This site is truly a Celtic cornucopia. The "Ceolas Archive" includes radio stations, magazines, events, and local information. There are good pamphlets from the Irish Traditional Music Archive: What is Irish Music?, Hearing Irish Music, Learning Irish Music, and Studying Irish Music. "Ceolas: Tunes" has links to GIF and "abc notation" formatted music. There are more links to tunes, listservs, newsgroups and mailing lists, festivals and concerts. And all those interesting Irish instruments, like Uiullean pipes, bodhráns, and tin whistles, have explanatory essays.

http://celtic.stanford.edu/ceolas.html

NET FILES

How many footballs are used in each NFL game?

Answer: According to the NFL Digest of Rules, "Twenty-four approved footballs will be used in each game (12 each half)." Visit the NFL's online library at http://nflhome.com/library/rules/diggame.html to find out more.

Lark In The Morning

Where could you buy a hurdy-gurdy, or an Italian bagpipe, or an eighteenth-century oboe? Lark In The Morning specializes in hard-to-find musical instruments, music, and instructional materials. They also sell recordings from all over the world, and have sound samples to entice you to buy. Their picture dictionary, describing music-makers strange only to us, is complete and fascinating. Read the articles on instrument repair, the interviews with musicians, the essays on various unusual instruments, humor, and dance, and other resources. Lark in The Morning is truly more than a music store. If you don't happen to live in Mendocino, California, you can still visit via the Net!

http://www.mhs.mendocino.k12.ca.us/MenComNet/Business/Retail/Larknet/larkhp.html

Maui Music Pages

Listen to beautiful classic and contemporary music from Hawai'i at this site. Definitely check out traditional slack key guitar music from Keola Beamer as well as the best-selling hits from Keali'i Reichel, who recently "swept" the Hawaiian Music Awards.

http://www.maui.com/~sbdc/music/

NATIVE AMERICANS AND OTHER INDIGENOUS PEOPLES

Arctic Circle: History and Culture

You'll find information here about many people who are native to the Arctic Circle region of the world. You'll not only learn about the Cree of Northern Quebec and the Inupiat of Arctic Alaska, but also the Nenets and Khanty of Yamal Peninsula, Northwest Siberia, and the Sámi of Far Northern Europe. Find out why the concept of "wilderness" is unknown to these people, who live in harmony with their natural surroundings.

http://www.lib.uconn.edu:80/ArcticCircle/
   HistoryCulture/index.html

A Guide to the Great Sioux Nation

The people of the Sioux Nation prefer to be called Dakota, Lakota, or Nakota, depending on their language group. On this South Dakota home page, you can learn about the languages, legends, and rich cultural traditions of these proud peoples. You'll see beautiful costumes, and maybe you can attend one of the pow-wows! There is a calendar of annual events here, so go get yourself some fry bread and enjoy the music and dance!

http://www.state.sd.us/state/executive/tourism/
   sioux/sioux.htm

Indian Lore Galore

The movie *The Indian in the Cupboard* is based on the culture of the Onondaga Nation, part of the federation of six eastern U.S. tribes known as the Iroquois or *Ho di no sion ni*. Jeanne Shenandoah, Turtle Clan Mother, shares Onondaga history, legend, and lifestyle. Read about the Great Law of Peace, and how the Creator's messenger united the original five Iroquois nations to be of one mind and cease their conflicts.

http://www.paramount.com/ILore.html

NET FILES

ACROSS the water, you see a distant fellow boater holding a yellow and red flag in each hand, out straight from his sides. Is he trying to tell you something?

ANSWER: He might be. If he is signaling you using the semaphore flag system, he is sending the code for the letter "R." Want to know what the rest of his message is? Better check *http://155.187.10.12/flags/semaphore.html* to find out!

National Museum of the American Indian

This particular Smithsonian Museum is in New York City, not Washington, D.C. Most of the one million objects in its collection represent cultures in the United States and Canada, although there are also items from Mexico and Central and South America. You can see many artifacts of ancient and contemporary native culture through the online exhibits of clothing, baskets, beadwork, and other objects. This museum displays sacred materials only with the permission of the various tribes, and returns these materials to the tribes on request. Chances are you've never seen things like this before! Imagine wearing a beautiful, eagle-feather costume as you dance. "When a Ponca singer sings, the singing and the music make you dance. Some singers don't move you, but a Ponca singer will move you in your heart and mind; they make it easy to dance longer. These eagle feathers are stripped so they can hang down and flutter in the wind, like the ribbons on our shirts."—Abe Conklin (Ponca-Osage).

http://www.si.edu/organiza/museums/amerind/nmai/
start.htm

NativeWeb Home Page

Did you know there are hundreds of federally-recognized Nations within the United States? Learn more about Native Americans at this site, which collects info on art, culture, government, languages, music, religious beliefs, and current tribal issues. You can read native newsletters and see a calendar of upcoming events. Particularly interesting are the rules you should follow when attending a pow-wow, a ritual celebration including dance, singing, and drumming. To help find one near you, this site has event listings for the U.S., Canada, and Mexico.

http://web.maxwell.syr.edu/nativeweb/

Oneida Indian Nation

The Oneidas were the first Indian nation to put up a Web page and claim territory in cyberspace. The Oneidas are located in central New York State, and they remain an unconquered nation. In fact, they were the only Indian tribe to fight on the side of the American colonists during the American Revolutionary war. This fact, often left out of history books, is detailed on this page. In 1777-1778, Washington's soldiers were enduring a hard winter at Valley Forge, Pennsylvania. Oneidas walked hundreds of miles south, carrying food and supplies, to come to their aid. Polly Cooper was an Oneida woman who helped the soldiers, teaching them how to cook the corn and other foods they had brought with them. Although offered payment, she refused, saying it was her duty to help friends in need. She was thanked for her assistance by Martha Washington herself, who presented Polly with a fancy shawl and bonnet. The shawl has been a treasured Oneida relic since then, and you can see a photo of it here. You can also hear some Oneida words, take a tour of the cultural museum, read original Indian treaties, and see some real wampum!

http://www.one-web.org/oneida/

Surf today, smart tomorrow.

OTA's Native American Resource Page

Recently, the U.S. Congress' Office of Technology Assessment released a report on the status of telecommunications and Indian nations. In the course of their investigation, they found many important Native Web resources. An annotated list of them is here. You'll find links to native music, arts, languages, tribal government information, and more.

http://www.ota.gov/nativea.html

Pueblo Cultural Center

In the American desert southwest, in New Mexico, nineteen Pueblo communities welcome visitors, both real and virtual. You can read descriptions of all of them here, as well as pick up some maps to the pueblos, calendars of events, and even some rules for attending dances (don't applaud; dance is a prayer, not a performance). Gaze at the stunning wall murals, with titles such as these: The One-Horned Buffalo Dance; The Sounds of Life and Earth as It Breathes; and Indian Maiden Feeding Deer. You can read biographies of the artists, too.

http://hanksville.phast.umass.edu/defs/independent/PCC/PCC.html#toc

Web Pages and Other Resources for Indian Teachers and Students

Want to learn about native astronomy or traditional foods, or read some stories written by kids at Indian schools? This page offers loads of annotated links to Mayan, aboriginal, and other resources. There's also an HTML tutorial for eight-year-olds! This page is a must for anyone interested in native issues and current events.

http://indy4.fdl.cc.mn.us/~isk/

NATIVE HAWAIIANS
Gods and Myths

Read about how the fire goddess, Pele, created the Hawaiian Islands, raising them with her volcanic power. If you visit Volcanoes National Park on the Big Island today, you will find flower leis and other offerings to this very powerful goddess. You'll also find out about the many other gods and goddesses of Hawai'i, sacred sites like ancient *heiau*, and other traditional practices.

http://hawaii-shopping.com/~sammonet/gods.html

A
B
C
D
E
F
G
H
I
J
K
L
M
N
O
P
Q
R
S
T
U
V
W
X
Y
Z

Arvol Looking Horse is the 19th generation *Keeper of the Sacred White Buffalo Calf Pipe* for the Lakota, Dakota, and Nakota Nations. He has called for a world day of prayer on June 21, 1996.

2,000 years ago, the pipe (or sacred bundle) was given to the People by **White Buffalo Calf Woman**. She taught seven sacred ceremonies, including the sweat lodge and sun dance ceremonies, before she left the nations. She made a prophecy that she would come back for the pipe someday, and that a sign of her coming would be the birth of a white buffalo calf. In 1994, a white buffalo calf was born in Wisconsin. You can read about the cultural and spiritual significance of this event at Web Pages and Other Resources for Indian Teachers and Students.

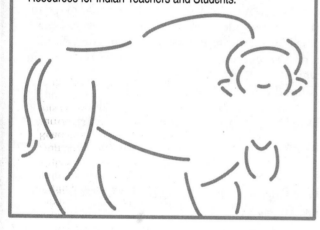

Nation of Hawai'i

In November, 1993, President Bill Clinton signed into law U.S. Public Law 103-50 which is "To acknowledge the 100th anniversary of the January 17, 1893 overthrow of the Kingdom of Hawaii, and to offer an apology to Native Hawaiians on behalf of the United States for the overthrow of the Kingdom of Hawaii." Some native Hawaiians are trying to restore Hawai'i to sovereign nation status. That means it would have its own leaders and could determine its own future. Read news about the Nation of Hawai'i, and find out about native island culture here.

http://hawaii-nation.org/nation/

Become one with the Net.

You Can With Beakman and Jax

Why do feet smell? What's JELL-O really made of? What direction is DOWN? Where are the latest Hubble Telescopespace photos? If it has something to do with science, you may find it collected here. Look for more Beakman information at the *Beakman's World* TV show home page at *http://www.spe.sony.com/Pictures/tv/beakman/beakman.html*.

http://pomo.nbn.com/youcan/

MAGAZINES
CyberKids

CyberKids magazine is chock-full of games, word searches and crossword puzzles, but—watch out!—you could learn something before you know it. All the stories and artwork have been created by kids, of course. They've told about the first African American woman in space, how one family came from Vietnam to the United States, and about Egyptian gods. Also pretty great are the reviews of computer stuff, like software and printers. You can contribute your own stories, enter contests, and comment on other kids' ideas.

http://www.mtlake.com/cyberkids/

Fish-Net

Fish-Net is an ever-changing gathering place for teens on the Web and its goal is to have you spend "quality time" on the Internet. This bills itself as a "high-performance magazine for students." Learn how to handle stress before a test, how to buy a backpack, how to recognize bogus advertising claims and more. Many of these articles are written by teenagers. You can send in your own story and earn money if your story's good enough to be published. You can also read what other kids think about different topics, and post your own responses.

http://www2.interpath.net:80/sbi/Open.html

Visit the stars in Astronomy.

MidLink Magazine: The Electronic Magazine for Kids in the Middle Grades

Design an alien or visit a virtual haunted house at *MidLink*, where kids ranging in age from 10 to 15 years gather to share news of their schools and cities. And speaking of cities, why not take a virtual tour of kids' homes around the world while you're there? Kids hanging out at *MidLink* are busy changing the meaning of the word "report" in their Electronic Portfolios section. They've written on subjects ranging from the atom bomb to surfing, but the really cool thing is all the reports have hypertext links to more information about the subjects in other places on the Internet. And don't miss the Cool-School Home Pages.

http://longwood.cs.ucf.edu/~MidLink/

Sports Illustrated for Kids Online

When was the last time you climbed a treacherous rock wall, shredded some ramps with the only pro female skateboarder in the country, or picked up some racing tips from the world's best BMX bicycle racer—all without leaving your computer? *Sports Illustrated for Kids Online* is all about athletic challenges—like climbing their sports trivia "rock wall." If you've been wanting to try your hand at a new sport, this is where you can find out all about the moves, the lingo, and the equipment. Don't miss the interviews with sports heroes, hilarious comics, and a whole lot more.

http://pathfinder.com/@@SYNR8pGQMgIAQAJQ/SIFK/

The Sun never sets on the Internet.

NET FILES

WHAT WOULD YOU BE LOOKING AT IF YOU WERE HOLDING A COPY OF THE ·DUNLAP BROADSIDE·?

Answer: You'd be looking at one of only 24 known surviving copies of the first printing of the Declaration of Independence, printed by Philadelphian printer John Dunlap on July 4, 1776. Read more interesting facts surrounding the creation of this famous document in the entry on Thomas Jefferson, in the "Specific Presidents" section of Presidents, *http://sunsite.unc.edu/lia/president/pressite/*

Time World Wide Home Page

Okay, okay, we know this is a news magazine for adults, but we've got a helpful homework hint for you. Say it's 9:00 P.M. and you've got a paper due tomorrow on how Russians and Americans are cooperating in space, or on hurricanes, or on computer hackers. Are you in big trouble or what? Well, here's what you can do. Go to this home page, where you can search through magazines for articles—and there's a whole lot more than just *Time* magazine. Don't forget: *Time* has a bunch of sister magazines, like *Fortune, Money,* and *People,* and they're all right here. Just type in a word or a phrase and let this Web site do the walking for the stories you need. You don't even have to spell the words right.

http://pathfinder.com/@@5U9HmOGxNwIAQANQ/time/timehomepage.html

A B C D E F G H I J K L M N O P Q R S T U V W X Y Z

U.S. News Online

Do we even need to mention that a magazine called *U.S. News* is going to bring you news, news, and more news every week? We don't think so. Want more than just the week's news? Click on "News You Can Use," a weekly feature, full of some really helpful tips, like how to order healthy food at a restaurant, how to buy a new computer, and which colleges are the very best in the country. Want to get into politics? Click on "Washington Infobank" to link to the White House, or your own senators and representatives, and to find out all about the people running for president in 1996.

http://www2.USNews.com/usnews/main.htm

USA Today

"Your news when you want it" is *USA Today*'s motto, and you're going to get exactly that at this site. You can go right to the sections you want by clicking on the buttons for News, Sports, Money, Life, or Weather. And speaking of weather, there's a ton of forecasts, fun facts, and other goodies here, from information on tornadoes and hurricanes, to tips on weather forecasting. Everything's just as readable and colorful as the actual newspaper. It's a whole lot more than a newspaper, though, because the news is updated every day and sports scores are freshened up every two minutes. Impress your family by downloading the interactive crossword puzzle and a special puzzle viewer so you can work it out offline.

http://www.usatoday.com/usafront.htm

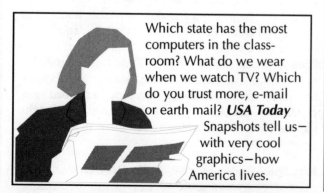

Which state has the most computers in the classroom? What do we wear when we watch TV? Which do you trust more, e-mail or earth mail? *USA Today* Snapshots tell us—with very cool graphics—how America lives.

NEWS SOURCES

Electronic Newsstand Homepage

The wind never blows the newspapers away, and browsing's always free at this virtual newsstand, where Reuters news service brings you the very latest news of the world and sports. Real news-hounds can link to excerpts from newspapers from South Africa, Russia, Singapore, or sign up for a free 30-day subscription to HeadsUp, an interactive daily news service that e-mails you only the news you're interested in. This is the best source on the Internet for articles from the world's leading newspapers, magazines, and catalogues. Keep in mind you're not getting the entire paper. For example, you'll find the *Wall Street Journal*'s Classroom Edition here, with information about the publication, and some sample articles from recent issues.

http://www.enews.com/

NewsLink

Wow! Stop the presses! Check this site: 705 newspapers, 444 broadcast stations, 669 magazines, plus 577 other special links. You ought to be able to get all the news here! Started wondering about which college is right for you? Maybe you've got a sister, brother, or friend who's already gone away to one. One of the best ways to find out about a college is to check out its newspaper. You can keep up with campus news by reading the online versions of college newspapers from the *Arizona Daily Wildcat* to *The Yale Daily News* at this site. About fifty college papers are there, with more being added all the time.

http://www.newslink.org/menu.html

Other RealAudio Sites

Now hear this! The news, that is. Yep, this site's for people who'd rather listen to the news than read it. You're going to want to grab your own version of the RealAudio player (it's free, courtesy of Progressive Networks) once you check out all the cool stuff you can hear. The RealAudio Player software enables users to access RealAudio programming and play it back in an on-demand audio stream, which means you don't have to download those gigantic files first, which gets a little boring. Not to be missed is the news from French, Italian, and Japanese public broadcast networks (not to mention our own National Public Radio), political speeches from C-SPAN, the evening news from ABC World News Tonight, and broadcasts from Greenpeace ships around the world.

http://www.realaudio.com/othersites.html

Pathfinder's News Now

Click on a headline in News Now and you'll be taken instantly to the complete story, whether it's the latest from Washington D.C., or the batting average of your favorite player. The news is updated hourly and sports is updated even more often. In fact, the sports news here is awesome: you can get stats, schedules, box scores, game recaps and previews, and the very latest transactions. Since Time Warner, Inc.—the people who publish *Time, People, Sports Illustrated, Money, Fortune,* and lots of other famous magazines—run this site, you can get the complete background on any subject right here.

http://pathfinder.com/@@q6KLAWF2NwIAQAhT/
News/news.html

NEWSPAPERS
CRAYON

Wouldn't it be great if you could design a newspaper with just the news YOU want to read? How about an all-sports newspaper? Or an all-music newspaper? How about adding the current weather map, or the current stock price on a share of Toys R Us? This interactive site lets you do just that, and "publish" an updated paper any time you want, with your very own Web browser.

http://sun.bucknell.edu/~boulter/crayon/

The Nando Times

What's a "Nando"? Are we talking about another planet here? Nope, "Nando" means News and Observer—the newspaper of Raleigh, North Carolina. The online edition keeps news of the world, sports, and entertainment coming around the clock, with updates from the Associated Press and lots of other places. While you're here, make sure you link back to the paper's online service, Nando.net, and check out NandoNext. It's a Web site created just for the interests and attitudes of the "next" generation, featuring stories and art from local high school students. Don't miss their music, movie, and concert reviews!

http://www2.nando.net/nt/nando.cgi

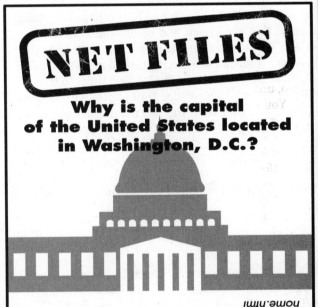

NET FILES

Why is the capital of the United States located in Washington, D.C.?

Answer: There weren't a lot of choices, back in the late 1700s. Some people though New York would be a good place, while others favored Philadelphia, Pennsylvania. George Washington finally selected a site on the Potomac River, about half-way between the original northern and southern states. The area was wilderness. It was marshy and full of mosquitoes. The area was drained and construction began. According to the White House for Kids home page, the French city planner, Pierre L'Enfant, "decided to place the Capitol Building on one hill and the 'President's House' on another hill. "In between, there were parks and grand boulevards. You can read more White House History at http://www.whitehouse.gov/WH/kids/html/home.html

OPTICAL ILLUSIONS

Illusions

Now you see them, now you don't! Optical illusions are given wide representation here. Open up the doors of perception and come on in. Maybe you'll even be able to find your way back out!

http://renoir.psych.nyu.edu:9999/~thebin/illusions/illusions.html

Optical Illusions

Bob Ausbourne, a commercial artist who loves optical illusions, has put together a page featuring a collection of classics, and occasionally includes one of his own design. He calls them "candy to the senses," and this is a great place to go to satisfy that sweet tooth. You will also find links to the M.C. Escher and Salvador Dali pages, with optical illusion artwork from the two master artists, and a stereogram page that leaps out at folks who have learned to use their "magic eye." Parental advisory: all links leading off this site have not been checked.

http://lainet3.lainet.com/~ausbourn/index.html

World of Escher

Waterfalls that flow up? Stairs that seem to keep going down, yet, suddenly, you're back on top of a building? These inexplicable drawings by M. C. Escher must be seen to be believed!

http://www.texas.net/escher/textonly.html

You Can Illusions

What you think you see is not always what's really there. Look at some famous optical illusions with Beakman and Jax, who explain things like whether that's a lady wearing a hat or a duck. Wait, she's not wearing a duck, she's wearing a hat. Maybe it's a duck. Oh, never mind!

http://pomo.nbn.com/youcan/illusion/illusions.html

ORGANIZATIONS

Children's Defense Fund

Being a kid in the 1990s can be tough. Poverty, abuse, and negligence are a few of the problems kids confront. The Children's Defense Fund is an organization designed to help kids with some of the difficult problems they face. To learn more about the Children's Defense Fund, take a look at their home page!

http://www.tmn.com/cdf/index.html

The InterNETional Scouting Page

Scouting is EVERYWHERE. Girl Scouts, Boy Scouts, Explorers, the college fraternity Alpha Phi Omega—these are all scouting organizations, and you can find them in just about every country in the world. Naturally, scouting groups are all over the Internet as well. To learn about scouting from A to Z, take a look at the InterNETional Scouting Page. You'll see a whole lot more about scouting than tying knots and selling cookies!

http://scout.strw.leidenuniv.nl/

NET FILES

What tiny critters can be found from twenty miles beneath Earth's surface to twenty miles overhead?

ANSWER: Microbes! Visit Dirt World at http://commtechlab.msu.edu/CTLprojects/dlc-me/zoo/ which is the DLC-ME Microbe Zoo! You'll find they inhabit almost every friendly corner on Earth. Be sure to check out the Snack Bar, too!

Make-A-Wish Foundation of America

Founded in the belief that lives are measured by memories, and not by years, the Make-A-Wish Foundation has granted more than 30,000 wishes to American children between the ages of two-and-a-half and eighteen who have terminal illnesses or life-threatening medical conditions. Since the first wish (granted in 1980 for a seven-year-old boy with terminal leukemia who wanted to be a policeman), 81 chapters have sprung up around the U.S. With the family's participation, the Foundation is committed to providing a memorable and carefree experience for these children, whose wishes are limited only by their own imaginations. If you know someone who would like to make a special wish, check the State listings to find the Make-A-Wish chapter nearest you.

http://www.wish.org/

National 4-H Council

What does it mean to be involved in 4-H? It can mean learning how to give a great speech, helping save the environment, raising animals, or working on a project with friends. From country lanes to city streets, kids are involved in 4-H activities, and 4-H kids are having fun and learning much. To get the inside scoop on 4-H, take a peek at the National 4-H Council home page.

http://www.fourhcouncil.edu/

National PTA

One hundred years ago, the National PTA was founded by Alice McLellan Birney and Phoebe Apperson Hearst, as the National Congress of Mothers. Alice McLellan Birney said, "Let us have no more croaking as to what cannot be done; let us see what can be done." Today, this large organization is doing many things. Here, you can get more information about educational initiatives, health and welfare programs, and legislative issues. Parents and teacher volunteers will meet in Washington, D.C. in June, 1996 to celebrate 100 years of advocacy for education.

http://www.pta.org/

Plugged In

Plugged In is an outreach program providing computer access to children and families in Palo Alto, California. Projects kids work on include fine arts, filmmaking, and storytelling, all via the computers. You can see the results here. This page describes Summer Drop-In Projects, and directs you to Cool Spots on the Internet and other fun Web things. Plugged In is also learning about student-run enterprise by creating Web pages for individuals, businesses and other non-profits. Check their rates!

http://www.pluggedin.org

YMCAs on the WEB

Why would you go to the "Y," the YMCA? You could go for all kinds of reasons. You could go for a game of B-Ball, swimming lessons, judo, or even basket weaving. The "Y" is a fun place for everybody in the family, and there are many YMCAs all over the Internet. Take a look at YMCAs on the Web to see if a "Y" near you has a presence in Cyberspace.

http://homepage.interaccess.com/~dhayward/index.html

OUTDOOR RECREATION

ARCHERY

Angus Duggan: Archery

Archery is hard! Making an arrow go where it's supposed to may seem easy, but it isn't. At the World Target Archery Records you'll see who is the best in bending bows and slinging arrows. You'll also learn something about the history of archery and its equipment.

http://www.dcs.ed.ac.uk/home/ajcd/archery/

Many common phrases originated in the sport of archery! "Point blank," "high strung," "straight as an arrow," "bolt from the blue," and "wide of the mark" are a few. Shoot over to **Angus Duggan's Archery Page** to learn more!

BICYCLES AND BICYCLING

Mountain Biking

You live in Kansas, but go on family vacations to California, and you love to go mountain biking there. Hey! You see on the news that there are wildfires in Pt. Reyes, and wonder what might have happened to your favorite seaside trails! Your local newspapers and bike shops don't have any info on trails that far away. What do you do? Connect to the Mountain Biking Web site and read updates about the trail damage, of course! Here, you'll find news, race information, and advice on riding and taking care of your mountain bike. You can also get information about cool mountain bike trails in the United States, Canada, Europe, Latin America, Asia, and Africa.

http://xenon.stanford.edu/~rsf/mtn-bike.html

The Stolen Bike Page

It's too bad, but plenty of bikes are stolen every year. You can pre-register your bike's description here, before it gets stolen. Or look for your bike in the database—maybe it's been found in the next city. You should know your bike's serial number, colors, decorations, and any other identifying equipment, dents, or markings.

http://www.nashville.net/cycling/stolen.html

CANOEING AND KAYAKING

See also: BOATS AND SAILING

Bruce's Paddling Page

Paddling is a fun and exciting adventure for the "real outdoors type." This site is from Delaware and there's some information of local interest, including some neat information on Chesapeake Bay. You can even get the local sea buoy meteorological readings! However, there is also extensive material for paddlers everywhere. Answers to frequently-asked questions, a list of resources, and a checklist of gear you really ought to have are all included. There's even a recipe page full of good "outdoor" eating. Paddle on over and go ashore.

http://ssnet.com/~bef/BrucesPaddlingPage.html

NET FILES

When was the planet Uranus discovered?

Answer: Uranus was discovered on March 13, 1781 by William Herschel. Check out the History of Astronomy at http://www.kaiwan.com/~ozma/mar.html for an astronomical list of facts.

FISHING

See also: FISH

GORP—Fishing Resources on the Internet

Looking for the right angle on fishing? GORP is where they're biting! This is no line, you'll find everything from general fishing, to fishing gear, to information on fishing trips. Stop by and catch yours today.

http://www.gorp.com/gorp/activity/fishing.htm

J.P.'s Fishing Page

Something smells FISHY here! That's because J.P.'s Fishing Page is full of fishy type information. Looking for places to go night fishing? Interested in learning about fly fishing, or just want to talk with others interested in this art? This is the place to go. Hurry, before this one gets away!

http://www.geo.mtu.edu/~jsuchosk/fish/fishpage

GOLF AND MINIATURE GOLFING
GolfMart University

Do you know how to improve your putting game for eight cents? Can you improve your swing by THROWING a golf ball, or by practicing with your eyes closed? These and other questions are answered at the GolfMart University site, where a teaching pro gives tips to make you a better golfer. By the way, if you practice your golf swing with your eyes closed, you will get a better idea of how your weight is balanced. If you fall down when you swing, you have some work to do!

http://chili.rt66.com/cyspacemalls/golf/tips.html

Golfweb—Library—Fun and Games

There's no doubt about it: golf is fun! But sometimes just keeping score isn't enough. At this site you can find the simple rules to dozens of different golf games. There are games for two, three, or four players, and there are team games for groups. And the best part is that they're all fun!

http://www.golfweb.com/glbb/index.htm

> ## Let balloonists take you to new heights in Aviation and Airplanes.

HIKING AND BACKPACKING
Hiking On The World Wide Web

This is a nice little annotated list for information on hiking the Appalachian Trail, or trails in many National Parks. There are pointers to gear reviews including boots and tents of the inexpensive kind. Take a hike up and down the trails this site recommends. Parental advisory: The Backcountry Home Page link off this page is generally excellent, but should be previewed.

http://moe.cc.utexas.edu/~susanw/inform/roe/index.html

LUMBERJACKS
The North American Guide to Lumberjack Entertainment and Sporting Events

There are world records for lumberjack sporting events. If you haven't heard of this sport, you will. It's growing like crazy. On this page, you can see who holds the world record in a variety of lumberjack competitions, as well as see other information about this unusual sport.

http://www.starinfo.com/ljguide/lumberjack.html

MOUNTAIN AND ROCK CLIMBING
Go Climb a Rock

Check the Climber's dictionary. They actually have an entry under "AAAAAAHHHHHHHH!!!" The definition is "a fall in progress!" Seriously, this is a site you need to traverse over to. Check climbing shoe ratings, technique tips, and a slew of links to climbing magazines and gear companies. There is a listing of the top climbers in the world, and big plans for expanding this site. They have an excellent start.

http://ic.net/~pokloehn/

A
B
C
D
E
F
G
H
I
J
K
L
M
N
O
P
Q
R
S
T
U
V
W
X
Y
Z

ORIENTEERING

Orienteering

Does this sound like fun? You and your friends use a very detailed map and a compass to visit various checkpoint flags hidden in the woods. When you reach a checkpoint, you use a special hole punch (usually hanging by the flag) to verify that you found the flag. The punches make different-shaped holes in your control card. This fast-growing sport can be enjoyed as a simple family walk in the woods, or as a competitive team race. Learn about getting started in orienteering here.

http://www.williams.edu:803/Biology/
  orienteering/o~index.html

ROLLER AND INLINE SKATING

Hardcore Inline Skating

There's "flatlanders" who love to inline skate. Then there's the "hardcore" skaters, who will try almost anything. This site is for all inline skaters and fans. It's packed! It has pages with skating techniques, video clips, safety tips, skating terms, product reviews, park listings—everything about inline! Go for that "mcflip" or a "farside missou," but maybe you should skate over to the "Hardcore..." page to see the pros do it first!

http://www.seas.smu.edu/~justin/inline.html

ROWING AND SCULLING

See also: BOATING AND SAILING

Rowing Frequently Asked Questions

"Stroke! Stroke! Stroke!" That's the call of the coxswain as the rowers propel the shell ahead in a race for the finish line. Rowing is a sport particularly enjoyed by college and university teams around the world. There are many amateur clubs as well. There are several variations on the sport, and the boats, equipment, and rowers are different in many cases. Did you know that there are heavyweight and lightweight classes of rowers? Learn all about the sport of rowing. "Stroke!"

http://riceinfo.rice.edu/~hofer/Rowingfaq.html

Origami: the fold to behold! Check out CRAFTS AND HOBBIES.

RUNNING

See also: SPORTS—TRACK AND FIELD

Road Runners Club of America

Runners can find a mile and a half of track at this site! Online articles and magazines about running are appearing all over the Internet. This site links you to them, and gives you a list of other resources, too. The club is involved in a wide range of activities, including events for women and children. There is general information on the club and their services, and an interactive map to let you find the local clubs and events in your own area. If you enjoy running, and you want to stay current on running and amateur sports news, then jog on over!

http://www.rrca.org/~rrca/

How about a fun run? Sounds great, but leave the tunes at home. Don"t wear headphones when you run. You need to rely on all your senses to be safe. Another rule is to tell someone where you'll be running and when you'll be back. Sprint over to the **Road Runners Club of America** for more tips about running, including how to run safely in hot or cold weather.

The Running Page

Running can be a sport, a hobby, or just an exercise. This is a nicely organized page for all kinds of runners: from casual to serious. There are many links to a wide variety of running sources, and even one to a chat site for runners. Serious runners can find race results, columns geared toward their level of interest, and lists of publications, frequently-asked questions and clubs. Basically, you can run in here to see what's new "out there." It's another way of getting from where you are to where you want to be!

http://sunsite.unc.edu/drears/running/running.html

SCUBA DIVING AND SNORKELING

Aquanaut

Swimming around for information on scuba diving? Dry off and sit down at the computer! This online magazine covers scuba from the serious diver's perspective. There is a treasure chest of information on scuba here. Online access to club listings worldwide, gear reviews, dive sites, and weather reports are always available. There's even a database of wrecks you can explore! And if you just can't get out on (and under) the water today, plenty of photographs will make you feel like you're there. But please, remove that gear and dry off before booting up your computer!

http://www.terra.net/aquanaut/

Welcome to CyberDIVE

An underwater adventure on land, in front of your computer? This must be some unusual way of scuba diving, if you don't even get wet! It is! You'll visit a database of great dive sites in Florida, read equipment reviews, and see underwater photos that must have been taken by fish! Confused about all the different types of certification courses you can take? Learn their differences here. Don't miss the info on snorkeling, either, or the live weather updates from marine buoys. Sure, there are the usual quizzes and win-free-stuff contests, since this is a site sponsored by commercial dive shops. But hey, who can't use a cool new T-shirt?

http://www.cyberdive.com/

SKYDIVING
C.S.P.A. | A.C.P.S.

Do you think that people who jump out of airplanes are just plain nuts? Or are you one of those who live to skydive off into the wild blue yonder? Skydiving may be the sport for you, and this page could be your jumping-off point. This bilingual (French and English) page includes information on how to get involved in skydiving, links to other skydiving Web sites, and an area for people to talk about their skydiving experiences. Some pretty funny stories there!

http://www.islandnet.com/~murrays/cspa.html

How do we know what time it is?

Answer: In the U.S., we ask the U.S. Naval Observatory. They have been keeping the nation's time since the 1800s. In 1845, they installed a time ball atop their telescope dome. According to their Web site, "the time ball was dropped every day precisely at Noon, enabling the inhabitants of Washington to set their timepieces. Ships in the Potomac River could also set their clocks before putting to sea." Times have changed since then. Now hydrogen maser clocks are used, which keep Atomic Time. There is a good correlation of Atomic Time to more traditional celestial observations, but every now and again the Atomic Clock has to be given a whack, known as a "Leap Second," to bring it into alignment with the heavens. If you have time and are interested, read more about it at http://tycho.usno.navy.mil/history.html

USPA and the World of Skydiving

This is the home page of the U.S. Parachute Association, and the first thing you need to know is that you can't skydive until you're eighteen. Some drop zones will allow it at sixteen with parental consent, but keep in mind that this is an expensive sport. Expect to pay $150 to $300 for your first instruction. It does get cheaper after you've convinced an instructor that you know what you're doing. You should find an accredited teacher, too, and there's a list here—find one near you.

http://home.worldweb.net/USPA/

SNOWBOARDING

Snwbrdr's Snowboarding Page

Snowboarding just keeps getting more popular, and more respected by athletes. It's fun, but not easy, and advanced boarders can do some amazing tricks. Find out who's ruling, where and how, at this great site in Finland. And check out these sweet action photos!

http://www.jyu.fi/snw/

SNOWMOBILES

The Snowmobile Homepage

Snowmobiling is one of the great escapes during the cold and snow season. Beginning and experienced snowmobilers are always interested in the latest models from the major snowmobile makers, the coolest pictures of snowmobile action, and the facts on all the equipment. At this Swedish site, you can even submit your questions and have them answered by the experts.

http://www.informatik.umu.se:80/~svph9419/
  snowmobile/

Yogatta try Yoga.

SNOWSHOEING

L.L. Bean Snowshoeing Information

Snowshoeing is a really cool (no pun intended) activity! It's a bit easier for most people than cross-country skiing, and it allows you to do a little more exploring. This page is where you can find out what you need, and how to get started. And after reading the helpful hints, maybe you still have a few more questions. Chances are the answers are only a mouse click away. For example, did you know you can make an emergency snowshoe repair with duct tape? (Is there anything you *can't* fix with duct tape?)

http://www.llbean.com/aos/snowshoeing/

It's like wearing tennis racquets on your feet! How do you get down a hill in these snowshoes, anyway? Whatever you do, don't jump down! That can damage the shoe and the webbing. There are specific techniques for snowshoeing. Things like going up and down hills, or walking backwards, can get a little tricky. Stop in at the **L.L. Bean Snowshoeing Information page** for the tips you need.

SURFING

Global Oceanic Surf Links

This is the real thing, not this waterless digital surfing we've all gotten used to. Big surf, land surfing, swells, it's all here. See a live picture of Sunset Beach on O'ahu, or check wave conditions in Australia. See some gnarly GIFs or check some equipment reviews. A lot of links here so we'll note there's a parental advisory on the site: we have not explored to the farthest ends of this page.

http://magna.com.au/~prfbrown/tubelink.html

Take a ride on a Carousel in AMUSEMENT PARKS.

Surfrider USA

This organization is working to protect our coastlines. But in addition to information on the group and its mission, there are numerous resources for surfers, and some nice pictures and music clips. You can even take a look at today's waves on the Southern California coast. The resource list of links can send you coast-to-coast (USA), off to Hawai'i, and all over the world. It's awesome, dude, hang ten!

http://www.sdsc.edu/SDSC/Partners/Surfrider/main.htm

NET FILES

The modern Olympics will celebrate its centennial with the Games of the XXVIth Olympiad, held in Atlanta, Georgia, July 1996. You'll see merchandise of all kinds with the special Olympic logo, and the mascot. What's an explanation of the symbols used in the logo, and what's the mascot's name? And how many medals will be awarded?

Answer: The mascot is named IZZY, a bright blue creature with Olympic rings on his tail, carring a torch, spinning off stars. The special centennial logo has a similar flame, rising from a base made of the Olympic rings, resting on the numeral 100. Athletes will compete for a total of 1,933 medals. http://www.atlantic.olympic.org/welcome/glance.html

SWIMMING AND DIVING

Open Water Swimming Tips

O.K., you like to go swimming. The school pool is good, when that kid in the other class isn't there to do cannon ball dives on your head. The backyard pool is nice, when the filter works. And you love the open water at the lake. But better yet, there's the ocean: the sand, the sun, and the surf. All of these are great, but open water swimming is not the same as swimming in a pool. For one thing, sometimes you can't even see the bottom under you! And there are other things to deal with, like the choppy water, the current, and those green slimy things floating by. Well, here's the page that tells you all about swimming in the open sea. There are tips on everything from getting ready to racing. And there's good common-sense information on how to deal with hazards. The number one rule is never swim alone (but you can visit this site alone).

http://rs733.gsfc.nasa.gov/~jntjw/swim/openwater.html

SWIMNEWS Online

Do you swim? We're not talking about an occasional wade through the baby pool here. We're talking about competitive swimming. You know: pruny-looking fingers, webbed toes, red eyes, and gills. If that's you, then you need to see this online magazine! Virtually every major swim meet in the world is here, and the results are updated regularly. There are features on the world's best swimmers. And all the world records are here. Links? You bet. This is the diving platform for your lane. On your mark ...

http://www.swimnews.com/

The Yellow Pages of Swimming

Are you a swimmer? Would you like to go to other swimmers' sites? Then this is the place for you—over 220 links to Web sites related to swimming and diving! You'll find governing bodies for swim competitions, college and high school swim team pages, swim club news, and more. Look for water polo, coaching, rankings, and international links here, too!

http://www.tcd.net/~jj/swimlinx.html

A B C D E F G H I J K L M N O P Q R S T U V W X Y Z

Alexander Popov, of Russia, swam the 100 meter freestyle in **46.74 seconds**, on March 19, 1994. Will the record be broken soon? Who's favored in the Olympics? Let's face it, the only good information is up-to-date information. Get the latest at SWIMNEWS Online.

WATER SKIING

Canadian Water Ski WWW Page

Remember when water skiing was just a boat, two skis, and a lake? Oh yeah, and a skier, too. You might be surprised to see all there is to water skiing these days! Luckily, this page covers many different aspects of water skiing, and answers so many questions. Sure, there's plenty of material on traditional skiing, including slalom and jumping. There are also links to barefoot and kneeboard sites. Did you think they would forget wake-boarding? It's there too! Could there possibly be pictures? Yes, there are, and they are pretty exciting! Could your picture be there? Yes! (But you have to submit it.) Now, how can you take a picture if you're holding that tow rope?

http://www.utoronto.ca:80/ski/water/

WIND SURFING

Mistral Welcome Page

This is a commercial page, from a company that wants to sell you their product. But, man, they have a great page! Not only can you take your first boardsailing lesson right here on the Net, you can watch some exciting videos and server-push animations of some of the world's best sailors! There are the usual tips and techniques, plus reviews and race results, too.

http://www.mistral.com/mistral_welcome.html

NET FILES

Who invented the microscope?

ANSWER: The first microscope was invented by Zacharias Jansen in 1595. Read all about the history of the compound microscope at http://www.duke.edu/~tj/hist/c2.html

windsurfer.com

If you're interested in boardsailing, you need to visit this site. There's the expected tips on sailing, race schedules, world rankings, and links to other Web pages on this topic. But you'll also find a list of user reviews of various boards, and user recommendations on the hottest travel destinations. Maps and other regional information will help you decide on where to beg mom & dad to take the next family vacation. You'll also find a handy calculator which will convert knots to mph, pounds to kilograms, feet to meters, and several other measurements.

http://www.windsurfer.com/

PARADES

Pasadena Tournament of Roses Parade and Rose Bowl Game

Alas, you won't be able to take time to smell the roses at this Web site, because there aren't any! But all the info is there about this traditional New Year's Day parade, held in Pasadena, California. All the floats must be completely covered with flowers or other natural, organic material.

http://www.geninc.com/geni/USA/CA/Pasadena/
chamber/rose_events.html

Trooping of the Colour

One of the largest military parades in the world, the Trooping of the Colour is held every June to celebrate the official birthday of Queen Elizabeth II of England. It's not on her real birthday, but on her "official birthday." It's a grand show of heraldry, music, prancing horses, and dashing soldiers. The presentation of the flag ("the colour") to Her Majesty is the highlight of the event. The soldier who carries the flag during the ceremony must train for months. The flag is weighty and cumbersome, but no one would turn down the honor of carrying it. The ceremony requires strict adherence to military regulations. Anyone falling from his horse could get three months in jail! See one of the most stirring parades in the world at this Web site.

http://secure.londonmall.co.uk/troop/

**Space Exploration is a blast.
Check out Astronomy.**

PEACE

1000 Cranes Project

Sadako and the story of the thousand cranes has touched hearts worldwide. An old Japanese legend says that if you fold 1,000 origami cranes, you can have a wish. Sadako was a survivor of the atomic bomb attack on Hiroshima, Japan. The radiation made her very ill, and she died before completing all her cranes. Her friends completed them for her. Sadako's story is not forgotten. Her inspiring statue stands today in the Hiroshima Peace Park. 1995 marked fifty years of peace between the U.S. and Japan, and many people around the world decided to fold cranes and send them to the Peace Park to honor Sadako and her gentle message of peace. Read the story of how many children's hands made these cranes, which flutter today over the park of peace. Similar project information is at Cranes for Peace, *http://www.he.tdl.com/~sparker/ cranes.html*.

http://www.csi.ad.jp/suzuhari-es/1000cranes/
index.html

"We are pleased to present nearly 20,000 paper cranes made by children in 42 states and 1 Canadian province. The children were linked to each other and to Japan through the Internet, and they were linked by love and a desire for peace," said teacher Sharon O'Connell. She had carried brilliantly colored origami cranes to Hiroshima, Japan for the 50th anniversary celebration of peace between the U.S. and Japan. Read about the program at the 1000 Cranes Project.

A
B
C
D
E
F
G
H
I
J
K
L
M
N
O
P
Q
R
S
T
U
V
W
X
Y
Z

Declarations of Peace

"The key to peace starts with each of us. Many times peace is defined as not fighting. However, broken feelings can be as painful as throwing a punch." This is one of the Peace Declarations published by an eighth-grade class at St. Julie Billiart School, Hamilton, Ohio. Go one level back, to *http://www.iac.net/~esimonds/julie.html* and choose to see what some seventh-graders say about peace.

http://www.iac.net/~esimonds/stjulie/eighthg.html

Line around the world

Here's something unusual. Its creator wants to draw a line around the world, connecting Web page to Web page, to show how we're all connected to each other on this little blue planet of ours. Register your home page, and within a few days, you'll receive the "line" to place on your page. You link back to the last person in the line, and the next person after you will link to your home page. Thus, you're standing in line between two strangers, but, oddly enough, it feels pretty good. By linking your home page, or your school's, into this big virtual "hug," you've agreed to perform a good deed. After you've done it, you can report back to this page and post a report about your deed and its results. How far has the line gone so far? Check this page to find out!

http://www-leland.stanford.edu/~dsedy/line.html

PEACE IN PICTURES

The project, located in Jerusalem, is both a contest and a collaboration. It invites kids to draw what they think "peace" looks like, and share those drawings with other kids all over the world. You can mail, fax, or ftp your drawing to this site. There are prizes, but no information yet on what these might be, or details about when the contest ends. But you can enjoy some of the pictures already entered.

http://www.macom.co.il/peace/index.html

> ## Surf today, smart tomorrow.

Seeds of Peace

This page is a year old, but it still carries a strong message. The organization, Seeds of Peace, brings young people from the Middle East (Egypt, Israel, Jordan, Palestine and Morocco) to the U.S. for a month of activities. Part of this month is spent at a summer camp where the kids participate in co-existence workshops. They learn about each other's cultures and discuss issues which concern them all. Their messages and drawings may be seen here.

http://www.itp.tsoa.nyu.edu/~peace/sop_home.html

PEN PALS

Pen Pal Request Form

There is a great service for kids called Schoolnet. The Schoolnet folks set up a service to help kids in Canada and elsewhere find pen pals. If you think you'd be interested in contact with kids from all over the world, take a look at the Pen Pal Request Form. All you need is e-mail and a willingness to make new friends. The top level of this gopher is at *gopher://schoolnet.carleton.ca:419/1*. You can also search their Web page and listserv archives at *http://schoolnet2.carleton.ca/*.

gopher://schoolnet.carleton.ca:419/00/K6.dir/pals

The Penpal Page!!!

Having a pen pal can be fun. You can make a new friend, see what it's like being a kid in some other part of the world, and get practice writing, all at the same time. A nice young lady named Debbie makes finding a pen pal easy and fun on the Penpal Page. All you have to do is submit your name, or look at those who have submitted their names, and then start communicating with your new pals. Be sure you are under 17, this is JUST for kids!

http://www.li.net/~edhayes/penpal.html

PEOPLE AND BIOGRAPHIES

Albert Einstein Online

Lots of people think Albert Einstein was the greatest physicist, ever. His famous Theory of Relativity includes the equation $E = mc^2$. He even had an element named after him! Einsteinium, element 99, was discovered in 1952. Einstein won the Nobel Prize for Physics in 1921. Although he urged President Roosevelt to consider making an atomic bomb (the letter is at this site), he believed in peace.

http://www.sas.upenn.edu/~smfriedm/einstein.html

Biographical Dictionary

Sometimes you get an assignment in school, or maybe you're curious, and you'd like to know some quick facts about a famous person. The Biographical Dictionary is the place to go for this type of info. Here you'll find several thousand people listed, from both historical and current times. In this simple alphabetical list, you'll learn when the famous person was born, the year of death (if applicable), and a very brief explanation of why the person is famous. There is no detailed information here, just the bare minimum of facts. Sometimes, though, even a little bit of info can be handy!

ftp://obi.std.com/obi/Biographical/

Carlos A. Pero

Carlos Pero is a Latino studying computers in graduate school at the University of Illinois. This very smart guy has some cool games you can play on the Internet, including Carlos' Coloring Book and HexLock. Take a look!

http://robot0.ge.uiuc.edu/~carlosp/

Become one with the Net.

The Sun never sets on the Internet.

Feynman Online

Richard Feynman was a physicist, bongo drum player, and engineer. He helped develop the atomic bomb in 1945, and also helped solve the mystery behind the Challenger space shuttle disaster. Learn about his most interesting life, including his fascination with Tuva, the land of triangular postage stamps and throat-singing.

http://users.aol.com/plank137/feyn.htm

Man of the Year Home Page

Need biographies of famous people? Cruise over to the "Man of the Year" home page for information about the man, woman, or idea considered the biggest influence on events each year since 1927. In 1982, the Computer was "Man of the Year." You may want to select the "Text only" version of this page, since the graphics take a long "time" to load.

http://pathfinder.com/@@5bslPXHlxQIAQHZQ/
    time/special/moy/moy.html

Martin Luther King, Jr.

In a thoughtful and moving Web site, the *Seattle Times* commemorates the life and legacy of Dr. Martin Luther King, Jr. You'll find a timeline of his life, along with many photos and audio files. Yes, you'll be able to hear part of the famous "I Have a Dream" speech as well as others. Check the sections on the history of the Civil Rights movement, and read about how the Martin Luther King, Jr. National Holiday was created in memory of this great leader, called "America's Gandhi."

http://www.seatimes.com/mlk/index.html

A B C D E F G H I J K L M N O P Q R S T U V W X Y Z

Dr. Martin Luther King Jr. has been called "America's Gandhi" because of his commitment to nonviolent struggle.

Written on a plaque in the hotel room in which he was killed are these words: *"Behold here comes the dreamer. Let us slay him, and we shall see what becomes of his dream."*

His dream lives on, despite the violent act that ended his life. Read about it at the Martin Luther King, Jr. Page.

MSU Vincent Voice Library

Wouldn't it be great to be able to hear the voices of some of these famous people? At this site, you can! Listen to sound files of many U.S. presidents, as well as brief conversations with people like George Washington Carver and Amelia Earhart. TEST! Teddy Roosevelt has left the building... he has left the building!

http://web.msu.edu/vincent/index.html

Pirates

"Shiver me timbers!" If you don't know a pirate from a buccaneer, better sail over to this page. You'll learn lots about famous pirates, legends, and perhaps locations of buried treasure!

http://tigger.cc.uic.edu/~toby-g/pirates.html

Visit the stars in Astronomy.

The World of Benjamin Franklin

Hey! Who's that guy on the one hundred dollar bill? Yeah, the hippie with the long hair. It's Benjamin Franklin—famous American scientist, statesman, and inventor. You remember him—he's the guy who flew the kite in the thunderstorm to learn about electricity. That wasn't a very smart idea, but here are some classroom activities to help you learn more about some of the things that interested Franklin. He was interested in lots of things, too. For example, he was one of the original signers of the Declaration of Independence! And you know where it was signed, right? At the bottom!

http://sln.fi.edu/franklin/rotten.html

BIRTHDAYS

Britannica's Lives

Ever wonder who shares your birthday? Sure, it might be your mom or your dad, or even your twin brother. But was anyone famous born on your birthday? (Besides you, of course!) Find out at this useful site! You can also discover which famous people in history share the same generation. For example, John McEnroe and Magic Johnson both turned 21 in 1980. Want to know more about each famous person? This site gives you short biographies and links to other resources about that person on the Internet.

http://www.eb.com/bio.html

WOMEN'S STUDIES

Biographies of Historical Women

Did you know a woman helped start the field of social work (Jane Addams)? Did you know a woman was one of the best guides for slaves fleeing to freedom (Sojourner Truth)? Did you know a woman was one of the world's first great novelists (Charlotte Brontë)? You can read brief biographies of these and other women here.

http://www.inform.umd.edu:8080/
  Educational_Resources/
  AcademicResourcesByTopic/WomensStudies/
  ReadingRoom/History/Biographies/

Women in Canadian History

Women have always been an important part of Canada's history. For example: Dr. Emily Jennings Stowe was the first woman to practice medicine in Canada. Lucy Maud Montgomery became known worldwide as the author of *Anne of Green Gables* as well as other books. Madeleine Jarrett Tarieu single-handedly defended an entire fort against invaders. To read more about these Canadian women, and many others, take a look at Women in Canadian History.

http://www.niagara.com/~merrwill/default.html

Women Mathematicians

These pages are an ongoing project by students in mathematics classes at Agnes Scott College in Decatur, Georgia. You'll find brief comments on over fifty women in mathematics, and expanded biographies, photos, and more information on at least ten of them.

http://www.scottlan.edu/lriddle/women/women.htm

Women's History Month Collaborative Encyclopedia

Kids noticed that there wasn't a site on the Web that brought together a list of famous women and their contributions to math, science, and the arts. So they decided to make one! You can submit biographical reports about famous women in history, and read what other kids have submitted so far. A lot of these reports are not spell-checked, but you'll get the idea.

http://www.teleport.com/~megaines/women.html

The Women's International Center

What are you going to do? Your next reading assignment is to read a biography—but you just don't know which book to pick—and whose life is really that interesting anyway? Here's a series of short biographies of interesting women who've won either an International Humanitarian Award or a Living Legacy Award. Look at this site and then head back to your library for more information. You can even find out names of famous women who were born on your birthdate here at *http://www.wic.org/cal/idex_cal.htm.*

http://www.wic.org/bio/idex_bio.htm

PETS AND PET CARE

Acme Pet—Your Guide to Pets on the Internet!

Pet enthusiasts welcome! Here you'll find a current and complete source of pet information, discussion lists, and resources all over the Internet. Send in your facts, views, or opinions about pet-related topics on this home page. Don't forget to visit today's Cool Pet Site or nominate your favorite pet site.

http://www.acmepet.com/

Brian's Hedgehog Page

Hedgehogs! The trendy pet of the 90s! Have you been considering getting a hedgehog as a pet, or are you just wondering what all the interest in those hedgehog things is about? Either way, Brian's Hedgehog Page is the place to go. Contrary to popular belief, hedgehogs are not related to porcupines! They make great pets, but some kinds make better pets than others. Find out which ones here. Some hedgehogs can even be trained to use a litter box! They eat a variety of food, such as cat food, hard-boiled eggs, cottage cheese, oatmeal, fruit, mealworms, crickets, grasshoppers, earthworms—well, you get the picture.

http://www.pci.on.ca/~macnamar/velcro.html

NetVet Veterinary Resources Home Page

The doctor is in! You'll find information here on animal care and behavior from breeders, vets, and researchers. NetVet Veterinary Resources Home Page features anything that walks, flies, hops, slithers, or swings through the trees. The NetVet resource contains some of the most respected and popular resources about pets on the Net.

http://netvet.wustl.edu/

Let balloonists take you to new heights in Aviation and Airplanes.

A B C D E F G H I J K L M N O **P** Q R S T U V W X Y Z

Hedgehogs of steel!

These cute critters have an amazing immunity to most things that are toxic. Toxins that would kill a human hundreds or even thousands of times over often have no noticeable effect on a hedgehog. Scientific research has even acknowledged that it is true! Visit Brian's Hedgehog Page to learn more about these adorable little creatures.

Pet Index Homepage

Ferret, fish, feline, fact—you'll find them all here. Crazy over chinchillas? Silly over snakes? Raving over rabbits? There's surely something for you on this page, where there are animals, animals, everywhere!

http://www.zmall.com/pet_talk/pet-faqs/

Pet Loss and Rainbow Bridge

It's so sad to lose a pet. This gentle site gives one beautiful idea of what happens when a beloved pet crosses "The Rainbow Bridge" and waits for his master to join him someday. You'll find pictures, poems, and thoughts about pets on this touching page. There are also numerous links to resources about dealing with grief over the loss of a companion animal.

http://www.primenet.com/~meggie/bridge.htm

Take a ride on a Carousel in AMUSEMENT PARKS.

Pets, Vets, You and Dr. Sue (Davis Virtual Market) vers 1.31

Did you know that a six-year-old dog or cat is equivalent to a 40-year-old human? This is based on tooth and bone growth and other items relating to maturity. This site offers additional interesting information such as pig and raccoon fun facts and seasonal pet care tips. Future topics will include iguana care, llamas as companions, and the new "flea pill." Stop by and see what Dr. Sue has to say.

http://promedia.net/dvm/DrSue/

Heat stress can be a big summertime problem for your furry friends. Your dog will enjoy a splash in a hard plastic wading pool instead of a walk on hot, burning pavement. Or, freeze water in a closed gallon jug and leave it for your pet to "snuggle up to." Keep your pets cool in the shade, give them plenty of water, and don't leave them in parked cars, even "for a minute." Summertime temperatures can soar in an enclosed space like your car. Know the signs and first aid tips for heat stress located at Pets, Vets, You and Dr. Sue. Be sure to call your own veterinarian in an emergency, though.

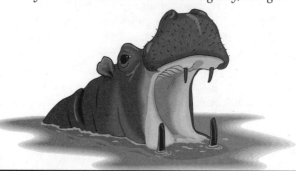

PHOTOGRAPHY

Center for Creative Photography

The University of Arizona maintains one of the largest and most accessible collections of fine photography in the world, with over 15,000 images. Renowned nature photographer Ansel Adams helped to found this institution, and his work, along with a who's who of other photographers, is well-represented at this site. Along with rotating selections from its archives, the Center's home page also features information on its educational programs, library, research facilities, publications, and museum shop. Parental advisory: not all photos have been previewed.

http://www.library.arizona.edu/branches/ccp/
  ccphome.html

George Eastman House

Explore the history of photography and view some very interesting early cameras and photographic experiments. George Eastman was the founder of the Eastman Kodak company, and this is a tour of his house and gardens in Rochester, New York, which has been preserved as a photographic museum.

http://www.it.rit.edu:80/~gehouse/

Kodak Home Page

You would expect Kodak to have an active home page, and they do indeed. There is all sorts of valuable information on photography to be found here, whether your interests lie in producing professional-quality photographs or simple snapshots. They have a "Kodak Link of the Week" that will keep you coming back regularly. One example is a section featuring the "Top Ten Techniques" for photographers to get good pictures.

http://www.kodak.com

Yogatta try Yoga.

UCR/California Museum of Photography presents... Hoffer Elementary School

For over five years, the California Museum of Photography has collaborated with the students and teachers of Hoffer Elementary School in Banning, California. Students learn how to use photography and other multimedia tools to express themselves. The results are displayed in this engrossing Web page, which features pictures, voices and written words of the student artists. They include a collection of their fun photos, montages, magazine collages, videos of motion toys, a collaborative e-mail "books project," and a history of the town of Banning in words and pictures. As more schools add their presence to the Internet, they would do well to follow this example. And as more high-powered graphic designers and ad agencies develop Web sites, it is heartening to see that one of the best pages around was designed by third-graders! Parental advisory: The UCR/California Museum of Photography has other exhibits may not be suitable for children. Proceed to links off this page with caution.

http://www.cmp.ucr.edu/exhibitions/hoffer/
  hoffer.homepage.html

PHYSICS

NYE LABS ONLINE

It's Bill Nye the Science Guy, and is he loaded with science goodies to show you! There are photos, sounds, and movies (caution—these are big files) in the Goodies area. Check out Today's Demo or visit the U-Nye-Verse to see what's happening in Bill's world of science. Lots of experiments and lessons on things scientific can be found here, plenty of fodder for your next science fair project! TV listings are also available if you want to find out when he's on the tube, and there is even a chat area where you can post comments and see if anyone replies!

http://nyelabs.kcts.org/nyelabs1.html

A
B
C
D
E
F
G
H
I
J
K
L
M
N
O
P
Q
R
S
T
U
V
W
X
Y
Z

Want to take great pictures at the next ball game?

Move in as close as you can! If you have a telephoto lens, use that, otherwise move yourself closer! Then, to freeze the sports action, use the fastest shutter speed your camera will allow. This will depend on the speed of the film you're using, so ask for some professional advice at the photo shop beforehand. It's also important to anticipate the peak of action: when the bat cracks against the ball, when the runner jumps the hurdle, when the basketball swishes through the hoop! Photos taken at the peak tend to be the most exciting! You can also freeze action by using a flash, but remember that your subject must be within about fifteen feet of you for this to work. Get more great photo tips at the Kodak Home Page!

Origami: the fold to behold! Check out CRAFTS AND HOBBIES.

9 out of 10 Internet users find this page shocking!

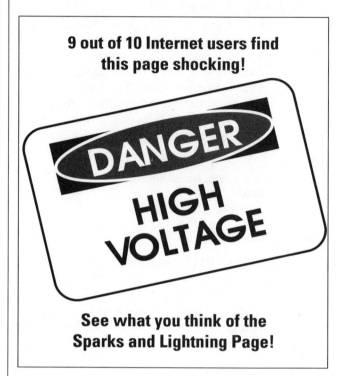

See what you think of the Sparks and Lightning Page!

ELECTRICITY
Sparks and Lightning

It's impossible to see a lightning bolt, it happens too fast. If you could only speed yourself up, while everything else went on at normal speed! This page helps you imagine what that would be like, as you examine a slow-motion lightning bolt strike on a nearby rooftop. Read this page and find out why lightning starts out as purple "St. Elmo's Fire." This page is not for the timid, though; you do get knocked unconscious by the near strike, but you learn a lot about electricity.

http://www.eskimo.com/~billb/tesla/spark.html

Lose yourself in a Museum. SCIENCE has them all.

Theater of Electricity

Did you ever get zapped from a metal doorknob at home? Where'd the electricity come from? Static electricity built up on your shoes as you walked across a carpet. Scientists who need a LOT of static electricity for an experiment use a Van de Graaff generator. The Van de Graaff generator makes electricity from a huge revolving belt inside one of its towers. Read about its history, construction, and all about lightning and electricity. You can see the huge original generator, built by Dr. Robert J. Van de Graaff, which now lives in the Theater of Electricity at the Museum of Science in Cambridge, Massachusetts, and on this World Wide Web site. You probably won't have a generator like this at home, but here, you'll find some experiments you can do with balloons, paper bunnies, and static electricity!

http://www.mos.org/sln/toe/toe.html

FORCES

Rocket Principles

This isn't exactly rocket science, but then again, this is where it all starts. Read all about Newton's first, second, and third laws of motion and forces, and how they relate to rocketry. These basic laws rule all motion, not just rocketry. They explain why a basketball bounces, why a baseball goes so far when you hit it with a bat, and why you go over the handlebars if you run into a tree with your bike. You don't have to try out the last one, just take our word on it! The top level of this page is at *http://www.lerc.nasa.gov/Other_Groups/K-12/TRC_activities.html* where you'll find some cool experiments to help you understand the laws of motion. Our personal favorite is the balloon-powered pinwheel!

http://www.lerc.nasa.gov/Other_Groups/K-12/
   activities_text/rockets/rocket_principles.html

SLN WaterWorks: Fountains

Oh, the magic of water fountains! Some are tall, some are wide, others squirt in many directions at once. Discover what makes a fountain work and the forces it takes to make water do its tricks. Pictures of different types of fountains are shown along with some that were made by students. There are even movies and sounds of the different fountains available—careful, the files are big!

http://www.omsi.edu/sln/ww/waterworks.html

LASERS

Frank DeFreitas Holography Studio

Lasers can do some pretty amazing things. Did you know they are used to make interesting 3-D pictures that allow you to "look inside" and see around objects? That's called holography. Although lasers are needed to make a hologram, you don't need a laser to view one. Scroll up to the top of this page to learn more about this terrific technology.

http://www.enter.net/~holostudio/
   intro.html#holokids

LIGHT

Bubbles

Bet you didn't know that soap bubbles can teach you a lot about light and optics, right? This site can tell you more, plus, it links to a page of other activities to explore light, refraction, lenses, and lasers. Practice tricks with bubbles, including how to make a bubble within a bubble! You'll also find the secret to making long-lasting "tough" bubble mix here!

http://www.scri.fsu.edu/~dennisl/topics/
   bubbles.html

MACHINES

You Can & Levers

The basic principles of levers are explained nicely here by Beakman and Jax. All three classes of levers are shown in easy to understand diagrams. Did you know that many household devices are levers? Nail clippers, pliers, nutcrackers, and fly swatters are just a few. See if you can tell which classes of levers each of these are after reading this page.

http://www.nbn.com/youcan/lever/lever.html

MAGNETISM

EPISODE 1-12: MAGNETISM

Here's an experiment that explores the world of magnetism. Bill Nye guides you through a simple project that shows you how to make your own compass out of a needle and bowl of water. Magic? No, magnetism!

http://nyelabs.kcts.org/nyeverse/shows/e121.html

Magnetism

What's the attraction? Magnetism helps us find our way with a compass. It's what makes electric motors run. Did you know it's also responsible for the Northern Lights? Read about the history of magnetism and how it works. Drawings show how magnetic fields are made up of invisible field lines. There are also facts about the contributions of Michael Faraday and James Maxwell to the "field" of magnetism. May the force be with you!

http://lepmp.gsfc.nasa.gov/Education/Imagnet.html

A
B
C
D
E
F
G
H
I
J
K
L
M
N
O
P
Q
R
S
T
U
V
W
X
Y
Z

SOUND

Characteristics of Sound

I'll bet you didn't know that the standard "A" note is 16.4 inches long. The calculation to prove it is right here on this page! There are comparison diagrams of a simple sine wave of Bart Simpson saying "Wow, cool man." There are also comparisons of different sound levels, a diagram of how the ear works, and a chart showing the range of human hearing. Sounds great, huh?

http://jcbmac.chem.brown.edu/scissorsHtml/sound/
  charOfSound.html

What are the major food groups? Isn't one of them chocolate?

ANSWER:
The Food Pyramid lists six food groups:
1 - bread, cereal, grains, pasta
2 - fruit
3 - vegetables
4 - meat, poultry, fish, dry beans
5 - milk, cheese, yogurt
6 - oils, fats, sweets (yes, that's chocolate, but eat only a little!)
Find out more at the International Food Information Council Foundation's page at http://ificinfo.health.org/adnukid.html

EPISODE 1-12: SOUND

Bill Nye the Science Guy has a sound project for you. It's not just educationally sound, it's ABOUT sound! With the help of a few household objects, learn how to make a sound-detecting device. You'll love the links to auditory experiments and demos elsewhere on the Web, too. Put on your lab coats and get out the fire extinguisher (just kidding) then prepare to sound off.

http://nyelabs.kcts.org/nyeverse/shows/e112.html

POLLUTION

About Kids F.A.C.E.

Kids can help end pollution and save the environment! Melissa Poe has shown what one child can do. When she was only nine years old, she started Kids For A Clean Environment. Only three years later, Kids F.A.C.E. chapters now number over 1,000, with a membership of over 50,000 eight- to eighteen-year-olds in ten countries. Membership is free, and you can find out how to join and get their educational materials here.

http://www.manco.com/kidsface.htm

Environmental Bill of Rights

Do you know your environmental bill of rights? There are five important points here that include controlling waste and pollution and preserving wildlife habitat. There are also links to the Sierra Club and The Wilderness Society. You can also check the Definition of Pollution Prevention at *http://www.snre.umich.edu/nppc/p2defined.html* for more information.

http://www.dtm-corp.com/~sven/bill_o_rights.html

Frisbee is the Ultimate in GAMES AND FUN.

AIR

Acid Rain Program's Home Page

Acid rain is a scientific puzzle that was not easy to solve. It takes years for acid rain to cause problems, so its existence remained unknown for years. It can cause acid levels in lakes to increase, so that fish and plant life cannot survive. Acid rain can also slowly eat away at buildings and structures, causing long-term damage. Where does it come from? What can be done about it? There are two major chemicals that combine to cause acid rain: sulfur dioxide and nitrous oxide. Although there are many sources of these two chemicals, coal-burning plants, cars, and trucks are the major contributors. This page, from the Acid Rain Program of the Environmental Protection Agency, describes some of the things that are being done to stop acid rain and its destruction.

http://www.epa.gov/docs/acidrain/ardhome.html

Burning Issues

If you live in a snow-bound part of the world, you may know that there's nothing like a nice warm fireplace fire. It feels so warm, and is so relaxing to view. Have you ever thought of how your wood smoke might be polluting the air? Particles from the smoke can drift far away before settling out of the air. Along the way, your smoke may be inhaled by anyone in the area. You have probably noticed the often pleasant-smelling smoke from a neighbor's fireplace yourself. Have you ever thought that your lungs may not think it's so pleasant? Read more about this issue here.

http://www.webcom.com/~bi/home.htm

> ## Lost your sheep? Count them in FARMING AND AGRICULTURE.

> ## Chase some waterfalls in EARTH SCIENCE.

NWF—Air Table of Contents

According to this site, "Americans make the equivalent of 3 million trips to the moon and back each year in cars, using up natural resources and polluting the air." Find out about the major kinds of air pollution, and what you can do to help. There's lots of classroom activities, too—how about putting on a play about pollution? Maybe you can get the part of reporter Connie Lung!

http://www.nwf.org/nwf/ed/air/

You Can & Acid Rain

Beakman and Jax answer the question "How can rain be acid?" They talk about acid rain and show you how to make an acid tester. Use the acid tester to check the rain in your town to see if your area's being affected. Oops, there's one small detail you should know. You need to boil some cabbage to make the tester. So what, you say. Well...I'll let you discover that one on your own. :-)

http://www.nbn.com/youcan/acid/acid.html

TOXIC WASTE

Ocean Planet: perils-toxic materials

Out of about 65,000 chemicals used by industry, do you know how many of them are toxic? No? No one else does, either! Only about 300 of them have been thoroughly tested to discover if they have a toxic effect on our environment. That leaves a whole lot of waste materials that could have an unknown effect on us and our future health. Read about how dredging harbors to make them deeper can stir up toxic problems that have long been "sleeping." There's also a success story about how oyster beds have recovered their vitality since a certain paint was banned from use on boats.

http://seawifs.gsfc.nasa.gov:80/OCEAN_PLANET/ HTML/peril_toxins.html

A
B
C
D
E
F
G
H
I
J
K
L
M
N
O
P
Q
R
S
T
U
V
W
X
Y
Z

*The water we have on Earth now
is all we will ever have,
so we'd better take care of it.
Did you know that one quart
of motor oil can contaminate up to
2 million gallons of drinking water?
Find out about the types of water
pollution at NWF: Table of Contents,
a National Wildlife Federation site.*

WATER

NWF: Table of Contents

These activities, for K-8, involve lots of fun activities to teach the sources of pollution, the reach of a watershed, and the problems of discarded plastics in the sea. There's also a quick tutorial on water pollution. Sure sounds like a fun way of learning!

http://www.nwf.org/nwf/ed/water/

Ocean Planet: Oceans in Peril

Did you know that U.S. sewage treatment plants discharge more oil into the ocean than spills from oil tankers? Medical waste, plastics, and other debris threaten not only water quality, but sea creatures. You can learn more facts about pollution of the ocean and waterways by taking a look at Ocean Planet: Oceans in Peril. The exhibit is presented by the Smithsonian Institution as part of a larger Internet exhibition on the ocean. You'll never think the same way about water draining from your kitchen sink!

http://seawifs.gsfc.nasa.gov:80/OCEAN_PLANET/
HTML/ocean_planet_oceans_in_peril.html

Lost your marbles? Find them in GAMES AND FUN.

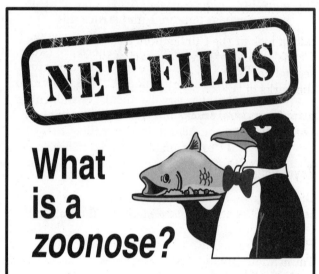

NET FILES

What is a zoonose?

ANSWER: No, it's not an elephant's trunk, an alligator's snout, or even a parrot's beak! A *zoonose* is a virus, infection, or disease that can be passed from an animal to a human. For example, there are lots of things you can get from your cat! The good news is that zoonoses are very hard to "catch." Read more about it at http://www.clock.org~ambar/
off/zoonoses.html

The Quality of Our Nation's Water: 1992

This is a report to Congress that defined the quality of U.S. lake, river, and stream water as it was in 1992. The report reveals its findings about the different types of pollutants, such as metals and pesticides. There are sections on the sources of water pollution, ocean waters, wetlands, and ground water. The information is presented in graphics and text, and contains good material for a school project on water pollution.

http://www.epa.gov/305b/sum1.html#SEC2

QUEENS, KINGS, ROYALTY

Curriculum vitae of H.M. King Albert II

Wouldn't it be great to be King? How do people get such a good job? You never see an ad in the paper that says "HELP WANTED: KING." Well, in most cases you have to be related, and there are other requirements. To see the background of one King, take a look at the Curriculum Vitae (that's Latin for life's work) of King Albert II of Belgium. You'll see it's not easy to become a King, but, then again, the perks of the job are probably really good!

http://www.belgium.be/belgium/eng/king-e/
king-e02.html

Royal Gallery

Did you know there are royal families from all over the world? Of course, there's the royal family in Great Britain, but have you ever heard of the Royal House of Araucania? Do you know about King Taufa'ahau Tupou IV of Tonga? To see pictures of royal families from many places, as well as see links to information about royal families and their countries, check out the Royal Gallery.

http://www.pitt.edu/~figtree/royal.html

QUOTATIONS

Bartlett, John. 1901 Familiar Quotations

Project Bartleby, from Columbia University in New York, is an easy way to look for "phrases, proverbs, and passages" from works of literature. Keep in mind you won't find anything contemporary here, just things prior to 1901. You can search for specific words, or for entries from various authors. Want to know some famous Ben Franklin sayings? Just click on his name! Hmmm—"Early to bed and early to rise, makes a man healthy, wealthy and wise." And you thought your dad made that up! According to the notes, Franklin didn't make it up, either, but he helped popularize it!

http://www.columbia.edu/acis/bartleby/bartlett/

"The web of our life is of a mingled yarn, good and ill together."

Was Shakespeare a psychic? Did he predict the growth of the Internet, almost 400 years ago? Check more of his quotes at the Bartlett, John. 1901 Familiar Quotations home page and decide for yourself!

Laws

Have you ever heard a saying and wondered who said it, or where it came from? For example—did you know that "When all else fails, read the instructions" is known as CANN'S AXIOM! How about: "A clean tie attracts the soup of the day." These quotes and sayings are fun to read and sometimes more fun to try to figure out. Remember—"Experience is something you don't get until just after you need it."

http://www.southern.edu/people/bnbennet/text/laws

Frisbee is the Ultimate in GAMES AND FUN.

A B C D E F G H I J K L M N O P Q R S T U V W X Y Z

Chase some waterfalls in EARTH SCIENCE.

Quotations Home Page

"A child of five could understand this. Fetch me a child of five." The comedian Groucho Marx said that! To find all kinds of quotes, from long ago and just yesterday, be sure to try this page. You'll find quotes from Miss Piggy to David Letterman here! There's a collection of the world's most annoying proverbs ("Haste makes waste!"), as well as student bloopers ("The Egyptians built the Pyramids in the shape of a huge triangular cube."). Don't miss "The Best of Anonymous" either ("Remember, a day without sunshine is like night."). You may want to download some of the inspirational color posters, too. For example, how about the photo of the cute kids with the text "We all smile in the same language." This site is highly recommended!

http://www.lexmark.com/data/quote.html

NET FILES

You see a shiny green dragonfly at the lake. How many of you does he see? How many lenses are in a dragonfly's eyes?

Answer: Dragonflies have as many as 30,000 lenses in each eye. Stop by and learn how insects use camouflage not only to hide from their enemies, but to catch their dinners. http://www.uky.edu/Agriculture/Entomology/ythfacts/entyouth.htm

NET FILES

Your brother always stands too close to the dart board when he plays. What's the rule about how far back you're supposed to stand?

Answer: According to the Darts Basics area of the CyberDarts page, "The official throwing distance, for most countries, is 2.37 meters, as measured along the floor, from the plane of the face of the dartboard. In feet, this is 7 feet, 9-1/4 inches. The height of the board, to the center of the bull, is 173 centimeters, or 5 feet, 8 inches." You can read more of the rules at http://www.cyberdarts.com/basics/DARTS BASICS.HTML#3

Lost your sheep? Count them in FARMING AND AGRICULTURE.

RADIO

Broadcasting History

Can you imagine driving in a car without tunes on the radio? Car radios weren't introduced until 1930. Radios were expensive back then, and not every home had one. In 1929, home radios were $120 each, which was a fortune! Before 1935, most radios broadcast only live music. After that, stations got record players and began spinning 33 1/3 or 78 RPM records. Don't remember records? Ask your parents! Radio plays were big, too; one of the biggest early successes was a western called *The Lone Ranger*. One of its sponsors was—Cheerios! Follow the amazing history of broadcast radio from the 1920s through the 50s at this site.

http://www.memst.edu/radio-archive/history1.html

NET FILES

Under Canadian Football rules, what does it mean when the referee turns his back on the players, and puts his right hand against his back?

Answer: He's either looking for his mom in the crowd, or he's signaling there was "unnecessary roughness" on the field. See more referee signals at **http://www.cfl.ca/ rules/signals.html**, on the Canadian Football League page.

The Sun never sets on the Internet.

Let balloonists take you to new heights in Aviation and Airplanes.

Marconi Centennial Celebration

Today, we think nothing of turning on the TV and seeing events happen, live, on the other side of the world. This was not always the case. Before the invention of fast communication technologies, news often took months to work its way across the globe. One of these great technological breakthroughs was radio—wireless communications. 1995 marked the 100th anniversary of its invention by Gugliemo Marconi. His first test radio experiments took place in Italy, in 1895. At first, radio communication was limited to a distance of about 100 miles from point to point. To make the invention a commercial success, long distance communication had to take place. The first stations that Marconi built to meet this goal were in Poldhu, Cornwall, England, and on Cape Cod, Massachusetts. According to this page, "Unfortunately, gales in the autumn of 1901 blew down the antennas of both stations, so Marconi had to improvise for his first transatlantic experiment with a temporary antenna at Poldhu and portable receiving equipment at St. John's, Newfoundland. In December, 1901, the first radio signals were transmitted across the Atlantic Ocean from Poldhu, and were received by Marconi at St. John's. This proved to Marconi (but not to everyone else!) that transatlantic radio communications were possible." The signal sent was in Morse code: "click—click— click." Marconi set about building his permanent stations, and settled on Nova Scotia as his western Atlantic radio terminus. On December 15, 1902, Marconi sent the first wireless transatlantic message to Cornwall, England, thus making Glace Bay, on Cape Breton Island, Nova Scotia, the birthplace of trans-ocean wireless communication. Read more and see historic photos of the stations and the original equipment at this most interesting site.

http://eagle.uccb.ns.ca/~kknoll/marconi/marc1.html

A B C D E F G H I J K L M N O P Q R S T U V W X Y Z

Old Time Radio (OTR) WWW Page

Many years ago, before cable TV, even before any TV, there was radio. Not just talk and music on the radio, like today, but radio "shows." Radio shows were like today's TV shows, without the pictures. There were comedies, dramas, mystery thrillers, and variety shows. It was a whole different kind of radio, at a whole different time, and now it is known as "old time radio." This page is entertainment and history all rolled into one, and it is packed with information, pictures and sounds. Hear clips from such radio greats as *The Lone Ranger*. (What kind of Indian was Tonto, anyway? Find theories here.) You can also take a fascinating virtual tour of the old NBC radio studios in Chicago's Merchandise Mart. Don't turn that dial!

http://www.old-time.com/

AMATEUR RADIO

Ham Radio Online Magazine

Licensed ham radio operators use high-tech radios for communications with others. It's sort of like using a cellular phone, but without the cost of air time charges. They also provide help to their communities during emergencies. Some systems even have "911" emergency access. Hams meet new friends and "visit" with hams in countries all over the globe. Hams have even talked with astronauts orbiting Earth! Many U.S. and Russian space missions carry astronauts who are also licensed hams. Sometimes they make contacts from space for educational uses and just for fun. If you're not already a ham, get in on this! If you are, here's where you'll keep up on all the newest amateur radio news and latest technological developments. Since hams often provide emergency communications in the event of a disaster, there are also real-time links to earthquake and other disaster monitoring sites all over the globe. Other unusual features are real-time forecasts for auroral, solar, and meteor shower activity. Don't forget to bring an umbrella if you're going out in a meteor shower!

http://pulm1.accessone.com/~vbook/hronline.htm

Welcome to the Amateur Radio Web Server

You knew "ham radio" was another name for amateur radio, didn't you? You didn't think there were knobs and buttons and an antenna sticking out of a ham, and that... no, of course you didn't. "Ham radio" is fun and exciting, and people of all ages have found it to be a useful hobby, as well. This site is a great home base to check up on the latest news and events in the world of amateur radio. You can also take a sample amateur radio licensing exam. How did you do?

http://www.acs.ncsu.edu:80/HamRadio/

What is Amateur Radio?

Amateur radio has long been an exciting hobby, for people of all ages, all over the world. From setting up your own equipment and broadcasting from your own home, to organizing a team to provide mobile communications at special events and festivals, the "ham" is always ready to be "on the air." Absolutely anyone can do it in most countries, so find out how. Even if you're already a ham, find out more!

http://www.acs.ncsu.edu/HamRadio/FAQ/

RADIO STATIONS

homepage@net.radio

Net.Radio was the first "radio station" just for the Internet! You can go to Net.Radio and listen to their music on your computer, even while you surf somewhere else! There's lots of good "music news" to read about while you listen. You can get the latest concert information, enter contests, win prizes, and vote in a monthly poll. It's all the fun stuff about radio right at your fingertips! Parental advisory: links from this site have not been viewed.

http://www.netradio.net/

J-WAVE Home Page

Japan has its share of rock music artists and fans, too. In fact, many of the most popular performers in the U.S. and Europe are just as big in Japan! There are English and Japanese versions of this page, right at your fingertips. So tune in J-WAVE on the Web, and you can learn about Japanese performers in pop music, as well as all the rockers. You can also find out what the top 100 CDs are in Tokyo. How many are your favorites, too?

http://www.infojapan.com/JWAVE/

Music question: who really is the best guitar player?

You decide! Every month there is a different poll to take part in at *http://www.netradio.net/*.
Besides that, there are links to music sites, and contests to enter. And most important, there's also a "radio" station to listen to, over the Internet! Tell your mouse to tune in and listen, and don't forget to cast your vote while you hum along!

KISS FM

Who's hot in music? What's the latest news on your favorite artists? Where can you "jump off" to the best music sites on the Web? KISS FM in Boston, Massachusetts has all the answers! This station plays the hottest music on the air, and gives you the weekly hit charts and music news you're looking for. The "Jump Station" takes you to everything from album covers to concert tickets. So stop spinning the dial and find the answers here!

http://www.kissfm.com/kiss/

KKLI Lite 106.3 FM

If yesterday's hits and today's lighter favorites sound like your kind of music, then this is your kind of radio station on the Net. "The Lite Site" is a fun place to surf around. Besides station information and events, you get great hot links to all your favorite artists, searchable by alphabet. There's dozens of other cool links too. You'll probably end up spending lots of time with "On This Day in Pop Music...", which gives you famous birthdays and events in pop history. Stroll into this southern Colorado radio station, and put your feet up.

http://www.usa.net/kkli/

NPR Online

Many people think that National Public Radio gives us the best news, feature stories, and music on the radio. "NPR Online" certainly gives you a lot of all these, and lets you know where on your local radio dial you can tune in. Like PBS on television, NPR is federally and privately funded programming that is commercial-free. This site has the same real "Breaking News" and "Story of The Day" as the NPR radio broadcasts. Yes, you can actually listen to the most recent NPR news report right on your computer. Tune in and see what public radio has to offer! You'll also want to check out Ira Flatow's NPR Science Friday Kids Connection (shortcut: *http://www.npr.org/sfkids/index.html*). You'll find study guides to some of Science Friday's cool topics: The physics of Star Trek, scientific toys, ocean acoustics, backyard astronomy, and more!

http://www.npr.org/

Q-92, KRQC Monterey Bay's Classic Rock

This station, in northern California, features "classic rock" music. This is the music that never seems to go away. KRQC even gives you "This Week in Classic Rock History," which tells you what happened in the world of rock music on this date years ago. Wow, in the same week in 1968, Big Brother & The Holding Company, Jimi Hendrix, and Steppenwolf were all in the top ten. If your music is driving your parents crazy, ask them about these old bands! See if your parents can remember what *their* parents thought about the music they listened to! (Hint: ask them about *Stairway To Heaven* by Led Zeppelin.) This page also lists the top 400 classic rock tunes of all time. Will your favorite song be there?

http://www.q92.com/

Space Exploration is a blast. Check out Astronomy.

A B C D E F G H I J K L M N O P Q R S T U V W X Y Z

Radio Aahs Online

Maybe you've heard of Radio Aahs, the 24-hour radio network for kids? Well, this site is for the eyes, not the ears. It's got the most eye-popping graphics of any magazine for kids on the Internet. Make sure you visit the Ka'Zoo Lounge: today you may see Bill Nye the Science Guy; tomorrow it could be Grandpa Munster, or just about any other star. Check out new games, books, music, CD-ROMs, and video games each month. Looking for a birthday present for your cousin? Search the reviews according to how much things cost or by the age of the birthday kid. The puzzles and mazes are worth printing out. And don't miss the joke of the day—each one contributed by a kid! And if you're on vacation and can't bear to be away from Radio Aahs—find out if there's a Radio Aahs station where you'll be.

http://pathfinder.com/@@H3oaerElMgIAQO1J/Aahs/

Radio Sweden's Virtual North

Radio Sweden broadcasts in several languages, including English. Luckily the Web pages are available in these languages too, because there is a lot of fascinating information here. Click on "Our Programs" and read up on (or listen to) the latest sports, media, money, science, and even environmental news. Hey, what's important in Sweden is important to everyone! Radio Sweden is useful current information, on the air, and on the Internet! A recorded daily broadcast is available either via RealAudio streaming, or you can ftp the entire file. A live broadcast occurs daily using Streamworks technology. Find out more here!

http://www.sr.se/rs/

U.S. Radio Stations on the Internet (K)

Is your favorite radio station on the Internet? How about that great station you listen to when you visit your cousin in Boston? This is the place to find out! This site lists radio stations all over the world that have home pages on the Web. So whether it's that country music station in Nashville or that hot rocker on the dial in the Netherlands, you can get there from here!

http://wmbr.mit.edu/stations/

Vatican Radio

Radio Vatican broadcasts on short wave, medium wave, FM, satellite, and the Internet! Staff from fifty countries prepare 400 hours of broadcast material every week, in thirty-seven different languages. You can download RealAudio files or ftp features in several languages. As they say "Listen, for heaven's sake!"

http://www.wrn.org/vatican-radio/about.html

Welcome to WCBS NEWSRADIO 88

In New York City, WCBS is the all-news radio station. On the Web, WCBS is also up-to-the-minute, with top news, sports, and weather stories. The feature series "Boot Camp" reports on the newest developments regarding computers and technology, and "Lifestyle" highlights travel and dining. The WCBS archives are all online, so if you missed a technology report, you can scan the archives for a computer topic that interests you!

http://www.newsradio88.com/

WNUR-FM JazzWeb

Hey, jazz-lovin' cats out there! This site is real cool, so breeze on in and chill awhile. The JazzWeb has a treasure chest of information for those who get into jazz music. There are sections on different jazz styles, individual musicians, musical instruments, and performances. Finding the info on jazz art, education, and resources is also a smooth ride. Linking up to jazz labels on the Net, and retail sellers, is a simple note. Brought to you by Northwestern University's radio station, if it's jazz, it's here.

http://www.nwu.edu/jazz/

SHORTWAVE

Amateur Radio FAQ (Shortwave subsection)

What is "shortwave radio"? Technically, that's the name for radio frequencies between 3 and 30 MHz. But what we really want to know is what we can use shortwave radio for. Shortwave broadcasts can be received over long distances, making it possible to communicate internationally. You can tune in radio broadcasts from around the world. Questions, anyone? The answers are here.

http://www.acs.ncsu.edu/HamRadio/FAQ/
  FAQ_Shortwave.html

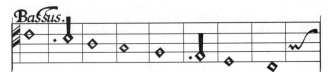

Hear the Aurora Borealis?
Listen to dawn break?
You can download these unusual .wav files at
*http://www-pw.physics.uiowa.edu/cgi-bin/
unzip-wav?mcgreevy/ak_vlf1.zip?kenaiwhi.wavn.*
These Very Low Frequency natural sounds
are part of the Shortwave/Radio Catalog.
To learn how to set up a "Dawn Chorus Patrol"
listening team in your school, travel to
*http://www.gsfc.nasa.gov/education/inspire/
listening_program.html*

The Internet Guide to International Broadcasters

This is a collection of links to major shortwave
broadcasters around the world. Want to request a
broadcast schedule? Some of the stations will mail
them to you. Others have home pages, or ftp
archives, and you can check the schedules yourself.
Want to know when you can hear rock music from
Estonia? Check the Eesti Raadio Home Page for
frequencies and times.

**http://www.cs.cmu.edu/afs/cs.cmu.edu/user/jblythe/
Mosaic/short-wave.html**

Numbers Stations on Shortwave

"So this is a shortwave radio. What do you guys listen
to on these things? Wait, turn the knob the other
way—slowly. Right there—stop! What in the world
is THAT? It sounds like counting, in a foreign
language. What IS that?" Could it be a math lesson
in Russian? A language class in the U.K.? A spy
sending secret code from some remote island
somewhere? Or maybe someone in the U.S.A. giving
someone in Germany their company's e-mail
address? Hmmm—the spy answer is definitely the
most fun—and it just might be the right one! The
so-called "numbers stations" heard on shortwave
radio make a fascinating topic. For many years,
listeners came across them now and again, never
really sure of their purpose. Even today, their origin
and meaning are mysterious. Can you find the
signals? What might they really be? This page helps
you track them down and uncover the truth. Listen in!

http://itre.ncsu.edu/radio/numbers.html

Take a ride on a Carousel in AMUSEMENT PARKS.

Shortwave/Radio Catalog

Shortwave radio enthusiasts can find lots of new
information in each new issue of this page. There
are always links to the basic information and
resources that the radio hobbyist will use again and
again. Hardware, software, and radio services are
covered in depth. Many familiar radio-related topics
are reviewed in each issue, but there are new ideas
being introduced all the time. There are plenty of
quality links to all kinds of radio information from
all corners of the globe. It really is a one-stop radio
information catalog for the Internet!

http://itre.uncecs.edu/radio/

RAILROADS AND TRAINS

See also: MODELS AND MINIATURES—
RAILROADS

The Great Northern Railway Page

All Abo-oard! Are you interested in trains? Who
isn't fascinated by these monstrous machines?
Whether it be diesel or steam engines, subway
systems, train photographs, games, or model
railroading, the Great Northern Railway Page has
a great collection of worldwide links to pages about
all of these subjects, and more. Expect to get a case
of railroad fever as you spend many hours exploring
these sites!

**http://www.prostar.com/~Lindsay.Korst/
gngoat.html**

Visit the stars in Astronomy.

A
B
C
D
E
F
G
H
I
J
K
L
M
N
O
P
Q
R
S
T
U
V
W
X
Y
Z

Interactive Model Railroad

Wow, that's a cool model train—too bad it's in Germany, bet you'd love to play with it. Guess what, you can! Through the magic of forms and server-push technology, you can select one of two trains to control. Then select which platform the train should travel to. Then press GO and watch your train speed along past the miniature Bavarian town! Oops, watch out for that alp!

http://rr-vs.informatik.uni-ulm.de/rr/

Jeremiah L. Toth Railroads Page

This site features information about Maryland railroad stations, Washington D.C.'s colossal and historic Union Station, railroading in Delaware, Pennsylvania, New York and Connecticut, and trolley, interurban and heavy rail resources. This is a good, fact-driven resource center for railroad buffs looking for on-track information.

http://www.clark.net/pub/jltoth/trains.html

North American Steam Locomotive Information

While a rarity today, steam trains have not entirely vanished from the American landscape. This page provides information about steamers of the past, and today's survivors, including schedules of currently running steam excursions, specifications of steam trains, and sections on trains that are "Lost Forever (but not forgotten)." There is also information on rail fairs, rail museums, and a special piece on the annual reenactment of the Golden Spike Ceremony in Utah, featuring some terrific photographs.

http://www.arc.umn.edu/~wes/steam.html

Yogatta try Yoga.

READING AND LITERACY

Children's Literature Web Guide

"If my cunning plan works, you will find yourself tempted away from the Internet and back to the books themselves!" says David K. Brown, children's librarian. He's collected links to many outstanding reading experiences. You can find information on fictional people and places in children's books. Play Virtual Poohsticks at the 100 Acre Wood! Look at the links to Arthurian legend. Series like Nancy Drew, the Hardy Boys, and *Goosebumps* also have their own pages. If you have a favorite author, like C.S. Lewis or Dr. Seuss, look here for links to their pages. There are online children's stories, and lists of award-winning books. And there's a whole section called "Children's Writings and Drawings." If you want to put your work on the Net for the world to see, start here. Also check the BOOKS AND LITERATURE section of this book for more!

http://www.ucalgary.ca/~dkbrown/index.html

CyberKids

This "cool place for kids to learn and have fun" is a free online magazine. Kids create the stories, articles, reviews and artwork. There are also puzzles and games to play. You can find keypals here as well.

http://www.mtlake.com/cyberkids/

NET FILES

Can you read this?
DOU12NO W@DDR?

Answer: UL 1/2 2CO2
http://reality.sgi.com/employees/
molivier_studio/license-plates.html
NCAURSLFI

IPL Youth Division

Some kids really like to go to the library and spend some time there—reading and rereading favorites, listening to CDs in the AV department, maybe even doing a little homework. Here's another library to explore, with guides like Dr. Internet to help you. Like any good public library, IPL has a good children's room. There are lots of things to read, a story time (with illustrated folk tales), homework help, and an Authors' Corner. If you go to story hour, some stories have audio or animations. Most of them are illustrated. If you like science, Dr. Internet will direct you to interesting sites on the Internet. You can explore Dinosaurs, Earthquakes, Geology, Volcanoes, and Weather. In the Authors' Corner, people like Matt Christopher, Jane Yolen, Avi, and Lois Lowry share their life stories and ways of writing. You can ask them questions too. If you like contests, there are links to many Internet contests. And the hours are great—this library is always open.

http://ipl.sils.umich.edu/youth

KidPub WWW Publishing

Here's a great place to share your stories, poems, and news about where you live. Kids from all over the world have their writing published on this Web page. You'll find stories mostly from the U.S., but there are also some from places like Tasmania, West Malaysia, Germany, and Singapore. Most of the young authors include their e-mail addresses, so you can write back to them. Writers also write a little bit about themselves. Contributors range in age from four to fifteen. Write on!

http://en-garde.com/kidpub/

Parents and Children Together Online

Part of the fun of reading and writing can be the sharing of it. This site is fun to explore with your mom or dad, or with a younger sister or brother. There are illustrated stories and articles for grades pre-6. Some of the stories and articles have links to resources on the Internet. You can follow the links to find information on koalas, cats, or Scottie dogs. The Scottie article even has a link to Franklin Delano Roosevelt (who had one)! If you like to write stories, hunker down around "The Global Campfire." There you can contribute your part to an ongoing story—science fiction, adventure, a family story, or a mystery. And if you want a keypal, look here. There are requests from like-minded sorts from Alaska to Zanzibar.

http://www.indiana.edu/~eric_rec/fl/pcto/menu.html

RECYCLING

COMPOST

This is the low-down on dirt (for those of you who have a sense of humus). It gives basic information about home composting. You can find out how to build compost heaps of every description, some even including worms. If you want to see a heap in action, there's a nationwide list of "Composting Demo Sites." It's a rotten Web site, and that's why we've included it!

http://net.indra.com/~topsoil/Compost_Menu.html

NET FILES

What are
**FELINE-L,
EXOTIC-L,**
and
SMLDOG-L?

ANSWER: Nope, not a rap group! They are all mailing lists for animal lovers. One is about cats, one is about birds, and one's about small dogs. Can you guess which is which? You'll find the answers at http://netvet.wustl.edu/e-zoo.htm, the Electronic Zoo.

recycle

This site will give you directions for making your own paper out of recycled materials. Making paper is fun, but it is pretty messy, so make sure an adult helps you!

gopher://schoolnet.carleton.ca:419/00/K6.dir/
trycool.dir/recycle

The Recycler's Bill of Rights

You recycle, right? But maybe you have questions about some things. Like those cryptic markings on the bottoms of plastic containers—what do they mean? You'll find a description of them here. Also, you can learn what to do with things like used motor oil, or spent nicad batteries. This is the one-stop answer place for recycling questions. It has good links, too.

http://www.best.com/~dillon/recycle/guides/
common.html

Your mom says this new juice is good for you, but you're not so sure you want to drink it. After all, the bottle has some other kid's name on it. There's this triangle with a "1" in it, and below that it says "PETE." Not to worry. That's a recycling symbol. It means the container is made out of Polyethylene Terephthalate (PET). Lots of soda and water containers, and some other waterproof packaging, have the same symbol. These markings help us know which plastics are recyclable and which are, well, trash. Find out more at The Recycler's Bill of Rights home page.

REFERENCE WORKS

The Scholes Library Electronic Reference Desk

Groan...your paperback dictionary has disappeared. Maybe it was the dog? Hmmm, well, here's the "A's" in the middle of the kitchen, and it's "B through F" headed down the basement stairs. Don't despair. You can use dictionaries online! This site also has encyclopedias, a thesaurus, maps, current news, historical documents, and more!

http://scholes.alfred.edu/Ref.html

ALMANACS AND GAZETTEERS
Events for ...

Ho hum, today is just another day, right? It seems there are so few special days—like Christmas, your birthday, or the Fourth of July. Actually, every single day has been important in history, or there is some momentous event taking place somewhere, or someone great was born. To see why today is important, take a look here. Maybe you can use the information here as a good excuse for a party!

http://astro.uchicago.edu/home/web/copi/
events.html

How Far Is It?

In the not too distant past, finding the distance from one part of the globe to another took a fair amount of work. It meant using complicated tables and converting map scales. Now, you have an alternative! On the How Far Is It page all you need to know is the names of two locations, and the distance between the two is calculated for you. This service provides distances for almost all places in the United States, and a good number of major cities elsewhere.

http://gs213.sp.cs.cmu.edu/prog/dist

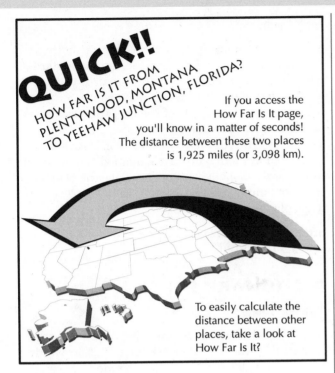

QUICK!!

HOW FAR IS IT FROM PLENTYWOOD, MONTANA TO YEEHAW JUNCTION, FLORIDA?

If you access the How Far Is It page, you'll know in a matter of seconds! The distance between these two places is 1,925 miles (or 3,098 km).

To easily calculate the distance between other places, take a look at How Far Is It?

The Old Farmer's Almanac

The *Old Farmer's Almanac* has been published ever since George Washington was president. This almanac gives the best time to plant crops, helps to determine the weather long in advance, and has lots of cool old sayings (these are called aphorisms). People have used and enjoyed the *Old Farmer's Almanac* throughout history. Now, parts of this publication are available on the Internet. You can see weather predictions, read some old-timey quotes, and there's a great history of the almanac. Whether you live on a farm or in a city high-rise apartment, you'll like the *Old Farmer's Almanac*!

http://www.xensei.com/ofa/index.html

U.S. Gazetteer

A quick way to find the county, state, area code, ZIP code, and longitude-latitude of a place in the United States (and a few world cities) is to check this resource. It is linked to the XEROX PARC Map Viewer, so once you find out that Prague, Arkansas is in Grant County, ZIP code 05053, latitude 34 17 12 N, longitude 92 16 50 W, you can click on these coordinates to view the map.

http://wings.buffalo.edu/geogw

The *World Factbook* 1995

Did you know that Kenya (569,250 sq. km) is twice the size of Nevada? What languages do the people of Denmark speak? They speak Danish, Faroese, Greenlandic and German. If you ever wanted to know facts like these about countries around the world, the CIA *World Factbook* is the place to look. By the way, did you know there are 193 million TV sets in the United States? A 1994 gopher version is also available at *gopher://hoshi.cic.sfu.ca/11/dlam/cia*.

http://www.odci.gov/cia/publications/95fact/index.html

AWARDS

The Academy of Motion Picture Arts and Sciences

If you're a movie fanatic, don't miss the Official Interactive Guide to the Academy Awards, designed to help you explore Oscar nominees and winners, past and present. Naturally, there are pictures and lots of information on all of them. Think you're a movie trivia expert? Play the Oscar Game and see just how good you are. You may be surprised to find out that the Academy of Motion Picture Arts and Sciences does a lot more than just give out awards: they have an amazing movie history library and sponsor Student Academy Awards, designed to recognize excellence among college students enrolled in film courses throughout the United States.

http://www.ampas.org/ampas/

Academy of Television Arts & Sciences

Have you ever heard the song by Bruce Springsteen, "Fifty-Seven Channels and Nothin' On"? Sometimes, there doesn't seem to be anything good on TV. There are many good shows, though. An organization called the Academy of Television Arts & Sciences selects some of the best programs, and gives the winning shows and actors an award called an Emmy. To see who the most current winners are, check out the Academy of Television Arts & Sciences Web page. You'll learn television history, see who is being nominated, and get a behind-the-scenes look at the annual Emmy Awards Show.

http://www.emmys.org/tindex.html

A B C D E F G H I J K L M N O P Q R S T U V W X Y Z

Children's Book Awards

Every year, thousands of books are written for kids. Most of the books are good, but trying to decide which books to borrow from the library can be difficult. Fortunately, there are several organizations that pick the finest books for children each year. These books are judged best by a variety of criteria, including which are best for young children, elementary-school-aged kids, etc. Some of the awards for the best children's books are listed on the Internet, and you can find convenient links to many of those lists here. Besides the Caldecott and the Newbery Awards, you'll find the Coretta Scott King Award, and the Laura Ingalls Wilder Medal winners. If you're looking for a good book to read, take a glance here!

http://www.state.lib.ut.us/awards.htm

Grammy Awards

Everybody likes music. Maybe you like pop sounds, rock 'n roll, rap, or R&B, but music is a universal language, liked by all people. Most music we listen to is recorded—either on tapes, CDs, the radio, or TV. The National Academy of Recording Arts & Sciences is an organization of recording specialists who decide what the best records are each year. The winning recording artists receive an award called a Grammy. To see (and hear) who has won in the past, and who is nominated for the upcoming awards, take a look at the Grammy Awards page. It's just the place to look if you like music, and who doesn't!

http://www.metaverse.com/grammy/index.html

Pulitzer Prizes presented by CJR

Joseph Pulitzer was an American newspaper publisher, known for his innovative ideas and bold reporting style. When he died, his will established the Pulitzer Prizes. The first ones were awarded in 1917. Each year, achievements in American journalism, letters, drama, and music are recognized. Fourteen prizes are given in journalism. The prizes in letters are for fiction, history, poetry, biography or autobiography, and general nonfiction. There are also prizes for drama and music. At this site, you can read about the 1995 winners; perhaps the site will expand to include 1996 and past years.

http://www.pulitzer.org/

Tony Awards

A live performance in a theater—there is nothing like it. Lights, stage props, music, and acting are all parts of what makes the theater great. If you've ever seen or participated in a play, you know it can be fantastic! Some of the best theatrical performances take place on Broadway in New York City. The Antoinette Perry (Tony) Award is presented annually for "distinguished achievement" in the professional theater. These are the best of the best, and if you like theater, take a look to see what plays have won!

http://artsnet.heinz.cmu.edu/OnBroadway/
    tony_index.html

DICTIONARIES

Acronym Lookup

Do you know what an acronym is? It's a word that is formed by the letters or syllables of other words. For example, let's say there was a made-up organization called American Children Reading Online Notes for Young Mothers—its acronym could be ACRONYM! If you want to look up what some real acronyms stand for (try UNESCO or PTA for fun), take a glimpse at this site! Be patient—the site is in Ireland, and there are a LOT of acronyms for it to look through!

http://curia.ucc.ie/cgi-bin/acronym

Casey's Snow Day Reverse Dictionary (and Guru)

Casey's an eleven-year-old girl in Los Alamos, New Mexico. One day, there was a lot of snow, and her school closed. She had to go to work with her dad. While she was there, she got this great idea. Sometimes you know what a word means, but you just can't think of the word! How about a reverse dictionary? Take a definition, and find a word that matches it. The whole process is backwards, but sometimes it can be helpful. The programmers thought Casey's idea was great, so they came up with a way to do it. All you do is type in the definition, and then see a list of choices that match it (to some degree or other). If words have a habit of escaping you, a reverse dictionary might be just what you need! They were so happy with it, they named it after Casey!

http://www.c3.lanl.gov:8075/cgi/casey/revdict

English-Estonian Dictionary

Estonia is a recently independent Baltic country with a very long and wonderful history. The English-Estonian Dictionary is a very well designed translator that can help you translate words from English to Estonian. You'll be one of about a million speakers of Estonian around the world!

http://www.ibs.ee/dict/

English-French Meeting Point

From Québec in North America, to Tahiti in the South Pacific, French is the primary language of about 124 million folks. At this Web page, you'll find a very nice translator for French to English and English to French.

http://mlab-power3.uiah.fi/EnglishFrench/
    avenues.html

English-Russian Russian-English Dictionary

Over 280 million people around the world speak Russian. The Russian language doesn't use the same alphabet as English. It uses Cyrillic characters, and you can find out more about this in the LANGUAGES AND ALPHABETS subject heading of this book. To be able to translate words from English to Russian requires special software for your computer. You'll find the software, and a good translator dictionary, at the English-Russian Russian-English Dictionary.

http://www.elvis.ru/cgi-bin/mtrans

Jeffrey's Japanese<->English Dictionary

About 126 million people speak Japanese. Many more know a few words, such as "Toyota," "karaoke," or "sushi." Those are Anglicized versions of the real Japanese words, because Japanese doesn't use the same alphabet English does. Since your computer is designed to display the letters in English and other Western languages, you have to obtain special software just to display Japanese letters (the Japanese call their letters characters). If you would like to translate some Japanese, take a look here. You'll find software to read Japanese characters, as well as a well-designed translation dictionary.

http://enterprise.ic.gc.ca/cgi-bin/j-e/

Spanish-to-English Dictionary

Spanish is a very important and beautiful language. In fact, there are about 380 million people who speak Spanish! The Spanish-to-English Dictionary will translate English words for any Spanish words you type, in an easy-to-use format. There are a very small number of words in this dictionary, but it works nicely.

http://www.willamette.edu/~tjones/forms/
    span2eng.html

Webster's Dictionary

Have you ever tried to actually read a dictionary? There's not much of a story! However, dictionaries are very useful when you want to know the meaning of a word. You can use this page to enter a word and have a computer at Carnegie Mellon look it up for you.

http://c.gp.cs.cmu.edu:5103/prog/webster?

ENCYCLOPEDIAS
The Best of Kidopedia

Lots of schools are starting their own kidopedias, encyclopedias written by kids for kids. This one pulls together the best entries from all the other kidopedias it knows about. Housed on a computer in Canada, this kidopedia is part of a worldwide effort to get kids not only to read great information, but also to contribute. See what other kids from all over the world are writing, and maybe you'll be inspired to write something yourself!

http://rdz.stjohns.edu/kidopedia/index.html

Britannica Online

The *Encyclopedia Britannica* is available on the Internet! All those great articles on science, history, and geography are obtainable by point and click—the whole enchilada is here! However (and this is a BIG however), it costs money to subscribe to this service. You can, though, sample the Britannica Online, to see if you want to purchase access. Use the "Sampler" area to get partial information in answer to any question. Sometimes that's enough! Also, all the details for cost and other subscription information are available. If you think you might be interested, take a look!

http://www.eb.com/

A
B
C
D
E
F
G
H
I
J
K
L
M
N
O
P
Q
R
S
T
U
V
W
X
Y
Z

Encyclopedia Smithsonian

For 150 years, the Smithsonian Museum collections have been a treasure trove. They house many wonders of history, science, and the natural world. Thousands of people visit the Smithsonian museums in Washington, D.C. everyday, and the staff there answer the same questions over and over. The Smithsonian folks took the answers to many of those questions, and put them in an encyclopedia format on the Internet. You can get information on the history of the U.S. flag, great lists of books on animals, the inside scoop on the Titanic, and loads of other info!

http://web1.si.edu/welcome/faq/start.htm

Vose Kidopedia Index

Imagine an encyclopedia written by kids for kids. Each article in the encyclopedia would feature the things kids are interested in, and kids could easily understand what's written. Well—you don't have to imagine this, Kidopedia is here! The Vose School in Beaverton, Oregon presents a nice encyclopedia with tons of articles on animals, famous people, space, and other topics. Every single word is written by elementary school students. If you're a kid—this is YOUR encyclopedia.

http://vose.demos.com/kidindex.html

POPULATION

Census Bureau Home Page

You know what Obi-wan Kenobi said to Luke Skywalker in *Star Wars*, when he had a question about the population of the United States? "Use the Source, Luke!" Go right to the source with questions like this—to the U.S. Census Bureau! How do they count how many people there are in the U.S.? Find out here, plus learn lots of statistical info on things like jobs, housing, health, crime, income, education, marriage and family, race and ethnicity, aging, transportation and travel, and recreation. Now you might think statistics are boring, but try this: 26% of the U.S. population is under 18! And if you don't have cable TV, tell Dad to get with the program: 61% of American households have it.

http://www.census.gov/

CERN/ANU—Demography & Population Studies WWW VL

The world is a mighty big place, and this is a mighty big Web page. From here, the intrepid internaut gathering data on population and demographics can click on over 150 links around the world, covering every aspect of the field. From tiny little sites dealing with local matters, all the way up to massive data banks at major colleges and government institutions, this site has it all.

http://coombs.anu.edu.au/ResFacilities/
DemographyPage.html

POPCLOCK Projection

The current estimated U.S. population is found at this site. They take the 1990 Census, add the births, and subtract the deaths. Then they factor in their best guesses about trends, and come up with this estimated result. In case you wondered, it counts only residents in the U.S and the District of Columbia, and not families of military serving overseas, or others living abroad.

http://www.census.gov/cgi-bin/popclock

Population Reference Bureau

The Population Reference Bureau has been providing the public with solid information on trends in world and U.S. population and demographics since 1929. This nonprofit organization has put together a useful and lively home page which enables visitors to query their extensive World Population Data Sheet and read current and back issues of their magazine "Population Today." There are also links to many other online population resources and a nifty game called "Population Jeopardy."

http://www.prb.org/prb

World POPClock

Quick! If you wanted to send a letter to everyone in the world, how many stamps would you need? Find an estimate of the world's current population at this site. You'll also find out how many births and deaths occur each minute.

http://www.census.gov/ipc-bin/popclockw

World Population

Every thirty seconds, the world population clock at this site clicks over with the latest figures. If you have Netscape 1.x, you can have the clock animated as well. From here, you can check out the U.S. Bureau of the Census's national and world POPClocks with just a click, and link onto other related sites.

http://sunsite.unc.edu/lunarbin/worldpop

Did you know Utah has the highest birth rate in the United States? Or that the country of Oman doubles its population every fourteen years? If you knew the answers to these population questions, you'd score well in Population Jeopardy, at the **Population Reference Bureau** home page!

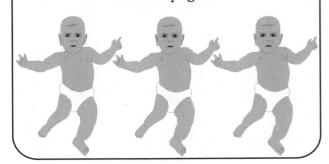

World Population Trends

Check this site for United Nations World Population statistics and trends. Included are population figures for countries, and a brief list of historical milestones in world population. For example, the estimated world population was one billion people in 1804. It took 123 years for it to double to two billion, in 1927. By 1974, 47 years later, it had doubled again to four billion. Estimates are that the world's population will double again, to eight billion, by 2021. Right now it's just under six billion people.

gopher://gopher.undp.org:70/11/ungophers/popin/ wdtrends

SUN AND MOON RISE CALCULATION
Sunrise/Sunset Computation

Sometimes you have to get up awfully early to watch the sun rise. When the sun or moon rises or sets depends on where you live and the time of year. You can take the mystery out of when old Sol (that's another name for the sun) takes off in the morning by using the U.S. Naval Observatory's Sunrise/Sunset Computation page. All you have to do is plug in a date and a place, and through the magic of computers, the time of sun (and moon) rise and set is provided. For fun, put in your birthday and birthplace, or pick an interesting date (like Dec. 31, 1999).

http://tycho.usno.navy.mil/srss.html

THESAURI
ARTFL Project: ROGET Form

Sometimes words can be so frustrating. Have you ever had a homework assignment, and found you were using the same word over and over again? To solve this very type of problem, a guy named Peter Roget came up with a list that grouped similar words together. This type of list of similar words is called a thesaurus, and Peter Roget's is considered one of the best. Type in a word. Now you'll be able to impress your teachers with your growing, ummm, make that expanding, ummm, make that increasing, ummm, make that enlarging vocabulary. Keep in mind this is the edition from 1911, so newer words will not appear.

http://humanities.uchicago.edu/forms_unrest/ ROGET.html

WEIGHTS AND MEASURES
The Beaufort Scale

The Beaufort scale is a way to estimate wind speed without the use of instruments. It's useful to know about this in case you want to fly a kite or go sailing. For example, the description of Beaufort force 3 is "Leaves and small twigs in constant motion; wind extends light flag." That translates to a wind speed of 7-10 knots (8-12 mph; 12-19 kph; 3.4-5.4 mps). Find out the other indicators here.

http://www.anbg.gov.au/jrc/kayak/beaufort.html

A
B
C
D
E
F
G
H
I
J
K
L
M
N
O
P
Q
R
S
T
U
V
W
X
Y
Z

Conversion of Units / Umrechnung von Einheiten

This is another HUGE measurement converter. Written in English and German, at this site you'll be able to convert everything from acres to yards. Included are electronic measures such as amperage and watts.

http://www.chemie.fu-berlin.de/chemistry/
general/units.html

Martindale's The Reference Desk: Calculators On-Line

Hotlist this one now. First off, it tells you what time it is. Not only where you live, but all over the world. It tells you what the weather is, where the earthquakes are, and where the surf's up. But move on to the calculators. Sure, it will convert the usual units for you: feet to meters, Celsius to Fahrenheit, and more. But then it moves from the commonplace to the exotic: automotive calculators, loan and budget calculators, math and engineering, medical, and even fabulous miscellaneous calculators (calculate the size of the fish tank you need). You can definitely count on this Web site!

http://sun2.lib.uci.edu/~martindale/
RefCalculators.html

Scales of Measurement

Ever wondered what the smallest thing is, compared to bigger things? This site lists various things in orders of magnitude. For example, Man is listed at about 1.8 meters long. On either side of that, we find an "unraveled human DNA strand" with a length of 0.068 meters, and a blue whale, at 30 meters. Grass grows at a faster rate than the sea floor spreads, but it's not as fast as the typical rate at which a glacier advances. Maybe they are checking the wrong grass. We seem to mow ours a lot around here.

http://xalph.ast.cam.ac.uk/public/niel/scales1.ascii

Unit Conversion Form

Provided by the University of Southampton in England, this great resource will convert distance (like miles to kilometers), mass (or weights, including pounds to kilograms), temperature (for example, Celsius to Fahrenheit), speed (such as kilometers per hour to miles per hour), and other types of measurements.

http://www.soton.ac.uk/~scp93ch/refer/
convform.html

NET FILES

True or False: Most cartoons we see on TV these days are created completely on computers.

Answer: False. Computer animation is still rare in the world of television cartoons. In fact, while you might assume that the pictures are the first things to "go digital," it's sound that is usually stored and played back on computers and special keyboards. Cool, huh? There's lots of info on how cartoons are made at http://pathfinder.com/@@algM69EIIAIAQOx5/KidsWB/cartoon/cartoon.html

WORLD RECORDS

See also: Name of Sport, or Subject

Hollywood GUINNESS World of Records

The Guinness Company has been collecting world records on just about everything. If you've ever seen a Guinness Book of World Records, or visited a Guinness Museum, you know they establish world records in a variety of categories. For example, they determine who is the biggest human being or what animal is the fastest. On this Web page you can sample a few of the Guinness records, including the lady with the longest neck!

http://www.ernestallen.com/TR/CA/
GuinnessWorldofRecords/

ZIP AND POSTAL CODES

Les Codes Postaux des Villes Françaises

In France postal codes are called "les codes postaux." At the Les Codes Postaux des Villes Françaises page, you'll see which postal codes are assigned to various towns in France. For anyone mailing letters to France, this is great, but be advised, the site is in French!

http://www.unice.fr/html/French/codePostal.html

Danske Postnumre

In Denmark, the postal codes are called "postnumre." If you're sending a letter to Denmark, get the right code first by checking out Danske Postnumre. It's a Great Dane Page, but be advised it's in Danish!

http://www.dk.net/misc/postnumre

Italian Zip Codes

You can easily find Italian postal codes on the Italian ZIP Codes page. All you have to do is type in a city or province, and you'll see the codes. Keep in mind, though, that this computer understands Italian only, so Rome, for example, is Roma!

http://www.crs4.it/~france/CAP/cap.html

PLZ Request Form (English)

Germany changed its system of postal codes a few years ago. This means if you want to send a letter to Germany, and you have an old code, it is best to convert from the old code to the new one. Fortunately, at the PLZ Request Form Page, your old number will be converted via the magic of software.

http://www.uni-frankfurt.de/plz/plzrequest.uk.html

Postal Code Lookup

If you need to send a message to Canada (or if you're Canadian and you need postal code info) take a look here. There's a neat graphic that shows you exactly how to address an envelope, and where everything goes. Toll-free 800 numbers are provided for assistance with looking up postal codes, and all sorts of info on the Canadian postal code system is available at this site.

http://www.canpost.ca/english/pclookup/
pclookup.html#pci

Postal Codes of the World

Ever wonder what all the letters and numbers mean in a Canadian postal code? Turns out that the first letter identifies the province, or region of a province. The rest of the letters and numbers have specific meanings, too. If you're interested in what postal codes might look like for Singapore, Estonia, or Vatican City, as well as many other countries, stop in here!

http://www.io.org/~djcl/postcd.txt

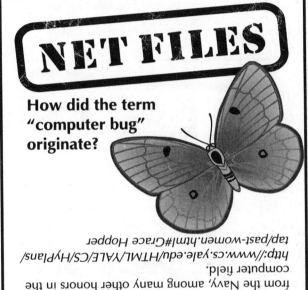

NET FILES

How did the term "computer bug" originate?

Answer: In 1951, Grace Hopper discovered the first computer "bug." It was a real moth, which she pasted into the UNIVAC I logbook. See a picture of it here! Admiral Hopper was a distinguished mathematician and programmer and received the Distinguished Service Medal from the Navy, among many other honors in the computer field.

http://www.cs.yale.edu/HTML/YALE/CS/HyPlans/tap/past-women.html#Grace Hopper

ZIP+4 Lookup

This is another U.S. ZIP code lookup service. Just like the National Address Service at *http://www.semaphorecorp.com/*, ZIP+4 Lookup will provide, in most instances, a ZIP code for a street and town address you provide. The difference here is that this service is provided by the U.S. Post Office! So, if one site is inoperable, you have yet another to use to find ZIP codes for all the important letters you have to send! If you don't know your nine-digit ZIP code, this site will tell you, based on your address.

http://www.usps.gov/ncsc/lookups/lookup_zip+4.html

A
B
C
D
E
F
G
H
I
J
K
L
M
N
O
P
Q
R
S
T
U
V
W
X
Y
Z

RELIGION

Religious and sacred texts

If you go to church or temple services, you probably know a lot about your own religion. But have you ever wondered about other people's beliefs? This site contains electronic versions of texts sacred to followers of many of the world's major religions, including Judaism, Islam, and Hinduism. Also explore links to early Christian texts, Zen gardens, and a thematic guide to world scripture.

http://www.marshall.edu/~wiley6/index.html

NET FILES

The Academy Awards statuette known as "Oscar" is 13 inches tall and weighs 8 pounds. It was born at a Hollywood banquet on May 11, 1927, one week after the Academy of Motion Picture Arts and Sciences was organized. At that meeting, Louis B. Mayer, president of Metro-Goldwyn-Mayer (MGM) Studios, urged that the Academy create a special film award. Cedric Gibbons, an art director for MGM, quickly sketched a figure of a knight holding a crusader's sword standing atop a reel of film, whose five spokes signified the five original branches of the Academy (Actors, Directors, Producers, Technicians, and Writers). Learn more about the award winners at *http://www.ampas.org/ampas/awards/history.html*

Frisbee is the Ultimate in GAMES AND FUN.

ANGELS
Mb's Angel Page

Have you ever had a close call? Did you wonder if you had a guardian angel who saved you from a mishap? This angel page has beautiful graphics and poems about angels, and lots of angelic links.

http://www.cs.iastate.edu/~gurski/Angels/angel.html

Welcome to Angels on the Net

Many people believe that angels, while invisible to the human eye, may be felt by the human heart. Did you know that there are nine different kinds of angels? This is the place to learn about angels, and share stories about how they have touched people's lives. The monthly newsletter will keep you up to date on new angel sightings. You'll also find many thoughtful links to similar Web pages.

http://www.netangel.com/

APPARITIONS AND MIRACLES
Catholic Apparitions of Jesus and Mary

An apparition? It's a supernatural sight. People have made various claims about apparitions all over the world. Did you ever wonder about which ones might have really occurred? Here's a list of reported apparitions, some of which are still ongoing! Some sites have been disproved by the Catholic Church, but others have been verified. Decide for yourself whether you are a skeptic or a believer in these happenings. There is also information about some saints, and the opportunity to download a current calendar with the saint's important dates.

**http://web.frontier.net/Apparitions/
  apparitions.html**

Shroud of Turin Home Page

In a cathedral in Turin, Italy, sits a silver chest. Inside the chest is the mysterious Turin Shroud, which many believe to be the burial cloth that covered Jesus Christ. You'll view amazing photographs and research about the famous shroud. Examining the evidence, what do you see? There are links to many Catholic sites on the Net, as well as a link to a Fatima Home Page.

http://www.cais.com/npacheco/shroud/turin.html

BAHÁ'Í

A Bahá'í Faith Page

One of the world's fastest-growing religions, Bahá'í was founded in the mid-nineteenth century by Bahá'u'lláh, a Persian nobleman from Teheran. He gave up a comfortable and secure lifestyle for a life of persecution and deprivation. Learn more about his life and teachings here, in many different languages.

http://www.bcca.org/~glittle/

Soc.Religion.Bahá'í

Could many of the world's religions be rolled into one? The Bahá'í believe that there have been many messengers from God, each one arriving during a different age. This online archive will show you other teachings, texts, sacred sites, and where to find more on the Bahá'í faith.

http://www.bcca.org/srb/

BUDDHISM

On-line Resources

Buddhism is a philosophy of life taught by Gautama Buddha, who lived and taught in northern India in the 6th Century B.C. The Buddha was not a god—"Buddha" means "enlightened one." The teachings of Buddhism are aimed solely to relieve beings from suffering. This meta-resource includes art, philosophy, meditation, and many fascinating links. Parental advisory: all links have not been checked.

http://www.psu.edu/jbe/resource.html

The White Path Temple

Visit a virtual Shin Buddhist Temple. You'll see intricate mandalas and other contemplative art. Learn about this religion by reading the beginner's guide, checking the online Buddhist dictionary, and visiting temples in Kyoto, Japan. To further investigate this religion, there's an extensive collection of links at W3C/ANU—Buddhist Studies WWW VL at *http://coombs.anu.edu.au/ WWWVL-Buddhism.html*. See the art, read the literature, and find out about the four great vows of Buddhism.

http://www2.gol.com/users/claude/shin.html

CHRISTIANITY

Distinctive Churches

Many churches have their own parishes in cyberspace these days. This site is trying to collect them all, and selects "distinctive" ones to highlight each month. There are churches from eight countries represented so far. It's interesting to drop in on many congregations and see what's happening. There are also (what else?) lots of links. Don't miss the Christian clip art, or the "Six Days of Creation" screen saver at *http://www.gospelcom.net/gf/ gallery/*.

http://www.rwf2000.com/church.html

Kingdom Surf

This site changes every week, so we won't even bother to describe what's on it! Here's your chance, though, to see what the Christian religion has to do with YOU. Look here first if you want a lift, because it's a timely, upbeat place that'll keep you on your toes! Other recent items have been Christian jokes, sermon clip art, readings from the Bible, and pen-pal lists. You don't have to be a Christian to enjoy this site.

http://www.crusade.org/surf/

Virtual Church Home Page

This virtual church has a room just for kids! There are Bible stories with colorful graphics to go along with them. If you want to read an exciting one, try "The Men in the Fiery Furnace." If you're a younger kid, you can ask a parent to download coloring pages, and then send them back after you've colored them on your computer. Explore the other rooms in this church, too. The library, for instance, contains crossword puzzles, trivia quizzes, and word jumbles.

http://www.connix.com/~kgeffert/vchome/ vcwelc.htm#open

Origami: the fold to behold! Check out CRAFTS AND HOBBIES.

A B C D E F G H I J K L M N O P Q R S T U V W X Y Z

> ## Chase some waterfalls in EARTH SCIENCE.

CHRISTIANITY—AMISH, MENNONITE

"The Plain People"

If you've ever been curious about the Amish, the Mennonites, the Brethren, or the other "Plain People" of the Pennsylvania Dutch Country, visit this page. You'll learn a little about their beliefs, their mode of dress, and their customs. Did you know that an Amish bride wears a blue wedding dress, or that kids attend school only through the eighth grade? There's also an opportunity for you to "Ask the Amish" and submit your own questions.

http://padutch.welcome.com/amish.html

CHRISTIANITY—CATHOLIC

Catholic Kiosk

The Archdiocese of Cincinnati, Ohio, has an extensive collection here. You can read the entire Catechism of the Catholic Church, as well as tour the Vatican and other Catholic art and architecture resources. You can also see a list of all the members of the College of Cardinals around the world, with links to their home pages, if they have them. That page's unusual counter reads "You are one of 1310 to have graced this page since the feast of SS. Simon and Jude, 1995." Many religious orders have opened up abbeys and cloisters on the Web, and you can visit them here. There are links to Saints' Lives, Marian resources, and sources of Catholic news. Many "Right-to-Life" links are included.

http://www.erinet.com/aquinas/arch/dio.html

> ## Lost your marbles? Find them in GAMES AND FUN.

The Holy See

The Vatican has established an official and attractive Web site under its own top-level country domain, ".va." The content is still being built, but there are several messages from Pope John Paul II, including his Christmas and World Day of Peace messages. You can read both in your choice of seven languages, and the page says it will soon provide info on all the Pope's daily activities, press releases, and official appearances. The definitive "Vatican" site is *Christus Rex* at *http://christusrex.org/www1/icons/index.html*. There is an annotation for it in the ART MUSEUMS section of this book. It contains not only pictures of the Vatican museums, but many more documents, and these items are in many languages. You may also want to check out Vatican Radio. "65 years of serving the unity of the Church and the peace in the world, night and day, every day, all over the world, in 37 languages... broadcasting on short wave, medium wave, FM, satellite, and the Internet." It's located at *http://www.wrn.org/vatican-radio/about.html*.

http://www.vatican.va/

The Marian Hour

Many Catholics around the world pray using a special set of beads called a rosary. They use the beads to count the various prayers they have said. You can learn about the Mysteries of the Rosary at this well-designed site, as well as hear the various prayers for yourself. This organization will send a free rosary to anyone who wants one.

http://netpage.bc.ca/marianhr/index.html

CHRISTIANITY—SAINTS

Catholic Cincinnati Info Web

At this site, you can read various Saints' Lives, and check the calendar to see whose feast day it is. Check Nicholas of Myra, the patron saint of children. You may know him as Santa Claus! Here's your chance to look up Saint Nick, Saint Valentine, Saint Patrick, and other Catholic saints. Still more information on Saints is at the Catholic Online Patron Saints Page, *http://www.catholic.org/saints/patron.html*.

http://www.erinet.com/aquinas/arch/saints.html

Home Page of the Immaculate

Mary, the mother of Jesus. What is the history of this woman who has been revered by so many? How did the prophets know that a virgin would bear a son, long before it happened? Find out about the miraculous events, and what some people think they mean. Here, too, you'll find the Little Internet Library of the Blessed Virgin Mary, and links to all over. You'll also want to visit The Mary Page at *http://www.udayton.edu/mary* for answers to frequently asked questions about Mary.

http://www.ici.net/cust_pages/ffi/index.html

CHRISTIANITY—THE CHURCH OF JESUS CHRIST OF LATTER-DAY SAINTS

World Wide Web First Ward

At this site you'll find a lively discussion of many topics of interest to Mormons, including what to do when your kids are disappointed they can't celebrate Halloween. Be inspired by the Daily Devotional and the scripture class for Sunday School teachers and interested others. There is a ton of geneaology resources, Church news, and sacred texts and resources. Don't miss the Salt Lake City, Utah Temple Square tour. Somewhat inexplicably, the "What Mormons Believe" resources are filed at the end of the tour, where you can also send e-mail to have a free *Book of Mormon* delivered to your house. The site is sponsored in part by clothier "Mr. Mac," the missionary's friend. If you've ever wondered how young Mormon missionaries always look so well-dressed, even in rustic situations, the secret is out! For still more links to LDS Information Resources try *http://wings.buffalo.edu/~plewe/lds.html* for links to sacred texts and commentary, family activities, clip art, and more.

http://www.uvol.com/www1st/homepage.html

Get your hobby off the ground! Try Rockets in MODELS AND MINIATURES.

Utah's state bird is the seagull, even though Utah is miles from any coastline! Seagull Monument stands in Temple Square, in Salt Lake City, as a reminder of a miracle that occurred there during the time of the Mormon pioneers. In the spring of 1848, their newly planted fields were being devoured by crickets. Without those crops, the settlers were sure to starve. However, seagulls appeared, gobbled up all the crickets, and saved the settlement. Read more about early Mormon history at the World Wide Web First Ward.

HINDUISM

Nine Questions about Hinduism

On July 4, 1990 the youth meeting of the Hindu Temple of Greater Chicago had a special visitor: Gurudeva, Sivaya Subramuniyaswami. He was asked to give "official" answers to nine questions, ranging from "Are Hindus idol worshippers?", to "What's this reincarnation thing?", to "Why do Hindu women wear the dot on the forehead?" It's a revealing look at what kids want to know about Hinduism. Hindu gods are explained and illustrated in one link from this page, and the top level (*http://www.spiritweb.org/Spirit/Veda/Overview.html*) includes numerous outside links. Parental advisory: links from this page have not been checked.

http://www.spiritweb.org/Spirit/Veda/nine-questions.html

A B C D E F G H I J K L M N O P Q R S T U V W X Y Z

Swami Chinmayananda

This is the home page of a great Indian spiritual master, who, in 1993, was chosen to act as the "President of Hinduism" at a meeting of the Parliament of World Religions in Chicago. Read his teachings and interpretations of the *Bhagavad Gita*, and learn why "Happiness depends on what you can give, not on what you can get."

http://WWW.tezcat.com/~bnaik/chinmaya.html

ISLAM
FAQ on Islam

This is a very easy-to-understand look at Islam and "Who's a Muslim?" Find out what Muslims believe, and read about their sacred text, the Quran. You'll also find answers to questions like "What do Muslims think about Jesus?" and "What about Muslim women?"

http://darkwing.uoregon.edu/~kbatarfi/islam_1.html

NET FILES

How many gallons of salt water are in the aquarium at Epcot's DiveQuest?

http://www.travelweb.com/thisco/wdw/wdwhome/epcot/ep105.html

Answer: Six million gallons! That's enough to fill Spaceship Earth (the giant geodesic golf ball) with room to spare.

Masjid of the Ether: Basic Information on Islam

Devout Muslims pray several times a day at specific times. You can use the "Prayer Calculator" and a ZIP code or city to find out the correct times, and the correct direction to face. See if your answers can be found in the Frequently-asked Questions area, and make a small visit to the Digital Tekke, a sufi lodge in Web space. Parental advisory: links off this site have not been checked.

http://www.uoknor.edu:80/cybermuslim/cy_masjid.html

USC Muslim Students Association Islamic Server

Explore the sacred pillars of this religion, its texts, and its practice. One interesting article states that the "Nation of Islam," among others, should not be calling itself that, based on its writings.

http://www.usc.edu/dept/MSA/

JUDAISM
Judaica web world

This is a terrific archive of spiritual and cultural Jewish knowledge. First off, we'll say we have not checked all these links. But there is a lot to like about these pages. For one thing, they promise (Real Soon Now) some special pages for Jewish kids. Right now, you'll find kosher Asian recipes, a Judaic calendar, GIFs of famous Rabbis, "the ultimate Jewish link-launcher," and a service that faxes (or e-mails) you a little daily Torah teaching.

http://www.nauticom.net/users/rafie/judaica-world.html

REPTILES

See also: PETS AND PET CARE

Mike's Herpetocultural Home Page

Here's a herp, there's a herp, everywhere's a herp, herp. It's not Old MacDonald and it's not a farm, but Mike's Herpetocultural Home Page is the place to go for information about reptiles. You'll learn about herpetoculture, the keeping and breeding of amphibians and reptiles. You'll find links to other herp home pages, research organizations, herp FAQs, journals and magazines, and much more.

http://gto.ncsa.uiuc.edu/pingleto/herp.html

Trendy's House of Herpetology

Snakes, amphibians, lizards, turtles, and iguanas. Everything you need to know is here, including lots of great photos. Learn how to treat your turtle, and how to coddle your chameleon. Whether you want to soothe your snakes, or animate your amphibians, this page will surely be of use. Parental advisory: there are two versions of this page. The URL listed is for the K-12 version. Even so, not all links off it have been checked.

http://web.bu.edu/~ldaly/herps/

CROCODILES AND ALLIGATORS

The Gator Hole

Much maligned and misunderstood, alligators have existed since the time of the dinosaurs. Hunted almost to extinction, they have made an astounding comeback. You will find an amazing collection of 'gator myth and fact lying around this virtual 'gator hole. Find out here if the stories you hear about alligators are true, or if it's just a crock.

http://magicnet.net/~mgodwin/#Myths_and_Facts

For happy hedgehogs see PETS AND PET CARE.

St. Augustine's Alligator Farm

CHOMP, CHOMP!! Be careful, don't get too close. Gomek is eating and you wouldn't want to become part of his dinner, would you? Gomek is the world's largest known reptile on exhibit. He's almost eighteen feet long and weighs over 1,700 pounds! Gomek wouldn't hurt me, would he? He certainly could! In the wild, alligators eat fish, turtles, and small mammals, but because Gomek has been fed by his innkeepers, he could be very dangerous to man. Feeding alligators causes them to lose their fear of man. They become bold, aggressive and expect more food. Visit Gomek and his other friends at the St. Augustine Alligator Farm and remember: you should never feed wild animals. Don't forget to pick up your discount admission ticket at this Web site too, should you ever visit the real zoological park in Florida!

http://pequin.aug.com/~oldcity/around/attractions/ gatorfarm/gator.html

LIZARDS
Heatherk's Gecko Page

Are you a "herper"? Perhaps you should stop by Heatherk's Gecko Page, just to be sure. Ask yourself the following questions and be careful how you answer them: Do you carry a moisture-mister and spray yourself three times a day? Do you lick your lips when a bug lands near you? Is your house the yearly field trip for the neighborhood school's science classes? Heatherk's Gecko Page also has links to other herp interest sites, herp home pages, and care sheets for other lizards, not just geckos.

http://www.wttf.com/~gecko/

Iguana iguana

You really want to raise a reptile, but can't stomach the thought of having to feed it icky insects. Then maybe you wanna iguana. These lovely lizards are very vegetarian, but will swiftly snarf your pepperoni pizza if left alone all night. Find out what makes these captivating creatures the most popular pet from the reptile race.

http://fovea.retina.net/~gecko/herps/iguanas/ index.html

A B C D E F G H I J K L M N O P Q **R** S T U V W X Y Z

Your First True Chameleon

That little statue-like lizard never moves, but you could swear those eyes follow you wherever you go. They do. Chameleons have globular independent eyes that can do almost a complete 360 degree turn without them ever moving their heads. The fascinating behavior, unusual body shapes, and changing color of these creatures have kept collectors intrigued for decades. However, they often face one major challenge. Delicate by nature, they tend to die easily. But the availability of quality information on raising chameleons, and new restrictions on importing them, has led to captive-bred lizards that are healthier and better adapted, increasing their chances of survival. Did you know you should buy food-quality crickets for your lizard, and not bait cricks, since they are often fed growth hormones? Lots of great info here for general lizard care, too!

http://www.skypoint.com/members/mikefry/
  chams.html

SNAKES

An Interactive Guide to Massachusetts Snakes

You found a snake you don't recognize sunning itself on your deck, and want to know if it's safe to move it. Answer a series of questions at this interactive site, and you can quickly identify that suspect snake. If you already know the snake's name, and want to know more about its lifestyle and habits, you can also find that here. But once you make an identification, remember it's usually best to let a sleeping snake lie.

http://klaatu.oit.umass.edu/umext/snake/

Jason's Snakes and Reptiles

Questions on housing for snakes, temperature control, feeding, diseases, or breeding snakes? Jason's Snakes and Reptiles page has the answers. Check out the care sheet for snakes, or get information on other snake sites, snake news groups, and snake gopher sites.

http://www.shadeslanding.com/jas/

NET FILES

How big is the world's largest kite?

Answer: This year, it's Peter Lynn's Trilobite. It's 165 feet long, 72.5 feet wide, and about thirty feet high. In fact, it's so huge, kids were flying other kites inside it! It has only a single line, and can be flown by one person! 20,000 yards of fabric make up the kite, but it's built in zippered sections. This makes it easier to carry around and repair. See some pictures of this awesome kite at the "Cool Links" area of http://www.kfs.org/kites/cool.html the Kite Flier's Site!

TURTLES

Turtle Trax—A Marine Turtle Page

Did you know that ALL species of marine turtles are either threatened or endangered? That's right, and a major reason for this is danger to their nests. These dangers include increased numbers of people on the beaches where the turtles dig their nests. Also, some people dig up the nests and sell or eat turtle eggs. Another problem is artificial lighting around beaches, which has a disorienting effect on little turtles, who can't find the safety of the sea. In addition to the nesting threats, don't forget about the environmental threats. These include water pollution and getting stuck in floating trash. These are just some of the most serious threats. For more information about marine turtles, their environment, and ways you can help, visit the Turtle Trax Page.

http://www.io.org/~bunrab/

RIGHTS AND FREEDOMS

The House of Representatives—Internet Law Library

Human rights may be inalienable, but it takes a lot of documentation to put them into law. This page includes literally hundreds of important documents pertaining to human rights from nations in every corner of the globe, and throughout history. If you're looking for the complete text of Thomas Paine's "Rights of Man" or the International Covenant on Civil and Political Rights, you'll find them only a click away here.

http://www.pls.com:8001/his/93.htm

The Human Rights Web Home Page

Certain human rights are guaranteed to everyone by United Nations declarations and other international agreements, but people in some countries have had to struggle to make those rights a reality. The very existence of the Internet has made it easier for those people to communicate with the rest of the world, and this page clearly and thoroughly spells out what human rights are and how to use the Net to help out in the cause. The resources section alone features links to groups like Amnesty International, PEN International Writer's Union, the U.S. State Department, and the Reebok Human Rights Awards Page, among dozens of others. Middle school and high school kids will find this page an endless source of thought-provoking information.

http://www.traveller.com/~hrweb/index.html

Have you hadrosaurus today? If not, try DINOSAURS AND PREHISTORIC TIMES.

Whooooooo will you find in BIRDS?

National Child Rights Alliance

It is startling that as we enter the twenty-first century, children have little more in the way of legal rights and status than they did in the nineteenth. The NCRA has a simple point of view—they feel that children have to be protected from abuse. Abuse takes many forms: both the more familiar overt physical kinds that are reported in the newspapers every day, and the more subtle forms, such as deprivation of safety, food, shelter, medical care, and dignity. Link here to a series of outrageous reports of children suffering under an antiquated legal system that often regards them as "property," and positive actions such as the NCRA's proposed Youth Bill of Rights. Parents should explore this site with their children.

http://www.ai.mit.edu/people/ellens/NCRA/ncra.html

Reebok and Human Rights

This well-designed page shines as an example of how corporations can become involved with more than just a ledger sheet. Since 1988, Reebok Shoes has been actively involved in the worldwide human rights movement. This isn't just a publicity stunt, either. They have been giving their Human Rights Awards to four young people every year and include a major cash donation to each recipient's organization of choice. They also have been promoting their Witness Program, which provides mass communications tools such as computers, video cameras, and fax machines to human rights groups, and their Project America has been responsible for getting thousands of people involved in community service organizations. Visiting this page would be worth it just to gawk at the graphics and movies. The fact that it's a significant place where things happen is just a bonus.

http://planetreebok.com/humanrights.html

A B C D E F G H I J K L M N O P Q R S T U V W X Y Z

The Religious Freedom Home Page

Beginning with the U.S. Bill of Rights, and continuing onward through the United Nations Universal Declaration of Human Rights, religious freedom has been a cornerstone of progressive government worldwide. This well-designed non-denominational Web site, sponsored by the Christian Science Committee on Publication, explores what religious freedom really means, and looks at the phenomenon both nationally and globally. It includes conflicting thoughts on controversial issues, but always takes the viewpoint that individuals should be informed and educated about their right to worship freely.

http://www.shore.net/rf

NET FILES

What are some words with no vowels, acceptable in Scrabble?

hmmm-hmmm

Answer: Here are a few: BRR, used to indicate coldness (brr); SHH, used to urge silence (sh); TSK, a scolding exclamation; PSST, used to attract someone's attention; and CRWTH, an ancient stringed musical instrument. Check http://www.yak.net/kablooey/scrabble.html for more from the San Jose Scrabble Club!

ROBOTS

Info on Hobby Robots (from comp.robotics.)

Why wait for George Jetson and Spacely Sprockets to build you a robot, when plenty of folks are building their own right now? This page gives you the lowdown on where to pick up inexpensive hobby kits for assembling your own robot! It also includes links to places where you can download hints and plans, information on building sensors, and the entire "6.270 Robot Builder's Guide," which is also available in hard copy from the Massachusetts Institute of Technology.

http://www.cs.uwa.edu.au/%7Emafm/robot/index.html

Lego Robot Info

You know those cute little Lego blocks that you keep finding under your sofa cushions? Those odd-shaped things are actually capable of being constructed into computer-driven, sophisticated robots! In 1994, the Boston Museum of Science had a robot design workshop and contest for 7th through 10th graders using Legos and Lego Dacta kits. The kids designed incredible machines, some using computerized interfaces, and this page has full-color photographs of their creations, as well as lots of information on how to build them yourself. Even if you don't particularly want to build a robot, you may want to drop in here and marvel at the kids who did.

http://legowww.itek.norut.no/robots

SCHOOLS AND EDUCATION

ARTSEDGE

This site aims to teach and learn what technology can do for education and the arts. "The arts" doesn't just mean drawing and painting, you know. There are also performing arts, like music, dance, and theatre. Since we don't know everything about how technology and the arts mix, think of this site as sort of an experimental lab. You'll find discussion areas for students and teachers, news flashes, curriculum guides, and even showcases of art by kids. There's a section for online exhibits, museums, and galleries, plus links to other Web arts sites.

http://artsedge.kennedy-center.org/

Cisco Educational Archive and Resources Catalog

OK, you've got this great new computer sitting in front of you, with a super-fast modem. Now, how do you actually use it for your day-to-day homework— or your teaching? Are you looking for information about the Dilophosaurus? Or perhaps you want to find out more about Civil Rights? Don't waste any time: go right to the door of the Virtual Schoolhouse! Investigate your questions here and "CEARCH" using a very fast search engine. Cisco's done an excellent job of collecting great resources for kids, teachers, and parents! You'll also find a list of online schools and links to their home pages. You may never have heard of Cisco, but your Internet Service Provider has, and chances are good that much of your Internet traffic travels through Cisco equipment. Cisco announces special grants and other opportunities for schools here, so check often.

http://sunsite.unc.edu:80/cisco/edu-arch.html

Take a ride on a Carousel in AMUSEMENT PARKS.

Lose yourself in a Museum. SCIENCE has them all.

Classroom Connect on the Net!

Classroom Connect is one of our favorite magazines. Their Web site doesn't disappoint, either. Check it out for info on upcoming conferences, a jumpstation to great Web links, newsgroups, ftp sites, a Web toolkit, and more. This is a commercial publisher, but they know their market, so stop in and browse!

http://www.wentworth.com/

EdWeb Home Page

Are you sick and tired of those endless clickable lists that seem to lead nowhere? How do you find out what it all means to your students and your school? Let's talk about the history and impact of technology, and the potential all this computer stuff has, for good and bad. The Center for Networked Information Discovery and Retrieval knows what you want. EdWeb is more than just a list of resources! Here you can also get the latest articles on technology and school reform. Find out how the World Wide Web relates to YOU and your classroom. Combine computers and kids in new, more exciting ways. This page will help you use the technology that's out there right now! Better hotlist this one, you'll want to come back.

http://k12.cnidr.org:90/

Global SchoolNet Foundation Home Page

"Where in the world is Roger?" "Roots and Shoots with Jane Goodall." "International CyberFair." "Global Schoolhouse Videoconferencing." Any of that sound interesting? The folks in charge of GSN just keep collecting and coming up with more terrific ideas all the time! Always fresh and exciting, this is where K-12 innovation lives on the Net!

http://gsn.org

A B C D E F G H I J K L M N O P Q R S T U V W X Y Z

NET FILES

What does All That mean?

Answer: It's "streetspeak," meaning "the big cheese, the top banana, the coolest person in the world." For example: Ever since she started playing in that band, she thinks she's all that." Find out more current slang, and submit new words you and your friends use! http://www.jayi.com/jayi/fishnet/streetspeak/SSdata.html

Global Show-N-Tell

You know how you can't find your refrigerator door anymore because of your pictures, paintings, and other stuff your Mom has hung up there? How about displaying your artwork on an electronic refrigerator door for awhile? Global Show-N-Tell showcases artwork of students worldwide. Visit the current exhibit, explore past ones, or search other kids' art sites on the Internet. You can enter your work to Global Show-N-Tell; the directions are right here. Some of the drawings are linked back to kids' personal home pages.

http://www.manymedia.com/show-n-tell/index.html

GNN Education Center Home Page

Try this site for more than links to great sites to support your curriculum. You'll find special-interest articles, the latest in K-12 Net-happenings, and a way to find out what projects are currently being conducted in other classrooms worldwide. As Frank Odasz of Big Sky Telegraph says, "When you hear that modem tone, you know you're not alone!"

http://gnn.com/gnn/meta/edu/index.html

Janice's K-12 Outpost

Janice is always sifting new Internet sites to find the best ones to show kids, parents, and teachers. Check her graphically delicious site for Internet treats.

http://k12.cnidr.org/janice_k12/k12menu.html

U.S. Department of Education

The Department of Education has a newly designed site with some useful and welcome features. Worth a look if you're concerned with any of the following: improving education on a local or national level, learning from other schools in other communities, application procedures for education grants, or student financial aid. The Picks O' the Month section highlights important resources you won't see everywhere else.

http://www.ed.gov/

Web 66

If your school has its own Web server, it should be linked here. It's the largest collection of all the schools with Web sites in the world! Don't have a Web site yet? There's a cookbook here that will give you the recipe to create your own: where to get the software, how to write the HTML, and more! Can't tell a LAN from a WAN? You just found out they want YOU to run ethernet around your building? No fear, stop here. You'll find technical info anyone can understand, plus acceptable use policies as well as other planning musts. You want links on top of all that? No surprise, they got 'em.

http://web66.coled.umn.edu/

WebEd k12 Curriculum Links

This page is the work of a librarian loose on the Web since 1993. The links are roughly categorized, but are not annotated. Still, a browse through here will unearth some pretty arcane stuff. Parental warning though: some of the sites are for older kids; explore this site with your kids, and preview if you can.

http://badger.state.wi.us/agencies/dpi/www/WebEd.html

Welcome to the ERIC Pages

Custom-build your own curriculum! The Educational Resources Information Center is a vast collection of data, ideas, research, lesson plans, literature, and more. It will be of interest to parents who want to supplement their child's education at home, or learn about parenting techniques. Teachers will find classroom ideas that go above and beyond textbook-type learning, as well as professional information. They can also use the renowned AskERIC service. If you're an education professional (librarian, teacher, administrator, homeschooler, and so on) you may e-mail questions to AskERIC's net-savvy information specialists. Within 48 hours, you'll have suggestions and solutions drawn from customized ERIC database searches, ERIC Digests, and Internet resources. If you've always wanted to talk to the Reference Librarian of the Internet, you can start with these folks. If you want to browse on your own, check AskERIC's Virtual Library, which contains over 700 lesson plans plus material drawn from the archives of *Newton's Apple*, *CNN Newsroom*, and The Discovery Channel.

http://www.aspensys.com/eric2/welcome.html

Yahoo—Education

Here's another searchable page chock-full of education resources. Everything from special education, to online teaching, to alternative education is accessible from Yahoo. As an aside, did you know that two graduate students started Yahoo as a hobby and developed it into the indispensable information service we know today?

http://www.yahoo.com/Education

Origami: the fold to behold! Check out CRAFTS AND HOBBIES.

Check Web 66: International WWW School Registry for a comprehensive list of schools with home pages. If your school starts its own home page, you'll want to get it listed here, too.

DISTANCE EDUCATION

Academy One

Get out your umbrella and your overcoat! You are now entering the "Classroom Without Walls." Academy One has students all over the globe. You and your school can participate in their simulations, including their "Virtual" Olympics. Compete in a track or math event at your own school, then post your score. You could even be the international winner! The site is an initiative of the National Public Telecomputing Network (NPTN). If you are not entering it from an NPTN-affiliated host, you will not be able to use all the information on this site. But everyone can get to some of the information offered!

http://www.nptn.org/cyber.serv/AOneP/index.html

The Cyberspace Middle School

"It's not just a school, it's an adventure." This is one of the best places on the Net for 6th to 9th-graders. Looking for excitement? Take a wild virtual bus ride to hook up with other schools. Or, you can get ideas for the science fair, research your projects, and ask questions of a real scientist. Are you an author or artist? Contribute to the Mid-Link magazine and see your work published for the whole world to see. Best of all, the Cyberspace Middle School is FREE!

http://www.scri.fsu.edu/~dennisl/CMS.html

A B C D E F G H I J K L M N O P Q R **S** T U V W X Y Z

KIDLINK: Global Networking for Youth 10-15

Wow! Kids from more than 77 countries have decided to answer these four basic questions: Who Am I, What Do I Want To Be When I Grow Up, How Do I Want The World To Be Better When I Grow Up, and What Can I Do Now To Make This Happen? Once you've answered those questions to introduce yourself, you can take part in any of the KIDLINK projects. You can even have a dialogue in the KidCafé in languages such as Spanish, Japanese, and Portuguese. Make the world a better place through KIDLINK!

http://www.kidlink.org/

NASA K-12 Internet Initiative

OK, everybody at your school wants to get hooked up to the Net. But not even the teachers know everything about how to do it! NASA will help you get started, with all the ins-and-outs of getting online. Then they've got links to online interactive projects—new ones every year! Past projects have included "Live from Antarctica," "Live from the Stratosphere," and "Live from the Hubble Space Telescope." Ask the scientists questions, order interesting materials, and help NASA decide what they will do next!

http://quest.arc.nasa.gov:80./index.html

VLC.Homepage

The Village Learning Center is a place where the future begins. If you're in grades seven through nine, you can learn at home on the Web. You even get your own cyber-teacher! While you learn, you begin to tie together different subject areas. Instead of spending one hour on math and then the next hour on social studies, make a model of a mosque and do both subjects at the same time! Note: there is a cost for subscriptions to the Village Learning Center, but you can look around for free.

http://www.snowcrest.net/villcen/vlchp.html

Frisbee is the Ultimate in GAMES AND FUN.

NET FILES

Were there any women pirates?

Answer: Aye, there were at least two, but they fought in men's clothing. One was Mary Read, and the other was Anne Bonny. They plied the waters of the Caribbean in the early 1700s and were known as tough, salty ladies. Sail on over to http://tigger.cc.uic.edu/~toby-g/whos.html to find out more.

HOME SCHOOLING

CIN's Christian Homeschool Forum WebPage

If you were to decide to homeschool, how would you get started? This information desk has tips to help you take the plunge. They also have have answers to questions you might ask, lists of books and magazines, links to support groups, and lots of tips. You'll find plenty of encouragement here!

http://199.227.115.30/homeschool/Index~1.htm

Home Schooling: Homespun Web of Home Educational Resources

Maybe your mom or dad would be interested in teaching you at home. The Homespun Web of Home Educational Resources has tips on getting started, where to find a support group, and (of course!) resources galore. Remember the time you built your own astronomy device? Want to share your experiences with others on the Net? Here's a list of people who'd like to hear from you!

http://www.ictheweb.com/hs-web/

Home Schooling for Unschoolers

As Mark Twain said, "I have never let my schooling interfere with my education." The Bedford family doesn't study "subjects," they follow their passions and interests as they "unschool." Now, you too can study and learn about what interests YOU! Lots of good links here with resources for homeschoolers and others.

http://www2.islandnet.com/~bedford/home_lrn.html

Famous people who have been home-schooled include Alexander Graham Bell, Agatha Christie, Sandra Day O'Connor, Albert Einstein, Wolfgang Mozart, astronaut Sally Ride, Mark Twain, and George Washington.
Read more at
Home Schooling for Unschoolers.

The Homeschool Page

Brrrr! Snow is falling all around and you're harnessing the dogs to the sled. Get ready for a trip to Alaska to visit the Teel family. There is no such thing as a typical homeschooling family, but you'll find out what interests the Teels on their homeschool Web page. See what curriculum they are working on this week, and explore some of their favorite links. Watch out for the polar bears, though!

http://www.alaska.net/~mteel/homesch/homeschl.html

Homeschool World

Some kids don't go to school. "What?" you say. "Isn't that illegal?" Actually, every state in the U.S., and many foreign countries, permit homeschooling in some form. If you're thinking of making the switch to more independent learning at home, or if you already learn at home, your parents will find lots of ideas at the Homeschool World site.

http://www.home-school.com

Who was Senator Bob Dole's boyhood hero?

Answer: He liked Ike! General and President Dwight "Ike" Eisenhower. See some of Dole's childhood photos at *http:// www.agtnet.con/ usnews/wash/doleyth.htm* while you read more.

Jon's Home-school Resource Page

If you could choose only one page on homeschooling, this would be it. Will you fit into the "real world" if you don't go to school? Will you do as well academically in homeschool? Will you be able to get into college? Research shows that the answer to all of these questions is a loud YES! Jon's Home-school Resource Page also has a collection of home pages and photos from families; check out what they're doing and learning.

http://www.armory.com/~jon/hs/HomeSchool.html

MIDDLE SCHOOL
Cool School Pages

If you want to find still more middle schools on the Web, here's a listing of sites pronounced "cool" by Midlink.

http://longwood.cs.ucf.edu/~MidLink/
   middle.home.html

First Colony Middle School Home Page

These middle-schoolers in Sugar Land, Texas invite you to become an official weather-watcher. They are collecting weather data from all over! You'll also want to have a look at their 'Netting The Butterfly project and their reports about animal migrations in Texas.

http://chico.rice.edu/armadillo/Ftbend/fcms.html

A B C D E F G H I J K L M N O P Q R S T U V W X Y Z

Highland Home Page

You may not know the word tessellation, but you've seen the results of it before. Ever seen those M. C. Escher drawings with repeating geometrical patterns, where a fish turns into a bird? That's tessellation! (If you have not seen these before, check "Sky and Water I" at *http://www.texas.net/escher/gallery/exhbt1.html*) But what does it have to do with MATH??? Look at the tessellation art done by students at Highland School; then you can download a Tesselmania Demo and try it out yourself! These students live in Libertyville, Illinois.

http://www.elk-grove.k12.il.us/schoolweb/highland/

Marion Cross School

The kids at this school in Norwich, Vermont will show you how to make your own home page. Go to their "MCS Easy Home Page Guide" for the scoop. Also check out the recommended reading lists, Web resources for schools and families, and much more!

http://picard.dartmouth.edu/~cam/MCS.html

Monroe Middle School

Take a tour of the historic Oregon Trail as it travels through Wyoming. Enjoy the scenery, and read the students' fictional journals, describing what life would have been like along the Trail. You'll also see lots of Wyoming wildlife, described by the kids in Green River, Wyoming, where Monroe Middle School is located.

http://monhome.sw2.k12.wy.us/

Vista Middle School Home Page

Join up with the students of Vista Middle School in Las Cruces, New Mexico to become a Knight in Space. They aren't real astronauts, but their school has the next best thing: a life-size space shuttle cargo bay! They go on "missions" to learn about space, and cooperation, too. Sometimes they have electrical problems (the teacher shuts off the lights) or a rough ride (if they are not secured when one of the hydraulic jack thrusters fires). Learn about their scientific experiments "in space." They've also got a great English as a Second Language Program. In fact, you can get to a Spanish/English dictionary right from their home page!

http://taipan.nmsu.edu/vista/vista_home.html

PRIMARY SCHOOL

Aloha!

Visit O'ahu in the Hawaiian Islands to see Lanikai School's page. You can even get a taste of their spot of heaven FROM heaven! (See a space shuttle photo of their location.) Learn some Hawaiian culture here!

http://www.doe.hawaii.edu/~lanikai/

NET FILES

You're making a recipe for dinner but the cookbook has some words you've never heard of. What, for example, is a roux?

Answer: According to Webster's Dictionary, it's a "cooked mixture of flour and fat," and it's pronounced "roo." Get out the butter! And learn more new words at http://c.gp.cs.cmu.edu:5103/prog/webster?

Hartsfield School's Home Page

This school is located in Florida. They were one of the very first schools to have a page on the Web! There are also links here to other fantastic sites in their home town of Tallahassee. Try DeSoto Trail and The Academic Resource Center for sure bets.

http://www.hartsfield.leon.k12.fl.us/ hartsfieldhome.html

Sister MacNamara School

Located in the heart of Winnipeg, Manitoba, Canada, this is a multicultural school. Check out the Monet reproductions by Miss Wallis's fourth-graders!

http://hal9000.wsd1.winnipeg.mb.ca/nnl/sister_m/
sismac.htm

Vose School

The students at Vose School in Beaverton, Oregon are actually writing their own encyclopedia! Click on "Vose Kidopedia" to check out their work in progress. They've already covered a lot of topics, with more to come in the future.

http://www.teleport.com/~vincer/info.html

Wangaratta Primary School

Wangaratta Primary School is in a rural city, North East Victoria, Australia. The school has 250 students ranging in age from five to twelve years. WOW, is this page FUN! Check the Aussie Activities! While you are learning about Australian animals, you can listen to a kookaburra laugh, search for the hidden Aussie animals in a word search puzzle, and learn how to make a kite like the sugar glider. You can also meet Michael, a cool kid with cerebral palsy and an Internet address, so be sure to write and say Hi!

http://www.ozemail.com.au:80/~ctech/wps.htm

Washington Magnet and Gifted School of Communication—Web Site

Wow! The graphics on this site will jump off the page at you! Find out what a magnet school is and how kids learn in this Rockford, Illinois school.

http://www.misha.net/~desktop/washschl.htm

Lost your sheep? Count them in FARMING AND AGRICULTURE.

STUDY AND HOMEWORK

CalRen Home Page

Something's clanking in the dryer. The dog is barking at a bike rider going by outside. You can smell dinner cooking, and you feel hungry. All of a sudden, a football whizzes by your bedroom window. So many distractions make it hard to study! Here are some tips to help you study better, listen, take notes, and take tests.

http://www.slc.uga.berkeley.edu/CalRENHP.html

How to succeed in math

Did you ever think that weird tricks might help you in math? Well, here are some weird and not-so-weird suggestions that just might make this subject easier for you! Some of these tips are common-sense ideas for studying at home or in the classroom, like "DO YOUR HOMEWORK" (ugh!). Others are novel ideas like "write your own test questions" or "dress up for the exam." Find out what works for you as you learn in your own style!

http://cedar.evansville.edu/~tv2/class/succesmt.html

SCIENCE

GENERAL WORKS AND MUSEUMS
AMATEUR SCIENCE

Are you into amateur science? If so, you just found a great place to bookmark! This site has lots of science links. Sites are grouped by categories such as Amateur Science, Science Projects, Kids Asking Scientists, Science Suppliers/stores, and others. If you're looking for a place to browse for science stuff, be sure to experiment with this one!

http://www.eskimo.com/~billb/

Exploratorium Home Page

What makes a fruit fly grow legs out of its head? How about teaching your duck to talk? He might have something interesting to say. The Exploratorium, in San Francisco, is a huge laboratory for kids of all ages. Discover the many interesting wonders that science has to offer here.

http://www.exploratorium.edu/

A B C D E F G H I J K L M N O P Q R **S** T U V W X Y Z

ION Science: Science and nature news and information

Keep up to date with what's happening in the world of science. Once a month, this site updates its collection of late-breaking science news stories. When we reviewed this site, one of the new stories was about the Ruffe in the Great Lakes. This fish was a stowaway that escaped from a European freighter. It's now a possible threat to the fish that naturally live there. Apparently, the Ruffe doesn't taste very good and has no natural predators here to keep it under control. Time will tell if the Ruffe will become an eco-disaster. There's more interesting news for inquiring minds. Also, check out their archive of older news stories.

http://www.injersey.com/Media/IonSci/

The Lost Museum of Sciences

No, they didn't lose the Museum, the idea here is for you to get lost. No, we don't mean GET LOST, just lose yourself amidst all the stuff you'll find here. Now you're starting to get it. By the time you do find your way back, if you find your way back, you're sure to have learned something. No, we don't mean you'll learn how to find your way back, we mean you'll learn something scientific. Oops! If you like to be challenged, you can always play "Find The Exhibit." The first one to find it gets his name displayed here for all to see!

http://www.netaxs.com/people/aca3/ATRIUM.HTM

Physics Around the World: History of Science & Science Museums

There are science history pages here for all to see. A few of the sites on this page include the History of Astronomy, the History of Computers, the History of the Light Microscope, Space History, and Women in Mathematics. There's a lot more, so be sure to get comfortable and grab a sandwich before you start—you might forget to stop to eat.

http://www.physics.mcgill.ca/physics-services/
  physics_history.html

Look up all kinds of historical and scientific facts at Physics Around the World: History of Science & Science Museums.

Subject Index

This is a no-frills site compiled by the Society for Amateur Scientists. No pictures or fancy graphics here, just lots of great sites. Here, you'll find links to sites on astronomy, chemistry, high altitude balloon launching, rocketry, amateur radio, suppliers for your projects, and more. A great place to find out more about your favorite science hobby, or to get info on starting one. Please be advised that this NOT just a kid's page. Grown-ups will find this stuff interesting, too! ;-)

http://www.cfn.cs.dal.ca/Science/SAS/sas-sub1.html

welcome

This is the *Newton's Apple* home page. This site is full of science-related lessons and experiments from the TV show. The lesson on "Arctic Nutrition" explains why arctic explorers need a diet rich in carbohydrates to maintain their strength. Another lesson explains why you don't get a strong smell from garlic until it is cut or crushed. You'll find lots more here to learn and experiment with. Have fun!

http://ericir.syr.edu/Newton/welcome.html

Yahoo—Science

This is Yahoo's Science list. It's big! There are lots of different sub-categories to browse through, from Acoustics to Zoology. Use the search function to get a list of things quickly. Hint—the default for the search is to search all of Yahoo. To narrow down the area for the search, click on the "Search only in Science" button. This limiting feature is available throughout Yahoo, so use it to your advantage.

http://www.yahoo.com/Science/

SHARKS

See Also: FISH

Beyond Jaws

Sharks have terrible eyesight, right? Wrong. OK, but sharks are brainless eating machines. Wrong again. Everyone knows the chances of being attacked by a shark are about the same as being struck by lightning, right? Your chances of being attacked by a shark increase if you spend five days a week in the ocean. Discover what is fact and what is fiction about these great ocean dwellers and learn shark no-no's when swimming in potentially shark-infested waters.

http://hockey.plaidworks.com/sharks/
  great-white.html

The Great White Shark

Carcharodon carcharias is the scientific name of the great white shark. It comes from the Greek *carcharos*, meaning "ragged," and *odon*, meaning "tooth." *Jaws* was a pretty scary movie, but it was just a story, after all. Discover the truth about great white sharks!

http://www.netzone.com/~drewgrgich/shark.html

Sharks page

SHARK! Good thing you're just surfing the Net and not the ocean. Actually, sharks do live in the ocean, but they can also be found in rivers, lakes, and other fresh water bodies. Sharks are salt water fish, but can live in fresh water for several days. Sharks are plentiful and can be found all over the world, so you must be careful when entering the water. Remember, the sea is the shark's natural environment, not yours. Stop by the Sharks page and learn about the different types of sharks, what they eat, and why they sometimes attack humans!

http://www.io.org/~gwshark/sharks.html

Chase some waterfalls in EARTH SCIENCE.

SHIPS AND SHIPWRECKS

See also: TREASURE AND TREASURE-HUNTING

Edmund Fitzgerald Bell Restoration Project

Surely you've heard the Gordon Lightfoot song commemorating the *Wreck of the Edmund Fitzgerald*. On November 10, 1975, the 729-foot freighter was hauling a heavy cargo of iron ore pellets across Lake Superior. She was caught in a severe storm that sent the ship suddenly to the bottom, killing her 29-man crew. This page describes the search for the wreck, the salvage effort, and the restoration of the ship's bell. Surviving family members asked that the bell be recovered as a memorial to the men who gave their lives in the maritime accident. A duplicate bell, inscribed with the names of the sailors, was left in the pilot house of the ship. The original bell was brought to the surface and dedicated July 7, 1995. At the ceremony, the bell was rung 30 times: once for each of the 29 Fitzgerald crew members, and once for all mariners who have lost their lives at sea.

http://web.msu.edu/bell/index.html

The Legend lives on from the Chippewa on down
Of the big lake they called 'Gitche Gumee'
The lake, it is said, never gives up her dead
When the skies of November turn gloomy
With a load of iron ore twenty-six thousand tons more
Than the Edmund Fitzgerald weighed empty.
That good ship and true was a bone to be chewed
When the gales of November came early.

Read about the history of this famous shipwreck at the **Edmund Fitzgerald Bell Restoration Project** page.

A B C D E F G H I J K L M N O P Q R S T U V W X Y Z

Mary Rose Homeport

19 July 1545. On a nearby flagship, the Tudor King, Henry VIII, was having a lavish dinner. The *Mary Rose* sailed nearby. She was a four-masted warship, built between 1510 and 1511. French ships appeared and fired on the fleet. A little while later, the *Mary Rose* was lying at the bottom of the Solent, a body of water between Portsmouth, England and the Isle of Wight. Most of her 500-man crew drowned. She was rediscovered in 1971, and raised to the surface in 1982. This site takes you on a tour of the museum artifacts found on board, as well as a dry dock containing what is left of the ship itself. You'll be fascinated at the technology used to raise the ship, and in the stories of shipboard life during those times.

http://www.synergy.net/homeport.html

Merchant Marine and Maritime pages

Ever wondered if you have what it takes to pass the Coast Guard Exam for a Marine Engineer License? Here's your chance to take a quiz! Examine many kinds of ship engines and ship designs. Maritime poems are interspersed with drawings and photos of all kinds of freighters in many world ports. Don't miss the Russian vessel in Kobe, Japan, "exporting" souvenir cars for each crew member. They sprout all over the deck, sticking out like porcupine quills! You'll find links to lots of other maritime sites around the Web, including virtual port authorities and research fleets. This Web site, written by a real merchant marine engineer, is a real winner!

http://pacifier.com/~rboggs/

Shipwrecks Around Nantucket

Since the 1600s, it's estimated that over 500 ships have sunk around the island of Nantucket, which is south of Cape Cod, Massachusetts. As far back as 1669, the town had laws regarding goods recovered from shipwrecks! A well-written, dramatic narrative concerning the town and the shipwrecks can be found on this beautifully designed Web page. Intrigued with the island of Nantucket and want to learn more? Click on the YI icon or type *http://www.nantucket.net/YI/Home.html*.

http://www.nantucket.net/YI/shoreline/home.html

The Titanic

For many years, the sinking of the *Titanic* was held to be a disaster of "modern" times. Now, the year 1912 seems long ago in the past. It has even become a distant memory for the dwindling handful of people who were alive both then and now. Web sites such as this have become excellent depositories for a great deal of information that could easily become lost. This page not only gives the hard facts of the sinking of the *Titanic*, but explores (through contemporary newspaper headlines, articles, and cartoons) how the average person of that time found out what was happening in the world. There was no cable TV satellite news back then! There's also information at another *Titanic* home page at *http://gil.ipswichcity.qld.gov.au/~dalgarry/*.

http://www.lib.virginia.edu/cataloging/vnp/titanic/titanic1.html

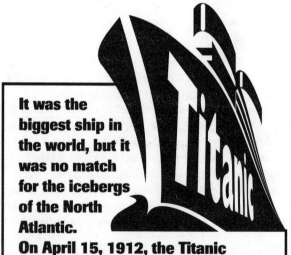

It was the biggest ship in the world, but it was no match for the icebergs of the North Atlantic.
On April 15, 1912, the Titanic struck an iceberg that caused enough damage to sink the ship off the coast of Halifax, Nova Scotia. Read about it at The Titanic page.

SPORTS

College Nicknames

Teams usually pick a nickname to describe themselves, like the Wolverines, or the Wildcats. Which names go with which U.S. colleges? Find out here! Did you know there's even a team nicknamed the White Mules? They're at Colby College, in Waterville, Maine.

http://grove.ufl.edu/~recycler/sports.html

You've picked a really cool name for your new team—

The Banana Slugs.

You figure **no one** will have thought of that one before. But you're wrong. It's the nickname for teams from the University of California at Santa Cruz! Try College Nicknames to find out more about team nicknames.

ESPNET Sports Zone

Get the latest in up-to-the-minute sports reporting, including scores, from the ESPNET Sports Zone. There are also columns and feature stories, too. Want to track Michael Jordan's progress since he came back to the NBA? Just do it. Or maybe you want to play Fantasy Football, or get some industry insider information. Then this site is for you, from the folks who brought you ESPN, the all-sports cable TV network. To get all the features of this site, you must be a paid subscriber, but much is available for free.

http://espnet.sportszone.com

Sports Illustrated

Have you ever wondered how *Sports Illustrated* picks people for its "Faces in the Crowd" section? Do you know a local high school or amateur athlete who deserves to be listed? Nominate him or her online! This site lets you read many of the magazine's articles, including special features like the College Basketball Preview or the NBA Preview.

http://pathfinder.com/@@m9vKXdFPtwIAQOFV/si/simagazine.html

Sports Spectrum

Who was the first NHL goalie to wear a mask? It was Jacques Plante of the Montreal Canadiens, who began wearing one in the late 1950s, after getting a head injury. What teams in the NFL have record single season scoring leaders who were NOT placekickers? Seven NFL teams have had this happen: the Packers, Forty-Niners, Bills, Cowboys, Vikings, Browns, and Colts. This is an example of the questions that are answered in the Web edition of Sports Spectrum Magazine. You can search for articles on lots of topics here!

http://www.gospelcom.net/rbc/ss/ssm

BADMINTON

Badminton

Current world rankings, results from major badminton tournaments, photos, and links to other major badminton sites are collected here. You can read stories from other badminton players, and even send in your own stories! If you want to organize your own tournament, why not use the Swiss Ladder System—the details are here, but there's a computer program also available to do the calculations for you.

http://huizen.dds.nl/~anita/badmint.html

Don't be a stick-in-the-MUD!

A B C D E F G H I J K L M N O P Q R **S** T U V W X Y Z

Badminton Olympic Page

What's the world's fastest and oldest racket sport? Badminton! The "bird," or shuttlecock, has been clocked traveling up to 200 miles per hour, and the sport goes back to the fifth century B.C. Yet, badminton only recently became an Olympic sport—first appearing at the 1992 Olympics in Barcelona. At the 1996 Games in Atlanta, 192 athletes are expected to compete in the sport of badminton.

http://www.atlanta.olympic.org/acog/sports/
   badminton/d-badminton.html

BASEBALL

Fastball

Do you love Major League Baseball, and hate it when the season is over? Then Fastball is the site for you! It is devoted to covering baseball during the off-season, and has discussion areas and the latest news for each team. If you are hooked on baseball, this is one site that will make it easier for you to wait for spring training!

http://www.fastball.com

Little League Baseball

Do you play Little League baseball? Did you know that the Little League Baseball organization has a Web site? This site gives you answers to frequently asked questions about Little League and its history. You'll also find summer camp information, Little League World Series news, and access to the Little League Gift Shop. No Little League near you? Talk Mom and Dad into starting one for you and your friends—contact names for starting the procedure are here!

http://www.littleleague.org

Major League Baseball : @BAT

All the information you'd ever need to settle any World Series argument is here. All the stats, all the teams, everything but the hot dogs. You'll need to hotlist this site right away because you'll need it all season. Here, you'll find official information on all the major league teams, expanded box scores for all the games, and a great photo gallery! There is a baseball team shop here too, but they were out of 1995 merchandise when we shopped.

http://www2.pcy.mci.net/mlb/index.html

NET FILES

Why are rainbows so frequently seen during summer and not so during winter?

Answer: To see a rainbow, you've got to have both rain and sunshine. In the winter, water droplets freeze into ice particles that do not produce a rainbow, but scatter light in other very interesting patterns. Learn more at About Rainbows, http://www.unidata.ucar.edu/staff/blynds/rnbw.html

National Baseball Hall of Fame

Visit the Baseball Hall of Fame in Cooperstown, New York! Get information on Hall of Fame exhibits and tours, and read "Around the Horn," the Hall of Fame newsletter. You'll read about Babe Ruth's bat, Mickey Mantle's locker, and Abbott and Costello's famous routine "Who's On First?". Unfortunately, the text to that routine isn't here, but you can get it at *http://www.ece.uc.edu/~pbaraona/stories/abbott_costello.txt* if you want to hear one of the funniest routines about baseball.

http://www.enews.com/bas_hall_fame

Professional Baseball in Japan

Let's go Yakult Swallows!! Look out for the Hiroshima Toyo Carp!! Baseball is HUGE in Japan and this page is the page for information and stats on Japanese baseball. You'll also find a search engine to look up Japanese and non-Japanese baseball stars. (Remember former NY Yankee Mel Hall? He's now a "hit" in Japan.)

http://www.inter.co.jp/Baseball/

YPN: Sports: Home Plate

This is a neat, annotated collection of Web sites, newsgroups, and graphics from all over the Net. You'll find links to baseball history, stats, Little League, coaching, and lots more here. Bring some peanuts and hot dogs, you'll be here all day!

http://www.ypn.com/sports/a270.html

BASKETBALL

College Basketball Page

This site gives news, scores, and stats about men's and women's college basketball, as well as info on TV schedules, rules changes, recruiting, and college basketball rankings. You'll find links to other basketball sites around the Web, too.

http://www.cs.cmu.edu/afs/cs.cmu.edu/user/wsr/Web/bball/bball.html

NBA.com

Who picks those All-Star teams, anyway? You can help—this year it's online for the first time! Get to the official NBA Web site and cast your votes for all your favorites. This site also gives you the latest news, schedules and results, and links to the home pages of your favorite NBA teams. You can also read reports in Spanish and French, as well as follow international hoop tournaments.

http://www.nba.com

The Unofficial Australian National Basketball League Page

It's not enough just to follow the NBA and the NCAA if you're a real basketball nut. You gotta follow the sport wherever it's played! Head for the Australian NBL home page. Get the latest information on all the Australian teams, including schedules, standings, statistics, rumors, results, and box scores from the most recent NBL playoff series.

http://natsem.canberra.edu.au/nbl/nbl.html

BOWLING

The Cyberspace Bowling Hall of Fame

Here, you can get bowling news from around the world, tournament dates and results, plus links to other bowling sites. But there's so much more—consider the archives of bowling horror stories, the lists of bowling organizations (including those for the disabled), and the history of bowling. There's also a link to information about the National Bowling Hall of Fame and Museum in St. Louis, Missouri!

http://members.gnn.com/bigbull300/index.htm

Bowling has been popular longer than you'd think! Artifacts for a game similar to bowling have been found in the tomb of an ancient Egyptian teen who died in approximately 5,200 B.C.

A
B
C
D
E
F
G
H
I
J
K
L
M
N
O
P
Q
R
S
T
U
V
W
X
Y
Z

PBA Tour

You're going to love the Professional Bowlers Association's Web site! Have a hard time finding the latest news stories and results from the PBA tour? At this site, you can get the latest results, tour schedules, and the history of the PBA. The PBA is popular all over the world: tournaments have been held in Canada, Puerto Rico, Japan, South America, France, and England. Chat with other bowling enthusiasts in the real-time chat emporium. Maybe you'll even get to talk to a pro!

http://www.pba.org

BOXING

The Boxing Page

If you want up-to-the-minute information on boxing, try this page full of boxing news. It will tell you how your favorite boxer did in his latest fight, and tell you the schedules for future fights. You'll find information on fights, and about boxing, including things like the top ten heavyweight boxers.

http://www.sportsnetwork.com/boxing/boxing.html

COACHING

Reebok Coaching Tips from Sports RX

You ask your mother to coach your basketball team this year. She says yes. As the season gets closer, she starts wondering about what she should do. How can you help? Check out this site that offers some basic tips about coaching kids in sports.

http://planetreebok.com/sptrx.html

CRICKET

An explanation of Cricket

What do rabbits, golden ducks, ferrets, and night watchmen have in common? No, it's not Grimm's fairy tales or the night shift at the local zoo. They are all terms used in the sport of cricket. This site provides a good starting point for learning about cricket, the distant cousin of baseball.

http://www.ida.com.au/sport/cricket/cricket_exp.html

CricInfo

This site is a gold mine of all things related to the sport of cricket, which has thousands of players and fans around the world. Here you'll find statistics, player profiles, news, match results, and even humor and history!

http://cricinfo.cse.ogi.edu/

Cricket on the Web

If you're curious about what happened in the world of cricket on your birthday, you'll want to check this site. There's also lots of interesting links to other cricket info, including one to *The Hindu,* India's national newspaper, where you can check up on Indian Cricket news!

http://www.ozmail.com.au/~reyre/cricket.html

CURLING

Brown Curling Club Home Page

What sport uses a 42-pound granite rock and a broom? No, it's not some Flintstones version of stickball...it's curling. You bowl this highly polished stone down an ice runway, you see, and try to knock your opponent's stone out of the house, and your teammates run in front of the hurtling stone and sweep ice crystals out of its way, and...well, maybe you'd be better off to go to this site for an explanation. You'll find a history of curling stones and info about the sport, including video clips of curling technique. It also gives links to other curling sites around the Net.

http://www.brown.edu/Students/
  Brown_Curling_Club/

Welcome to ICING (International Curling Information Network Group)

Curling is a game played on ice only in northern countries, right? Wrong! Curling is also played in the Southern Hemisphere. In fact, Australia will participate in the 1996 World Curling Championships! This site offers information about curling history, rules, and equipment, as well as links to organizations and clubs around the world. This is the best site yet for information on the sport of curling.

http://www.netaccess.on.ca/icing/icehome.htm

EXTREME SPORTS
Ultramarathon World

What is an ultramarathon? Imagine people running races of 50 miles, 100 miles, even more! How about running in the Sri Chimnoy ultramarathon, 1300 laps around a one mile loop? How about the Trans America Footrace, Los Angeles to New York? Find out all this and more at the Ultramarathon World site.

http://fox.nstn.ca/~dblaikie/index.html

The Comrades Marathon, in South Africa, may be the greatest ultramarathon in the world. It was first run in 1921 and now more than 10,000 runners annually participate. The route varies, but the distance is 55.89 miles (90km). There is an elevation change of 2,500 feet (762 meters) along the course. Read more about it at Ultramarathon World.

FENCING
Art of Fencing

Everyone likes a great swordfight in the movies. Peter Pan, Zorro, the pirates, and those shiny knights, all jumping here and there, swiping at the opponent, while all the time avoiding the other guy's sharp sword. Sometimes it's scary. But it's always exciting. The sport of fencing is exciting, too. Fencing is an Olympic sport that is practiced almost everywhere. There may even be a fencing club near you! Find out!

http://www.ii.uib.no/~arild/fencing.html

FIELD HOCKEY
Field Hockey Canada

Want to know who won the eighth World Cup in field hockey? How long will it be until the next World Cup? This site covers field hockey from Canada and the international scene, and has links to other field hockey sites on the Web.

http://www.cdnsport.ca/~snichols/

Hockey

What is field hockey? It's an ancient game that began in Egypt, and today it is much like soccer, except that you carry sticks! The Olympics will give you a good chance to see field hockey in action. In the 1996 Games, there will be eight women's teams and twelve men's teams competing for the gold.

http://www.atlanta.olympic.org/acog/sports/
   hockey/d-hockey.html

FOOTBALL
NCAA Football: Awards

Each year, outstanding college football players are selected for a slew of awards by the National Collegiate Athletic Association. The most famous of these is the Heisman Memorial Trophy, but there are many others. To see who won what award when, make an end run to this site.

http://www.sportsnetwork.com/ncaa-football/
   awards.html

Team NFL

Want to let the National Football League know what you think? Send in a response to the NFL Fan Survey on the Net. The official NFL site provides the latest headlines and league statistics, and even offers an NFL Kids page where you can meet the stars or learn about the Punt, Pass, and Kick Contest! Coming soon, you'll be able to talk to other kids interested in football! You'll also find a complete digest of NFL rules, and a library of historical facts and timelines.

http://nflhome.com

A B C D E F G H I J K L M N O P Q R S T U V W X Y Z

FOOTBALL—AUSTRALIAN RULES

Bouncedown—The Australian Rules Football Home Page

What is the oldest form of "football"? Australian rules football dates back to the 1850s and predates American football, rugby, soccer, and Gaelic football. This site provides an overview of Australian rules football, and lets you take a look at Australian football trading cards. It also answers a burning question—what is the Australian equivalent of hot dogs, eaten at American football games? The answer is: Aussie meat pies! This site also provides a link that allows you to listen to a live radio broadcast of the Australian Football League Finals over the Internet!

http://www.uwa.edu.au/student/graymice/afl.html

Ultimate Australian Rules Football Homepage

This game resembles rugby. There are eighteen people on a side, they use an oval ball, and score by kicking it. This site is a virtual photo scrapbook of your favorite Australian rules football players in action! You can get dozens and dozens of pictures, and links to other Aussie rules sites!

http://www.odyssey.com.au/sports/afl.html

FOOTBALL—CANADIAN RULES

Canadian Football League

Visit the official Web site for the Canadian Football League! Read the latest CFL news, look at a list of CFL records and awards, see the CFL Hall of Fame, and read a history of the CFL! There are also links to other sites about the CFL.

http://www.cfl.ca

The Very Unofficial Canadian Football League Home Page

Canadian rules football differs from American football in many ways. There are 12 people on a side, and the field is set up in a different way. There are lots of other scoring and rules differences, too, so check it out! Want to learn about the Canadian Football League? This site has CFL news, stats, schedules, team rosters, and links to other sites about the CFL. You can even get a CFL screen saver for your computer!!

http://alf.usask.ca/~cgm133/cfl.html

NET FILES

Which large, plated dinosaur is known for having a brain the size of a walnut?

Answer: The Stegosaurus. This plant eater was really a strange combination of parts. Were those bony plates for protection, or to help his body stay cool? And how about those spikes on the tail, what did they do? Check all the dinos out at http://www.cuug.ab.ca:8001/VT/tyrrell/index.html

GYMNASTICS

Gymn

Know the results of the gymnastics world championships, and other current events, by tumbling over to this site! Like to read articles about gymnasts? Want a list of gymnastics magazines with order forms? It's here! There are gymnastics trivia tests, too! This is an excellent site for the gymnastics fan, and received a "Best of the Net" nomination for 1995.

http://rainbow.rmii.com/~rachele/gymnhome.html

Have you hadrosaurus today? If not, try DINOSAURS AND PREHISTORIC TIMES.

Lisa's Gymnastics Archive

Do you love gymnastics? Sometimes it helps to see photos of people performing the routines. Would you like to be able to get pictures of your favorite gymnasts? This site has a huge archive of photos, clip art and ASCII art, as well as links to other gymnastics sites on the Web!

http://humper.student.princeton.edu/
  ~lcozzens/index.html

GYMNASTICS—RHYTHMIC GYMNASTICS

Sherwin's Rhythmic Gymnastics Page

Do you have trouble spelling "Rhythmic Gymnastics," but love the sport anyway? Would you like to get pictures of your favorites in action? For current results from World Cup and European Cup competitions, start here. All the pages here are packed with pictures and information, and links to other interesting sites.

http://www.geopages.com/colosseum/1082/
  rhythmic.html

ICE AND SPEED SKATING

Amateur Speedskating Union of the United States

When you take up this sport, you are guaranteed to be hanging out with some "cool people"! It's speedskating! Fast? You'd have to be crazy to go this fast! How crazy? Well, let's see—ice, blades, power, speed—sounds just crazy enough to be fun! And it is; fun for everyone, from kids to seniors. If you're just thinking about starting, this page fills you in, and gives you advanced details on clubs and special events if you're already a diehard skater. It's great exercise, and it makes those long winters (and you) go really fast!

http://web.mit.edu/jeffrey/speedskating/asu.html

> ## Whoooooooo will you find in BIRDS?

> ## Read any good Web sites lately?

Figure Skater's Home Page

Hang on to your wooly hats, you're about to slide into a major rink full of ice skating info. This page has material on both the basic and competition levels. You can look up skating clubs and upcoming competitions from around the world. Check out the Skater's Challenge crossword puzzle, and word searches on skating terms and famous skaters, if you want to test your skating knowledge.

http://www.webcom.com/~dnkorte/sk8_0000.html

Recreational Figure Skating FAQ

Have you often wondered what's the difference between a "crossover" and a "progressive"? Do you need to know how to execute a "closed mohawk"? How do you know when your skates need sharpening? Chances are you'll find answers to most of your skating questions here, including those mentioned above. If ice skating's your game, you've found the answer page.

http://www.crc.doc.ca/~kbryden/
  recreationalSkating/

ICE HOCKEY

National Hockey League Players' Association

You and a friend are talking hockey, but you disagree on the number of goals your favorite player has scored this season. Where do you go for the answer? The NHLPA site provides player stats for each NHL player, and these stats are updated each day! You can find pictures, personal information, stats for this season, and stats from past seasons…just like online hockey trading cards! And there's even more. Check this site for the weekly hockey trivia challenge. Answer the questions correctly and you may win an autographed NHLPA replica jersey.

http://www.nhlpa.com

A B C D E F G H I J K L M N O P Q R S T U V W X Y Z

WWW Hockey Guide

This site pulls together information about hockey from all over the Web, linking to over 400 other hockey sites. Would you like a list of all Stanley Cup Finalists since the Stanley Cup started in 1893? How about a visit to the Hockey Hall of Fame? It's here, as well as all official and unofficial home pages for your favorite National Hockey League teams. You can see the latest hockey news from ESPN or *USA Today*, too! If you can't get enough information about hockey, start with this site!

http://www.hockeyguide.com

MARTIAL ARTS

Black Belt Magazine

Brought to you by the publishers of *Black Belt Magazine*, *Karate Kung-fu Illustrated Magazine* and *Martial Arts Training Magazine*. This site has interesting articles, schedules of events, lists of martial arts schools, and links to other sites. It even has a Black Belt for Kids page. Remember, though, the empty-handed master defeats another warrior with his most powerful weapon—his mind.

http://www.blackbeltmag.com

Judo Information Site

Are you interested in Judo? Maybe you'd like to learn more about its history, or see the results of tournaments like the World Judo Championships? Then this site is for you! There are also links to *dojo*s and judo schools, and e-mail addresses of other people who are interested in judo.

http://www.rain.org/~ssa/judo.htm

The Martial Arts Menu Page

Parental advisory: this site has hundreds of links to other martial arts sites on the Web, and you should explore this with your child. A very comprehensive starting point for information about martial arts around the world. You'll find sites for Judo, Karate, Aikido, Jujutsu, Ninpo, Wing Chun, Tai Chi, and much more!

http://fly.hiwaay.net/~mcgee/martial.arts.html

Martial Arts Resource Site

Are you interested in martial arts, but don't know where to start? Then head for MARS—the Martial Arts Resource Site. This site may not have everything, but it comes close! It has links to martial arts books and articles, online magazines like *Black Belt* Magazine Online, information on how to choose a martial art, and many other good martial arts sites.

http://www.lehigh.edu/~sjb3/martial.html

WOW! YOUR FIRST MARTIAL ARTS CLASS! LEARN THE CORRECT WAY TO PUT ON THE GI, THE STANDARD UNIFORM FOR STUDYING JAPANESE MARTIAL ARTS SUCH AS AIKIDO, JUDO, AND KARATE, AT **HTTP://WWW.HAL.COM/ ~LANDMAN/AIKIDO/GI.HTML**, OFF THE MARTIAL ARTS RESOURCE SITE! REMEMBER TO FOLD THE LEFT SIDE OF THE JACKET OVER THE RIGHT SIDE—THE OTHER WAY IS ONLY FOR DEAD PEOPLE.

Tae Kwon Do Reporter

Want to read articles about Tae Kwon Do, Karate, Hapkido, and other martial arts? The Tae Kwon Do Reporter is an online magazine that has martial arts news from around the world, and articles on training and techniques.

http://www.tenerten.com/tkdrpt

NETBALL

Netball at the Australian Institute of Sport

The most popular women's sport in Australia is netball! The sport started in England way back in 1898. It's like basketball, except it's played with something more like a soccer ball. It can be played on wood flooring, grass, cement, or artificial surfaces, which may be either indoors or outdoors. Today there are more than 2 million netball players in the world. Australia has won six world championships, more than any other country. Find out the history and rules of netball here!

http://www.ausport.gov.au/aisnet.html

OLYMPICS
1998 Nagano Olympic Winter Games

Seems like a long wait for the next Winter Olympics, doesn't it? It will be in Nagano, Japan. Guess what, they have already picked out the official mascots for the games—snowlets! These four birds represent the owls found in the forests of Nagano. Owls are found throughout much of the world, and they are a Greek symbol of wisdom. The snowlets each have a unique character, but we'll all have to wait to find out more about that. Read more plans and ideas about the 1998 Winter Games here, and keep watching this site !

http://www.linc.or.jp/Nagano

Guide to the 1996 Olympics

Where will you be in July, 1996? Probably glued to the TV watching highlights of the Summer Olympics in Atlanta, Georgia! Can't wait until then? You can scope out the various events, venues, and schedules right now. Mountain bike racing is the newest Olympic sport, but there are 216 others that might catch your interest, too. This multimedia site features a fly-through tour of the Olympic Stadium as well as audio and video files. You can also look over the selection of official souvenirs, find out how to get tickets, and volunteer to help (but you must be 18).

http://www.atlanta.olympic.org/index.html

Salt Lake City Olympic Organizing Committee Home Page

Did you go to the 1996 Olympics in Atlanta? Did you enjoy the experience? Are you wondering when the Olympics will come again to North America? The XIX Olympic Winter Games will be held in Salt Lake City, Utah! This site already gives information on where the events will be held, and where the Olympic Village will be located. If you live in the Salt Lake City area, there is even information on how to join the volunteer program for the 2002 Olympics.

http://slc2002.org/olympics

Sydney 2000 Olympic Games Official Home Page

After the 1996 Summer Olympic Games in Atlanta are over, what's next? In the year 2000, athletes will gather in Sydney, Australia! The official Sydney Olympics 2000 site is the place to go for early information. Approximately 5.5 million tickets will go on sale in 1999, and this site will be the first to provide information about ordering tickets.

http://www.sydney.olympic.org

RACQUETBALL
United States Professional Racquetball Association

You've wanted a racquetball racquet for a long time, and finally you spot one at a garage sale. It needs new strings, but you're not sure if it can be restrung, or if it's junk. What do you do? The USPRA Web site provides handy tips on restringing racquets, and offers links to information about Olympic racquetball, official rules, and the schedules for televised racquetball on ESPN, the all-sports cable network. You'll also find tips on improving your backhand stroke, and be able to ask a certified referee all your tricky rule questions.

http://emporium.turnpike.net/~cyberguy/uspra.html

RUGBY
The Unofficial Official Rugby Webpage

Don't know anything about rugby? It's a fast-moving team sport played with a ball that looks like a football, only slightly larger. You also can't pass forward! This site is a good place to start. It gives you basic information about rugby, a short history of the sport, and a little bit about rugby in the U.S., as well as a link to the official World Cup site.

http://icarus.uic.edu/~jgrzes1/rugby/rugby.html

Women's Rugby

Learn all about women's rugby in Italy, Canada, and the United States. All the rules of rugby are here in an easy-to-use format, as well as links to other sites on the Web that have information about rugby. There's a great GIF of the dimensions of a rugby playing field, too.

http://vail.al.arizona.edu/rugby

A
B
C
D
E
F
G
H
I
J
K
L
M
N
O
P
Q
R
S
T
U
V
W
X
Y
Z

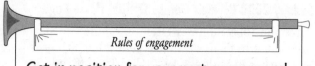

SKIING
The Consummate Skiing List

They stay up all night, working in the freezing cold. They mix proteins into water and make "whales." Nothing pleases them more than the sight of fresh powder. Who are they? They are the folks who run the snow-making equipment at ski resorts! Did you know that dirty water makes better snow than clean water? Check the "Miscellaneous" topic to find out about the snow-making process. When you've satisfied your curiosity about that, look around. This site is packed with information about skiing and equipment, articles, and links to hundreds of other skiing and snowboarding sites.

http://ski.websmith.ca/ski

SNOWEB

You gotta snowboard—but there's no snow! You can at least dream about it! See how much snow is on the ground at ski resorts across the U.S.! This site offers pictures taken daily at ski resorts, as well as weather forecasts. Find links to great stories about skiing and snowboarding, explore trail maps, and much more, all awaiting you at this site. Come in out of the cold and ski the Net!

http://www.snoweb.com/

SLIME is a polymer, as anyone who's read CHEMISTRY knows!

Surface Conditions

You're reading the ski reports for your favorite slopes, and the descriptions just don't make any sense! What the heck is "frozen granular"? What about "corn snow"? Is it even worth getting out your equipment? Check that report against the definitions provided at this site! Corn snow, typical in spring conditions, is made up of large ice granules, which are loose when the temperature is above freezing, but freeze together if the temperature gets any colder.

http://www.sportsite.com/mac/remote/sany/
info/surf.html

SKIING—ALPINE SKIING AND SKI JUMPING
Jump

Welcome to "Jump," a site created by a ski jumper! Get up-to-date information on the World Cup and other ski jumping competitions, and check out the links to other ski jumping sites.

http://www.cdnsport.ca/jump

SkiNet

Get the latest in skiing techniques, reports on snow conditions, and skiing news, from the editors of *Ski* magazine and *Skiing* magazine. You can even read articles from the pages of these magazines, and join the SkiNet mailing list. There's a list of the top 100 ski instructors in the U.S.—see if your dad is listed!

http://www.skinet.com

SKIING—FREESTYLE
Owens Corning World Cup Freestyle

Imagine ballet on a tilted stage that's almost three football fields long, where the dancers turn cartwheels and do handsprings wearing skis and ski poles!! Welcome to the strange world of freestyle, or ballet skiing! This site gives a good description of this winter sport.

http://www.freestyleski.com/

SKIING—MOGUL SKIING
Mogul Lingo

What sport has back scratchers, double uprights, helicopters, mule kicks, twisters, and zudniks? Mogul skiing!! That's when the only thing between you and the bottom of the hill is a steep, frozen landscape of bumps, jumps, and tricky twists. This site does a good job of explaining how the sport works and how it is judged. The explanation of mogul slang will definitely help you follow the action the next time you watch this strange sport on TV!

http://turnpike.net/~tjohnsto/Moguls.html

SKIING—NORDIC SKIING
Cross Country Ski World

Are you interested in cross country skiing, but don't know how to start? Cross Country Ski World is packed with information on the world's oldest skiing sport, including a special section just for junior skiers! You'll find out how to choose equipment, how to wax for various conditions, and how to handle "botanical brakes"—TREES!

http://www.weblab.com/xcski

If you don't know your klister from your kick wax, better glide on over to Cross Country Skiing World! Lots of tips for skiing families about waxing and ski technique.

Crack open CODES AND CIPHERS.

SOCCER
Soccer for kids

This soccer cybertour was created for kids, by a kid! Use the Soccer Worldwide Penpal Connection and read soccer tips and ideas from kids in other countries. Send in your own soccer photos and illustrations, and find a pen pal of your own! See what interests kids when it comes to soccer, and link to news of lots of international soccer teams.

http://www.charm.net/~jsent/kid.html

The Soccer Homepage

Why is the sport called "soccer" in some countries and "football" in others? The sport started as "football" in England. By the time it became popular in other parts of the world, some countries already had sports known as football: the U.S. had American football, and Australia had Australian rules football. In countries where "football" was already played, the sport became known as "soccer," short for "Association Football," the original name for the sport in England. This site also has links to the Olympics soccer page, World Cup soccer facts and records, and soccer rules.

http://www.distrib.com/soccer/homepage.html

SPECIAL OLYMPICS
Massachusetts Special Olympics

"Let me win, but if I cannot win, let me be brave in the attempt." This is the oath of the Special Olympics. What great inspiration for all athletes, not just "special" kids with physical, mental, or other challenges! The first International Special Olympic Games was held in 1968, at Soldier Field in Chicago, Illinois. It was organized by Eunice Kennedy Shriver. Since then, the Special Olympics have become the world's largest year-round program of physical fitness, sports training, and athletic competition. In the U.S., games at the local and chapter levels are held every year, with special summer and winter events held every four years. Check out two California Special Olympic sites at *http://se.saic.com/home/mary/spoly/soabout.html* and *http://meer.net/users/taylor/specolym.htm* for more information.

http://www.gran-net.com/olympics/mso_home.htm

SQUASH

Internet Squash Federation

Do you love squash? Yum—Hubbard, Summer, Acorn—even Zucchini! But we're not talking veggies here, we're talking about the fast-paced game of squash ball, sort of like racquetball except the court, equipment, and rules are different! All the rules are here, including those governing clothing, equipment, and more! Player profiles, tournament schedules, even satellite broadcast schedules are here. This site also featured an online broadcast of the 1995 U.S. Open squash competition, and will probably have more broadcasts in the future.

http://www.ncl.ac.uk/~npb/

World Squash Federation

The WSF currently estimates there are fifteen million squash players in the world today, and over 125 million who just like to watch the game. If they could all log into this site on the Net, they would! Want to look at a copy of *International Squash* magazine? It's here, along with information on squash programs worldwide. Squash isn't an Olympic Sport—yet—but fans are trying to get it into the 2000 Olympic games in Sydney, Australia.

http://www.ncl.ac.uk/~npb/WSF/index.html

How did a space-borne spider's web influence the design of earthly tennis racquets? Find out at the WWW Tennis Server, under equipment tips!

TABLE TENNIS

The Belgian TT Page

Ever wonder if anyone actually makes a living playing ping-pong? Well, Kong Linghiu of China won $33,000 for winning the 1995 World Cup in table tennis. But you might want to ask the folks in Hungary. Hungary has won the most world titles with 73, although China is close behind with 71 titles. For answers to questions about table tennis, try here!

http://othello.ulb.ac.be:1024/tt/

The Table-Tennis Table

You're finally going to beat your big brother! You go down into the basement to play ping-pong. Everything's cool and you're ready to start, but the only balls you can find have dents in them. Don't worry—there's a way to fix dented ping-pong balls! Put the balls in a pan, pour hot water over them, cover with a towel, and let them sit for about an hour. There—good as new! This is just one of many interesting tidbits from The Table-Tennis Table. You can also find official rules, 1996 Olympic information, and a history of table tennis. Around 1900, the game was also called Gossimar and Whiff-Whaff.

http://www.epix.net/~gandalf/pingpong

TENNIS

Tennis Worldwide Magazine

This "Net" magazine offers a world of information on tennis. Television schedules for tournaments, sources of supplies, and rankings are all here. There are also feature articles, like how hard a junior player should practice! You'll also find info on wheelchair tennis, tennis camps, racquet repair, jokes about tennis, and more.

http://www.xmission.com/~gastown/tennis

See what's shakin' in EARTH SCIENCE—GEOLOGY—EARTHQUAKES.

WWW Tennis Server

Would you like free tips from a tennis pro? Would you like to know how to avoid tennis elbow? Would you like information on tournaments, players, rankings and equipment? How about links to other tennis sites? You get all this and more with the WWW Tennis Server.

http://www.tennisserver.com

TRACK AND FIELD

See also: OUTDOOR RECREATION—RUNNING

Athletics Home Page

Who is the world's fastest Norwegian? Who is the best overall Italian athlete? What's the Morrocan record in the high jump? If you are a track and field statistics nut, then this is the site for you. It lists world's records, indoor and outdoor, for men and for women, as well as track and field records for many nations.

http://www.hkkk.fi/~niininen/athl.html

USA Track & Field

USA Track and Field is the governing body for track and field in the United States. This site gives you news on the latest happenings in track and field, and has links to other track and field sites. You'll really enjoy seeing the U.S. Track and Field Hall of Fame, and reading about record performances and the athletes who made them! This is a great source for short sports biographies, too!

http://www.usatf.org

> ### Find your roots in GENEAOLOGY.

> ### People are the true treasures of the Net.

TRACK AND FIELD—POLE VAULT

Minnesota Pole Vault Association

What is the single most important thing in pole vaulting? Pole vaulters and coaches answer this and other questions at this site. You can even give your own answers to these questions. By the way, even though the vaulters don't agree on THE most important thing, most of them agree that it is speed! You'll also find the top 100 vaulters, some great animations, and a place to trade used poles!

http://condor.stcloud.msus.edu/~khanson

VOLLEYBALL

NCAA Women's Volleyball

The *USA Today* women's volleyball page provides the latest information on the sport, including tournament schedules. Want to know the latest National Collegiate Athletic Association (NCAA) volleyball rankings? How about information on volleyball win streaks? Check the sport's stars, check tournament schedules—it's all here!

http://www.usatoday.com/sports/other/sowvbn.htm

Volleyball Worldwide

Is beach volleyball an Olympic sport? Yep, it will be, for the first time, in the 1996 Atlanta Olympics. Twenty-four countries will send men's teams, and there will be sixteen women's teams. What is wallyball? Where can you find information on international volleyball? What teams will play in the volleyball World Cup? If you love volleyball, start with this site, with general volleyball info, including TV schedules and links to organizations like USA Volleyball, Federation Internationale de Volleyball, and professional and college volleyball.

http://www.volleyball.org

A B C D E F G H I J K L M N O P Q R S T U V W X Y Z

WATER POLO
The H2O Polo Home Page

Water polo is your favorite game and you love to watch a college game every week. But mom says you're moving, and you're worried there won't be a water polo club where you're going. What do you do? Check this site, and find one! If one's not listed, maybe you can talk mom into moving someplace else! This page offers links to college and club teams, and other information, including the Olympic water polo schedule. You'll also find results from European Water Polo Championships here. Don't get in over your head, but there's plenty water polo info here!

http://www.h2opolo.com

WRESTLING
The Mat, the home page of Amateur Wrestling!

This site will get a hold on you, if you're into wrestling. Find info on the international, collegiate, high school, and youth wrestling scenes, including current results and news. Check the Wrestling Mall for info on books, equipment, videos, and links to photo archives.

http://www.coe.uncc.edu:80/~jrlareau/

Welcome to InterMat!—The Ultimate Amateur Wrestling Resource

You know, you don't have to look like Hulk Hogan to wrestle. Lots of people participate in this sport, in all different weight classes. For the latest in international, collegiate, and high school wrestling, including rankings, try this site!

http://www.netins.net/showcase/intermat/

> **Never give your name or address to a stranger.**

> **Ask not what the Net can do for you, ask what you can do for the Net.**

STAR TREK

The Klingon Language Institute

How many languages do you speak? Have you checked the batteries in your universal translator? If you saw a snarling Klingon warrior, what would you say? Are you worried that your opportunities on the Klingon homeworld are limited because of the language barrier? The Klingon Language Institute is the place for you!

http://www.kli.org/KLIhome.html

Star Trek: Deep Space Nine

Are you a *Deep Space Nine* fan? Who's your favorite character? Check out Paramount's official *DS9* page! It offers a brief description of the next episode, with a cast photo and a list of actors in the episode. You can also download a QuickTime video preview of the episode to play on your computer.

http://www.paramount.com/DS9Home.html

Star Trek: Voyager

Have you been to the Delta Quadrant lately? Visit the official home page of *Star Trek: Voyager*, and discover hot news about the show. This site is complete with crew profiles, episode descriptions, and information about the U.S.S. Voyager.

http://voyager.paramount.com/VoyagerIntro.html

SUMMER CAMPS

Peterson's Education Center Summer Jobs

Get your older brother or sister to apply for a job at camp! From winter through mid-spring, Peterson's (the educational directory publisher) posts lists of summer jobs here, mostly at summer camps, for both older teenagers and young adults. Phone numbers and e-mail contact addresses are included, making this a good place to look for that first-time job. Your parents may want to explore the rest of the items at this comprehensive educational directory. They will find everything from K-12 schools to colleges, from studying abroad to career information.

http://www.petersons.com/summerop/sumjob.html

A knotty problem: What's the difference between a hitch and a bend?

Answer: Know the ropes! A hitch is a knot that ties a line onto something else, and a bend ties two lines together. If tying knots leaves you in a snarl, then be sure to drop in on http://www.pcmp.caltech.edu/~tobi/knots for a new twist in learning.

U.S. Space Camp

It's light years away from any other camp experience! You can visit Space Camp here on the Web, and see pictures of some of the things kids (and adults) get to do. How would you like to ride a space shuttle simulator, or build your own satellite? Beam yourself up to this site, there is definitely intelligent life here!

http://www.spacecamp.com/

United Camps, Conferences & Retreats Camp & Conference Homepage

Any search of the Web will bring up well over a thousand summer camp home pages in the U.S. and elsewhere. What's nice about this site is that they feature a highly organized listing of many top-notch camps, organized by region, type, or even alphabetically. You might be looking for a performing arts camp in northern California, a ranch camp for girls in Texas, a space camp in Florida, or a listing of the dozens of Boy Scout camps in Virginia. Whatever particular kind of summer camp experience you're trying to find, there are detailed listings for each of the camps on the list, including phone numbers, addresses, and sometimes even photographs. There's a "Camp-O'-The-Week" featured here every seven days, as well, plus links to environmental and outdoor educational centers, retreats, associations, online magazines, and a detailed calendar.

http://www.camping.org

Welcome to National Computer Camps

Way back in 1977, Dr. Michael Zabinski established the first "computer camp" in an effort to familiarize young people with the use and workings of computers. Soon after, the nation was awash with them, but as the fad wore off, Dr. Zabinski continued to develop the concept and curriculum of these summer camps to encompass all aspects of computer literacy. Today, he has camps strategically placed in California, Connecticut, Ohio, and Georgia. Students are given the option of an all-computer agenda or half computer/half sports. This page contains information on the entire program, schedules, staff, locations, and dates.

http://www.corpcenter.com/ncc/

TELEPHONE

Anatomy of a telephone call

Ever wonder how your telephone works? Why do the lights on your phone dial usually keep working, even when the power goes out? What happens if you press two touch-tone keys at the same time? This site answers these questions and more, giving you an overview of what takes place when you make that call to your great-grandma in Cleveland. You did remember to thank her for sending those cool handkerchiefs for your birthday, right?

http://www.att.com/talkingpower/map.html

Telephony/Media History

If you're like most people, all you know about how a telephone works is that you talk in one part and listen through another. The rest of it is magic. When you're through checking out everything on this page, you'll know more than you ever dreamed there was to know about the telephone! It contains links to the Alexander Graham Bell Home Page, the History of the Telephone page, and an antique phone page. There are sites on telephone and communication technology from Sweden and France, plus the Smithsonian Information Age exhibit page. Home pages for virtually all of the long distance carriers and the big "baby bells" are collected here at the Media History Project.

http://spot.colorado.edu/~rossk/history/phone.html

TELEPHONE BOOKS

AT&T Internet Toll Free 800 Directory

You have a suggestion for a new toy, so you want to call up the new products division at Mattel. How do you get the number? No problem. Fire up this Web site and search for the name Mattel, or look in the category "Toys and Games." While not quite as thorough as AT&T's voice directory assistance, this handy Web tool features an easy-to-use interface. Search for toll-free numbers by category or name with a simple click.

http://www.tollfree.att.net

Toll-free phone numbers can be very useful, but did you know there is one "800" number that is not free?

It's the "information" number for getting the listings in the first place! Now you can dig up these listings from the **AT&T Internet Toll Free Directory** page.

Bell Atlantic Interactive Yellow Pages: Government Information

Bell Atlantic is the local phone company for the Washington, D.C. area, and that makes them the company of choice for most of the United States federal government. This Web page offers not only every listed federal phone number in the D.C. area, but if a listed agency or department has a Web page, you can click on their listing to get there. A very handy page! The top level, if you want to see the entire resource, is at *http://yellowpages.badg.com/*.

http://yellowpages.badg.com/cgi-bin/pageDisplay.
  high?S8933:governmentPageUS

Central Source Yellow Pages

Need to look up a business somewhere? Why drag out that hefty yellow telephone book when this Web page is available? Let your mouse do the walking as you scour through over ten million business listings in the U.S., organized by company names, categories and even phone numbers. There's also a handy separate listing for Dial-up Access Providers, and links to phone directories for other countries.

http://www.telephonebook.com

NTC Phone Phinder

Need an area code for a city? Need a city for an area code? This page not only lets you find one with the other, but it also will narrow searches down to three number phone prefixes. If you want another country's dialing code (or vice versa), this is the place to look.

http://www.natltele.com/form.html

TELEVISION

NETWORKS AND CHANNELS

Broadcast Networks

A collection of all U.S. broadcast networks is here. If there is a home page, there is a link to that. If there is e-mail, you'll find that, as well as fax and voice phone numbers and addresses. The cable broadcast channels are all collected at: *http://tvnet.com/tv/us/cable.html* but you should peruse this list with your children.

http://tvnet.com/tv/us/networks.html

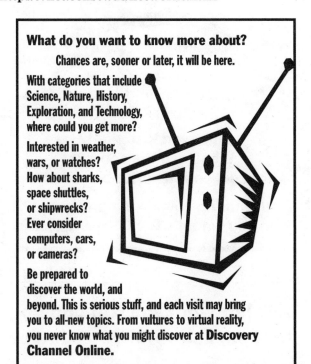

What do you want to know more about?

Chances are, sooner or later, it will be here.

With categories that include Science, Nature, History, Exploration, and Technology, where could you get more?

Interested in weather, wars, or watches? How about sharks, space shuttles, or shipwrecks? Ever consider computers, cars, or cameras?

Be prepared to discover the world, and beyond. This is serious stuff, and each visit may bring you to all-new topics. From vultures to virtual reality, you never know what you might discover at **Discovery Channel Online.**

For breaking news, we can't steer you anywhere else but CNN Interactive. Go here for updates on news as it happens. But you can also look over a video archive of cool QuickTime movies. You can see a virtual fly-over of Bosnia, or see a demo of that hot Web application, Java, or maybe you'd prefer some video about the great Pyramid, or some elephants, or some sports event. It's here! Wish it was indexed, but for now, you'll just have to explore. Don't miss the special reports in the **Interactive Time Line**. CNN has produced some in-depth resources on such things as the Rabin assassination and the Million Man March.

C-SPAN

If you want to see the U.S. government at work, you'll see it here. Hearings, meetings, legislative sessions: this site will tell you what C-SPAN will be showing, and when. There are also classroom activities and lesson plans for the teachers among you. And aren't we all teachers, really? Even you kids are teachers, and every truly great adult teacher knows that.

http://www.c-span.org/

See what's shakin' in EARTH SCIENCE—GEOLOGY— EARTHQUAKES.

CNN Interactive

CNN, the 24-hour news channel, has made it easy and fast to get the news of the moment over the Internet. And that up-to-the-minute news is put together in a multimedia format that brings you lots more than words: QuickTime movies and sound turn up in the most amazing places, ranging from stories about belly-flop contests to space shuttle dockings. And if you want to know more about the news CNN's covering, you can link to thousands of newspapers, magazines and broadcasts from all over the world. Don't forget that CNN covers entertainment, sports, style, and other fun stuff. Check out Billboard's weekly Top Ten list, featuring sound clips of each song.

http://www.cnn.com/index.html

Discovery Channel Online

You'd expect to find background stories on many of the Discovery Channel's programs here, and you'd be right. There are stories and pictures from shows on history, nature, science, and people. But there's more: how about a magic knapsack that travels the Web for you, looking for things you want, even if you're not online? When it finds something, it sends you e-mail. Maybe they will invent one that does your homework for you and then send you e-mail when it's done ;-) ! Be sure to enter the weekly contests, too.

http://www.discovery.com/

ESPNET SportsZone

Heeeeey, sports fans! If you're really into sports, then you probably already know about ESPN, the all-sports cable network. They do the same great job on their home page as they do on their network! This site offers the latest (up-to-the-minute) sports news, scores, and game summaries. Let's say your favorite team is in Seattle, and you live all the way 'cross country, on the other coast. Chances are, it's a pain in the neck to get the latest news, stats and player profiles on your favorite team. Hey, relax. Tune in to the "zone" and get it all right here: college, amateur, pro. They cover it all, and, they let you talk back. After all, you have to put your two cents in, right?

http://espnet.sportszone.com/

Will Keiko, the *Free Willy* whale, go free again?

Animal experts hope so. Keiko is now in a more spacious aquarium in Oregon. Trainers there will teach him skills wild orcas need to survive. If Keiko's native pod (family of whales) can be found, and his skills are relearned, Keiko may someday be released. Read regular updates on Keiko at **Discovery Channel Online**.

Who won last night?
What was the score?
How did your favorite player do?

You want up-to-the-minute sports?
Then you want **ESPNET SportsZone.**

Ask not what the Net can do for you, ask what you can do for the Net.

Find your roots in GENEAOLOGY.

History for Kids

Do you say, "History? Yes!", or do you say, "History? Oh, no!" Well, either way, sooner or later you have to know what happened when, and where, and why. Get it? This is history that's made for your entertainment. Yep, history can be interesting. Find out what else happened on your birthday. Learn fun historical facts. If you like history, or you just have to do a report, this is a great place to get started. And besides, where else can you learn while entering contests for free prizes? And if you're someone who can't get enough history, then there's lots more on the main pages (*www.historychannel.com*). Take a break from that history book and tune in!

http://www.historychannel.com/kids/kids.html

Kids' WB

It seems like Warner Brothers has been making cartoons forever! Here's where you'll find their latest shows, the schedules, and even a historical look at the some of the most famous cartoons ever made. But that's only part of this site. There are games to play and download, and a fascinating look at how cartoons are made. Stop in whenever you want to see, hear, or watch your favorite cartoon characters online, because the pictures, sounds and video clips are right here! Shows included are: *Animaniacs*, *Freakazoid!*, *Pinky & The Brain*, *The Sylvester & Tweety Mysteries*, and *Earthworm Jim*.

http://pathfinder.com/@@a1gM69EIIAIAQOx5/
KidsWB/home.html

NASA Television on CU-SeeMe

You can watch broadcasts from the space shuttle mission, or whatever else NASA is broadcasting today. And if you have the right kind of Internet connection, you can watch this stuff right on your computer! All you need to know is right here on this home page. There is also a programming schedule.

http://btree.lerc.nasa.gov/NASA_TV/NASA_TV.html

PBS Online®

It seems that if it's on PBS, it's either educational, entertaining, excellent, or all of the above. Viewers support their local public stations, and these stations bring viewers quality local programs, as well as programs from PBS (Public Broadcasting Service). From Muppets to money, PBS brings us important issues and delightful special events. The Web site invites you to investigate what's on the schedule, what's going on inside the network, and what to try on in the network store. The online news reports keep you up-to-date, and links to your local station keep you in touch. Did you know that you're the public? So it's your network!

http://www.pbs.org/Welcome.html

Sci-Fi Channel: The Dominion

If it's not of this world, then it must be from the sci-fi zone. It's UFOs, monsters, vampires, that kind of stuff. It's *Star Wars*, Buck Rogers, *The Twilight Zone*, and all that cool stuff. It's far out. It's waaaaayyyy far out. And it's all out there on the Web. Can you get there? Can you get program schedules, highlights, and series information? Affirmative! Are there pictures, landscapes, sounds, and science fiction video clips? The sky isn't even the limit. There's an autobot that KNOWS what's on the Sci-Fi Channel right now, and scrolls that across your screen! You'll also find a live chat area, where you can talk to famous actors, such as James Doohan, from the original *Star Trek*. Explore the site beyond all others. Set your coordinates. Warp factor seven. Engage....

http://www.scifi.com/

People are the true treasures of the Net.

A B C D E F G H I J K L M N O P Q R S T U V W X Y Z

TV Land

This could be one of the most unusual (and fun) sites on the Web! It's a home page. It's a television museum. It's an amusement park! How can this be? It just is! It's the best of classic television presented in a fun and interactive way. "Turn" the channel (ask a parent or other "old" person to find out why you "turn" the channel) and then play a wacky game based on a classic TV show, such as *Bewitched*, or *I Dream of Jeannie*. The games weren't all working right when we tried; maybe you'll have better luck! Take the time tunnel to the history of American television. Look at the classic old toys, and check out the ads! Your parents ate this cereal? Pass the Quisp!

http://www.ravenet.com/tvland/index.html

The Weather Channel® Home Page

How's the weather where you are, or anywhere else for that matter? Actually, anyone can find out just by visiting this page!. Sure, there is up-to-date weather information from around the world. But that's only the beginning. There's more weather stuff here than anyone could imagine! It includes shareware to download, maps, video clips, tips on getting started as a meteorologist, and special forecasts for sports fans. This site is really cool (in the North) and hot (down South)!

http://www.weather.com/weather/

Welcome to the FOX Kids Network!

This network is a favorite for Saturday morning and after-school entertainment. Here you'll find the latest info on your favorite shows with schedules, summaries, and the "kids countdown." What shows? How about *Taz-Mania*, *X-Men*, or *Mighty Morphin Power Rangers*? Heard of any of those? Don't forget our personal favorite, *The Tick*. There's the "Kid's Club" and the "Totally Kids Magazine" too! But it keeps on going, gang! There's contests, games, and tips on getting the most out of the Internet. Here, the links are only for kids, not grown-ups (unless you supervise them). This sounds like just the place for you!

http://www.foxnetwork.com/kids/index.html

Welcome to Nick at Nite

Everyone loves this stuff. *The Munsters*, *The Mary Tyler Moore Show*, *Bewitched*, *I Dream of Jeannie*.... Good ol' classic TV! If you have an opinion about classic TV, take the survey and tell them what you think. Vote for other classic TV shows that you want to see. Get the classic TV lineup and download the clever and funny ads used on the network! It's fun TV you can watch at night, and now you can visit those wacky characters on the Web. Lucy, I'm home!

http://nick-at-nite.com/

NET FILES

What is likely to happen right after you do an Air Kedidi?

Answer: You'll fall down. Come on, admit it. Anytime you catch THAT much air, and your legs start to bicycle without a bicycle, you're probably going to hit the ground. Hey, we're talking inline skating here! And whether you're hardcore or just a flatlander, skate over to http://www.seas.smu.edu/~justin/inline.html It's radical (and vertical)(

PROGRAMS
Beakman's World Home Page

Beakman is a kid's personal scientist. He answers questions that kids can't get the answers to in school. Stuff about embarrassing bodily functions. Stuff like why cats purr. There are lots of zany characters on the show, which makes science FUN! See video clips from the show and learn about your favorite cast member! For answers to some of your science questions, try the companion home page, You Can With Beakman and Jax at *http://pomo.nbn.com/youcan/* . *http://www.spe.sony.com/Pictures/tv/beakman/beakman.html*

Clarissa Explains it All

We love to listen to Clarissa explain her rather strange life. It sounds more and more like ours all the time! They only made sixty-five of these shows at Nickelodeon, but we never tire of watching them. We've even been to the set complex at Universal Studios, Florida! OK, so we're fans, but we think perhaps you are too.

http://www.ee.surrey.ac.uk/Contrib/
  Entertainment/Clarissa/

Encyclopedia Brady

The Brady Bunch is one of those TV shows that just seems to go on forever. Just about everybody has seen at least a few of the original episodes featuring Marcia ("Marcia, Marcia, Marcia!"), Greg, and all the rest as they struggle through life in suburbia. If you're a Brady Bunch fan, this site is just for you. Included here are details about the Brady Bunch that would inform even the most dedicated Brady follower! For example, although the series was filmed on a sound stage, the exterior shots are of a real house. The address (near Los Angeles) is here, along with real Brady trivia, like the mysterious connection between the show and *Gilligan's Island,* another popular show.

http://www.primenet.com/~dbrady/index.html

Ghostwriter—welcome Page

What is Ghostwriter, anyway? The kids don't really know, but he "talks" to them by rearranging whatever printed words happen to be around. Or, he can use the computer keyboard. Naturally, his next jump was to get a Web page. Here, you can meet the rest of the Ghostwriter team and learn how they solve mysteries! There's a description of the shows, and teachers will like the classroom activity suggestions which correspond to the shows. There is a complete list of all the Ghostwriter books and videos, too. The only surprise is that Ghostwriter doesn't have an e-mail account. You have to send him snail mail, and the address is here.

http://www.pbs.org/ghostwriter/welcomepage.html

> **Never give your name or address to a stranger.**

I come from the 'net

Reboot lives inside Mainframe with all the other subroutines and sprites. Outside, there's something called User, and *Reboot* is trying to find who the mysterious "User" is. The cartoon is way cool, and so is this site! Download some fun games, and explore your computer from the inside! Feel what a program feels! Where do you want to click today?

http://alliance.idirect.com/reboot/title.html

Lamb Chop's Play-Along

Shari Lewis, "the lady who works for Lamb Chop," has a sweet home page here, with suggestions on how to help kids get the most out of the show, which is aimed at three- to seven-year-olds. You'll find knock-knock jokes, coloring pages, and classroom activities. Don't miss those, they have very silly jokes in them! Here's an example: Shari: "Did you know it takes three sheep to make a sweater?" Lamb Chop: "I didn't know sheep could knit!"

http://www.pbs.org/lambchop/intro.html

Mister Rogers' Neighborhood

This beloved TV show has entertained three generations of neighborhood visitors, and has won every broadcast award there is. Little ones have fears, dreams, hopes, and feelings—just like everyone else. Fred Rogers has always understood that, and his Web site shows that care in detail. He has everything from play activities (just right for preschoolers), to his favorite song lyrics, to an annotated booklist. Read Rogers' biography and hear a message from him. Don't miss the history of the show, and learn what happened when viewers were invited to the studio to celebrate Daniel Striped Tiger's birthday.

http://www.pbs.org/rogers/mrr_home.html

A B C D E F G H I J K L M N O P Q R S T U V W X Y Z

NET FILES

When was U.S. President Bill Clinton born?

Answer: It was August 19, 1946, and you can find out more vital statistics and biographical information here:
http://pathfinder.com/@@@p00R@yGg8AMAQDtT/
pathfinder/politics/1996/clinton.html

Newton's Apple

This insanely great science program covers everything from earthquakes to garlic, from the Hubble telescope to the Redwoods. We wish they listed the programs by topic so that all the "Astronomy" topics, for example, were together. Maybe they will think of that if they read this. You'll love the Science Try-it section, where you can learn to make your own barometer, and have fun with a Möbius strip.

http://ericir.syr.edu/Newton/welcome.html

Shining Time Station—Introduction

Do you know *Thomas the Tank Engine & Friends*? If you're a fan of *Shining Time Station,* then you'll love the pictures and information on Thomas and the whole gang. And listen to those sounds! Thomas toots, Bertie shouts "All aboard!" and off you go out of the station. There are lots of activities here to go with the popular series. For even more pictures of Thomas and info on all the "Friends," check the *Shining Time Station* page at *http://www.catt.ncsu.edu/users/gkeeper/HTML/my.useless.pages/STS/*.

http://www.pbs.org:80/shiningtime/intro.html

The Ultimate TV List

Are you a big fan of *Bewitched,* or *Lost in Space*? Maybe you just love TV! If only you could find a Web site listing all the TV shows from the old days, and all the TV shows from today, and all the Web pages that are dedicated to them, and—STOP! That would have to be the grandest TV list of all. That would have to be the ULTIMATE TV list! That's it! This list has over 3,000 links for over 600 TV shows. Wondering if there's a Web page, FAQ, or newsgroup devoted to your favorite show? If there is, you can get there from here! Parental advisory: just as you guide what your kids watch on TV, guide them in using this site. Not all shows are appropriate, and not all links have been checked. WARNING: there are no suitable sites on the Net about *Barney and Friends.* There just aren't. The ones we found are, well, pretty disturbing (you will find a few of them as links on this site). Some of them start out looking OK, but about half-way through they become unsuitable (trust us). We think it's OK to do an "I hate Barney" page, but people should label those Web pages accordingly, not draw kids in with misleading titles, then abuse their trust. We happen to like dinosaurs, especially purple ones. And we wish we could have listed a Web site for kids who love Barney; maybe someone will build one by the next edition of this book. At least you can safely listen to the theme song while we wait for a better world: *http://themes.parkhere.com/themes/sounds/children/barney.au.*

http://www.tvnet.com/UTVL/utvl.html

The Web Site of Pete & Pete

What could be crazier than two brothers, both named Pete? The surreal adventures they get into, that's what! This unofficial fan page has everything you've always wanted to know about the Wrigley family, including speculation on where they live. Don't miss the quotes from superhero Artie, the Strongest Man in the World, fond of such words of wisdom as "Physics makes me strong!"

http://www.cs.indiana.edu/entertainment/pete-and-pete/

Where in the World is Carmen Sandiego?

It was late, on an evening with snow coming down like caramel corn. Shaking the stuff off of my mukluks, I headed over to warm my hands by the hot computer. Yes, Acme Crimenet was still booted up from this morning. It seemed so long ago. Like so many times before, I looked at the Most Wanted Criminals list between bites of cold pizza. Hmmm, "Wonder Rat," "Patty Larceny," "Robocrook." I knew I'd have to stay on the lookout for them. I got out my well-thumbed atlas and entered the latest online contests. I had to laugh out loud when I read the stuff about behind-the-scenes mistakes on the set. They make it all look so easy on TV! Suddenly, I heard a noise! I looked up and saw my face reflected in the dark monitor screen. Wait, was that Wonder Rat behind me? Later, gumshoes....

http://www.boston.com:80/wgbh/pages/
carmensandiego/carmenhome.html

Wishbone Content List

How can a little dog know so much about literature? This new PBS series features a Jack Russell Terrier with a BIG imagination. You'll find descriptions of all the shows, the classic literature on which they are based, and suggested activities. One QuickTime movie completes the offerings so far.

http://www.pbs.org/wishbone/introduction.html

The X-Files

Are UFOs and extraterrestrials for real? *The X-Files* is a make-believe TV show about two FBI agents trying to answer that question. Join Special Agents Fox Mulder and Dana Scully as they investigate UFOs and extraterrestrial sightings, and many other bizarre cases. This Web site has in-depth character sketches, episode descriptions and information about the show. Warning—some of the show descriptions are graphic.

http://www.delphi.com/XFiles/index.htm

> ## Not everything on the Net is true.

REVIEWS
Television Reviews

Everyone is talking about that new show on Thursday nights. But is it really funny? Is it OK for the kids to watch? And what about that made-for-TV movie based on that great book? Did they do a good job, or will everyone say, "The book is way better!" Don't waste two hours finding out that tonight's shows are boring! Check out the reviews from some of the most respected entertainment and news magazines. Read past and present opinions on what's on the tube. Want to put in your own two cents? Then post it on the message board.

http://pathfinder.com/@@94HxkpEGJQIAQIZ@/
pathfinder/hitcity/tvrev.html

SCHEDULES
TV1 What's on Tonite!

What's on the tube tonight? Deciding what to watch is one problem. Finding out when your favorite show is on is another. They keep switching it to different nights! There has to be a way to find out what's on tonight, and where they moved your favorite program this time. There is! At this site you can look at tonight's line-up, look ahead at the week's offerings, or search for something you're interested in. Searching can be done by time, network, or category. Now finding out what's on TV is almost more fun than watching it!

http://tv1.com/wot/index.html

SOUNDS AND THEMES
WWW TV Themes Home Page

If it's been on TV in the last thirty years or more, then the theme song is probably here. This collection is so extensive, it's impossible to describe. Themes for shows are categorized by: Comedy, Drama, Action-Adventure, Action-Sci-Fi, Westerns, Children's Shows, Cartoons, Other Shows, and even Commercials! Don't argue over the words to *Gilligan's Island*, listen to them! Want to see Mom and Dad act nostalgic? Play them some tunes like the theme song from *Captain Kangaroo* or *The Mickey Mouse Club*. Looking for a great TV sound bite for your computer's start-up sound? Then get here and start browsing! How about this one, can you guess the TV show? "Here's the story..."

http://themes.parkhere.com/themes/

A
B
C
D
E
F
G
H
I
J
K
L
M
N
O
P
Q
R
S
T
U
V
W
X
Y
Z

You just found out your family's going to visit Great Auntie Gwen in Great Britain!
You're pretty excited, but then you realize you're going to miss two weeks of your favorite shows on Nickelodeon!

What do you do?

Before you get depressed, check the World Television page. It will tell you what TV stations and networks are available, all over the world! Nickelodeon is broadcast on cable channels in the United Kingdom, so hope that Great Aunt Guinevere has cable! But, you know, you should get out more.

STATIONS
U.S. Local TV

Is your favorite local television station on the Internet? Maybe you can e-mail them with your complaints and compliments! Maybe they have a Web page full of information on their news team. Maybe you can find out what's on tonight. Never mind maybe! This is the place to find out if they are on the Net! This site lists U.S. television stations that have Internet addresses. In many cases mail addresses, fax and voice phone numbers, and Web pages are included. TV stations are there to entertain and serve you, so keep in touch! For World Station information, see *http://tvnet.com/WORLDtv/worldtv.html*.

http://tvnet.com/TV/localtv.html

World Television

Where in the world can you find a television station that has an Internet address? Right here! A growing number of television stations and resources around the world are joining the Internet and "logging in." Some have e-mail capabilities and even Web pages! Find your favorite station, or just look around for someplace interesting. What's on TV in Iceland? You could find out here! For U.S. Stations see *http://tvnet.com/TV/localtv.html*.

http://tvnet.com/WORLDtv/worldtv.html

TIME

CALENDARS
The Aztec Calendar

The Aztecs lived in the fourteenth century, in the area now known as Mexico. Scholars disagree on exactly how the Aztec calendar works. There are really two different calendars, one for sacred uses and one for everyday use. The sacred year had 260 days, while the "regular" year had 365! Think of that, you could have two different birthdays a year! There are free software programs here that will translate a modern date into the Aztec pictograph system. These include stylized icons of flowers, crocodiles, and other things. What will your birthday look like in Aztec pictographs?

http://napa.diva.nl/~voorburg/aztec.html

Calendar

If you've ever needed a quick calendar, for, say, the year 1753, or maybe the year 3000, or anything in-between, you'll love this site in Norway. Key in the year you want, perhaps the year you were born, and like magic, a calendar is generated. Be sure to read the technical information on how the calendar program works.

http://www.stud.unit.no/USERBIN/steffent/kalender.pl

VNLich—Vietnamese Calendar

The Windows software found at this site will generate a Vietnamese calendar entirely in that language, with all important holidays noted. It indicates the lunar months as long, short, or leap. The documentation is in Vietnamese.

http://www.webcom.com/~hcgvn/software/win/vnlich.html

You Can Calendar

Check this cool calendar by Beakman and Jax. Look up any month and find out how it got its name. Look up the interesting things that happened in each month throughout history, and more! Did you know Saturdays are the only day of the week named after a Roman god? Saturn also got a planet named after him!

http://pomo.nbn.com/youcan/calendar/calendar.html

CLOCKS

Directorate of Time

The U.S. Naval Observatory in Washington, D.C. is the Official Timekeeper for the United States. And this site is tied into the official clock. Clocks, actually. U. S. Naval Observatory timekeeping is based on several unusual clocks: cesium beam and hydrogen maser atomic clocks. You can find out more about these at this site. They also use a network of radio telescopes to make sure they are always right on time. Why is that so important? Well, if you burn a rocket engine a second too long, you may end up miles from where you want to be. And if one computer sends a message, but the other computer isn't "on" to receive it yet... there's a problem. These clocks are correct to the nanosecond level, which is a billionth of a second! At this site, you can also calculate the sunrise, sunset, twilight, moon rise, moon set, and moon phase percentages and times for a U.S. location.

http://tycho.usno.navy.mil/time.html

Earth Viewer

This isn't really a clock, but it will show you where it's day and where it's night—right now—all over the planet. Besides, this is one of our favorite places on the Internet. We hope you think so, too!

http://www.fourmilab.ch/earthview/vplanet.html

Make a Two-Potato Clock

We just can't resist putting this page in the book. Be sure to have an adult help you with this, though. Will it work with other vegetables or fruits?

gopher://schoolnet.carleton.ca:419/00/K6.dir/trycool.dir/clock

World Clock

Hey, what time is it, anyway? Curious about the clocks in Copenhagen? Or maybe you want to make inquiries in Istanbul? This page gives you the current time in over 100 locations on the globe! If you keep watching it, the page will automatically update every minute. If you want to know how much time is left before the year 2000, have a look at the same author's countdown clock at *http://stud.unit.no/USERBIN/steffent/aar2000.pl*.

http://www.stud.unit.no/USERBIN/steffent/verdensur.pl

If you ever wonder if tomorrow will ever come, just check the World Clock. You can find out where it's already tomorrow, in time zones all around the world!

GEOLOGIC TIME

Geology Entrance

Just when is the paleozoic? Is it anywhere near the mezzanine? Find out here as you learn about how geologic time is measured, and how the science of geology began. Remember, the oldest rocks are on the bottom!

http://ucmp1.berkeley.edu/exhibittext/geology.html

A B C D E F G H I J K L M N O P Q R S T U V W X Y Z

TIME MACHINES

PM TIME MACHINE

Popular Mechanics is *the* magazine for anyone interested in machines. Now, they have built an Internet time machine to help you see how machines have improved over the last ninety or so years. See high-flying French balloons from the early 1900s, and crazy car designs from 1960. It's a walk through history, and you won't even have to leave the chair in front of your computer! Your time machine comes with a lot of shiny buttons, and there's even an owner's manual. Let's see, what happens if we press this button right here? That's right, the one that says "Do Not Press."

http://popularmechanics.com/popmech/time/
   1HOMETIME.html

The Time Machine by H. G. Wells

Probably the best story about time machines is one of the first—it was written by H.G. Wells, in 1898. This story, titled *The Time Machine*, has inspired a countless number of books, movies, and articles on time travel. Read a copy of the story right here on the Internet, and maybe you'll decide to write your own time travel tale!

http://www3.hmc.edu/~jwolkin/hum1/
   TimeMachine.html

A Time Travel Into History, Turkey

Traveling through time has been a dream of many people. Imagine being able to see what life was like when your grandparents were kids. Or maybe you could experience life more than a thousand years ago! We haven't been able to figure out how to travel through time yet, but on the Internet you can get a sense of what time travel would be like. Turkey has been at the center of human history for thousands of years. From Troy, to Caesar, to an emerging modern country, Turkey is an historical gold mine. You can travel back into its amazing history on a time machine designed by Mehmet Kurtkaya. See how people have evolved from dwelling in caves to building some of the most beautiful structures of all time. You'll also learn about the actual locations of places we know mainly in legend!

http://www.xmission.com/~gastown/
   ebb/timetrav.htm

The Sun never sets on the Internet.

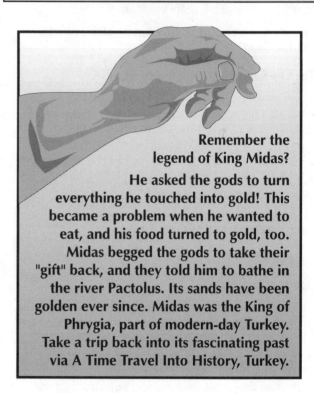

Remember the legend of King Midas?
He asked the gods to turn everything he touched into gold! This became a problem when he wanted to eat, and his food turned to gold, too. Midas begged the gods to take their "gift" back, and they told him to bathe in the river Pactolus. Its sands have been golden ever since. Midas was the King of Phrygia, part of modern-day Turkey. Take a trip back into its fascinating past via A Time Travel Into History, Turkey.

TOYS

LEGO Information

Your dog chewed all the little bitty pieces and now you need some new ideas for other LEGO projects to make with what's left! On the LEGO Information page, you can see pictures of other people's creations, and discover how to make and play LEGO games. How about the world's largest LEGO car? Or LEGO fighter jets? LEGO robots? Don't stop until you've built a walking elephant, a mousetrap, a cannon, a bobsled…. How do you suppose they make all those parts in a LEGO factory? Find out here!

http://legowww.homepages.com/

> ## Surf today, smart tomorrow.

Official Teenage Mutant Ninja Turtles Web Page!!!

Cowabunga Dudes! It's the official Teenage Mutant Ninja Turtle page! It's totally awesome! Michelangelo, Leonardo, Raphael, and Donatello want you dudes and dudettes to send them some fabuloso mail with your thoughts and opinions, so they can have the coolest place on the Net. Don't forget to enter their totally rad coloring contest and make sure you have a totally Turtly day!

http://www.ninjaturtles.com/

DOLLS AND DOLLHOUSES

Dollhouse Central

You finally own the house of your dreams! You built it with your own two hands. You don't plan to live in it or sell it. But you are using this site to get ideas on furnishing it, to find a solution to the wallpaper problem you were having trouble with, and to meet other people in similar situations. Why go to all that trouble? Because you want your dollhouse to be the best-looking dollhouse in the neighborhood!

http://www.iii.net/users/donna/dollhous/
    dollhous.htm

Kachina Collection, Brandon Pierce

Kachina dolls are an important part of the religion of the Hopi Indians of northern Arizona. They are given to the children not as toys, but to be treasured and studied so that they may become familiar with the various spirits. This site showcases an eight-year-old's growing collection and relates the history and meaning behind these stunning creations.

http://wpl.lib.oh.us/docs/Kachina/home.html

TEDDY BEARS

Bear Page

Germany and the United States each have laid claim to the fame of having the originated the "teddy bear" back in 1903. Check out both stories, but you'll have to decide for yourself which one was bear first.

http://www.bucknell.edu/~thuber/bear.html

Parabears

Is it a bird, a plane, a weather balloon? No, it's PARABEARS! These ever-daring bears thrill the masses at kite festivals with their exploits of parachute jumping from kites. You can meet the crew, view their home movies, and gather tips and techniques for forming your own parabear squadron. Very uplifting!

http://www.interlog.com/~lepkites/parabear/
    pb_menu.htm

YO-YOS

AYYA Yo-Yo Page

What should you say to your friends if they tell you last night they "walked the dog," "rocked the baby," "hopped the fence," went "around the corner," saw a "flying saucer" and a "tidal wave," and entered into a "time warp"? Congratulate them on some great yo-yo tricks and then check out the official American Yo-Yo Association site. And maybe you'll find yourself "reaching for the moon" and perfecting a "warp drive."

http://www.pd.net/yoyo/index.html

> ## Space Exploration is a blast.
> ## Check out Astronomy.

A B C D E F G H I J K L M N O P Q R S T U V W X Y Z

World of Yo

Beginners are welcome in the World of Yo. Learn the ten basic yo-yo tricks shown here, study the history, memorize the ten reasons why you'd rather have a yo-yo, and soon you will be on the way to being a yo-yo man (or woman).

http://www.socool.com/socool/yopage.html

On July 31, 1992, a yo-yo made its debut in space! NASA Astronaut Jeffrey Hoffman put it through some zero-G tricks. The yo-yo traveled 3,321,007 miles and went around the world 127 times during the flight. On Earth, the Around-The-World record is 102 times in a row. Read more at the World of Yo.

TRAVEL

See also: COUNTRIES OF THE WORLD—TOURISM, UNITED STATES—STATES

City.Net

If your family wants to travel and is looking for a fun place, surf to City.Net. City.Net is a well-organized list of great places to go. There's a random destination link if you don't know where you want to go, or if you just want to find out about someplace new. You might even find information about what's happening in your own home town.

http://www.city.net/

GNN Travelers' Center Home Page

Do you need a vacation? How about some sunshine? At GNN Travel you can enter a vacation contest, and read travel reports, stories and reviews. There are regular travel columns, and a whole lot of great vacation ideas. If you're ready for a trip and looking for something fun, see all there is to offer. Parents, this is a page more for you than for your kids.

http://gnn.com/gnn/meta/travel/

GORP—Great Outdoor Recreation Pages

Do you love to play in the great outdoors? Is there anything more fun than hiking, camping, climbing, or seeing wildlife? GORP has it all. Check out the sections on places to go, things to do, good food to take, and staying healthy while traveling. If you are trying to get in the mood to go camping, enjoy the outdoor art, photography, cartoons, and best of all, traveler's tales. Parental advisory: links off this page have not been checked.

http://www.gorp.com/

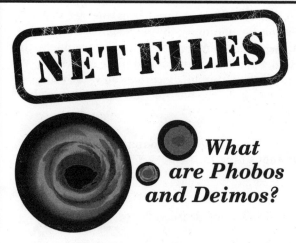

NET FILES

What are Phobos and Deimos?

Answer: Phobos and Deimos are the moons of Mars. Get the inside scoop on all planets and their moons, the Sun, comets, and asteroids at

http://seds.lpl.arizona.edu/nineplanets/nineplanets/nineplanets.html

Become one with the Net.

Hawaii's Living History—Voyaging into New Horizons

Did you know that "Aloha" means "hello" and "good-bye" in Hawaiian? Hawai'i was first discovered by some very brave people over 2,000 years ago. They navigated across the ocean in small boats and settled on the islands. Now Hawai'i is one of the most exotic places in the world to visit. Come to "Hawai'i's Living History" and see the beauty of America's 50th state.

http://www.aloha-hawaii.com/a_history.html

HEALTHY FLYING With Diana Fairechild

Have you ever flown on an airplane? Flying takes less time than going by car, but it can be less comfortable. The airplane air is drier. The pressure changes quickly as the plane takes off and lands. Flying to places in different time zones can leave passengers with jet lag, that tired feeling that you may be someplace new, but your body is still someplace else! The solutions to most of these problems are inexpensive and can be brought with you on the plane! Read Diana's secrets for comfortable flying and share them with your parents. She should know, she's a retired flight attendant!

http://www.maui.net/diana/

The Penny Whistle Traveling With Kids Book

If you could go anywhere in the world, where would you go? How would you get there? What will you need to take with you? There's a lot of stuff that you want to take, but there isn't room to pack it all. How do you decide what to bring and what to leave? The Penny Whistle has tons of great ideas for you and your parents. For example, how about making your own "passport" to keep track of your travels? Or maybe you'd like to try some of the take-along snacks and recipes—and there's even a handy recipe conversion chart. Or try some of the backseat travel games to pass the time. Are you there yet?

http://family.starwave.com/funstuff/pwtravel/
  pwttoc.htm

Rec.Travel Library: Worldwide Travel and Tourism Information

Where in the world can you go to have fun? If you are asking yourself this question, check out the Rec.Travel Library. The Rec.Travel Library is a collection of posted articles from the Usenet news section called rec.travel. There are recommendations for places to go, how to get there, what to do there, and much more! Parental advisory: links off this page have not been checked.

http://www.remcan.ca/rec-travel/

Recreation and Travel

Whether you're traveling by car or by plane, don't miss the great information here on how to keep your brothers and sisters entertained. There are activities and games, travel snacks (what would any family trip be without food?), packing tips, and lots more.

http://family.com/Features/Recreation/
  Travel&Rec.HTML

U.S. State Department Travel Warnings

Have you ever pretended you were an international spy? This site has links to all sorts of cool stuff! There are travel advisories and maps of all of the different countries. Check out the Central Intelligence Agency (CIA) Publications and Handbooks. Look in on what's going on in different countries, what is necessary to get across the border, and what to take with you to be safe. Besides your passport, that is.

http://www.stolaf.edu/network/
  travel-advisories.html

Visit the stars in Astronomy.

A
B
C
D
E
F
G
H
I
J
K
L
M
N
O
P
Q
R
S
T
U
V
W
X
Y
Z

TREASURE AND TREASURE-HUNTING

See also: SHIPS AND SHIPWRECKS

The Home Page of The Armchair Treasure Hunt Club

Some years ago, publication of Kit Williams' beautifully illustrated book, *Masquerade*, caused an international sensation. Williams had buried a valuable Golden Hare and provided a series of cryptic visual clues and riddles in the book that revealed where the treasure was hidden. Intrepid treasure hunters did not have to go skulking about back yards and parks with shovels (although some did). Instead, they simply had to send in the correct location to the publisher to win the golden statue. This could feasibly be done without leaving home—hence the advent of the phrase "armchair treasure hunting." Since then, similar puzzling treasure hunts have popped up with enough regularity that a home page has become essential to sort them all out. You'll find lists of and links to an assortment of new and ongoing hunts, the solutions to old ones, and an invitation to join an Internet mailing list where armchair treasure hunters around the globe compare notes with each other.

http://sunacm.swan.ac.uk/~milamber/treasure

NET FILES

What national park has more geysers than any other place on Earth?

geyser.html

ANSWER: Don't get steamed up, but it's Yellowstone, in Wyoming/Montana/Idaho. There are over 400 geysers there. Yellowstone was the first national park in the world! It was established in 1872! http://www.wku.edu/www/geoweb/

International Treasure Hunters Exchange

Do you think the days of digging up buried treasure are over? Does the idea of stumbling onto a chest of pirate gold or digging up Genghis Khan's fabled lost tomb seem like something from storybooks? Well, it doesn't happen daily, but there are many people out there every day looking for fabulous treasures, and finding them more often than you'd think! The International Treasure Hunters Exchange covers the worldwide treasure-hunting scene with a thoroughness that makes dropping in on their site a true joy for anyone who has ever fantasized themselves with armloads of pieces of eight. If you actually want to go out and hunt up some treasure, then this page is a must for you. Some solid information can be found here on metal detecting, shipwrecks, and online research sources. The "Treasure Hunting Shopping Mall" is a virtual paradise for folks looking to equip their hunt, and there is online messaging and a regularly published newsletter. Perhaps most interesting is the "Treasure Hunting in the News" section, which features incredible stories of treasure hunters around the world.

http://www.treasure.com

The On-Line Treasure Hunter

There are some exciting stories of real treasure finds at this site! Sometimes the best place to look for treasure is where others have already looked. With today's modern computerized, electronic equipment, treasure hunters can often revisit sites that were "cleaned out" many years ago and walk off with riches! This site offers plenty of detailed information for folks who would like to find wealth in the ground or the ocean, as well as solid equipment data, classified ads, question and answers, and links to other related pages.

**http://cyberatl.net/~infosvc/treasure/html/
  index.html**

TREASURE NET

There is so much treasure-hunting activity on the Web these days that it must seem that there is a gold rush going on! As a matter of fact, there is! This site has all the usual resources for equipment and advice, plus a nice assortment of maps and historical photos. There are also links to sources of old state and county maps, which could be a bonanza for treasure hunters. It's especially useful, though, for the message forums, where you can discuss treasure sites and technical tips with others interested in this hobby.

http://www.halcyon.com/treasure

TRUCKS AND HEAVY MACHINERY

EMERGENCY—Emergency Service Vehicles

This comprehensive Australian site offers over 150 images of fire trucks, ambulances, rescue aircraft and boats, and other emergency equipment. Parental advisory: if you stay on this page you should be OK. If you go back to the top level of the home page, do not choose "Action Photos." There are accident photos that may be disturbing for sensitive children and adults, so use with care. The top level does have links to many fire companies on the Web, some shoulder patch pictures, and information on fire safety. The "Safety" area has some coloring pages for kids, as well as printed and audio safety information.

http://www.catt.citri.edu.au/emergency/equip/
  es-vehicles.html

The Firehouse Museum's Home Page

Did you ever wonder how they fought fires in grandpa's day? They didn't have the sleek, powerful fire trucks we have today! See some historic photos and memorabilia from this museum in San Diego, California, dedicated to firefighters all over the world. Check the steam fire engines, and old fire extinguishers, and don't miss old La Jolla #1, a hand-drawn chemical fire truck. See more contemporary machinery at The FireWeb Apparatus Museum at *http://fireweb.com/nav/apparmus.html*.

http://www.globalinfo.com/noncomm/firehouse/
  Firehouse.HTML

NET FILES

What's the world's largest insect?

Answer: According to the Insect Home Page, the longest insect in the world is the Stick insect (*Phasmacia serritypes*), the females of which can be over a foot long! To find out more incredible facts check *http://linfo.ex.ac.uk/~glframe/six.html*

George Hall/Code Red Fire Trucks in Action

This photographer is trying to sell you his calendar, and what exciting fire truck photos he has! You almost need sunglasses to look at some of these shiny trucks! And the action photos—step back from the heat and smoke! Parental advisory: the fire links from this page have not been checked.

http://www.code-red.com/calendar.html

NET FILES

Which would you rather be in the middle of

•MILLS MESS•
or
"Burke's Barrage"?

Answer: Actually, if you aren't a juggler (and a good one at that), you better not get in the middle of either one! These are two difficult juggling tricks. Hey, don't worry! Even if you're just starting out, there's juggling help and information for everyone at the Juggling Information Service site, *http://www.batcon.org/congress.html*

NET FILES

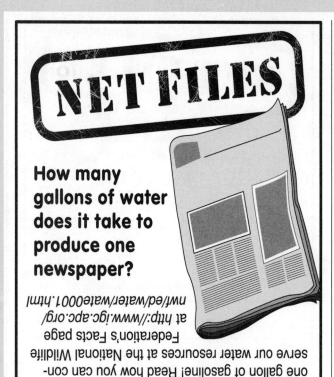

How many gallons of water does it take to produce one newspaper?

Answer: Through the whole process, it takes 280 gallons of water to produce one Sunday newspaper! It takes 7 to 25 gallons of water to produce one gallon of gasoline! Read how you can conserve our water resources at the National Wildlife Federation's Facts page at http://www.igc.apc.org/nwf/ed/water/wate0001.html

The Pickup Truck Homepage

This is the place to go for the latest scoop on pickup trucks. Get up-to-the-minute news on what's going on in the industry, check out profiles and stats on all the sharpest rigs out there, and gaze at color snaps of cool custom trucks, factory beauties, and NASCAR sport truck and off-road races. When you're done with all that, there are looks at pickup trucks around the world, and even a section with pickup truck accessory software!

http://www.rtd.com/~mlevine/pickup.html

Space Exploration is a blast. Check out Astronomy.

Origami: the fold to behold! Check out CRAFTS AND HOBBIES.

NET FILES

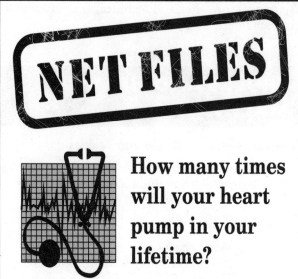

How many times will your heart pump in your lifetime?

Answer: According to the Franklin Institute's "The Heart: A Virtual Exploration," it will beat two and a half BILLION times. That's a lot of ba-bump, ba-bump. If you want to learn just about everything there is to know about the heart, take a look at http://sln.fi.edu/biosci/heart.html

Racing Truck Photos

Here's a multitude of the coolest big boss rigs ever collected on one Web site! Slick, customized racing trucks itching to chew up the track are displayed here as a series of thumbnail images. Click on them and get huge downloadable color photos for your collection. NASCAR SuperTruck Series schedules, standings, and results are at *http://www.primenet.com/~thomasj/suptrk.htm.*

http://www.primenet.com/~thomasj/trkimage

UFOS AND EXTRATERRESTRIALS

The Bermuda Triangle

There are two sides to every story, and this page takes the skeptic's side of the mysteries of the Bermuda Triangle. This page explains, in factual terms, why many of the mysterious events attributed to the Bermuda Triangle may be no more than products of "over-active imaginations."

http://tigger.cc.uic.edu/~toby-g/tri.html

The Roswell Centre

Have you ever seen a flying saucer? No, not the one your little sister threw on the floor! Although there is very little evidence to prove it, a lot of people believe that Earth has been visited by aliens. Roswell, New Mexico, is the location of one of the most well-known and controversial "encounters." According to some accounts, a flying saucer crash-landed in the desert near Roswell in 1947. It was near a military base, and the U.S. Army is said to have quickly hidden all of the evidence. Some say they actually found a live alien! Sort through the documents at "The Roswell Centre" and decide for yourself whether the story is true.

http://www.paragon.co.uk/ros/ros.htm

UFO Sightings by Astronauts

Read what thirteen astronauts have to say about UFOs. These people aren't just average citizens with unbelievable stories. They are trained astronauts that have reported seeing various UFOs while in flight. Transcripts of their "live" reports are included, so that you can read what they actually said when they first spotted the strange sights. Were they being checked out by aliens while making their historic flights? Were they "warned off" the moon by aliens? You be the judge.

http://www.cs.bgsu.edu/~jzawodn/ufo/
　astro-sightings.html

UNITED STATES

CITIES, COMMUNITIES, REGIONS
City.Net United States

City.Net combines the features of an atlas, gazetteer, and almanac, plus the best material from local guidebooks and newspapers. This page starts with a list of all the states and territories. Within each state, you'll find links sorted by city, county, or subject. Subjects include arts and entertainment, education, events, government, and more. Use the search function to find out if anything is available for a specific city or town. This is great for probing through local community Web pages to help you with that history or geography homework. Check it out!

http://www.city.net/countries/united_states/

NET FILES

DID you know that sunspots rotate around the sun? How long does a sunspot take to go completely around and get back to where it was?

ANSWER:
A sunspot takes 27 days to rotate around the sun's surface. Read all about sunspots at http://www.sel.bldrdoc.gov/primer/primer.html

The USA CityLink Project

Homework can be fun with a resource like this to help! This is a nicely organized site, sorted by state. Within each state are links to general state pages, city pages, and regional pages. So, if you needed to find information on places of interest in Syracuse, N.Y., you could click on New York and select one of the Syracuse links for more info. You can also search the Lycos index from the CityLink home page for even more Net links on that city.

http://banzai.neosoft.com/citylink/

USA United States Community Page Index

This site specializes in collecting local community pages. Check out the index and find out if your town is on the Net. It's a great way to keep up with your local events and organizations. Take a trip to Anytown, U.S.A. and see what's happening in their neck of the woods. Look up your next vacation spot and find out what's fun to do there! Since each community publishes its own pages, the information you'll find will vary, but there's a lot of valuable local info out there.

http://www.nsbol.com/nsbol/comindex/us_index.htm

NET FILES

In the latest Star Trek series, what class of ship is the U.S.S. Voyager, *and how many like it have been built? You'll need to be a real trekker to answer this one!*

Answer: Voyager is an Intrepid class ship; it is the second of four such ships in Starfleet. It was launched Stardate 48038.5 (the year 2371). Find out more about Star Trek trivia at http://voyager.paramount.com/VoyagerTechOl.html

FEDERAL GOVERNMENT
CapWeb—A Guide to the U.S. Congress

Did you know that you have representatives in Washington? They are supposed to be working for you, but they are so far away, how can you check up on them? One way is across the Internet! Type in your ZIP code and find out how your representatives voted on recent legislation. You'll also find address books here so you can write to your congresspeople and express your opinions! If you're a little hazy about how all this government stuff works, this site will get you up to speed.

http://policy.net/capweb/congress.html

Federal Courts Home Page

Order in the court! Hmmm—but which court? Supreme Court, Court of Appeals, bankruptcy court—more courts than a tennis tournament! This site is a clearinghouse of information on the U.S. Federal Judiciary system, and the hypertext links will give you a brief overview, plus contact information for more in-depth help.

http://www.uscourts.gov/

FedWorld Home Page

This is your "one-stop location" for finding information that's available online from the U.S. Government. It's a master list of all the Net servers and resources, bulletin boards, and electronic documents the government has to offer. For example, check the new design and the new "security features" of the 1996 $100 bill. You'll find GIFs and a press release at the U.S. Treasury server. You can find lots of cool stuff here, if you take time to look! If you want to look something up by keyword, try a search from National Technical Information Service (NTIS) area of FEDWORLD. You can also browse by subject area, such as "Health Care" or "Space Technology." Download (or order) a number of free catalogs, ranging from Environmental Highlights to Occupational Safety & Health Multimedia Training Programs. Government documents are a gold mine of information, "pick" some today!

http://www.fedworld.gov/

Library of Congress World Wide Web Home Page

Did you know that the first American "postcards" were souvenir mailing cards sold at the Columbian Exposition in Chicago, all the way back in 1893? They didn't become popular, partly because you couldn't write on the back. What did people mail to their friends back home when they went on vacation? Luckily, on May 19, 1898, Congress passed a law which allowed private printers to publish and sell cards. The postage rate was 1 cent back then. This began the postcard era in the United States. This information was found in the American Memory Collection of the Library of Congress on the World Wide Web. This site has access to newspapers around the world, and thousands of historical postcards, photographs, motion pictures, manuscripts, and sound recordings. Many Library of Congress exhibits are also online for viewing.

http://lcweb.loc.gov/homepage/lchp.html

Supreme Court Decisions

Prepared by the Cornell University Law School, these hypertext Supreme Court decisions date from 1991. Also included are a few famous historical cases that took place before this time.

http://www.law.cornell.edu/supct/

THOMAS: Legislative Information on the Internet

It's Congress at your fingertips—lots of information here! Read a detailed account of how laws are made, find out what happened at the 103rd Congress, or get the scoop on the hot bills now under consideration at the 104th Congress. Did you know there is a bill in the Senate right now to declare English to be the official language of the U.S. Government? It's bill number S.175. If this bill gets passed, all official U.S. documents would only be available in English. The full text of the Constitution of the United States is also available here. Most of the information is also searchable by keyword, which makes your search easier.

http://thomas.loc.gov/

Welcome to the White House

Besides a tour of the White House, you can learn a lot about President Bill Clinton and the First Family. You can even hear Socks, the First Cat, meow! This is also a gateway to information about the executive branch of the U.S. Government, its cabinet offices, and independent agencies.

http://www.whitehouse.gov/

NATIONAL PARKS
The National Park Service Home Page

This site, offered by the U.S. National Park Service, is loaded with facts! It includes visitor information, statistics, conservation practices, and park history. You can find information on a specific park or historic site in a variety of ways. Try the alphabetical list, or use a clickable map to select from a list of sites for that state. A selection sorted by theme or keyword is also available. They even include a list of keywords to use to make the selection easier.

http://woodstock.rmro.nps.gov/parks.html

USDA Forest Service Recreation Home Page

America's National Forests belong to you, but when was the last time you visited one? To find out how, visit the USDA Forest Service graphical guide, a map showing every national forest, grassland, and park in the country. Clicking on any one of them tells you all about the area, including what kind of wildlife you can see and what there is to do, whether it's fishing, skiing, biking, kayaking, or camping. Once you've decided where you'd like to go, reserve your spot by downloading a reservation application.

http://www.fs.fed.us/recreation/welcome.htm

Surf today, smart tomorrow.

POLITICS

Campaign '96

How can you keep track of the race for the Presidency? Every day something changes. Each candidate says that he is the right person for the job. *Time* magazine has a very good collection of information about the campaign. Attention has been given to all parties, including independent candidates. See news, the latest polls, commentary, humor, and links to REALLY important documents, like the Declaration of Independence and the Constitution of the United States of America.

http://pathfinder.com/@@p0OR@yGq8AMAQDtT/
   pathfinder/politics/1996/

NET FILES

What insect is being used to help design fighter jets?

Answer: Dragonflies are able to change direction very quickly in flight. Engineers at the University of Tennessee are trying to find out how to make jets do the same by studying dragonfly wings. They "fly" large models of these insects in wind tunnels to study how their wing shape keeps them up. Read about the project at: http://loki.ur.utk.edu/utZkids/dragonfly/dragonfly.html

CNN Political News Main Page

No matter where you live, your life is affected by these people. They are everywhere! Politicians make laws about a lot of different things every day. CNN is one of the world's most trusted news sources, and offers these pages dedicated to political news. From the federal budget to the 1996 presidential elections, look here for great leads on today's top stories.

http://www.cnn.com/POLITICS/index.html

Election '96

Do you want to be president? What would you tell voters to get them to elect you? What things would you change if you got the job? This is *U.S. News & World Report* magazine's online page dedicated to the candidates. Each page lists a short biography and has a link to the candidate's Web page.

http://www.agtnet.com/usnews/wash/election.htm

Election '96 Homepage

How many decisions do you make a day? You may pick out your own clothes, or you might even get to choose what to have for lunch. What if you had to select the next person to be president? How would you make up your mind? Election '96 is a complete guide to the candidates, the issues, and the race for the presidency.

http://dodo.crown.net/~mpg/election/96.html

Vote Smart Web

Have you ever seen a politician? Ever wondered how the U.S. Government works? Politicians are everywhere, and they are constantly making important decisions. Vote Smart keeps track of what politicians are doing. If you have to write a paper about a candidate, a political issue, or even a project that requires a cartoon or an audio clip, try Vote Smart. It has links to the '96 presidential campaign, educational material, and a political humor section.

http://www.vote-smart.org/

STATES

You need information about each state? We've found it for you! General information about each state can usually be found at the sites we've picked. Other common resources can include travel, historical, cultural, and statistical data. Most state home pages are run by their respective state governments. The "official" home pages of each are included, if one was available at the time. Otherwise, we've included a good source of general, "unofficial," information for that state. Some of these are hosted by universities or local businesses within the state.

Yahoo—Regional: U.S. States

Yahoo has just about everything available when it comes to U.S. states. If you don't mind wading through lots of links to find just what you're looking for, try here. To your advantage, though, each state's links are also sorted by category. You can ask for just the links on education, sports, outdoors, cities, government, and more. There's also a search field that you can use to narrow down your selection.

http://www.yahoo.com/Regional/U_S__States/

Alabama

Located in the Deep South, Alabama is the 22nd state. Alabama is an Indian name for "tribal town." The state bird is the Yellowhammer, and the flower is the Camellia.

AlaWeb!:
http://alaweb.asc.edu/

AlaWeb—Tourism HomePage:
http://alaweb.asc.edu/ala_tours/tours.html

Emblems and Symbols:
http://www.asc.edu/archives/emblems.html

The Sun never sets on the Internet.

Alaska

Alaska is the largest state in area, and is home to the tallest mountain, Mount McKinley (20,320 ft). It's both the westernmost and easternmost state at the same time! This curiosity is possible because, technically, part of the Aleutian Island chain of Alaska is located in the Eastern Hemisphere, while the rest of Alaska is in the Western Hemisphere. Alaska gets its name from an Inuit word for "great lands." It is the 49th state, and some of it lies above the Arctic Circle.

aboutalaska:
http://info.alaska.edu:70/0/Alaska/aboutalaska

State of Alaska's Home Page:
http://www.state.ak.us/

Tourism Information:
http://www.state.ak.us/local/akpages/COMMERCE/tourtran.htm

Arizona

The 48th state, Arizona, is home to the largest gorge in the U.S.: The Grand Canyon. It is 277 miles long and one mile deep. The name Arizona is from the Aztec word *arizuma* meaning "silver bearing." The official state bird is the Cactus Wren and the flower is the Saguaro Cactus. This western desert state has LOTS of cactus!

Key Attractions:
http://www.state.az.us/ep/natmrk/attrac.shtml

State of Arizona Services via World Wide Web:
http://www.state.az.us/

Arkansas

Rice grows in much of the lowlands of the 25th state. Midlands Arkansas is home to Hot Springs National Park, where people come from miles around to relax and soothe their tired muscles in the hot mineral baths. Arkansas' name is from the Quapaw language and means "downstream people." The official state bird is the Mockingbird.

Arkansas Home Page:
http://www.state.ar.us/

Arkansas Parks and Tourism Page:
http://www.state.ar.us/html/ark_parks.html

A B C D E F G H I J K L M N O P Q R S T U V W X Y Z

California

California, the 31st state, was once part of Mexico. It is known for its National Park, Yosemite. Also, the lowest point of land in the United States is Death Valley, at 282 feet below sea level. Located on the west coast, California is known as The Golden State. The state tree is the California Redwood, and its flower is the Golden Poppy.

California Insignia:
http://library.ca.gov/california/cahinsig.html

California State Home Page:
http://www.state.ca.us/

Traveling & Vacationing in the Golden State:
http://www.ca.gov/gov/tourism.html

Colorado

One of the Rocky Mountain states, Colorado has the highest average elevation of all the states, and over 50 of the highest mountain peaks in the U.S. are found here. Yes, skiing is popular in Colorado! The 38th state has had over 20,000 years of human habitation. Its state flower is the graceful Rocky Mountain Columbine.

Colorado's Homepage:
http://www.state.co.us/

Visitor's Guide to Colorado:
http://www.state.co.us/visit_dir/visitormenu.html

Connecticut

Settled by the Dutch in the early 1600s, Connecticut was one of the original thirteen colonies. It is the 5th state. The name of this east coast state comes from a Mohican word meaning "long river place." The official state song is "Yankee Doodle."

Connecticut Tourism Guide:
http://ctguide.atlantic.com/vacguide/

Random facts:
http://ctguide.atlantic.com/info/facts.html

State of Connecticut Home Page:
http://www.ctstateu.edu/state.html

Become one with the Net.

Delaware

Delaware was the first state, becoming one in 1787. It's the second smallest state in area, ahead of only Rhode Island. Delaware was named after Lord De La Warr, a governor of Virginia. The motto of this eastern seaboard state is "Liberty and Independence."

Delaware Facts:
http://www.state.de.us/facts/history/delfact.htm

Delaware Tourism:
http://www.state.de.us/tourism/intro.htm

State of Delaware Internet Information Server:
http://www.state.de.us/

District of Columbia

Although it's not a state at all, the District of Columbia is well known for its city of Washington, D.C. It's the special place where the United States Government buildings and leaders are. The President lives here, and you can visit the White House and other historic buildings either in person or over the Net. The District of Columbia has its own "state" motto, "Justice for all," as well as an official flower (American Beauty Rose), tree (Scarlet Oak), and bird (Wood Thrush).

Nomius Eye : Tourism—Washington DC:
http://www.nomius.com/~dc/washdc.htm

The Washington DC City Pages:
http://dcpages.ari.net/

Florida

Florida has the distinction of being the flattest state. It is also home to the southernmost spot in the continental United States. Its peninsula divides the Atlantic Ocean from the Gulf of Mexico. Florida was named by Ponce de León in 1513. It means "Flowery Easter." Lots of oranges and grapefruit grow here due to the mild, sunny climate. The 27th state's official flower is the orange blossom!

Communities of Interest:
http://fcn.state.fl.us/cgi-bin/wow/
  www_index.show?p_searchkey=168

Fact Sheet:
http://hammock.ifas.ufl.edu/text/original/facts.html

Florida Communities Network:
http://www.state.fl.us/

Visit the stars in Astronomy.

Georgia

Georgia is named after King George II of England. The Cumberland Island National Seashore is a coastal wilderness area located in Georgia, also famous for its sea islands. The 1996 Summer Olympics will be held in Atlanta. The 4th state's official tree is the Live Oak.

Georgia DOAS Home Page GO Network:
http://www.state.ga.us/

Georgia Secretary of State Department of Archives and History:
http://www.state.ga.us/doah/

NET FILES

Dad says I can eat dessert first "once in a blue moon." What's a Blue Moon, and when is the next one?

ANSWER: Calendar months are either 30 or 31 days long. But the lunar month is twenty-nine and a half days. Every now and again, there are two full moons in the same month. The second full moon in the same month is called a Blue Moon. According to the Old Farmer's Almanac, the next one will be in June of 1996. Both June 1 and 30 will have a full moon, so get your dessert spoon ready! Look for more interesting weather lore at http://www.nj.com/weather/faq.html

Hawai'i

Hawai'i's Mt. Waialeale, on the island of Kauai, is the rainiest place in the world, with an average rainfall of over 460 inches a year. Also within this tropical state is the southernmost spot in the U.S., at Ka Lae on the Big Island of Hawai'i. Hawai'i comprises over 130 Pacific islands, but there are eight main islands. Its name is believed to have come from the native word "Hawaiki," meaning homeland. It is the 50th state, and its state tree is the Candlenut. Some people in Hawai'i are trying to return the state to sovereign nationhood. Please see the entry for the Nation of Hawai'i in the Native Americans and Other Indigenous Peoples section.

Hawai'i State Government Home Page:
http://www.hawaii.gov/

Hawai'i Overview:
http://www2.hawaii.edu/visitors/overview.html

Visitor Information:
http://www.hawaii.net/hawaiihome/vis.html

Idaho

Idaho is known for its farming, and its most famous crop, the Idaho potato. The deepest gorge in North America is in Hells Canyon, along the Idaho-Oregon border, measuring 7,900 feet deep. This Rocky Mountain state's official bird is the Mountain Bluebird. It is the 43rd state.

Idaho Recreation and Tourism Initiative Home Page:
http://www.IDOC.state.id.us/

Other Idaho Information:
http://www.state.id.us/other.html

The State of Idaho's Home Page:
http://www.state.id.us/

Illinois

Illinois is the Algonquin word for "warriors." The 21st state was the birthplace of Abraham Lincoln. The tallest building in the United States is the Sears Tower in Chicago, Illinois. The official bird of this midwest state is the red Cardinal.

Illinois Tourism:
http://www.state.il.us/CMS/HP0060.HTM

State of Illinois:
http://www.state.il.us/

State Symbols of Illinois:
http://www.museum.state.il.us/1/exhibits/symbols

A B C D E F G H I J K L M N O P Q R S T U V W X Y Z

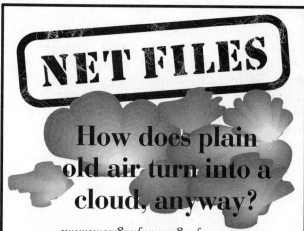

NET FILES

How does plain old air turn into a cloud, anyway?

Answer: Those magical, fluffy castles in the sky are caused by a process of air rising, expanding, and cooling to its saturation point, where it becomes visible as a cloud. Find out more, and see great cloud photos, at http://www.atmos.uiuc.edu/covis/modules/clouds/cloud_listing/html/listing_home.html

Indiana

Indiana means "land of the Indians." Indianapolis is its capital and largest city, and is the site of the Indianapolis 500 auto race is held every year. The 19th state, midwestern Indiana's official tree is the Tulip Tree.

Indiana State Government Page:
http://www.state.in.us/

Iowa

A major producer of corn and soybeans, midwestern Iowa is a Native American name for "beautiful land." It is the 29th state. Its state bird is the colorful and jaunty Eastern Goldfinch.

Iowa Tourism:
http://www.state.ia.us/tourism/index.html

State of Iowa Home Page:
http://www.state.ia.us/

Table of Contents for Iowa State Symbols:
http://lwvia.cornell-iowa.edu/Iowa/LSB/StateSymbols/TOC.html

Kansas

The geographical center of the lower 48 states is located near Lebanon, Kansas. Kansas is a Sioux word meaning "south wind people." Famous for farming and wheat fields, the 34th state is also known as the mythical home of Dorothy and Toto of *The Wizard of Oz.*

Kansas Government:
http://skyways.lib.ks.us/kansas/kan_govt.html

Kansas Sights:
http://falcon.cc.ukans.edu/~nsween/europa.html

Nature Watch, Vol. 5:
http://ukanaix.cc.ukans.edu/~seec/naturev5.html

Kentucky

Kentucky, the "land of tomorrow," has possibly the largest cave system in the world, Mammoth Caves. The 15th state is also known for its many thoroughbred horse farms. Its state flower is the Goldenrod.

Commonwealth of Kentucky—Virtual Tour:
http://www.state.ky.us/tour/symbols.htm

Commonwealth of Kentucky Web Server:
http://www.state.ky.us/

Commonwealth of Kentucky Web Server—Virtual Tour:
http://www.state.ky.us/tour/tour.htm

Louisiana

This southern state is where the mighty Mississippi River enters the Gulf of Mexico. Its largest city, New Orleans, is famous for its Mardi Gras celebration, held every year on the last day before Lent. The 18th state's bird is the Brown Pelican, which also appears on the state flag.

Culture, Recreation and Tourism:
http://www.state.la.us/crt/crt.htm

Info Louisiana: Main Page:
http://www.state.la.us/

Miscellaneous Facts about Louisiana:
http://www.state.la.us/crt/profiles/lafacts.htm

> **Space Exploration is a blast.**
> **Check out Astronomy.**

Maine

This is the state where the lobster is king. It's also the easternmost point of the U.S. mainland. The 23rd state is also famous for Acadia National Park and its rugged coastline. The state bird is the playful Black-capped Chickadee, and the official tree is the Eastern White Pine.

Maine State Government (WWW) Home Page:
http://www.state.me.us/

Maine Tourism—Maine Facts:
http://www.state.me.us/decd/tour/facts.html

The Maine Tourism Web:
http://www.state.me.us/decd/tour/welcome.html

Maryland

East coast Maryland is where the District of Columbia, the capital of the United States, is located. The national anthem, *The Star Spangled Banner,* by Sir Francis Scott Key, was inspired by a battle in 1814 at historic Fort McHenry. Surrounding the Chesapeake Bay, much of eastern Maryland is known for its fishing industries, particularly for soft-shelled crabs. You may have read the horse story *Misty of Chincoteague* by Marguerite Henry. These stories were set at the Assateague National Seashore, which Maryland shares with neighboring Virginia. The 7th state, Maryland's state bird is the Northern Oriole.

Maryland POGs:
http://www.inform.umd.edu:8080/
  UofMd-System_and_State_of_Maryland/
  UMD-Projects/MCTP/Technology/
  School_WWW_Pages/pogs/index.html

State of Maryland Main Page:
http://www.maryland.umd.edu/

Tourism in the State of Maryland:
http://www.maryland.umd.edu/tourism.html

NET FILES

How do you play "Chicken Skins"?

Answer: "Chicken Skins" refers to a version of competition golf where players play for points on each hole. In the popular "skins game," players get a point for each hole they win. If any two players tie, the point is added onto the next hole (now worth two). In "Chicken Skins," the points do not carry over to the next hole. Do you just love playing golf? Don't be chicken, try http://www.golfweb.com/glbl/index.htm to learn the rules of any golf game you can imagine!

Massachusetts

The Pilgrims landed at Plymouth Rock, near Boston, on December 21, 1620. They started one of the most traditional American feasts, Thanksgiving. Native Americans helped them to survive. Famous folks from Massachusetts include John F. Kennedy and Louisa May Alcott. The 6th state's official flower is the Mayflower.

Commonwealth of Massachusetts—MAGNet:
http://www.state.ma.us/

Massachusetts Vacation Information:
http://www.magnet.state.ma.us/travel/travel.html

Michigan

Henry Ford's Detroit auto factory began an industry that has made Michigan the center of U.S. car manufacturing. Michigan gets its name from *mici gama,* the Chippewa words meaning "great water." Michigan is in two parts, the Upper and Lower peninsulas. It has shoreline on four of the Great Lakes: Lake Michigan, Lake Huron, Lake Erie, and Lake Superior. The 26th state's official bird is the Robin.

State of Michigan:
http://www.migov.state.mi.us/

A B C D E F G H I J K L M N O P Q R S T U V W X Y Z

Minnesota

The Mississippi River starts here! Minnesota is from the Sioux word meaning "cloudy water" of the Minnesota River. This northern border state has over 15,000 lakes, left there by glaciers. The 32nd state's official bird is the Common Loon and its flower is the Pink and White Lady's Slipper.

All About Minnesota Page 5:
http://www.state.mn.us/aam/aamp5-6.html

Minnesota Office of Tourism:
http://tccn.com/mn.tourism/mnhome.html

North Star Main Menu:
http://www.state.mn.us/mainmenu.html

Mississippi

Southern Mississippi's history dates back to the 1500s when Spanish explorers visited the area. The French were the first to settle it, however, in 1699. The 20th state was a center of attention in the 1960s with the activities of the Civil Rights movement. The state flower is the sweetly scented Magnolia.

Mississippi Gulf Coast:
http://www.datasync.com/trebor/index.html

State Of Mississippi:
http://www.state.ms.us/

Governments have lots of laws and rules for people and businesses to follow. When a new law is needed, it goes through a maze of committees and meetings. The proposed new law is called a bill. The following page contains a nice chart that shows all the steps that it takes for a bill to become a law in Mississippi.

The Life of a Bill in Mississippi:
http://www.peer.state.ms.us/LifeOfBill.html

Yogatta try Yoga.

Missouri

Two major rivers, the Missouri and the Mississippi, meet here in the 24th state. Samuel Clemens, also known as Mark Twain, lived in Hannibal, Missouri, on the Mississippi River. The Ozark Mountains in this state contain more than four hundred caves. A dam on the Osage River holds back the Lake of the Ozarks, one of the largest man-made lakes in the world. The official state tree is the Hawthorn.

MO-EDODEV Tourism Homepage:
http://www.ecodev.state.mo.us/tou/home.htm

State of Missouri Home Page:
http://www.ecodev.state.mo.us/

NET FILES

What is an afuche drum? What does it look like?

Answer: It's a small, squat cylinder with a handle and a corrugated metal surface. A long string of beads wound loosely around it makes a scrabbly, swishy note when you shake it. There's a great picture at http://www.cse.ogi/Drum/encyclopedia/a.html. You can also find out what a shekere is, among other things.

Montana

This is "Big Sky Country," a nickname that came from the wide open spaces that dominate the eastern grasslands. However, the Rocky Mountains in the west are responsible for its name, *montana,* the Spanish word for mountain. The 41st state's official tree is the Ponderosa Pine.

STATE OF MONTANA:
http://www.mt.gov/

Travel Montana's Home Page:
http://travel.mt.gov/

> ## Let balloonists take you to new heights in Aviation and Airplanes.

Nebraska

Nebraska's name is from the Omaha word meaning "broad water," referring to the Platte River. The Agate Fossil Beds National Monument contains bones from animals over twenty-two million years old. This Great Plains state is known for farming and grazing land. The official tree of the 37th state is the Cottonwood.

Nebraska State Government:
http://www.state.ne.us/

Nebraska Travel & Tourism:
http://www.ded.state.ne.us/tourism.html

Nebraska's State Symbols:
http://www.ded.state.ne.us/tourism/report/
  symbols.html

Nevada

Nevada's Hoover Dam on the Colorado River is one of the tallest dams in the world. Tourists from around the world visit Las Vegas for its gambling and entertainment. The official flower of the 36th state is the pungent Sagebrush.

City of Las Vegas Welcome Page:
http://gate.vegas.com/CLV/

Reno/Tahoe Territory:
http://www.reno.net/territory/

New Hampshire

This state's motto is "Live Free or Die." Although New Hampshire was the 9th state to be admitted into the United States, it was the first colony to declare its independence from Britain. Its state flower is the sweetly scented Purple Lilac.

New Hampshire at a Glance:
http://www.nh.com/politics/firstntn/nhglance/

NH Access Internet—Vacation & Tourism:
http://www.nh.com/tourism/

WELCOME TO WEBSTER:
http://www.state.nh.us/

New Jersey

The 3rd state admitted to the Union was New Jersey. Northeastern New Jersey is densely populated with close ties to New York City. It is also known for Atlantic City, a popular seaside resort. The state flower is the Purple Violet.

E-deZign Group: New Jersey Information:
http://www.ezweb.com/local.html

Official Symbols of the State of New Jersey:
http://www.state.nj.us/njfacts/njsymbol.htm

State of New Nersey:
http://www.state.nj.us/

New Mexico

The 47th state has many natural wonders. Carlsbad Caverns National Park has caves that are over 11,000 feet deep and twenty miles long. This western desert state claims the Yucca as its official flower, and the Roadrunner as its bird.

Bienvenidos a Nuevo Mexico:
http://www.nets.com/tourism.html

State of New Mexico Services via World Wide Web:
http://www.state.nm.us/

New York

From New York City, to the Adirondack Mountains, to Niagara Falls, New York has a diverse array of sights. Its history dates back to the 1620s when the Dutch colonized Manhattan Island. The Baseball Hall of Fame is located in Cooperstown. The 11th state's official tree is the Sugar Maple. This state also has an official muffin!

gov-agencies:
gopher://unix2.nysed.gov:70/11/gov-agencies

NY State Emblems:
http://unix2.nysed.gov/library/emblems/
  emblems.html

Welcome to New York:
http://www.state.ny.us/

> ## Take a ride on a Carousel in AMUSEMENT PARKS.

A B C D E F G H I J K L M N O P Q R S T U V W X Y Z

Check out CRAFTS AND HOBBIES.

North Carolina

Orville Wright made his historic first flight at coastal Kitty Hawk, North Carolina. The first English settlement in the Americas was made on Roanoke Island in 1587, but three years later, the village was found abandoned and in ruins. What happened to these people remains a mystery to this day. The 12th state's official tree is the Long-leafed Pine.

North Carolina Interstates:
http://interstatelink.com/isl/inc.html

Official State Symbols of North Carolina:
http://hal.dcr.state.nc.us/NC/SYMBOLS/
   SYMBOLS.HTM

State of North Carolina:
http://www.state.nc.us/

North Dakota

This state is known for uneven territory known as the Badlands. The Badlands were justly named by early travelers because they are almost impossible to cross. Dakota is a Sioux word meaning "friend." A 2,063-foot TV tower in Blanchard, North Dakota is the tallest man-made structure in the country. North Dakota's official flower is the Wild Prairie Rose. It is the 46th state.

State of North Dakota:
http://www.state.nd.us/

Ohio

Ohio is an Iroquois word for "good river." This was one of the ancient homes of the Mound Builders, who built thousands of earthen burial and ceremonial mounds, many of which can be seen today. The Pro Football Hall of Fame is located in Canton. The 17th state's official tree is the Buckeye.

State of Ohio Web Servers:
http://www.state.oh.us/

Welcome to TR@VEL.OHIO!
http://www.travel.state.oh.us/

Oklahoma

The deepest well in the U.S. is located in Washita County. This gas well is 31,441 feet deep! Oklahoma gets its name from a Choctaw word meaning "red man." The 46th state's official tree is the Redbud. Yahoo! The National Cowboy Hall of Fame is in Oklahoma City.

Oklahoma Home Page:
http://www.oklaosf.state.ok.us/

Oklahoma Tourism and Recreation Department:
http://www.oklaosf.state.ok.us/~odt/

State of Oklahoma, Statistics:
http://www.oklaosf.state.ok.us/osfdocs/gen-facts.html

Oregon

The deepest lake in the United States is Crater Lake, in Crater Lake National Park, Oregon, with depths to 1,932 feet. This lake is located inside an ancient volcano and has no water flowing in or out. West coast Oregon is known for its dense woods and beautiful, mountainous scenery. Its state tree is the Douglas Fir. It is the 33rd state.

Oregon Home Page:
http://www.state.or.us/

Pennsylvania

Pennsylvania was settled by Quakers from Great Britain in the 1680s. In 1863, during the Civil War, a famous battle was fought in Gettysburg. You'll also find the Liberty Bell in Philadelphia. Pennsylvania, which is the 2nd state, has a small border on one of the Great Lakes, Lake Erie. Its official bird is the Ruffed Grouse.

Commonwealth of Pennsylvania:
http://www.state.pa.us/

PENNSYLVANIA STATE HISTORY:
http://www.state.pa.us/PA_History/symbols.htm

Pennsylvania's Visitor's Guide—Table of Contents:
http://www.state.pa.us/Visit/index.html

Rhode Island

Rhode Island is the smallest state in the U.S. It is also the 13th of the original thirteen colonies, and the 13th state. The first factory in the U.S. was built here in the 1790s. This east coast state's official bird is the Rhode Island Red Chicken.

RI State Government:
http://osfn.rhilinet.gov/

Welcome to Rhode Island:
http://ets.cis.brown.edu/Student_Services/
    Rhode_Island/welcome.html

South Carolina

The Civil War started in South Carolina, at Fort Sumter in Charleston harbor. This historic east coast city is very well preserved. Hilton Head and Myrtle Beach are well-known and popular seaside vacation sites. The 8th state's official bird is the Carolina Wren.

**State of South Carolina—Public Information Home
    Page:**
http://www.state.sc.us/

State Symbols:
http://lis.leginfo.state.sc.us/scinfo/info.html

South Dakota

Famous Mount Rushmore is located in the Black Hills of South Dakota. Four sixty-foot heads of U.S. presidents have been sculpted on the side of a mountain. The Black Hills look "black" from a distance because they are covered with dense pine forests. The 40th state's official bird is the Ring-necked Pheasant.

Signs and Symbols of South Dakota:
http://www.state.sd.us/state/sdsym.htm

State of South Dakota:
http://www.state.sd.us/

Tennessee

Tennessee, the 16th state, is known for the Great Smoky Mountains National Park. Nashville is famous as a world center for country music. The state flower is the Iris.

Tennessee's WWW Home Page:
http://www.state.tn.us/

NET FILES

How did the chipmunk get her stripes?

Answer: In a Native American tale, it's told that, because the winters were cold and people were starving, Coyote went to the mountians to steal fire from the Fire Beings. As he was returning with it, the easily annoyed Fire Beings ran after him. Coyote threw the fire to Chipmunk, who began to run with it. One of the Fire Beings reached out to grab her, but the rodent was too fast, and she got away. However, the clawed white burn marks can be seen on Chipmunk's fur to this day. Read more about this story at http://www.ece.ucdavis.edu/
~darsie/hcst.html

Texas

Cattle and oil dominate the economy of Texas. It's the largest state in area, except for Alaska. A famous battle in 1836, between thousands of Mexicans and a few hundred Texans, took place at an old Spanish mission called the Alamo, located in San Antonio. "Remember the Alamo" is a famous battle cry. Texas is the 28th state, and its flower is the Bluebonnet.

State of Texas Government World Wide Web Server:
http://www.state.tx.us/

TravelTex:
http://www.traveltex.com/

A B C D E F G H I J K L M N O P Q R S T U V W X Y Z

Utah

Utah comes from a Navajo word meaning "upper." Salt Lake City is the center of the Church of Jesus Christ of Latter-day Saints (Mormon) religion. The Great Salt Lake in Utah is eight times saltier than the ocean. Utah is the 45th state; its official bird is the California Gull.

Information about Utah:
http://www.state.ut.us/utinfo/

State of Utah WWW Homepage:
http://www.state.ut.us/

Utah Travel Guide:
http://www.netpub.com:80/utah!/

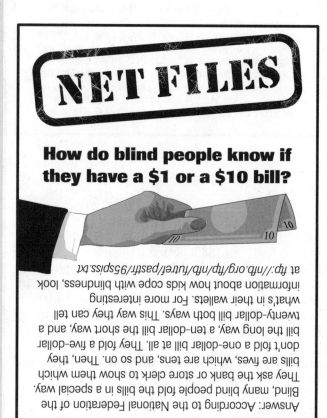

NET FILES

How do blind people know if they have a $1 or a $10 bill?

Answer: According to the National Federation of the Blind, many blind people fold the bills in a special way. They ask the bank or store clerk to show them which bills are fives, which are tens, and so on. Then, they don't fold a one-dollar bill at all. They fold a five-dollar bill the long way, a ten-dollar bill the short way, and a twenty-dollar bill both ways. This way they can tell what's in their wallets. For more interesting information about how kids cope with blindness, look at ftp://nfb.org/ftp/futref/pastrf/95spiss.txt

---

Frisbee is the Ultimate in GAMES AND FUN.

Chase some waterfalls in EARTH SCIENCE.

Vermont

Vert and *mont* are French for "green " and "mountain," respectively. The Green Mountains are located in Vermont. One interesting fact about Vermont is that there are no major cities. This makes it the most rural state in the country. Its official flower is the Red Clover and it is the 14th state.

State of Vermont Home Page:
http://www.cit.state.vt.us/

State of Vermont: State Treasures:
http://mole.uvm.edu/Vermont/vttres.html

Virginia

Virginia has been home to both George Washington and Thomas Jefferson, and you can tour their homes today. Jamestown became the first permanent English settlement in 1607. It is the 10th state, and the Dogwood is both its official tree and flower.

Welcome to Virginia:
http://www.state.va.us/

Washington

Coastal Washington state is known for its many natural features. The Cascade Range is where Mount St. Helens erupted in 1980. Olympic National Park contains vast sections of ancient rainforest. It is the 42nd state, and the Rhododendron is the official flower.

Home Page Washington—Home:
http://www.wa.gov/

Symbols of Washington State:
http://www.tourism.wa.gov/general/students/
  symbols.htm

Travel in Washington:
http://www.travel-in-wa.com/

West Virginia

West Virginia's natural features are dominated by the Appalachian Mountains. Mining in these mountains is a major industry here, where coal is the main product. The 35th state's official bird is the brilliantly colored Cardinal.

West Virginia Library Commission Home Page:
http://www.wvlc.wvnet.edu/

West Virginia State Symbols:
http://www.wvlc.wvnet.edu/WVA_Symbols.html

Wisconsin

Wisconsin is a state with over eight thousand lakes, carved out by glaciers long ago. This state has more dairy cows than any other state, so it's no wonder that milk and cheese are its major products. Bordered by two Great Lakes, Lake Superior and Lake Michigan, Wisconsin is the 30th state. Its official flower is the Wood Violet.

State of Wisconsin Web Page:
http://www.state.wi.us/

Welcome to the Wisconsin Tourism Division:
http://badger.state.wi.us/agencies/tourism/places/Cover.html

Wyoming

Wyoming means "large prairie place" in Algonquin. Yellowstone National Park is famous for its geysers and hot springs. Fictional "Jellystone Park" is where Yogi Bear and Boo-Boo live. This rugged Rocky Mountain State was the 44th to be admitted to the Union. Its official flower is the Indian Paintbrush.

The Windy Wyoming Web:
http://www.uwyo.edu/Lib/Wyoming/index.html

Welcome to the State of Wyoming:
http://www.state.wy.us/state/text_welcome.html

Lost your sheep? Count them in FARMING AND AGRICULTURE.

TERRITORIES AND FREE ASSOCIATION NATIONS

American Samoa

This 76-square-mile island group sits in the middle of the South Pacific Ocean, 2,600 miles from Hawai'i. Its citizens are considered U.S. nationals and can freely enter the United States. Many American Samoans live in Hawai'i. They have a large tuna fishery there; other exports include coconuts, taro, yams, bananas, and breadfruit. You can't make a sandwich out of breadfruit, by the way. Well, maybe you can in the Sandwich Islands, but not on American Samoa! If you go to this site, you'll hear a greeting in Samoan! You may want to check *http://www.ic.gov/94fact/country/4.html* for further details.

American Samoa:
http://prel.hawaii.edu/prel_sites/am_samoa/am_samoa.html

Baker Island

This is a teeny low-lying atoll in the North Pacific Ocean, about one-half of the way from Hawai'i to Australia. It was mined for its guano deposits until 1891. The birds are still there, the guano is still there, but you'll need a permit to visit. There's only offshore anchorage, and be advised there are no malls or fast food restaurants.

Baker Island:
http://www.odci.gov/cia/publications/95fact/fq.html

Guam

Guam, located near the International Date Line, is "where America's Day Begins." This island is in the West Pacific, 3,700 miles from Hawai'i. Guamanians are U.S. citizens. You can find more information at *http://www.ic.gov/94fact/country/98.html* or at *http://prel-oahu-1.prel.hawaii.edu/prel_sites/guam/guam.html*.

Welcome to Guam:
http://www.gov.gu/

A B C D E F G H I J K L M N O P Q R S T U V W X Y Z

Howland Island

This tiny sandy island is in the North Pacific Ocean, about one-half of the way from Hawai'i to Australia. It's another National Wildlife Refuge, and you need permission from the U.S. Department of the Interior to visit it. The island is famous because of someone who never made it there. In 1937, an airstrip was constructed there as a refueling stop on the round-the-world flight attempt of Amelia Earhart and Fred Noonan. They had they left Lae, New Guinea, for Howland Island, but something happened, and they were never seen again. Their disappearance is truly one of the world's great unsolved mysteries. Earhart Light, on the Island's west coast, is a day beacon built in memory of the lost aviatrix. The airfield is no longer serviceable.

For a possible solution to the mystery, see *http://msowww.anu.edu.au/~dfk/magazine/mpi/july95/tighar.html* about recent expeditions and findings on Nikumaroro. If you want to read the lyrics to a folk song about Earhart, try *http://web2.xerox.com/digitrad/song=AMEARHRT*, and you can download a 540K audio file of Earhart discussing technology's impact on women at *gopher://gopher.msu.edu:70/ss/libraries/collections/main/voice/sounds/Amelia_Earhart.au*. The Smithsonian Institute has one of her leather flying jackets; see it at *http://web1.si.edu/resource/150th/150trav/discover/d513a.htm*. A nice illustrated biography is at *http://141.224.128.4/mdot/amelia.html*. For some brief background info, try *http://web1.si.edu/resource/150th/150trav/discover/d513a.htm*. It includes the incredible disclosure that Earhart may have invented the world's first skateboard!

Howland Island:
http://www.odci.gov/cia/publications/95fact/hq.html

Lost your marbles? Find them in GAMES AND FUN.

Jarvis Island

This tiny coral island is in the South Pacific Ocean, about one-half of the way from Hawai'i to the Cook Islands. It is a favorite nesting and roosting area for seabirds, and until the late 1880s, guano was actually mined there. Bird droppings are a rich source of fertilizer, but it seems like a long way to go to import some. You can't visit this place without permission of the Department of the Interior, since it is considered a National Wildlife Refuge.

Jarvis Island:
http://www.odci.gov/cia/publications/95fact/dq.html

Johnston Atoll

This strategically located atoll group is in the North Pacific Ocean, about one-third of the way from Hawai'i to the Marshall Islands. It's closed to the public, and has been used for testing nuclear weapons. There are about 300 people there, working on military and other projects. All food and other equipment has to be imported, but they do have excellent communications through an underwater cable link. Maybe they will get a home page on their own server soon!

Johnston Atoll:
http://www.odci.gov/cia/publications/95fact/jq.html

Sirena loved to swim in the sea!

One day, she forgot her chores, and spent the day swimming. When she did not come home, her angry mother said she should just become a fish, if she loved the sea so much! Sirena's god-mother quickly said "But let the part of her that belongs to me remain." Sirena, still swimming, suddenly felt strange. She looked down and realized the lower part of her body had become a fish! The legend of Sirena is from Guam. Read more about the story, and see a statue of Sirena, at the Welcome to Guam home page.

Kingman Reef

We're talking VERY tiny here—only one square kilometer of land area. This reef is in the North Pacific Ocean, about one-half of the way from Hawai'i to American Samoa. It's only about a meter in elevation, so it's often awash with waves! If you go, bring your boots, but you'll need permission from the U.S. Navy. This reef was used as a waystation by Pan American Flying Boats in 1937 and 1938. Now, it's basically famous as a maritime hazard.

Kingman Reef:
http://www.odci.gov/cia/publications/95fact/kq.html

Marshall Islands

This group of atolls and reefs is in the North Pacific Ocean, about one-half of the way from Hawai'i to Papua New Guinea. The group has a population of over 56,000 people. It has had a free association agreement with the U.S. since 1990, and became an independent nation in 1991. One of the atolls is Bikini, famous for the first military atomic bomb tests. You can read an account of these tests, and see a photo, at *http://magic.geol.ucsb.edu/~fisher/bikini.htm*. The bikini swimsuit, a very explosive new fashion, was invented about the same time as the weapon, and was named for this atoll. Nearby islands with indigenous people were evacuated in 1948, some of them, and their descendants, are asking to be repatriated to their traditional homelands. This is difficult due to residual radiation in the soil and food sources. You can read a report about that at *http://www.nas.edu/onpi/pr/marshall/*. More information about the Marshalls is at *http://prel-oahu-1.prel.hawaii.edu/prel_sites/marshalls/marshalls.html*.

Republic of the Marshall Islands:
http://www.odci.gov/cia/publications/95fact/rm.html

Micronesia, Federated States of

This island group is in the North Pacific Ocean, about three-quarters of the way from Hawai'i to Indonesia. Its landscape varies from low coral atolls to high forested mountains. About 123,000 people live there, and they achieved independent nation status in 1991. They have a Compact of Free Association with the U.S., which means that the nation is fully responsible for its internal government, while the U.S. retains responsibility for external affairs. The Island of Yap has a home page at *http://prel-oahu-1.prel.hawaii.edu/prel_sites/yap/yap.html*. The Island of Chuuk is a famous destination for scuba divers who want to explore a sunken Japanese fleet. Its home page is at *http://prel-oahu-1.prel.hawaii.edu/prel_sites/chuuk/chuuk.html*. Rural Kosrae's map and home page is at *http://prel-oahu-1.prel.hawaii.edu/prel_sites/kosrae/kosrae.html*, while Pohnpei—famous for gourmet pepper—has a home page at *http://prel-oahu-1.prel.hawaii.edu/prel_sites/pohnpei/pohnpei.html*.

Federated States of Micronesia:
http://www.odci.gov/cia/publications/95fact/fm.html

Midway Islands

This is an atoll group in the North Pacific Ocean, about one-third of the way from Hawai'i to Tokyo, Japan. There are over 400 U.S. military personnel here, and the area is closed to the public. This was a famous battle site during WWII.

Midway Islands:
http://www.odci.gov/cia/publications/95fact/mq.html

Navassa

This Caribbean island is strategically located, about one-fourth of the way from Haiti to Jamaica, and south of Cuba. Haiti disputes the U.S. claim to the territory. Haitian fishermen often camp on the island, which has steep cliffs and is populated by goats and cactus.

Navassa:
http://www.odci.gov/cia/publications/95fact/bq.html

A B C D E F G H I J K L M N O P Q R S T U V W X Y Z

Northern Mariana Islands

Between Guam and the Tropic of Cancer lie the seventeen volcanic islands that make up this Commonwealth. Its inhabitants are U.S. citizens, and tourism is becoming a major industry. For more information about its people and culture see *http://www.ic.gov/94fact/country/180.html*.

Commonwealth of the Northern Mariana Islands:
http://prel.hawaii.edu/prel_sites/cnmi/cnmi.html

Palau

This island, and its 16,000 people, is less than 500 miles from the Philippines. It consists of several hundred volcanic islands and a few coral atolls, but only eight islands are inhabited. It has mineral resources, including gold, but its main industry is tourism. This republic entered into a free association relationship with the United States in 1994.

Republic of Palau:
http://prel-oahu-1.prel.hawaii.edu/prel_sites/
   palau/palau.html

Palmyra Atoll

Administered by the U.S. Department of the Interior, this atoll group lies in the North Pacific Ocean, about one-half of the way from Hawai'i to American Samoa. It's only 12 square kilometers in land area, and its many tiny islets are densely covered with vegetation and coconut palms.

Palmyra Atoll:
http://www.odci.gov/cia/publications/95fact/lq.html

Puerto Rico

The island of Puerto Rico is the smallest and the most eastern island of the Greater Antilles, in the Caribbean. Puerto Rico is Spanish for "rich port." Puerto Ricans are U.S. citizens. You may have heard of these famous Puerto Ricans: musician Pablo Casals, sports figure Roberto Clemente, and actress Rita Moreno. Even more facts about Puerto Rico are located at *http://www.odci.gov/cia/publications/95fact/rq.html*.

Commonwealth of Puerto Rico: PUERTO RICO:
http://www.prairienet.org/~maggy/pr.html

Virgin Islands

The Caribbean islands of St. Thomas, St. John, and St. Croix are known as the U.S. Virgin Islands. Columbus stopped there in 1493, and since then, tourism has become a huge industry. Residents of the Virgin Islands are U.S. citizens. Still more can be found at *http://www.odci.gov/cia/publications/95fact/vq.html*.

American Paradise: U.S. Virgin Islands Tourist, Vacation, Business & Shopping Guide:
http://www.usvi.net/

NET FILES

What tree, whose wood and flowers have been revered by the Chinese and Japanese for centuries, has been discovered growing in Washington, D.C.?

Answer: It's called the Paulownia. According to Chinese legend, the tree meant good luck because of its association with the mythical phoenix bird. The story told that the phoenix would only roost in the very best Paulownia trees, and only when a very excellent ruler was in power. See http://www.si.edu/organiza/museums/zoo/homepage/zooview/plants/paulowni.htm for more legends and stories associated with this tree.

Wake Island

This almost flat volcanic island group is in the North Pacific Ocean, about two-thirds of the way from Hawai'i to the Northern Mariana Islands. About 300 people live there, and there is a U.S. Military base. It is also used as an emergency stopover for transpacific commercial aviation.

Wake Island:
http://www.odci.gov/cia/publications/95fact/wq.html

Don't be a stick-in-the-MUD!

U.S. PRESIDENTS AND FIRST LADIES

A Day In The Life Of A President

Did you ever think about growing up to be President of the United States? If you think you have a busy schedule now—with school and sports and errands and homework—you should check this out! Taken directly from former President Gerald Ford's daily diary, read what a typical day in the life of the President is really like. The day is Monday, April 28, 1975. The day begins with breakfast at 6:50 A.M. and goes non-stop from there with staff meetings, press conferences, and various other meetings with important people from all over the world. At 9:15 P.M., the President and First Lady have dinner…hey, whatever happened to lunch? Then, phone calls and more phone calls, and some pretty serious decision-making in the "Situation Room." At 12:05 A.M., the President finally returns to his second floor bedroom so he can catch a few hours of sleep and then do it all over again.

http://www2.sils.umich.edu/FordLibrary/
DayInTheLife.html

Hillary Rodham Clinton, First Lady of the United States

Bet you didn't know that Mrs. Clinton is a SERIOUS baseball fan! That's right! Her father used to take her to all the Cubs games at Wrigley Field in Chicago when she was young. She was even invited to throw out the first ball of the Cubs' 1994 season. Check out this site for more interesting facts about the First Lady of the United States. Her speeches are also included here. Take time to tour the Ladies' Garden of the White House and see the special twentieth-century sculpture exhibit, an idea of the First Lady herself.

http://www.whitehouse.gov/White_House/
EOP/First_Lady/html/ HILLARY_Home.html

Presidents

You know that old story about George Washington chopping down the cherry tree? Ever wonder if that really happened, and if it did, where it happened? Find out at this site, which is loaded with information about many of the U.S. presidents. Take a tour of Woodrow Wilson's historic home in Washington, D.C. The Presidential Portrait Gallery provides links to each Presidential Library, beginning with Herbert Hoover and continuing through to President Bill Clinton. And, in recognition of the significant contribution to American history made by many of the presidents' wives, the First Ladies Web site is also under construction at
http://sunsite.unc.edu/lia/president/firstladies/.

http://sunsite.unc.edu/lia/president/pressites/

The U. S. Presidents: Welcome Page

What a great way to learn American history and master presidential trivia all at once! Which U.S. president said, "The only thing we have to fear is fear itself"? (Franklin Roosevelt). Which president was responsible for starting the National Park Service in 1916? (Woodrow Wilson). Who initiated the United Nations? (Harry Truman). How about the Peace Corps? (John F. Kennedy). You can find answers to these questions and much more as you zip through more than 200 years of American history. Read the brief biographies of each U.S. president. The entry for each president includes a description of his administration, its chief concerns, highlights of his years in office and links to his inaugural speeches. Be sure to type the address correctly—there is no "e" in ~presidnt! :-)

http://chestnut.lis.utk.edu/~presidnt/USPres1.html

WIC Biography—Hillary Rodham Clinton

From her close-knit family in Park Ridge, Illinois, to Yale Law School, to First Lady of Arkansas, to the White House, Hillary Clinton has demonstrated her special concerns for protecting children and their families. Read about her many activities and the programs she has pioneered.

http://www.wic.org/bio/hclinton.htm

A B C D E F G H I J K L M N O P Q R S T U V W X Y Z

VIDEO AND SPY CAMS

The Amazing Fish-Cam

Yes, from wherever you are on the Web, you can watch fish swim around a tank in someone's office. These fish can be viewed by two different cameras (you get to pick), or you can choose the "Continuously Refreshing Fish-Cam" if you have Netscape 1.1. Ah, a nice salty glass of refreshing fish-cam! Nothing quite like it!

http://www1.netscape.com/fishcam/fishcam.html

Big Brother is Watching

From this one site, you can watch an observatory being built in Hawai'i, check out the traffic in Hong Kong, or watch the planes at airports in San Diego and Denver. Indoor cams more your style? OK, how about spying on the employees at Berkeley Systems? Watch them eat lunch or go down the slide. That's right, there is a slide in the employee lunchroom—sounds like a fun place to work! If you want to watch someone else's pets, try the piranha fish tank (especially entertaining when they clean it—any volunteers?). You can also monitor satellite weather, and other forecasting models. Be sure to check real-time traffic reports for many cities, too! This is a very useful site, with thoughtful and current reviews.

http://www.pitt.edu/~sbrst4/html.camtitle

Buckman School, Room 100

What are the kids doing in Room 100 of the Buckman Elementary School in Portland, Oregon? What are they looking at under their video-equipped microscope? This spy cam will show you a current view of the classroom, and maybe you'll get a picture of "the bee that just stung Ted" or something equally interesting.

http://buckman.pps.k12.or.us/picturecam.html

For happy hedgehogs see PETS AND PET CARE.

SLIME is a polymer, as anyone who's read CHEMISTRY knows!

Giraffe Cam

Check out the giraffes at the Cheyenne Mountain Zoo in Colorado Springs, Colorado. You can view the giraffe's entrance to their giraffe house. They are normally visible from 10 A.M. to 4 P.M. Mountain Time. This zoo is famous for their success in breeding giraffes in captivity!

http://www.ceram.com/cheyenne/giraffe.html

Hawaiian Eye, Oahu, Hawaii

Ah—another perfect day in Honolulu, on the Hawaiian Island of Oahu! That's the Aloha Tower market in the distance, and you can almost taste the shave ice from here! You have some control over which way you want the camera to point, but it's all beautiful, and a real contrast to the Mawson Station image from Antarctica!

http://planet-hawaii.com/ph/he.html

Iguana Cam

Check out Dupree the green iguana as he lazes the day away. By the way, he's probably the only iguana on the Web with its own home page! The best time to visit is between about 9 A.M. and 6 P.M. Pacific Time, Monday through Friday. Otherwise, he's out partying, and you'll just see a typical image, not a live one.

http://iguana.images.com/dupecam.html

Interactive Model Railroad

This one is pretty cool. You get to give commands to an actual model train at the University of Ulm in Germany! You pick the train you want to control, tell it which station to go to, and if you're quick (and lucky) enough, you're in charge. A box on the page gives the domain name of whoever happens to be controlling the train at the time.

http://rr.vs.informatik.uni-ulm.de/rr/

Mawson Station, Antarctica

Extremely, er, "cool" to get a live image of Antarctica! This picture is usually updated automatically each hour. The date/time on the picture shows local Mawson time, which is six hours ahead of UTC (GMT). Gee, it's 1 A.M. there and the sky's pretty bright! Also, extremely depressing to find out that it's warmer at Mawson Station than it is outside our window!! :-) To find out how your local temperature compares, use the Celsius/Fahrenheit conversion tables at *http://www.soton.ac.uk/~scp93ch/refer/convform.htm*l or others listed under "REFERENCE—Weights and Measures."

http://www.antdiv.gov.au/aad/exop/sfo/mawson/ video.html

Parrot-Cam

Keep track of the activities of Webster the Senegal parrot, and as the FAQ says, if you see him hanging off his perch upside-down, "he just likes to do that." At night they cover his cage with a blanket, and on weekends, a staff member takes him home, so if you miss Webster, drop in again. Lots of parrot links off this page, too! Webster's in Mississauga, Ontario, Canada.

http://www.can.net/parrotcam.html

Pikes Peak Cam

Lt. Zebulon Montgomery Pike discovered the mountain in 1806, but he never climbed it—seems the snow was too deep. This page shows a live image of Pikes Peak, elevation 14,110 feet, near Colorado Springs, Colorado. The tourist info here says the best viewing time is from sunrise to noon. They say the sunsets are magnificent, too, and "If you want to see the most spectacular lightning storms in the world, view the mountain between 3:00 P.M. and 5:00 P.M. (Mountain Time) in July and August."

http://www.softronics.com/peak_cam.html

Rome Lab Snowball Camera III

Another fun thing to try is the Rome (NY) Lab's Snowball-Cam. See that engineer at his keyboard? Try to aim a virtual snowball at him! You may get a "hit"! If not, you can view recent attempts. Last time we looked, we saw Elvis! A classic spy-cam— be sure to read the description of the engineers (and others) so you'll know who moves slow enough to hit, and what his/her/its trophy value is in points! To throw a snowball, just click the picture of the lab.

http://www.rl.af.mil:8001/Odds-n-Ends/sbcam/ rlsbcam.html

Visit Pikes Peak, Colorado!

In 1893, Katherine Lee Bates did! A Massachusetts author and teacher, she was so inspired by the view that she composed the lyrics to "America the Beautiful," one of the most-beloved patriotic songs.

You remember it: spacious skies, amber waves of grain, etc. You can see a live view of the mountain behind the song at the Pikes Peak Cam!

What is VRML?

It's virtual reality (VR) on the world wide web, and stands for Virtual Reality Modeling Language. You can experience the look and feel of VR at The Web Gate to VR.

A B C D E F G H I J K L M N O P Q R S T U V W X Y Z

San Francisco City Cam

Ah, the City by the Bay, where every nightclub crooner always manages to leave his heart. Now you can visit San Francisco over the Net, and see a new view every five minutes! KPIX's camera is high atop the Fairmont Hotel on Nob Hill. Since the camera pans from the Golden Gate Bridge to the Bay Bridge, you may be able to catch video of both bridges, plus views of downtown, the famous Coit Tower, Fisherman's Wharf, the Marina district, and other attractions. Better hold onto your heart, though!

http://www.kpix.com/live/

See the Live Ants!

Every time we visit this site the view reminds us of Auntie Em's farm, in *The Wizard of Oz*. The cyclone's just struck, carrying Dorothy off, everybody else is hiding in the root cellar. Yet, below the ground, the ants go on, industriously making molehills out of mountains. Check their activity, or lack of it, but keep an eye on the weather!

http://sec.dgsys.com/AntFarm.html

Traffic to and From Russia at Vaalmaa Border Crossing

There's something satisfying about watching traffic waiting to cross the Finnish border. Check the map to see where this particular crossing is located. What's in that truck? Hey, that lady in the car—she looks just like Carmen Sandiego! What stories can you make up about the people and vehicles you see? This picture is only updated twice an hour, so don't hang around, someone might ask to see your passport!

http://www.ktt.fi:8001/eindex.htm

Curl up with a good Internet site.

NET FILES

Did you know that the Antarctica contains 90 percent of Earth's ice and has regions drier than the Gobi Desert?

Find out more about Antarctica at
http://quest.arc.nasa.gov/livefrom/teacherguide.html
Select Program 1: The Coldest, Windiest, Iciest Place On Earth.

VIDEO GAMES

GameGuide

Do you want the scoop on your favorite game? GameGuide is there for you. The Guide has connections to the big names in home gaming. There are regularly updated articles about popular games, game techniques, and solutions to technical problems in the games. Check out the reviews of the "month's best shareware games." Who knows? You might even find free stuff to download.

http://techweb.cmp.com/ng/gameguide/
   gameguid.htm

Games Domain Review

Are you stumped deciding which computer or video game you want next? Do you wish you could find out about the games available for your system? This online magazine covers reviews, news, previews, and an opinion section for games on PC and Macintosh computers, as well as dedicated game systems. Add to the review database!

http://wcl-rs.bham.ac.uk/gdreview/

NewType

Do you ever wish there was free video game stuff waiting for you somewhere? Free secrets, free gear, and free games? Did you hear us? FREE!!! *NewType* magazine is dedicated to keeping you informed about your games. There's information about every gaming system. Warning: this site contains large graphics files.

http://www.newtype.com/NewType/

Welcome to Computer Gaming World

How much do you know about video games? Do you know it all, or do you want to know more? *Computer Gaming World* has a very well-written collection of information about home computer video games. It has in-depth reviews, cheat codes, hints, tips, and previews of beta release versions of games. You can never have enough great sources of gaming information. There are also links to almost every game manufacturer's home page. *Computer Gaming World* also features a text-only mode.

http://www.zdnet.com/~gaming/

Never give your name or address to a stranger.

Ask not what the Net can do for you, ask what you can do for the Net.

What is Santa Claus's postal code?

Codes of the World! information on Postal postcd.txt for more http://www.io.org/~djcl/ holidays. Try around the Christmas special promotion used it's H0H 0H0. This is a Answer: In Canada,

Crack open CODES AND CIPHERS.

A
B
C
D
E
F
G
H
I
J
K
L
M
N
O
P
Q
R
S
T
U
V
W
X
Y
Z

WEATHER AND METEOROLOGY

The Weather Channel Home Page

Serious weather watchers and meteorologist wannabes should head over to the Weather Channel Home Page. Grab your own heat index or wind chill charts from the Meteorologist's Toolbox. Find out how to become a meteorologist, a storm chaser for the National Weather Service, or maybe just a backyard observer. And if you've still got questions about the weather, you can ask the Weather Channel meteorologists. They pick the best ones to answer online.

http://www.weather.com/metnet.html

WeatherNet

Tired of surfing the Internet? OK, then is it a good day for surfing in Maui? What's the latest view from above that hurricane swirling around in the Gulf of Mexico? And how does the weather look—right now—on the slopes of your favorite ski resort or on the streets of Hollywood? The answers can be found right here, along with links to over 200 great meteorology sites.

http://cirrus.sprl.umich.edu/wxnet/

CLOUDS
UIUC Cloud Catalog

If you can say "cumulonimbus" or "cirrostratus" and point out these kinds of clouds in the sky, you can call yourself a cloud expert! If you'd like to be one, check out the University of Illinois Cloud Catalog. Of course, there are some really great pictures to go along with all these huge words. You may be surprised to find out how much difference there is between clouds close to earth and clouds much higher in the sky.

http://www.atmos.uiuc.edu/covis/modules/clouds/html/cloud.home.html

In medieval times, knights wore suits of armor as protection in battle. Since all knights looked alike with their armor on, they needed some way to tell each other apart at a distance. A coat of arms was originally a silk T-shirt worn over the armor. This garment had a picture of things important to the knight's family, arranged in specific ways, and in various colors, which also had meaning. Everyone in the same family wore the same coat of arms. In the Bible, Adam was the first man and Eve was the first woman. Did either have a coat of arms?

Answer: Heralds in medieval times thought every important person should have a coat of arms. So, although it was thousands of years later, they decided to assign arms to Adam and Eve. Adam's shield is plain red and Eve's plain silver. See the shields at
http://www.fred.net/jefalvey/jeffhera.html
You can also find out more about Heraldry at
http://www.outfitters.com/~helm/heraldry.html

HURRICANES
Explores! Tropical Hurricane Information

Print out this site's handy tracking chart map and keep an eye on this year's 'canes in the Atlantic, Caribbean, Gulf of Mexico, and Eastern Pacific. See up-to-the-minute satellite pictures of tropical storms or even full-blown hurricanes. Maps of hurricane tracks are available for the past 100 years. What was happening the year you were born?

http://www.met.fsu.edu/explores/tropical.html

Miami Museum of Science—Hurricane Main Menu

During Hurricane Andrew in Florida in 1992, the Benitez family huddled together in a closet while their whole farm was destroyed in 150-mile-per-hour winds. "The part I thought was the worst was when we heard the windows break," says 11-year-old Patrick, whose family had nothing to eat for two days! Read this family's story and find out how they survived. Or maybe you'd like to try flying into the eye of a hurricane with a special storm hunting plane. Check out Hurricane Andrew with 3-D glasses you can make, or learn how to create a model of a hurricane spiral.

http://www.miamisci.org/hurricane/

RAINBOWS

About Rainbows

The spectacular light shows known as rainbows are really just spread-out sunlight. People have been wondering about rainbows for a long time, but the first scientist to study them was René Descartes, over 350 years ago. He found out about rainbows by looking at just one drop of water and observing what happened when light fell on it. Learn all about the optics behind the magic of rainbows at this page, along with some fascinating facts. Did you know that no two people see the same rainbow? In fact, each of your two eyes sees its own rainbow!!

http://www.unidata.ucar.edu/staff/blynds/rnbw.html

SNOW

Current Snow Cover

So you think you're sick of shoveling the snow out of your parents' driveway? See where kids have it worse than you do! Check out how deep the snow is all over the U.S. today with this snow cover map.

http://thunder.atms.purdue.edu/gopher-data/
  surface/snow_cover.gif

Surf today, smart tomorrow.

Become one with the Net.

Kids Snow Page

If you lived in the frozen North, you might have as many different words for snow as the Inuit do. There are words that mean falling snow, ground snow, smoky snow, and wind-beaten snow. Use the list of all the different kinds of snow and see how many you can find where you live. If you'd like to keep your snowflake finds, learn how you can do it with a piece of glass and some hairspray. Make an edible glacier, cut and fold paper snowflakes, and learn that soap bubbles won't pop if you blow them outside when it's −40° F, as it is pretty often where the Teel family kids live—in Alaska.

http://www.alaska.net/~mteel/kids/kids.html

THUNDERSTORMS AND LIGHTNING

See also: PHYSICS—ELECTRICITY

Lightning Gallery

It's hard to see lightning. For one thing, the flash happens so fast. For another thing, you're probably hiding in bed with the covers pulled up over your head! To get a good look at lightning, check the spectacular images at this site!

http://www.StrikingImages.com/lightnin.htm

Space Shuttle Observations of Lightning

Everybody's seen lightning from down here on Earth, but not many people get to see it from outer space. Lightning bounces around in some very weird ways out there. For a long time, pilots had been saying that they saw lightning that started at the tops of clouds and shot out into space, but nobody believed them. In 1989, Space Shuttle astronauts helped solve this mystery when they took pictures of this "vertical lightning." Check out their pictures and movies of some wild storms as seen from space.

http://rimeice.msfc.nasa.gov:5678/skeets.html

A B C D E F G H I J K L M N O P Q R S T U V W X Y Z

The Sun never sets on the Internet.

Storm Chaser—Warren Faidley's Homepage

Thunderstorms, monsoons, and waterspouts are all just part of the incredible day's work of photographer Warren Faidley, the world's only full-time, professional storm chaser. His storm pictures have appeared in *National Geographic* and *USA Today*, in commercials and music videos, and even in Michael Jordan's latest sports video. His severe weather slide show will amaze you!

http://www.indirect.com/www/storm5/

You Can & Thunder

Wow! That was a LOUD storm! You can come out now. Let Beakman and Jax answer your questions about thunder. What's it made of, anyway? Is it hot? Is it cold? What does it look like? Try these simple experiments to help you learn more about thunder.

http://pomo.nbn.com/youcan/thunder/thunder.html

NET FILES

Your grandpa sent your dad a ticket for a lottery drawing out of state. How can you find out if your family won?

Answer: Good luck! Check the USA Today web site: http://www.usatoday.com/sports/other/solor.htm for lottery winners in over 30 states.

TORNADOES
NWSFO Norman WWW Home Page—Spotter Guide

See what happens to a car during a tornado and why it's a bad idea to stay in yours when these violent storms—some of them have winds of up to 300 miles per hour—come your way. (Hint: the car left the ground and never came back!) This storm spotter's guide explains how these long-lasting storms, called "supercell" thunderstorms, cause most of our really bad weather, including tornadoes and big hail. Learn how you can stay safe during all the different kinds of bad storms.

http://www.nssl.uoknor.edu/nws/spotterguide.html

TSUNAMIS
Tsunamis

Tsunamis—walls of water, sometimes more than 100 feet high—are caused by earthquakes or big storms at sea. When you check out this collection of tsunami pictures, you'll see huge boats that have been thrown onto the shore like toys and amazing before-and-after pictures. See what happened to a five-story lighthouse that sat 40 feet above the sea when a tsunami came crashing ashore. Read about tsunamis one level up, at *http://www.ngdc.noaa.gov:4096/cgi-bin/sed/men2html?/export/home/html/seg/menus/slide2.men+MAIN+MENU.*

http://www.ngdc.noaa.gov:4096/cgi-bin/sed/men2html?/export/home/html/seg/menus/slide2.men+Tsunamis

WEATHER FORECASTING
The Lighthouse

Your picnic basket's packed, you've got your Frisbee, but Mom's trying to make you wear your raincoat. Will it rain or not? Fast and reliable weather forecast service for 250 U.S. cities and summary data from many locations around the world are at this site. You'll need to know the airport code for the city you're interested in, but don't worry, this site has a button to locate that for you.

http://the-tech.mit.edu/Weather/

WORDS

Words, Wit and Wisdom

Evan Morris picked up the reins on this syndicated newspaper column that has been running since 1953 from his father, William Morris. A short while after the columns run in newspapers, he posts them on this page. Morris answers readers' questions about the English language and its odd words and phrases, such as "busting chops," "lame duck," or "eyes peeled," and he does this adroitly, with wit and humor. He also has a sampling of "The Word Detective," a newsletter that "aims for the large grey area between the Oxford English Dictionary and Monty Python."

http://www.users.interport.net/~words1/index.html

ANAGRAMS

Inert Net Grave Near Mars

Do you know what an anagram is? Take all the letters in a word or phrase, scramble them, and come up with a new word or phrase! For example, "Inert Net Grave Near Mars" is an anagram for "Internet Anagram Server." Type in ten or fewer letters and see what mysterious phrase you'll get. For anagrams of more than ten letters, use the "anagram by email" service.

http://lrdc5.lrdc.pitt.edu/awad-cgibin/anagram

MNEMONICS

Chapter X Remembering Numbers

Mnemonics are handy little devices for jogging our memories. For example, the first letters of "My Very Educated Mother Just Served Us Nine Pickles" gives the initials, in order, of the nine planets. "Lucy Can't Drink Milk" provides the Roman numerals in order for 50, 100, 500, and 1000. Some of these mnemonics have been helping students breeze through tests for years, now it's your turn to use them! Have trouble remembering dates in history class? Try this mnemonic alphabet system, which replaces numbers with consonants. Maybe you can make up some of your own, too.

http://www.curbet.com/speedlearn/chap10.html

Get Mnemonic With A Personalized Vanity License Plate

Parental advisory: some of these license plates are somewhat racy. Once you get the hang of it, figuring out the messages on personalized "vanity" license plates is pretty easy, especially after consulting the list on this page. In addition to a key listing of basic plate codes, there's a few tricks and tips, a long list of clever plates spotted on the road, and even links to a handful of other license plate lists on the Web. BCNUONDNET!

http://reality.sgi.com/employees/molivier_studio/
   license-plates.html

NET FILES

The comic strip "Peanuts" was first printed on October 2, 1950. In what year did Snoopy the beagle first appear standing on two legs instead of four?

Answer: Snoopy first stood on two legs in 1958. There are more Snoopy facts at the Comic Strip.

TONGUE TWISTERS

Tongue Twister

Somehow, it seems appropriate that a real get-down-to-business English language tongue twister page would be from Japan. There's a couple of dozen or so of these here, from the banal—"How much wood could..."—to the short and clever—"Unique New York" or "Truly Plural" (go ahead—say them a few times).

http://www.edu.ipc.hiroshima-cu.ac.jp/~b11074/
   CLASS/rest.html

A
B
C
D
E
F
G
H
I
J
K
L
M
N
O
P
Q
R
S
T
U
V
W
X
Y
Z

Welcome to the Grade Four Student Page

The fourth grade kids of Stony Mountain Elementary (Manitoba, Canada) write their own tongue twisters about different subjects. Some weather-related ones include "Hard hail hit heavily on a hawk's hollow head," or "The twirling tornado twisted its way to Texas." There's plenty more here—download them and have a tongue twister party!

http://www.mbnet.mb.ca/~stonymtn/student.html

WRITING

District WEB.KIDS

Write a science fiction story with up to 50 other kids! Get in on the start of a story, and you might even be the one to give it a title. Or, see how creative you can get in the actual story-writing. Help to weave a tale of adventure!

http://www.hoofbeats.com/

KidPub WWW Publishing

Got the itch to get published? Here are poems, stories, and more from kids your age! New stories appear every day, and yours can be one of them. The last time we checked, there were titles like "Great Excuses for Not Cleaning Your Room," or "Being the New Kid," or "The Revenge of the Slime Monsters." There's also a story to which you can add—it's called a collaboration!

http://www.en-garde.com/kidpub/

Kids' Space

Every kid's home page! Want other kids to see your paintings? Want them to be able to hear you play your trombone? How about letting kids all over the world read your story or poem? Send your multimedia to this site for publication! Also, you can look for a pen pal to write to on the Internet, and if you don't have a mailbox, use the bulletin-board feature to let other kids know what you're thinking about, looking for, or dreaming. Menus are in both Japanese and English.

http://plaza.interport.net/kids_space/

> ## Let balloonists take you to new heights in Aviation and Airplanes.

Purdue On-Line Writing Lab Web Server Home Page

Are those commas confusing? How about nouns, verbs, and adjectives? Are apostrophes getting you mixed up every time? And what's a preposition, anyway? Come to this Writing Lab to figure out how you should use all these things. Your reports, letters, and tests will look impressive!

http://staff4.sla.purdue.edu/

GREETING CARDS

Build a Card

Picture this. You're at school and suddenly realize today is your Mom's birthday. No problemo. Just Web over to this site and create a card online. Select a background, choose a font, and type your own message. Then mail the card to your Mom's e-mail account—it will be there the next time she reads her mail. To keep your creation forever, download it as a GIF file from your browser; the directions are included on the page.

http://holodeck.maxonline.com/cgi-win/
   cardnew.exe?

The Electric Postcard

Hey, it won't even cost you the price of a stamp, and you won't get writer's cramp! Instead, you can send a postcard to anyone who has an Internet address and access to the Web! First, you choose a piece of art or a graphic for the front of your postcard; then you fill in your message (even links if you want!); next, type in your friend's e-mail address. They will get a message by electronic mail, giving them a code number and asking them to go to the Web site pick-up window. Imagine their surprise when they go to pick up their very own postcard from you!

http://postcards.www.media.mit.edu/postcards/

A
B
C
D
E
F
G
H
I
J
K
L
M
N
O
P
Q
R
S
T
U
V
W
X
Y
Z

NET FILES

Where is the world's largest colony of bats?

Answer: The largest known colony is at Bracken Cave, Texas. The 20 million Mexican free-tails eat 250 tons of insects nightly. The largest known colony in a city is in Austin, Texas, under the Congress Avenue bridge. The Austin bats eat from 10,000 to 30,000 pounds of insects per night, including mosquitoes and numerous agricultural pests. "This is the largest urban bat colony in North America. With up to 1.5 million bats spiraling into the summer sunset, Austin now has one of the most unusual and fascinating tourist attractions anywhere." See the bats at
http://www.batcon.org/congress.html

JOURNALS AND DIARIES

The Diary Project

Do you have fears that you don't want to discuss with anyone? Or maybe you have a secret dream that you'd like to see happen one day? You can write about these in your diary or journal; it is your personal and private business. But here in The Diary Project, kids from all over the world have decided to share their journals with YOU! Contribute an entry from your diary (only your first name will be used if you wish, or you can write anonymously). Entries will be printed as a book in the near future.

http://www.well.com/user/diary/

Take a ride on a Carousel in AMUSEMENT PARKS.

X-RAYS

MPTEACH.HTML

Most of us have had our teeth x-rayed. That's so the dentist can "look inside" our teeth to see if any cavities are hiding there for her to fix. X-rays are also used by doctors to look inside us to see if we are healthy. Did you know x-rays are also used to check mechanical parts like airplane engines? Technicians can see if there are any cracks that might cause problems later on! Check out this site to discover what makes x-rays work and read about the different types of x-ray machines.

http://www.mcw.edu/medphys/mpteach.html

X-Ray Tomographic Microscopy

Here's a 3-D x-ray technology that doctors and scientists use to help them look inside things in a special way. With x-ray tomography, a series of x-rays are taken of an object. The object is moved a tiny bit between each picture. All the images are stored in a computer. The pictures from the computer can show the object from different angles. Also, it can show various depths inside the object. This can often reveal hidden things that would normally go undetected. This page describes the process in more detail and has some pictures that help show how it all works.

http://www.llnl.gov/IPandC/opportunities93/08-NDE/X_Ray_Tomo.shtml

---

Space Exploration is a blast. Check out Astronomy

YOGA

Giri's Home Page

One of the first things you will learn in yoga class, besides where to take off your shoes, is the word namasté. Your instructor will say it to you, and you're expected to say it back. Namasté is derived from the Sanskrit word namaskaar, meaning "I bow to the divine in you." Yoga is from the Sanskrit word Yug, meaning union with the divine. This site is a great overview of major yogic disciplines, although it's kind of wordy. You'll also get an introduction to Hinduism, and tips on learning Sanskrit.

http://www.geocities.com/RodeoDrive/1415/

Yoga Paths

Parental advisory: this site covers many spiritual topics besides yoga, so you should explore this site with your child. When you think of yoga, do you think of impossible body postures and unusual breathing patterns? Maybe you think of burning incense, or chanting Sanskrit mantras over and over. But yoga is less, and more, than that. Did you know there are many kinds of yoga, and the physical postures or *asanas* are only one small part? This site explains many yogic paths, and provides links to Web sites which will help you choose a yoga center, if you're interested in learning more.

http://www.spiritweb.org/Spirit/Yoga/Overview.html

ZOOLOGY

Australian A to Z Animal Archive

Do you know how the kangaroo got its name? When European explorers first saw a strange animal jumping around, they asked the Aborigines what it was. The Aborigines replied "kangaroo," which to them meant "I don't understand," but the Europeans thought that was the strange animal's name—kangaroo. Check out this site and learn about other Australian animals.

http://www.com.au/aaa/A_Z/home.html

NWF Home Page

What's for lunch at the National Wildlife Federation Home Page? Flamingos eat algae, and that's where they get their beautiful pink coloring. Wait, isn't algae green? Well, algae has a special chemical that turns the birds' feathers pink! Koala bears are very picky eaters. They only eat one kind of food, eucalyptus (yoo-kuh-LIP-tus) leaves. Tree squirrels eat nuts, pine cones, and other foods that they bury to prepare for winter. When winter arrives, they search for the food they have buried. Squirrels have an excellent sense of smell and can sniff out food that has been buried in a foot of snow! Did you know that up to 100 species become extinct every day? You can help. Visit the National Wildlife Federation Home Page and find out how you can get involved in a project or organization working to help endangered species. You may even be able to "adopt" an endangered animal.

http://www.nwf.org/nwf/

Phylum Level Index

You may know a sponge as something you use to wash Dad's car, but do you know about the sponge sea animal? That's right, though it may look like a plant, the sea sponge is really an animal. Check out the Phylum Level Index site where you'll learn all about sponges, and other sea animals such as flatworms and comb jellies. You'll also make your way through to sealife with backbones, including various types of fish.

http://www.mbl.edu/html/MRC/HTML/phylum.html

Zoological Information by Animal Group

Did you know that you're a *Homo sapiens*? That's the scientific classification name for humans. All life can be organized and classified this way, using a system of scientific naming or nomenclature. Visit the *Zoological Record* Home Page, where you'll find information on the ordering of organisms into groups based on their relationships. You'll find the order, class, and kingdom for everything here, from people to dinosaurs. In addition, there are reports containing the symbol, scientific name, common name, and family for each member of the animal kingdom.

http://www.york.biosis.org/zrdocs/zoolinfo/
  gp_index.htm

NET FILES

You've always wondered if your brother is an alien from outer space. Now you get your photos back and sure enough, he's got glowing RED eyes! What should you do?

Answer: Don't call NASA yet. According to Kodak, this effect occurs sometimes when you use a flash. It's actually the reflection of light from the flash off of the blood vessels inside your brother's eyes. To reduce red-eye, you need to reduce the size of your subject's pupils so there won't be so much reflective surface available. There are several ways to do this: increase the light level in the room by turning on all of the lights, or have your brother look at a bright light just before you take the flash picture. Also, some cameras have a red-eye reduction feature. To eliminate red-eye from pictures you have already taken, you need to manipulate the image electronically. If you have the equipment available to you, you can do it yourself, or you can take the prints to a Kodak Digital Enhancement Station at a retail store. Call Kodak for locations, and visit http://www.kodak.com:80/cgiHome/tags/tag.shtml for answers to more frequently asked questions about film and photography!

MIGRATION

Journey North

Can you imagine a hummingbird flying 600 miles, non-stop, and in a matter of hours? It takes ships days to travel that far! These tiny birds can burn up to half their body mass making this kind of trip. Migration occurs every year with all kinds of animals. Even your grandma and grandpa like to go south for the winter! Visit the Journey North site and learn about wildlife migration sightings from school kids around the globe.

http://www.ties.k12.mn.us/~jnorth/

ZOOS

The Birmingham Zoo

Look at the Kudu antelope with a pair of oxpecker birds on her back. They're eating ticks and other "bugs" off of the antelope, bringing her relief from an irritating source of discomfort. What's that black spot in the corner of that Dik Dik's eye? It's a gland with black sticky stuff that Dik Dik antelopes rub on tree branches to mark their territory. Have you ever been on an African safari? Well, these are some of the things you will see while taking a "virtual safari" through the Birmingham Zoo home page in Alabama. Have fun, and watch out for the leopards hiding in the rocks and trees!

http://www.bhm.tis.net/zoo/

The Electronic Zoo

Let a veterinarian loose on the Internet and what do you get? A Web site filled with information on all kinds of animals, plus resources on veterinary medicine, agriculture, biology, environment and ecology—and the list goes on and on. Do you think this guy loves his job AND knows his stuff? You bet!

http://netvet.wustl.edu/e-zoo.htm

NET FILES

In the Pasadena Tournament of Roses Parade, each float must be completely covered with flowers or other organic material. What's the average number of flowers on each float?

Answer: An average float requires up to 100,000 blossoms. More than one-half million roses are used in each parade, according to the home page at http://www.geninc.com/geni/USA/CA/Pasadena/chamber/rose_events.html

DLC-ME The Microbe Zoo

There is a fabulous Microbe Zoo running wild around your yard, in your food, even on your clothes! They are so small, you can't see them without a microscope, but they affect your life daily, in a big way. Zoom in on the invisible world of these small creatures and learn how they interact with the larger world around them. And don't forget to thank them for that last chocolate bar you ate, or root beer you drank—they helped make it!

http://commtechlab.msu.edu/CTLprojects/dlc-me/zoo/

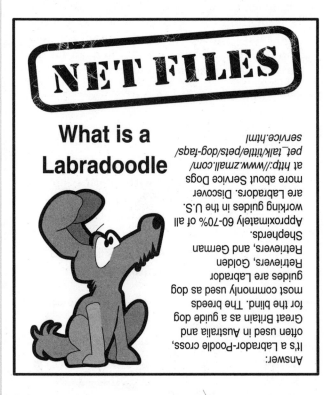

NET FILES

What is a Labradoodle

Answer:
It's a Labrador-Poodle cross, often used in Australia and Great Britain as a guide dog for the blind. The breeds most commonly used as dog guides are Labrador Retrievers, Golden Retrievers, and German Shepherds. Approximately 60-70% of all working guides in the U.S. are Labradors. Discover more about Service Dogs at http://www.zmall.com/pet_talk/title/pets/dog-tags/service.html

National Zoological Park Home Page

Admission: Free. Rules: Don't feed the animals (and don't smudge the computer screen with your nose!). Have you ever wondered what goes on behind the scenes at the National Zoo in Washington, D.C.? People, animals, and plants all play a part! How do cheetahs get their exercise at the zoo? Cheetah calisthenics! Yes, the cats actually warm up by playing ball, and then they run through a ropes course. Visit your favorite animal at the National Zoo home page.

http://www.si.edu/organiza/museums/zoo/ homepage/nzphome.htm

Rhinos and Tigers and Bears—Oh My!

What's that hippo doing with a watermelon? And why is that tiger rolling a barrel? Those are special toys and enrichment activities for the zoo animals. Find out more about animal toys, and learn lots of other interesting information about the diet and conservation of the animals at the Knoxville, Tennessee Zoo.

http://loki.ur.utk.edu/ut2kids/zoo/zoo.html

ZooNet

ZooNet doesn't collect animals, they collect zoos! Their goal is to link to every zoo in the world, and they're doing a great job. They can link you to official home pages for private and specialized zoos, or for zoo-related organizations. They also provide the latest on zoos in the news! Don't forget to download some animal screensavers while you're here! The animal galleries offer herds of animal photos and images for your pleasure. Also, check the endangered species info, and the links to many animal pages across the Net.

http://www.mindspring.com/~zoonet/

Your report on giraffes is just about finished. It still needs some finishing touches, though. For example, it would be nice to have a picture! Hike over to the animal galleries at **ZooNet**, and download or print your choice!

Index

*Main subject headings are shown in **bold***

*Main subject headings are shown in **bold***

*Main subject headings are shown in **bold***

*Main subject headings are shown in **bold***

*Main subject headings are shown in **bold***

*Main subject headings are shown in **bold***

*Main subject headings are shown in **bold***

*Main subject headings are shown in **bold***

*Main subject headings are shown in **bold***

*Main subject headings are shown in **bold***

Main subject headings are shown in **bold**

*Main subject headings are shown in **bold***

*Main subject headings are shown in **bold***